Benchmark Papers
in Ecology

Series Editor: Frank B. Golley
University of Georgia

PUBLISHED VOLUMES

CYCLES OF ESSENTIAL ELEMENTS / *Lawrence R. Pomeroy*
BEHAVIOR AS AN ECOLOGICAL FACTOR / *David E. Davis*
NICHE: THEORY AND APPLICATION / *Robert H. Whittaker and Simon A. Levin*
ECOLOGICAL ENERGETICS / *Richard G. Wiegert*
ECOLOGICAL SUCCESSION / *Frank B. Golley*
PHYTOSOCIOLOGY / *Robert P. McIntosh*
POPULATION REGULATION / *Robert H. Tamarin*

RELATED TITLES IN OTHER BENCHMARK SERIES

STOCHASTIC MODELS IN POPULATION GENETICS / *Wen-Hsiung Li*
EUGENICS: THEN AND NOW / *Carl Jay Bajema*
DEMOGRAPHIC GENETICS / *Kenneth M. Weiss and Paul A. Ballonoff*
GENETICS AND SOCIAL STRUCTURE: MATHEMATICAL STRUCTURALISM IN POPULATION GENETICS AND SOCIAL THEORY / *Paul Ballonoff*

**Benchmark Papers
in Ecology / 7**

A BENCHMARK® Books Series

POPULATION
REGULATION

Edited by

ROBERT H. TAMARIN

Boston University

Dowden, Hutchinson
& Ross, Inc.

STROUDSBURG, PENNSYLVANIA

Copyright © 1978 by **Dowden, Hutchinson & Ross, Inc.**
Benchmark Papers in Ecology, Volume 7
Library of Congress Catalog Card Number: 77–16178
ISBN: 0–87933–324–3

80 79 78 1 2 3 4 5
Manufactured in the United States of America.

LIBRARY OF CONGRESS CATALOGING IN PUBLICATION DATA
Main entry under title:
Population regulation.
  (Benchmark papers in ecology ; 7)
  Includes indexes.
  1. Population biology—Addresses, essays, lectures. I. Tamarin, Robert H.
QH352.P63   574.5'24   77–16178
ISBN 0-87933-324-3

Distributed world wide by Academic Press,
a subsidiary of Harcourt Brace Jovanovich,
Publishers.

SERIES EDITOR'S FOREWORD

Ecology—the study of interactions and relationships between living systems and environment—is an extremely active and dynamic field of science. The great variety of possible interactions in even the most simple ecological system makes the study of ecology compelling but difficult to discuss in simple terms. Further, living systems include individual organisms, populations, communities, and ultimately the entire biosphere; there are thus numerous subspecialties in ecology. Some ecologists are interested in wildlife and natural history, others are intrigued by the complexity and apparently intractable problems of ecological systems, and still others apply ecological principles to the problems of man and the environment. This means that a Benchmark Series in Ecology would be subdivided into innumerable subvolumes that represented these diverse interests. However, rather than take this approach, I have tried to focus on general patterns or concepts that are applicable to two particularly important levels of ecological understanding: the population and the community. I have taken the dichotomy between these two as my major organizing concept in the series.

In a field that is rapidly changing and evolving, it is often difficult to chart the transition of single ideas into cohesive theories and principles. In addition, it is not easy to make judgments as to the benchmarks of the subject when the theoretical features of a field are relatively young. These twin problems—the relationship between interweaving ideas and the elucidation of theory, and the youth of the subject itself—make development of a Benchmark series in the field of ecology difficult. Each of the volume editors has recognized this inherent problem, and each has acted to solve it in his or her unique way. Their collective efforts will, we anticipate, provide a survey of the most important concepts in the field.

The Benchmark series is especially designed for libraries of colleges, universities, and research organizations that cannot purchase the older literature of ecology because of costs, lack of staff to select from the hundreds of thousands of journals and volumes, or from the unavailability of the reference materials. For example, in developing countries where a science library must be developed *de novo*, I have seen where the Benchmark series can provide the only background literature available to the students and staff. Thus, the intent of the series is to provide an authoritative selection of literature, which can be read in the original form, but that is cast in a matrix of thought provided by the editor. The volumes are designed to explore the historical development of a concept in ecology and point the way toward new developments, without being a historical study. We hope that even though the Benchmark Series in Ecology is a library oriented series and bears an appropriate cost it will also be a sufficient utility so that many professionals will place it in their personal library. In a few cases the volumes have even been used as text books for advanced courses. Thus we expect that the Benchmark Series in Ecology will be useful not only to the student who seeks an authoritative selection of original literature but also to the professional who wants to quickly and efficiently expand his or her background in an area of ecology outside his special competence.

Population regulation, the subject of the present volume, has been a major focal point for ecology almost continually since the science became an identifiable discipline. The dynamic and sometimes even explosive nature of populations has a mirror image in their regulation and relative constancy. Regulation may be a function of the environment outside the population or come from within. Robert Tamarin, an Associate Professor in the Department of Biology at Boston University, is well equipped to explore this important topic. Dr. Tamarin received his doctorate from Indiana University for research on the population genetics of field mice *(Microtus)*, where he worked with Charles Krebs. He did further post doctorate study on genetics with Ashton in Hawaii and on community ecology with McArthur at Princeton. His current research is on regulation of field mice populations on small islands.

FRANK B. GOLLEY

PREFACE

The scientific study of population regulation began at the very beginning of the twentieth century with the work of economic entomologists, who were trying to control the unwanted outbreaks of natural and introduced insect pests. From these beginnings, acerbic controversies have raged over which factors in the environment or within the organisms themselves lead to the control of numbers. Although these controversies are not yet settled, they have become much more tempered. Rather than arguing over whether density-dependent or density-independent factors are regulating a population, population researchers seem to be devoting more interest to determining which density-dependent factor regulates populations, since (1) almost all factors in the environment are density-dependent and (2) regulation by density-independent factors is by far less interesting. Most of the controversies have historical roots, so historically important papers are included here along with up-to-date articles.

As with most areas of ecology, there is a three-pronged approach to population regulation: from the field, from the laboratory, and from the armchair. The field is where the phenomenon of population regulation actually occurs. If field observation and mathematical model disagree, the model is wrong. I do not mean to belittle math modeling or laboratory studies, however. The ultimate goal of any science is to develop a comprehensive, quantitative description, which is—of course—the math model. The laboratory allows us to isolate phenomena and study them in detail with reference to specific aspects of the field situation. And good science is predictive science; good hypotheses, by definition, can be falsified by observation or experimentation. Without the criterion of falsifiability, we are dealing with vague metaphysical concepts, not theories of population regulation. The many untestable hypotheses and the vague use of terminology have been—and, to some extent, still are—major causes of difficulty in this branch of ecology.

Progressing through these papers, the reader may note two of my biases: theories of self-regulation and population cycles. My own research has concerned these two areas, so I have taken the liberty of ending this book with a section on each of them. Although few species undergo population cycles, an inordinate amount of study of cycles is carried on. Here there is the real challenge of trying to ferret out the causes of a still mysterious phenomenon. I have tried to justify this section by suggesting that the study of cycles is a microcosm of the general field of population regulation.

For a reader to get the most of this book, he should have acquaintance with the general field of ecology, but an educated layman can understand almost all the articles. The basic concepts are not very difficult: the difficulty comes from proving which ideas are correct. At some points the reader is assumed to be familiar with the statistical technique of regression analysis, and at other points, a basic knowledge of genetics is assumed. At still other points, graphical analysis is presented.

I am pessimistic that a general theory of population regulation can be achieved. I believe, however, that there is some hope that the study of population cycles will produce a comprehensive theory. Additionally, the study of the interactions between any species with its environment is inherently interesting, and these sorts of studies are an outcome of the search for a general theory of population regulation.

I am most grateful to Charles Krebs of the University of British Columbia and the late Robert Mac Arthur of Princeton University, both of whom influenced my views profoundly. I would also like to thank Frank Golley for giving me the opportunity to present my views. My wife Ginger devoted many hours of constructive criticism on the Editor's Comments sections. Linda McGettrick typed the manuscript. All errors are my own.

ROBERT H. TAMARIN

CONTENTS

Contents

PART VII: THEORIES OF SELF-REGULATION

PART VIII: POPULATION CYCLES

CONTENTS BY AUTHOR

POPULATION REGULATION

INTRODUCTION

All animal populations have the reproductive capacity to increase without limit, yet none do. The study of the factors that prevent unlimited growth—population regulation—is the topic of this book. What is superficially a very simple problem turns out to be a very difficult problem that has been compounded by confused terminology, studies of taxononomically unrelated organisms, and a lack of communication among field workers, lab workers, and theoreticians. In the face of all these problems, however, valuable research has been done, and a fair insight into the workings of natural populations has been achieved. In my own view, a study is complete when an adequate theory exists that not only explains all the facts that we know but also predicts what we do not yet know. I do not believe that the study of population regulation is at that stage yet. I do not know whether it will ever reach that stage, but at the moment I am pessimistic. (I elaborate on this problem in the "Concluding Remarks" section of this book.)

The study of population regulation has evolved from the classic work of the Reverend Thomas Malthus. Concerned with the prospect of human overpopulation, he wrote in 1798:

> I think I may fairly make two postulata.
>   First, that food is necessary to the existence of man.
>   Secondly, that the passion between the sexes is necessary and will remain in its present state.
>
> . . . .
>
>   Assuming then, my postulata as granted, I say, that the power of population is indefinitely greater than the power in the earth to produce subsistence for man.

1

> Population, when unchecked, increases in a geometrical ratio. Subsistence increases only in an arithmetical ratio. A slight acquaintance with numbers will show the immensity of the first power in comparison of the second.
>
> By that law of our nature which makes food necessary to the life of man, the effects of these two unequal powers must be kept equal.
>
> This implies a strong and constantly operating check on population from the difficulty of subsistence. This difficulty must fall some where and must necessarily be severely felt by a large portion of mankind.

Drawing on the work of Malthus, Charles Darwin took the problem of population regulation into account with the theory of evolution. He assumed that competition for limited resources caused the regulation of numbers; thus not all offspring could survive to reproduce, and only the fittest would survive. Neither Darwin nor Malthus was investigating causes of regulation, however; Malthus already knew what factors caused humans to die. He was interested in encouraging people to restrain from reproducing in order to lower the birth rate to the level where all could be fed. It was not until investigators started to inquire about animal populations to determine what regulated their numbers that the current field of population regulation was born.

Controversies over the mechanisms of population regulation began in the 1930s. They have not been settled yet, although a good deal of compromise has taken place. There is still a "school-of-thought" approach to much of the study of the factors that limit population growth, and there is still the controversy of single-versus multiple-factor regulation (Lidicker 1977). We have much more data, however, and many valuable studies can support or refute various ideas that were held back in the thirties. Historical papers are thus useful when we seem doomed to repeat past errors.

From the beginning, the study of population regulation has been plagued by several types of problems. The first is one of confounding of terminology. To this day, terms such as "density dependent" and "regulation" bring shudders to the hardened population biologist. Rather than redefine such terms, I will merely point out that when reading many of the papers in this volume a wary eye is necessary to be sure that terms are explicitly defined or understood in the same way to both the reader and writer. But as several of the authors in this volume point out, the basic problems are not merely semantic. Rather, terminological problems are the result of other, deep-rooted problems mainly involved with totally different ways of viewing the same world.

The second problem, or class of problems, is the basic difficulty in population biology of doing decisive experiments or gathering data to unequivocally prove or disprove a hypothesis. There are several reasons for this problem. First, this is a general difficulty one faces when dealing with relatively long-term phenomena in nature. One habitat differs from another, one year differs from another, and so on. Thus the repetition and control of experiments are often difficult in the ecological end of the hard sciences. Whether these problems are eventually overcome will tell us whether certain areas of ecology will join the ranks of truly predictive science. Another major area of difficulty comes from the complexity of the problems themselves. That is, we often do not know the relevant parameters that need controlling in any given experiment. For example, in Paper 25 in this collection, Krebs and his students serendipitously demonstrate the importance of dispersal to population processes when fenced experiments failed to work properly. Thus we now know that when one attempts to manipulate a natural population of rodents, one must account for dispersal. It took five years to discover that.

The next problem is the difficulty of generalizing from one organism to another. For example, some workers study insects while others study mammals and birds. Insects are cold-blooded and have very steretyped behaviors. Mammals and birds, on the other hand, are warm-blooded and have very flexible, complex behaviors. Insects are often regulated directly by food or weather, whereas mammals and birds tend to be regulated by complex social interactions and behaviors.

Another source of difficulty is the fact that the umbrella term "population biologist" refers to people trained as ecologists, geneticists, endocrinologists, mathematicians, ethologists, and so on. Often the language of one is not the language of the other, which fosters problems. To some extent we are making advances here, and many people with dual training are making substantial contributions. As Jonathan Roughgarden (1977) wrote in his review of Caughley's article in Robert May's (1976) book *Theoretical Ecology*: ". . . He writes that he awaits the time when population geneticists 'grow weary of their pivotal assumption that a population has no dynamics' and when population dynamicists 'abandon the belief that a population has no genetics.' One need wait no longer; there already is a rich and growing literature that has answered this challenge."

Finally, problems arise because some population biologists work in an armchair, some in the lab, and some in the field. The armchair ecologist tends to talk in a dialect of matrix algebra, the

laboratory ecologist tends to talk of perfectly controlled experiments, and the field ecologist tends to talk about the vagaries of
nature. Inevitably, problems in communication arise. However,
as with the previous problems of subspecialization, strides are being made to overcome these communication problems. Especially
helpful have been symposia designed to overcome these problems such as those edited by Lewontin (1968), Cody and Diamond
(1975), and Snyder (1977).

In collating this collection of readings, I decided to include
papers giving a historical outlook to the study of population regulation as well as those marking the frontiers of current research.
It was difficult to accumulate a series of readings adequately covering both the past and the present within the page limits of this series. This is partly because many of the papers written are lengthly
either because of style or because of the voluminous amounts of
data that population studies tend to amass. Another problem that
I confronted in gathering these readings was determining at what
point one draws the line between what material is and what material is not actually "population regulation" in scope. Since population regulation is an interface area of ecology, virtually all
areas of ecology deal to some extent with population regulation.
For example, many view population distribution as an aspect of
density. That is, zero abundance occurs at the edge of a species
range. I have chosen to avoid the literature of biogeography and
systematics by dealing strictly with the control of numbers of a species well within the borders of its range. (For a discussion of these
particular issues see Mac Arthur 1972 and Krebs 1972.)

In addition, I am very interested in mechanisms. That is, it is
more important for me to know the environmental factor that
causes a population to decline than to have an elaborate mathematical description of the decline. Nevertheless, I do believe that
mathematical theory is of the utmost importance. As a matter of
fact, the ultimate goal of the study of population regulation is to
establish a strong mathematical framework of theory around which
field and lab studies gain perspective. As of this writing, however,
there is still a fair separation of mathematical theory and empirical
mechanistic studies, and in this volume I am bent well over to the
mechanistic side. A good introduction to much of the current theoretical literature can be found in May's *Theoretical Ecology*. Let
me give a brief description of the sections that will follow in this
book.

Paper 1, by L. C. Cole, gives a general overview of the study of
demography (and thus in itself constitutes Part 1 of the book). The

next two parts include papers by the proponents of the biotic and the abiotic schools of population regulation. The biotic school is concerned with competition, predation, disease, and parasitism as mechanisms of population regulation. The abiotic school is primarily concerned with weather as a regulating agent. We usually associate the term "density-dependence" with the biotic school and the term "density-independence" with the abiotic school. That is, biotic regulating mechanisms tend to increase their effects as the density of the regulated population increases, whereas abiotic factors tend to exert their effects regardless of the density of the regulated population, or so the proponents of the biotic school have claimed. Andrewartha and Birch (Paper 5), however, present an argument that weather can certainly be a density-dependent factor. Part IV deals with compromise theories and critiques of theories, with many papers offering both. These papers give a view of population regulation involving many factors, both biotic and abiotic.

Part V deals with predation and competition, the two most commonly studied biotic mechanisms. Here the papers discuss the theory of the way a mechanism should work, along with some practical observations about how the mechanisms can and do work. Although in any particular case a good deal of controversy exists about whether competition or predation regulates a given population, the study of both factors provides important insight about how two-species systems tend to interact. Parasitism and disease are cited the least as distinct mechanisms of population regulation. To some extent, they can be regarded as types of predation where the predator is smaller than the prey. (In Part VII, however, we see that some of Pimentel's—and others'—ideas are easily applicable to parasitism.)

Part VI deals with key-factor analysis, which is not a theory of population regulation but rather a method of deciding which factors are acting in a density-dependent fashion in influencing the numbers of a population from one generation to the next. It basically involves a regression-analysis technique. Part VII is a collection of papers that discuss self-regulatory mechanisms. Self-regulation can be one of the more interesting areas of population regulation, for it combines genotypic and phenotypic mechanisms that take into account the behavior and physiology of a population's individuals and the evolution of populations.

Part VIII, the last section, covers population cycles. Although this field deals with a specific problem of population regulation (the regular three- to four-year cycles of a limited number of species), it provides a good summary of the field in general because it is a microcosm of the study of population regulation.

In this volume, I am treating the study of population regulation as a science, and science involves hypotheses that are predictive and testable (Popper 1959; Kuhn 1962; Platt 1964). Although I return to this point in the concluding remarks, let me state here that it is possible that a good deal of the study of population regulation may not lend itself to bold generalizations. Thus the reader should keep two questios in mind: What does this theory predict, and how do I test it? Much of the controversy may stem from these questions. Perhaps the basic question in population studies is not What regulates this population? but rather, How do we determine what regulates this population? As Charles Darwin said: "Looking back, I think it was more difficulty to see what the problems were than to solve them."

REFERENCES

Cody, M. A., and J. M. Diamond (eds). 1975. *Ecology and Evolution of Communities*. Cambridge, Mass.: Harvard Univ. Press.

Krebs, C. J. 1972. *Ecology*. New York: Harper & Row.

Kuhn, T. S. 1962. *The Structure of Scientific Revolutions*. Chicago: University of Chicago Press.

Lewontin, R. C. (ed.). 1968. *Population Biology and Evolution*. Syracuse, N.Y.: Syracuse Univ. Press.

Lidicker, W. Z., Jr. 1977. Regulation of Numbers in Small Mammal Populations. In D. Snyder (ed.), *Pymatuning Symposium in Ecology*, no. 5. Ann Arbor, Mich.: Edwards Brothers.

Mac Arthur, R. H. 1972. *Geographical Ecology*. New York: Harper & Row.

Malthus, T. R. 1798. *An Essay on the Principle of Population as It Affects the Future Improvement of Society*. London: Johnson.

May, R. M. (ed.). 1976. *Theoretical Ecology*. Philadelphia: Saunders.

Platt, J. R. 1964. Strong Inference. *Science* **146**:347–353.

Popper, K. R. 1959. *The Logic of Scientific Discovery*. New York: Harper & Row.

Roughgarden, J. 1977. Review of R. M. May (ed.), *Theoretical Ecology*. *Science* **196**:51.

Snyder, D. (ed.). 1977. Populations of Small Mammals under Natural Conditions. *Pymatuning Symposium in Ecology*, no. 5. Ann Arbor, Mich.: Edwards Brothers.

Part I

PARAMETERS OF POPULATION STUDY

Editor's Comments
on Paper 1

1   COLE
Sketches of General and Comparative Demography

At the Cold Spring Harbor Symposium on Quantitative Biology of 1957—whose subject was "Population Studies: Animal Ecology and Demography"—L. C. Cole gave the introductory talk entitled "Sketches of general and comparative demography." This paper is an excellent entry to the terminology of population studies. Cole points out that animal ecology and human demography are really aspects of the same thing, because prior to the twentieth century, virtually all population work was done on humans anyway. Thus the historical roots of population studies are with humans. As a matter of fact, both "population" and "demography" essentially mean "people."

Two of Cole's points are extremely important. First, he points out the three-pronged approach to population biology: field studies, lab studies, and theoretical studies. He praises the innovation of the biologists who have been capable of bringing intractable problems into the laboratory, where they can be tackled at a much simpler level. He rightly points out and emphasizes that our ultimate goal is to understand populations in nature. That is, when theory or lab studies are contradicted by the results of a study in nature, the theory or the lab study must be modified. It is the population in nature that must be understood, with theory and lab studies only means to that end.

The second point is that population biology is highly interdisciplinary. The expert population biologist is often required to know not only population ecology, but also mathematics, demography, evolutionary biology, population genetics, physiology, nutrition, climatology, taxonomy, parasitology, and much more. This is not meant to frighten off the novice, but merely to warn him that the study of the regulation of natural populations draws from many disciplines. The better researchers in this area tend to be generalists.

Let me turn from Cole for a few words on the measurement of density. In the study of population regulation, the basic unit of measure is density, or number per unit area. Population density is usually measured either by enumeration or by sampling. Enumeration techniques attempt to count every animal in the population; they are usually successful with humans and with large, easily observable organisms, such as herbivores, that can be counted by means of aerial surveys. For example, in his classical work on the wolf–moose interaction on Isle Royale, Mech (1966) used aerial reconnaissance techniques to enumerate both species.

Many sampling procedures use a random portion of a population to estimate the density. With these methods, it is important to keep in mind the problem of randomness, or more precisely, the problem of the dispersion of organisms throughout their habitat. If organisms tend to occur in a patchy fashion, then sampling procedures must take this into account.

The best known method of sampling is the capture-recapture technique, also known as the Lincoln or Peterson index, where a sample is withdrawn from a population, marked, and then returned to the population. Later the population is resampled with the proportion of marked animals and the size of the sample indicating the density by way of the formula

$$N = \frac{S}{P}$$

where N = estimate of density

S = size of the marked population

P = proportion of the total population that is marked.

Other techniques make use of removal trapping, estimations from catch per unit effort, random subsampling of sessile organisms, singing male bird counts, and others. Many ecology lab manuals describe these various techniques (Cox 1976; Brower and Zar 1977; Benton and Werner 1972; Rolan 1973; Darnell 1971).

Further detail in the study of population growth can be obtained from Deevey's classical paper on life tables (1947). The basic parameters, birth and death rates, are calculated from these life tables; they then determine population growth. Leslie (1945; 1948) pioneered the use of matrix algebra in the study of population growth; in fact, the "Leslie matrix" is still widely used. May (1975) discusses more up-to-date accounts of population growth theory as well as analyses of the complex behavior that simple difference equations can exhibit. General treatments of these topics are available in most elementary books on ecology, population ecology, or population biology (see, for example, Mertz 1970; Wilson and Bossert 1971; and Poole 1974).

REFERENCES

Benton, A. H., and W. E. Werner, Jr. 1972. *Manual of Field Biology and Ecology,* 5th ed. Minneapolis: Burgess.

Brower, J. E., and J. H. Zar. 1977. *Field and Laboratory Methods for General Ecology.* Dubuque, Ia.: Wm. C. Brown.

Cox, G. W. 1976. *Laboratory Manual of General Ecology.* Dubuque, Ia.: Wm. C. Brown.

Darnell, R. M. 1971. *Organism and Environment.* San Francisco: Freeman.

Deevey, E. S., Jr. 1947. Life Tables for Natural Populations of Animals. *Qt. Rev. Biol.* **22**:283–314.

Leslie, P. H. 1945. On the Use of Matrices in Certain Population Mathematics. *Biometrika 33:* 183–212.

Leslie, P. H. 1948. Some Further Notes on the Use of Matrices in Population Mathematics. *Biometrika 35:* 213–245.

May, R. M. 1975. Biological Populations Obeying Difference Equations: Stable Points, Stable Cycles, and Chaos. *J. Theor. Biol.* **51**:511–524.

Mech, L. D. 1966. *The Wolves of Isle Royale.* Washington, D.C.: U.S. Govt. Printing Office.

Mertz, D. B. 1970. Notes on Methods Used in Life-History Studies. In J. H. Connell, D. B. Mertz, and W. W. Murdoch (eds.), *Readings in Ecology and Ecological Genetics,* pp. 4–17. New York: Harper & Row.

Poole, R. W. 1974. *An Introduction to Quantitative Ecology.* New York: McGraw-Hill.

Rolan, R. G. 1973. *Laboratory and Field Investigations in General Ecology.* New York: Macmillan.

Wilson, E. O., and W. H. Bossert. 1971. *A Primer of Population Biology.* Sunderland, Mass.: Sinauer Assoc.

Reprinted from Cold Spring Harbor Symp. Quant. Biol. **22**:1–15 (1957)

Sketches Of General and Comparative Demography

LaMont C. Cole

Department of Zoology, Cornell University, Ithaca, New York

Introduction

We are gathered here to discuss a branch of biology that can almost be described as a new field of science despite the fact that man has been studying it and writing about it for more than 3,000 years. Population study as a truly scientific discipline is new in the sense that there are large and obvious gaps in our fundamental knowledge, our concepts, and our techniques. And there are still some notable conflicts in our interpretations of the facts we do possess.

My commission for this opening session is to set the stage for the presentations that are to occur here during the next nine days, and I undertake the task well aware of the fact that some of these sessions may be illuminated by brilliant fireworks and that I run the risk, while setting the stage, of also setting off premature explosions.

I believe that the risk is worth while. The field of population studies is the branch of science that lies at the heart of the most crucial problems currently facing mankind. If we can discover no more than our actual areas of agreement and disagreement within the next few days this will have been an invaluable Symposium.

I suppose that many of our colleagues, in looking over the list of participants and subjects in this Symposium, will wonder just what it is that has brought together such a strangely assorted group of people, drawn, as we are, from the lists of anthropologists, mathematicians, zoologists, and even economists. I assume that it is part of my task to explain this phenomenon, so, before sketching modern concepts, I am going to try to trace the historical course of events that has made it meaningful at this time to assemble a group such as this.[1] My task will be easier if I suggest at the very outset that this Symposium is not as heterogeneous as our subtitle suggests, that we are not really here to discuss the two subjects of "animal ecology" and "demography" but are all here to talk about the same thing.

Terminology

My dictionary tells me that the word "population" is derived from the Latin *Populus*, meaning people. However, as everyone knows, this word has taken on a much wider meaning and I do not think that anyone is now offended by references to non-human populations. Even abstract quan-

[1] I must acknowledge indebtedness to the historical surveys of Strangeland (1904), Bonar (1931), and Pearl (1940) for much guidance in my searches of the literature on populations.

tities can form populations such as the very large population of possible bridge hands from which small samples are drawn in every game of bridge. The phrase "human population" is not to be regarded as redundant in a scientific age when our statistician colleagues feel it necessary to refer to "biological populations" in order to be specific (*e.g.* Chapman, 1954).

In another place my dictionary tells me that the word "demography" comes from the Greek *Demos* which also means people and which can be translated into *Populus*. Hence, it appears that "demography" may be synonymous with "population study". It is true that a cult of purists has tried to confine *Demos* to man and I have colleagues who would recoil with horror from the thought that anyone would speak of "epidemics" in non-human populations. But, on the other hand, biogeographers have apparently gained respectability for the term "endemic species". Very gingerly I would like to take the next step and declare that we are all demographers. Some of us study populations in general while others largely confine their attention to particular species, including man. Specialists and generalizers should both be able to profit from the opportunity to exchange ideas and concepts and information.

Population study, or demography, is a discipline young enough to permit us profitably to examine the general characteristics and phenomena that are common to all populations. If, as specialists, any of us have developed habits of thinking about populations in terms of particular factors such as predation, egg cannibalism, susceptibility to drought, monetary problems, or contraception, then the next days should enable us to broaden our perspective by illuminating our problems with the light of "comparative demography". This, incidentally, is the original form of the term introduced by Guilliard in 1855 and which is now commonly shortened to plain "demography".

In introducing the Symposium on Quantitative Biology two years ago Professor Dobzhansky (1955) found it necessary to define what was meant by the word population and I believe that this year also we shall have need of a working definition. The abstract populations of the mathematician are too generalized for our purposes and Dobzhansky's "Mendelian population", which is composed of individuals sharing a common gene pool, is not general enough, since this definition would exclude asexual and parthenogenetic forms from the population concept. Perhaps each of us will have to give our own definition but I propose, in this contribution, to use the word "population" for *a biological unit at the level of ecological integration where it is meaningful to speak of a birth rate, a death rate, a sex ratio, and an age structure in describing the properties of the unit.* This definition excludes the fortuitous aggregations of animals, which may have supraorganismic properties and advantages in natural selection, but which do not have meaningful birth rates and death rates, and it excludes also the so-called "interspecies populations" which must be treated quite differently by the ecological theorist and which I, therefore, regard as a higher level of integration. I leave open the question of whether or not there is such a thing as "the human population of the world"

HISTORICAL SKETCH

Although demography can be regarded as a branch of general biology it must be admitted that its historical development up until very recent times has been largely the work of human demographers. It seems certain that early man must have counted at least his domestic animals and have thought about ways of regulating their numbers, but whatever records may have been made of such endeavors are not available. The history of population studies prior to the twentieth century could be written almost without reference to non-human populations.

With respect to techniques for population measurement, the ancient Egyptians and Babylonians may have conducted some sort of a census, and King David counted the Israelites in approximately 1000 B.C. The Greek city-states seem to have known the sizes of their populations and the Romans were worried by unfavorable census returns before the birth of Julius Caesar. We learn from Marco Polo that by 1277 A.D. the Chinese registered vital statistics and population movements by a system that would seemingly be a credit to a modern nation. Then there is a long gap, and the modern practice of making periodic complete censuses of national populations only began in Canada in 1666 and, as is well known, this movement has not yet extended to all countries of the world.

Quantitative work on non-human populations came much later in the history of demography. In 1816 the Arctic explorer William Scoresby (1820) constructed a sampler for collecting water from the depths of the sea and this sampler incidentally collected plankton organisms. Scoresby was impressed by the numbers of these organisms and attempted numerical estimates. He published a drawing of what is clearly a calanoid copepod which he identified as the food resource of the whale population and he tried to estimate the magnitude of this resource. In the literature there are doubtless other scattered instances of population estimates made before the 1890s when Petersen and his school of Danish oceanographers began the systematic sampling of marine populations and made attempts to estimate the sizes of fish populations. It is, however, only within the twentieth century, with the rise of statistical thought and the blossoming of statistical techniques for interpreting the results of sampling, that any considerable body of information about the sizes of natural populations has been accumulated.

With respect to the conceptual side of demography, Plato, and probably Solon before him, had a definite concept of an optimum population size and an understanding of factors regulating population size. Population growth could be stimulated by compulsory and early marriages and by rewards for high fertility, while overpopulation could be prevented by abortion, infanticide, and, as last resorts, celibacy and emigration. From the time of these Greek philosophers 2000 years had to elapse before the literature of demography began to show any important advances in the major concepts of populations and the factors regulating them.

The Roman attitude toward population was dominated by the need to breed soldiers for their armies of conquest and it was axiomatic with them that this could be done by stimulating the birth rate. Julius Caesar arranged fines for bachelors and even prohibited childless women from wearing jewelry. These seemingly foolproof schemes, however, did not work, and Augustus and later emperors continued, also without notable success, to try to stimulate population growth by law. All aggressive nations since Rome have made similar attempts with patent lack of success. In 1767 Dr. Adam Ferguson ridiculed the statesman who claimed that he had succeeded in stimulating population growth by likening him to " . . . the fly in the fable, who admired its success in turning wheels and in moving carriages: he has only accomplished what was already in motion; he has dashed with his oar to hasten the cataract; and waved with his fan to give speed to the winds".

Yet even today modern nations are trying to stimulate the growth of their populations for one avowed purpose or another and they are encountering the same inertia felt by Caesar and alluded to by Ferguson. This inertia, it should be added, has for the last hundred years been frustrating man's efforts to improve fishing and hunting by operating hatcheries for fishes and game birds. These facts I interpret to mean that population study, as a scientific discipline concerned with some of man's most pressing problems, has not yet succeeded in gaining proper recognition.

The generalizations of the Athenians, attributing population regulation to the balance between fertility and immigration on the one hand, and, on the other, mortality and emigration due to wars and pestilence, and relative sterility due to social conditions, were not superseded by any other conceptual scheme for twenty centuries. Then, in his book on "The Greatness of Cities", first published in the year 1588, the Italian Giovanni Botero (1588) clearly enunciated a distinctly different concept of population regulation. Mankind, he concluded, was potentially as fertile in his day as in ancient times but populations did not grow because the resources of the environment were insufficient to support larger populations. He realized that one man and one woman could in 3,000 years have become the ancestors of more people than then existed and he considered that the human population of the world had rapidly grown to a maximum and then ceased to grow despite the fact that generative powers had not decreased. Population growth was halted, sometimes by famine, sometimes by contagious diseases abetted by crowding, and sometimes by wars, earthquakes, floods, and other accidents, but, generally, the basic limitation was that "the fruits of the earth do not suffice to feed a greater number".

Here, two centuries before Malthus, we find the concept of a population potentially capable of geometric (multiplicative) growth but actually restrained from growing by the finite carrying capacity of its environment. We also find a discussion of the effects of increased population density in increasing mortality by contagion and by aggressive behavior, in this case expressing itself in piracy, vandalism, and warfare. In terms of broad concepts of population regulation how little has been added since Botero's day!

A series of successors to Botero spoke of the limitation of population growth by the finite carrying capacity of the environment. For example, Sir Walter Raleigh (1650) noted that Spain could send large numbers of men to wars and to colonies without altering the size of the parent population and he reasoned that this must be because the size of the population in Spain was adjusted to what the country "can well nourish". Some 190 years later Malthus (1798) considered himself original in recognizing "a persistent force resisting depopulation". And it was not until his second edition, which appeared five years after the original, that Malthus caught up with Raleigh, who had recognized moral restraint and "artificial sterility" as possible forces resisting overpopulation, in addition to the miseries of hunger, pestilence, crime, and war which dominated the first edition of the essay on population.

The analytical side of demography, which was developed largely for actuarial purposes, is also characterized by a long gap between ancient and modern times, and in some ways this hiatus is even more curious than the long one in conceptual schemes between Plato and Botero. The Romans sold annuities and set values on lifetime rentals. A table attributed to Ulpian in the third century A.D. clearly recognizes that an elderly person should pay less for an annuity than a younger one. This principle, however, is apparently not self-evident because it eluded both Isaac Newton

(1686) and the English government, which, in 1692, was trying to raise spending money by selling life annuities at a fixed rate independent of the age of the purchaser.

If Newton failed to grasp the basic concept that life expectancy is a function of age, there were, however, predecessors and contemporaries of his who understood this very well. John Graunt's (1662) table of mortality, listing both the number of deaths and the number of survivors by decades for a cohort of 100 persons, appeared in 1662 and was read and appreciated in that same year by Christiaan Huygens (1662). Graunt's contribution entitles him to be recognized as the father of demography, if we follow the usual definition of demography as the statistical study of populations.

Graunt had some conception of the relationship between a frequency distribution and the probability of the occurrence of an event. This appears, for example, in his offer to insure any sane man at 1000 to 1 against dying as a lunatic in Bedlam within seven years, "because", he says, "I find that not above one in about one thousand five hundred have done so".

Graunt obviously recognized that for a proper analysis of vital statistics one should know the size of the population he is studying and should have a classification of the deaths and of the living population members by age and sex. However, there were no reliable census data for London and the bills of mortality did not specify the age of the deceased. Graunt complained of these deficiencies (p. 20) and tried to estimate age-specific death rates indirectly by computation (p. 84). Life tables of a more modern type, that is to say, based on the frequency distribution of age at death, were drawn up by De Witt in Holland sometime before his death in 1672 and by Halley in England in 1693, but even in these cases no accurate census data were available.

Although Graunt seems to have possessed considerable statistical intuition he apparently knew nothing of formal probability theory. The calculations of Huygens in 1669, based on Graunt's work, seem to represent the earliest application of relatively sophisticated probability theory to problems of demographic interest such as the computation of the "probable lifetime" remaining for a person of known age.

Although Botero and other scholars had implied that populations grow geometrically, that is by successive doublings in successive equal time intervals, Graunt went a step farther and estimated the potential rate of population growth. He concludes (pp. 85–86) that the population of London could double in sixty-four years without immigration and he points out that at this rate Adam and Eve could, in the 5610 years of the age of the earth, have given rise to a population much larger than the actual one. In 1677 Hale concluded that population could double in thirty-five years but that at this rate it would long before have exceeded the means of subsistence. He attributed population limitation to famine, disease, war, and accidents such as floods and earthquakes.

I shall not here dwell upon the subsequent crude attempts of Sir William Petty to compute rates of population doubling or upon subsequent refinements of census methods and life tables. Graunt had initiated the empirical study of vital statistics, had shown the need for census data and better statistical reporting, and had estimated the geometric rate of population increase. Huygens had shown that formal mathematics and probability theory could be applied to such studies. Three-quarters of a century earlier Botero had concluded that the capacity of the environment to support population is finite. The works of Graunt, and Petty, and Botero all went through several editions and must have been widely known, yet their essential elements of interest to us would appear very novel when they came from the pen of Malthus more than a century later.

Thus, many essentials of human demography were established before the beginning of the eighteenth century but the principles had not been generalized to other species. Perhaps the first comparative demographer, the first man to anticipate the subject matter of this Symposium, was the Reverend William Derham (1713) whose "Physico-theology" was first published in 1713. In this pious age Derham was one of those intent on proving that all acts of outrageous fortune are really demonstrations of a Divine Wisdom, yet the ninth and tenth chapters of his book seem to entitle him to a place in the history of ecology. He asserts that the various species of animals differ in their organs and ways of life because "the surface of the . . . globe is covered with different soils, with hills and vales, with seas, rivers, lakes, and ponds, with divers trees and plants, in the several places"; and that the various species of animals are "manifestly adapted" for the places in which they live and for the ways in which they live.

Further than this: "The whole surface of our globe can afford room and support only to such a number of all sorts of creatures. And if by their doubling, trebling, or any other multiplication of their kind, they should increase to double or treble that number, they must starve, or devour one another". This is prevented by "*balancing the number of individuals* (his italics) of each species of creatures, in that place appointed thereto".

This balance of numbers, Derham concludes, is kept even because the length of life in each species is adjusted to its ability to increase. "Voracious beasts and birds" have long lives but their rate of increase is small so that they do not "overstock the world", while insects exemplify animals with great reproductive ability but short lives. He cites Graunt's table and presents a table of his own compiled to give the ratios of marriages to births and of births to burials in various parts

of Europe. Human longevity, like that of other animals, he believed, is adjusted to the available space. From the creation to Noah's time the world was underpopulated and a man might live 900 years. Then, when the world was depopulated by the flood, each species of animal doubled at its natural rate and restocked the earth. Soon after the time of Abraham, human longevity had been reduced to the prevailing sixty or seventy years at which level "life and death keep an equal pace", and other species had also ceased to double. There is nothing mechanistic and no notion of natural regulation in Derham's argument which attributes everything to the wisdom of a Divine Providence, but the fundamentals of comparative demography are there.

Graunt and Derham were the pioneers who charted the course for Buffon and Malthus. After Derham much of the remainder of the eighteenth century was marked by the development of techniques which are now used by demographers; in particular by the work of Süssmilch on the vital statistics of human populations and by the work of DeMoivre on probability theory. Linnaeus (1740? 1743?)[2] and Benjamin Franklin (1751) recognized that even plant populations are potentially capable of growth by geometric progression and DeMoivre (1724) apparently became the first to try to fit a mathematical formula to mortality data when he proposed that human survivorship after the age of twelve could be assumed to decrease in arithmetic progression.

In the latter half of the eighteenth century we encounter Buffon (1756, 1758) on comparative demography and Malthus (1798) on human demography. Malthus, so far as I can discover, said nothing of importance to demographers that had not been said before but he is important for having brought the questions to general attention. He was noticed because of the circumstances of the time in which he wrote—a time when England was worrying about overpopulation, while Prime Minister Pitt was studying proposals for increasing the birth rate.

Buffon was listened to because of the great weight of his prestige and the popularity of his encyclopedic treatise on natural history. He also deserves to be regarded as the intellectual ancestor of this Symposium. He considered that populations of man, of other animals, and of plants are subject to the same types of control by a balance of physical forces. "An unbounded fertility of every species" is counter-balanced "by the innumerable causes of destruction which are perpetually reducing the produce of that fecundity . . . so as to preserve nearly the same number of individuals in each species". This, however, is not a fixed number, so populations oscillate in

[2] Thompson (1942) gives the date 1740 for this interesting essay of Linnaeus and this is also the date given on the English translation by F. J. Brand in the British Museum. I have not seen the first Latin edition but the second and later editions date this essay 1743.

size between limits. An excess of fecundity in one year is followed by relative sterility in the next. If this were not the case the fruits of the earth would be decimated. Some insects, for example, produce several generations per year and so are potentially capable of multiplying more than their food plants, which have only one generation per year.

Buffon disagreed with Aristotle's contention that heavy rains cause the decline of populations of field mice and he leaned toward control by biological agents. "Contagion", he says, is "a necessary consequence of too great a mass of living matter assembled in one place". Intraspecific strife he recognized in reference to the ". . . field mice, whose prodigious increase is checked solely by their cruelties to each other when provisions become scarce". But first place among controlling factors he attributed to predation. Of rabbits, he says that ". . . if it were not for dogs and ferrets, they would reduce the country to a desert". He regarded predation as necessary and beneficial both to predator and prey populations as evidenced by his account of the herring (1758, p. 6), which, he says:

"present themselves in millions to our fishermen, and after having fed all the monsters of the northern seas, they contribute to the subsistance of all the nations in Europe for a certain part of the year. If prodigious numbers of them were not destroyed, what would be the effects of their prodigious multiplication? By them alone would the whole surface of the sea be covered. But their numbers would soon prove a nuisance; they would corrupt and destroy each other. For want of sufficient nourishment their fecundity would diminish; by contagion and famine they would be equally destroyed; the number of their own species would not increase, but the number of those that feed upon them would be diminished. As this remark is alike applicable to any other species, so it is necessary they should prey upon each other . . . "

Buffon was a skilled mathematician and was familiar with probability theory[3] but he did not attempt to deal with population phenomena quantitatively. His understanding of population regulation as a general organic phenomenon, however, was distinctly modern.

In the nineteenth century, interest in population phenomena ran high as a result of the controversy stirred up by Malthus. There is not time here to review this controversy, which is not yet dead, so we shall note only some selected contributions to the development of general demography. This was the century in which mathematical statistics was maturing under the tutelage of Laplace and Gauss, and in which it was applied to demographic problems by DeMorgan (1838). In 1825, almost exactly a century after DeMoivre, Gompertz (1825) made the next significant at-

[3] His scheme for measuring the value of π experimentally by tossing a needle of known length onto a ruled surface and counting the times that the needle crosses a line is the prototype of the "Monte Carlo Method" which assumed importance in modern physics during World War II.

tempt to find a mathematical formula that would express a law of mortality. The Gompertz curve was derived from the postulate that the ability of individuals to resist destruction decreases as a geometric progression with age, and this curve still finds uses in population studies.

In 1835 Quetelet (1835) became perhaps the first biometrician. He proposed that population growth is regulated by the balance between a potential ability to grow by geometric progression and a resistance to population growth which increases as the square of the rate of growth. A century later the term "environmental resistance" was brought into general ecological use through the work of Chapman (1928, 1931) and it is my present feeling that this concept may have had an unfortunate influence. A population growing according to Quetelet's postulates would eventually attain a "terminal velocity" of growth, but growth would never cease; inhibition rather than resistance must enter into models of population growth.

In 1838 Quetelet's student and colleague Verhulst (1838) derived the logistic equation as a model for population growth and this equation still occupies a prominent position in population theory. Thirty years later, with the work of Galton (1869), biometry became a self-conscious field which grew rapidly during the remainder of the nineteenth century, culminating in the work of Karl Pearson and his associates, and with the first publication of Biometrika in 1901.

Meanwhile, other developments essential to modern demography were taking place. The study of vital statistics was taking on a modern form in the hands of William Farr who in 1843 reached the conclusion that human mortality in English towns increases as the sixth root of the population density; Darwin (1859), stimulated by Malthus, had found in the mortality necessary to regulate population growth the mechanism of evolution; and Mendel (1866) had accomplished the unparalleled scientific achievement of inferring a scientific law with a probabilistic basis from numerical data.

Early in the twentieth century, as everyone knows, much of science underwent a complete revolution. It has often been said, probably correctly, that the revolution in the physical sciences was made possible because pure mathematicians had been laboring for years out of sheer curiosity to develop systems that seemed to be of no practical significance. When the conceptual side of physics reached the point where it could use them, the physicists found the non-Euclidean geometries of Lobachewsky and Riemann and the invariance principle of Cayley, among others, developed and ready for their use.

The early twentieth century revolution in science extended to demography. Perhaps no development here is more significant than the technique of moving populations into the laboratory where they can be studied under controlled, or at least specifiable, conditions. For this innovation demographers are, I believe, more than to anyone else, indebted to Raymond Pearl. The powerful tools of modern mathematical analysis were also brought to bear on our subject and in this connection we think of Alfred J. Lotka and Vito Volterra.

At this point I shall discreetly stop mentioning names. Without the leverage provided by perspective it is hard to tell just where we are or what is important and I have no desire to set off explosions by my sins either of omission or commission.

However, here at the end of this historical sketch I wonder if there may not exist somewhere the tools to initiate a new era in demography. Modern analysis has been applied to the theory of our subject and we no longer retreat from differential equations, matrices, and stochastic processes. High speed computing machines have entered the picture and, in their tedious, moronic way, they are solving in hours problems that would take a man a lifetime of computing. Perhaps, though, the analytical techniques that demographers really need to bring the subject to maturity have been developed in some obscure place. I know that I am not the only one among those present who has gone back to nearly forgotten literature to study the calculus of finite differences in the hope that this neglected branch of mathematics would answer our needs. It is even possible, I believe, that ours is the field of science that awaits important discoveries in what has been called "the last great unexplored continent of mathematics"; namely, the theory of numbers. At least, enough of the problems that have interested me are recognizable as problems in the composition and partition of numbers to lead me to offer this suggestion.

In any case, here we are, past the middle of the twentieth century, and mankind is still engaged in demographic controversies, many of which would be appropriate to the time of Malthus. We live at a time when Asiatic countries are just beginning to give serious thought to ways of relieving their problems of overpopulation and excessive birth and death rates, while some Latin American statesmen are boasting of the prospect that their populations may catch up with those of Asia. Proposals for regulating human populations are, as usual, opposed by an influential group of persons who maintain that human misery is part of a grand plan which must not be obstructed, and they are now joined by a new group composed of visionary physical scientists who can see man sending his armies of conquest throughout the universe.

Ours is the most irresponsible era in history when it comes to the poisoning of environments, and our policies with respect to pests and game animals sometimes still leave much to be desired from the standpoint of the demographer. The operation of hatcheries seems to be based on the implicit assumption that game birds and fishes lack adequate fertility, while our programs of trapping, and poisoning, and hunting various allegedly noxious species seem to be singularly uninfluenced by demographic considerations. We spend money to destroy predatory animals and more money to destroy herbivores of types which were formerly eaten by those very predators, and we usually do this without inquiring as to whether such destruction, by carnivores or by man, will actually exercise control of population size.

Yet, we have at our disposal the tools to deal with population problems more intelligently and effectively than has ever been possible in the past. Many population phenomena can now be studied in the laboratory employing species that go through many generations in the time required for a single generation of those forms that interest us in nature. Laboratory forms are available with very simple life histories or with very complex patterns of reproduction and survival, so that laboratory studies can have general validity. For field studies we have methods of collecting vital statistics and conducting censuses, such as the "mark and recapture" methods, which are developments of this century. And we have the potentiality for fruitful collaboration among the demographers working in the experimental laboratory, in the field, and in theory.

No demographer should make the mistake of disparaging any of these three basic approaches to knowledge of his subject. Our ultimate purpose, of course, is to understand population phenomena in nature, that is, in the field, but there are very real possibilities for dissecting the complex situations encountered in field studies into simpler components that can be studied experimentally in the laboratory. The phenomena observed in the field and laboratory determine the postulates that go into theoretical studies and, when the postulates can be realistically defined, the analytical methods of the theorist can often move rapidly ahead suggesting new experiments and new observations to be made in the field. Theoretical models of populations and actual populations will behave alike when the correct postulates are put into the model. It is, therefore, a matter of the utmost importance to compare the results of empirical and theoretical studies.

When theory and observation fail to agree it is usually assumed that some postulate of the theory is wrong either because the field or laboratory observations suggested incorrect assumptions or because the theorist resorted to oversimplification for the sake of ease in handling. This indictment, if we can call it that, is usually justified, although the observation may be important in showing what simplifications must be avoided, but there is an alternative possibility that should not be overlooked. Populations are statistical entities, and biological populations are always finite and quite limited in size. Two actual populations governed by the same statistical "laws" need not follow identical paths, for approximately the same reasons that no two bridge tournaments come out alike. The deductive method of predicting the course of a particular population from general theory may be more often correct than the method of analogy in which one uses a knowledge of the history of one particular population to predict the fate of another.

SKETCHES OF QUANTITATIVE DEMOGRAPHY

Comparative Life Histories

It has been obvious, at least since the time of Derham, that the more fertile species must suffer greater mortality than less fertile species because, otherwise, they would quickly overflow the earth. No individual organism is immortal so there is one death corresponding to each birth. But it is not always easy to draw up a balance sheet of births and deaths when populations are changing in size and moving in space, and when life histories are complicated.

Many species of animals are semelparous, that is, they reproduce once in a lifetime as do annual plants. Since succeeding generations do not overlap in these species it is easy to evaluate their potential rate of population growth. In the iteroparous species, those that reproduce more than once per lifetime, matters become more complicated and a population may consist of a mixture of many generations.

It is, however, possible to take any combination of life history features and compute how rapidly a population would grow if these features did not change with time (see review by Cole, 1954). It turns out that any pattern whatsoever of life history features which is consistent with growth will eventually lead to a rate of population growth such that population size (N_t) at any time (t) can be adequately represented by the equation of exponential growth:[4]

$$N_t = N_0 e^{\rho t}$$

where N_0 is the initial population size and where the constant exponent (or "compound interest rate"), ρ, is a parameter with various names, the most common of which is "the intrinsic rate of natural increase". Since e^ρ is a constant this equation can be regarded as the formula for a geometric progression, showing that the pioneers who spoke of geometric growth were on the right track, and we can make a case for speaking of the rate of population doubling by writing 2^{ct} for $e^{\rho t}$.

This formula for exponential growth implies that all populations of a particular species would follow identical growth curves and would be immune to accidents. This is what we want to imply when we are trying to appraise the maximum potentiality of a species or to compare the relative merits of two life history patterns. The exponential (or "geometric") form of potential population growth can, however, be derived under much more general assumptions (cf. Skellam, 1955). In a stochastic model where each individual is allowed a finite probability of dying without reproducing and where litter size is allowed to vary at random, the exponential formula will still describe the *most probable* course of population growth, or the *average* size at a given time of a large number of initially similar populations.

It is obvious that in order for a species to survive, its life history features must provide for a sufficient reproductive potential to maintain population size and provide a margin of safety adequate to cope with all exigencies that are encountered. Probably the number of species that have escaped extinction to the present time is but a small fraction of the number that has existed during the earth's history[5] and we reason, accordingly, that the ability to support population growth is subject to natural selection. Species that have to surmount drastic obstacles to population replacement must have the potential for high intrinsic rates of natural increase, and selection will favor these high rates even at the expense of efficiency in other respects. Gametes contain energy and protein, and an increased production of gametes can only be obtained at the expense of increasing nutritional requirements, that is, by reducing the efficiency with which food is utilized for promoting individual survival.

For this and other reasons selection pressure would necessarily work against the production of a wasteful profusion of gametes or offspring. Evidence that natural selection has not pushed reproductive potentials to their attainable extremes is provided by domestic and laboratory animals where artificial selection is effective in increasing fertility. It has been noted, however (Smith, 1954), that this "gain" is purchased at the expense of other traits that would be important for survival in nature.

Continuing in this vein, we conclude that the normal maximum value of the intrinsic rate of natural increase found in a species can be considered to measure an adaptive characteristic which should perhaps be identified with what Chapman (1928) called "biotic potential" and which he defined as "the inherent property of an organism . . . to increase in numbers".

It is necessary to emphasize that the biotic potential or maximum intrinsic rate of increase is here regarded as a species characteristic depending on the capabilities of the organisms but not on the characteristics of any particular environment to which a specific group happens to be exposed at any particular time. For this parameter it is correct to say that the housefly, *Musca domestica*,

---

[4] Strictly, of course, any enumerable population can only assume integral values. However, one could argue that a nearly mature individual should count for a fraction more than a new-born individual since the former is nearer to multiplication. For all practical purposes the argument is irrelevant.

[5] According to the "guesses" by Simpson (1952), the number of living species is on the order of 2 million and the number of extinct species is on the order of 500 million.

has a higher biotic potential than does the African elephant, *Elephas africanus.* This figure tells us how rapidly a population could grow in an optimal environment of infinite extent but not how rapidly a given population is actually growing. The latter value is most commonly zero for both elephants and houseflies. The concept referred to by Andrewartha and Birch (1954) as the "innate capacity for increase" seemingly tries to embrace both meanings but I find it advantageous to distinguish between prevailing and maximum potential growth rates.

There are a number of ways in which natural selection might alter the life history of a species to increase biotic potential. Larger litters of young, closer spacing of litters in time, earlier maturation, increased survivorship until the end of reproductive life, and biasing of the sex-ratio in favor of females would all be effective. The potential effectiveness of a change in a particular life history feature, however, depends upon the pattern of other features already present in the species. Species that reach maturity early can gain more from increasing litter size than from living longer and producing more litters, and the increase will be greatest where the initial litter size is small. The relative importance of these two factors may be altered in species that mature slowly and here it may be more advantageous to live longer and produce more litters than to increase litter size (Cole, 1954).

Life history changes that involve a biasing of the sex-ratio are peculiar in their evolutionary advantages and in the payment exacted for these advantages. Shifting to an excess of females in a species with biparental inheritance will obviously raise biotic potential but it may decrease the probability that females will find mates and it makes population survival dependent on the persistence of a minority group which may become liable to accidental extinction. An answer to this problem can be found in asexual reproduction or parthenogenesis which makes males unnecessary and at the same time improves the possibilities for dispersal, since only one individual is required to start a new population. But for this the species must pay what appears to be a high price in the currency of survival, namely, the reduction of genetic recombinations.

Corals, cladocerans, and aphids, among others, appear to do very well by retaining the abilities for both uniparental and biparental reproduction, and from the demographic standpoint this is an admirable arrangement which permits rapid population growth under favorable circumstances without sacrificing all of the advantages afforded to the species by sexual reproduction.

From the evolutionary standpoint the biotic potential of a species is of particular interest and it is easy enough to compute the value of ρ when we have enough information to estimate the age at which females first reproduce, the rapidity with which they can produce successive litters, the sizes of the litters, and the length of time for which the females retain the potentiality for reproduction. The sex-ratio can usually be ignored on the grounds that the male portion of the population will be "carried along" parallel to the number of females. ρ can be used as a basis for comparing the potentials of different species (*e.g.* Smith, 1954) and for lending support to such general conclusions as that there is a tendency for small organisms to have higher biotic potentials than larger forms, and that species where the young face exceptional hazards to their establishment have evolved very high biotic potentials. For example, it would not take many generations of oysters or tapeworms to overflow the earth if all could survive.

The concept of the intrinsic rate of increase has a wider utility if, instead of confining it to the measurement of a species characteristic, we extend it to individual populations. When this is done the exponential rate becomes a statistic, which is usually designated as r, and its value depends upon the prevailing age-schedule of fertility and survival. It can be positive or negative and can fluctuate in time, in fact it can assume any value from $-\infty$ to ρ. To compute its value we need the empirical data to construct a life table and an age schedule of fertility; that is, for each interval of age we need to know the probability that a female will be alive and the mean number of female offspring produced per female.

When used in this way the intrinsic rate of increase can become a measure of the difference between two populations of the same species growing under different conditions (see especially Birch, 1948; Andrewartha and Birch, 1954). It becomes an indicator of the suitability of an environment and gives some insight into the relationships between populations and their environments. When r is negative the population will decrease, and it will become extinct if this condition continues.

We can express every possible influence of any environmental factor in terms of its effect on the probability of survival and on age-specific fertility, and any change in either of these is reflected in the value of r. In a climatic region that is, say, entirely too cold for a given species the probability of a female surviving to reproductive age is zero and the species does not occur except perhaps as a temporary immigrant. In a slightly less harsh environment there may be some years or sequences of years when there is a positive probability of females surviving and reproducing, and some may do so. In this region the species is sometimes present and sometimes absent. In this or a slightly more favorable environment r may be positive in some years and negative in others so that, once the species establishes itself locally, the population will alternately increase and decrease. There may be "sanctuaries" within the region where some representatives of the species will always persist, or there may be repeated immigration from outside to provide a population nucleus. Under these conditions we derive a picture of a safely established source of new individuals regularly sending excess individuals as emigrants into marginal environments where they can sometimes, but not always, persist and multiply; into sub-marginal environments where they occasionally persist temporarily; and into intolerable environments. This, I hope, is a fair summary of the gist of the comprehensive theory of the distribution and abundance of organisms which has been developed in detail by Andrewartha and Birch (1954).

Population Regulation

The theory just described gives the appearance of clashing with some widely held concepts of the control or regulation of population size, and we cannot avoid the necessity for examining the reality of this conflict. Some of the troublesome differences are obviously of semantic origin and I think we can best avoid semantic pitfalls if we approach this subject in a formal manner.

We have already indicated that the equation of exponential growth, $N_t = N_0 e^{rt}$, is applicable to the population growth of any species, whatever its life history pattern may be. Then, if the length of time between successive generations is T, the population will grow in each generation by a factor e^{rT}, which is called the "net reproductive rate", R_0. This "rate" can be defined as the ratio of female births in two successive generations, say generation x and generation $x + 1$. In terms of discrete units, if the population increases by a factor R in each generation, we have:

$$N_{x+1} = RN_x.$$

Now, if R is a constant, this equation gives:

$$N_x = N_0 R^x$$

from which it is apparent that the value of the constant must be very precisely unity. If it was as large as 1.01 a "population" of a single individual weighing one gram would grow to equal the mass of the earth in 6200 generations. Any constant value of R less than unity would lead to the rapid extinction of any existing population.

It would, of course, be hopelessly unrealistic to believe that populations are so precisely regulated and immune to accidents that the net reproductive rate could always be precisely unity. A second thought on the matter might lead us to suggest a stochastic approach; perhaps R has an expected value of unity but is subject to fluctuations about this mean value. Perhaps it exceeds unity in favorable years and is less than unity in unfavorable years. Models like this are now classical in probability theory (Feller, 1950). In the simplest case the population is regarded as "playing a game" where, in each generation, it has equal probability of gaining or losing capital .to an "infinitely rich opponent". If one feels intuitively

that under these conditions the population will merely show moderate fluctuations about a mean value he will be surprised by the dizzy heights to which such a population is likely to soar. The game may have a very long expected duration but the final outcome is certain; the population will "random walk" itself to exhaustion and become extinct.

Now, this is not the way actual populations behave. As has often been noted, small populations and rare species are much more frequent than large populations and common species, but extinctions seem to be rare events and populations exhibit much greater stability than appears to be consistent with random-walk processes. Exchanges of status between rare species and common species are almost always identifiable with observable environmental changes, and repeated reversals of status seem to be excessively rare.

All of this leads us to conclude that populations must possess some autoregulatory mechanism which tends to raise the net reproductive rate above unity before a declining population reaches zero and which halts excessive population increase by reducing the net reproductive rate. The intrinsic rate of increase r differs from the biotic potential ρ in some systematic way. We might write something like:

$$N_{x+1} = RN_x g(x)$$

where $g(x)$ represents a "governor" or controlling influence which must be something more than a random variable.

Continuing for a moment in this abstract vein, what kinds of governors could be attached to populations? Several types are theoretically possible. For example, $g(x)$ might be a function of time alone. Here, a young population would have a high net reproductive rate which would decline with age. In the history of biology there have been put forth doctrines of "racial senescence" but, to the best of my knowledge, no one today gives serious thought to such oversimplified systems; there is too much evidence that populations that have ceased growing can be made to grow again by altering something in the environment.

As a next thought we might assume, $g(x) = f(N)$, the ability of a population to increase is a function only of population size. Something like this, I believe, is often implied when we speak of populations as "self-regulating systems", but this is obviously a tremendous oversimplification. Similar populations placed in different environments cannot be expected to grow alike or to reach the same steady-state size. The simplest model worthy of consideration is $g(x) = f(N, E)$ where the governor is a function of both population size and environment, which we here understand to refer to everything except population size.

The governing function will be zero in an intolerable environment and can climb to unity in an optimum environment, provided that its dependence on population size is such that this is possible. We know that in very crowded populations there are deleterious effects that may cause the governing function to approach zero no matter how favorable other conditions may be. There are limits to the extent to which we can crowd any population even with all of the tender care that is possible in the laboratory.

For analytical purposes it is desirable to find some one expression that will contain both the effects of population size and environmental limitations. The most obvious procedure is to make use of the concept of carrying capacity which, as we have seen, has been recognized since the time of Botero. If carrying capacity is defined as the maximum population (N_{max}) that can be supported in a given habitat, then we have in the expression

$$\left[1 - \frac{N_x}{N_{max}}\right]$$

a possible governing factor that will be essentially unity when N_x is very small and which will drop to zero when the carrying capacity is attained. This is the way in which we might postulate that population increase should behave, so we might write for the change in population size per generation:[6]

$$\Delta N = RN_x\left[1 - \frac{N_x}{N_{max}}\right].$$

The equation is intractable in this form but the corresponding continuous case must give a good approximation, and this differential equation is easily solved. It is, in fact, the logistic equation of Verhulst and, in its modern applications, of Pearl and Reed (1920).

I do not here wish to discuss either the merits or the faults of the logistic curve as a model of population growth. The point that I do consider important in the present context is that the governing term,

$$\left[1 - \frac{N_x}{N_{max}}\right],$$

is commonly referred to as "population density" when it really represents the proportion of the "occupiable spaces" which are still unoccupied in the particular environment (cf. Slobodkin, 1953). "Density", in this sense, is not number of organisms per unit area or volume but is the difference between this actual density and that which would prevail at carrying capacity. The concept includes both the effects of crowding as a governing factor, which have been stressed so particularly by Nicholson (1933

[6] This is equivalent to writing:

$$g(x) = 1 - \frac{N_x}{N_{max}} + \frac{1}{R}$$

and later), and the effects of environmental inadequacies.

Here, in my opinion, we have the crux of many of our recent controversies. Two populations of identical size occupying equal areas can differ in this type of "density", and an unvarying population can change in density when the weather changes. If this governing term which is appropriate to the logistic theory, or some generalization of it (cf. Slobodkin, 1953a), is an appropriate type of governor to be considered in population theory—and it seems to me highly probable that it is—then population size can, in general, be under the influence of any factor that affects the number of individuals directly or that affects carrying capacity.

Now, there seems to be nothing in this scheme that would imply that populations cannot be regulated by climatic factors, and I suspect that the population students who are supposed to hold such a view have been misunderstood by both opponents and supporters. Thus, we read in Nicholson (1933, p. 172) that: "The distribution and densities of all animals are ultimately dependent upon the physical environment". This dependence, however, is indirect. All animals ultimately depend upon plants for food and "the physical environment ultimately limits the distribution of all plants". "Physical factors that are uninfluenced by the densities of animals cannot directly determine those densities" but (p. 173) "competition forces the surplus animals into unsuitable portions of the environment, where they are destroyed by the physical factors".

Nicholson's usage of the word "competition" has been the subject of much criticism (cf. Thompson, 1939; Birch, 1957), but that is a question of semantics, as is the question of whether population regulation by physical factors is "direct" or "indirect". The above statements and more recent views (Nicholson, 1954) do not seem to justify the interpretations of more casual students of population dynamics who suggest that populations would "increase without limit" if it were not for the "action of enemies". Similarly, H. S. Smith (1935), who introduced the term "density dependent", recognized the fact that physical factors can operate in a "density dependent" manner because excess individuals are forced out of the "more or less limited number" of "protective niches in the environment". Incidentally, there is much persuasive evidence that a great deal of predation operates in this same way (cf. Errington, 1946), and one may be justified in wondering if the distinction between density dependent and density independent factors is not a potential source of confusion.

Whatever view we may hold regarding the terminology of regulatory factors, it is clear that in a given environment of constant carrying capacity the governing factors must, at some level, exert greater restraint on a dense population than is exerted on some less dense population which is still able to grow. It is equally clear that the simple linear relationship between intensity of regulation and population density, which is implied by the logistic formula, is too simplified to be generally valid. The late W. C. Allee devoted a large part of a productive scientific career to collecting examples of underpopulation effects to match the better-known deleterious effects of overpopulation (Allee, 1951; Allee *et al.*, 1949, Chap. 23) and he has conclusively shown that it is a widespread phenomenon for very small populations to be suboptimal for survival and growth.

Small populations lack genetic variability, and hence adaptability, and this may be aggravated by inbreeding. They face an increased risk of random extinction and of failure of the sexes to meet, and there is often a need for "unconscious cooperation" among the individuals in some sort of "conditioning" of the environment. Hence, any analytical formula which is capable of representing what I have here been calling the governing function must be capable of assuming a minimum value at some population density greater than zero (*i.e.* $Rg(x)$ must be able to have at least one inflection point which is a maximum). Some interesting results, including the prediction of oscillations in population size under certain conditions, have already been obtained by Ricker (1954) who has examined the consequences of "reproduction curves" of this general shape without, however, attempting to give analytical form to the functions studied.

Any suitable function will necessarily require the formula describing population growth to contain at least one more constant than is present in the logistic formula. But one of the persistent criticisms of the logistic (Feller, 1939; Smith, 1952) has been aimed at its versatility which provides the fitter of empirical curves with three arbitrary constants to be manipulated. Provide him with more than this, and the versatility will be further increased so that the formula will tend to become a mere "graduating" formula that will fit many sets of data but defy any meaningful interpretation.

The answer to this dilemma, I believe, is to be found in collaboration between the theorist and those working in the field and laboratories. Some of the biological parameters must be estimated directly so that they do not enter the growth formula as arbitrary constants.

Much remains to be done on the analysis of population growth and regulation and I feel that generalizations to the effect that food supply, or disease, or predation, or a shortage of "protected niches", is the "most usual" factor regulating population size are premature. One thing is certain; potential population growth is so rapid that no non-extinct population can ever be very many generations removed from the possibility of mass starvation. It may, however, be even nearer to a shortage of some resource other than food which it requires of the environment.

Fluctuations

The preceding discussion is barely an introduction to the problems connected with the regulation of population size and I cannot go more deeply into the subject here. I suppose, however, that the author of an introductory survey should show that he is aware of the fact that populations do not just grow to some maximum size and remain there, but that they fluctuate in size with time.

There are many causes of population fluctuation. In a species where individuals require more than one year to reach reproductive age, annual censuses will show fluctuations in each age class that is studied.[7] If there is some fairly critical population density at which the population ceases to grow and begins to decrease, an oscillatory tendency may appear (*cf.* Ricker, 1954). The "classical oscillations" are produced when one population is dependent upon the exploitation of another and when the exploiter population can grow more rapidly than that of the "host". Then there are fluctuations in physical factors such as temperature and rainfall that affect reproduction, mortality, and carrying capacity, and there are occasional events such as fires, floods, frosts, and droughts that may profoundly influence population size.

Acting alone any one of the biological causes of fluctuation might be expected to lead to regular cycles of population size, and it is possible that under carefully controlled laboratory conditions such cycles have actually been observed (*e.g.* Utida, 1955). In nature, however, all of the factors making for population change are interacting in complex ways and random components are brought into the system through the vagaries of weather plus the fact that an environmental condition may be innocuous or beneficial at some times and represent a disaster at other times because of the seasonal incidence of many biological activities.

In systems with so many interacting components we begin to approach the complexity of the causal system that determines the positions in which a set of rolling dice finally come to rest. Palmgren (1949) seems to have been the first to suggest in public that the apparent regularity, which has been said to be "the only peculiar feature of the fluctuations of the cyclic species" (Lack, 1954, p. 223), is actually consistent with random variation. I have elsewhere recorded the results of my study of this problem (Cole, 1951, 1954, 1957) which have led me to

[7] This, incidentally, appears to be the simplest possible example of a "time-lag" effect (Hutchinson, 1948, 1954) where there is a delay between a population effect and the factor inducing it. Such delays are another formidable source of difficulty in the analysis of population regulation.

essential agreement with Palmgren; at least I am convinced that the burden of proof has been handed back to those field workers who persist in seeing something mysterious in the fluctuations of natural populations.

We can trace a nice parallel here with the efforts of physical scientists to explain the structure of matter. As described by Zacharias (1957), the mathematical problems of systems involving two particles can be solved with great accuracy, but the slightly more complicated cases are still beyond the best calculating machines—until we come to "those cases in which there is enough chaos to make things simple again". Perhaps it is fortunate that natural populations are not subject to alteration only by two or three interacting factors but are affected by a large enough number to encourage us to look for secondary simplicity; the highly acclaimed regularity of population cycles seems to be no greater than that which is encountered in a sequence of random numbers.

Age Structure

One final feature of quantitative demography demands mention in our sketch of the field. I refer to the troublesome problems connected with the age structure of a population, problems that still seem to go entirely unnoticed by non-demographers, including intelligent administrators. So much has been said about population size that there has been a tendency to overlook the fact that two populations of equal size may be entirely different in many of their properties and prospects; one may contain the potentiality for eruptive growth while the other is destined by its structure for inevitable decline.

Such paradoxes arise from the fact that the ratio of reproductive females to total population is not only a determiner of the birth rate but is also a consequence of the birth rate. Any population living under conditions where the age schedules of mortality and fertility are fixed will gradually assume a constant age structure such that there is a constant proportion of the population in each age class. Also, as first proved by Sharpe and Lotka (1911), this structure is "stable" in the sense that it will tend to become re-established following any accidental or deliberate displacement, provided, of course, that the age-specific birth and death rates are unchanged.

Problems involving age distribution in natural populations are among the most important and least elementary matters with which demographers have to deal, and it would not be appropriate here for me to attempt a detailed discussion of these problems. The importance of the matter, however, is easily indicated.

If we begin fishing, or hunting, or otherwise exploiting a population that has not previously been subjected to such exploitation we will necessarily change the life expectancy of members of the population. We are also likely to operate selectively against certain age classes. Senile individuals may fall most easily before the hunters, or young, inexperienced, individuals may be the most vulnerable. The size of the mesh in our nets may let some age classes escape or we may legislate protection for certain age classes. All of these things change the age-specific death rates and, therefore, tend to cause the age structure of the population to shift. The shift in age structure will usually cause a secondary change in population birth rates.

In many species, including man and our important fellow travelers of the genus *Rattus*, the youngest and oldest members of a population are non-reproductive. Subject such a species to a hazardous environment and life expectancy will be reduced, that is to say, the probability of reaching the age of post-reproductive sterility is reduced. In a harsher environment then, a larger proportion of the population automatically comes to fall in the reproductive age classes, and this automatically increases the birth rate. When this phenomenon is observed in nature the population is said to "compensate" for the increased mortality.

It will eventually come to the attention of field biologists generally that a great deal of information about the status of a population can be obtained from the study of its age distribution, and that changes in this distribution may be preludes to more dramatic changes in population size. Up to the present, however, the subject has not received adequate attention even in human populations.

In primitive human cultures life expectancy must be low. I have thought, while looking at cliff dwellings in our Southwest, that great longevity must have been very rare among a people who had to climb precipitous cliffs to get home at night. Their adult populations must have consisted primarily of persons of reproductive age. This condition promotes high birth rates and it follows that they must also have had high death rates.

Let us try to imagine what would have happened if these people had been provided with elevators, modern sanitation, and other advantages such as modern medical care. Life expectancy would have increased and, with increased infant survival, the population would have tended to "explode" in size. Gradually, however, a larger part of the adult population would have passed over into the post-reproductive age classes and, as the population exhausted the possibilities for growth, the birth rate would have fallen. In modern language we would say that the population had undergone "the demographic transition" (*e.g.* see Putnam, 1953).

Sundbärg (1900) seems to have been the initiator of the serious study of age distribution in human populations and he reached at least one generalization which still is not widely recognized but which seems to me to be of the greatest importance for human demography. He concluded that 50 per cent of the individuals in a human population are aged from 15 years to 50 years and that this ratio is independent of whether the population is growing, shrinking, or remaining stationary in size. Recent figures from the United Nations (1954) show, for example, that as of July 1, 1953, the proportion of the population of the United States aged between 15 and 50 years was 49.00 per cent. For France, as of December 31, 1953, the corresponding figure is 47.97 per cent, while Sweden in 1952 had 49.42 per cent of its people in this age range. On the other side of the demographic transition we find that, as of 1950, the persons in this age range accounted for 48.13 per cent of the population of Venezuela and 47.35 per cent of the population of Mexico, and in India in 1951 this proportion was 50.47 per cent.

Now, no one here needs to be told of the contrasts among the populations mentioned. France, with 28.49 per cent of its population aged 50 or above, and Venezuela, where only 9.97 per cent of its population members have reached their fiftieth birthdays, stand at opposite extremes, but the populations of Sweden and the United States resemble that of France, while those of Mexico and India resemble that of Venezuela.

Like the cliff-dwellers, the population of Venezuela can be expected either to grow rapidly or to be under the pressure of very high birth and death rates, or both, while in France there is actually concern over the low birth rate. The improvements in modern sanitation and medical care that I spoke of for the cliff-dwellers will, if adopted in Venezuela, work in the right direction to cause first a population explosion and then the demographic transition in age structure toward the condition already attained in France. Whether the explosion can be contained without employing such artifices as contraception and delay in the age at marriage are questions totally outside of my field of competence.

There are numerous important corollaries of these differences in age structure which should hold the attention of demographers. It is obvious that in that statistical El-Dorado where other things are equal a pediatrician would do better as a Venezuelan than as a Frenchman, while it might be difficult to interest the people of Venezuela in geriatric medicine.

Causes of death, notably cancer, that are highly selective for older individuals are certain to be more prominent in the more elderly populations. In the United States we have seen cancer climb from eighth place to second place among causes of death, paralleling a shift in our age distribution between 1900 and 1946 (Dublin, Lotka, and Spiegelman, 1949).

In dealing with non-human populations we have still, as Bodenheimer (1938) complained in 1938, paid all too little attention to these matters. The predator or parasite that selectively kills superannuated individuals may be our friend in helping to increase the productivity of game animals. Such a species, however, will work against our efforts to control noxious species even though he may pose as our friend by providing ample evidence that he is killing the things we want to control.

CONCLUSION

In this sketch, or series of sketches, I have tried to touch upon as many of the things that we do and do not know about populations as I could possibly excuse myself for including within a single paper. I have tried to emphasize the areas that are important to all of us despite our diverse backgrounds, research techniques, and terminologies.

The population, to my mind, is one of the natural levels of ecological integration. Past generations of ecologists have solved many of the problems of the ecology of individual organisms and the way in which nature selects the fit. But, beyond the level of individual survival, there are a host of obvious adaptations related to survival of the population. The evolution of structures such as mammary glands was never promoted by any benefits conferred on the individuals that actually possess them. And social life has been independently evolved several times among various groups of insects in ways that can only be explained when we recognize that the group behaves as a unit which is selected on its merits.

I think it is undoubtedly correct to extrapolate and assume that communities composed of interacting populations of several species may also behave as units in natural selection, and that later generations of ecologists will be working to understand evolutionary processes at that higher level. My present conclusion, however, is that much remains for us to do at the population level if we are to qualify as fit intellectual ancestors of those later generations.

REFERENCES

ALLEE, W. C., 1931, Animal Aggregations. A study in general sociology. Chicago, Univ. of Chicago Press.
ALLEE, W. C., EMERSON, A. E., PARK, O., PARK, T., and SCHMIDT, K. P., 1949, Principles of Animal Ecology. Philadelphia, Saunders.
ANDREWARTHA, H. G., and BIRCH, L. C., 1954, The Distribution and Abundance of Animals. Chicago, University of Chicago Press.
BIRCH, L. C., 1948, The intrinsic rate of increase of an insect population. J. Anim. Ecol. 17: 15-26.
1957. The meanings of competition. Amer. Nat. 91: 5-18.
BODENHEIMER, F. S., 1938, Problems of Animal Ecology. Oxford, Oxford Univ. Press.
BONAR, J., 1931, Theories of Population from Raleigh to Arthur Young. London, George Allen and Unwin.
BOTERO, G., 1588, "A treatise concerning the causes of the magnificency and greatness of cities." Translation by Robert Peterson, 1606. Reprinted in 1956. London, Routledge and Kegan Paul.
BUFFON, L. L., DE, 1756, Histoire naturelle, général et

particuliére avec la description du cabinete du roi. Vol. 6.

1758, Les animaux carnassiers. *Ibid.* Vol. 7.

CHAPMAN, D. G., 1954. The estimation of biological populations. Ann. Math. Stat. *25:* 1–15.

CHAPMAN, R. N., 1928, The quantitative analysis of environmental factors. Ecology *9:* 111–122.

1931, Animal Ecology with Especial Reference to Insects. New York, McGraw-Hill.

COLE, L. C., 1951, Population cycles and random oscillations. J. Wildlife Manage. *15:* 233–251.

1954, Some features of random population cycles. J. Wildlife Manage. *18:* 2–24.

1954a, The population consequences of life history phenomena. Quart. Rev. Biol. *29:* 103–137.

1957, Population fluctuations. Proc. Tenth Intern. Cong. Entomol. (in press).

DARWIN, C., 1859, The origin of species by means of natural selection or the preservation of favored races in the struggle for life. London, Murray.

DeMOIVRE, A., 1725, Annuities upon lives; or the valuàtion of annuities upon any number of lives; and also of reversions. London.

DeMORGAN, A., 1838, An essay on probabilities and on their application to life contingencies and insurance offices. In Lardner's Cabinet Encyclopedia.

DERHAM, W., 1713, Physico-theology, or a demonstration of the being and attributes of God from his works of creation. A new edition 1798. London, printed for A. Strahan; T. Cadell Jun. and W. Davies, in the Strand; and W. Creech, Edinburgh.

DOBZHANSKY, TH., 1955, A review of some fundamental concepts and problems of population genetics. Cold Spring Harbor Symposia Quant. Biol. *20:* 1–15.

DUBLIN, L. I., LOTKA, A. J., and SPIEGELMAN, M., 1949, Length of life. A study of the life table. Rev. ed. New York, Ronald Press.

ERRINGTON, P. L., 1946, Predation and vertebrate populations. Quart. Rev. Biol. *21:* 144–177, 221–245.

FARR, W., 1943, Causes of mortality in town districts. Fifth Ann. Rept. Reg. Gen. of births, deaths and marriages in England, Pp. 406–435.

FELLER, W., 1939, Die Grundlagen der Volterraschen Theorie des Kampfes ums Dasein in Wahrscheinlichkeitstheoretischer Behandlungen. Acta Biotheretica *5:* 11–40.

1950, An Introduction to Probability Theory and its Applications. Vol. 1. New York, J. Wiley and Sons.

FERGUSON, A., 1767, An Essay on the History of Civil Society. 4th. ed. 1773. London, Printed for T. Caddel, in the Strand; and A. Kincaid, W. Creech, and J. Bell, Edinburgh.

FRANKLIN, B., 1751, Observations concerning the increase of mankind and the peopling of countries. In: The works of Benjamin Franklin, ed. J. Sparks, 1836, Vol. 2: 311–321. Boston, Hilliard, Grey.

GALTON, F., 1869, Hereditary Genius. London, Murray.

GOMPERTZ, B., 1825, On the nature of the function expressive of the law of human mortality. Phil. Trans. Roy. Soc. *36:* 513–585.

GRAUNT, J., 1662, Natural and political observations mentioned in a following index and made upon the bills of mortality . . . London, Printed by T. Roycroft.

GUILLIARD, A., 1885, Éléments de statistique humaine ou démographie comparée. Paris, Guillaumin et Cie Libraires.

HALE, M., 1677, The primitive origination of mankind. London, Shrowsberry.

HUTCHINSON, G. E., 1948, Circular causal systems in ecology. Ann. N. Y. Acad. Sci. *50:* 221–246.

1954, Notes on oscillatory populations. J. Wildlife Manage. *18:* 107–109.

HUYGENS, C., 1662, Letter No. 1022, Christiaan Huygens à R. Moray. In: Oeuvres Completes de Christiaan Huygens, 1895. Tome IV: 148–152. LeHaye, Martinus Nijhoff.

1669, "En examinant le calcul de Mon Frere Louis." *Ibid.* VI: 526–531.

LACK, D., 1954, The Natural Regulation of Animal Numbers. Oxford, Clarendon Press.

LINNAEUS, C., 1743, Oratio de telluris habitabilis. In, Amoenitates Academicae seu Dissertationes Varie . . . Editio tertia curante. J. C. D. Schrebero, 1787. Vol. 2: 430–457. Erlange, J. J. Palm.

MALTHUS, T. R., 1798, An essay on the principle of population as it effects the future improvement of society . . . London, Printed for J. Johnson in St. Paul's Churchyard.

MENDEL, G., 1865, Versuche über pflanzenhybriden. Verhandlungen des Naturforschenden vereines in Brünn IV.

[NEWTON, I.], 1686, Tables for renewing and purchasing of the leases of Cathedral-Churches and colleges, . . . Also tables for renewing and purchasing of lives . . . Cambridge, Printed by John Hayes, printer to the University.

NICHOLSON, A. J., 1933, The balance of animal populations. J. Anim. Ecol. *2:* 132–178.

1954, An outline of the dynamics of animal populations. Australian J. Zool. *2:* 9–65.

PALMGREN, P., 1949, Some remarks on the short-term fluctuations in the numbers of northern birds and mammals. Oikos *1:* 114–121.

PEARL, R., 1940, Introduction to Medical Biometry and Statistics. 3rd. ed. Philadelphia, W. B. Saunders.

PEARL, R., and REED, L. J., 1920, On the rate of growth of the population of the United States since 1790 and its mathematical representation. Proc. Nat. Acad. Sci. Wash. *6:* 275–288.

PUTNAM, P. C., 1953, Energy in the Future. New York, Van Nostrand.

QUETELET, A., 1835, Sur l'Homme et le Développment de ses Facultés ou Essai de Physique Sociale. Paris, Bachelier, Imprimeur-Libraire.

RALEIGH, W., 1650, (First published in his essays.) A discourse of the original and fundamental cause of natural, arbitrary, necessary, and unnatural war. In: The works of Sir Walter Raleigh, Kt. now first collected. 1829. Oxford, Oxford Univ. Press.

RICKER, W., 1954, Stock and recruitment. J. Fish. Res. Bd. Canada *11:* 559–623.

SCORESBY, W., 1820, An account of the arctic regions, with a history and description of the northern whalefishery. Edinburgh, printed for Archibald Constable and Co.

SHARPE, F. R., and LOTKA, A. J., 1911, A problem in age distribution. Phil. Mag. *21:* 435–438.

SIMPSON, G. G., 1952, How many species? Evolution *6:* 342.

SKELLAM, J. G., 1955. The mathematical approach to population dynamics. In: The Numbers of Men and Animals. Ed. by J. B. Cragg and N. W. Pirie. Edinburgh, published for the Institute of Biology by Oliver and Boyd.

SLOBODKIN, L. B., 1953, An algebra of population growth. Ecology *34:* 513–519.

1953a, On social single species populations. Ecology *34:* 430–434.

SMITH, F. E., 1952, Experimental methods in population dynamics: a critique. Ecology *33:* 441–450.

1954, Quantitative aspects of population growth. In: Dynamics of Growth Processes. Ed. E. J. Boell. Princeton, N. J., Princeton Univ. Press.

SMITH, H. S., 1935, The role of biotic factors in the determination of population densities. J. Econ. Ent. *28:* 873–898.

STRANGELAND, C. E., 1904, Pre-Malthusian doctrines of population; a study in the history of economic theory. Columbia Univ. Stud. Hist. Econ. Pub. Lab. Vol. 21, No. 3.

SUNDBÄRG, A. G., 1900, Sur la répartition de la population parâge et sur les taux de mortalité. Bull. de l'Inst. Internat. de Statistique *12:* 89–94.

THOMPSON, D'ARCY W., 1942, On Growth and Form, a New Edition. Cambridge, Cambridge Univ. Press.

THOMPSON, W. R., 1939, Biological control and the theories of the interactions of populations. Parasitology *31:* 299–388.

United Nations, 1954, Demographic Yearbook, 1954. New York , Statistical Office of the United Nations.

UTIDA, S., 1955, Population fluctuations in the system of host-parasite interaction. Mem. Coll. Ag. Kyoto Univ. No. *71.*

VERHULST, P. F., 1838, Notice sur la loi que la population suit dans son accroisissement. Corresp. Math. Phys., A. Quetelet *10:* 113–121.

ZACHARIAS, J. R., 1957, Structure of physical science. Science *125:* 427–428.

Part II

THE BIOTIC SCHOOL
OF POPULATION
REGULATION: HISTORICAL

Editor's Comments
on Papers 2 and 3

2 HOWARD and FISKE
Excerpt from *The Importation into the United States of the Parasites of the Gipsy Moth and the Brown-Tail Moth: A Report of Progress with Some Consideration of Previous and Concurrent Efforts of This Kind*

3 NICHOLSON
Excerpt from *The Balance of Animal Populations*

With this section we begin to look at the opposing points of view that have dominated the study of population regulation: the biotic, abiotic, compromise, and self-regulation schools of thought. Although the situation today may be more rational, the extensive controversies of the recent past are by no means completely resolved. The proponents of the biotic school believe that animal populations are regulated by interactions with other organisms through either competition, predation, disease, or parasitism. These interactions produce their effects in a density-dependent manner. That is, as a population increases in density, its rate of increase slows proportionately until finally it stops growing. The higher the density, the greater the pressure to stop growing. Later, in a section on compromise theories, we shall look at some of the terminological problems. At this point, however, it is necessary only to keep in mind the range of new terminology devised. To this day there are disagreements about and errors in the use of such words as "regulation" and "density-dependent" (McClenaghan and Gaines 1976; Lidicker 1977).

The study of the regulation of animal populations was begun in this country by economic entomologists who were interested in controlling the outbreak of pest species of insects. The first significant study was by L. O. Howard and W. F. Fiske (Paper 2), who were interested in using imported parasites of the gipsy and brown-tail moths to control these pests. At the time (1911), Howard was the chief of the Bureau of Entomology of the U.S. Department of Agriculture, and Fiske worked directly under him. Both had earlier, and independently, worked on parasitic control of insect pests

(Howard 1897; Fiske 1903). They believed in the balance of nature, a view prevalent among those who believe in density-dependent population regulation. Howard and Fiske coined the terms "facultative" and "catastrophic." According to them, for a population to be regulated, at least one factor in the environment would have to be facultative—that is, more effective—as favorable conditions for the species increase. They preferred parasitism but also believed that predation could be an effective facultative agent. An example of a catastrophic agent is climate, whose relative effect on the species is independent of the species' abundance.

The next paper, Nicholson's "Balance of Animal Populations" (1933), is probably the most important single paper published in the field of population regulation, having sparked the many controversies in this field. Nicholson's two basic precepts are similar to Howard and Fiske's, with whom he agreed. First, there is a balance of nature, and second, ". . . the action of the controlling factor must be governed by the density of the population controlled."

There are several places of difficulty in this paper. First, Nicholson differentiates between destruction and control; when the weather knocks out 99 percent of a population, the competition that knocks out the 1 percent is the real controlling element. Obviously, 1 percent is well within experimental error and outside our ability to measure. Second, by assuming a balance of nature, Nicholson can disregard any factor that does not conform to that balance-of-nature view. His reasoning that competition is the only factor that can regulate populations comes almost directly from his definition of competition. Nicholson proceeds to develop the idea that competition is the main regulating factor for natural populations. He derives 76 verbal conclusions that deal with entomophagous insects.

The terms "density-dependent" and "density-independent" were coined by Harry S. Smith (1935), another economic entomologist. He was in charge of biological control in California from 1913 to 1951, at first in the State Agriculture Department and then at the University of California. He used the terms in a manner similar to Howard and Fiske's "facultative" and "catastrophic"; the effects of agents were either dependent (facultative) or independent (catastrophic) of the density of the controlled populations. Trying to present more of a compromise theory, Smith added the idea that climate can act in a density-dependent manner.

Nicholson continued and amplified his 1933 theory, first with the collaboration of the physicist V. A. Bailey (Nicholson and Bailey 1935), and then in a series of singly authored papers continuing into the 1950s (1954a; 1954b; 1958). Nicholson makes a point that will be important later, in our discussion of self-regulation schools

29

of thought: Natural selection cannot adjust local population density—in fact, it acts in a disruptive manner.

REFERENCES

Fiske, W. F. 1903. A Study of the Parasites of the American Tent Caterpillar. *Tech. Bull. N.H. Agric. Exp. Stat.* **6**:183–230.

Howard, L. O. 1897. A Study in Insect Parasitism. *Tech. Ser. U.S. Dept. Agric.* **5**:5–57.

Lidicker, W. Z., Jr. 1977. Regulation of Numbers in Small Mammal Populations. In D. Snyder (ed.), *Pymatuning Symposium in Ecology*, no. 5. Ann Arbor, Mich.: Edwards Brothers.

McClenaghan, L. R., Jr., and M. S. Gaines. 1976. Density-dependent Dispersal in *Sigmodon*: A Critique. *J. Mamm.* **57**:758–759.

Nicholson, A. J. 1954a. Compensatory Reactions of Populations to Stress, and Their Evolutionary Significance. *Aust. J. Zool.* **2**:1–8.

Nicholson, A. J. 1954b. An Outline of the Dynamics of Animal Populations. *Aust. J. Zool.* **2**:9–65.

Nicholson, A. J. 1958. The Self-Adjustment of Populations to Change. *Cold Spring Harbor Symp. Quant. Biol.* **22**:153–173.

Nicholson, A. J., and V. A. Bailey. 1935. The Balance of Animal Populations. *Proc. Zool. Soc. Lond.* **3**:551–598.

Smith, H. S. 1935. The Role of Biotic Factors in the Determination of Population Densities. *J. Econ. Ent.* **28**:873–898.

2

Reprinted from *U. S. Dept. Agr., Bur. Ent., Bull.* **91**:105–109 (1911)

THE IMPORTATION INTO THE UNITED STATES OF THE PARASITES OF THE GIPSY MOTH AND THE BROWN-TAIL MOTH: A REPORT OF PROGRESS WITH SOME CONSIDERATION OF PREVIOUS AND CONCURRENT EFFORTS OF THIS KIND

L. O. Howard and W. F. Fiske

[*Editor's Note:* In the original, material precedes this excerpt.]

PARASITISM AS A FACTOR IN INSECT CONTROL.

In reviewing the results of these studies, the fact is strikingly evident that parasitism plays a very different part in the economy of different hosts. Some habitually support a parasitic fauna both abundant and varied, while others are subjected to attack by only a limited number of parasites, the most abundant of which is relatively uncommon. No two of the lepidopterous hosts studied, unless they chanced to be congeneric and practically identical in habit and life history, were found to be victimized by exactly the same species of parasites. Neither are the same species apt to occur in connection with the same host in the same relative abundance, one to another, year after year in the same locality, nor in two different localities the same year.

At the same time there are certain features in the parasitism of each species which are common to each of the others, whether these be arctiid, liparid, lasiocampid, tortricid, saturniid, or tineid, one of the most common of which is that each host supports a variety of parasites, oftentimes differing among themselves to a remarkable degree in habit, natural affinities, and methods of attack. Departures from this rule have not been encountered among the defoliating Lepidoptera as yet, and while exceptions will probably be found to exist, they will doubtless remain exceptions in proof of the rule. From this the rather obvious conclusion has been drawn, that to be effective in the case of an insect like the gipsy moth or the brown-tail moth, parasitic control must come about through a variety of parasites, working together harmoniously, rather than through one specific parasite, as is known to be the case with certain less specialized insects, having a less well-defined seasonal history. To speak still more plainly, it is believed that the successful conclusion of the experiment in parasite introduction now under consideration depends upon whether or not we shall be able to import and establish in America each of the component parts of an effective "sequence" of parasites. This belief is further supported by the undoubted fact, that in every locality from which parasite material has been received abroad, both the gipsy moth and the brown-tail moth are subjected to attack by such a group or sequence of parasites, of which the component species differ more or less radically in habit and in their manner of attack.

In the case of the gipsy moth and the brown-tail moth abroad, as well as in that of nearly every species of leaf-feeding Lepidoptera studied in America, there are included among the parasites species which attack the eggs, the caterpillars, large and small, and the prepupæ and pupæ, respectively. Frequently, but not always, there are predatory enemies, which, through their ability to increase at the immediate expense of the insect upon which they prey, whenever this insect becomes sufficiently abundant to invite such increase, are to be considered as ranking with the true facultative parasites when economically considered.

It is, therefore, our aim to secure the firm establishment in America of a sequence of the egg, the caterpillar, and the pupal parasites of the gipsy moth and brown-tail moth as they are found to exist abroad, and until this is either done or proved to be impossible of accomplishment through causes over which we have no control, we can neither give up the fight nor expect to bring it to a successful conclusion.

It was stated a page or two back that some species of insects support a parasitic fauna both numerous and varied, while others are subjected to attack by only a limited number of parasites, none of which can be considered as common. Notwithstanding the fact that somewhat similar differences are discernible between the parasitic fauna of the same insect at different times or under different environment, it is perfectly safe to elaborate the original statement still further and to say that some species are habitually subjected to a much heavier parasitism than others. Unquestionably the average percentage of parasitism of the fall webworm in eastern Massachusetts, taken over a sufficiently long series of years to make a fair average possible, is the same as the average would be over another similar series of years in the same general region. This could be said of the larvæ of any other insect as well as of that of the fall webworm, but the average percentage of parasitism in another would most likely not be the same, but might be very much larger or very much smaller. To put it dogmatically, each species of insect in a country where the conditions are settled is subjected to a certain fixed average percentage of parasitism, which, in the vast majority of instances and in connection with numerous other controlling agencies, results in the maintenance of a perfect balance. The insect neither increases to such abundance as to be affected by disease or checked from further multiplication through lack of food, nor does it become extinct, but throughout maintains a degree of abundance in relation to other species existing in the same vicinity, which, when averaged for a long series of years, is constant.

In order that this balance may exist it is necessary that among the factors which work together in restricting the multiplication of the species there shall be at least one, if not more, which is what is here termed facultative (for want of a better name), and which, by exerting a restraining influence which is relatively more effective when other conditions favor undue increase, serves to prevent it. There are a very large number and a great variety of factors of more or less importance in effecting the control of defoliating caterpillars, and to attempt to catalogue them would be futile, but however closely they may be scrutinized very few will be found to fall into the class with parasitism, which in the majority of instances, though not in all, is truly "facultative."

A very large proportion of the controlling agencies, such as the destruction wrought by storm, low or high temperature, or other climatic conditions, is to be classed as catastrophic, since they are wholly independent in their activities upon whether the insect which incidentally suffers is rare or abundant. The storm which destroys 10 caterpillars out of 50 which chance to be upon a tree would doubtless have destroyed 20 had there been 100 present, or 100 had there been 500 present. The average percentage of destruction remains the same, no matter how abundant or how near to extinction the insect may have become.

Destruction through certain other agencies, notably by birds and other predators, works in a radically different manner. These predators are not directly affected by the abundance or scarcity of any single item in their varied menu. Like all other creatures they are forced to maintain a relatively constant abundance among the other forms of animal and plant life, and since their abundance from year to year is not influenced by the abundance or scarcity of any particular species of insect among the many upon which they prey they can not be ranked as elements in the facultative control of such species. On the contrary, it may be considered that they average to destroy a certain gross number of individuals each year, and since this destruction is either constant, or, if variable, is not correlated in its variations to the fluctuations in abundance of the insect preyed upon, it would most probably represent a heavier percentage when that insect was scarce than when it was common. In other words, they work in a manner which is the opposite of "facultative" as here understood.

In making the above statement the fact is not for a moment lost to sight that birds which feed with equal freedom upon a variety of insects will destroy a greater gross number of that species which chances to be the most abundant, but with the very few apparent exceptions of those birds which kill for the mere sake of killing they will only destroy a certain maximum number all told. A little reflection will make it plain that the percentage destroyed will never become greater, much if any, as the insect becomes more common, and, moreover, that after a certain limit in abundance is passed this percentage will grow rapidly less. A natural balance can only be maintained through the operation of facultative agencies which effect the destruction of a greater proportionate number of individuals as the insect in question increases in abundance.

Of these facultative agencies parasitism appears to be the most subtle in its action. Disease, whether brought about by some specific organism, as with the brown-tail moth, or through insufficient or unsuitable food supply without the intervention of any specific organism, as appears at the present time to be the case with the gipsy moth, does not as a rule become effective until the insect has increased to far beyond its average abundance. There are exceptions to this rule, or appear to be, but comparatively only a very few have come to our immediate attention. Finally, famine and starvation must be considered as the most radical means at nature's disposal, whereby insects, like the defoliating Lepidoptera, are finally brought into renewed subjugation.

With insects like the gipsy moth and the brown-tail moth disease does not appear to become a factor until a degree of abundance has been reached which makes the insect in question, *ipso facto*, a pest. Whether in the future methods will be devised for artificially rendering such diseases more quickly effective, remains to be determined through actual experimental work continued over a considerable number of years.

In effect, the proposition is here submitted as a basis for further discussion that only through parasites and predators, the numerical increase of which is directly affected by the numerical increase of the insect upon which they prey, is that insect to be brought under complete natural control, except in the relatively rare instances in which destruction through disease is not dependent upon super-abundance.

The present experiment in parasite introduction was undertaken and has been conducted on the assumption that there existed in America all of the various elements necessary to bring about the complete control of the gipsy moth and the brown-tail moth, except their respective parasites. Believing that this stand was correctly taken, much time has been devoted to a consideration of the extent to which these pests are already controlled through natural agencies already in operation. The fact that both insects have increased steadily and rapidly in every locality in which they have become established and where adequate suppressive measures have not been undertaken, until they have reached a stage of abundance far in excess of that which prevails in most countries abroad, renders superfluous further comment upon the present ineffectiveness of these agencies. The difference between the rate at which they have averaged to increase in localities where they have become established and their potential rate of increase as indicated by the number of eggs deposited by the average female should indicate very accurately the efficiency of such agencies, and the difference between the actual rate of increase and no increase similarly indicates the amount of additional control which must be exerted by the parasites if their numbers are to be kept at an innocuous minimum.

[*Editor's Note:* In the original, material follows this excerpt.]

3

Reprinted from *J. Anim. Ecol.* 2:132–148, 178 (1933)

THE BALANCE OF ANIMAL POPULATIONS

By A. J. NICHOLSON, D.Sc.

(*Division of Economic Entomology, Commonwealth Council for Scientific and Industrial Research, Canberra, Australia.*)

(*With eleven Figures in the Text.*)

FOREWORD.

FOR some years the writer, with the generous collaboration of Prof. V. A. Bailey[1], has been investigating the problem of competition in animal populations. An endeavour has been made to investigate the influence of competition on animal populations in all the principal kinds of situations known to exist between animals, and between animals and their environments, and to examine the major types of other factors known to influence populations, in order to see whether these are capable of nullifying, or otherwise influencing, the effects of competition. The scope of the work is thus very wide, and a full presentation of the conclusions, and of the arguments upon which they are based, cannot be given here.

The present paper forms an introduction to later and more detailed publications. Its object is first, to show why it is believed that the competition existing between animals when searching is of fundamental importance in the limitation of animal populations, and secondly, to give an outline of the major conclusions of biological interest that have been reached. Nothing more is attempted at present than to show the reasonableness of these conclusions, rigorous proof being postponed to future publications. It is thought that the "bird's-eye view" of the subject thus given will not only prepare the way for the more detailed work to be presented later, but will also provide biologists with useful hypotheses, the proof or disproof of which by experiment and observation should materially advance our knowledge of animal populations and their natural control.

PART I. THE NATURAL LIMITATION OF POPULATIONS.

THE EXISTENCE OF BALANCE.

It appears to be usual at present to deny the existence of the "balance of nature," about which there has been so much vague talk. Therefore, before considering the question of the balance of animal populations, we must examine the arguments for and against the existence of such balance.

There is an outstanding feature of animal populations with which all must be familiar. In any given place the population densities of animals are ob-

---

[1] Associate Professor of Physics, University of Sydney.

served to change in close association with the changing seasons. Similarly, for any given species of animal, the population density differs in different places, and usually there is a fairly evident relation between the differences in the population densities and the differences in climate, or other environmental conditions. These observations clearly indicate that animal populations must exist in a state of balance, for they are otherwise inexplicable.

Let us take a simple analogy. A balloon rises until the weight of air displaced exactly balances the weight of the balloon, but if ballast be then discarded the balloon again rises until it reaches a new position of balance. Because a balloon in the air is a balanced system, there is a relation between the weight it carries and the height it reaches; without balance, the height reached would be indeterminate.

The balance of animal populations is similar to that of a balloon acted upon by the changing temperatures of night and day. Such a balloon rises and falls in relation to the change in temperature, for this varies the volume of the balloon and the density of the surrounding air. The balloon is continually in a state of tending towards a position of stationary balance, but continues to rise and fall because the position of stationary balance is changing all the time. It may be remarked that even when moving uniformly the balloon is in a state of balance, friction with the air making up the deficiency either in the weight of the balloon or in the weight of air displaced, so governing the speed with which the balloon rises or falls.

The observed fact that there is a relation between the population densities of animals and environmental conditions can be explained only in terms of balance, just as the relation between the weight carried and the height reached by a balloon can be explained only in this way. Without balance the population densities of animals would be indeterminate, and so could not bear a relation to anything.

The evidence for the existence of balance is not confined to logical deduction from the known facts about animal populations existing in a state of nature. Experiments dealing specifically with populations prove that the latter do reach a state of stationary balance under constant environmental conditions. Thus Pearl (**18**, ch. 2), working with *Drosophila melanogaster* bred on banana-agar in milk bottles, showed that the density progressively approaches an asymptotic population, which is clearly a population in a state of balance. However, owing to difficulties of manipulation, his experiments mostly ended when the asymptotic population was closely approached. It is of particular interest that different races of *Drosophila*, bred under identical conditions, have different asymptotic populations.

Chapman (**3**), working with the flour-beetle, *Tribolium confusum*, showed that populations of this beetle grow until a particular density is reached, beyond which there is no further growth. This density is independent of the absolute quantity of flour available. In other words, the number of beetles is directly proportional to the quantity of flour available, when a state of balance is reached.

MacLagan (**15**, p. 126), working with *Smynthurus viridis*, has shown that increasing density progressively decreases the rate of population growth, and this is the essential mechanism for the production of balance in populations.

The most satisfactory experimental demonstration of the production of balance in animal populations is given by Holdaway (**9**). He shows that under given conditions populations of *Tribolium confusum* reach and maintain a particular density; and also that when the conditions are varied (he varied humidity) the density reached is also varied. He brings out clearly the important point that it is the interaction of the insects themselves that produces balance and so limits density, while physical factors, by modifying this interaction, influence the position at which the insects themselves limit their population.

ARGUMENTS USED TO DISPROVE THE EXISTENCE OF BALANCE IN NATURE.

Having very briefly considered the evidence provided by observation and experiment for the existence of balance in animal populations, let us now examine the arguments that have been used to support the contention that there is no such balance.

The claim that animal populations are not in a state of balance is usually based upon the observation that animals do not maintain constant population densities. Clearly this argument is illogical, for, if a population is in a state of balance with the environment, its density must necessarily change in relation to any changes of the environment. A population density that does not change with the environment is evidently not in a state of balance, but is fixed independently of the environment.

Another argument, which has received much prominence in recent years, is that, because a close association between variations in the population densities of animals and changes in climate has been demonstrated, therefore climate is almost wholly responsible for the determination of the densities of animals—while other factors, such as the availability of food and space, and the presence of natural enemies, are of negligible importance (cf. Bodenheimer (**2**) and Uvarov (**23**)). The fallacy of this argument is made evident by the following analogy: If we examine the surface of the ocean, we observe that it rises and falls in relation to the position of the moon. From this we do not conclude that the depth of the ocean is determined by the position of the moon, but merely that change in depth is associated with the position of the moon. The depth of the ocean is determined by the shape of the ocean bottom, by the quantity of water present, and by the balance of the surface, governed by gravity. Similarly, the observed association between changes in the population densities of animals and changes in climate does not show that the densities are determined by climate, but merely that climate may vary the densities. These, it will be shown, are determined by other factors besides climate, and are limited and held in a state of balance by competition.

Climate, by itself, cannot determine the population densities of animals, for it does not possess the property necessary for the production of balance; and it has already been shown that, unless there is balance, densities are indeterminate and cannot be related to anything. For the production of balance, it is essential that a controlling factor should act more severely against an average individual when the density of animals is high, and less severely when the density is low. In other words, *the action of the controlling factor must be governed by the density of the population controlled.* Clearly no variation in the density of a population of animals can modify the intensity of the sun, or the severity of frost, or of any other climatic factor. The necessity for this interdependence of population densities and the action of the controlling factors has been pointed out by several writers (cf. Howard and Fiske (**11**, p. 107), Nicholson (**17**, p. 83), Fisher (**7**, p. 42), Martini (**16**)), but its paramount importance in the study of the population problem has generally been lost to sight by biologists.

A moment's reflection will show that any factor having the necessary property for the control of populations must be some form of competition. If the severity of its action against an average individual increases as the density of animals increases, the decreased chance of survival, or of producing offspring, is clearly brought about by the presence of more individuals of the same species in the vicinity. This can only mean that the decreased chance of survival is due to increased competition of some kind.

In recent years the importance of the influence of climate on the activities of animals has been demonstrated by many workers. They have shown that changes in population densities are associated with changes in climate; but, for the reasons just given, this does not support the hypothesis many of them stress so strongly, namely, that the climate is mainly, if not wholly, responsible for the determination of the population densities of animals. The point of view of these workers is well expressed by Uvarov in the following passages: "…the evidence collected in this section, as well as in the whole of this paper, should go far towards proving that the key to the problem of balance in nature is to be looked for in the influence of climatic factors on living organisms" (**23**, p. 161). "It is a balance resembling that of a cork floating on the surface of a running stream, with its whirlpools, eddies and back currents, while the wind blowing with varying force now ripples the surface gently, now causes it to rise and fall in great waves. The cork rises and falls with them, comes into collision with other floating objects, now rides on a calm surface and is dried by the sun, now is again rolled over and over by a storm and is beaten by rain, but always continues its journey with ever-changing velocity and along a fantastically tortuous course" (**23**, p. 162).

This simile is apt, and forcibly illustrates the vicissitudes of an animal population. But stress is placed on the agitation of the cork, whereas its balance on the surface of the water is fundamentally important. Were it not for this balance, the cork would simply fall out of the system, and its interesting career would be brought to an untimely end. So it is with animal populations. Were it not for the fact that competition holds populations in a state of balance with their environments, there would be no limited populations for physical factors to vary. The populations would either disappear altogether or increase without limit.

In support of the contention that climate is mainly, if not wholly, responsible for the limitation of animal populations, much stress is commonly placed upon the fact that climate is known to destroy large numbers of animals. Quantitative observations in the field have proved that climate sometimes destroys far more individuals of a species than all other factors put together (cf. Bodenheimer (2)). However, the belief that this proves the important part played by climate in determining the densities of animals is based upon the confusion of two distinct processes, namely, destruction and control.

Let us take an example to illustrate the distinction between these processes. We will suppose that the animals in a certain population would increase one hundredfold in each generation if unchecked, and also that, on the average, climate destroys 98 per cent. of the animals. It is clear that the number of animals would be doubled in each successive generation if no other factors operated. Climate could never check this progressive increase, for it would continue to destroy only 98 per cent., its action being uninfluenced by the density of the animals. If, however, there is some other factor, such as a natural enemy, the action of which is governed by the density of animals, the destruction of the remaining 1 per cent. necessary to check increase would soon be accomplished. If this example were observed in nature, one would be tempted to conclude that, because climate destroys 98 per cent. of the animals while the natural enemy destroys only 1 per cent., the limitation of the population is mainly due to the influence of climate. However, it is clear that the natural enemy is wholly responsible for control, because climate, by itself, would permit the density of the population to become indefinitely great. It is not even necessarily true that the destruction caused by climate reduces the density of animals. Considerations will be given later which show that in such a situation the effect of climate is almost as likely to increase the number of survivors in an average generation as to decrease this number!

If an attempt be made to assess the relative importance of the various factors known to influence a population, no reliance whatever must be placed upon the proportion of animals destroyed by each. Instead, we must find which of the factors are influenced, and how readily they are influenced, by changes in the density of animals.

Investigations on the influence of climate on the life and activity of animals are in themselves of great interest. Also, they are of great economic importance, for they enable us to predict the possible limits of distribution of pests, and under what conditions increases or decreases in abundance may be expected. But, until such time as they take balance into account, they cannot give us any information about the values at which the densities of animals will be limited under given conditions, and this is the most important problem of all in economic biology.

VIEWS ON THE MECHANISM OF BALANCE.

Having shown that the evidence for the existence of balance in animal populations is overwhelmingly great, and that the arguments commonly used when denying balance are unsatisfactory, we will now examine the views generally held about the mechanism of balance.

In almost all discussions of the "balance of nature" there is a strong implication that evolution is responsible for this. It seems generally to be considered that natural selection is the mechanism of evolution that produces and maintains balance, though how it can do so is never clearly stated. This common belief that natural selection has two distinct functions, namely, selection and the production of balance, appears to be responsible for most of the criticism to which the theory of natural selection has been subjected. Elton clearly recognises the difficulty, and remarks (5, pp. 24–5): "We have had to abandon the simple idea of the balance of nature, which was supposed to be produced by the natural selection of more or less fixed instincts, physiological reactions and structures....I do not wish to cast doubt here on the general ability of natural selection to produce adaptations. I am merely raising the question whether it is able to account for the regulation of numbers in an animal community."

The function of natural selection is to select—not to produce balance. Its mechanism is very simple. All animals produce a surplus of offspring, which is somehow destroyed. Natural selection merely causes a greater proportion of the more perfectly adapted individuals than of the less perfect ones to be amongst the survivors. This tends progressively to improve adaptation, but it has nothing whatever to do with the production of balance or the limitation of populations.

The idea that natural selection produces balance appears to be due to a misconception about the meaning of "adaptation." It seems generally to be thought that adaptation is the precise adjustment of the properties of species so that they balance the inherent resistance of the environment. This idea is expressed by Fisher (7, p. 38) in the following passage: "An organism is regarded as adapted to a particular situation, or to the totality of situations which constitute its environment, only in so far as we can imagine an assemblage of slightly different situations, or environments, to which the animal would on the whole be less well adapted; and equally only in so far as we can imagine an assemblage of slightly different organic forms, which would be less well adapted to that environment. This I take to be the meaning which the word is intended to convey, apart altogether from the question whether organisms really are adapted to their environments."

Observation and experiment show that such precise adjustment of the properties of animals to those of their environments does not exist. Thus Uvarov (23, p. 152) points out that "The common, though never proved, assumption that every organism is perfectly adjusted to its environment, requires a complete agreement between the environmental relations of the insect and its natural enemies, particularly parasites," and investigation has shown that this complete agreement is often lacking. Similarly, MacLagan (15, p. 144) has recently shown that no one set of conditions provides the optima of all the physiological processes of *Smynthurus viridis*, so that clearly this insect can never be precisely adjusted to its environment. Also, we know that species range over environments differing markedly from one another. Therefore, if a species be assumed to be perfectly adjusted to one kind of environment, it clearly cannot be so adjusted to the other kinds of environment in which it also occurs.

Adaptation is not the exact balancing of the properties of the environment by those of a species. It is simply the possession by animals of properties that enable them to exist in a given environment. If individuals with improved properties appear, this type ultimately displaces the original normal type of the species, so improving adaptation; but this adaptation has nothing to do with perfect adjustment or balance.

Even if we assume that adaptation is the qualitative balance of the properties of animals and those of their environments, and that this balance can be produced by natural selection, this does not help to explain the limitation of populations—for qualitative balance would be maintained whatever the density of a species might be. That is to say, there would be a neutral equilibrium, leaving the population densities indeterminate.

However, natural selection cannot produce even this neutral equilibrium. A number of arguments in support of this contention might be given, but it is sufficient at present to mention just one. We will assume that a population is in a state of qualitative balance with its environment, and that within the population there are some individuals having a greater survival value than the average. Clearly natural selection should tend to preserve such individuals at the expense of the others. But, if it does so, the properties of the population are improved, so over-balancing those of the environment and permitting a progressive and indefinite increase of the population. If natural selection is to produce and maintain balance, in such a situation it must preserve the normal individuals at the expense of those that have the greatest survival value! It is thus evident that natural selection is not only incapable of producing and preserving qualitative balance, but actually, by altering the properties of populations, must continually tend to destroy any such balance that may already exist.

Lotka (**12** and **13**), and later Volterra (**24–28**, and see Chapman (**4**, pp. 409–48)) and Bailey (**1**), give mathematical theories which conclude that the interaction of animals may itself lead to a condition of balance, and that the position of stationary balance depends upon the properties of the animals, the nature of their interaction and the properties of the environment. They also conclude that this interaction causes an oscillation about the steady density. However, consideration of the mathematical papers of these and other authors must be postponed to subsequent publications, though it may be mentioned that a brief account of the relation of Volterra's work to the present investigation has already been given (Bailey (**1**, p. 76)).

OTHER VIEWS ON THE LIMITATION OF POPULATIONS.

Another mechanism of balance is sometimes described, though it is generally put forward as an alternative to what is considered to be the untenable hypothesis of balance in nature. This mechanism is made clear in the following passages: "The organism considered may increase in numbers for a considerable time but it obviously cannot go on increasing indefinitely. As it increases in numbers it necessarily spreads, both in space and time, and during its spread it moves to points outside its optimum environment, when its rate of multiplication immediately diminishes" (Thompson (**22**, p. 57)). "When the population increases seriously far above its optimum, there is a shifting of the animals to other places, so that the abnormal density is relieved....If the population is less than it might be, the gaps soon fill in from the outside by a similar process of adjustment. Migration in response to an innate sense of harmony with the habitat makes possible a solution of the animal population problem" (Elton (**5**, p. 61)).

It will be observed that the migration referred to here is not necessarily a concerted movement of a large section of a population to a distant place, but is more likely to be a diffusion of individuals within, or beyond, the normal area of distribution of the species. The migrating animals may reach new and incompletely stocked places suitable for their existence, but in general they are likely to spend their time in unsuitable places, so that their chance of survival is reduced. In short, pressure of population induces migration, and this in turn decreases the chance of survival of an average individual. Thus this mechanism possesses the property essential for the limitation of populations, and automatically causes a population always to tend towards a position of balance.

It is of interest to note that with this mechanism it is possible that the whole of the surplus animals may be destroyed by climatic factors, and yet climate is not responsible for control. If increasing pressure of population in favourable areas leads to migration, the degree of migration is governed by the severity of competition. The proportion of individuals destroyed by climate is dependent on the proportion competition forces out of the favourable parts of the environment. Therefore it is competition, not climate, that regulates the fraction of animals destroyed, and so limits the density and holds the population in a state of balance with the environment.

Mention needs to be made of Chapman's concept of "biotic potential," which he defines as "the inherent property of an organism to reproduce and to survive" (4, p. 182). His idea appears to be that biotic potential, when pitted against environmental resistance, determines the density of a species; and that, as biotic potential and density can be measured, environmental resistance can be expressed quantitatively in terms of these factors. Space does not permit of detailed discussion of his arguments, so attention will be confined to his main thesis, namely, that the resistance of the environment to organisms is similar to the resistance of a conductor to an electric current. The reader is expected to see a striking resemblance between electrical potential (i.e. work done on a unit electric charge) and biotic potential (i.e. *possible* rate of increase). The whole argument seems to depend upon this double use of the word "potential."

Chapman continually reiterates the importance of his hypothesis in enabling us to express biotic factors in a quantitative way. However, he makes only one attempt to give an example of such quantitative expression. Having experimentally determined the density of *Tribolium confusum* under certain conditions, he proceeds to calculate environmental resistance by means of his formula. A glance at this example (3, p. 120) shows that the only use made of the experimentally determined density is to multiply *both* sides of the equation by it. Clearly the result is independent of density, and Chapman's hypothesis completely fails to help us to deal quantitatively with animal populations.

Competition.

It has already been shown that competition is capable of producing balance, and so of limiting animal populations. Indeed, any factor that produces balance is almost necessarily some form of competition, for balance can be produced only if increasing density decreases the chance of survival of an average individual. There is, of course, nothing new in the idea that competition is the major factor limiting populations, for this idea is fundamental to the epoch-making work of Malthus (14) on the population problem.

Many organisms alter the chemical and physical nature of their environment, and, generally, the increase in density of such organisms causes the character of the environment to become progressively less suitable for themselves. This clearly is a form of competition and provides the mechanism necessary for balance. It appears to be of major importance in the control of plants and micro-organisms, and not only limits the densities of species but also plays an important part in determining what other species may exist in the same environment. Competition of this type is sometimes also of importance to animals. For example, by destroying vegetation grazing animals alter the light, humidity and other physical factors near the ground, so making the environment unsuitable for many animals and plants that live on or close to the ground, while making it suitable for other animals and plants that would have been unable to live in the shade of the vegetation. Thus the alteration of the physical qualities of the environment by the activities of animals may be of the utmost importance in determining what kinds of animals can live together in any given environment.

Though a species may sometimes limit its own density by altering the chemical and physical qualities of its environment, such limitation seems to be unusual amongst animals. Generally speaking, animals appear to be limited in density, either directly or indirectly, by the difficulty they experience in finding the things they require for existence, or by the ease with which they are found by natural enemies. We are thus faced with the problem of the competition that exists amongst animals when searching, and the whole of the investigation that follows is concerned with this important problem.

Examination of the problem of searching shows that it is fundamentally very simple, provided the searching within a population is random. Before further investigation, therefore, we must find if it may safely be claimed that the searching within animal populations is actually random.

It is important to realise that we are not concerned with the searching of individuals, but with that of whole populations. Many individual animals follow a definite plan when searching. For example, a fox follows the scent of a rabbit, and a bee systematically moves from flower to flower without returning on its course. However, there is nothing to prevent an area that has been searched by an individual from again being searched systematically by another, or even the same, individual. If individuals, or groups of individuals, search independently of one another, the searching within the *population* is unorganised, and therefore random. Systematic searching by individuals improves the efficiency of the individuals, but otherwise the character of the searching within a population remains unaltered. Therefore, when investigating the problem of competition, we may safely assume that the searching is random.

We will now examine this question of random searching. The area searched by animals may be measured in two distinct ways. We may, as it were, follow the animals throughout the whole of their wanderings and measure the area they search, without reference to whether any portions have already been searched, and so measured, or not. This we will call the area *traversed* by the animals. On the other hand, we may measure only the previously unsearched area the animals search. This we will call the area *covered* by the animals. Thus the area *traversed* represents the total amount of searching carried out by the animals, while the area *covered* represents their successful searching, i.e. it is the area within which the objects sought have been found.

Suppose we now take a unit of area, say a square mile, and consider what happens at each step when animals traverse a further tenth of that area. When the animals begin to traverse the first tenth of the area, no part of the area has already been searched, so in traversing one-tenth the animals also cover one-tenth of the area. At the beginning of the next step only nine-tenths of the area remains unsearched, so, as the animals search at random, only nine-tenths of the second tenth of the area they search is previously unsearched area. Consequently after traversing two-tenths of the area the animals have covered only 1·9-tenths. Similarly, after traversing three-tenths of the area the animals have covered only 2·71-tenths. The calculation may be continued in this way indefinitely, and it is clear from the character of the problem that, at each step of one-tenth of area traversed, the animals cover a smaller fraction of area than in the preceding step. Also, because at each step the animals cover only one-tenth of the previously unsearched area, the whole area can never be completely searched. This, however, is true only if the total area occupied by the animals (not the unit of area considered) is very large. When the results of such a pro-

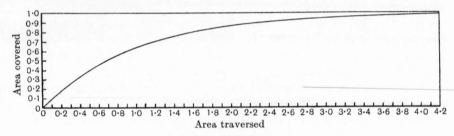

Fig. 1. The "competition curve."

gressive calculation are plotted, they are found to approximate to the curve shown in Fig. 1.

Such a calculation gives the general character of the effects produced by progressively increasing competition, and the original work on the present investigation was based on a curve calculated in this way. However, such a curve only approximates to the true form. Thus, when the animals have nearly completed their search of the first tenth of the area, only slightly more than nine-tenths of the area remains unsearched. Consequently even while traversing the first tenth of the area the animals spend some small part of the time searching over areas that have already been searched, and the same type of error runs through the remainder of the calculation. The calculation could give the correct result only if it were based upon indefinitely small steps. For this reason I approached Prof. V. A. Bailey, who gave me the formula (see Bailey (**1**, p. 69)) upon which the "competition curve" shown in Fig. 1 is based. This curve was then used throughout the investigation.

It may be mentioned that Fiske (**8**) used a curve, based on arithmetical calculations, which was essentially similar to the "competition curve," and that

Thompson (**21**) made use of a formula (given him by Prof. Deltheil of Toulouse) virtually the same as that on which the "competition curve" is based. However, both these authors were concerned only with the problem of superparasitism, a very specialised form of competition, and neither attempted to use the curve or formula for the investigation of the general problem of competition.

Examination of Fig. 1 shows that as the area traversed increases there is a progressive diminution in the rate of increase of the area covered. That is to say, the searching animals have progressively increasing difficulty in finding the things they seek. This is shown more directly in Fig. 2, which is easily derived from Fig. 1. Thus there is a definite relation (expressed in Fig. 2) between

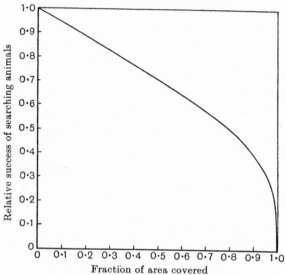

Fig. 2. Curve showing how increasing intensity of competition decreases the success of an average individual in finding the things it seeks. The success of an individual when free from competition is represented by unity.

the reduction of the success of the searching animals and the increase of the intensity of competition; and, with random searching, this relation is perfectly general, and so is independent of the properties of animals and those of their environments. Consequently, the "competition curve" has a general application to all problems of random searching.

It should be noticed, however, that the "competition curve" represents a probability. If small numbers of animals and small areas are taken, it is likely that the relation between the area traversed and that covered will not be found to be exactly as shown in Fig. 1. This does not indicate that there is anything wrong with the "competition curve," but merely that small samples of a statistical population are not necessarily completely representative of the large population from which they are taken. As in the present investigation we are always concerned with large populations, it is safe to conclude that the probability represented by the "competition curve" corresponds closely to what actually takes place in nature.

Before making use of the "competition curve" to investigate the limitation of the densities of animals it is necessary to define certain properties.

The number of times a population of animals would be multiplied in each generation, if unchecked, will be referred to as the *power of increase* of the species under the given conditions. The value of this property determines the fraction of the animals that needs to be destroyed in each generation in order to prevent increase in density.

The area *effectively* traversed by an average individual during its lifetime will be referred to as the *area of discovery* of the species under the given conditions. For example, if an average individual fails to capture, say, half the objects of the required kind that it meets, then the area of discovery is half the area traversed. The value of the area of discovery is determined partly by the properties of the searching animals, and partly by the properties of the objects sought. Thus it is dependent upon the movement, the keenness of the senses, and the efficiency of capture of an average individual when searching, and also upon the movement, size, appearance, smell, etc., and the efficiency in resisting capture of an average object of the kind sought. Consequently, under given conditions, a species has a different area of discovery for each kind of object it seeks. The value of the area of discovery defines the efficiency of a species in discovering and utilising objects of a given kind under given conditions, and determines the density of animals necessary in order to cause any given degree of intraspecific competition.

It is particularly important to recognise that these two properties respectively embrace all those things that influence the possible rate of increase of the animals, and all those that influence the efficiency of the animals in searching. Thus they are not merely properties of species, but properties of species when living under given conditions—the same species may have different properties in different places, or in the same place at different times. Also, it is important to notice that climatic conditions and other environmental factors play their part in determining the values of these properties, for they influence the vitality and activity of animals. Consequently, though such factors may not be specifically mentioned, they appear implicitly in all investigations in which values are given to the powers of increase and areas of discovery of animals.

Further increase of a population is prevented when all the surplus animals are destroyed, or when the animals are prevented from producing any surplus. When this happens the animals are clearly in a state of stationary balance with their environments, and maintain their population densities unchanged from generation to generation under constant conditions. This will be referred to as the *steady state*, and the densities of the animals when at this position of balance as their *steady densities* under the given conditions.

It is a relatively simple matter to determine the steady densities of animals when we know the values of their areas of discovery and powers of increase. Let us take a simple example. We will suppose that an entomophagous parasite attacks a certain species of host, that one host individual provides sufficient food for the full development of one parasite, that the area of discovery of the parasite is 0·04, that the power of increase of the host is 50, and that no factors operate other than those specifically mentioned. Clearly the steady state will be reached when the parasites are sufficiently numerous to destroy 49 out of every 50 hosts, and when there are sufficient hosts to maintain this density of parasites.

The parasites, then, are required to destroy 98 per cent. of the hosts, and so to *cover* 0·98 of the area occupied by the animals. To do this, it is necessary for the parasites to *traverse* an area of 3·91, as will be seen from examination of the "competition curve" (Fig. 1).

The required density of parasites, therefore, is 3·91/0·04, i.e. 98 (approx.).

But, in order that the density of the parasites may be maintained exactly, each parasite is required to find on the average one host[1].

Hence, the parasites are required to find 98 hosts in the area of 0·98 they cover, so that the steady density of hosts is 98/0·98, i.e. 100.

The steady densities calculated, of course, are the number of animals per unit of area. It is always convenient to choose a large unit for the measurement of area, so that the areas of discovery of the animals are represented by fractions, for the densities of animals can then be given in whole numbers. If small units of measurement are used the character of the results obtained is actually unaffected, but the densities calculated have to be expressed as small fractions of an animal per unit of area, which is undesirable.

It should also be noticed that the densities calculated are those within the areas in which the animals interact, and not necessarily within the whole countryside. Thus, if the animals can live only in areas containing a certain kind of vegetation, then the calculated densities are those within such areas, while the intervening areas in which the vegetation is unsuitable for the animals are ignored. Other things being equal, then, the density of a species within the whole countryside varies directly with the fraction of the countryside that provides suitable conditions for the species. It will be shown later that this is only approximately true.

The example just given is an exceptionally simple one, but it illustrates how the problem of the competition of animals may be investigated arithmetically. By assuming different properties for the animals, and different kinds of association between animals, or between animals and their environments, it is possible in this way to investigate how competition influences the

---

[1] Though only the female parasites search for hosts, it is convenient to consider the searching of an average individual, both males and females being included when making the average, and so establishing the value of the area of discovery.

densities of animals in all the principal types of situation known to exist in nature. Originally this arithmetical method was used for the investigation of almost all the problems that are here presented, but it is cumbersome and makes an adequate presentation of the subject very difficult. I therefore placed the problems before Prof. V. A. Bailey, who undertook the onerous task of investigating them mathematically[1]. The results obtained arithmetically were confirmed by the mathematical investigation, and the work was extended to certain problems that were not amenable to the arithmetical method.

In order to make any progress it was clearly necessary first to investigate ideally simple situations, even though these may have no counterpart in nature. Later, new factors were introduced, one at a time, in order to see how these influence the results already obtained. In this way the major types of factors known to influence animals were investigated. Unless some important factor capable of nullifying the effects of competition has been overlooked, which seems unlikely, the results should correspond to the facts of nature, for we know that animals do search for the things they require, and that competition does exist. It will later be seen that in their general features the results obtained in this investigation correspond to the observed facts, but more detailed observation and experiment is necessary in order to show whether there is a similar correspondence in detail.

The more important conclusions that have been obtained by a study of the problem of the competition that exists between animals when searching are given in Part II of this paper. These conclusions inevitably follow from the formulation of the problem already given, but for their rigorous proof much use needs to be made of mathematics, and it is thought desirable to postpone this to subsequent publications. However, when possible, brief general arguments are given to show that the conclusions are entirely reasonable.

PART II. THE EFFECT OF COMPETITION ON THE DENSITIES OF ANIMAL POPULATIONS.

In this part we shall investigate the way in which competition may determine the densities of animal populations in the types of situation that are believed to be of greatest importance under natural conditions. It must be realised, however, that though natural enemies and the availability of food and of suitable locations are factors that *may* control the densities of populations, they are not *always* control factors. For example, a species that is controlled by the availability of suitable locations is unaffected by the attack of a natural enemy if the latter merely destroys some of the surplus individuals that otherwise would die for lack of suitable places in which to live.

---

[1] Though arithmetic is a branch of mathematics, it is convenient in this paper to speak of *arithmetical* work when the arguments are conducted on definite numerical examples, and of *mathematical* work when the reasoning is by means of mathematical symbols.

(1) TWO CONCLUSIONS OF FUNDAMENTAL IMPORTANCE.

It has been shown (pp. 135 and 142) that intraspecific competition acts to populations in the way necessary to produce balance, and it is clear that the position of stationary balance is that at which the surplus animals are destroyed, or at which no surplus of animals is produced. This leads inevitably to the following conclusion:

C 1. Intraspecific competition automatically regulates the severity of its action to the requirements of each population, provided the inherent resistance of the environment is sufficiently low to permit the species to exist.

This means that, if animals find an environment suitable for their existence, they will increase in density until such time as the severity of competition, together with the inherent resistance of the environment, just counterbalances the innate tendency of the animals to increase in density. For example, let us suppose that conditions are suitable for the existence of a certain species of natural enemy. In this situation competition influences the density of prey available to the natural enemies. Starting with few natural enemies, their density (and consequently competition) increases until the density of prey is such that the surplus natural enemies fail to find sufficient prey for survival. Clearly, then, if individual natural enemies require large numbers of prey, decrease in the density of prey is arrested when there is a just sufficiently high density of prey for the requirements of the natural enemies. Similarly, when individual natural enemies require very small numbers of prey, balance is reached when the density of prey is very low. This is only one of a number of apparently paradoxical conclusions that follow immediately from C 1.

C 2. For the steady state to exist, each species must possess some advantage over all other species with respect to some one, or group, of the control factors to which it is subject.

A *control factor* is one which responds to increase in the density of a given species either (1) by increasing the severity of its action against the species (as do natural enemies), or (2) by causing intraspecific competition to decrease the chance of survival of individuals (as do limited supplies of food or of suitable places in which to live). It should be noticed that (1) is actually a special case of (2).

When the conditions of C 2 are not fulfilled, other species maintain the action of all the control factors to which a given species is subject at a greater severity than this species can withstand. Moreover, even when these conditions are fulfilled the given species may not be able to exist in the steady state, for its special advantage with respect to certain of its control factors may be more than counteracted by special disadvantages with respect to other control factors. However, if the species is not so affected by disadvantageous characters, its density tends to reach such a value that intraspecific competition, together with environmental resistance (which includes that due to the

10–2

presence of other species), just balances its natural tendency to increase in density.

[*Editor's Note:* In the original, material follows this excerpt.]

REFERENCES.

(1) **Bailey, V. A. (1931).** "The interaction between hosts and parasites." Q. J. Math. 2, 68–77.

(2) **Bodenheimer, F. S. (1928).** "Welche Faktoren regulieren die Individuenzahl einer Insektenart in der Natur?" Biol. Zbl. 48, 714–39.

(3) **Chapman, R. N. (1928).** "The quantitative analysis of environmental factors." Ecology, 9, 111–22.

(4) **Chapman, R. N. (1931).** "Animal ecology." New York and London.

(5) **Elton, C. (1930).** "Animal ecology and evolution." Oxford.

(6) **Elton, C. (1932).** "Territory among wood ants (*Formica rufa* L.) at Picket Hill." J. Animal Ecology, 1, 69–76.

(7) **Fisher, R. A. (1930).** "The genetical theory of natural selection." Oxford.

(8) **Fiske, W. F. (1910).** "Superparasitism: an important factor in the natural control of insects." J. Econ. Entom. 3, 88–97.

(9) **Holdaway, F. G. (1932).** "An experimental study of the growth of populations of the Flour Beetle, *Tribolium confusum* Duval, as affected by atmospheric moisture." Ecol. Monographs, 2, 262–304.

(10) **Howard, H. E. (1920).** "Territory in bird life." London.

(11) **Howard, L. O. and Fiske, W. F. (1912).** "The importation into the United States of the parasites of the gipsy-moth and the brown-tail moth." U.S. Dept. of Agric., Bureau of Entom., Bull. 91.

(12) **Lotka, J. A. (1920).** "Analytical note on certain rhythmic reactions in organic systems." Proc. Nat. Acad. Sci. 6, 410–15.

(13) **Lotka, J. A. (1925).** "Elements of physical biology." Baltimore.

(14) **Malthus, T. R.** "On the principle of population." London.

(15) **MacLagan, D. S. (1932).** "An ecological study of the 'Lucerne Flea' (*Smynthurus viridis* Linn.)." Bull. Ent. Res. 23, 101–45.

(16) **Martini, E. (1931).** "Zur Gradationslehre." Verh. Deuts. Ges. Angew. Ent., Mitglieder-Versamml. Rostock, Aug. 1930, 19–26. Berlin.

(17) **Nicholson, A. J. (1927).** "A new theory of mimicry in insects." Australian Zoologist, 5, Part 1. Sydney.

(18) **Pearl, R. (1926).** "The biology of population growth." London.

(19) **Russell, E. J. (1927).** "Soil conditions and plant growth." Rothamsted Monographs on Agricultural Science, London.

(20) **Strickland, E. H. (1928).** "Can birds hold injurious insects in check?" Scientific Monthly, 26, 48–56.

(21) **Thompson, W. R. (1924).** "La théorie mathématique de l'action des parasites entomophages et le facteur du hasard." Ann. Fac. Sci. Marseille, Ser. 2, 2, 69–89.

(22) **Thompson, W. R. (1930).** "The biological control of insect and plant pests." Publ. Empire Marketing Board 29, H.M. Stationery Office, London.

(23) **Uvarov, B. P. (1931).** "Insects and climate." Trans. Ent. Soc. London, 79, 1–247.

(24) **Volterra, V. (1926).** "Variazioni e fluttuazioni del numero d'individui in specie animali conviventi." Mem. Accad. Naz. Lincei (Sci. Fis. Mat. e Nat.), Ser. 6, 2, No. 3.

(25) **Volterra, V. (1927).** "Sulle fluttuazioni biologiche." Rend. R.A. dei Lincei, Ser. 6, 6.

(26) **Volterra, V. (1927).** "Leggi delle fluttuazioni biologiche." Rend. R.A. dei Lincei, Ser. 6, 6.

(27) **Volterra, V. (1927).** "Sulla periodicità delle fluttuazioni biologiche." Rend. R.A. dei Lincei, Ser. 6, 6.

(28) **Volterra, V. (1931).** "Leçons sur la théorie mathématique de la lutte pour la vie." Cahiers scientifiques, No. 7. Gauthier-Villars et Cie, Paris.

Part III

THE ABIOTIC SCHOOL
OF POPULATION
REGULATION: HISTORICAL

Editor's Comments
on Papers 4 and 5

4   **UVAROV**
     Excerpt from *Insects and Climate*

5   **ANDREWARTHA and BIRCH**
     A General Theory of the Numbers of Animals in Natural Populations

The economic entomologists were foremost in the abiotic school as well as in the biotic school. F. S. Bodenheimer (1928) suggested that only abiotic factors (climate) were important in the regulation of animal species. He believed that weather acts directly on survival and development in insects. He also believed that parasitism has less of an effect on population processes than it appears because eggs, larvae, and imagoes that are parasitized would often die anyway from effects of climate.

In 1931, B. P. Uvarov published "Insects and Climate" (Paper 4), which was commissioned by the British government to summarize the literature on insects and climate. We reprint here the final portion, which concerns forecasting and pest control. According to Uvarov, "Climate . . . is the ever-present factor in insect life."

The most important work representing the climate school is *The Distribution and Abundance of Animals* by Andrewartha and Birch (1954). We reprint their Chapter 14, "A General Theory of the Numbers of Animals in Natural Populations," as Paper 5.

Andrewartha and Birch made several extremely important contributions to the study of population regulation. First, They rejected the density-dependent/density-independent division of parameters, claiming that the division is not useful because any agent can be density dependent. Second, they rejected the balance-of-nature concept of natural populations; they commented that virtually no data support Nicholson's ideas.

In their empirical view of the world, Andrewartha and Birch divide the factors that determine the numbers of an animal population into weather, food, other organisms, and a place in which to live. Although generally, their theory may be classified as comprehensive, its main thrust is that weather is the only environmental factor that regulates both the distribution and the abundance of animals. As Birch, in "The Role of Weather in Determining the Distribution and Abundance of Animals" (1958), stated, "weather is a component of the environment of animals which effectively determines the limits to distribution and the abundance of some species." Birch repeated this basic thesis in a paper coauthored with P. R. Ehrlich (Paper 12). Later, however, in 1960 (Paper 19), Birch published an important paper regarding the influence of genetic factors in determining population density. This paper supports the self-regulation school of thought.

REFERENCES

Birch, L. C. 1958. The Role of Weather in Determining the Distribution and Abundance of Animals. *Cold Spring Harbor Symp. Quant. Biol.* **22**:203–218.

Bodenheimer, F. S. 1928. Welche Faktoren regulieren die Individuenzahl einer Insektenart in der Natur? *Biol. Zentralbl.* **48**:714–739.

4

INSECTS AND CLIMATE

B. P. Uvarov

[*Editor's Note:* In the original, material precedes this excerpt.]

(*d*) Forecasting.

The economic entomologists of the present day are mainly historians of insect pests, in so far as they record and describe their outbreaks, and sometimes attempt to analyse their causes. They are, however, also expected to be prophets and to forecast the seasonal appearance of pests, the years of outbreaks and the ability of an introduced pest to survive in a new country. This can be done only on the basis of a most intimate knowledge of the pest and of its relations to its environment, *i.e.* of a thorough understanding of the whole bewildering complex of environmental factors and of the responses thereto of the insect. We have seen in the preceding sections how limited and fragmentary is our knowledge on these points. It is not surprising, therefore, that it is only quite recently that the first, almost timid, attempts at entomological forecasting were made. These are reviewed in the following pages, and it will be seen that, though the results actually attained are as yet very modest, the outlook for the future is promising.

The basis for entomological forecasting of any kind is the physiological life-history of the pest and the climatic conditions of the area, or the season, though some successful work in this direction has been done even without exhaustive physiological studies. The main data which should be known for

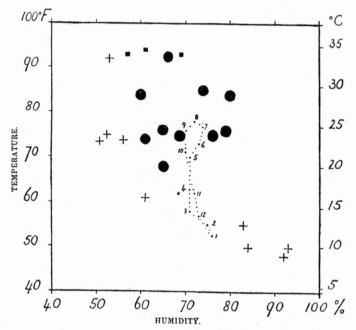

FIG. 53.—Graph showing the conditions of temperature and humidity which are favourable and unfavourable for the survival of rat fleas. Black circles signify more than 50 per cent. of survivals; a square signifies less than 50 per cent. of survivals; a cross, mortality of 100 per cent., or nearly so (data derived from Bacot, 1914). The dotted line is a climatograph for Jaffa, Palestine. It will be seen that the favourable area of the graph is fairly well defined and that the climate of Jaffa falls within that area for the summer months, but quite outside it for the winter months. (After Buxton, 1923.)

forecasting are the limiting values of the climatic factors (see p. 120) and the influence of the latter on the rate of development (see pp. 19, 72) and on the abundance of the insect studied (see p. 136).

(i) *Forecasting of distribution.*

One of the first attempts at entomological forecasting was that of Gill (1921), in which he defined the areas where malarial epidemics are possible. On the basis of the temperature and humidity factors limiting the distribution of mosquitos and necessary for the development of the malarial parasite, he concluded that the meteorological conditions of a large part of England and Wales, and of the whole of Scotland and Ireland are definitely unfavourable to the transmission of malaria by mosquitos.

An outbreak of bubonic plague in Jaffa caused Buxton (1923) to analyse the local climatic conditions in relation to the survival of the eggs and larvae of fleas, by constructing a climatograph (Fig. 53) which proved that the climate of Jaffa may be favourable to fleas in summer but not in winter.

Mansfield (1924) analysed the climatic conditions of the areas of distribution of the Colorado potato beetle in North America and those in Germany, and reached the conclusion that the German type of climate is probably not wholly suitable to the pest.

A series of papers dealing with the forecasting of distribution has been written by Cook (1924, 1925, 1928, 1929), who based his work not on physiological studies of insects, but on actual observations of their relative abundance in different years and different areas and on parallel studies of the meteorological data represented by hythergraphs. The following example will make this method clear.

The pale Western cutworm, *Porosagrotis orthogonia*, Morr., was very injurious in Montana during the period 1915–1920, and the data on the damage (percentage of crops destroyed), on the monthly mean temperatures and monthly mean totals of precipitation for all meteorological stations within the infested area (including the stations where no damage occurred), were obtained. From the climatic data, and by weighting each entry with figures representing the percentage of damage at the respective station, computations were made of the monthly means of temperature and rainfall side by side with the means for non-infested stations (see Table XXXIX).

TABLE XXXIX.

	Temperature (F.°).			Precipitation (inches).		
	Cutworm stations.	All stations.	Difference.	Cutworm stations.	All stations.	Difference.
July	69·2	68·4	0·8	1·48	1·48	−0·43
August	67·0	66·7	0·3	1·00	1·06	−0·06
September	55·7	55·5	0·2	1·00	1·35	−0·35
October	42·8	44·4	−1·6	1·07	0·85	0·22
November	28·3	32·0	−3·7	0·47	0·57	−0·10
December	22·6	22·4	−0·2	0·45	0·54	−0·09
January	25·0	23·2	1·8	0·44	0·38	0·06
February	24·1	20·7	3·4	0·50	0·51	−0·01
March	28·4	30·6	−2·2	0·69	0·73	−0·04
April	40·2	40·3	−0·1	1·46	1·21	0·25
May	51·0	51·5	−0·5	1·54	1·89	−0·35
June	61·9	63·6	− ·17	1·52	1·79	−0·27
Annual (mean and total)	43·0	43·3		11·19	12·36	

The data for the infested stations served to construct a hythergraph representing the optimum conditions for the insect (Fig. 37, p. 123). This optimum hythergraph showed a semi-arid condition throughout the year, with moderate rainfall in each of the three spring months. The summer was hot and dry, and the autumn drier than the spring. The snowfall during the entire winter was light.

The next step was to compare the hythergraphs for various stations with the optimum hythergraph, and, by noting the resemblances and differences, to determine whether the station is suitable for the insect to become abundant. On the basis of these comparisons a map was constructed (Fig. 38) showing the areas where the Pale Western cutworm can be " normally present," " occasionally present," or " absent " as a pest though occurring as a species.

An examination of all the available records of the outbreaks of the cutworm was then undertaken, and none have been found outside the zone of possible occurrence, while all major outbreaks were confined to the inner zone.

Similar work on purely climatological lines has been done by Cook (1929) on the army worm, *Cirphis unipuncta*, Haw., and on the alfalfa weevil, *Phytonomus posticus*, Gyll. (Cook, 1925). In both cases maps were constructed on the basis of hythergraphs, and the actual records of economic distribution were found to agree closely with the maps.

In contrast with Cook's work, that of Bodenheimer (1925) on the Mediterranean fruit-fly, *Ceratitis capitata*, Wied., was based primarily on physiological data for the insect. An equilateral hyperbola derived from Blunck's formula (see p. 25) of the thermal constant was constructed on the bases of the experimental data on the length of development at different temperatures. This curve, and the mean annual temperatures made it possible to calculate the possible number of annual generations in any given locality. As a result, it was possible to classify the countries where the fruit-fly occurs as follows :—

(1) Countries where a permanent acclimatisation is impossible, since the number of days in a year with effective temperatures is not sufficient for a single generation to develop. Example : England.

(2) Countries where *C. capitata* is established permanently but the continuity of generations is interrupted by winter, when the development of a single generation takes about 110 days. Examples : The Mediterranean region, the cooler parts of Australia, California.

(3) Countries where generations follow each other continuously, the average temperature never being below 13·5°. To this class belong the tropical regions.

The data derived from the hyperbola were then tested by comparing them with the number of generations actually developing in the different areas of Palestine, where the local climatic conditions vary considerably. It was found that in every case the actual number of generations agreed with that calculated. Since the number of annual generations in the case of the fruit-fly is an index to the degree of its economic importance, the method has proved to be of value in determining the areas of economic distribution.

Work on the same lines has been done by Bodenheimer on a number of insects transmitting diseases (1925a), on two species of *Sitophilus* (1927), and on *Sitotroga cerealella* (1926).

A very interesting and promising, though little studied method of determining areas suitable for a certain insect is the *phytometer* method (Clements, 1920 ; Clements and Goldsmith, 1924 ; additional references will be found in these two fundamental books). This method is based on the idea that

" every plant is a measure of the conditions under which it grows. To this extent it is an index of soil and climate, and consequently an indicator of the behaviour of other plants and of animals in the same spot."

The use of plants as indicators of certain conditions of soil and climate is, of course, not new, since the zonation of plant associations is commonly correlated with soil and climate. Similarly, ecoclimatic conditions can be judged by the presence, or absence, of certain plants.

Clements, as a botanist, developed the phytometer method for the study of the ecology of plants only, although his general definition quoted above suggests the possibility of using plants in studies of animal ecology. He even suggested, though in a very general way, that certain animals can also be used for the same purpose as *zoometers.*

A practical application of the phytometer idea to the ecological study of insects was made independently by Vinokurov, who used it in his work on the ecological distribution of grasshoppers in Siberia (Vinokurov and Rubtsov, 1930). Analyses of a number of plant associations were made, parallel with the study of their grasshopper population, and coefficients of common occurrence of certain species of plants and of grasshoppers were calculated. In this way, plant indicators for the occurrence of each grasshopper species were determined. Since grasshoppers do not depend directly on their plant indicators, the connection must be purely environmental, and, most probably, ecoclimatic, so that a plant may be utilised in this way as an indicator of an ecoclimate suitable for a species of insect. Further work in this direction should be very interesting.

(ii) *Forecasting of outbreaks.*

General considerations on the question of whether certain types of weather are favourable to a given pest have been expressed by many authors, but there are very few definite attempts at forecasting outbreaks on the basis of weather conditions.

The problem is certainly a very complex one, as has been pointed out by Stear (1928) and by Hinds (1928). Its study in each particular case involves quantitative work on the pest, studies of its physiological life-history, and an exact evaluation of the meteorological conditions and of their influence on the insect. The main difficulty lies, of course, in the fact that it has to be done some time before the beginning of the outbreak. This requires a theoretical evaluation of meteorological factors some time ahead, which amounts largely to guesswork, since the long-range forecasting of weather is still unreliable. However, with regard to many insect pests of temperate regions, the number of individuals entering hibernation bears a more or less definite relation to the number surviving the winter. Thus, the conditions of one year determine, to some extent, the probability of an outbreak during the next.

For example, the conditions favourable for an outbreak of the nun-moth have been defined by Sedlaczek (1915, 1916) as follows. The eggs, which hibernate from September to April, are very resistant to weather conditions. Winter weather has therefore no influence on the abundance of the insect. The development of larvae and pupae continues through May, June and July, and requires an accumulation of about 1500° of effective temperatures. In a warm summer the development is accomplished more rapidly, and the difference in the time of the emergence of the moths may amount to a month. The copulation flights of moths are possible only during still and rainless evenings with air temperature above 15°. The number of such evenings after the emergence of the moths and until the autumn depends on the time of their emergence. When there are more than twelve such evenings, the year is favourable for an increase and a gradation may be expected to begin in the following year.

Cook (1926, 1928*b*) applied the method of analysing weather conditions by means of hythergraphs to forecasting outbreaks of the pale Western cutworm, *Porosagrotis orthogonia*, Morr. Studies of hythergraphs for a series of years showed that the main factor in the abundance of the insect is the rainfall in spring and summer (May to August) of the year preceding the outbreak, the critical amount of the precipitation being between four and five inches. When it was over five inches, the cutworms decreased in the following year. When it was under four inches, an increase usually followed. Thus it is possible to predict the probability of an outbreak from the rainfall data of the preceding spring and summer. Essentially the same idea has been expressed by Seamans (1923) with regard to this species of cutworm. A few other examples can be found in entomological literature in which the study of conditions preceding an outbreak has made it possible to formulate conclusions as to its causes. These conclusions may often serve as a basis for forecasting outbreaks. So far, however, there has never been any actual forecasting, apart from the warnings issued by local entomologists based on the actual abundance of a pest. The first step towards organised forecasting may be seen in the annual surveys of the abundance of insect pests parallel with the meteorological conditions. This service is particularly well organised in the United States (Hyslop, 1922), where the weather data for each year are tabulated, presented graphically, and correlated with the insect outbreaks. In the temperature and precipitation studies departures from the normal, instead of the mean, are used, since acute outbreaks are considered as reflecting abnormal meteorological conditions. An arbitrary year is adopted starting with September, since insect outbreaks are considered as predetermined by the conditions prevailing during the late autumn and the early winter of the year preceding the actual outbreak and culminating before the end of the calendar year in which the outbreak occurs. Presumably a large amount of valuable data has been accumulated in this way, but so far this material has not been made public.

In England annual fluctuations in the abundance of the more common pests are recorded in the reports of the Ministry of Agriculture (Fryer, 1928), but no attempt is made to correlate these fluctuations with meteorological conditions, or to utilise the data for forecasting.

The collection of statistical data on the abundance of insect pests is particularly well organised in Germany, where since 1893 this work has been centralised in the " Sonderausschuss für Pflanzenschutz der Deutschen Landwirtschafts-Gesellschaft " (special section of the German Agricultural Society), but it is only quite recently that the enormous mass of data accumulated for the period have been summarised by Schnauer (1929). This author has presented a general survey of the course of the outbreaks of the main pests, viz. *Blitophaga* spp. (sugar-beet beetles), *Chlorops pumilionis*, Bjerk., *Jassus sexnotatus*, Fall., and *Hylemyia coarctata*, Fall. Apart from the data collected by the Agricultural Society, he has made use also of the entomological literature, agricultural reports, crop statistics, etc. The distribution of each species by years and by areas is given in a series of maps, while graphs representing the fluctuations in numbers from year to year are accompanied by diagrams showing the course of the main meteorological factors. With regard to each of the species treated, it was found possible to elucidate the probable connection of the outbreaks with a definite type of weather condition, and this conclusion can be used as a basis for forecasting in future. (Schnauer's paper contains a very extensive bibliography of the pests in question, as well as of the meteorological aspects of insect outbreaks generally and it should be consulted in the original.)

(iii) *Forecasting of seasonal events.*

The definition of areas suitable, or unsuitable, for a pest, and the forecasting of coming outbreaks are extremely important practical problems, but they do not arise as regularly as does the forecasting of the seasonal appearance of pests. Modern economic entomology includes a number of control measures which, in order to be effective, should be applied just before the appearance of the injurious stage. This involves continuous observations on the course of the development of the pest under natural conditions, but this is often not practically possible for an agriculturist who does not notice the pest until the damage is done. In practice, therefore, it is customary to recommend the application of certain control measures at more or less definite dates, and calendars of control measures in orchards, etc., are published for the guidance of agriculturists. It is scarcely necessary to point out that this practice is fundamentally wrong.

The realisation of the impossibility of correlating natural events with calendar dates has suggested to practical entomologists the idea of a *phenological* method, and control calendars have been evolved in which the times of the application of control measures are determined by some conspicuous events in the development of the host plant, *e.g.* the bursting of buds, the end of flowering, leaf-fall, etc. A typical example of this method is offered by the usual recommendation to spray apple trees against the codling moth immediately after the petals have fallen and before the calyx cups are closed. There is no doubt that the use of plants as indicators of the seasonal development of an insect may be carried much farther than is the practice at present (this point of view was strongly advocated, *e.g.* by Hopkins, 1918, and by Filipjev, 1928), but the problem has never been investigated in a sufficiently broad aspect. It must be realised that the plant most suitable as an indicator for an insect need not necessarily be its food-plant. Very careful and prolonged phenological observations on the insect and all plants usually occurring in its habitat are necessary to find the plant with the seasonal cycle most closely correlated with that of the insect. It must be always borne in mind, however, that the responses of every organism to external conditions are an integral part of its specific, and often its racial, characteristics, and no two organisms can be expected to respond to changes in all factors in exactly the same way. While, therefore, the flowering, for example, of a certain plant may normally coincide with the emergence of a certain insect, abnormal weather may in any given season affect the two organisms in a different way, in which case there will be a discrepancy in their development.

The *ecoclimatic* method of seasonal forecasting appears more reliable, at least on theoretical grounds, than those reviewed above. This is a term which may be conveniently applied to the method based on the physiological life-history of the insect, on one hand, and on the actual seasonal course of the weather, on the other. This method was originally suggested by the idea of the thermal constant for development (see p. 22). If the time necessary for the insect to complete a stage in its development depends on the accumulation of a definite amount of heat energy, as expressed by the sum of effective degrees of temperature, the actual observations on the temperatures from the beginning of the stage would show when that sum is approaching the constant, and when the stage may be supposed to be near its end.

The idea of the thermal constant, or of a constant sum of the effective day-degrees, has been used successfully by Glenn (1922, 1922*a*, 1922*b*; also Headlee,

1928) for forecasting the times of the appearance of various generations of the codling moth and for spraying against them. Experimental work carried out through several seasons enabled Glenn to estimate the average number of the effective day-degrees necessary to complete each stage. On the basis of these data a spraying calendar was prepared in which the time for the application of spraying against the larvae of each successive generation is indicated by the accumulation of the effective day-degrees. To compute the effective day-degrees, accurate thermograph records should be kept, and only the degrees above 10° taken into account. A correction must be introduced for temperatures above 30°, since they retard the development. Approximate determinations of the effective day-degrees may be made also from the maximum and minimum temperature according to a special formula.

Glenn's work has been continued by Shelford (1927), who introduced a number of important modifications and corrections. In his physiological investigations Shelford has taken into account not only the temperature, but all factors which may influence the duration of development, viz. variations in the temperature, humidity, etc. The investigations, partly described elsewhere (see p. 85), led to the evaluation of the rate of development at different conditions not in " day-degrees," but in developmental units (see p. 23). A total of 6480 developmental units was found to be necessary to complete the pupal stage, while 3864 units were necessary for the development of the eggs, and 18,000 units for the development of the larva. The practical procedure recommended for determining the times of spraying is as follows. The date of the first pupation of hibernating larvae kept out of doors, under conditions similar to those in the orchard, must be found by direct observation. From that date onwards, hygrothermograph records should be kept and the readings of the temperature and humidity for each hour should be tabulated. These readings should then be translated into developmental units, by means of a table showing the velocity values for each combination of temperature and humidity (see Table XL).

TABLE XL.

VELOCITY VALUES (NUMBER OF DEVELOPMENTAL UNITS PER HOUR) FOR VARIOUS TEM-
PERATURES AND HUMIDITIES, APPLICABLE TO THE PUPAE AND EGGS OF THE CODLING
MOTH. (After Shelford; only a small section of the original table is reproduced here.)

F.°.		Per cent. humidity.									
		32.	34.	36.	38.	40.	42.	44.	46.	48.	50.
75°	. .	22·1	22·1	22·2	22·3	22·3	22·4	22·5	22·6	22·7	22·8
74°	. .	20·7	20·9	21·1	21·2	21·2	21·3	21·3	21·4	21·5	21·6
73°	. .	19·7	19·9	20·1	20·2	20·4	20·5	20·6	20·6	20·7	20·8
72°	. .	18·9	19·0	19·1	19·2	19·2	19·3	19·4	19·5	19·7	19·8
71°	. .	18·0	18·1	18·2	18·3	18·4	18·5	18·6	18·7	18·9	19·0

Hourly values are then summarised, and when the sum approaches 6480 units, the time of the emergence of the moths may be predicted a week or more in advance (a correction may be necessary for the retardation or the acceleration of development caused by the autumn rainfall, and a special table is provided for the purpose). After this, if temperatures above 16·6° occur after sunset, the moths will begin laying eggs two days after emerging. From the date on which the first moth is estimated to have begun laying eggs, hygrother-mograph records should be continued until 3864 developmental units are accumulated which will correspond to the hatching of the eggs. The time of the development of the larvae in apples is further estimated. It should take 18,000 units. The procedure is continued throughout the season for successive generations, so that the time of the appearance of each one can be predicted some days in advance.

It is unfortunately not known whether Shelford's method has ever been applied for practical forecasting, although an example from actual observations is analysed by means of the method, and practically all calculated times fall within a day or so of the actual event.

There is no doubt that Shelford's method of developmental units is theoretically well founded and very exact. It has, however, some very serious drawbacks. It should be realised that the preliminary work on the physiological life-history of the codling moth, necessary for the preparation of the table of velocity values, has taken ten years. This means that work on a similar scale has to be carried out in the case of each insect for which the basic data for practical forecasting are desired. Of course, some parts of the work on the codling moth were of a pioneer character, and the corresponding data for other insects can be now obtained in less time, but the programme of work on physiological life-histories, as outlined by Shelford himself (see p. 169), is still sufficiently formidable. Consequently, the method can be applied in practice only with regard to pests of exceptional economic importance, in the case of which an accurate forecasting is absolutely essential for control.

Further, the practical application of the method, when the table of velocities is prepared, is not devoid of serious difficulties. The keeping of hygrothermo-graph records and the calculation of hourly velocity values, with various corrections, would not commend itself favourably to an average fruit-grower. Moreover, the initial date of all computations, that of the pupation of the hibernating larvae, has to be determined by direct observation, and the probability of an error here is very great, while the whole season's forecasting depends on the accurate determination of this date.

All these considerations raise serious doubts as to the practical value of Shelford's method of seasonal forecasting.

An interesting example of the possibility of forecasting seasonal events in the life of a pest for the purpose of its control is offered by the work of Prinz (1928) on the larvae of *Polyphylla olivieri*, Zap., damaging roots of vine in Trans-caucasia. In autumn the larvae burrow to a depth of 30–40 cm., when the soil temperature at 20 cm. reaches 10–12°, and move to the upper layers of the soil in spring at the same soil temperature (see p. 89). The use of carbon bisulphide against larvae is effective only when they are in the deeper layers of the soil. Collecting them by digging out is possible only when they are near the surface. Thus the knowledge of the soil temperature makes it possible to forecast the movements of the larvae and to determine the time for the application of one, or other, method of control. A similar connection was found by Prinz between the soil temperature and the seasonal movements of the vine *Phylloxera*. This knowledge again can be utilised for control.

(e) The Utilisation of Climatic Factors for the Control of Pests.

(i) *Phenological methods of control.*

Under this heading may be included the methods of controlling insect pests that aim at destroying the normal seasonal adjustment in the life-history of the pest and of its food-plant.

The best-known method of this kind is the control of the Hessian fly by the late sowing of winter wheat. This method is based on the fact that the life of an adult fly, which cannot feed, only lasts a few days. If the winter wheat is sown after the mass flight of the insect the crop will escape injury. The " fly-free " date can be established only by observations at an entomological station, and applies, of course, only to areas with the same climatic conditions. The necessity of making direct observations on the flight in every climatic area has been partly eliminated in the United States with the help of the, so-called, *bioclimatic law* developed by Hopkins (1918, 1919, 1921). This law, or, rather, this empirical rule, refers to the differences in the date of seasonal events according to latitude, longitude and altitude. The main clause of the rule is that " other conditions being equal, the variation in the time of occurrence of a given periodical event in life activity in temperate North America is at the general average rate of four days to each one degree of latitude, five degrees of longitude and 400 feet of altitude, later northward, eastward, and upward in the spring and early summer, and the reverse in late summer and autumn."

A map for North America was constructed showing the *isophanes*, that is, the theoretical lines along which all seasonal phenomena should occur at the same date, and this map can be used for the determination of the date of sowing winter wheat so as to escape infestation by the Hessian fly. Local conditions, however, cause considerable departures in the actual dates of seasonal events from those indicated by isophanes.

Znamenskiĭ (1924, 1925, 1926), in attempting to apply the bioclimatic law to conditions in Russia, had to introduce several important modifications. Instead of basing the isophanal map on degrees of latitude and longitude, he made use of the mean annual isotherms, and shifted the safe date of sowing four days later for each extra degree of the mean annual temperature. Another correction was introduced for precipitation, viz. for every 25 mm. of annual rainfall above the normal the date was shifted one day later.

Geissler (1927) found that climatic and phenological conditions of the European continent are such that an application of Hopkins' law to them is impracticable, and he suggested that, instead of the theoretical isophanes, maps of actual isophanes based on empirical data should be constructed.

The correlation between the stage of the development of maize at the time when eggs are laid by the corn-borer moths and the survival of the resulting larvae is very close (Huber, Neiswander and Salter, 1928). Therefore, an alteration in the date of planting, or the introduction of varieties developing at a different rate, presents a good phenological method of control. The principle of this method is, however, well known to every economic entomologist, since it has been recommended with regard to a number of insect pests, and there is no need to give other examples.

(ii) *Ecoclimatic methods of control.*

The cultural methods designed to alter unfavourably the climatic environment of a pest may be classified as ecoclimatic methods of control.

The fact that tsetse flies are very sensitive to air humidity suggested the idea of controlling their distribution by clearing infested forests so as to create conditions of temperature and evaporation unfavourable to the insects (Roubaud, 1909; Fiske, 1920; Swynnerton, 1921). This method is being studied at present in all its aspects by the recently established Tsetse Research Department in Tanganyika Territory (1929).

Essentially the same principle applies to the prevention of injury by borers in forests. For example, the injury by the white-pine weevil, *Pissodes strobi*, Peck., is invariably greater in open pure stands of white pine growing in full sunlight. In mixed stands, where hardwoods shade the pine, the injury is much less and decreases inversely with the intensity of shade until it reaches the zero point under a shade corresponding to that cast by an average stand of oak or maple. It is recommended, therefore, that white pine should be grown under a shelter-wood system that will provide a light shade for the young trees (Graham, 1926). A similar recommendation has been made for the prevention of attacks by *Cyllene robiniae*, Forst., on locust trees (Craighead, 1919).

The importance of the proper water balance in the food-plant for the insects feeding on it has been pointed out elsewhere, particularly with regard to bark-beetles (see p. 150), which develop best in trees having a water content below the normal. Craighead (1928) recorded that treatments aimed at increasing the water content of trees, such as defoliation (*i.e.* the reduction of the transpiration), or the supply of water to the roots, tend to check the development of bark-beetles and of the wood-staining fungi (*Ceratostomella*, sp.) associated with them.

Other examples of ecoclimatic and microclimatic methods of controlling insect pests can be found in the economic entomological literature, but the principle is sufficiently clear from the above cases. There is no doubt that, with the advance of knowledge regarding the ecoclimates and microclimates of insect habitats, methods of controlling insects by influencing their immediate climatic environment will be still further developed.

(iii) *Direct control by climatic factors.*

The use of radiant heat for the direct destruction of certain insects has been recommended more than once. Cunningham (1911) experimented with carpets infested with fleas and found that no live fleas remained after an exposure to sunlight for 60 minutes when the temperature under the carpet reached 27·8° and that over it was 29·5°. Reeves (1917) suggested controlling the alfalfa weevil by covering the surface of the field with something like a dust-mulch. On a bright hot day such a surface was heated by the sun to a degree sufficient to kill all stages of the pest. Craighead (1920) and Graham (1925, 1929) developed a method of controlling wood-borers in logs by exposing them to direct sunlight and turning them from time to time Patterson (1930) elaborated this method in great detail. Graham (1929) also recommended some methods of controlling borers in logs by a modification of the moisture content, *e.g.* by piling, barking and sun-curing, which reduce the water content, or by sprinkling the wood with water, or floating the logs, to increase the moisture content to a degree unfavourable for the pests. The possibilities of directly utilising climatic factors for the destruction of insects are very great, and the advantages of control methods in which the killing agency does not cost anything are obvious. It is to be hoped, therefore, that microclimatic investigations leading to such methods will find favour with economic entomologists.

Control methods which rely on the destruction of insects by high or low temperatures artificially produced do not come within the scope of the present work, and it will be sufficient to quote only some of the papers dealing with the subject, as follows :—

High temperature against insects in logs : Craighead and Loughborough, 1921 ; Graham, 1929 ; Snyder, 1923 ; Snyder and St. George, 1924 ; Welch, 1924 ; do., against grain, mill and household pests : Back and Duckett, 1918 ; Dean, 1911 ; Dean and Schenk, 1929 ; Gibson, 1916 ; Goodwin, 1914, 1922 ; Mills, 1836 ; Scott, Abbott and Dudley, 1918 ; do., against bedbugs : Gibson, 1918 ; Harned and Allen, 1925 ; W. Ross, 1916 ; E. Scott, Abbott and Dudley, 1918 ; do., against termites : Snyder, 1929 ; do., against the pink bollworm : Gough, 1916 ; Storey, 1916, 1917.

Low temperature : Back and Duckett, 1918 ; Back and Pemberton, 1916 ; Howard, 1896, 1897 ; Larson and Simmons, 1924 ; De Ong, 1921.

Vacuum : Back and Cotton, 1925.

Artificial light in orchards (apart from light traps, the literature on which is very voluminous) : Herns, 1929 ; D. Collins and Nixon, 1930.

(iv) *Effects of weather and climate on controlling insects by artificial methods.*

Weather conditions are a factor of outstanding importance in the application of a number of methods of chemical control.

Rains constitute one of the greatest obstacles to successful spraying with stomach poisons, through washing away the poison from plants and thus necessitating repeated spraying. Even a heavy dew has the same effect. Strong wind also affects spraying and dusting operations very unfavourably. The successful use of bait-traps and light-traps for catching moths is more dependent on weather conditions than is any other method, since the flight activities of moths are greatly affected by all weather factors. Poisoned bran baits for locusts and grasshoppers must be used with due regard to weather conditions, because the feeding on baits and the period during which the baits are effective depend on the temperature and humidity. The same applies to the control of locusts by barriers and trenches, since the behaviour of locust hoppers is an almost direct response to weather conditions. The method cannot be used, for example, in cool, or in very hot weather, when locust hoppers do not march and cannot be driven.

The toxicity to insects of stomach poisons and fumigants greatly depends on the temperature, as does that of contact insecticides (Shafer, 1915 ; Brinley and Baker, 1927). The possibility of injury to the foliage by sprays is also determined by weather conditions (Fernald and Bourne, 1922).

Meteorological factors are of exceptional importance in the biological control of pests, though it must be admitted that, so far, most of the work in connection with the introduction of the natural enemies of insect pests from one country into another has been, and still is, conducted without any serious attention to the climatic aspect of the problem. It is not known what percentage of the failures of introduced parasites to establish themselves in a new country is due to the climatic conditions being unsuitable. There is, however, one recent case of an unsuccessful attempt at biological control which has been well investigated climatically. I refer to the introduction into Egypt and Palestine of a Coccinellid,

Cryptolaemus montrouzieri, Muls., for the control of the sugar-cane mealy-bug, *Pseudococcus sacchari,* Ckll. Nearly 250,000 beetles were introduced into Egypt in the course of seven years; but without any success. Hall (1926) explained this mainly on climatic grounds, and Bodenheimer and Guttfeld (1929) confirmed his conclusions with regard to Palestine, where the climate closely resembles that of Egypt and where an attempt has been made to introduce the same beetle for the control of the citrus mealy-bug, *Pseudococcus citri,* Risso. The last two authors have thoroughly investigated the problem by studying the physiological life-histories of both species under the actual climatic conditions of Palestine. The rate of development of both insects in different months, *i.e.* under different mean temperatures, was determined and the curves (hyperbolae) of development as dependent on the temperature were constructed. It was found that *Pseudococcus citri* in the coastal zone produces 7 to 8 annual generations, while *Cryptolaemus* has six. A study of the limiting factors proved that the beetle suffers greatly both in winter from cold and humidity, and in summer from the excessive heat and dryness. *Cryptolaemus* can only effectively control *Pseudococcus* with mean temperatures of about 18–23° for 3 to 5 months, which are never found either in Palestine or in Egypt. On the contrary, the same beetle proved to be able to establish itself in California and on the Riviera, where the climatic conditions are more favourable to it.

Bodenheimer and Guttfeld studied by the same method several native natural enemies of the citrus mealy-bug and found that the Hemerobiid, *Sympherobius amicus,* Navas, and a Cecidomyid are much better adjusted to the local climate than *Cryptolaemus,* and they are very effective as controls.

These investigations are of great general interest, since they prove the possibility of determining the chances of a predator or a parasite to establish itself when introduced into a new country, and of evaluating their probable controlling influence on the pest, by studying the physiological life-histories of the insects concerned in their relation to the actual climate of the country. The method deserves the serious attention of all entomologists and institutions engaged in biological control.

The practical necessity for similar bioclimatic studies in all cases of proposed introduction is made clear by the fact that the greatest percentage of successful introductions of parasites falls to Hawaii, a country where the monthly means of temperature and rainfall are practically the same throughout the year and no extremes of any factor occur. On the other hand, there are scarcely any cases of successful biological control in countries having a temperate climate and pronounced seasonal fluctuations in weather (Stellwaag, 1929*a*).

It is hardly necessary to quote examples illustrating the importance of weather conditions for the use of parasitic fungi in insect control. Wherever the practical utilisation of fungi for control has been attempted, it has been invariably found that no results can be obtained if the weather is unfavourable to the development of the fungus. On the other hand, suitable weather (abundant humidity and sufficiently high temperature) results in spontaneous epidemics, and the artificial dissemination of pathogenic fungi becomes unnecessary.

BIBLIOGRAPHY

[*Editor's Note:* Bibliography has been abridged to include only those references cited in the excerpt.]

Back, E. A., and Cotton, R. T. 1925. The use of vacuum for insect control.—*J. Agr. Res.,* **31**:1035–1041, tab.

Back, E. A., and Duckett, A. B. 1918. Bean and pea weevils.—Farmers' Bull. U.S. Dept. Agric., **983**:24 pp., 24 figs.

Back, E. A., and Pemberton, C. E. 1916. Effect of cold-storage temperatures upon the Mediterranean fruit fly.—J. Agric. Res., **5**:657–666, 1 tab.

Bacot, A. 1914. A study of the bionomics of the common rat fleas and other species associated with human habitations, with special reference to the influence of temperature and humidity at various periods of the life-history of the insect.—J. Hyg. (Plague Suppl.), **3**:447–654, 8 pls., 60 tab.

Bodenheimer, F. S. 1925. On predicting the developmental cycles of insects. i. *Ceratitis capitala,* Wied.—Bull. Soc. ent. Egypte, **1924**:149–157, 3 tab.

———. 1925a. Ueber die Voraussage der Generationenzahl von Insekten. ii. Die Temperaturentwicklungskurve bei medizinisch wichtigen Insekten.—Zbl. Bakt. (i) **93**:474–480, 9 figs.

———. 1926. Ueber die Voraussage der Generationenzahl von Insekten. iii. Die Bedeutung des Klimas für die landwirtschaftliche Entomologie.—Z. angew. Ent., **12**:91–122, 7 figs.

———. 1927. Über die ökologischen Grenzen der Verbreitung von *Calandra oryzae,* L., und *Calandra granaria,* L.—Z. wiss. InsektBiol., **22**:65–73, 3 Figs., 4 tab.

Bodenheimer, F. S., and Guttfeld, M. 1929. Über die Möglichkeiten einer biologischen Bekämpfung von *Pseudococcus citri,* Risso, in Palästina.—Z. angew. Ent., **15**:67–136, 24 figs., **17** tab.

Brinley, F. J., and Baker, R. H. 1927. Some factors influencing the toxicity of hydrocyanic acid for insects.—Biol. Bull., **53**:201–207.

Buxton, P. A. 1923. On predicting the seasonal prevalence of an insect.—Trans. Soc. Trop. Med. Hyg., **16**:465–468, 1 fig.

Clements, F. E. 1920. Plant indicators. The relation of plant communities to process and practice.—Publ. Carnegie Instn. Washington, **290**:388 pp., 92 pls.

Clements, F. E., and Goldsmith, G. W. 1924. The phytometer method in ecology. The plant and community as instruments.—Publ. Carnegie Instn. Washington, **356**:106 pp., 11 pls.

Collins, D. L., and Nixon, M. W. 1930. Responses to light of the bud moth and leaf roller.—Bull. N. York Agric. Exper. Sta., **583**:32 pp.

Cook, W. C. 1924a. Climatic variation and moth flights at Bozeman.—Canad. Ent., **56**:229–234.

———. 1925. The distribution of the alfalfa weevil (*Phytonomus posticus,* Gyll.). A study in physical ecology.—J. Agric. Res., **30**:479–491, 12 figs.

———. 1928. A note regarding temperature curves.—J. Econ. Ent., **21**:510–511.

———. 1928b. Weather and probability of outbreaks of the pale western cutworm in Montana and near-by states.—Mon. Weather Rev., **56**:103–106, 1 fig., 3 tab.

Cook, W. C. 1929. A bioclimatic zonation for studying the economic distribution of injurious insects.—Ecology, **10**:282–293, 3 figs., 2 tab.

Craighead, F. C. 1919. Protection from the locust-borer.—Bull U.S. Dept. Agr., **787**: 12 pp., 3 pls.

———. 1920. Direct sunlight as a factor in forest insect control.—Proc. Ent. Soc. Wash., **22**:106–108.

———. 1928. Interrelations of tree-killing bark-beetles (*Dendroctonus*) and blue stains.—J. Forestry, **26**:886–887.

Craighead, F. C., and Loughborough, W. K. 1921. Temperatures fatal to larvae of red-headed ash-borer as applicable to commercial kiln drying.—*Loc. cit.*, **19:** 250–254.

Cunningham, J. 1911. The destruction of fleas by exposure to the sun.—Sci. Mem. Med. Sanit. Depts. Ind., **40:**27 pp., 3 figs., 8 tab.

Dean, G. 1911. Heat as a means of controlling mill insects.—J. Econ. Ent., **4:**142–158, 9 charts.

Dean, G. A., and Schenk, G. 1929. The control of stored grain and flour mill insects.—Trans. 4th Int. Congr. Entom. Ithaca, **2:**203–228, 2 figs.

De Ong, E. R. 1921. Cold storage control of insects.—J. Econ. Ent., **14:**444–447.

Fernald, H. T., and Bourne, A. I. 1922. Injury to foliage by arsenical sprays.—Bull. Mass. Agric. Exper. Sta., **207:**19 pp., 23 figs; **210:**89–98, 14 figs.

Filipjev, I. N. 1928. [Phenology and injurious insects.] (In Russian).—Izvest. Gosud. Inst. Op. Agron., Leningrad, **1927:**441–456, 1 tab., 7 charts.

Fiske, W. F. 1920. Investigations into the bionomics of *Glossina palpalis.*—Bull. Ent. Res., **10:**347–463.

Fryer, J. C. F. 1928. Insect pests of crops 1925–1927.—Misc. Pub. Min. Agric. Fish. Lond., **62:**47 pp., 1 diagr.

Geissler, A. 1927. Das "Bioklimatische Gesetz" von Hopkins und der Versuch seiner Nutzbarmachung für die Landwirtschaft.—NachrBl. deuts. PflSch-Dienste, **7:**35–36, 43–44.

Gibson, A. 1916. Superheating as a control method for insects which infest stored products.—Proc. Ent. Soc. Brit. Columb., **9:**83–84.

——. 1918. The value of high temperature for controlling the common bed-bug.—Agric. Gaz. Canada, **5:**949–951, 2 figs., 1 tab.

Gill, C. A. 1921. The influence of humidity on the life-history of mosquitoes and on their power to transmit infection.—Trans. Soc. Trop. Med. Hyg., **14:**77–83.

Glenn, F. W. 1922. Codling-moth investigations of the State entomologists' office, 1915, 1916, 1917.—Bull. Illinois Nat. Hist. Surv., **14:**219–288, 8 figs, 7 graphs, 51 tab., 3 charts.

——. 1922*a*. Relation of temperature to development of the codling moth.—J. Econ. Ent., **15:**193–198, 6 tab.

——. 1922*b*. A problem in the relation of temperature to rate of insect development.—Kansas Univ. Sci. Bu:l., **14:**317–323, 1 fig.

Goodwin, W. H. 1914. Some factors affecting results in the use of high temperatures for the control of insects injuring cereal products.—J. Econ. Ent., **7:**313–322, tab.

——. 1922. Heat for control of cereal insects.—Bull. Ohio Agric. Exper. Sta., **354:** 18 pp., tab.

Gough, L. 1916. Note on a machine to kill *Gelechia* larvae by hot air and the effects of heat on *Gelechia* larvae and cotton seed.—Bull. Min. Agric. Egypt, **6:**18 pp., 3 pls., 4 tab.

Graham, S. 1925. The felled tree trunk as an ecological unit.—Ecology, **6:**397–411, 19 figs.

——. 1926. Biology and control of the white-pine weevil, *Pissodes strobei*, Peck.—Bull. Cornell Univ. Agric. Exper. Sta., **449:**32 pp., 14 figs.

——. 1929. Principles of forest entomology. London. 339 pp., 149 figs.

Hall, W. J. 1926. The introduction of *Cryptolaemus montrouzieri*, Muls., into Egypt.—Bull. Ent. Res., **17:**385–392, 2 pls.

Harned, R. W., and Allen, H. W. 1925. Controlling bedbugs in steam-heated rooms.—J. Econ. Ent., **18:**320–331, 2 figs.

Headlee, T. J. 1928. Some data relative to the relationship of temperature to codling-moth activity.—J. N.Y. Ent. Soc., **36:**147–163, 6 tab.

Herms, W. B. 1929. A field test of the effect of artificial light on the behaviour of the codling moth, *Carpocapsa pomonella*, Linn.—J. Econ. Ent., **22:**78–88, 4 tab.

Hinds, W. E. 1928. Is there any definite basis for forecasting insect outbreaks and ascertaining if control measures are practical? A discussion from a research standpoint.—J. Econ. Ent., **21**:559–563.

Hopkins, A. D. 1918. Periodical events and natural law as guides to agricultural research and practice.—Mon. Weather Rev. Suppl., **9**:42 pp., 24 figs.

———. 1921. The bioclimatic law and its application to research and practice in entomology.—J. Wash. Acad. Sci., **11**:141–142.

Howard, L. O. 1896. Some temperature effects on household insects.—Bull. Div. Ent. U.S. Dept. Agric., (n.s.) **6**:13–17.

———. 1897. Temperature experiments as affecting received ideas on the hibernation of injurious insects.—*Loc. cit.*, **9**:18–19.

Huber, L. L., Neiswander, C. R., and Salter, R. M. 1928. The European cornborer and its environment.—Bull. Ohio Agric. Exper. Sta., **429**:196 pp., 85 tab., 20 figs.

Hyslop, J. A. 1922. Summary of insect conditions throughout the United States during 1921.—Bull. U.S. Dept. Agric., **1103**:51 pp., 28 figs., 11 tab.

Larson, A. O., and Simmons. P. 1924. Insecticidal effect of cold storage on bean weevil.—J. Agric. Res., **27**:99–105, 5 tab.

Mansfield, K. 1924. Der Koloradokartoffelkäfer im Klima Deutschlands.—NachrBl. deuts. PflSchDienst., **4**:45–46.

Mills, W. 1836. Observations upon the corn weevil.—Trans. Ent. Soc. Lond., (1) **1**: 241–242.

Patterson, J. E. 1930. Control of the mountain pine beetle in lodgepole pine by the use of solar heat.—Techn. Bull. U.S. Dept. Agric., **195**:19 pp., 11 figs.

Prinz, I. Y. 1928. [On the pests of the vine.] (In Russian).—Ent. Cab. Agric. Cooper. Soc. Concordia, Tiflis, **2**:127 pp., 3 maps, figs., tab.

Reeves, G. I. 1917. The alfalfa weevil investigations.—J. Econ. Ent., **10**:123–130.

Ross, W. A. 1916. Eradication of the bedbug by superheating.—Canad. Ent., **48**: 74–76.

Roubaud, E. 1909. Recherches biologiques sur les conditions de viviparité et de vie larvaire de *Glossina palpalis*, R. Desv.—C.R. Acad. Sci. Paris, **148**:195–197.

Schnauer, W. 1929. Untersuchungen über Schadegebiet und Umweltfaktoren einiger landwirtschaftlichen Schädlinge in Deutschland auf Grund statistischer Unterlagen.—Z. angew. Ent., **15**:565–627, 24 figs.

Scott, E. W., Abbott, W. S., and Dudley, J. E. 1918. Results of experiments with miscellaneous substances against bedbugs, cockroaches, clothes moths, and carpet beetles.—Bull. U.S. Dept. Agric., **707**:36pp.. 10 tab.

Seamans, H. L. 1923. Forecasting outbreaks of the pale western cutworm in Alberta.—Canad. Ent., **55**:51–53.

Sedlaczek, W. 1915. Einflüsse der Witterung auf die ortsweisen Lebenserscheinungen der Nonne *(Lymantria monacha).*—Zbl. ges. Forstwesen, **41**:321–342.

———. 1916. Einwirkung des Klimas auf die Entwicklung der Nonne.—Verh. zool.-bot. Ges. Wien, **66**:28–33.

Shafer, G. D. 1915. How contact insecticides kill.—Tech. Bull. Michigan Agric. Exper. Sta., **21**:67 pp., 1 pl., 8 tab., 3 figs.

Shelford, V. E. 1927. An experimental investigation of the relations of the codling moth to weather and climate.—Bull. Illinois Nat. Hist. Surv., **16**:307–440, 34 figs., 28 tab.

Snyder, T. E. 1923. High temperature as a remedy for *Lyctus* powder-post beetles.—J. Forestr., **21**:810–814.

———. 1929. Damage by termites causes modification of building codes.—Trans. 4th Int. Congr. Ent., Ithaca, **2**:268–277, 3 figs.

Snyder, T. E., and St. George, R. A. 1924. Determination of temperature fatal to the powder-post beetle, *Lyctus planicollis*, Leconte, by steaming infested ash and oak lumber in a kiln.—J. Agric. Res., **28**:1033–1038, pl.

Stear, J. R. 1928. Insect prediction hazards with particular reference to the leaf-hopper, *Empoa pomaria,* McA.—Proc. Penn. Acad. Sci., Harrisburg, **2:**54–58.

Stellwaag, F. 1929a. Neue Erfahrungen in der biologischen Bekämpfung schadlicher Insekten.—Verh. deuts. Ges. angew. Ent., **7:**15–32.

Storey, G. 1916. Simon's hot-air machine for the treatment of cotton seed against pink boll worm.—Bull. Min. Agric. Egypt, Tech. Sci. Serv., **11:**77 pp., 3 tab.

———. 1917. Machines for the treatment of cotton seed against pink boll worm (*Gelechia gossypiella,* Saund.).—*Loc. cit.,* **14:**30 pp., 3 tab.

Swynnerton, C. F. M. 1921. An examination of the tsetse problem in North Mossurise, Portuguese East Africa.—Bull. Ent. Res., **11:**315–386, 9 pls., 1 map.

Vinokurov, G. M., and Rubtzov, I. A. 1930. [Studies on the ecology of grasshoppers in the Irkutsk district.] (In Russian).—Bull. Irkutsk Plant Prot. Sta., **2:**3–86, 1 fig.

Welch, M. B. 1924. Note on the effect of temperature on borers attacking seasoned and unseasoned timber.—J. Proc. Roy. Soc. N.S. Wales, **57:**227–230.

Znamenskii, A. V. 1924. [The importance of agricultural and climatic conditions on the mass appearance of the Hessian fly and the frit-fly in 1923, and prospects for 1924.] (In Russian).—Bull. Ent. Dept. Poltava Agric. Exper. Sta., **3:**27 pp., 7 figs.

Znamenskii, A. V. 1925. [On methods of controlling the Hessian fly.] (In Russian).—Protect. Plants Ukraine, Kharkov, **1–2:**41–51, 1 fig., tab.

———. 1926. [Insect pests of field crops. I. Pests of grain crops.] (In Russian).—Trud. Poltav. Selskokhoz, Op. Sta. **50:**296 pp., 118 figs., 7 pls.

5

Reprinted from pp. 648–665 of *The Distribution and Abundance of Animals*,
H. G. Andrewartha and L. C. Birch, Univ. Chicago Press, 1954, 782 pp.

A General Theory of the Numbers of Animals in Natural Populations

From my early youth I have had the strongest desire to understand or explain whatever I observed,—that is, to group all facts under some general laws. These causes combined have given me the patience to reflect or ponder for any number of years over any unexplained problem. As far as I can judge, I am not apt to follow blindly the lead of other men. I have steadily endeavoured to keep my mind free so as to give up any hypothesis, however much beloved (and I cannot resist forming one on every subject), as soon as facts are shown to be opposed to it.

DARWIN, *Autobiography*

14.0 INTRODUCTION

IN THIS chapter we have to build a general theory about the distribution and numbers of animals in nature. This should summarize in general terms as many as possible of the facts which we have discussed in the empirical part of the book and so provide a general answer to the questions we propounded in section 1.1: Why does this animal inhabit so much and no more of the earth? Why is it abundant in some parts of its distribution and rare in others?

Elton (1949, p. 19) wrote: "It is becoming increasingly understood by population ecologists that the control of populations, i.e., ultimate upper and lower limits set to increase, is brought about by density-dependent factors either within the species or between species (see Solomon, 1949). The chief density-dependent factors are intraspecific competition for resources, space or prestige; and interspecific competition, predators or parasites; with other factors affecting the exact intensity and level of these processes." Elton said quite precisely what he meant by "density-dependent factors"; in section 2.12 we discussed some of the other meanings which have been attributed to the same phrase; like many other ecological terms, this one lost most of its strength shortly after it was coined. We hope that Elton overstated the case. We believe that it would be nearer the mark to say that the various assertions about "density-dependent factors" and "competition" which are familiar to ecologists are just about the only generalizations available in this field. The student of ecology may either accept or reject them. Hitherto if he rejected them, he has had nothing to put in their place.

The statement that the ultimate upper and lower limits set to increase in a population can be determined only by "density-dependent factors" may be taken as axiomatic for the highly idealized hypothetical animals of the sort which may be represented by the symbols in a simple mathematical model. In this case the limits which are referred to are theoretical quantities which must be deduced by mathematical argument. They cannot, by their very nature, be related to the empirical quantities which are got by counting the numbers of animals in natural populations. There are two chief reasons for this: (*a*) the idealized hypothetical populations are very different from what is actually found in nature, and (*b*) one would not expect to come across a limiting density in any finite number of observations.

Yet this mistake is commonly made, as Elton has pointed out. The usual generalizations about "density-dependent factors," when they refer to natural populations, have a peculiar logical status. They are not a general theory, because, as we have seen, especially in chapter 13, they do not describe any substantial body of empirical facts. Nor are they usually put forward as a hypothesis to be tested by experiment and discarded if they prove inconsistent with empirical fact. On the contrary, they are usually asserted as if their truth were axiomatic. A good example of this approach is seen in the passage from Smith (1935; quoted in sec. 2.12), where he argued that since weather is known to "regulate" the numbers of animals, it must therefore be a density-dependent factor. These generalizations about "density-dependent factors" and competition in so far as they refer to natural populations are neither theory nor hypothesis but dogma.

We often find the expressions "balance," "steady-density," "control," and "regulate" used in theoretical discussions of populations. Their meanings may be obscure, especially when they are used in relation to natural populations. They stem from the dogma of "density-dependent factors," and they are allegorical. Unless their meanings are made very clear, it is best to be cautious about any passage in which they are used.

Our theory is not concerned with these rather allegorical properties of populations but with numbers that can be counted in nature. In each of the sections which follow we first state the principles of the theory in general terms and with the aid of simple diagrams. Then we refer back to the natural populations which have been discussed in earlier chapters and show how particular empirical observations may be fitted into the general theory; for the theory may be regarded as sound only if it serves to explain all, or most, of the empirical observations that may be brought forward to test it.

14.1 COMMONNESS AND RARENESS

If we say that species A is *rare* or that species B is *common*, we can only mean that individuals of species A are few relative to some other quantity which we can measure, and individuals of species B are numerous relative to the same or some other quantity. We might arbitrarily choose a number relative to a certain area and decide to call a species rare if they are, say, fewer than one (or one million) individuals per square mile. This approach may be necessary for the hunter or fisherman, but it does not, at this stage, help us to think clearly about the theory of ecology. So we shall put it aside for the present.

Another meaning for this sentence might be that in a certain area individuals of species A are few relative to the individuals of species B. Certain mathematical expressions have been developed to describe the relative numbers of different species found in large communities or large samples from communities. The size of the community is measured by the number of individuals of all species that are counted. Williams (1944) gave the name "index of diversity" to the coefficient $\alpha = n_1/x$ derived from the series

$$n_1, \frac{n_1}{2}x, \frac{n_1}{3}x^2, \frac{n_1}{4}x^3, \ldots, \text{etc.},$$

where n_1 is the number of species represented in the sample by one individual and x is a positive number less than 1. Large values of α indicate diversity in the community. Preston (1948) fitted a "truncated" normal curve to the frequencies of species represented in the sample by 0–1, 1–2, 3–4, 5–8, 9–16, $\ldots$, $(2^{n-1} + 1)$–2^n, individuals per species. In this expression the diversity of the community is measured by the mean and the variance of the normal curve and the position of the "truncation."

Both expressions depend on the assumption that in any large community there will be a few species represented by many individuals and many species represented by few individuals. This assumption is confirmed by the goodness of the fit obtained when the theoretical curves are tested against empirical records. In other words, most communities seem to be dominated by a few species. This may be an important fact for students of "community ecology." It is, indeed, on facts of this sort that they base their theory of "dominance" and other important theories about communities and the relationships of the species which constitute them. But this way of looking at commonness and rareness and the studies which stem from it have little to contribute to the general theory of ecology, using "ecology" in the narrow sense defined in section 1.0. So we say no more about them.

A third way of considering commonness and rareness is to relate the number of individuals in the population to the quantities of necessary resources, food, places for nests, etc., in the area that it inhabits. This is the common-sense way for the theoretical ecologist and the practical farmer to look at the matter. The farmer is not interested in whether the caterpillars in his crop of wheat are more or less numerous than, say, the mites which eat the dead grass on the surface of the soil. He wants to know whether the caterpillars are numerous enough to eat much of his crop. The ecologist has the same point of view, but his interest goes deeper. If the caterpillars are so few that they eat only a small proportion of the stock of food available to them, the ecologist has to inquire what other environmental components may be checking their increase.

14.11   *The Conditions of Commonness in Local Populations*

A population of a certain species, living in a certain area, may consistently use all the stocks of a particular resource, say food or places for nesting, that

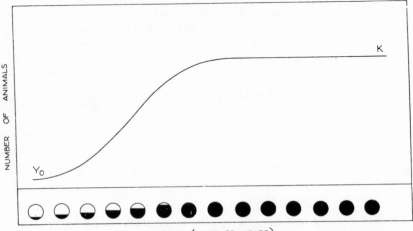

Fig. 14.01.—The growth of a "local population" (i.e., the population in a "locality") whose numbers are limited by the stock of some nonexpendable resource, such as nesting sites. The initial numbers (i.e., the number of immigrants who colonize the locality) are represented by Y_0; the maximal numbers that the resources of the locality will support are represented by K. The circles repeat the information given by the curve. The proportion of the circle shaded represents the number of animals at the specific time as a proportion of the maximum.

occur in the area. The simplest case of this, though perhaps the most unusual in nature, may be found when there is no interaction between the resource and "other animals of the same kind." This happens when the animals can use the resource without destroying it. Such was the case in the imaginary example we gave in section 2.121. The bees in that example did not destroy their nesting places by using them. There was the same number of holes for nest-building generation after generation, irrespective of the numbers of bees in each generation. If nothing else checked the bees, their numbers would be determined entirely by the number of holes for nests. We have illustrated this principle in Figure 14.01. The asymptote for the curve represents the number of bees in a local situation when all the nesting places are used. The shaded parts of the circles represent the population as a proportion of what the total resources of the area will support. A natural population which comes very close to the simplicity of the imaginary one is the population of great tits mentioned by Kluijver (sec. 12.31) as living in a wood where there was a shortage of holes for building nests. Another one, which is nearly as simple, is the one described by Flanders (sec. 12.23) for *Metaphycus helvolus* living on oleanders. In this case living food in the form of migrating scale insects was the resource in short supply. It was fed into the population of *Metaphycus* at a

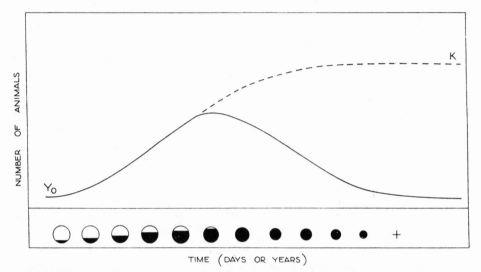

FIG. 14.02.—The solid line represents the growth of a local population whose numbers are limited by a diminishing resource, such as living food, which becomes less, the more animals there are feeding on it. The symbols have the same meanings as in Fig. 14.01; the circles grow smaller because the plant (or population of prey) grows smaller and eventually dies out because there are too many animals eating it. The cross indicates that this is the place where a local population recently became extinct (see Figs. 14.07 and 14.08).

fairly steady rate, which was largely independent of the numbers of animals waiting to eat it. But there were always enough *Metaphycus* to eat all the food that was provided.

When living food is the resource that is fully used up, there may be certain complicated interactions between "food" and "other animals of the same sort"; the result may be a reduction not only in the total stocks of food but also in the proportion of it that is effectively used (sec. 11.22). The sequence of events usually culminates in the complete destruction of localized stocks of food. This accentuates the patchiness of the distribution of food; and the animal's chance of finding food comes increasingly to depend on its powers of dispersal. A characteristic sequence of events was described for *Cactoblastis cactorum* in section 5.0. The general case is illustrated in Figure 14.02. A horizontal line drawn through K would represent the maximal number of animals that could live in this locality if they used up all their resources. The curve represents the rise and fall in the number of animals from the time that they first find the place to the time that they die out from lack of food. The diminution in the amount of food and its ultimate extinction from this place are indicated by the diminishing size of the circles from left to right. The cross indicates a place from which a local population has recently died out. The food becomes less and ultimately disappears, because there are too many animals feeding on it. We mentioned *C. cactorum* feeding on *Opuntia* spp. as an example of this (sec. 5.0); *Ptychomyia remota* is a carnivore for which the same sequence of events was described in section 10.33; other examples were given in section 10.321; we can think of many more examples from carnivorous species than from herbivorous ones. It is unusual to find herbivorous animals eating out their stocks of food, even in local situations. Animals which are living in the circumstances which we have described in this section must be counted as common, no matter how few they may be per square mile. Conversely, animals which are living in the circumstances which we describe in section 14.12 must be counted as rare with respect to their stocks of food, etc., no matter how many of them there may be per square mile.

14.12 *The Conditions of Rareness in Local Populations*

Very few of the natural populations which were described in chapter 13 ever became numerous enough to make use of all their stocks of food, etc. Most natural populations are like this. The numbers fluctuate, perhaps widely; but they do not become numerous enough, even during periods of maximal abundance, to use more than a small proportion of their resources of food, nesting sites, and so on.

The general case for this condition is illustrated in Figure 14.03. The curves and the symbols have the same meanings as in Figures 14.01 and 14.02; note that the size of the circles remains the same from start to finish, because the stocks of food, etc., are not appreciably reduced by the activities of the animals; the circles, of course, never become completely black. The circle with a cross in it provides an alternative to the one above it. These alternatives indicate that the population in a locality runs a risk of being extinguished but also has a chance to survive as a small remnant. In the latter case the population may increase again when circumstances become favorable once more.

The numbers continue to increase while births exceed deaths, that is, while r remains positive; they begin to decrease when r becomes negative. A large part of this book has been devoted to a discussion of the ways that environment may influence the three components of r—fecundity, speed of development, and duration of life. We do not need to reiterate here that any environmental component may have its appropriate influence and that, at any one time, some may be more influential than others. We single out weather and discuss it in section 14.13, partly because its influence is more subtle than that of the other components, and partly because this is a subject that has been much misunderstood.

In section 14.2 we discuss, in relation to the general theory, the way that weather, food, predators, and a place in which to live may influence the value of r and hence determine the numbers in natural populations which occupy substantial areas and which may, or may not, be short of some necessary re-

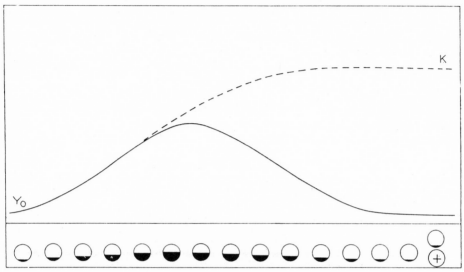

TIME (DAYS OR YEARS)

Fig. 14.03.—The solid curve represents the growth of a local population which never uses up all the resources of food, etc., in the locality because its numbers are kept, by weather, predators, food (in the relative sense of sec. 11.12), or some other environmental component, at a level well below the maximum that the resources of the locality could support. The symbols have the same meanings as in Figs. 14.01 and 14.02. The two symbols at the end indicate alternative conclusions to the history of this local population on this occasion: it may be extinguished (*circle with a cross in it*), or a remnant may persist, perhaps to increase again when circumstances change (*circle with a remnant of shading*).

source. We choose these components because they are often important in nature. The reader can readily fit other environmental components into the general theory.

Figure 14.03 refers generally to any population which is not short of any resource, no matter whether r is chiefly influenced by weather, food, predators, or some other environmental component. But it lacks generality in one respect: it does not cover the special case of the population in which a more or less constant proportion is sheltered from a danger which is likely to destroy all those that are not so sheltered. A good example of this was provided by the artificial population of *Ephestia*, which was kept in check by a predator (sec. 10.222). A natural example, which was nearly as good, was described by Flanders for a population of scale insects *Saissetia oleae*, living on the shaded parts of oleander (sec. 12.23). This exception to the general rule is covered by Figure 14.04. The meanings of the curves and symbols are self-evident.

14.13 *The Way in Which Weather May Determine Commonness or Rareness in Local Populations*

We build up our theory about weather from a simple beginning with Figure 14.05. The abscissae are in units of time—days, years, or generations. The

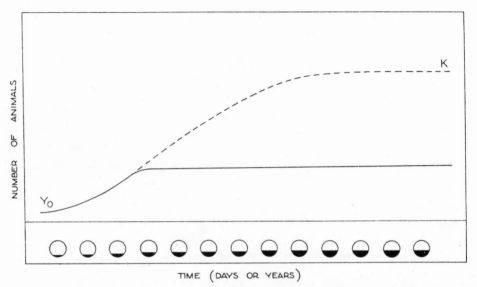

FIG. 14.04.—The solid curve represents the growth of a local population in which a more or less constant number of the individuals are sheltered from some danger which destroys all those which are not so sheltered. This number is not enough to use up more than a small proportion of the total resources of food, etc., in the locality.

ordinates for each curve are numbers of animals; K represents the number of animals which the area could support if the total resources of food were fully used up. The number indicated by Y_0 is the remnant left when the unfavorable period ends and is also the nucleus for multiplication during the next favorable period. The rate of increase which pertains during the favorable period is called r.

Let us suppose that the three pairs of curves represent three ways in which the weather may determine the number of animals in a local population. The curves on the left relate to a place where the weather is favorable, and those on the right relate to a place where the weather is severe. In the top pair the two curves start from the same level at the beginning of the favorable period (Y_0 is constant); and they rise at the same rate because r is constant. But the curve for area A rises farther because the favorable period lasts longer. With the middle pair, the two curves rise at the same rate (r is constant); they continue rising for the same interval of time (favorable period, t, is constant). But the curve for area A rises farther than that for B because it started from a higher level (Y_0 is greater for A). This means that in A the unfavorable period was shorter or else the catastrophe that caused it was less severe, or for some other reasons the population was still relatively large when the weather

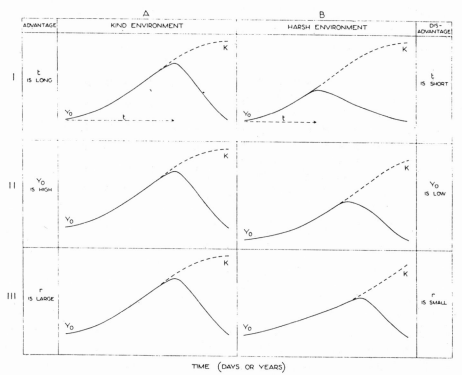

Fig. 14.05.—Three ways in which weather may influence the average numbers of animals in a locality. The numbers in the locality are increasing during spells of favorable weather and decreasing during spells of unfavorable weather. Two areas A and B are compared with respect to three qualities. Quality I determines the duration of the favorable period; quality II determines the severity of the unfavorable period; and quality III determines the rate of increase of the population during the favorable period. The numbers which would be attained if all the resources of food, etc., in the area were made use of are indicated by K; the numbers to which the population declines during the unfavorable period is represented by Y_0. For further explanation see text.

changed and allowed the animals to start increasing again. With the bottom pair, the two curves start from the same level (Y_0 is constant); they continue rising for the same interval of time (favorable period, t, is constant). But the curve in area A rises higher because it is steeper (rate of increase, r, is greater for A). Taking all three curves into account, one can easily see that the animals would be more numerous, on the average, in area A than in area B. This principle has been stated in completely general terms. The model which we describe in section 1.1 provides a particular example of it.

14.2 THE PRINCIPLES GOVERNING THE NUMBERS OF ANIMALS IN NATURAL POPULATIONS

Each of Figures 14.01–14.05 represents the trend in numbers in one locality. A natural population occupying any considerable area will be made up of a number of such local populations or colonies. In different localities the trends may be going in different directions at the same time. It is therefore feasible to represent the condition of the population in a large area by drawing a col-

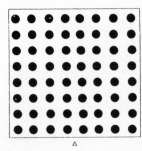 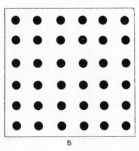

Fig. 14.06.—The populations of large areas are made up of a number of local populations. In the two areas which are compared in this diagram the resources of every locality are fully used up (as in Fig. 14.01), but there are more favorable localities in area *A* than in area *B*.

lection of circles, each one of which represents the condition in a local population. Since we are now considering larger areas, we must take into account, in addition to the principles set out in section 14.1, the dispersive powers of the animals and their food. Also we are now in a position to widen the meaning in which we use "common" or "rare" so that it includes the number of animals in the population relative to the area over which they are distributed (sec. 14.0). We do this in the examples which follow.

To start with the simplest case first, we make up an example directly from Figure 14.01. Let us suppose that in Figure 14.06 area *A* includes many localities where fenceposts have many holes suitable for the bees to build their nests in. And suppose that area *B* is like *A* in every respect except that there are few localities where the fenceposts carry many holes that are suitable for nests. Every hole will be used. All the circles are completely blackened in both areas. The two areas are alike, in that the bees are equally common with respect to their stocks of nesting sites. But the areas are different, in that the bees will be more numerous in *A* than in *B;* this is indicated by the numbers of circles in the two areas. This example brings out the two meanings of "common" quite nicely. Which one you emphasize will doubtless depend on whether your interest lies in having empty auger holes or many bees to pollinate your lucerne. The wood where Kluijver put additional nesting boxes for *Parus* was like *A*, except that some were not used; and the other more natural wood, which he described as lacking a sufficiency of tree-holes for nests, was like *B* (sec. 12.31).

The next example is more complex because it deals with living food instead of a lifeless nonexpendable resource like nesting sites. Suppose that, in Figure 14.07, *A* and *B* are two areas where prickly pears grow in colonies; the two areas are alike in climate, soil, distribution of suitable places for *Opuntia* to grow, and every other respect except that *A* supports a population of *Cactoblastis cactorum*, whereas in *B* there is a variant which has very much poorer powers of dispersal. Say we call it *Cactoblastis blastorum*. Area *C* is like the

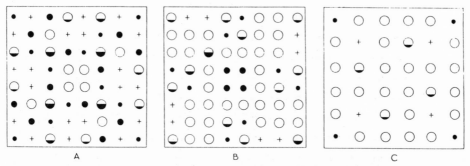

A   B   C

Fig. 14.07.—The populations of the large areas *A*, *B*, and *C* are made up of a number of local populations. Not all the favorable localities support local populations (*hollow circles*). Favorable localities are distributed equally densely in *A* and *B* but more sparsely in *C*. Area *A* is occupied by a species with high powers of dispersal; *B* and *C* are occupied by a species which is similar except that it has inferior powers of dispersal. The symbols are taken from Fig. 14.02. In Area *A* the number of animals is chiefly limited by the stock of food in the absolute sense. In *B* and *C* there is no absolute shortage of food, but the numbers of animals in these areas are limited by a shortage of food in the relative sense (sec. 11.12). This is related to the poor powers of dispersal of the species that lives in these areas. For further explanation see text.

other two except that, for physiographical reasons, colonies of prickly pears must remain very sparsely distributed, irrespective of whether any are destroyed by *Cactoblastis* or not. Area *C* supports a population of *C. blastorum*. The distributions of the circles and the shading in them indicate: in area *A* there are few colonies of prickly pears, but *C. cactorum* is making good use of what are there. Its numbers are clearly being limited chiefly by the absolute amount of food in the area; and the numerous crosses indicate that there is definitely less food in the area as a result of the presence of *C. cactorum*. In area *B* there are more colonies of prickly pears. Relatively few of them harbor local populations of *C. blastorum*. The numbers of *C. blastorum* are not being seriously limited by an absolute shortage of food. Nevertheless, by virtue of their poor powers of dispersal, they are suffering from a relative shortage of food. In area *C* the circumstances are much the same as in *B*, only more so. The food is even harder to find; the death-rate is therefore higher still; and the numbers of *C. blastorum* in the area are few indeed. The presence of a few crosses in both *B* and *C* shows that relative shortage of food (sec. 11.12) is the real cause of the trouble, because, once *C. blastorum* has found a colony of prickly pears, the insects increase rapidly and, in due course, destroy all the food, just as the real *C. cactorum* does in area *A*.

We need not have invented *C. blastorum* for area *B*. Several natural examples have been described, for example, *Chrysomela gemellata* (sec. 11.12) and *Rhizobius ventralis* (sec. 10.321). The fact that the latter feeds on animals instead of plants does not alter the principle. We do not know of an exact parallel for area *C*, but *Thrips imaginis* near Adelaide during summer are kept

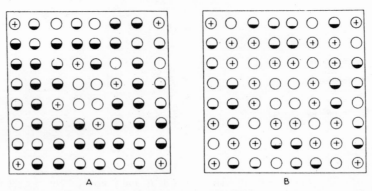

Fig. 14.08.—The populations in the large areas *A* and *B* are made up of a number of local populations. There is an equal number of suitable places where the animals may live in each area. In area *B* there is an active predator whose powers of dispersal and multiplication match those of the prey. This predator is absent from *A*, where its place is taken by one which is more sluggish. Relatively more of the suitable places are occupied by the prey in *A* than in *B*, and the local populations are, on the average, larger. There are more local situations in *B* from which the prey has recently been exterminated. Altogether, the animal is more common in *A* than in *B*. The symbols have the same meaning as in Fig. 14.03.

scarce by a relative shortage of food as *C. blastorum* is in area *C*, but they do not destroy their food so thoroughly as *C. blastorum* is supposed to do.

Let us consider next the case of an animal which has an active predator in its environment. We take the symbols from Figure 14.03 to make Figure 14.08. The two areas, *A* and *B*, have the same number of circles, because the presence of the animals does not influence the stocks of food, etc., in the area. Both *A* and *B* support populations of the same sort of herbivores. But in *B* there is also a species which is an active predator, with powers of dispersal and rate of increase which match those of the prey; in area *A* these predators are replaced by another species with equivalent capacity for increase but inferior dispersive powers. In *B* many localities which are quite favorable are empty; some have become empty only recently (circle with cross in it), and in most of those which are occupied the numbers are low. Either the herbivores have only recently arrived at the place and have not yet had time to become numerous, or else, if they have been there longer, the predators have found

84

them and are in the process of exterminating the local colony. In *A*, relatively more of the favorable places are occupied, and the numbers in the local populations are, on the whole, larger. There are relatively few places from which the prey have been recently exterminated. All this can be explained simply by saying that the prey, being superior to the predators in dispersive powers, enjoy, on the average, a relatively long period of freedom from attack in each new place that they colonize. Several natural examples of this principle were discussed in section 10.321.

A similar diagram may be drawn to illustrate the case in which the numbers

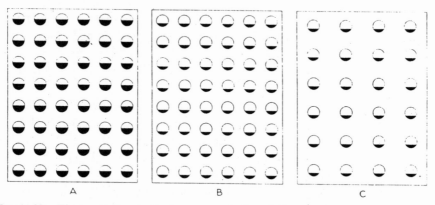

A   B   C

Fɪɢ. 14.09.—The populations in the large areas *A*, *B*, and *C* are made up of a number of local populations. The climate in *A* is more favorable than that in *B* or *C*; so the numbers (indicated by the shaded part of the circle) are, on the average, larger in each locality in *A* and in the area as a whole. There are fewer favorable localities in *C* than in *B*; so there are, on the average, fewer animals in area *C* than in *B*, where the climate is the same but the number of places greater.

in the area are determined largely by climate. In Figure 14.05 the two areas *A* and *B* were considered to differ only with respect to climate. The circles in Figure 14.09 may be related to Figure 14.05. In Figure 14.09 there is the same number of suitable places where the animals may live in *A* as in *B*, but the climate is more favorable in *A* than in *B*, so the animals are more common relative to their stocks of food, etc., in *A* than in *B*; there are also more of them in the area. Area *C* is inferior to *B* with respect to the number of places, and it is inferior to *A* with respect to both the number of places and the climate. The animals are uncommon in *C* relative to *A* in both meanings of the word. The natural population of *Porosagrotis orthogonia* (sec. 13.13) is a particular example of this principle, except that the difference between *A* and *B* in that case referred to the difference between the same area before and after it had been developed for agriculture.

The reader may have anticipated the general conclusion that we have been leading up to. The numbers of animals in a natural population may be limited in three ways: (*a*) by shortage of material resources, such as food, places in which to make nests, etc.; (*b*) by inaccessibility of these material resources relative to the animals' capacities for dispersal and searching; and (*c*) by shortage of time when the rate of increase *r* is positive. Of these three ways, the first is probably the least, and the last is probably the most, important in nature. Concerning *c*, the fluctuations in the value of *r* may be caused by weather, predators, or any other component of environment which influences the rate of increase. For example, the fluctuations in the value of *r* which are determined by weather may be rhythmical in response to the progression of the seasons (e.g., *Thrips imaginis*, sec. 13.11) or more erratic in response to "runs" of years with "good" or "bad" weather (e.g., *Austroicetes cruciata*, sec. 13.12). The fluctuations in *r* which are determined by the activities of predators must be considered in relation to the populations in local situations (Figs. 14.03 and 14.08). How long each newly founded colony may be allowed to multiply free from predators may depend on the dispersive powers of the predators relative to those of the prey.

With respect to the second way in which numbers may be limited, the food or other resource may be inaccessible either because it is sparsely distributed, like the food of *Thrips imaginis* during late summer (sec. 13.11), or because it is concealed, like the food of *Lygocerus* (sec. 10.321). In either case the inaccessibility is relative to the animals' capacities for dispersal and searching. We emphasize, in section 11.12 and elsewhere, that it is the inaccessibility of the resource which is important; the argument is independent of whether the stocks of food, etc., are scarce or plentiful, in the absolute sense of so much per square mile.

Of course, it is not to be supposed that the ecology of many natural populations would be so simple that their numbers would be explained neatly by any one of the principles described in this and the preceding two sections. A large number of systems of varying complexity could be synthesized, in the imagination, from various combinations of the principles set out in these sections. But this is not their purpose: they are intended to help the student to analyze the complex systems which he finds in nature into their simpler components, so that he may understand them better.

14.3 SOME PRACTICAL CONSIDERATIONS ABOUT THE NUMBERS OF ANIMALS IN NATURAL POPULATIONS

Darwin in chapter 3 of *The Origin of Species* wrote: "The causes which check the natural tendency of each species to increase in numbers are most obscure. Look at the most vigorous species; by as much as it swarms in numbers, by so much will its tendency to increase be still further increased. We know not what the checks are in one single instance. Nor will this surprise any one who reflects on how ignorant we are on this head." A little further on he wrote: "It is good thus to try in our imagination to give any form some advantage over another. Probably in no single instance should we know what to do, so as to succeed." In chapter 11 he stated: "Rarity is the attribute of a vast number of species of all classes in all countries. If we ask ourselves why this or that species is rare, we can answer that something is unfavourable in its conditions of life; but what that something is we can hardly ever tell."

During the century that has passed since these passages were written, we have learned enough about "the conditions of life" of at least a few species to be able, at will, to alter their numbers greatly. And we have, unwittingly, altered the "conditions of life" for a great many more species, so that their numbers have increased, or decreased, sometimes to our advantage, sometimes to our disadvantage.

With species that are pests of crops, foodstuffs, clothing, etc., it is to our advantage if we can insure that they never become numerous enough to eat a considerable proportion of their total resources of food. The majority of such species are insects. With respect to most of them, our ignorance is still abysmal, and the only way we know how to alter their "conditions of life" to our advantage is to poison as many of them as we can with insecticides. The chief disadvantage of the method is its costliness; but as the insecticides increase in number and complexity, we run an increasing risk of poisoning ourselves as well as the insects.

Ecologically, the use of insecticides fits into the principle illustrated by Figure 14.03. The difference between a good insecticide and a poor one is illustrated, in Figure 14.05, by the middle pair of curves. The difference between an insecticide applied frequently and one used infrequently is shown by the top pair of curves in Figure 14.05. And the difference between an insecticide applied thoroughly and one applied less well is shown in Figure 14.09. It is incorrect to say that, because an insecticide is not a "density-dependent factor," it cannot "regulate" the numbers in a population. There are millions of farmers who could testify that the proper use of insecticides makes a big difference to the size of the populations of certain insects. Many people all over the world would starve if this were not so.

"Biological control" (that is, the introduction of new sorts of predators into the area) is the next most popular way of altering the "conditions of life" of an insect pest. But other methods may be suggested by the principles set out in Figures 14.05 and 14.09. Modifications in husbandry might be thought out which would shorten the period available to the insect for multiplication or reduce the value of r (Fig. 14.05). Or other methods might be tried which would reduce the number of suitable places for the insects to live in or alter the distribution of such places in a way that would be detrimental to the pest (Fig. 14.09).

87

With animals that are valued for their flesh or fur or for some other quality, it is necessary to take quite a different point of view. It matters hardly at all whether the populations use up much or little of their total resources of food, etc., so long as the individuals are numerous enough to be hunted or fished with profit. If it so happened that the population conformed to Figure 14.01 or Figure 14.02, then the numbers per square mile might be increased by adding to the stocks of the limiting resource in the area. This method seems to have been greatly successful with the muskrat in North America (sec. 12.31). But if it happened that the population conformed to the principles illustrated by Figures 14.03–14.05, then other methods would be required.

14.4   SOME REFLECTIONS ON THE GREATLY MISUNDERSTOOD SUBJECT OF "EXTINCTION"

We conclude this chapter with an anticlimax. The reader may regard it as an appendix if he likes. However rare they may be with respect to the proportion of their total resources that they use up, most of the species that are studied or observed are common in terms of the number of individuals per square mile. This is easily explained by a number of practical reasons. But the fact that we usually study unusual populations is far too frequently overlooked. The truth is that the vast majority of species are rare, by whatever criterion (sec. 14.1) they are judged. Smith (1935, p. 880) commented on this: "The fact that the number of species which become sufficiently abundant to damage crops is *relatively* small, and that such species form only an insignificant fraction of the total number of phytophagous insects is ignored." Bodenheimer (1930, in Smith, 1935) commented in the same vein: "It is only in rare borderline cases that the food is used up to the possible limit. Any meadow, field, or orchard will prove this sufficiently." And, of course, Darwin was well aware of the fact. In a slightly different context he wrote (chap. 11 of *The Origin of Species*): "To admit that species generally become rare before they become extinct, to feel no surprise at the rarity of the species, and yet to marvel greatly when the species ceases to exist, is much the same as to admit that sickness in the individual is the forerunner of death—to feel no surprise at sickness, but, when the sick man dies, to wonder and to suspect that he died of some deed of violence."

Nevertheless, the misconception prevails that the extinction of a population is a very rare event. This leads our colleagues who hold to the dogma of "density-dependent factors" to propound this riddle. On hearing us expound our views on ecology, they ask: "How is it, if there is no density-dependent factor in the environment, that the population does not become extinct?" This places us in a position like that of the man in the dock who was asked to answer Yes or No to the question: "Do you still beat your wife?" We cannot answer the question until we have cleared up the misconception in the mind of the questioner.

First of all, it is indeed true that the species which we study are less likely than most to become extinct, because invariably we choose for study those in which the populations are large. Elsewhere in this book, and especially in sections 13.11 and 13.12, we explain why certain species of insects did not become extinct during the period that they were studied and infer that they are not likely to become extinct during the immediate future. A quotation from Stevenson-Hamilton (1937, p. 258) shows that the same principles apply to mammals which commonly maintain large populations: "The extermination, under natural conditions, of one indigenous species by another, whether directly through carnivores consuming herbivorous types, or indirectly by one herbivorous type proving too strong for its associates in the same area, except as a final culmination, after Man, or one of the other factors cited above, has first played the principal part, is unknown in natural history so far as our experience extends, and may be safely ruled out in any wild-life reservation *of adequate extent where room exists for seasonal migration* [our italics]."

But the risk of extinction for species in which the populations are small is greater. Darwin in the fourth chapter of *The Origin of Species* wrote: "Any form which is represented by a few individuals will run a good chance of utter extinction during great fluctuations in the nature of the seasons, or from a temporary increase in the numbers of its enemies." A quotation from Ford (1945*a*, p. 143) shows how this risk operated in the particular case of the butterfly known as the "Wood White":

Any species can survive such periodic fluctuation provided that its numbers are large enough, and that it is somewhere sufficiently well established to tide over the dangerous period when it is reduced to its lowest level. Clearly, a "normal" cycle of this kind may be disastrous to a butterfly which maintains itself precariously, whether in an isolated locality or in the country as a whole. The Wood White survived in Westmorland until about 1905 when it disappeared and has never been seen there again. At that time the species was in general becoming rare, and in the south retracting its range to a few favoured places. From these it could, and did, spread once more; but not in the north, where the one isolated colony was wiped out by a process which had no serious consequences elsewhere. Similarly, it disappeared from the New Forest early this century and has not returned. It was said at the time that this was due to overcollecting, and probably that was true. But I suspect that the butterfly was reduced to dangerously small numbers by natural causes, operating there as elsewhere, and for that reason the activities of the collector were fatal.

Ford quoted several other examples of butterflies which have recently become extinct in Britain.

There is evidence from paleontology to show that extinction of species is commonplace in the time scale of that science. Simpson (1952) estimated that there might now be 2,000,000 species of plants and animals in the world and that the total number of species that have existed since the "dawn of life" may be of the order of 500,000,000. On this estimate, more than 99 per cent of the species that have ever existed are now extinct. Mayr (1942, p. 224) pointed out that many of the species that are known to have become extinct during modern times have lived on small islands, where the terrain would be more uniform and the opportunity for dispersal less than in a larger area.

There is no fundamental distinction to be made between the extinction of a local population and the extinction of a species other than this that the species becomes extinct with the extinction of the last local population. We can witness the extinction of local populations, of even the most abundant species, going on all around us all the time. So if the extinction of a population were proof that the "environment" lacked a "density-dependent factor," we would have ample evidence of the absence of "density-dependent factors" from the "environments" of the animals in local populations of most species.

Species are likely to be "rare" near the margins of their distributions, and outside the distribution they are "extinct." Because distribution and abundance are but two aspects of one phenomenon, the study of abundance in different parts of the distribution is itself a study of the causes of rareness and commonness in species.

BIBLIOGRAPHY

[*Editor's Note:* Bibliography has been abridged to include only those references cited in the excerpt.]

Bodenheimer, F. S. 1930. Über die Grundlagen einer allgemeinen Epidemiologie der Insektenkalamitäten, Ztschr. f. Angew. Ent., **16**:433–50.

Elton, C. 1949. Population interspersion: an essay on animal community patterns, J. Ecol., **37**:1–23.

Ford, E. B. 1945a. Butterflies. London: Collins.

Mayr, E. 1942. Systematics and the origin of species. New York: Columbia University Press.

Preston, F. W. 1948. The commonness, and rarity, of species, Ecology, **29**:254–83.

Simpson, G. G. 1952. How many species? Evolution, **6**:342.

Smith, H. S. 1935. The role of biotic factors in the determination of population densities, J. Econ. Ent., **28**:873–98.

Solomon, M. E. 1949. The natural control of animal populations, J. Anim. Ecol., **18**:1–35.

Stevenson-Hamilton, J. 1937. South African Eden: from Sabi game reserve to Kruger national park. London: Cassell & Co., Ltd.

Williams, C. B. 1944. Some applications of the logarithmic series and the index of diversity to ecological problems, J. Ecology, **32**:1–44.

Part IV

THE COMPROMISE SCHOOL
OF POPULATION
REGULATION: HISTORICAL
(INCLUDING CRITIQUES OF THEORIES)

Editor's Comments
on Papers 6 Through 12

In this section the biotic and climate schools of population regulation are compared. Aside from self-regulation theories, which will be discussed later, most theories of population regulation are really compromises, each in its own way giving some measure of importance to both climate and to biotic factors (competition, predation, disease, parasitism). By thus being compromises, they are also to some extent critiques of both the original theories.

W. R. Thompson and A. Milne, two British entomologists, present modifications of a basic compromise mechanism of population regulation. In 1929, Thompson (Paper 6) presented a view where animal populations are regulated by what he calls the intrinsic limitations of the organisms themselves. (I might add that I have treated Thompson's 1929 work as a compromise theory of

Nicholson and Andrewartha and Birch, even though he predates them. This is merely a didactic convenience.) Thompson's basic meaning is that a whole host of agents in the environment can regulate a population, and whether a population increases or decreases depends on the totality of these agents making the environment more or less optimal. In a later paper (1939), Thompson dispenses with the problem of the use of the term density-dependence by noting that the whole universe is a density-dependent factor. In his 1929 paper (Paper 6) he refutes ideas of Charles Elton (1927), who suggested that one single factor regulated populations. Thompson in this paper also predates the current arguments of group selection by stating that there was no optimal density that a species tended to—again as Elton (1927) suggested—but rather that organisms multiply without regard to the species as a whole. After the publication of Nicholson's 1933 work (Paper 3), Thompson published a series of papers outlining and criticizing Nicholson (and others) well into the mid-1950s (Thompson 1939; 1956).

Milne in 1957 combined the best of Thompson, Nicholson, Andrewartha, and Birch, and then added his own modification. The modification came from Milne's idea of the ultimate factor of population regulation, the one perfectly density-dependent factor: intraspecific competition. This is the only factor affected solely by numbers and therefore having an unfailingly exact response to numbers. Most of the time, however, populations are at density levels below which competition is significant; at those times they are held in check by density-independent factors or "imperfectly" density-dependent factors (i.e., anything else). In 1962 Milne published a paper (Paper 7) restating his theory and answering the various criticisms, both direct and indirect, that had been levelled at his theory. On Professor Milne's urging, I have reprinted excerpts of that paper, rather than his 1957 paper.

Paper 8, by Varley, is a special review of several of F. Schwerdtfeger's papers in the German literature. It is presented for two reasons. First, it is a summary and introduction to the German forest workers, of whom Schwerdtfeger was a leader. Second, it serves as a critique of this work and of Schwerdtfeger's theory. Schwerdtfeger favored the concept of the gradocoene , which is the sum of all factors affecting the species. Thus the gradocoene determines a population's density. Varley points out that this is obviously a truism. Using his data from pine-feeding moths, Varley criticized Schwerdtfeger for failing to use statistics and to gather critical mortality and fertility data.

Other comprehensive theories have been put forth, most of

which are variants of each other. Of special note are the writings of M. F. Solomon, another British entomologist (1949; 1964), and of C. B. Huffaker and P. S. Messenger (1964), two Americans. Basically, Huffaker and Messenger support Thompson's view, but they also stress the importance of genetic changes for population regulation. [Debach (1964) which includes the Huffaker–Messenger article, is a good introduction to the formal study of biological control. The term "density-dependent" is specifically discussed in the exchange between Varley (1958) and Solomon (1958).]

Paper 9, by H. S. Horn, a former student of G. H. Orians (Paper 10), is an interesting attempt to bring together the ideas of density-dependence and density-independence by developing a model in which they are opposite ends of a spectrum. Horn shows how density-dependent and density-independent agents can interact to regulate numbers. This paper will also interest those who are unfamiliar with the techniques of graphical analysis, where arguments are constructed based on the shape and intersection of plotted curves (see also Paper 14).

The next two papers in this section (Papers 10 and 11) are solid critiques of the various schools of thought. Both papers refer to David Lack's *Natural Regulation of Animal Numbers* (1954). Lack was a proponent of competition for food as a regulating mechanism; his main research concerned birds (Lack 1966). Lack was also a leader in the field of evolutionary ecology with his *Darwin's Finches* (1947), and *Ecological Adaptations for Breeding in Birds* (1968), among others.

Paper 10 is by G. H. Orians, who analyzes the density-dependent versus density-independent controversy by comparing Andrerwartha and Birch's book (see Paper 5), representing the density-independent school, with Lack's 1954 book, representing the density-dependent school. Orians points to several possibilities for the dichotomy between the two schools of thought, based on the fact that Andrewartha and Birch studied insects whereas Lack studied birds. However, he believes that the fundamental difference is one of approach; that is, the climate people do not really have a theory because they need to look at each case by itself, and the evolutionary people are more interested in adaptation than in regulation. Orians concludes that no general theory can exist without considering evolutionary pressures.

Bakker summarizes both current controversies, as well as Orians' comments, in his 1964 paper (Paper 11), and he comes up with close to a dozen areas of disagreement in types of organisms used, use of terminology, unjustified extrapolations of analogies, etc. He concludes with a general ecosystem-web type of model of his own. The lesson from these papers, to me at least, is that the controversies are to a great extent influenced by circumstances that should not necessarily be determinants, such as terminology, verbosity, choice of taxon, and a distinct lack of data.

The last paper in this section (Paper 12) is one in a series of exchanges that took place over an original article by Hairston, Smith, and Slobodkin (1960) entitled "Community Structure, Population Control, and Competition." The arguments of this paper were as follows: Since the accumulation of fossil fuels is negligible at present, all organisms, especially decomposers, are food limited. Because herbivores don't deplete green plants and because meteorological catastrophes are exceptional, producers are neither herbivore limited nor catastrophe limited and thus must be resource limited (light, water, minerals, etc.). Herbivores can at times deplete vegetation, especially when protected by humans, who remove their predators and allow them to build up in density. Herbivores are thus not usually food limited, so that the only remaining method is predator limitation (including parasitism, etc.). Since herbivores are limited by predators, predators must be food limited. The general conclusions of the paper are that decomposers, producers, and predators, as whole trophic levels, are resource limited and thus compete in the classical density-dependent manner.

Murdoch (1966) published the first critique of this paper. The major thrust of that critique is that Hairston, Smith, and Slobodkin's hypothesis was not formulated in a testable way. That is, it may or may not be correct; it simply cannot be tested because there are no criteria for rejection and because the hypothesis was not stated in a way to generate falsifiable statements. This critique was followed by Ehrlich and Birch's (Paper 12) and later followed by a rebuttal by Slobodkin, Smith, and Hairston (1967). The published exchange more or less ended there. I have chosen to reprint only Ehrlich and Birch's contribution. The 1960 paper by Hairston, Smith, and Slobodkin is easily summarized, and we shall talk later about the testability of hypotheses, which is the thrust of Murdoch's paper.

REFERENCES

DeBach, P. (ed.). 1964. *Biological Control of Insect Pests and Weeds.* London: Chapman and Hall.

Elton, C. 1927. *General Ecology.* London: Sidgwick and Jackson.

Hairston, N. G., F. E. Smith, and L. B. Slobodkin. 1960. Community Structure, Population Control, and Competition. *Am. Nat.* 94:421–425.

Huffaker, C. B., and P. S. Messenger. 1964. The Concept and Significance of Natural Control. In P. DeBach (ed.), *Biological Control of Insect Pests and Weeds*, pp. 74–117. London: Chapman and Hall.

Lack, D. 1947 (1961 edition in Harper Torchbooks) *Darwin's Finches.* New York: Harper.

Lack, D. 1954. *Natural Regulation of Animal Numbers.* London: Oxford University Press.

Lack, D. 1966. *Population Studies of Birds.* London: Oxford University Press.

Lack, D. 1968. *Ecological Adaptations for Breeding in Birds.* London: Methuen.

Milne, A. 1957. The Natural Control of Insect Populations. *Can. Ent.* **89**: 193–213.

Murdoch, W. W. 1966. Community Structure, Population Control, and Competion—a Critique. *Am. Nat.* **100**:219–226.

Slobodkin, L. B., F. E. Smith, and N. G. Hairston. 1967. Regulation in Terrestrial Ecosystems, and the Implied Balance of Nature. *Am. Nat.* **101**:109–124.

Solomon, M. E. 1949. The Natural Control of Animal Populations. *J. Anim. Ecol.* **18**:1–35.

Solomon, M. E. 1958. Meaning of Density-Dependence and Related Terms in Population Dynamics. *Nature* **181**:1778–1780.

Solomon, M. E. 1964. Analysis of Processes Involved in the Natural Control of Insects. *Adv. Ecol. Res.* **2**:1–58.

Thompson, W. R. 1939. Biological Control and the Theories of the Interactions of Populations. *Parasitology* **31**:299–388.

Thompson, W. R. 1956. The Fundamental Theories of Natural and Biological Control. *Ann. Rev. Ent.* **1**:379–402.

Varley, G. C. 1958. Meaning of Density-Dependence and Related Terms in Population Dynamics. *Nature* **181**:1780–1781.

6

Reprinted from *Parasitology* **21**:269–281 (1929)

ON NATURAL CONTROL.

By W. R. THOMPSON, Ph.D., D.Sc.

Imperial Bureau of Entomology.

I.

THERE can be no doubt that reasoning by analogy contributes enormously to the progress of Science by suggesting the hypotheses which form the basis of experimental investigation. But although it is useful, it is also dangerous and it is not infrequently the source of plausible but inaccurate and misleading catchwords.

An example of this is to be found in the comparison of the Universe with a machine. In this comparison, there is no doubt some value and certainly more truth than there is in the notion, which periodically reappears in biological and philosophical literature, that the Cosmos is an organism. Nevertheless, the idea that the Universe is a machine is in many ways inadequate and inexact, and like other plausible but inadequate conceptions, it has given rise to a good deal of confused thinking in regard to natural processes. This seems to be particularly true in regard to what is commonly known as natural control.

By *natural control*, we mean the check exerted on the multiplication of organisms by natural, as opposed to artificial environmental factors. Ever since the work of Malthus on population, the enormous disproportion between the reproductive powers of organisms and the multiplication that actually occurs, has been among biologists a theme for commentary and discussion. Huxley calculated that the progeny of a single Aphis, would, in the course of ten generations, supposing all survived, "contain more ponderable substance than five hundred millions of stout men; that is, more than the whole population of China." The third chapter of the "Origin of Species" is largely devoted to questions of this kind, the consideration of which formed an important part of the argument of Darwin in favour of the hypothesis of Natural Selection.

The fact that the variation in numbers of the larger and more striking elements of a fauna or flora is not obvious and escapes attention, unless it is made the object of special study, gives rise to the idea that their numerical and specific composition is approximately constant over long periods. An analogy with physical systems, which has recently been embodied in the terms, proposed by Chapman[1], of "biotic potential" and "environmental resistance," has led naturally to the conception of organic groups as constellations of forces in equilibrium. Any unusual increase in the numbers of a species is commonly

[1] *Animal Ecology*, Minneapolis, Minn., 1925.

said to be due to a *rupture of the Natural Equilibrium*. When a reduction in numbers occurs, it is considered to be due to the operation of forces which tend to *the restoration of the Natural Equilibrium*. That there are in fact in Nature certain special "regulatory" forces or agents is a common belief which finds expression in many standard works. Thus Caullery[1] describes entomophagous insects as by far the most effective natural regulatory agent in regard to the multiplication of a very large number of insects. Elton[2] suggests that there is for most organisms one special "limiting factor," by which their ability to reproduce and spread is primarily conditioned, the organism being excessively susceptible to variations in the intensity of this factor, but more or less indifferent to variations in the intensity of others.

Whatever be the real origin of these ideas, it is certain that they have a logical connection with the conception of the Universe as a mechanical system. If the equilibrium of such a system be disturbed by the application of a force at a certain point, a force of equal intensity, acting in exactly the opposite direction, is required to restore it. Similarly, in a moving mechanism, irregularities in action are provided for by regulatory arrangements, designed to compensate for certain special defects. Thus "racing" in engines is checked by "governors" acting in such a way that an increase in speed of the flywheel causes a gradual application of brakes and, consequently, a reduction of speed. "Control" in mechanisms is thus due in any given case to the action of some positive regulatory factor exactly adapted to a given end, and, consequently, of a very definite and restricted type. The conception of the Universe as a machine, or as a system in equilibrium, leads naturally to the idea of positive regulatory mechanisms or, in other words, to the idea that the natural control of a given organism is due to some specific agency, in the absence of which an outbreak naturally occurs. Some of the recent proposals to investigate "the causes of insect outbreaks" seemed to be based principally upon this idea.

II.

However, this conception of natural control does not agree with the facts. Few really extensive studies of the natural control of organisms have been made; but during the period from 1919–1928, the writer with assistants carried on, on behalf of the United States Bureau of Entomology, a general study of the European Corn Borer (*Pyrausta nubilalis* Hubn.) and its controlling factors, in all the main bioclimatic regions of Europe, in which the species occurs. The results of this study have been published elsewhere in detail. The conclusions reached were, briefly, that the control of *Pyrausta nubilalis* in Europe is not due to any simple cause, but is produced by a complex group of agricultural, meteorological and parasitic factors. The composition of this group of factors is not constant over the whole range of the Corn Borer but varies both quantitatively and qualitatively in the different zones

[1] *Le Parasitisme et la Symbiose*, Paris, 1922.
[2] *Animal Ecology*, London, 1927.

inhabited by the insect, and also, though to a lesser degree, in different generations and years in the same zone. No real outbreaks were observed during the
period covered by the investigations. Control was thus maintained, but there
was no evidence that it was in all regions or even in the majority, the work of
any one factor. Certain factors, indeed, were more consistently important than
others, but no one factor was definitely and demonstrably capable of controlling the Corn Borer in the absence of the others.

The information available concerning the natural control of numerous
other insects, though less complete in most cases, tends in general to support
the results obtained from the study of the European Corn Borer, so that we
see insects controlled in one season or in one district mainly by drought, in
another by excessive cold, in another by fungous disease, and in a fourth by
parasites, though several of these and others as well generally act together in
many regions.

III.

Elton has suggested in his excellent book on Animal Ecology that there is
for most species one particular "limiting factor," in relation to which the
organism is extremely sensitive, though variations, even of considerable
amplitude, in the intensity of other factors, affect it very little. "Animals are
not completely hemmed in by their environment in any simple sense," says
Elton (l.c. p. 41), "but are nearly always prevented from occupying neighbouring habitats by one or two "limiting factors" only.

It would be extremely convenient and would simplify to an enormous
degree the work of the ecologist and of the practical entomologist, if this view
were correct, but there is, unfortunately, no very solid ground for supposing
that it is. It may be true that when the effect of variations in the various environmental factors of a given organism is tested under laboratory conditions,
it is found to be intolerant of variations of relatively few of these factors and
tolerant of large variations of the majority of them, or intolerant of small
variations of a very small number. Nevertheless, this information would not
necessarily enable us to determine with certainty the actual distribution of
the species in nature, nor would it necessarily provide the true explanation of
its variations in numbers. An area within the limits of distributions as determined by the alleged limiting factor will not necessarily contain the species
considered at all points within its borders. The species may not be able to exist
outside the area considered, but on the other hand, it will not necessarily exist
everywhere within it, and even where it does exist it may vary very greatly
in numbers owing to the action of factors to whose variations it is indeed
comparatively tolerant but which exert a marked effect upon it either because
of the extreme intensity of their action over large areas or because of their
numbers, the combined action of several factors, each of which taken
separately, cause only a slight mortality, being as important as that of one of
the so-called "limiting factors."

It must be remembered that the combination of one "limiting factor" with a group of indifferent factors, though relatively easy to produce in the laboratory, is not likely to occur again with any uniformity in nature simply because of the tremendously complex variations in environmental conditions from point to point, even in comparatively small areas.

The idea that the distribution of an organism is chiefly determined by the action of one or two "limiting factors" is, it seems, an *a priori* conception which is not in agreement with the facts. The reduction of reproductive rate preventing an increase or determining an actual decrease in numbers seems due in the vast majority of cases to complex combinations of factors, of which different members dominate in different times and places.

IV.

It is true, as I have explained in detail in a previous paper[1], that the effect of certain lethal factors may be much less than it appears to be, because, even if these factors were absent, they would be, to a large extent, automatically replaced by others. Thus, suppose we have an insect population of which 50 per cent. succumbs owing to low temperatures during the winter months. If, previous to the winter a predator kills off 30 per cent. of the population, the total kill effected by the two factors working together will be

$$0\cdot3 + (1 - 0\cdot5)\, 0\cdot3 = 0\cdot3 + 0\cdot35 = 0\cdot65.$$

The disappearance of the predator would mean a fall of not 30 per cent., but only 15 per cent. in the mortality; while in other cases the elimination of factors of this type would have even less effect. Nevertheless, the effect, though less than it appears, is quite real and though it may be slight would make just the difference between stability and increase of population, or, in other words, between control and an outbreak. It is thus quite safe to say that when we examine the actual causes of mortality in a given case, and find that there are a number of these acting together in a given region, control really is effected by the combination of these factors and not by one particular factor which would be effective whether the others were present or not.

There can be little doubt that the majority of organisms are kept in control by a complex of factors, varying in composition both quantitatively and qualitatively in different geographical areas or even localities. The idea of specific limiting factors can hardly provide us with a *general* solution of the problem of natural control.

The notion that the natural control of a given organism is not necessarily produced by any specific controlling or limiting factor, but by a heterogeneous assemblage of different factors, is at first sight rather confusing. If control results in different places from the action of different factors, it is obviously impossible to express the facts concerning it in any definite formula of general application; and if no specific agent of control can be found for a given species,

[1] *Parasitology*, 20, 90, 23 April 1928.

how can we arrive at any general solution of the problem of insect outbreaks? Again, it is not surprising that in a given district, a certain combination of factors should produce control, but that different combinations should also produce control at other points seems remarkable. Supposing that a certain factor F_1 acting at a certain intensity is actually responsible for a certain fraction of the mortality necessary for control, one would expect that the disappearance of this factor, or a diminution in its intensity, would result in an outbreak, that in a district where F_1 is absent, it should be replaced by another factor F_2, also acting at an intensity sufficient to prevent increase, is singular; and that such an exactly calculated assemblage of different factors should occur at a large number of different points seems, on the face of it, extremely unlikely. One would be led by this chain of reasoning to suspect that the diversity of the complexes of controlling factors is more apparent than real and that the disappearance of many of them from the field of action might not have any noticeable result. In other words, one would be led back to the idea that control is produced by certain specific limiting factors, whose essential importance is merely masked by the action of other factors, apparently effective, but really unnecessary for the maintenance of control.

V.

But these and kindred difficulties arise simply from a misconception of the problem and from a failure to recognise what is, in the last analysis, the fundamental cause of natural control.

The simple truth is that the natural control of organisms is primarily due, not to any complex cosmic mechanisms or regulatory factors, but rather to the intrinsic limitations of the organisms themselves.

Every organism has certain specific characteristics which, though they actually oscillate about a mean, may be considered for practical purposes as fixed. These specific characteristics imply and indeed include specific needs. An environment which meets these specific needs is, for a given species, the optimum environment. Given this optimum environment, indefinite increase at a specific rate is possible.

But the environmental conditions of the globe vary from point to point and are probably in no two places exactly alike. From this it follows that at a given moment, in a given area, the precise environmental complex constituting the optimum for a given species will be found at relatively few points.

This is the real reason why organisms and, in particular, injurious insects do not often increase to the point where they are devastating plagues. The fundamental constitution of the universe, composed of a multitude of specifically different and interacting things, living and non-living, necessarily implies a limited possibility of existence for any particular one of them. The fact that there are *species*, i.e., a variety of essentially limited things, means that their ability to increase is necessarily limited.

The world being what it is, *control*, or in other words, a condition under which an organism *cannot* realise all of its potentialities is therefore *normal* and outbreaks *abnormal*.

VI.

An excessive reverence for the idea of adaptation and the assumption that organisms are indefinitely plastic and capable of fitting themselves into almost any situation at relatively short notice, has led to some rather inaccurate statements on this subject. In his introduction to Elton's *Animal Ecology*, Julian Huxley suggests (p. 14) that there is for any given species an optimum density of numbers and that there are, as it were, cosmic mechanisms whereby "the actual density of population is regulated toward the optimum." Elton himself affirms that "every animal tends to have a certain suitable optimum which is determined by the habits and other characteristics of the species in question." It is clear that no such inherent tendency toward an optimum density of population can possibly exist. One reason is, that there is no such thing as an absolute optimum density of population. The density best suited to the species depends upon circumstances. When food is abundant we may have a thriving and healthy population of a thousand individuals for each unit of area; when it is rare, a population of five hundred might produce premature exhaustion of the available food supply, having as a consequence the local extermination of the species. But a diminution or increase in the food supply might come about in a great many ways through the complex action and interaction of a great multitude of diverse causes. In fact, in order to maintain the population of the species at an optimum density, the inherent tendency would have to adjust matters in relation to future contingent events. Now we are ready to admit and have indeed maintained that instinct is a very marvellous thing and involves the disposition of things in relation to ends as yet unknown, but no instinct however remarkable is able to arrange matters in regard to future events brought about through the play of pure chance.

It is therefore quite impossible to admit that organisms possess any instinct or inherent tendency to the maintenance of their populations at a density advantageous to them, or that there are any cosmic mechanisms working to this end. The examples cited by the authors we have mentioned in support of their hypothesis indeed demonstrate this clearly. Thus Elton states that a lighthouse keeper in Berlenga Island, off the coast of Portugal, introduced cats to kill off the rabbits, which they did so effectively that they ultimately ate every single rabbit on the island, after which they starved to death.

There is nothing in this which supports the idea of an inherent tendency toward an optimum density. What the example really shows is that organisms multiply without any regard to the interests of the species as a whole. Whether the rate of multiplication, having regard to actual circumstances, is harmful, indifferent or beneficial to the species is entirely a matter of chance.

VII.

When conditions in a locality inhabited by a given species approach the optimum, the species automatically increases in numbers. This increase constitutes what we call, technically, an *outbreak*, which is of necessity, as we have already said, an *abnormal* phenomenon. The organism considered may continue to increase in numbers for a considerable time, but it obviously cannot go on increasing indefinitely. As it increases in numbers it necessarily spreads, both in space and time. As it spreads, it moves to points outside its optimum environment, when its rate of multiplication immediately diminishes. Furthermore, as the population of the species becomes more numerous, the action it exerts upon its environment, both indirectly and directly, increases in intensity, producing changes which are on the whole, in so far as they depend purely and simply on the numerical increase, disadvantageous, since they consist to a great extent in the progressive exhaustion of the nutritive power of the environment in relation to the species considered. It must also be remembered that the condition of the globe at any point is never constant. A region which to-day presents conditions optimum for a given species may depart from optimum conditions in the direction X next year and in the direction Y in the year following.

Thus, under even most favourable conditions, there cannot be a continuous and uninterrupted increase in numbers, but simply an oscillating movement whose amplitude will vary according to circumstances, but is more likely to be feeble than extensive, because of the narrowly circumscribed optimum and restrictive adaptive powers of the majority of species.

Whether the change in numbers of a species will take the form of an oscillating movement about a mean value, depends, however, on chance. Some species go on increasing for long periods of years. Others, in consequence of environmental changes producing conditions with which they cannot cope, decrease in numbers and disappear completely. Numberless catastrophes of this kind have occurred in the past and, though the majority of them escape notice, still continue to occur. The only reason why oscillation about a mean population value is on the whole more frequent than a steady increase or decrease, is that on account of the great complexity of the natural environment, changes unfavourable to a species do not usually occur simultaneously in all the localities it inhabits, so that although its numbers diminish at one point they increase at another.

VIII.

Let us now consider more particularly the factors of natural control.

It will be clear from what has preceded, that there are not in nature any specific regulatory agencies, *i.e.*, any cosmic mechanisms specifically working to regulate the numbers of organic beings. Factors of control are such only in a *relative* sense, in relation to certain particular species. Thus a temperature which is inimical or fatal to one species may be optimum for another. This is true even for parasites and predators, whose attack on one phytophagous insect may prevent it from exhausting the food supply and thus favour the increase for another which arrives on the scene somewhat later in the season. What we call controlling factors are, in general, only the ordinary environmental factors, whose controlling influence depends primarily upon the specific limitations and needs of the organisms upon which they act.

There is thus an almost infinite variety of controlling factors differing not only according to the organic species, but also according to the particular point in space and moment in time considered. Nevertheless, for practical purposes the natural factors of control may be divided into two great classes—the biotic or organic factors comprising living organisms and the abiotic or inorganic factors comprising physico-chemical forces and influences of various kinds.

IX.

The interrelation between living organisms falls into two main categories—the indirect and the direct. Every organism has an effect upon its fellows through its general action upon the common environment, which it both impoverishes and enriches in a manner peculiar to its species. The effect of such indirect relations on the formation and development of biological associations is undoubtedly enormous. During the course of its ordinary existence and in the pursuit of its own ends, the organism prepares an environment in which certain of its associates will flourish, but from which others will be excluded. For example, the larvae of some mosquitoes are apparently unable to live in water containing certain species of Chara[1]. This is what may be termed indirect biological control.

Any organism which habitually injures or destroys others is a factor of biotic control. Since all animals and many protozoa, bacteria and fungi, as well as certain of the higher plants, prey upon and develop at the expense of living things, the number of controlling factors of this group is very large. However, since they are without exception essentially limited in character and distribution, only a very few at most come into play in any given case.

The vast majority of parasites, predators and pathogenic organisms require for their continued existence and propagation, not merely the presence of certain hosts, but also a certain definite complex of environmental conditions quite independent of the host. The distribution of these organisms in space and time therefore does not necessarily coincide with that of the species on which they are found acting at certain points at certain seasons. This is true not only in the case of fungous, protozoal and bacterial diseases, whose influence is notoriously limited, sporadic and uncertain, it is also true of the predaceous and parasitic enemies of insect pests. Biologists have long been accustomed to ascribe to entomophagous parasites and predators the principal rôle in the limitations and suppression of insect invasions. "Les Insectes

---

[1] Matheson and Hinman, abstr. in *Rev. of Appl. Ent.*, 16, B.

Entomophages," writes M. Caullery (*l.c.*), whom we may cite again on this point, "sont aussi l'agent regulateur naturel de beaucoup le plus efficace, de la multiplication d'un très grand nombre d'Insectes, avant tous des Lepidoptères. En particulier ils constituent un facteur de première importance dans la lutte contre leur propagation excessive." That this estimate of the part played by insect parasites in the prevention and the control of the outbreaks of their hosts corresponds to the general belief is certain. The real facts are, however, that parasites and predators play very little or no part in the economy of many insect pests, that even when they are present their action is often purely local, and that the cases in which control can be definitely ascribed uniquely or even principally to their action, are rather uncommon.

The fundamental reason for natural control, as we have already stated, is simply the fact that every insect pest, like every other organism, requires at every moment of its life-history a special habitat which exists only at a few points.

X.

One character of the optimum habitat, in species having parasites and predators, is of course the absence of these enemies. But the physical factors of the environment are equally important. In order to persist, reproduce and multiply, the organism requires not only its food, but also a precise delicately adjusted combination of the physico-chemical qualities. The optimum combination for any species is definite and irreplaceable. Abnormal heat is not corrected by abnormal moisture, nor abnormal drought by abnormal cold. One combination alone is perfectly suitable for a given species. An organism has therefore only to emerge at any moment in its life-history from its specific habitat to be exterminated or at least weakened by environmental influences. The more complex and elaborate the life-history, the less chance of survival, other things being equal.

The reason why the control of insect pests is principally effected by the physico-chemical factors, instead of by entomophagous insects, as is commonly believed, is at first sight, perhaps, not obvious, but it is a very simple one. It is that parasitic and predaceous control is effected by specific organisms whose distribution in time and space is limited by their specific requirements, of which the presence of the host organism is only one. Only a few of such organisms are capable of acting upon any given host because only a few are attracted by it. The organic factors of control are thus strictly limited both in number and in distribution. [The physical factors of control, on the contrary, are simply intensities of omnipresent physical and chemical influences above or below the limits between which a given species can subsist. Their distribution, or, in other words, the range over which they will be found acting, is obviously far more extensive than that of the biotic factors. Thus, daily temperatures above the limit of toleration for a given species may occur in a long band of territory at practically every point in which the food plant of a given organism exists;

but the conditions favourable to the development of a given parasite or predator will be found only at certain points in such areas. Furthermore, the number of physical factors of control is for practical purposes unlimited, since any departure in either the positive or negative direction of any physical factor from the intensity which a given species can tolerate will eliminate it. Thus supposing that a given species can survive and remain active only between temperatures of 60° F. and 80° F.; in such a case control will be effected not simply by temperatures of 81° F. and 59° F., but by *any temperature below* 60° F. *and by any temperature above* 80° F. The same thing will be true of any physical factors. These factors are therefore, as has been said, unlimited in number.

It is also necessary to remember that in order to be lethal, physical factors need not be of extraordinary intensity. Physical factors are indeed seldom lethal in themselves—we mean, in respect to *all* organisms. They are lethal only in respect to *certain organisms*, whose reception of their action specifies them as lethal. An environment which is practically normal for species in certain stages of development may be full of dangers at other periods of their existence. Young stages and transition periods in organisms with complicated metamorphoses are often particularly susceptible. For example, in practically every environment in which *Pyrausta nubilalis* Hubn. has been studied, a mortality of from 85 per cent. to 95 per cent. of the younger larvae has been observed. This mortality can be ascribed to nothing but the ordinary physical factors which are lethal because of the extreme fragility of the *Pyrausta* larvae in the initial phases of development.

From what has preceded, we may conclude that although physical control is everywhere important, it is not everywhere of equal importance. The regions in which it is most effective are naturally those in which general conditions are least favourable to life in general, such as the polar zones, deserts, rocks and the like. The regions in which it is the least effective are those like the tropical rain forests, where conditions are constantly and uniformly favourable to life in general. Between these extremes are regions like the temperate zones, where favourable and unfavourable periods alternate in both the diurnal and annual cycle.

The importance of the biological factors (*i.e.*, the parasitic and predaceous enemies) varies, other things being equal, in an exactly inverse manner. Since the factors are themselves organisms, they are less likely to be present and abundant in regions where the conditions are unfavourable to life and most likely to be present and flourishing in regions where conditions are constantly and consistently favourable to life in general. In intermediate regions we may expect them to be moderately abundant like their hosts. It must also be noted that one of the most important factors in determining the status of the parasites and predators is the relative abundance of the food supply, *i.e.* of their hosts. The more perfectly uniform and continuous the distribution of the hosts, the more likely are the parasites to flourish. Furthermore, since the essential characteristic of the parasite or predator is that it increases at the *expense of its host* the regions in which the host is abundant are those *in which it is likely to be most effective as a controlling factor.*

We may thus conclude that such tropical regions as are favourable to life in general will be those in which the biological factors of control will be of the greatest importance as compared with physical factors; that in regions unfavourable to life they will be quite unimportant; and that, in the intermediate regions, in which are included the great temperate zones comprising the areas most heavily populated by and most suitable to the human race, they will be of only moderate importance. What part biological factors and physical factors respectively play in the control of any given organism in any region can of course be determined only by careful investigation, since the general rules just formulated are not always applicable. Certain species and groups of species, such as the Heteropterous Hemiptera, have, as far as we know, relatively few parasites in any region[1].

Certain species are heavily attacked by parasites and predators in one locality, but suffer very little in this way at other points in the same geographical or even biogeographical area.

XI.

In short, as a general rule, the complex of factors which actually effects control in the case of any species differs in composition from point to point and from year to year in the area of distribution.

It follows that there is not in general any regulating factor responsible for the natural control of a given species. Investigations undertaken with the object of discovering the "limiting factor" of an insect pest, *i.e.*, some influence which keeps the species in check over the whole area of distribution, are therefore unpromising. The same thing is true of studies of "the causes of insect outbreaks," if by this we are to understand an attempt to discover some general underlying influence effective in preventing the increase of all species. Insect outbreaks, considered in general, have no uniform and common cause in any environmental condition, or combination of environmental factors. The only absolutely general statements that can be made in regard to them is that they arise because the environment has for a time approached the optimum for the species concerned.

Since the environments in which the organism is in control may be of many different types, the approximation to the optimum may be from many different directions and may differ in degree. Thus, in an environment which is too dry, a little more moisture may give rise to an outbreak; in one which is too cold, a little more heat will have the same effect. It is extremely difficult to pick out, from the immense multitude of varying and interacting factors, those

---

[1] This is sometimes considered to be due to the possession of protective devices of certain kinds, but the explanation is not satisfactory. Neither systems of colorations, nor nettling hairs, nor an armour of chitinised plates, nor rapidity of movement, nor the existence of toxic principles in the blood prevent insects from being decimated by parasites.

whose variations have been important. If there is a simultaneous excess or deficiency in two or more factors, an approximation of one of these to the intensity characteristic of the optimum environment may not be advantageous, but the reverse. For example, if the climate is both too cold and too dry an increase of temperature alone or of moisture alone may have a detrimental effect. The simultaneous return to normal intensity of both factors may be necessary for increase.

On the other hand, all environments in which outbreaks occur will not necessarily be similar. A numerical increase may take place in regions in which conditions are not, absolutely speaking, optimum, but which approximate to the optimum, though in different respects. Thus, suppose that a certain species is kept in control in one region by the combined action of several parasites and some form of agricultural control, and in another by an absence of moisture together with an unfavourable distribution of the food plant. The disappearance of one of the parasites from the first environment and an increase in moisture in the second, might lead to a simultaneous outbreak of equal intensity, the rate of multiplication in both cases being considerably below that occurring in an absolutely optimum environment, but nevertheless sufficient to cause extremely serious damage. It is obvious that from such cases, which are those ordinarily encountered in practice, it would be very difficult to extract information of really general value, permitting one to understand or predict other outbreaks.

XII.

We may therefore conclude that attempts to determine the causes of natural control and the reasons for outbreaks simply by a study of the environmental conditions are not likely to be successful, unless the species studied is sensitive to some one particular factor and unaffected by variations in any of the others. Since cases of this kind are very rare, the most promising method of attacking the problem is to determine the ecological optimum for the species considered by a careful laboratory study of its physiology and habits. It is of course sometimes difficult to provide, under laboratory conditions, an environment exactly suited to the living organism. The difficulty one often experiences in inducing certain insects to mate and reproduce in captivity under conditions which appear, as far as one can tell, to differ very little from those in the natural habitat, shows clearly that we still have much to learn in this field. On the other hand, the rate of increase of many species under laboratory conditions so greatly exceeds what is observed under natural conditions, that they may be considered as being a nearer approximation to the optimum, than those which the organism is accustomed to encounter in the field. With the development of suitable apparatus our ability to control, vary and combine the various environmental factors is steadily increasing. By the careful study of an injurious insect under controlled laboratory conditions, we can, I believe, even now, determine the optimum environment more accurately and rapidly than would be possible by attempts to analyse the natural environments of the species.

At all events, it is along these lines that the problem of the natural control and outbreaks of injurious insects must be attacked. Outbreaks of species are simply due to the fact that conditions momentarily correspond or approximate to the ecological optimum; control means simply a departure in one or many directions from optimum conditions to the point where the species is just able to maintain itself, and below which it decreases in numbers and disappears. The organism with its specific behaviour and requirements is the centre of the problem, and it is not until we understand it that we shall find a clue to the fluctuations in its numbers.

7

Reprinted from J. Theoret. Biol. 3:19–26, 32–42, 48–50 (1962)

On a Theory of Natural Control of Insect Population †

A. MILNE‡

Durham University School of Agriculture,
King's College, Newcastle upon Tyne, England

(*Received* 11 *September* 1961)

This paper re-states, elaborates, and answers criticisms of, a theory of natural control of insect population which is summarized as follows: For the most part, control of increase of population of any species X is due to the combined action of density-independent and imperfectly density-dependent environmental factors. In the comparatively rare cases where this combined action fails, increase to the point of collective suicide is prevented by the one and only perfectly density-dependent factor, namely, intraspecific competition of X. On the other hand, decrease of numbers to zero is prevented ultimately by density-independent factors alone.

1. Introduction

The mechanism of natural control of population is undoubtedly the most controversial problem in animal ecology today. In 1956 at Montreal, I pointed out the shortcomings (as they seem to me) of previous theories of the mechanism and then proposed a new theory for insects (Milne, 1957a and b). The time has now come to consider the inevitable criticism which my theory has aroused.

2. Questions of Definition and Classification

In ecology a technical term or concept seldom has exactly the same meaning for all students—see, for example, the varied notions even of basic terms such as "population dynamics" and "effective environment" (Milne, 1957b) and "competition" (Milne, 1961). Therefore, before re-stating my theory briefly, it is necessary to deal with relevant matters of definition and classification as follows:

Population is the number of individuals of a particular species existing in a particular place. Population, of course, changes in time.

The *ultimate* capacity of a place for a species is the maximum number of individuals that the place could carry without being rendered totally

---

† Substance of a paper requested by the International Union of Forest Research Organisations for discussion at Zurich in August 1960.

‡ Agricultural Research Council Unit of Insect Physiology, 24 Leazes Terrace, Newcastle upon Tyne, England.

uninhabitable by utter exhaustion or destruction of resources (food and/or living-space in their various forms), i.e. without causing the species to succumb in or quit the place entirely. The *environmental* capacity of a place for a species is the maximum number of individuals that the species could maintain in the place. Obviously, environmental capacity cannot be greater than ultimate capacity; it could, conceivably, be equal to ultimate capacity but laboratory experiments with populations suggest that it is usually somewhat smaller. The two capacities are related, and both vary in time (see later under "Solomon's Criticism").

Population dynamics is that branch of ecology which investigates (1) the causation of change in population and (2) the mechanism of natural control of population.

In population dynamics, the effective environment must be defined with respect to the individual because the population is itself an environmental factor having effect on the individual according to density.† This presents no difficulty since what happens to a population is simply the sum of what happens to each of its individuals. Let us regard the individual as fulfilling itself when it fully realizes its maximum potentials for speed of development, amount of reproduction, and length of survival. The effective environment is then everything else in the universe which helps or hinders fulfilment of the individual.

Population change is, of course, increase or decrease of numbers (with or without variation in age-composition). It is clearly due to the sum of the actions of all effective environmental factors on all individuals of the population.

Natural control is best defined from the viewpoint of the continuing existence of the population itself. In nature, insect density fluctuates irregularly between variable higher and lower values. Obviously, if a population is to continue its existence, two conditions must be met: (a) the highest densities must never exceed ultimate capacity and (b) the lowest densities must always be above zero. Control simply means the unfailing arrest of increase and decrease somewhere short of these two extinction levels. The question is whether natural control is due to one, some or all of the effective environmental factors.

Clearly the first step in the problem of the mechanism of natural control is to classify effective environmental factors according to their response to density. The common view has been that there are only two groups of factors, namely density-independent and density-dependent, the latter having increasing intensity of action (percentage effect) with rising density and decreasing intensity with falling density. This dual classification, the basis of Nicholson's theory (1933 and later), is inadequate.

† Hence *environmental*, as distinct from *ultimate*, capacity.

I recognize three kinds of environmental factor capable of causing changes in the population of any particular insect species. These three kinds, A, B and C, are defined thus: with respect to any species X, and at (= during the reign of) any given capacity for X,

A the density-independent factor is one in which intensity of action is entirely independent of density of X;

B the imperfectly density-dependent factor is one in which intensity of action is determined partly by density of X and partly by other variables which vary independently of the density of X;

C the perfectly density-dependent factor is one in which intensity of action is determined solely by density of X.

And hence, according to justifications already given fully (Milne, 1957a, pp. 258–9, 262–3 and 1959a, pp. 532–3), classification of the effective environment is as follows:

A. Density-independent factors: (1) Physical circumstances, mainly, or basically, weather. (2) Actions of other species, such as their indiscriminate browsing, grazing, fouling and treading on vegetation, or casual predation and parasitism.

B. Imperfectly density-dependent factors: actions of other species competing for the same resources (interspecific competition), and of predators, parasites and pathogens in general.

C. The one and only perfectly density-dependent factor: competition (for food, space, etc.) within the population itself, i.e. intraspecific competition. In order to avoid misunderstanding (see Milne, 1961) let it be said now that competition is the endeavour of two (or more) animals to gain the same particular thing, or to gain the measure each wants from the supply of a thing when that supply is not sufficient for both (or all); and that this endeavour may take various forms and have various direct or indirect deleterious effects on the fulfilment of the animals concerned.

Collectively, the A(1) factors alternate between providing depressive conditions and conditions favourable to increase of population. When acting, the A(2), B and C factors are always depressive to some extent.

From a study of small mammal predation on the European Pine Sawfly, Holling (1959a) seeks to re-introduce the notion of a fourth kind of factor, namely, a factor with inverse density-dependence (see also MacLellan, 1959). If the population of a predator is fixed or has a temporary limit then, as prey density rises, the percentage of prey taken will obviously (tend to) increase up to a point, then decrease. The latter phase, when percentage kill is decreasing, occurs simply because there is a limit to the number of prey that the individual predator can deal with in unit time, no matter how dense (i.e. easy to find) the prey becomes. To call it a phase of inverse density-dependence is unhelpful and in fact misleading so far as natural control is concerned. Actually it is a form of density-independence: predation, having reached its maximum intensity, no longer responds to increase in prey density. When both phases are taken into account, the predation is still imperfectly density-dependent.

Note: In my previous papers, I did not distinguish the two kinds of capacity, ultimate and environmental.

3. The Theory

Since control of population increase means that the highest densities must never exceed ultimate capacity and since this capacity varies through time, it follows that a natural factor, in order to control, must be able to arrest increase before it exceeds ultimate capacity at all possible ultimate capacities or, in other words, at any given (possible) ultimate capacity.

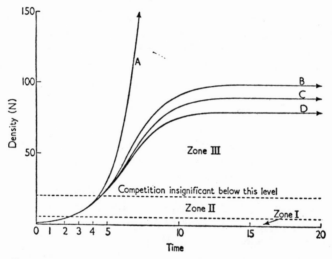

FIG. 1. Exponential (A) and logistic (B, C, D) growth of population (see text).

Mathematically, it can readily be shown that a variable depressive factor will control population increase of species X on two conditions: I. the factor's intensity of action must be perfectly density-dependent; II. the intensity at density equal to, or less than, ultimate capacity for X must be sufficient to stop population growth, i.e. reduce rate of growth to zero. A very simple and therefore rather limited demonstration of this was given earlier (Milne, 1957b, page 258). More adequate demonstrations are given below with the so-called logistic curve (of which the 1957 demonstration is a special case) and modifications of that curve. The corresponding exponential curve (Fig. 1A), the curve of unrestricted growth, is included for comparison.

Let N be the population at any moment, t the time measured as time or generations, b a constant representing the maximum reproductive rate per individual (i.e. the rate if individuals were completely fulfilled) and K a constant representing ultimate capacity. The logistic curve is then derived from the differential equation for rate of growth

$$\frac{dN}{dt} = bN \frac{(K - N)}{K} \tag{1}$$

as

$$N = \frac{K}{1 + e^{(a-bt)}} \tag{2}$$

Using equation (2) with $b = 2$, $K = 100$, $N = 1$ at $t = 0$, and 0·3515 as unit of time, the result is Fig. 1B which shows population growth arrested at 100, i.e. at K level. It scarcely requires adding that no matter what values are allotted to b and K, the same type of curve (the logistic) results, with arrest always at K level. The arrest at this level is due to a "factor" which meets both the conditions I and II stated above, as can be seen by studying equation (1). This equation says that rate of growth is a variable fraction $[(K - N)/K]$ of the potential multiplication $[bN]$ per generation. The fraction $[(K - N)/K]$ is the "factor". Obviously this "factor" reduces $[bN]$ by a constant amount $[1/K]$ for each individual added to the population; that is, the intensity of action of the "factor" increases with, and is determined solely by, density $[N]$ at ($=$ during the reign of) any given capacity $[K]$. In other words, the "factor" is perfectly density-dependent (condition I). The equation also says that rate of growth is reduced to zero by the "factor" $[(K - N)/K]$ when density $[N]$ equals capacity $[K]$. In other words, the intensity of the "factor" at density equal to capacity is sufficient to stop population growth (condition II).

Finally, let c be a constant of value >1. Two modifications of the logistic may then be written thus: First

$$\frac{dN}{dt} = bN \frac{(K - cN)}{K} \tag{3}$$

which integrates to

$$N = \frac{K/c}{1 + e^{(a-bt)}} \tag{4}$$

and second

$$\frac{dN}{dt} = bN \frac{(K - N^c)}{K} \tag{5}$$

which integrates to

$$N = \left\{ \frac{K}{1 + e^{(a-bct)}} \right\}^{\frac{1}{c}} \tag{6}$$

Using $c = 1 \cdot 1$, Fig. 1C illustrates equation (4) for the same values of b, K and time-unit as in Fig. 1B; and using $c = 1 \cdot 05$, Fig. 1D illustrates equation (6) similarly. In both these modifications the "factor" again meets conditions I and II. The relation between density and intensity of the "factor" is linear in the first modification (as in the logistic proper) but curvilinear in the second. Arrest is below K level in both cases.

It should be noted that the asymptote of Fig. 1B is ultimate capacity (because, by definition, $K =$ ultimate capacity); and the asymptote of Fig. 1C or Fig. 1D represents environmental capacity when that is less than ultimate capacity, as it usually is.

Now, obviously, neither an imperfectly density-dependent nor a density-independent factor can alone control increase of numbers indefinitely, because neither fulfils even condition I. Nor, since there are numerous instances of insect "outbreak" despite a formidable array of inimical species, can it be argued that several imperfectly density-dependent factors might add up to a perfectly density-dependent process, let alone that such a process would necessarily meet condition II. In other words, competing species, predators, parasites and pathogens, whether acting singly or in concert, can no more be expected alone to control increase of species X unfailingly than weather can alone.

Equally obviously, intraspecific competition does meet condition I. The question is: does it also meet condition II? This depends on whether the reduction of [bN] per added individual is (i) equal to or (ii) greater or (iii) less than [$1/K$]. If circumstances (i) or (ii) apply, then intraspecific competition can arrest population increase at or below K level (see equations 2, 4 and 6 and Figs. 1B, 1C and 1D). If circumstance (iii) applies, then it cannot do so (as can be seen by entering $c < 1$ in equations (3) and (5)). Now it is unthinkable that circumstance (iii) should apply because, if it did, Nature would have no unfailing means of preventing suicidal multiplication of a species when conditions militate against its enemies. It certainly does not apply in the case of plants, as any gardener knows from experience with seed beds and seed boxes. Nor does it apply in the case of animals. Laboratory experiments have indicated again and again that intraspecific competition for resources prevents collective suicide, i.e. arrests population growth at or below the level of ultimate capacity (references too numerous for individual mention here—see text-books like Allee et al., 1949, and Andrewartha & Birch, 1954); and so also have observations on natural populations (see e.g. Bodenheimer, 1937; Bitancourt, 1941; Davidson, 1944). In the few instances where intraspecific competition has apparently failed to control (see Andrewartha & Browning, 1961), the reason is an unnatural situation such as lack of alternative prey or of opportunity for the partial emigration which is one of the reactions of some, though by no means all, animal species to competition (see e.g. Elton's, 1927, record of the castaway cats multiplying until they all starved to death on a small island).

Intraspecific competition, then, must be the ultimate controlling factor for population increase. But in Nature, most insect species, in most places for most of the time, are held fluctuating at population levels low enough for this kind of competition to be absent or insignificant. In other words, control by intraspecific competition itself is seldom evoked. It follows that control of increase is, for most of the time if not almost endlessly, a matter of the combined action of factors which are imperfectly density-dependent and factors which are density-independent, each supplying the lack of the other in controlling effect.

Density-dependent factors (both perfect and imperfect) obviously must relax their depressive action as density falls, but, equally obviously, density-independent factors are not tied to do so, simply because their action is independent of density. Clearly, therefore, the ultimate control of decrease of numbers rests with the density-independent factors alone. For, unless the density-independent factors change at the appropriate time from causing decrease to permitting increase, then the remnant of individuals left by the imperfectly density-dependent factors must continue to dwindle towards zero.

Briefly, then, my theory of natural control of insect population is this: For the most part, control of increase of population of any species X is due to the combined action of density-independent and imperfectly density-dependent environmental factors. In the comparatively rare cases where this combined action fails, increase to the point of collective suicide is prevented by the one and only perfectly density-dependent factor, namely, intraspecific competition of X. On the other hand, decrease of numbers to zero is prevented ultimately by density-independent factors alone.

This theory is illustrated in Fig. 2, which is a slightly modified form of the original conception (cp. Diag. 2 of Milne, 1957a or Fig. 3 of Milne, 1957b). It will be noted that the range of population density for a species is divided into three zones, indicating Zone III $>>>$ Zone II $>$ Zone I. This is in accordance with frequency distribution of density in long series of field population data such as the 60-year Letzlingen observations on four forest moths published by Schwerdtfeger (1935, 1942), e.g. the case of *Bupalus piniarius*:

Number per 100 sq m	Frequencies of years
0·1– 0·9	10
1·0– 149·9	42
150·0–2549·0	8

Of necessity, the above account is very compressed. Fuller argument and evidence for some aspects of the theory are to be found in previous papers (Milne, 1957a and b; 1958; 1959a and b).

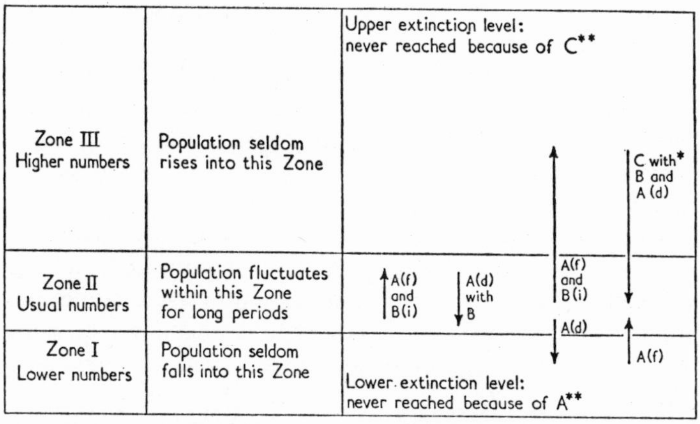

FIG. 2. *Illustration of the author's theory of natural control of an insect population.*
Left-hand pair of arrows represents fluctuation of population within Zone II; the amplitude of this fluctuation varies. Right-hand pairs of arrows represent departure and return of population from and to Zone II; the magnitude of departure varies. Factors causing fluctuation within, and departure from and return to, Zone II are represented by letters beside the arrows.

A   = Density-independent factors.
A(f) = A having favourable sum-effect.
A(d) = A having depressive sum-effect.
B   = Imperfectly density-dependent factors. These, when acting, are always depressive to some extent in sum-effect.
B(i) = B having inadequate depressive sum-effect.
C   = The one perfectly density-dependent factor (intraspecific competition).
*   = If population rises sufficiently high, C may be able by itself to send population back to Zone II (see p. 36) but usually it acts in conjunction with B and A(d).
**   = NEVER, if the area is not too small or if emigration/immigration is not precluded.
Note: C is absent or insignificant in Zone II, and B similarly in Zone I.

[*Editor's Note:* Material has been omitted at this point.]

117

5. Solomon's Criticism

Solomon (1958a, and see, partly, Milne, 1958) argued that since intensity of intraspecific competition varies at any given density, its intensity is not determined solely by density and therefore this competition (like the "B" factors) is not perfectly density-dependent. My reply (Milne, 1958) may be summarized as follows: Solomon's conclusion is false because the variation to which he refers is caused by variation in environmental capacity which is expressly ruled out in my definition of perfect density-dependence. A factor is perfectly density-dependent not because its intensity of action is determined solely by density but because its intensity is so determined at any given environmental capacity. When the capacity alters, the "curve" of competition intensity is bound to change in regard to its slope (so that competition intensity varies at any given density), but it does not cease to be a function solely of numbers at any given capacity, i.e. perfectly density-dependent. Alteration of environmental capacity can be absolute, that is, independent of the organisms concerned, as when weather favours or retards the growth of vegetation for food or shelter; or it can be relative, that is, due to modification of average individual needs brought about, for example, by weather increasing and decreasing activity, or by some change in age-distribution or genetical composition of the population.

Solomon's rejoinder (1958b), unanswered until now, is reproduced verbatim in the sequence of inset sections (i)–(iii), below:

> (i) "I objected to Dr. Milne's proposed term 'perfectly density-dependent' because neither intraspecific competition nor any other factor to be observed in the field is likely to preserve (in the words of his definition) 'an exact linear (or curvilinear) relationship between increasing action of the factor and increasing density of the species'."

Solomon here gives not my definition but my supplementary mathematical illustration of it omitting the premise of constant environmental capacity (see Milne, 1957b). In the field, the relationship in the case of intraspecific competition could not be a "simple" linear or curvilinear relationship because environmental capacity is not constant there. Solomon goes on:

> (ii) "The logic of his argument can be made clearer by re-stating it as follows. If all causes of variation were removed, there would be a simple and exactly maintained relationship between the intensity of intraspecific competition and the population density. Let us relegate all sources of variation to a category for which we shall borrow the term environmental capacity. Then we are left with a perfectly density-dependent factor, intraspecific competition."

This is not my argument. There is no relegation. As noted earlier, the variation to which Solomon refers has only one cause, namely, variation in environmental capacity for population. It is variation in environmental capacity which has a number of causes. It is also illogical to say that the term environmental capacity has been borrowed for use in connection with competition. Environmental capacity is an integral part of the concept of competition as an effective factor since competition owes its very existence to the fact that this capacity is finite or limited. Solomon ends:

> (iii) "I see no objection to this argument [(ii) above] as an exercise in logic or as a step in the development of a simplified mathematical theory. I only wish to point out that the perfection achieved in this way bears little relationship to what we can expect to find in studying the dynamics of actual populations, and that therefore the term seems inappropriate for use by the practical ecologist. It should perhaps be added that, by a similar process of abstraction, the relationships expected to hold between a parasite or predator population and the density of its host can also be made to appear simple and regular, as in the mathematical theories, although imperfect in Milne's sense."

As noted above, the "logic" and the "perfection achieved" by it are Solomon's, not mine. Of course the removal of all causes of variation in predation other than variation in prey density (his "process of abstraction") would result in predation intensity being determined solely by prey density (his "simple and regular relationship"). But this abstract relationship is not perfect density-dependence according to definition. Predation is not perfectly density-dependent simply because its intensity on species X at any given capacity for X is not determined solely by density of X but partly by density of X and partly by other variables which vary independently of density of X. Examples of these "other variables" are the actions of enemies peculiar to the predators of X, weather which does not change environmental capacity for X either absolutely or relatively but which affects the functioning of the predators, and etc. Intraspecific competition is perfectly density-dependent according to definition, and is the only effective environmental factor that is so. Solomon's criticism arises from misunderstanding of the definition and is therefore irrelevant.

The distinction between perfect and imperfect density-dependence is perhaps subtle but it must be of practical value to ecologists in the question of natural control of increase because it is a real and relevant distinction between certain effective environmental factors in the field. The argument for it is hinged on environmental capacity for the very obvious reason that this capacity is the all-important circumstance to organisms in the matter of their population increase. The argument is in no sense a "process of

A. MILNE

abstraction". It is analytic. For example, if the intensity of action of a factor on X does depend solely on density of X at any given capacity for X (analysis) then it does so at all capacities (synthesis).

Some of the points in this section can be illustrated by simple graphs based on equation (1), assuming now that K = environmental capacity. If individuals are all identical (i.e. all "Q" individuals) then, when K is fixed, the intensity of intraspecific competition is increased by $1/K$ for each individual added to the population. Hence at any density N the

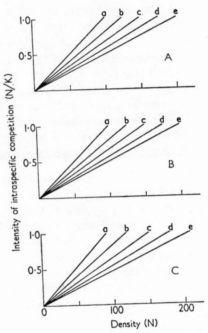

FIG. 3. The relation between intensity of intraspecific competition and density (see text).

A.	B.	C.
All Q		All $Q:P::1:2$
(a) $K = 100$	(a) All Q $K = 100$	(a) $K = 90$
(b) $K = 125$	(b) $Q:P::3:2$ $K = 125$	(b) $K = 120$
(c) $K = 150$	(c) $Q:P::1:2$ $K = 150$	(c) $K = 150$
(d) $K = 175$	(d) $Q:P::1:6$ $K = 175$	(d) $K = 180$
(e) $K = 200$	(e) All P $K = 200$	(e) $K = 210$

intensity of competition is N/K, a linear relation in which N/K obviously must be unity when $N = K$. Figure 3A illustrates this linear relation for K between 99 and 201, showing clearly how the slope of the "curve" (in this case a straight line) of competition intensity changes as capacity changes. (Incidentally it also shows, like Figs. 3B and 3C, Solomon's irrelevant point that competition intensity varies for any given density.)

Now the first graph in Fig. 3A is designated "all Q, $K = 100$". This means that amount of living-space† and rate of generation of food are constants such that 100 individuals is the capacity when they are all Q individuals. But individuals in a natural population are never identical. They vary as to age and genotype and therefore their needs vary accordingly. For maximum ease in calculation, let us imagine that there are only two kinds of individuals, P and Q, such that the same constant conditions of living-space and rate of food generation provide a capacity of 100 for Q and 200 for P. Then the utmost capacities for mixed population of P and Q

TABLE 2

Composition of population			Capacity
Q	P	$Q:P$	
100	0	All Q	100
99	2	99 : 2	101
98	4	49 : 2	102
97	6	97 : 6	103
96	8	12 : 1	104
.	.	.	.
.	.	.	.
.	.	.	.
75	50	3 : 2	125
.	.	.	.
.	.	.	.
.	.	.	.
50	100	1 : 2	150
.	.	.	.
.	.	.	.
.	.	.	.
25	150	1 : 6	175
.	.	.	.
.	.	.	.
.	.	.	.
1	198	1 : 198	199
0	200	All P	200

under these conditions are as in Table 2. The relation between competition intensity and density at five of the one-hundred-and-one capacities in Table 2 is shown in Fig. 3B. It should be noted that, with mixed population, N can be read only for multiples of the least value of $(x + y)$ in which x and y are whole numbers related by the proportion $x:y::Q:P$, but the ninety-nine possible graphs, giving one to fifty multiples each, cover all relevant contingencies. Figure 3B exemplifies the situation where capacity changes relatively due to change in population composition while amount of living-space and rate of generation of food remain unaltered.

Similarly, Figs. 3A and 3C exemplify the situation where capacity

† In Nature, living-space is a variable fraction of the area (or volume) of the "place" inhabited by the animals constituting a population.

changes absolutely due to change in amount of living-space and/or rate of generation of food while population composition remains unaltered.

The important circumstances to note in Fig. 3 are that the relation between intensity of intraspecific competition and density is always linear at any given capacity, and that the intensity always has the same value when density equals capacity, namely, the arresting value. In any place in Nature, capacity varies both absolutely and relatively, often both simultaneously, through time. However, at any instant there is a "given" capacity, determined by amount of living-space and/or rate of generation of food at that instant, for population with the same proportional composition as at that instant. Thus it follows from Fig. 3 that as population increases in Nature it is always on the way (i.e. on one or other of the innumerable graphs leading) to appropriate arrest by intraspecific competition.

Figure 3 is based on equation (1) merely for simplicity. Essentially the same results would be got with equations (3) and (5) (in which, of course, $K =$ ultimate capacity), although with (5) the graphs would be curvilinear. The question is: which equation represents intensity of competition in relation to density? Since (1) is the special case of both when $c = 1$, consideration is narrowed down to (3) in which the key variable is cN and (5) in which it is N^c. On the analogy that the number of collisions per unit time between gas molecules is proportional to the square of the density of molecules, i.e. to N^2 (compare N^c), the much more likely answer to the question is equation (5). Unlike gas molecules, however, animals do not move at random; having senses, they can avoid harmful "collisions" (interferences) to some considerable extent (as when the weaker avoid the stronger, or when ovipositing females avoid hosts already used by their kind); hence the constant c must be considerably less than 2 and tend nearer to 1 the more "sessile" the animals. Equation (5) seems to be more plausible than the equations suggested by Andersen (1957, 1960).

Finally, it must not be concluded from Fig. 1 that intraspecific competition necessarily maintains population at an asymptote if it is the only depressive factor acting. In fact, either the asymptote, or an oscillation of which the upper limit corresponds to it, may result from intraspecific competition (as any text-book of ecology shows). The work of Albrecht et al. (1959) and of Chitty (1960) suggests that oscillation is due to the impairing effects of intraspecific competition (at "asymptotic" level) being not only severe but also transmissible for one or more generations in declining degree.

6. Nicholson's Criticism

In his lengthy criticism (1958), Nicholson pronounces me "careless", my arguments "illogical" and my theory "a chaos hypothesis" for which I provide "no supporting evidence". No useful purpose would be served by going into all the details of this intemperate criticism. It is sufficient to deal reasonably with the main points (omitting the unfounded accusation of carelessness which has already been rebutted, see Milne, 1959a).

On my conclusion that neither parasites nor predators can control by themselves Nicholson says my

> "argument seems plausible, but it is wrong as the following considerations show. Let us suppose that nonreactive modifying factors directly or indirectly increase the mortality of the parasites. This would favour growth of the host population. As the hosts increase in number the chance of any parasite contacting a host necessarily improves, and so the parasite population also grows, in spite of the fact that some fraction of it is destroyed by the modifying factors. Consequently, more and more of the occupied area is effectively searched collectively by the surviving parasites, and so the fraction of the hosts attacked by the parasites increases progressively. Growth of both populations inevitably ceases when this fraction, together with that destroyed in any other way, equals the surplus fraction of host offspring."

Being density-independent, the "nonreactive modifying factors" can "increase the mortality of the parasites" at any level of host numbers. Thus these factors can "favour growth of the host population" when the latter equals environmental capacity, i.e. when any further growth would mean extinction of the host. Of course there would be no further growth because of intraspecific competition, but obviously the logical end to the first two sentences of Nicholson's argument is that parasites cannot control alone. The remainder of his argument is no less vulnerable. The "nonreactive modifying factors" can not only "increase the mortality of the parasites" but also reduce "the chance of any parasite contacting a host". For example, sunless, windy or rainy periods may occur during any season in a way that on the average reduces mating-opportunity, searching-efficiency or searching-time for the parasite (see, e.g., Schwerdtfeger, 1942, Beirne, 1955, among many others) so that although there are more hosts the proportion of them "contacted" (attacked) is not increased and may even be reduced. Accordingly, "the fraction of hosts attacked" does not "necessarily" increase "progressively", as Nicholson imagines. Progressive increase in the fraction requires both the numbers and the functioning of the parasite to be determined solely by host density. This requirement is clearly unattainable in Nature. If ecological research has shown one thing more clearly than all else, it is surely the fact that no organism's numbers, nor its functioning, are determined wholly by one

123

circumstance. Whatever response the parasite might make to host density is inevitably modified by other factors (1) peculiar to the parasite itself and (2) common to itself and host but affecting each to a different degree (see Milne, 1957b). In short, intensity of parasitic attack is imperfectly density-dependent and so parasites cannot alone control their host. It is not denied that in general the intensity of enemy attack tends to increase with host density, but no amount of specious reasoning can transmute that tendency into the perfect density-dependence necessary in a factor before it can control by itself.

Nicholson asserts that I give no "supporting evidence" for my claim that "the ultimate controlling factor for increase, intraspecific competition, is usually seldom evoked". This is not so. I cited the Schwerdtfeger data (1935, 1942) on four pine-forest moths at Letzlingen over 60 consecutive years as the best of all examples (see Milne, 1957a, page 210). Simple calculation reveals that for many years (60 of the 60 years in the case of *Panolis*, 50 in *Sphinx*, 46 in *Dendrolimus* and 15 in *Bupalus*) each moth species was present at no more than one pair of adults per 3–400 sq m, i.e. per three or four trees at least. Since much higher densities occurred at other times (incomparably higher in all except *Panolis*) and since average potential production is no more than 35–100 eggs per female, it is unlikely that moth larvae suffered appreciable intraspecific competition during those years and quite certain that population growth was not then being arrested by such competition. In fact, Schwerdtfeger provides the best available evidence (best because it is the longest of reliable records) for the general conclusion that among insects at large the ultimate controlling factor for increase, namely the arresting power of intraspecific competition, is seldom evoked. I could give further quantitative evidence from ecological studies on several insects by myself and colleagues over the past 21 years. Actually there is no need to give any evidence at all. One should not have to give evidence of a fact of Nature so obvious that it is now a truism. Long ago Darwin (1859) observed that "rarity is the attribute of a vast number of species of all classes, in all countries" ("Origin of Species", Chapter 11). Practising ecologists and those familiar with the literature well know the massiveness of the evidence that intraspecific competition, of a degree capable of arresting population growth, is extremely uncommon in the field.

Nicholson tries to demolish my conclusion that when insect populations are low for long periods they are being held low during those periods by the combined action of density-independent (A) and imperfectly density-dependent (B) factors, each supplying the lack of the other. But this conclusion is the only one possible because intraspecific competition (C) cannot control increase at low density-levels (and indeed is virtually absent or ineffective at such levels) and neither A nor B factors are able to control increase by themselves. Nicholson also asserts that I give "no indication of a mechanism" whereby A and B could supply the lack of each other in controlling effect. This is not so. I do give a sufficient general indication (see Milne, 1957a, pp. 210–211). Details of the "mechanism" are obviously infinitely variable, differing in every place and period for every species (cp. Thompson, 1929, 1939, and Milne, 1957a, page 195).

Nicholson has little to say on my conclusion that the ultimate controlling factors for decrease in numbers are the density-independent factors. He dismisses it with the comment that

> "he (Milne) considers that it is mere chance which prevents adverse factors from causing extinction of species. . . ."

This is misunderstanding. My theory deals with persisting populations, i.e. offers an explanation of the fact that such populations do not decrease to zero. I know of no factor with intensity of effect varying at random in time (see later under Wilbert). Therefore I said nothing about "chance" preventing adverse factors from causing extinction. There is no chance attached to the matter in the case of a persisting population. Clearly, a population cannot persist except in a place where the (density-independent) adverse factors are such that they can never extinguish it though they may from time to time come more or less near to doing so.

Nicholson rejects my conclusion that the "balance" is not between population and environment (as he claims) but is in the environment itself, i.e. that through space and time, favourable conditions are balanced by unfavourable conditions in such a way that populations continue to exist where they do (continued existence being control), as follows:

> "He (Milne) provides no factual evidence for such qualitative environmental balance, he does not suggest any mechanism which could possibly produce or maintain it and, even if it did operate, it would not itself cause the numbers of animals to be low."

But I do give factual evidence, namely, the fact that populations generally continue to exist (see Milne, 1957a, page 193). Obviously, continued existence is possible only if favourable conditions (those permitting increase) are somehow or other balanced in their incidence and intensity by unfavourable conditions (those causing decrease). And I do suggest a mechanism producing and maintaining this environmental balance which enables a population to persist (there being, or course, no such mechanism where a population does not persist). It is in fact my theory and it is no "chaos hypothesis"! The suggested mechanism is simple. It is comprised of only two devices. The first consists in unfavourable conditions having a natural limit to their severity such that they can reduce the population down to a certain point but not down to the point of extermination. The second consists in favourable conditions being turned into unfavourable by the population itself before its numbers can surpass environmental capacity. These devices together curtail the incidence and intensity of favourable and unfavourable conditions so that the latter are balanced despite the irregularity of their alternations. Moreover, I did not claim that balance in environmental conditions would "itself cause the numbers of animals to be low". On the contrary I pointed out that control could occur at any level, high or low, according to the conditions (see Milne, 1957a, page 193, paragraphs 2 and 3).

Nicholson nevertheless insists on his own view. He avers that

> "the densities of animal populations bear a relation to the environmental conditions to which they are subject, and the existence of this relation shows that populations must be in a state of balance with their environments."

Now the relation referred to here is simply that densities become high in good conditions and low in bad. No one would deny the existence of this relation. But the existence of a relation does not show (prove) that it must be one of balance. There can be relations other than balance between two things. For instance one relation between E and P could be E pushing P up or down all the time with P powerless to resist. Here there would be no balance between E and P but it would still be a relation—a simple cause and effect relation. Let us extend this: Imagine two limits, the lower being L_o and the upper L_u, both of which, if reached, mean extinction of P. Now E can cause P to move towards L_o and also permit it to move towards L_u at irregular rates for irregular periods alternately. But E always gives up somewhere short of L_o while P itself can modify E in the vicinity of L_u (only) so that E always retracts its permission somewhere short of L_u. Here there is still a relation between E and P, a less simple relation, but certainly not one of balance. This obviously is my theory of natural control if P is read as population, E as environmental conditions in $toto$, L_o and L_u as lower and upper extinction limits respectively for P, and the factual observation accepted that for most of the time E is operating so that P is much nearer L_o than L_u and seldom comes very near L_o and even less often very near L_u. It is a theory of cause (environmental conditions) and effect (population density).

In addition to his criticism, it is worth looking at the evidence Nicholson puts forward for his own theory. For an example of "self-regulation" in the field he quotes his junior colleague Carne (1956) at Canberra to the effect that *Aphodius howittii* Hope is controlled by intraspecific competition. This is flatly contradicted by Andrewartha's junior colleague Maelzer (in the press) at Adelaide who studied the same beetle. But Carne and Maelzer were in the field at different times and only for a very short period of years in either case. Working on the ecology of a somewhat similar pasture scarab in North England, *Phyllopertha horticola* L., I found some evidence of intraspecific "strife" in 1947–48 but numbers fell very low in 1949 and have not so far (spring 1961) risen again. Hence I imagine the case with *A. howittii* is really that it suffers intraspecific competition only occasionally (cp. my theory). For his other example in the field Nicholson contradictiously attempts to show that the data of Davidson and Andrewartha (1948a and b) on *Thrips imaginis* Bagnall furnish "unusual and very important evidence of population self-regulation"! Perhaps the best comment on that is Andrewartha's own reply (1957): "It seems that Nicholson does not understand how the equation for partial regression was calculated." For regulation by enemies in the field, Nicholson rests his case on successes in biological control. This is wishful thinking. Such successes do not prove that the introduced enemies are controlling by themselves but merely that they have reduced the level at which control occurs (see my reply, 1959a, to DeBach, 1958).

Nicholson also gives laboratory examples of self-regulation and regulation by enemies. All his examples of single species populations show (as agreed in my theory) that intraspecific competition can control increase. But it is unrealistic to decide from such experiments that intraspecific competition plays a sustained part in Nature. The experiments are so constructed that intraspecific competition is unavoidable! As his sole example of control by an enemy, Nicholson cites a laboratory population study by Utida (1950). He ignores the fact that with Utida (1950, as with Utida, 1955) control collapsed in 50% of the replicates although the experiments were designed to give a maximum approach to the unvarying environment demanded by the Nicholson-Bailey equations.

Clearly, none of Nicholson's evidence supports his theory with respect to his particular beliefs about enemies or about intraspecific competition in Nature. I venture to think that, objectively interpreted in the light of physiological/ecological knowledge and experience, his evidence is in accordance with my theory of natural control.

Finally, it is appropriate here to correct two misunderstandings by the Nicholson School (private correspondence, and also DeBach, 1958): (1) My theory does not deny successes in biological control (see Milne, 1957a, page 204; 1957b, page 259). It merely denies the Nicholsonian interpretation of these successes, namely, that enemies are able to control alone. Such interpretation hinders progress in understanding the principles of biological control. The point is very well taken in the latest book on biological control (Franz, 1960). Nor (2) does my theory under-rate the importance of the contributions of enemies, and of intraspecific competition, to control of population increase (see Milne, 1957a, pages 206, 209–211, and also at length in Milne, 1957b). Enemies in action are always depressive factors, can sometimes take a very severe toll and, if possessing any tendency to density-dependence, can, according to the degree of imperfection of it, help to reduce the number of occasions on which the ultimate arresting power of intraspecific competition would be required in their absence

[*Editor's Note:*   Material has been omitted at this point.]

REFERENCES

ALBRECHT, F. O., VERDIER, M. & BLACKITH, R. E. (1959). *Nature*, **184**, 103.

ALLEE, W. C., PARK, O., EMERSON, A. E., PARK, T. & SCHMIDT, K. (1949). "Principles of Animal Ecology". W. B. Saunders, Philadelphia and London.

ANDERSEN, F. S. (1957). Annual Report 1954–1955, Government Pest Infestation Laboratory, Denmark, pp. 56–78.

ANDERSEN, F. S. (1960). *Biometrics*, **16**, 19.

ANDREWARTHA, H. G. (1957). *Cold Spring Harb. Symp. Quant. Biol.* **22**, 219.

ANDREWARTHA, H. G. & BIRCH, L. C. (1954). "The Distribution and Abundance of Animals". University of Chicago Press.

ANDREWARTHA, H. G. & BROWNING, T. O. (1961). *J. Theoret. Biol.* **1**, 83.

BEIRNE, B. P. (1955). *Ent. Gazette*, **6**, 21.

BIRCH, L. C. (1960). *Amer. Nat.* **94**, 5.

BITANCOURT, A. A. (1941). *Arch. Inst. Biol.* **12**, 229.

BODENHEIMER, F. S. (1937). *Biol. Rev.* **12**, 393.

CARNE, P. B. (1956). *Austral. J. Zool.* **4**, 259.

CHITTY, D. (1960). *Can. J. Zool.* **38**, 99.

CHRISTIAN, J. J. (1957). Lecture and Review Series No. 57–2. Naval Medical Research Institute, Bethesda, Maryland.

CLEMENTS, F. E. & SHELFORD, V. E. (1939). "Bio-Ecology". John Wiley, New York.

DARWIN, C. (1859). "The Origin of Species by Means of Natural Selection or the Preservation of Favoured Races in the Struggle for Life". Murray, London.

DAVIDSON, J. (1944). *Austral. J. Exp. Biol. & Med. Sci.* **22**, 95.

DAVIDSON, J. & ANDREWARTHA, H. G. (1948a). *J. Anim. Ecol.* **17**, 193.

DAVIDSON, J. & ANDREWARTHA, H. G. (1948b). *J. Anim. Ecol.* **17**, 200.

DAY, M. F. (1955). *J. Austral. Inst. Agr. Sci.* **21**, 145.

DEBACH, P. (1958). *J. Econ. Ent.* **51**, 474.

ELTON, C. (1927). "Animal Ecology". (New Impression with additional notes, 1935.) Sidgwick & Jackson, London.

FENNER, F. (1953). *Cold Spring Harb. Symp. Quant. Biol.* **18**, 291.

FENNER, F., MARSHALL, I. D. & WOODROFFE, G. M. (1953). *J. Hyg.* **51**, 225.

FORD, E. B. (1956). *Endeavour*, **15**, 149.

FRANZ, J. M. (1949). *Z. angew. Ent.* **31**, 228.

FRANZ, J. M. (1956 (1958)). *Proc. Tenth Internat. Congr. Ent.* **4**, 781.

FRANZ, J. M. (1960). "Biologische Schädlingsbekämpfung. Handbuch der Pflanzenkrankheiten" (Eds. O. Appel, H. Blunk, B. Rademacher, H. Richter), Vol. 6, Pflanzenschutz, Part 3. Paul Parey, Berlin and Hamburg.

HOLLING, C. S. (1959a). *Canad. Ent.* **91**, 293.

HOLLING, C. S. (1959b). *Canad. Ent.* **91**, 385.

HURST, H. E. (1957). *Nature*, **180**, 494.

KENDALL, M. G. (1943, 1946). "The Advanced Theory of Statistics". Charles Griffin, London.

LABEYRIE, V. (1960). Entomophaga, No. 1, pp. 1–193. Institut Pasteur, Paris.

LEROUX, E. J. & REIMER, C. (1959). Canad. Ent. 91, 428.

LI, C. C. (1955). "Population Genetics". University of Chicago Press, Chicago.

MACLELLAN, C. R. (1959). Canad. Ent. 91, 673.

MAELZER, D. A. (In press). "An Ecological Study of Aphodius howittii Hope in the South-east of South Australia". Ph.D. Thesis lodged at the University of Adelaide, 1958.

MARSHALL, I. D. (1958). J. Hyg. 56, 288.

MILLER, C. A. (1959). Canad. Ent. 91, 457.

MILNE, A. (1943). Ann. appl. Biol. 30, 240.

MILNE, A. (1957a). Canad. Ent. 89, 193.

MILNE, A. (1957b). Cold Spring Harb. Symp. Quant. Biol. 22, 253.

MILNE, A. (1958). Nature 182, 1251.

MILNE, A. (1959a). J. Econ. Ent. 52, 532.

MILNE, A. (1959b). Nature, 184, 1582.

MILNE, A. (1959c). Biometrics, 15, 270.

MILNE, A. (1961). Symp. Soc. exp. Biol. 15: Mechanisms of Biological Competition, pp. 44–61. Cambridge University Press.

MORRIS, R. F. (1959). Ecology, 40, 580.

MORRIS, R. F. (1960). Ann. Rev. Ent. 5, 243.

MORS, H. (1942). Monogr. Z. angew. Ent. 15, 535.

NEEDLER, A. W. H. & LOGIE, R. R. (1947). Trans. Roy. Soc. Canada, 3rd Ser., Sect. V 41, 73.

NEYMAN, J. (1939). Ann. math. Statist. 10, 35.

NICHOLSON, A. J. (1933). J. Anim. Ecol. 2, 132.

NICHOLSON, A. J. (1958). Ann. Rev. Ent. 3, 107.

NICHOLSON, A. J. & BAILEY, V. A. (1935). Proc. Zool. Soc. Lond., Part 3, 551.

PAINTER, R. H. (1951). "Insect Resistance in Crop Plants". MacMillan, New York.

PAINTER, R. H. (1954). J. Econ. Ent. 46, 295.

PIMENTEL, D. (1961). Amer. Nat. 95, 65.

RICHARDS, O. W. (1961). Ann. Rev. Ent. 6, 147.

SCHWERDTFEGER, F. (1935). Z. Forst- und Jagdw. 67, 15–38, 85–104, 449–482, 513–540.

SCHWERDTFEGER, F. (1942). Z. Angew. Ent. 28, 254.

SKELLAM, J. G. (1955). "The Number of Man and Animals". Oliver & Boyd, Edinburgh and London, pp. 31–46.

SOLOMON, M. E. (1958a) Nature, 181, 1778.

SOLOMON, M. E. (1958b). Nature, 182, 1252.

THOMPSON, H. V. (1954). Ann. appl. Biol. 41, 358.

THOMPSON, W. R. (1929). Parasitology, 21, 269.

THOMPSON, W. R. (1939). Parasitology, 31, 299.

UTIDA, S. (1950). Ecology, 31, 165.

UTIDA, S. (1955). Reprinted from "Memoirs of the College of Agriculture", Kyoto University, No. 71, 1–34.

VARLEY, G. C. (1947). J. Anim. Ecol. 16, 139.

WATT, K. E. F. (1959). Canad. Ent. 91, 129.

WATT, K. E. F. (1960). Canad. Ent. 92, 674.

WATT, K. E. F. (1961). Canad. Ent. 93, Supplement 19, 1–62.

WAY, M. J. (In press). Proc. Eleventh Internat. Congr. Ent.

WELLINGTON, W. G. (1960). Can. J. Zool. 38, 289.

WILBERT, H. (1959). Verhandlungen der Deutschen Zoologischen Gesellschaft in Münster Westf. 57, 510.

ERRATUM

Figure 2 (page 26) suggests that Zone I is equal to Zone II in size. Actually, as stated in the text (p. 25) and shown clearly in Figure 1 (p. 22), Zone I is smaller than Zone II.

Reprinted from *J. Anim. Ecol.* **18**(1):117–122 (1949)

POPULATION CHANGES IN GERMAN FOREST PESTS

By G. C. VARLEY

(With 1 Figure in the Text)

F. Schwerdtfeger (**1935**). 'Studien über den Massenwechsel einiger Forstschädlinge'. Z. Forst- und Jagdw. 67: 15–38, 85–104, 449–482, 513–540.

F. Schwerdtfeger (**1942**). 'Uber die Ursachen des Massenwechsels der Insekten'. Z. Angew. Ent. 28: 254–303.

Census work on certain insect pests of the German State Forests has been continued for a total of 60 years, and the results are of very great interest to ecologists. An important account was published in 1935, and this was followed by a further review in 1942. The data concern the population densities of four species of moths, all of which feed as larvae on the needles of the pine *Pinus sylvestris* L. The populations were estimated annually in December by counting pupae or larvae in the surface soil of selected localities. The results are given by Schwerdtfeger as graphs of the numbers found per 100 sq.m. Since the population densities varied between 0·1 and 2500 per 100 sq.m. the direct plotting employed by Schwerdtfeger has disadvantages. His data from Letzlinger Heide have therefore been read off his graphs, or taken from the actual figures where these have been given, and have been replotted on a logarithmic scale. This has the advantage that the enormous peaks of population are easily plotted on the same graph. Also relative changes in population density show clearly at all population densities. The very lowest values were difficult to read accurately from the original graphs, but any inaccuracies introduced here by the reviewer are of small importance, as the statistical errors are also very large when the population density is estimated to be as low as 1 per 1000 sq.m.

Panolis griseovariegata (Goeze), pine beauty, Noctuidae. (Called by Schwerdtfeger the Eule, or Forleule, *P. flammea* Schiff.). This species showed small peaks of population density in 1883, 1888, 1893 and 1897, which begins to suggest regular oscillations with a 5-year period. But oscillations apparently ceased between 1899 and 1910, when changes were rather small and irregular. In 1912 there was a

definite peak, when the population density reached its maximum value of 40 per 100 sq.m. Further peaks in 1919 and 1931 led up to the much larger populations between 1937 and 1939.

Hyloicus pinastri (L.), pine hawk, Sphingidae (Kiefernschwärmer, *Sphinx pinastri*). The data for this species were omitted by Schwerdtfeger in his 1942 paper, and have been taken from his paper of 1935, which gives data only up to 1930. The population change from generation to generation in this species was rarely as great as fourfold, and was often much less. Also the population density tended to remain rather low. Only in 1887 did its population density rise as high as 38 per 100 sq.m. This peak, and smaller ones in 1899, 1915 and 1927 all coincided with periods when the population of *Bupalus* was also high.

Dendrolimus pini L. (Kiefernspinner) is a large Lasiocampid moth, not found in Britain. It was seldom a pest at Letzlinger Heide and had only two major outbreaks (gradations) during the period. In the outbreak of 1886–9 the population density rose to a maximum of 18 per sq.m., and in 1937 it rose to 3 per sq.m. From 1890 to 1927 the population remained below six larvae per 100 sq.m., and was often far below this. Two minor peaks of population density in 1927 and 1932 suggest increasing oscillations with a 5-year period, leading up to the major outbreak of 1937.

The picture for *Bupalus piniarius* (L.), bordered white, Geometridae (Kiefernspanner) is quite different from the other species considered. Letzlingen is in the centre of the main area of damage by this species, and outbreaks were both frequent and severe. Never did the population density settle to an approximately steady state, as sometimes happened with the other three species. Seven small or large outbreaks were recorded in the period of observation: in 1888, 1894, 1900, 1905–6, 1917, 1928, and 1936. Up till 1905 there were peaks of population density every 5 or 6 years. Then there were gaps of 12, 11 and 8 years.

Schwerdtfeger's two papers are largely devoted to detailed discussions of the causes of the striking population changes observed. In the earlier paper the

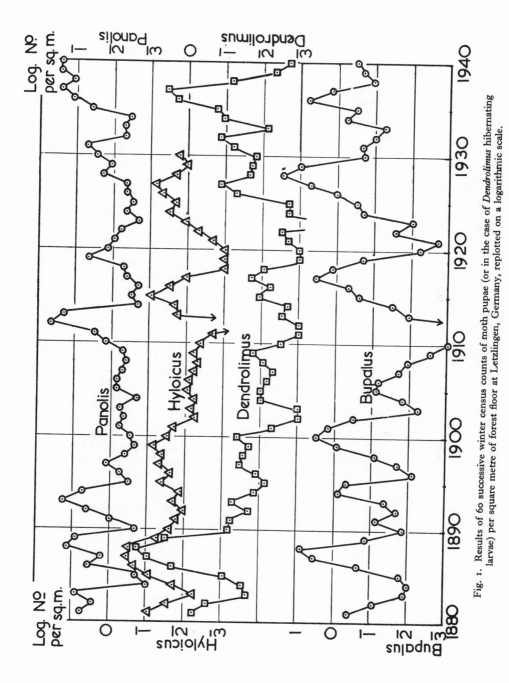

Fig. 1. Results of 60 successive winter census counts of moth pupae (or in the case of *Dendrolimus* hibernating larvae) per square metre of forest floor at Letzlingen, Germany, replotted on a logarithmic scale.

data are analysed in relation to a theory of *gradations*. Between gradations the population is in a kind of dynamic equilibrium, and fluctuates up and down at a low level, termed the 'normal Bestand', or less appropriately the 'eiserne Bestand'. The upper limit of this 'normal' population density is defined as 10 per 100 sq.m. for *Bupalus*, and 5 per 100 sq.m. for the other three species. Below this limit of the 'normal Bestand' Schwerdtfeger points out that 40-fold changes in the population density can occur. These changes show very clearly when the data are plotted, as in Fig. 1, on a logarithmic scale. When plotted as numbers on a normal scale such that the tops of the peaks can be shown on the graph, points within the limits of the 'eiserne Bestand' are so near the zero line that a superficial appearance of stability is given. How far this method of plotting has been responsible for the popularity of this theory in Germany and elsewhere is open to speculation.

If the population density should increase above this limit, it is supposed to be in equilibrium no longer, and a gradation begins. The population rises for a few years at a great rate, and a serious outbreak of the pest is the result. For reasons which seem obscure, Schwerdtfeger divides the gradation into four phases, two of increase, and two of decrease, and tabulates for each species the number of generations spent in each phase, and the number of years between each gradation.

The basic causes of the changes are not explained, but they are discussed in considerable detail in the 1942 paper. It must be said at the outset that a proper understanding of such changes requires reasonably complete knowledge about the mortality and fertility of the species. For certain years of exceptional insect abundance Schwerdtfeger does indeed give most of the data required for some of the species. On p. 286 of the 1942 paper the mortality and fecundity of *Panolis* are given for four different localities for one whole season. Had there been comparable data for a whole gradation some at least of the fundamental problems of population ecology might have been far better understood.

It is a pity that such valuable work should suffer from a serious omission of this kind; but this is unfortunately rather characteristic of ecological work at the present time. The cause in this case is not far to seek. Only when an insect is exceptionally abundant can data be easily accumulated. At the low population densities, of the order of 1 per 100 sq.m. or less, Schwerdtfeger very naturally found it quite impossible to get enough material for study.

In the absence of this crucial information Schwerdtfeger (1942) brings forward much other relevant data from the literature (mostly German papers, many of which are not readily available in this country) and reviews at some length the various theories which

have been advanced to account for such population changes.

(a) Parasite and biocoenosis theories

By the parasite theory is to be understood the idea that specific parasites alone are responsible for population changes. Schwerdtfeger rightly considers this view far too simple, although it is well known that a high percentage of pests are at times destroyed by parasites, and that parasites have been successfully used in biological control. He emphasizes that since many parasites have a variety of alternative hosts, the whole biocoenosis must be considered; but that even this is not enough.

(b) Weather theory

Schwerdtfeger examines in detail the possibility that climatic factors may be responsible for the changes in population from year to year, and finds the evidence against this view. Bodenheimer's claim that in general climatic factors cause a mortality of 85–90 % in the egg and larval stages of insects is shown to be untrue for *Panolis*, in which this mortality was estimated to be as low as 25 %.

(c) Overpopulation theory

Eidmann's idea that in its main area of damage a pest shows regular outbreaks every 10–12 years is examined. Eidmann's figures were obtained from a variety of insect pests, such as locusts in South America, and *Dendrolimus* at Schweinitz in Germany. Originally, in 1931, Eidmann had interpreted these results in terms of the well-known 11-year sunspot cycle. Later (Eidmann, 1937) he abandoned this view, and explained them in terms of overpopulation. When for a number of years the population increases, the trees are eventually defoliated, food supply is reduced, and the pest brings about its own destruction by the reduction of its 'Lebensraum'. The critical factors here are reduced fertility, reduced resistance to disease, and death from starvation. These factors are density dependent. On this view no outbreak should come to an end without severe defoliation of the trees. But the data in Fig. 1 show various small peaks of abundance, such as that of *Panolis* in 1919, and *Bupalus* in 1905, which are far too small for this explanation to be tenable.

(d) The factors of population dynamics

Under this heading there is a very long discussion of factors which influence sex ratio, fertility and mortality, from which the following conclusions emerge:

(1) In no case is any single factor predominant, as

is suggested by the parasite theory, or the weather theory.

(2) Many factors operate, and each changes widely in its intensity from year to year.

(3) Factors may be either biotic, or abiotic. Hence neither parasite theory nor weather theory can be accepted alone.

(4) The importance of any single factor changes with time, place, species, etc.

(5) The only common factor is the variability of the factors which cause the population changes.

Thus, after a useful critique of a number of theories, Schwerdtfeger seems to relapse into obscurantism.

(e) The gradocoene

The changes in population density have been interpreted by Friederichs as due to the operation of the 'holocoene' (Holocön), defined as the sum total of environmental factors of all kinds. Schwerdtfeger rightly regards this concept as too wide, since neither *all* species of the community, nor *all* the attributes of the physical environment have any significant effect on the numbers of one species. Only a part of the holocoene, called the *gradocoene*, is important. The gradocoene is the sum of the factors which affect the numbers of the species. That the gradocoene is therefore responsible for changes in the numbers of a species would appear to be a truism; but it is a point which perhaps needs emphasis, as it seems sometimes to be forgotten.

However, for Schwerdtfeger the gradocoene seems to have some mystic significance, and is a system of factors which regulate themselves to form an organized unit. The pest itself is regarded as the centre of an organized network, which strives to reach equilibrium. Nevertheless, it is clear from the data that stability is not achieved.

The cause of gradations remains obscure. Impressed by the big changes even when population densities are low, Schwerdtfeger suggests that a gradation is merely an unusually strong swing of the ever-moving pendulum of population density. But the changes are by no means random. Periods in which there is population increase for a number of years are followed by almost equally long periods of decrease, as is particularly clear for *Bupalus*.

Nowhere in his papers does Schwerdtfeger make any use of statistical methods, either to estimate the variance of numerical data, or in other ways. Yet various questions quickly come to mind which can profitably be studied in this way. For instance, examination of Fig. 1 shows that the peaks of abundance of *Dendrolimus* and *Bupalus* often seem to be coincident or nearly so. Are the numbers of these two species correlated? Calculation shows that the correlation coefficient is $r = 0.20$, with a probability of

between 0.1 and 0.2 that the observed degree of correlation is due to chance. Similarly, the correlation coefficient between the numbers of *Bupalus* and *Hyloicus* has been found to be $r = 0.18$, with a probability of 0.2 that the resemblance might be due to chance. Moran (1949) has shown that correlation coefficients calculated in this way from oscillatory time series may easily give misleading high values of significance. But as the correlation is low, the data lend no support to the view that a common factor may be responsible for the changes of more than one species.

Various broad ecological issues raised by these long-continued observations are hardly touched on by Schwerdtfeger. Here we have four species of moth, each belonging to a different family, all living together and eating the same food. Under the simplest conditions of interspecific competition for food, only one species should survive (Gause, 1934); and this has been confirmed experimentally *in vitro* by Crombie (1947) and Park (1948). What are the conditions which permit the continued coexistence of four species in nature?

It might be that Letzlingen is a place where two or more geographically separated species, each adapted to a different climate, happen to find conditions equally suitable, and hence overlap in just this region. The climatic requirements of the species have been studied in detail by Schwerdtfeger (1935), and are in fact very similar, although the localities where *Dendrolimus* is a major pest tend to be slightly warmer and less humid than those where other species thrive. *Panolis* and *Bupalus* are major pests in areas of identical mean monthly temperature, humidity and precipitation, except that *Panolis* seems most abundant where April temperatures are higher. It is then that this moth is on the wing. Schwerdtfeger (1935, fig. 10) gives a map of the areas of damage of the species, and there is little or no difference in their distribution. The evidence gives no support at all to the idea that Letzlingen is a unique locality where separate areas of distribution happen to meet.

Another possibility lies in the fact, which Schwerdtfeger hardly mentions, that the life cycles of the four species are different. This is shown in Table 1, based on information in Spuler (1908–10), where l indicates small and L fully grown larvae.

The main emergence periods of the moths varies between April for *Panolis*, and July for *Dendrolimus*. The weather conditions during the adult stage, in which mating and oviposition occur, must be very critical for each species. Heavy rain or high winds might also cause heavy mortality in the very small larvae. The differences between the species is so great that their individual critical periods scarcely overlap at all. This isolation in time is the sort of thing to be expected as a mechanism preventing the inter-

Table 1

	Apr.	May	June	July		Aug.	Sept.	Oct.	Winter
Panolis	Moth	Eggs l	l	L	L	Pupa..			
Hyloicus	Pupa.............................		Moth Eggs			l	L	Pupa	
Bupalus	Pupa .... Moth		Eggs	l		l	L	L Pupa.........	
Dendrolimus	l	L	Pupa ......Moth			Eggs	l	l	Hibernating

breeding of closely allied species, but cannot be supposed to have this function here. On the other hand, Lack (1944) has shown that closely allied species of birds can live together if they are of different sizes, and therefore take rather different foods. Is it possible that competition between species is reduced if their feeding and growing stages are of different sizes at the same time, which is one result of the differences between the life histories?

Schwerdtfeger gives no clear picture of the extent to which the four species compete for food. Defoliation certainly occurs in the worst outbreaks, but which outbreaks caused defoliation and which did not is not clearly stated. But food supply was at times limiting, and a footnote to Schwerdtfeger's table 2 (1942) states that adults of *Panolis* migrated away from a defoliated area in 1932.

The effects of defoliation on the pine is much more severe than on a deciduous tree such as oak, which puts forth new leaves in the same season. Marcus (1942) shows photographs of sections of pine trees which had been heavily damaged by an outbreak of *Panolis* between 1928 and 1930 in another area. They show a minute growth ring in 1930, none at all in 1931 or 1932, small rings in 1933–5, and the first year of normal growth was 1936. This disastrous effect on tree growth is related to the fact that each pine needle normally lives for 3 years before it drops. New leaves are not immediately put forth after defoliation, and a full series of new leaves will require at least 3 years to grow.

When the trees are defoliated the various species of caterpillar presumably compete for the reduced food supply. The increase of one species to abundance may then inhibit the increase of another. Perhaps this may explain some of the small peaks of *Hyloicus* when *Bupalus* was already far more abundant. But other factors must be at work, since none of the species was at all abundant between 1903 and 1911, and there was no major outbreak, and hence no likelihood of defoliation, between 1890 and 1925. The four species compete for a limited amount of food only on rare occasions.

The most likely hypothesis to explain the coexistence of the four species is that the population densities of each species are separately controlled by different factors at such low population densities that

direct competition for food is very uncommon. The parasites of the caterpillars may be the main factors. Schwerdtfeger gives an inadequate idea of the position, but the parasite catalogue of Thompson (1943–) gives useful lists. Neglecting the records for 'Europe' and taking only those for Germany, one finds 33 species listed as parasitic on *Panolis griseovariegata*, 26 of which have not been recorded from the other three hosts. Of the 19 species parasitic on *Bupalus piniarius*, 13 are not recorded from the other three hosts. Two of the four species on *Dendrolimus pini*, and three of the four species on *Hyloicus pinastri* do not attack the other species. No species of parasite was found on all four hosts, although the ubiquitous egg parasite *Trichogramma evanescens* Westw. and the chalcid *Dirhicnus alboannulatus* Ratz. each attacked three hosts, and five species of parasite attacked two hosts.

Clearly the different species of hosts are to a very large extent attacked by effectively specific parasites. If these parasites are the agents responsible for the control of the population density of the pests (and one is left in doubt as to how far this may be so by the lack of data) then the numbers of each of the four species may be controlled independently. The only common factors would be general predators such as birds, and occasional food limitation when one or more of the four species happened to have an outbreak.

There is some indirect evidence that parasites themselves may be responsible for the gradations. Schwerdtfeger shows that the catastrophic fall of the population at the end of a gradation is accompanied by a very high percentage of parasitism, if it is not indeed so caused. This amounted to 98·5 % parasitism by tachinid flies at the end of a gradation of *Panolis*. Details are given also for *Dendrolimus* between 1934 and 1935 at Malterhausen where in two successive generations the percentage of parasitized pupae rose from 20 % in 1934 to 58 % in 1935, and was accompanied by a heavy fall in population. Unfortunately there are no data about the percentage of parasitism when the population density is rising from very low values. The theory of Nicholson & Bailey shows that regular oscillations in population density may be expected if a species is controlled by a specific parasite. The percentage of parasitism is very low as the host increases, and rises to very high values as the population falls.

134

Furthermore, Nicholson & Bailey (1935, p. 585) give a formula for the period of the oscillations in the population of host and parasite, the value of which depends solely on the rate of increase of the host in the absence of the parasite. The figures below have been computed from this formula:

Rate of host increase per generation	1·5	2·0
Period of oscillation in generations	10·2	8·2

These figures are valid only for oscillations of small magnitude. If the amplitude is large, then the period of oscillation is longer, so that the change in population can be achieved with unrestricted increase of the host in half the period of oscillation.

It will be seen that the calculated period of oscillation is little affected by changes in the rate of host increase, once this is greater than fourfold. We shall not require a very accurate estimate of host increase to get a satisfactory estimate of the period of oscillation. For this purpose we do not require the mean number of eggs laid per moth, but the net rate of increase of the host with the effects of all mortality factors included, except the parasites. Assuming that the effect of the parasites can be neglected during periods of rapid host increase, this can be estimated from the data in Fig. 1.

For *Bupalus* the mean value of the net rate of increase per generation, when increase is rapid, is given by the antilog of 0·85 = 7, and estimates for the other species are similar, except for *Hyloicus*, which increases about threefold per generation. Hence, according to Nicholson & Bailey, the period of oscillation should be between five and six generations for three of the species, and about seven generations for *Hyloicus*, always assuming that the effective parasite in each case has one generation to each generation of the host.

At various times *Dendrolimus*, *Panolis* and *Bupalus* show three or four consecutive peaks of population indicating oscillations of about this period. But there are also times in which there are oscillations of a much longer period (e.g. the very strong swings of population in *Bupalus* after 1905), or no sign of

3	4	7	10	20	100
7·0	6·3	5·6	5·4	5·0	4·7

oscillation at all, as is the case for three of the species between 1895 and 1910.

Where the change in population density is small, can it be that it is close to the *steady density* of Nicholson? If this were so, once oscillations re-started, the population density should rise above and then fall below the previous level. Examination of the curves in Fig. 1 gives no support to this idea. Thus *Dendrolimus* remains at a low population density from 1901 to 1925 and then shows three clear peaks, the first two being 10 times and the last 100 times the previous maximum. But the minima in between are well above the average of the previous period of low density. There is something happening here which does not fit with the theory of Nicholson and Bailey.

Superficially at least the attempts of Schwerdt-feger, and later of Voûte, to explain the long periods of low population density as a stable state, and to find separate explanations for the onset and ending of gradations are attractive. And this present attempt to see how far the facts can be explained in terms of Nicholson's theory meets with no more than partial success. But the nature of the data on which interpretation must be based remains inadequate. Let us hope that further work will be concentrated on producing the detailed mortality and fertility data which may eventually help to provide a proper explanation of these fascinating problems.

REFERENCES

Crombie, A. C. (1947). 'Interspecific competition.' J. Anim. Ecol. 16: 44–73.

Eidmann, H. (1931). 'Zur Kenntnis der Periodizität der Insektenepidemien.' Z. Angew. Ent. 18: 537–67.

Eidmann, H. (1937). 'Zur Theorie der Bevölkerungsbewegung der Insekten.' Anz. Schädlingsk. 13: 25–6, 47–52.

Gause, G. F. (1934). 'The struggle for existence.' Baltimore.

Lack, D. (1944). 'Ecological aspects of species-formation in passerine birds.' Ibis, 86: 260–86.

Marcus, B. A. (1942). 'Über das Wachstum der Kiefer nach starkem Eulenfrass.' Z. Angew. Ent. 29: 31–84.

Moran, P. A. P. (1949). 'The statistical analysis of the sunspot and lynx cycles.' J. Anim. Ecol. 18: 115–16.

Nicholson, A. J. (1933). 'The balance of animal populations.' J. Anim. Ecol. 2: 132–78.

Nicholson, A. J. & Bailey, V. A. (1935). 'The balance of animal populations. Part 1.' Proc. Zool. Soc. Lond. 551–98.

Park, T. (1948). 'Experimental studies of interspecies competition. I. Competition between populations of the flour beetles *Tribolium confusum* Duval and *Tribolium castaneum* Herbst.' Ecol. Monogr. 18: 265–307.

Smith, H. S. (1935). 'The rôle of biotic factors in the determination of population densities.' J. Econ. Ent. 28: 873–98.

Spuler, A. (1908–10). 'Die Schmetterlinge Europas.' Stuttgart. 3 vols.

Thompson, W. R. (1943–). 'A catalogue of the parasites and predators of insect pests.' Belleville, Ontario.

9

REGULATION OF ANIMAL NUMBERS: A MODEL COUNTER-EXAMPLE

Henry S. Horn

Department of Biology, Princeton University, Princeton, New Jersey

(Accepted for publication January 24, 1968)

Abstract. Data resembling either density dependent or density independent "control" of animal numbers may be generated by models that differ in degree but not in kind.

INTRODUCTION

The nature of mechanisms regulating the sizes of animal populations is a central problem in modern ecology. During the history of the formulation of this problem, workers and their ideas have become so polarized that new students are introduced to the problem as a "controversy." Students who lack the historical and philosophical perspective of their mentors are apt to judge the controversy as sterile, and consequently to regard the problem as insignificant.

The following model presents the regulation of animal numbers in such a way that the controversy becomes an aspect of the problem, rather than *vice versa*. The model shows in a generalized, but none the less analytical, way how the data of both sides of the controversy may be generated by plausible mechanisms that differ in degree, but not in kind. It also demonstrates that "density dependence" and "density independence" are not mutually exclusive alternatives. Finally, the flexibility of the model as a didactic tool is limited only by the imagination of the student and the diversity of nature. I am here concerned only with mechanism. The philosophy behind the positions taken by those engaged in the controversy is no less important, but it has been reviewed recently by Birch and Ehrlich (1967), Lack (1966), and Orians (1962). Techniques for analyzing censuses of animal populations have been presented by Salt (1966), Southwood (1967), and Tanner (1966).

This paper results from discussions with R. H. Mac-Arthur. Critical comments by J. M. Emlen, D. J. and E. G. Horn, E. G. Leigh, and G. H. Orians were very helpful.

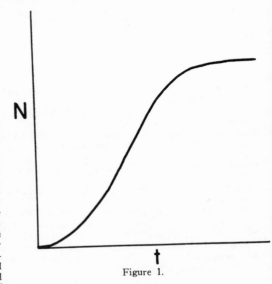

Figure 1.

THE MODEL

The "growth curve" of any animal population in a benign but finite environment will generally take the sigmoid form of Figure 1, where N is the size of the population and t is time. The well-known logistic is a special case of such a curve, but we need not be limited by stringent assumptions as to the formal shape of our curve; any biologically reasonable curve for which d(logN)/dt decreases monotonically with N will give the same qualitative result. We may now plot the slope of the sigmoid curve, dN/dt, against N for a benign environment, and use the resulting graph (Fig. 2) to examine the stability of each population size. Where dN/dt is positive N will increase, while where dN/dt is negative N will decrease. N will converge on a stable population equilibrium, N_e, where dN/dt = 0. We shall call the curve of Figure 2 "g," as it represents a net growth rate in response to "density dependent" factors. "Density depen-

dence" here means simply that the particular contribution to population growth rate is not a linear function of N.

In a more rigorous environment, of course, the death rate will be increased at all population sizes by factors that are "density independent." Strict "density independence" implies a linear relationship between N and the particular component of dN/dt. A density independent factor, however, is somewhat more vaguely defined as a factor whose major component is linear. To present most forcefully the effect of a strictly density independent factor on changes in population size, I shall assume that the effect of density independent factors is indeed linear, but the model tolerates large departures from linearity before the qualitative results are appreciably changed. The death rate due to density independent factors is

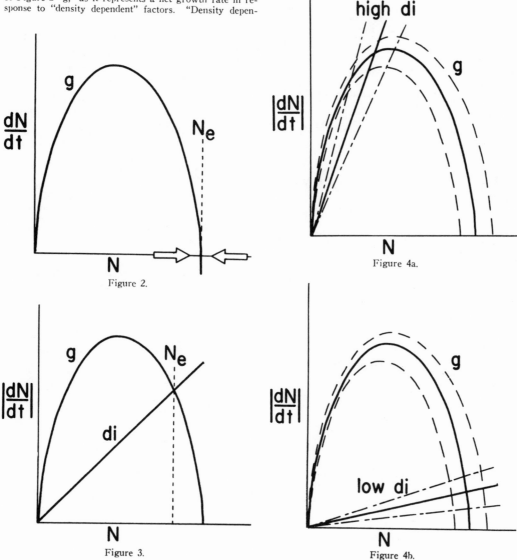

Figure 2.

Figure 3.

Figure 4a.

Figure 4b.

plotted as "di" in Figure 3. The population size at which the curves g and di intersect is now the population of stable equilibrium, N_e.

We may now represent fluctuations in density dependent factors by movement of the peak and N-intercept of curve g. Similarly, fluctuations in density independent factors may be represented by changes in the slope of curve di (see Fig. 4). If g and di fluctuate independently and the average di intersects g near its peak (Fig. 4a), the resulting fluctuations of the equilibrium population will follow the fluctuations of di more closely than those of g. If, on the other hand, the average di intersects g in its steeply descending region (Fig. 4b), fluctuations of the equilibrium population will follow fluctuations of g more closely than those of di.

As an exercise to illustrate these results graphically, we may take relative positions of the g and di curves from a table of random digits. In Figure 5 we plot, as time series, the relative values of g and di, along with the resultant fluctuations in the equilibrium population taken from Figures 4a and 4b. It is clear from Figure 5 that fluctuations in the equilibrium population with a high sensitivity to the environment (high di) follow fluctuations in the density independent factors (di) more closely than they follow fluctuations in density dependent factors (g). Conversely, the population with a low

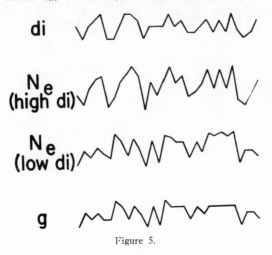

Figure 5.

sensitivity to the environment (low di) is closely tied to density dependent factors (g).

DISCUSSION

The vehemence of the controversy over the regulation of animal numbers suggests that there is some natural polarity in the mechanisms regulating the number of animals. Such a polarity may be generated by considering the effect of natural selection on the model. Natural selection is here defined to favor those individuals in each generation whose offspring form the greatest proportion of the breeders in the next generation.

If the density independent sensitivity to the environment is high, the average equilibrium population is far below that which the biotic environment is capable of supporting, and populations are always fluctuating in response to a varying environment. Under these conditions selection favors those individuals with the highest intrinsic reproductive rate, even at the expense of a slightly greater sensitivity to the environment. As a result of such selection, the g and di curves should tend to become high and narrow if the di curve originally had a great slope. If, on the other hand, the density independent sensitivity to the environment is low, the average equilibrium population is very close to the maximum number that the biotic environment can maintain. Selection will then favor the production of fewer, more vigorous offspring. Consequently, the g and di curves should tend to become flattened if the di curve originally had a low slope. Thus we might expect that animals would conform to the extreme models more often than to an intermediate model.

The suggested effect of selection is speculative and may be wrong, but the model itself allows some conclusions that are relatively independent of stringent assumptions about the form of the curves. The model shows analytically how "density independent" factors may affect animal numbers in such a way that the best predictor of these numbers is a measurement of the value taken by the appropriate density independent factor. But the model also suggests cautious interpretation of data that show, for example, a close correlation between some animal numbers and weather records. Given such data, we cannot conclude that density dependent factors (e.g. predation and competition for space) are irrelevant to the regulation of numbers of these animals.

LITERATURE CITED

Birch, L. C., and P. R. Ehrlich. 1967. Evolutionary history and population biology. Nature 214: 349–352.

Lack, D. 1966. Population studies of birds. Oxford University Press, London. 341 pp.

Orians, G. H. 1962. Natural selection and ecological theory. Amer. Naturalist 96: 257–263.

Salt, G. W. 1966. An examination of logarithmic regression as a measure of population density response. Ecology 47: 1035–1039.

Southwood, T. R. E. 1967. The interpretation of population change. J. Animal Ecol. 36: 519–529.

Tanner, J. T. 1966. Effects of population density on growth rates of animal populations. Ecology 47: 733–745.

10

1962 by The University of Chicago Press

from Am. Nat. 96(890):257–263 (1962)

NATURAL SELECTION AND ECOLOGICAL THEORY

GORDON H. ORIANS

Department of Zoology, University of Washington, Seattle, Washington

A long and intense controversy over the mechanisms of control of animal populations in nature has accompanied the development of ecology as a vigorous science during the past two decades. While admitting that this has stimulated a great deal of research, I shall argue that much of the controversy has involved peripheral issues and that its perpetuation will continue to result in wasted efforts on the part of ecologists and will add to the confusion among interested non-ecological biologists as to what ecologists are really concerned about. Many share the view of Dobzhansky as expressed during one of the discussions at the Cold Spring Harbor Symposium on Population Studies (1957). "To a non-ecologist, the controversy which has made our session so lively is, I confess, somewhat bewildering. I have had a feeling for several years now that this is a controversy chiefly about words, about 'semantics,' to use a fashionable word. Having tried to the best of my ability to understand the issue involved, I still continue to feel that way."

In advancing the view that there is really a basic issue involved, which is much deeper than its peripheral manifestation in the form of the argument over density-dependence and density-independence, I shall base my case largely on two important books on population ecology, those of Lack (1954) and Andrewartha and Birch (1954). Recognizing that no two books can effectively speak for an entire field, I still select this course because of the great impact of these books on current thinking and because their views are clearly stated. As with most arguments, the most critical portion concerns the initial assumptions upon which theories are erected. Hence, attention will be concentrated upon these fundamental assumptions, rather than upon corollaries which follow if the assumptions are granted.

The basic goals of ecology are seldom stated clearly by ecologists, if, indeed, most ecologists even have opinions about them, but Andrewartha and Birch are characteristically explicit on this point. To them it is the job of the ecologist to explain why a certain animal is found in one place and not in another, why it is more numerous in one place than another, and why there are fluctuations in its numbers. To accomplish this, a three-pronged approach is proposed—the physiology and behavior of the animal must be investigated; the physiography, climate, soil, and vegetation of the area must be studied; and the numbers of individuals in the population in question must be measured as accurately as possible. Other organisms are to be investigated as they appear important in the ecology of the species under special investigation.

This method of study is not only presented as being extremely profitable, but also as being definitely preferable to other methods commonly employed by ecologists. Community studies, which are motivated by the hope that predictable relationships between the relative abundance and interactions of species can be discovered leading to insights into community structure, are rejected as having contributed nothing, and as being unlikely to contribute anything in the future, to general theory. When too much attention is put upon the community, too little attention is paid to the species whose distribution and abundance are to be explained. Moreover, the community studies are said to stress the importance of other plants and animals to the neglect of other components of the environment.

In my view, the rejection of community ecology by Andrewartha and Birch is the corollary of a still more basic position, namely, that evolutionary concepts have no place in ecological theory. The importance of natural selection is not disputed, for the final section of the book is devoted to evolutionary aspects of ecology, and Birch (1955, 1961) has made important contributions to the study of evolution. Rather it is claimed that a general and satisfying theory of ecology can and should be constructed without recourse to evolutionary thinking and concepts. This view is clearly illustrated by the now famous case of the bees in the auger-holes (page 23). It is the job of the ecologist to count auger-holes and so to predict the number of bees to be found and the job of the evolutionist to measure genetic change as a result of competition. Conceptually, the two fields are kept quite distinct.

Their general theory of ecology states that the numbers of animals in natural populations may be limited in three ways: (1) by shortage of material resources, (2) by inaccessibility of resources, and (3) by the short period of time in which the intrinsic rate of natural increase (r) is positive. The fact that the third of these factors belongs to a category quite distinct from the first two need not be pursued now. For the present it is sufficient to note that, unfortunately, the current controversy is centered around the relative importance of these factors and not upon the assumptions which have led to them.

Lack does not attempt to state a formal theory of ecology but his approach to ecological problems is clearly outlined in the introduction to the the book. Since the book is oriented toward population control, Lack does not consider community studies, but there is an implicit acceptance of their fundamental importance. On points other than those pertaining to communities, he is clear. The distinguishing feature of his approach to ecology is an emphasis upon the need to recognize the distinction between proximate and ultimate factors. Believing that ultimate factors provide the key to the understanding of current population adaptations, Lack has oriented his own research toward the elucidation of evolutionary mechanisms in ecology. Andrewartha and Birch are, of necessity, concerned only with proximate factors and it is at this point that the most fundamental dichotomy exists.

Lack also strongly supports the belief that controlling mortality factors must be density-dependent. He thus rejects climate *per se* as a controlling mechanism and discusses climate only with respect to changes in range and not with respect to population regulation. In contrast, Andrewartha and Birch ascribe major importance to control of populations by climate and regard distribution and abundance as two aspects of the same problem.

Given these striking differences in viewpoint, it remains to analyze their significance. Since Lack has studied primarily birds and Andrewartha and Birch, insects, it is fruitful to consider whether the differences in viewpoints might be attributable to their choice of organisms since it is to be expected that different organisms will have differing autecologies. It is important to note, however, that Andrewartha does not believe this to be the case, for in his recent book (1961) he is at great pains to cite vertebrate examples, conspicuous by their absence in the earlier book, to substantiate views derived from studies of insects.

Despite this, however, several major possibilities immediately suggest themselves. First, insects are heterothermic and therefore more at the direct mercy of climatic variations than homeothermic birds which can stand wide variations in climate provided resources are available, especially in desert or near-desert environments. Second, a large proportion of insects which have been intensively studied are herbivores, whereas most birds are insectivores or carnivores. Since the apparent inability of herbivores to make effective use of the primary productivity in most terrestrial ecosystems is a puzzling problem, it could be argued that control mechanisms in herbivores are basically different (Hairston, Smith and Slobodkin, 1960). From this it might follow that orderly predictions about insect populations are more difficult to make and, hence, such populations are more appropriately treated by different methods (MacArthur, 1961). Moreover, most birds exhibit well-defined territorial behavior which may act strongly as a density-regulating factor (Orians, 1961), thus modifying the impact of the population upon its resources to a much greater degree than in insects with less highly developed intrapopulational control mechanisms. However, this argument ignores the complexity of the problem of utilization of primary productivity in terrestrial ecosystems. The assumption of different control mechanisms for herbivores and carnivores is based upon inadequate evidence and fails to consider the problem of food quality, often of prime importance to herbivores (Cowan et al., 1950; Taber, 1956, Harlan, 1956; Orians and Pitelka, 1960). Moreover, though the action of natural selection may be more difficult to trace in insect populations than birds, this provides no convincing basis for rejecting an evolutionary approach.

Further, we may consider differences in the nature of the communities studied by field ecologists. As economic entomologists, primarily concerned with insect pests of croplands and their predators, Andrewartha and

Birch work in the highly artificial and recently derived communities of pure-stand crops. One result is that most insects are studied not in the native vegetation to which they have been evolutionarily adapted but in recently colonized habitats many of which are geographically remote from the natural range of the species. In most cases nothing is known of the ecology of the species in diversified natural communities so that the adaptive significance of many life history features is obscure. It is at present impossible to assess the impact of these circumstances in relation to empirical results on population fluctuations in cropland pests, but there is clearly sufficient ground for caution in generalizing from these results to natural communities. Moreover, the growth of economic entomology has been stimulated by particular practical demands, namely the prediction of outbreaks of pests and their control, either through predators or through the discovery of a particularly vulnerable stage of the life history. Since correlation may permit prediction, these goals can often be achieved by obtaining climatic correlations with population fluctuations, despite the fact that the correlation need not imply causation.

However important the differences in the autecologies and environments of organisms studied by ecologists of different schools of thought may be, I believe that the fundamental dichotomy in modern ecology, as illustrated by the books under consideration, can only be understood as a manifestation of the fundamental division of biology into two major categories — functional biology and evolutionary biology (Mayr, 1961). The differences in method and basic concepts of these major fields is sharply focused in this controversy though its roots have apparently not been grasped either by the participants or interested observers. As functional ecologists, Andrewartha and Birch are concerned with the operation and interaction of populations and one of their major concerns is with experimental control of environmental variables. This approach leads to the rejection of results directed toward the elucidation of the action of natural selection upon populations, such as the distribution of chaffinches (*Fringilla coelebs* and *F. coerulea*) in the Canary Islands (Lack and Southern, 1949) and character displacement (Vaurie, 1951; Brown and Wilson, 1956). To the evolutionary ecologist, this rejection is quite inconsistent with their easy acceptance of climatic correlations that appear far less critical and may easily be misinterpreted through improper application of statistics (Smith, 1961).

As an evolutionary ecologist, Lack is primarily concerned with the causes behind observable ecological adaptations and has made his major contribution in the subject of the evolution of reproductive rates. This approach leads to the rejection of climate as a significant regulating factor for populations, a rejection which the functional ecologist finds incomprehensible.

It is pointless to debate the validity of these contrasting approaches to ecology as both have clearly justified their usefulness in all fields of biology. However, it is of great importance to consider the claim of Andrewartha and Birch that general ecological theory can and should be built solely upon the functional approach. Just as many physiologists treat the animal body as a highly interesting and complex mechanism which has not been and

142

is not going anywhere, Andrewartha and Birch treat ecology as the study of complex relationships between animal populations and their environments which are to be best understood as neither having evolved nor continuing to evolve.

It is becoming increasingly apparent that a complete answer to any question should deal with physiological, adaptational and evolutionary aspects of the problem (Pittendrigh, 1958). The evolutionary process of becoming yields the most profound understanding of biological systems at all levels of organization (Simpson, Pittendrigh and Tiffany, 1957). The non-evolutionary answer to the question of why an animal is abundant in some parts of its range and rare in others is of necessity incomplete. The functional ecologist can and does make an important contribution to the understanding of the dynamics of populations, but for the formulation of theory it is essential that the approaches be combined. The functional approach by itself cannot provide a basis for theory and, in fact, the "theory" of Andrewartha and Birch really states that no general theory of ecology is possible and that each case must be considered individually, which is really a statement of research technique rather than theory.

The application of selectionist thinking to natural populations has already led to deeper insights about the proximate relationships of populations. In fact, it is difficult to think about populations without considering the selective advantage of various life history features. Lack's work on avian reproductive rates is an excellent example of ecological insight derived from selectionist thinking. Another is R. A. Fisher's theory on the evolution of sex ratios, originally proposed in 1930 and recently amplified by Kolman (1960) and Bodmer and Edwards (1960). To this we may add Medawar's (1957) stimulating discussion of the evolution of death rates, a fundamental ecological and physiological problem; all competition studies; the ecology of vertebrate social organization (Pitelka, 1959; Orians, 1960, 1961); and the nature of animal niches (Hutchinson, 1959; MacArthur, 1961). Recent studies of species abundance and diversity (Kohn, 1959; MacArthur, 1957, 1960; MacArthur and MacArthur, 1961) are also producing promising results, but it still is too early to evaluate them adequately. Also, animal ecologists are adopting more widely the community approach which has been intensively and extensively used by plant ecologists for decades (Elton, 1949).

On the other hand, Lack and others of similar viewpoint probably overstate the case for density-dependence when they assume that regulation and evolution cannot occur unless there is so-called biological control and competition. The role of climate as a controlling mechanism is often doubted on this ground alone, but Birch (1960) has made a valid claim for the operation of natural selection through climate. Moreover, environments do fluctuate and may do so regularly enough to prevent competition from proceeding to its conclusion (Hutchinson, 1953).

Finally, it may be asked whether or not there is any such thing as a general theory of ecology, satisfying or unsatisfying. Is there a theory of behavior or comparative anatomy or embryology or physiology? Whereas there

143

are descriptive generalizations in all of these fields, the only general theory which now seems possible is that of natural selection. Ecology, too, has its descriptive generalizations, such as the principle of competitive exclusion, but as in other fields, evolution would seem to be the only real theory of ecology today. Even if one strongly believes in the action of natural selection it is exceedingly difficult, as Darwin pointed out, to keep it always firmly in mind. Neglect of natural selection in ecological thinking is, therefore, understandable though regretable. However, its deliberate exclusion in these years following the Darwin centennial would seem to be exceedingly unwise.

CONCLUSIONS

The roots of the current controversy which so deeply divides ecology lie much deeper than their peripheral manifestations in the argument over density-dependence and density-independence. Rather, they stem from the division of the field into two major categories — functional ecology and evolutionary ecology. Both of these approaches are valid and useful and it is a mistake to erect general ecological theory exclusively on either.

ACKNOWLEDGMENTS

The development and clarification of the ideas presented here has been greatly helped by discussions with students in my advanced ecology class during the past two years, and I gratefully acknowledge their substantial contributions. Also, F. A. Pitelka, W. T. Edmondson and A. J. Kohn read the manuscript and made helpful suggestions.

LITERATURE CITED

Andrewartha, H. G., 1961, Introduction to the study of animal populations. Univ. Chicago Press, Chicago. 281 pp.
Andrewartha, H. G., and L. C. Birch, 1954, The distribution and abundance of animals. Univ. Chicago Press, Chicago. 782 pp.
Birch, L. C., 1955, Selection in Drosophila pseudoobscura in relation to crowding. Evolution 9: 389-399.
        1960, The genetic factor in population ecology. Am. Naturalist 94: 5-24.
        1961, Natural selection between two species of Tephritid fruit fly of the Genus Dacus. Evolution 15: 360-374.
Bodmer, W. F., and A. W. F. Edwards, 1960, Natural selection and the sex ratio. Ann. Human Genet. 24: 239-244.
Brown, W. J., Jr., and E. O. Wilson, 1956, Character displacement. Systematic Zool. 5: 49-64.
Cowan, I. McT., W. S. Hoar and J. Hatter, 1950, The effect of forest succession upon the quality and upon the nutritive values of woody plants used as food by moose. Canadian J. Research 28: 249-271.
Dobzhansky, Th., 1957, Mendelian populations as genetic systems. Cold Spring Harbor Symp. Quant. Biol. 22: 385-393.
Elton, C., 1949, Population interspersion: an essay on animal community patterns. J. Ecol. 37: 1-23.

Fisher, R. A., 1958, The genetical theory of natural selection. Dover, New York. 291 pp.

Hairston, N. G., F. H. Smith and L. B. Slobodkin, 1960, Community structure, population control, and competition. Am. Naturalist 94: 421–425.

Harlan, J. R., 1956, Theory and dynamics of grassland agriculture. Van Nostrand, Princeton, N. J. 281 pp.

Hutchinson, G. E., 1953, The concept of pattern in ecology. Proc. Acad. Nat. Sci., Phil., 105: 1–12.

1959, Homage to Santa Rosalia or Why are there so many kinds of animals? Am. Naturalist 93: 145–159

Kohn, A. J., 1959, The ecology of *Conus* in Hawaii. Ecol. Monographs 29: 47–90.

Kolman, W. A., 1960, The mechanism of natural selection for the sex ratio. Am. Naturalist 94: 373–378.

Lack, D., 1954, The natural regulation of animal numbers. Oxford Univ. Press, Oxford. 343 pp.

Lack, D., and H. N. Southern, 1949, Birds on Tenerife. Ibis 91: 607–626.

MacArthur, R. H., 1957, On the relative abundance of bird species. Proc. Natl. Acad. Sci. U. S. 43: 293–295.

1960, On the relative abundance of species. Am. Naturalist 94: 25–36.

1961, Population effects of natural selection. Am. Naturalist 95: 195–199.

MacArthur, R. H., and J. W. MacArthur, 1961, On bird species diversity. Ecology 42: 594–598.

Mayr, E., 1961, Cause and effect in biology. Science 134: 1501–1506.

Medawar, P. B., 1957, The uniqueness of the individual. Methuen, London. 191 pp.

Orians, G. H., 1960, Social stimulation among blackbird colonies. Condor 62: 330–337.

1961, The ecology of blackbird (*Agelaius*) social organization. Ecol. Monographs 31: 285–312.

Orians, G. H., and F. A. Pitelka, 1960, Range management for the animal ecologist. Ecology 41: 406.

Pitelka, F. A., 1959, Numbers, breeding schedule, and territoriality in Pectoral Sandpipers of Northern Alaska. Condor 61: 233–264.

Pittendrigh, C. S., 1958, Adaptation, natural selection, and behavior. *In:* A. Roe and G. G. Simpson [eds.], Behavior and evolution. Yale Univ. Press, New Haven, Conn. 557 pp.

Simpson, G. G., C. S. Pittendrigh and L. H. Tiffany, 1957, Life. Harcourt, Brace and Company, New York. 845 pp.

Smith, F. E., 1961, Density dependence in Australian thrips. Ecology 42: 403–407.

Taber, R. D., 1956, Deer nutrition and population dynamics in the North Coast Range of California. Trans. Twenty-first North American Wildlife Conf.: 159–172.

Vaurie, C., 1951, Adaptive differences between two sympatric species of Nuthatches (*Sitta*). Proc. X Intern. Ornithol. Congr. 1950: 163–166.

11

Copyright © 1964 by Verlag Paul Parey
Reprinted from *Z. angew. Ent.* **53**:187–208 (1964)

Backgrounds of controversies about population theories and their terminologies

By K. Bakker

With 1 figure

Since the appearance of the book of Andrewartha and Birch in 1954, which initiated a turbulent period in population dynamics, we have witnessed a veritable outburst of papers on theoretical population problems. All the fundamental concepts of population dynamics have been criticized and revised again and again by a large number of authors which hold very different opinions. As a result, violent controversies and heated arguments have dominated the discussions on theoretical problems in the last decade.

It is recognized lately that these controversies stem from various sources, and it is widely felt that population dynamics would profit from "more light and less heat" (Richards, 1961) in future discussions. Peaceful coexistence of the various investigators seems to me a prerequisite for a healthy growth of our science. This does not, of course, preclude lively discussions among them.

Apart from the fact that the disagreement is certainly partly due to the scantiness of our knowledge of natural populations – a disadvantage which can and has to be cured by increased effort devoted to practical studies – it is obvious that another part of the disagreement originates from differences in the empirisms, the evaluation of the various scientific methods, and the ideals of knowledge of the adherents of the different population theories. Furthermore, a lot of confusion has certainly arisen from terminological difficulties.

In the following an attempt will be made to show some backgrounds of the current controversies. The literature on the subject is so vast and extensive that I can hardly hope to add anything new. Most of what I could possibly say, will have been discussed at length before. This paper will therefore become an example of the thesis that when one copies only one book or paper, it is plagiary, but when one cites ten or twenty authors it becomes "science". However, it may be useful to summarize the different opinions and to order them from a particular viewpoint.

My first problem was to decide how to set up this paper. I have deliberately refrained from giving a chronological annotated list of theories and terms with their definitions and their authors. Such a list, though perhaps very useful, would help little to clear the confusion and would be unbearably dull to read. Instead, I have tried to summarize the various causes of controversies and to propose a terminology which may perhaps give no reason for misunderstanding.

One of the outstanding characteristics of ecology in general is the lack of agreement as to what the subject is really concerned with (RICHARDS, 1939). The divergence in subject matter and point of view is enormous: ecologists are, so to say, a mixed lot. This is partly due tot the vague circumscription of "ecology", because practically everybody who studies animals or plants in nature, as well as a number of investigators who study artificial populations in the laboratory, call themselves "ecologists", independent of their point of view, which may be purely typological, causal or teleological. Investigators who describe and classify grassland communities, analyse fluctuations in spruce budworm populations or study the adaptive significance of territories in birds are all "ecologists" according to the broad definition (PEARSE, 1939): "Ecology is the branch of biological science that deals with relations of organisms and their environment". According to RICHARDS (1939) this definition "would provide the title for an encyclopaedia, but not delimit a scientific discipline".

Characteristic for this broad view is the following quotation of OOSTING (1948): "Since all plants and animals, including man, are organisms, and since environment can at times include almost everything in the universe, the subject matter of ecology is almost unlimited". To this, EGLER (1951) in a very critical paper, remarks: "This nebulous unlimitedness . . . seems to delight the ecologists, . . . (though it) has not yet gained the respect of other biologists". EGLER's paper, which is a commentary on (American) plant ecology, remains an extremely valuable reexamination of ecology in general, of its subject matter, methods, point of view, and purpose. In an (unusual) editor's note, LAWRENCE stated that it needs to be thought through by all ecologists.

It is sometimes argued that ecology, being a relatively young science, lacks for this reason a sound theoretical foundation. This would be the cause of the vagueness of the definition. I believe that the vagueness is especially a consequence of differences of opinion as to what the problems are.

It is not my aim to discuss here at length the delimitation of "ecology" or its subdivisions, interesting though this problem may be. The only point I want to stress is that several authors have split up "ecology" in a more or less similar way (GAMS, 1918; DU RIETZ, 1921; VAN DER KLAAUW, 1936; SCHWENCKE, 1955). According to them, the whole of biology can be divided into two main branches: one is called "idiobiology" and here the unit which is studied is the individual organism or parts of it. To this branch belong the "classic" subdivisions as morphology, physiology, taxonomy, etc. Here also belongs ecology in so far as the individual organism is studied in its relation to the environment. VAN DER KLAAUW (1936) considers the point of view from which these relations are studied in this (aut)ecology as far as zoology is concerned as basically non-causal. Though the method of analysis may be (and will be) entirely causal, the ultimate questions (ideals of knowledge) in (aut)ecology are teleological in the modern sense. Physiological or morphological properties and behavioural characteristics of the organism are hence studied in relation to the environment from *the point of view of their adaptive significance*. Focus is on their importance for the preservation of life, for reproduction, for dispersal, etc. Causal problems concerning the reaction of organism to environmental factors belong, according to him, to the domain of physiology, albeit that in this "ecology" the functions are investigated on the entire organism instead of on certain organs. A causal autecology would be only a crude kind of physiology. Strictly spoken, this is certainly true. However, in practice there are many "causal autecological" investigations which would never be undertaken by physiologists.

The other main branch of biology next to idiobiology has been called biosociology, biocoenology, synbiology or synecology. Here the unit studied is the biocoenosis. According to some authors each of the subdivisions in idiobiology has an analogous subdivision in biocoenology. In this way we have studies on the qualitative and quantitative composition of the bio-coenosis, on the role which the different organisms play in the biocoenosis (niche-study), on the delimitation and classification of communities, on succession etc. These are respectively analogous with morphological, physiological, taxonomical and embryological studies in idiobiology.

To return to our subject, we could now ask where in this framework we should place population-dynamics. An answer to this question is indispensable for our discussion. The first thing to do is to make clear what we will call a population. On this point we should realize that there exist various opinions as regards the reality of the very unit we want to study: the population of some animal species. THOMPSON (1956) holds the opinion that "the only real beings that exist in the real world are individual organisms" and that "the population is referred to (by NICHOLSON) as if it were an entity, but as an entity it exists only in the mind, having merely the status of a concept". The difficulty here lies in a failure to distinguish abstract concepts like "individual organism" and "population" from concrete examples which bear the same name. EGLER (1951) says that "this idea of the 'concrete' and the 'abstract' ... is one of the most basic precepts of logical reasoning, one that should exist as a second nature to all scientists. It is hardly an idea that should form the subject of discussion ... in the twentieth century". Populations have characteristics of their own, as a genetic structure, sex ratio, birth rate, death rate, density, age structure, social structure and distribution pattern, and on this ground can be considered as entities, though admittedly of a less easily circumscribed nature as individual organisms. This, however, does not defeat scientific analysis of processes which take place in them.

Moreover, THOMPSON's reliance on "individual organisms" as real beings seems to imply that here there are no difficulties. THOMPSON seems to overlook the fact that the "individual organism" is also a concept, of which a certain beetle, elephant or fish may be a concrete example. In contrast to the population, this distinction between the "abstract" and the "concrete" is here much easier overlooked, because the "concrete" individuals are so obviously present and can generally be physically isolated from their environment. However, here the problem may become increasingly more difficult when we study colonies of hydrozoa, siphonophora, bryozoa, etc. A population of individuals of a certain species is an entity on a higher level of integration than the individual organism and on a lower level than the biocoenosis. The increasing complexities of these entities renders the analysis more difficult, but this makes these entities none the less real, in spite of the fact that a physical isolation of these entities from others is often impossible.

To do justice to THOMPSON, we must consider that the reason for his attack on the population as a real entity was, that NICHOLSON (1954), according to him, had hypostatized the population and attributed to it the power of self-regulation. I wonder whether this criticism applies in this case, but it is certainly important to warn against a very dangerous procedure in science: unwarranted extrapolation of analogies. Too often a certain analogy, e. g. between an individual organism and a community, is taken as a fundamental identity and a misleading extrapolation from the individual to the community takes place. This happened in the ecological theories of CLEMENTS (1905, 1916, 1931) to a very high degree, a fact which has been recognized and criticized by various workers as, e. g. GAMS (1918), DU RIETZ (1919), BRAUN-BLANQUET (1928), EGLER (1951). Remnants of this reasoning by analogy reappear now and then in the literature and there is every reason to remain cautious.

Though we will consider populations as entities with characteristics of their own, this does not mean that the delimitation of populations does not present an important and difficult problem. The delimitation and size of a particular animal population which is chosen as an object of a certain study is extremely important and may even influence the interpretation of the observed facts as is clearly pointed out by KUENEN (1958). When this fact would be realized more fully, some of the misunderstanding among population ecologists would certainly disappear. A definition of "population" can hardly be very narrow, since the delimitation of a population we want to study depends on the problem we want to solve. As a definition I would suggest:

A population of a certain species is a group of individuals of this species, which possesses certain quantitative properties, and which is separated from other groups of this species by discontinuities in the frequencies of interactions, the magnitude of these discontinuities being dependent on the nature of the group, and hence on the problem chosen for study.

Our next question, logically, is: "What are the problems in population-dynamics?" Unfortunately we cannot be satisfied with a definition like: "Population-dynamics is the science which is concerned with the explanation of the distribution and abundance of animals and the changes which take place in their numbers".

I will give some examples to show where such a definition gives rise to controversy. The first can be found in the recent paper by KLOMP (1962), where he discusses SCHWERDTFEGER's (1958) interpretation of the findings of HEERING (1956) on the population-dynamics of the barkbeetle *Agrilus viridis*, which oviposits on the trunks of beech. Healthy trees can defend themselves against penetrating larvae but this ability is upset during periods of drought. During the years 1946–1951 weather had been extremely dry and *Agrilus* became a pest. An enormous decrease in numbers occurred, however, when as a result of a large precipitation in 1952 the trees regained their vigour and killed the larvae. This led SCHWERDTFEGER to the conclusion: "Consequently, it was the weather which, influencing the brood fitness of the host plant, indirectly determined the increase as well as the decrease in the abundance", and thus, under these conditions weather regulated population density. To this interpretation, KLOMP remarks: "In fact, weather does not *regulate* the number of animals, but *determines* the number of suitable habitats (trees). It is the *regulation* per unit of suitable habitat which *interests us*, but not the total quantity of suitable habitats, how interesting the latter question may be from the *viewpoint of the forester*" (italics mine).

In this case, KLOMP is certainly right when he claims that the weather did not regulate this population. It simply cannot do so, as the severity of the weather is generally independent of the density of the animals, and *regulation*, according to the (implicitly given) definition can only be brought about by density-dependent mechanisms. This does not mean that the mortality caused by a given severity of the weather is always independent of the density of the animals. However, if there is a density-dependent mortality in which the weather acts as the direct destructive agency, the real density governing mechanism is always an underlying competition for favourable places (shelter), as NICHOLSON (1954) clearly pointed out.

Here, it seems the place to say something about a similar difficulty which can be encountered in literature. Some authors seem to struggle with the idea that e. g. "competition for food" and "sheer starvation" are *alternative* causes of death (ULLYETT, 1950). Here, again, there is a confusion of regulating processes and direct causes of death, which do not exclude each other, as has been rightly pointed out by HUFFAKER (1958).

Returning to the disagreement between SCHWERDTFEGER and KLOMP, we may ask, whether the issue (determination versus regulation) is relevant to the interest of both authors. Here we come much nearer to the roots of the disagreement. RICHARDS (1961) wrote: "Perhaps one of the greatest real sources of controversy at the moment is the division of interest between those for whom the most important or interesting phenomena are those of balance, and those who are more interested in explaining fluctuations". In a very interesting paper WILBERT (1962) states that "Massenwechsel" and "Regulation" are not always clearly distinguished, no more than are "Regulation" and "Determination", and that the basis of the misunderstanding lays here.

A similar difference of opinion as that between KLOMP and SCHWERDTFEGER can be found between LACK (1954) and ODUM (1953). Here the issue is the "importance" of the increase and decrease of animal populations. LACK, being interested in the "natural regulation of animal numbers", places emphasis on the decrease, arguing that the increase is not nearly as interesting because most animals are capable to increase enormously in numbers. In contrast with this view, ODUM considers the negative phase "merely a secondary result of overpopulation" and recommends that more attention should be paid to the positive growth phase.

The problem is also raised by NICHOLSON (1954) and THOMPSON (1956) when they discuss the relative importance of the various factors known to influence the population. In NICHOLSON's opinion "no reliance whatever must be placed upon the proportion of animals destroyed by each. Instead we must find which of the factors are influenced and how readily they are influenced by changes in the density of the animals". This means, says THOMPSON, that "the factual evidence we can obtain at any particular moment in nature has not necessarily any significance in regard to the problem we are trying to solve", which is clearly not acceptable to him. Here, again, I would say that the *problems* are not entirely the same.

Now that we have arrived at the point that we realize that there is no agreement about the problems, it becomes very clear that there cannot be agreement as to their solution. The first thing to do now is to seek a common ground for the distinction of the different problems in population ecology.

Last year, a thought-provoking paper by ORIANS appeared in The American Naturalist, entitled: "Natural selection and ecological theory". In this paper, ORIANS argues that the intense controversy over the mechanisms of control of animal populations is only a peripheral manifestation of a much more basic issue, which is not clearly understood. According to him, the real disagreement stems from the division of the field of ecology into two main parts, i. e. functional ecology and evolutionary ecology[1]. To elucidate his view he compares the two important animal ecology texts of ANDREWARTHA & BIRCH (1954) and LACK (1954) who represent clearly the two different "schools". I will give his arguments with some additions of my own[2].

For ANDRWARTHA & BIRCH it is the main task of the ecologists to explain "the distribution and abundance of animals". The approach is through a study of the physiology and behaviour of the individual animal and a study of the environment. Community studies are rejected as contributing next to nothing to the solution of the problem. Evolutionary concepts have no place in this type of ecological work. Their often quoted example of the bees in the holes may serve as a clear expression of their view. They expressed serious doubts concerning the importance of competition in animal ecology, because "the student of ecology" has only to count the holes in order to know how large the bee population can be. To "the student of evolution" the intensity of competition which takes place is of the utmost interest as it determines genetic changes in the populations.

The approach to the problems of distribution and abundance is thus through the study of *proximate* factors which influence population densities, the individual animal is taken as the basic entity, the problem is causal.

On the other hand, LACK is interested in "the natural regulation of animal numbers" and hence the focus in his book is mainly on *ultimate* factors which may provide the key to the understanding of current population adaptations. Therefore, LACKS's attention is directed towards the elucidation of evolutionary mechanisms in ecology. The problem here is teleological in the modern sense[3], as VAN DER KLAAUW sees it, and its solution is attempted according to a causal analysis. The ultimate aim of the study is to try to get an answer to the problem of adaptation and evolution, and the causal analysis is only the means to acquire this answer.

ORIANS discusses further the possibility that the difference between the two schools may also be caused by the organisms (insects versus birds) and the nature of the communities which are primarily studied by their adherents. Though this may have a very important impact on their mode of thought, it is not the fundamental cause of the disagreement, which is the dichotomy in functional and evolutionary ecology.

The functional ecologists' answer to the question of distribution and abundance is incomplete, important and indispensable though his contribution to the understanding of the dynamics of populations may be. However, functional ecology cannot provide a "general theory" of populations

---

[1] These terms are derived from MAYR (1961). See Appendix.

[2] The concept and term "teleology" is not used by ORIANS.

[3] Or historic-causal when the origin of the adaptations is studied.

– if such a thing exists at all – which is clear from the attempts of ANDRE-
WARTHA & BIRCH and MILNE (1962)[4].

Evolutionary ecologists will study ecological adaptations, the significance of territories, the evolution of reproductive rates in relation to
parental care, niche relations, diversity of species, competition, social organization and similar problems.

A few critical remarks on ORIANS' important paper are appropriate.
When he states that the *basic* issue involved is much deeper than its peripheral manifestation in the form of the argument over density-dependency
and density-independency, he refers to the books of LACK (1954) on the one
side and ANDREWARTHA & BIRCH (1954) on the other. In these books the
difference in viewpoint is very clear. Now the controversy about the problem is much older and for a *historical* base ORIANS should have turned to
NICHOLSON (1933) and THOMPSON (1929, 1939). Then he would not find
such a clear difference between the two authors as regards an "evolutionary"
versus a "functional" point of view. NICHOLSON nor THOMPSON have a
clear "evolutionary" approach to the problem of natural control of animal
populations. However, if ORIANS has not the *historical* base in mind, but
merely wants to stress that there is a strong relation between the selectionist
and regulationist way of thinking, and that therefore evolutionists will
generally be interested in regulating mechanisms, he is certainly right. For
instance, competition, being one of the manifestations of the struggle for
existence, which leads to natural selection, is also one of the important
mechanisms in the regulation of population density. It is, however, possible
to focus on one of these aspects only.

A second remark concerns the *terms* "evolutionary" and "functional"
ecology[5], which are somewhat unfortunate. As has been argued, not all
regulation problems have *evolutionary* aspects though *selection* plays always a role. On the other hand, the term "functional" ecology has a teleological ring, which is certainly not intended: on the contrary I would say.

In the following I have nevertheless retained the terms.

According to ORIANS, the evolutionary ecologists are "primarily concerned with the causes behind observable ecological adaptations". This is
exactly the point which THOMPSON had in mind when he, ironically, objected
to NICHOLSON's remark about the relative importance of factors[6]: "To
discover the inner meaning of the facts, a very lengthy and arduous investigation has to be made. In cases where this investigation has not been made,
we simply have to rely on faith". If "faith" is here identical with logical
interpretation of facts through inferential reasoning, I may argue that this
remark would apply also to the wealth of factual evidence for evolutionary
theory, derived from paleontology. THOMPSON remarks further: "In the
operations of the economic entomologist the principle (that the importance
of a mortality factor is determined by the degree of its density dependence)
is not and cannot usually be applied". This difficulty is caused by the fact
that the regulation is super-imposed on the fluctuations (Massenwechsel).
An inductive *practical* study of the former problem is therefore only possible
if enough is known of the latter and this is seldom the case in natural popu-

[4] Some of their ideas are sound enough, but they do not make a comprehensive "theory".

[5] A further discussion on these terms can be found in the Appendix.

[6] Cited on p. 191.

lations of insects. However, it does not follow that a deductive *theoretical* approach of regulation is without significance (WILBERT, 1962). The deductive method is a powerful tool in clarifying thinking. We should not be infatuated by a theory which does not fit the facts, nor believe that facts without a theory can make a science.

A next issue on which opinions diverge (or collide, depending on the temperament of their holders) concerns the usefulness of mathematical models. In my opinion this usefulness depends on what is expected from them. Sometimes they may serve for the illumination of certain processes, like parasite-host fluctuations, competition or predation, in other cases they may only provide a reasonable basis for the prediction of the density of the population studied. If they fulfil the purpose for which their inventors made them, it is rather pointless to object that they do not provide satisfactory answers to the problems of others. It is not a question of right or wrong. As long as the fundamental limitation of the usefulness of models in general is realized, it seems to me that this issue need not give rise to any serious disagreement. However, then one condition must be fulfilled: the model should not be presented as a "general theory". I think nobody will deny the value of mathematics as a tool in ecology, nor on the other hand will believe that it can replace investigations on natural populations themselves.

Though it may be called "stressing the over-obvious" I want to mention here for the sake of completeness the great difference in the kinds of animals and the nature of the environments studied as major sources of different views concerning the importance of density dependent processes in natural populations. It is meaningless to combat a conclusion derived from work on territorial insectivorous birds in the tropics with arguments derived from work on phytophagous insects in the temperate region, to give an extreme example. Animals are so different in their life histories, their requirements and their adaptations, etc., that any attempt to give a useful "general theory" of population-dynamics must necessarily fail, or it becomes so vague that it largely looses its meaning. Further, there is such an enormous difference between the environments in which animals live and the complexity of the communities of which they are a member that any generalization is bound to be unjustified (SCHWERDTFEGER, 1941). On this last point the distinction between hazardous and salubrious environments, made by HUFFAKER (1958) is very useful. In the former, "fortuitous changes in the levels of the requisites as e. g. caused by weather" is dominant and may short-circuit or obscure the tendency for competition to establish balance, while in the latter "competition for all practical purposes dominates and exerts the conspicuous action over such changes in density as are observed" because the levels of the requisites are relatively constant.

Finally, there have been a number of authors who suspected that a lot of confusion has arisen from an inconsistent and loose use of terms. This is certainly true, but in my opinion it is not the only or even the major cause of confusion. The terminology is certainly a reflection of the underlying theory, and hence discussions on terminology will always be discussions on these theories as well (LABEYRIE, 1963). I will have to return to this subject later on, but will mention here the vehement discussion on terms like "density dependent" (e. g. SOLOMON, 1958; VARLEY, 1958) and "competition" (BIRCH, 1957; KLOMP, 1960; BAKKER, 1961; MILNE, 1961). VARLEY (1958) prefers to use terms according to their original definition. In my opinion this is certainly advisable if the original definition is clear-cut and if it is useful. However, if the old definition is vague or does no longer fit modern views, it should be rejected and replaced by a new definition. There is certainly nothing sacrosanct about them, and it seems to me unjustified to introduce "priority rules" here. It may be advisable to mention always the author of a certain term, e. g. "competition in the sense of X (19...)".

A very important source of disagreement concerns the use of the word "factor" (HUFFAKER, 1958; NICHOLSON, 1960). Competition, temperature, drought, reproductive capacity, predators, tolerance, food, sex ratio, and habitat have all at some time or other been called "factors". We should be careful to avoid this loose usage. "Competition" is a kind of interaction, "temperature" is a physical component of the environment, "drought" is a particular range of another physical component, "reproductive capacity" and "tolerance" are properties of the individual animals, "food" and "predators" are biotic components of the environment, the one belonging to the resources, the other to the enemies, "sex ratio" is a property of the population, and "habitat" denotes the place where the animal lives. Now all of these may *become* "factors", namely when they enter an equation which describes a certain process. For instance, the rate of feeding is a property of an organism, but in an equation describing growth it becomes a "factor".

Another source of misunderstanding is the unclear distinction between the numerical value of a certain mortality factor and the effect of its action (VOÛTE, 1946; KUENEN, 1954). This gives rise to difficulties when the "factor" is to be classified in the "density-dependent" or "density-independent" category. The numerical value of a mortality factor is measured in factor units (degrees centigrade, millimeters precipitation, number of predators). The effect of its action is measured in the population affected (e. g. percentage killed by the factor). When the effect of the factor increases with increasing population density, while the numerical value remains the same, we speak of the "functional response" of the factor to population density (SOLOMON, 1949). A "numerical response" of the factor occurs when the effect increases through an increase in its numerical value.

If we now try to summarize the different sources of disagreement before making an attempt to determine our position, we get the following list[7]. It should be noted that many points are related.

1. A very vague circumscription of ecology, its subject matter and point of view.
2. A difference of opinion regarding the reality of populations, stemming from a failure to distinguish abstract concepts from concrete examples.
3. Unjustified extrapolation of analogies.
4. A difference in the main field of interest of the various workers (called by ORIANS [1962] functional or evolutionary ecology), which manifests itself in a number of points regarding:
   a. the importance of evolutionary or selectionist concepts for ecology;
   b. the delimitation of populations, notably their size;
   c. the emphasis which is laid on ultimate or on proximate factors;
   d. the problem of regulation as compared to fluctuation;

---

[7] The philosopher would have divided these points in another way, namely in empirisms, methods and ideals of knowledge.

    e. the nature of the problem, namely whether it is basically causal or
teleogical;

    f. the emphasis which is laid on long-term or short-term processes.

5. Differences in the evaluation of deductive methods.
6. Disagreement about the usefulness of (mathematical) population models.
7. Controversies about the importance of the study of community relations.
8. Enormous differences in the properties of the organisms and the nature of
the environments studied by the various workers.
9. Misunderstanding through inconsistent and loose use of terms.

On this point we may now try to clear the position of the applied entomologist as regards these controversies. His main task is the prevention of
pests. He is confronted with a particular problem, and, as the pest insect is
inherent in the problem, he is in a way at a disadvantage as compared to the
worker who can select an animal to suit the interesting problem he wants
to study, because the pest insect may have an extremely inconvenient life
history[8].

His initial approach will be mainly functional and his interest will be
directed primarily towards the causes of fluctuations. Correlation analysis,
substantiated by causal analysis carried out with the aid of field and (or)
laboratory experiments may serve to clarify the population-dynamics of
the insect in its environment.

After a number of years this may enable him to indicate "key factors"
(VARLEY & GRADWELL, 1960) and perhaps also to predict with a reasonable
degree of accuracy what is going to happen with the population density the
next generation.

The applied entomologist may construct (or adopt) a model which facili-
tates the approach to certain phenomena, and then this model can be tested.
Again, it may prove to be either useful for the understanding of the process
involved or only suitable for prediction. He may discover that single-factor
analysis (MORRIS, 1959) gives him most of the information he needs for
the measures he wants to take, and as long as it is not pretended that
this gives him a complete picture of the population-dynamics of the
species in question, nobody can object that it is an over-simplification. We
should not be dogmatic but pragmatic in these matters.

I feel strongly, however, that a notion of the web-like structure of the
environmental relations will be indispensable from the beginning, even when
it cannot be tackled immediately.

If the investigator is allowed to study the fluctuations of his pest population and their causes long enough, he may be able to discover whether the
regulating mechanisms which will undoubtedly be present do indeed have a
decisive influence on the fate of the population, or whether the restriction
of the density fluctuations are mainly attributable to the stabilizing influence
of random fluctuations in the numerical values of environmental components known to influence reproduction and mortality of the population
independent of its density, a standpoint which is taken by SCHWERDTFEGER
(1958) and DEN BOER (1963) and which is disputed by WILBERT (1959) and
KLOMP (1962).

In contrast with workers who start with a theory which is to be tested,

---

[8] On the other hand this has the advantage that it will prevent the investigator to look in
nature only for those phenomena which illustrate his preconceived ideas.

the applied entomologist may form a theory at some moment during his study, after having accumulated a reasonable amount of facts. His need for a terminology will therefore be different from that of the worker just mentioned. He will benefit most of a clearcut set of terms which are not loaded with concepts derived from particular population models. I therefore agree entirely with the views of FRANZ (1960, 1961) in this matter. It should be avoided to build a classification of processes, to be used in practice, on the basis of the *results* they will produce. How are we going to name a process which obviously takes place before we know its short-term or long-term result? In an eventual synthesis of the complex of environmental components and their properties, the population and its individuals with their characteristics, and the interactions and processes which take place between and within them, terms can be used which denote the effect on, or the relation with population density, if this is required.

I am not sure, however, whether it is necessary to be a perfectionist and to try to invent different terms for all the conceivable complex interactions and processes which occur in all different species populations in all natural communities. I am afraid that this "pigeonholing of nature" will overshoot its purpose, which is (or should be) to clarify the representation of an intricate web. Instead of this, it is not improbable that it will lead us to such splitting of categories that we will ultimately get the same interrelations and processes we already knew before we started to classify, as EGLER (1951) remarked when discussing CLEMENTS' (1949) classification of plant communities. Moreover, a too finely detailed classification will let us down, because the finer the classification becomes, the more will remain which does not fit in the different categories (since it is still different). On the other hand, a too crude classification does not help us either. We apparently have to look for an optimal number of terms, which describe large groups of environmental components, interactions and processes, sufficiently different and easily recognized to merit separate terms.

With these points in mind, on what bases are we going to classify? We certainly have an embarrassing choice among the existing systems.

The system of CLEMENTS & SHELFORD (1939) is based on the nature of the processes which take place within a population or community and between a population or community and the environment. Here we meet such terms as action, reaction, coaction, cooperation, disoperation, competition, destruction, aggregation, migration, succession, etc. The system is fairly consistent and the terms are reasonably well defined. In my opinion they provide a very useful and practical set of terms for the different processes.

SCHWERDTFEGER (1941) gives a system in which not the processes are classified, but in which the environmental components which influence the population are represented in a web-like structure. The different possible interactions are indicated with the aid of arrows. Since his system emphasizes the web-like structure of the environmental relations of the population studied, I consider it as a very useful representation.

PARK (1949) gives a scheme in which the interplay of factors that affect populations are represented. The major division is in "responses" favouring increase, and those favouring decrease. Both of them are influenced by genetic and ecologic factors, and the latter consist of density-independent and density-dependent factors. This system is, in fact, an extension of

CHAPMAN's (1951) ideas about a biotic potential and an environmental resistance.

A system which is very similar to that of SCHWERDTFEGER, though it is somewhat more elaborated, is that of SOLOMON (1953, 1955). It also emphasizes the web-like nature of the interrelations. SOLOMON did not distinguish clearly processes which take place within the individual and properties of the population.

The classification of "factors" given by NICHOLSON (1954) is based on:

a. the influence of the population density on the numerical value of the "factors" (responsive and unresponsive "factors");

b. the absence or presence of a modification in the influence of the "factor" in the population as a result of a change in density (non-reactive and reactive "factors");

c. the effect of the "factor" on population density (density-governing, -disturbing, -legislative and -inactive "factors" or processes).

The different density-governing processes are further classified.

Though NICHOLSON certainly sometimes recognizes the danger of attributing certain qualities like "density-dependency" to environmental components like "food" or "predators" as if these qualities were innate characteristics (1957), he gives rise to serious confusion about his real views because he uses a host of different terms which are not always clearly defined (1954, 1957, 1960). For instance he uses nouns like "factor", "requisite", "agent", "property", "mechanism", "process", "interference", etc., combined with adjectives like "density-related", "-governed", "-legislative", "-adjustive", "-triggered", "-conditioned", etc., which makes one wonder whether we really know so much about populations that we are justified to apply such a precise nomenclature. No sooner have we discovered that there is a lot of synonymity and inconsistence in his use of these terms and that he in his paper of 1960 pleads for "a shift of emphasis from factors to mechanisms and properties", than we realize that his system is inadequate and premature. NICHOLSON (1960) recommends:

"I urge ecologists to abandon the cumbersome practice of attempting to describe population regulation in terms of different kinds of factors, and, should they wish to use the word factor, to give this precision by restricting its use to attributes of environmental elements, or to properties, which directly influence population densities. However, factors are essentially the concern of mathematicians and it is generally best to avoid reference to them in verbal discussions." "The straightforward way to discuss the self-adjustment of populations to their environments is to refer to the operative governing mechanisms and processes, which can be specified readily as food depletion, competition for favourable space, cannibalism, intraspecific strife, environmental contamination, predator-prey interaction or by any other appropriately descriptive term. In brief, experience has shown that attempts to identify, to define and to classify the factors which influence populations, lead to unnecessary difficulties and to confusion in verbal discussions. It is therefore recommended that we should think instead in terms of properties, influences and governing mechanisms."

Though I do not agree entirely here, it cannot be denied that this is a serious reappraisal of the old Nicholsonian terminology, which is certainly an improvement. The rejection of the old nomenclature does not mean that I have no great admiration for NICHOLSON's theoretical and experimental work. I think we all agree that he has stimulated population ecology tremendously, including the work of his opponents.

The system of ANDREWARTHA & BIRCH (1954), modified by ANDREWARTHA & BROWNING (1961) and BROWNING (1962) takes the individual organism as the central unit and analyses environment into five components (BROWNING, 1962): weather (s. l.), resources, members of the same species, members of other species and hazards. Explanation of the numbers in any population would, according to BROWNING, be possible by measuring the influence of these components on the average individual's chance to survive and reproduce. The system is not based on the web-like structure of the environmental relations and hence does not show "hierarchy" in the influence of the different components on the population.

MILNE's (1957, 1962) classification is noteworthy for its extreme simplicity. He recognizes three categories of factors: density-independent, imperfectly density-dependent and perfectly density-dependent. The first category comprises mainly weather and actions of other species, as indiscriminate grazing etc., and casual predation and parasitism. The second category comprises inter-specific competition, and the actions of predators, parasites and pathogens. The "one and only perfectly density-dependent factor" is intra-specific competition. According to MILNE, natural control of insect populations is attained by a combination of these groups of factors.

WILBERT (1962) uses the same terms as MILNE does, but discusses the action of the different factors with the aid of terms derived from cybernetics. Like MILNE, he attributes much value to intra-specific competition as a regulating mechanism. In my opinion, WILBERT has succeeded in saying what NICHOLSON has always wanted to say on the subject of population fluctuation, determination, and regulation. NICHOLSON has not always been very fortunate in the choice of his illustrative examples (balloon, ship on stormy sea, equestrienne, tight rope artist) nor in his terminology. Moreover, he has evoked so much criticism because of certain aspects of his theory, especially the rather irrealistic premises, that his very realistic views on the influence of his "density-legislative factors" were ignored by his opponents.

The different systems do obviously overlap to a certain degree, but in some emphasis is laid on the description of the components of the environment, in others on the nature of their action on the individuals of the population, and in yet others on their effect in relation to population density. Now this clearly correlates with the purpose of the different systems, which is, respectively, to provide: (1) a system of terms for description of environmental components and their possible interactions with the population, (2) a system which is suitable for the description of succession in biotic communities, and (3) a system which is adapted for the description of population regulation.

In the first type, the web is given as a generalized cross-section of the relations of the population with its environment. A time scale is absent. The importance of the different relations will change with time (SCHWERDTFEGER, SOLOMON). In the second and third type a time scale is implicit (CLEMENTS & SHELFORD, NICHOLSON, PARK, MILNE).

In my opinion the model and the accompanying terminology should fulfil the following requirements:

1. It should take the population of one animal species as the central unit of study and not the individual, nor the community.

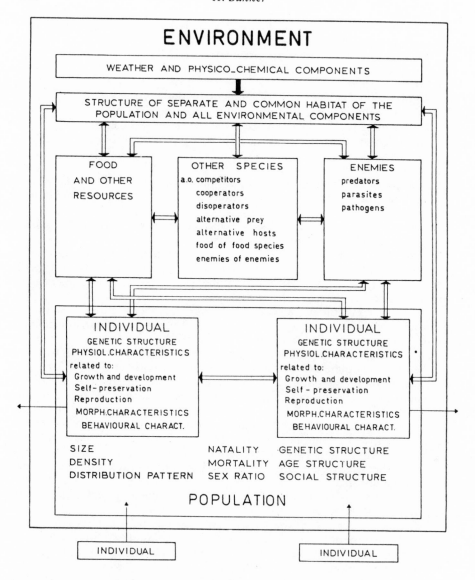

2. It should emphasize the web-like nature of the relations between the population and its environment.
3. It should be able to grow with the needs of the investigator from a purely descriptive frame of terms denoting components and properties, to one in which the (inter)actions are included and named, to one in which the quantitative aspects of the various interactions are summarized in mathematical equations, and *finally* to one in which the whole population-dynamics is synthetized and considered as regards the problem of regulation.
4. It should not be too detailed, especially as regards the nomenclature of the interactions.

5. It should be flexible so as to be easily adapted and elaborated for a certain investigation.
6. It should clearly differentiate between
   a. components of the environment,
   b. their properties,
   c. interactions between the components of the environment,
   d. the largely one-sided action of the superimposed component of the environment (weather and other physico-chemical components) on all other components through the influence on the structure of the habitat (see figure),
   e. properties of the population,
   f. properties of the individual organisms constituting the population,
   g. interactions within the population, i. e. among its constituent individuals,
   h. interactions which take place between components of the environment and the individuals of the population,
   i. the effect of all these interactions on the properties of the population.

The accompanying figure gives what I consider to be an easy and useful picture. The system distinguishes the population and its environment. The population and its properties are represented as an integration of the properties of its constituent individuals. The environment is analysed in five groups of components, of which "weather and other physico-chemical components" as a group is superimposed on the others.

The action of the "weather s. l." on the individual of the population and on the other components will almost always be modified by the structure of the habitats of the population and those of the other components of the environment. Only rarely will the action of the weather be direct. Therefore "structure of the habitats" is linked between "weather" and the population, and between "weather" and the other components. It should be noted, that for instance the food of a certain species population may shape at the same time the structure of its habitat. Feeding will thus lead to a change in this structure and hence to a change in the impact of the weather on the population.

All the possible (inter)actions between the elements of the scheme have been indicated by arrows.

For the reasons given above (4) it should not be attempted to invent special names for all the conceivable (inter)actions. I would favour a set of terms which clearly and directly denote the nature of the (inter)action. I will give a few examples: the direct interactions between individuals of the population comprise: aggregation, mating, parental care, fighting, cannibalism, mutual disturbance, etc. Indirect interactions between individuals of the population are possible through the habitat structure (disoperation, cooperation), through food and other resources (competition), or through enemies. (For this last indirect interaction I have not been able to find a suitable term. KLOMP [1960] proposes to use the term "competition" also in this case, but I do not agree, because the mechanism is quite different.)

The different interactions between individuals and the resources and their possible effects can be analysed further, for instance in the way ANDREWARTHA & BROWNING (1961) have done this. The same applies for the interactions between the individuals of the population and their enemies. The various complications, which arise through the other species in the environment (alternative prey or hosts, competitors, disoperators, etc.) can be introduced and mathematical models can be constructed for such interactions as predation, parasitism, competition, disoperation, etc. From these models a tremendous improvement of our insight in the effect of these particular interactions can be expected. It is impossible to generalize about these effects, as they depend largely on the composition of the specific web of interactions, which is different for each population and in each environment.

The scheme lacks a time scale: it is a generalized cross-section through the system in which the change in the numerical values of the different components and in the importance of the different (inter)actions in time are not shown. Time must be visualized as an axis which runs vertically on the plane of the scheme.

From the scheme it can be seen which possible (inter)actions there are, and with what possible disturbing (inter)actions we have to reckon when we study a certain part of the problem. It is easy to see which interactions may have "density-depent" effects, and in which ways such governing negative feed-back mechanisms may operate and may be upset. Particularly, the possible consequences of the introduction or removal of enemies, competitors, alternative prey, etc., the application of selective insecticides, or changes in the habitat can be taken in at a glance with the aid of the scheme.

It is, however, an illusion to believe, that a verbal discussion and explanation of these complicated interactions can replace mathematical treatment as regards its quantitative precision. The scheme provides the basis of the investigation: it shows the components, their properties, and possible interactions, and supplies the terms. The investigation has to provide the parameters to be used in the models and finally the integration of the whole dynamics can be attempted. It remains to be seen whether "catastrophe and adjustment phases" dominate the history of the particular population, whether long-term restriction of density fluctuations are caused by random fluctuations in the action of a great number of environmental components, or whether the various negative feed-back mechanisms are able to govern population density to a reasonable degree.

For the study of the last problem, I believe we should consult cybernetics. In this science problems similar to ours have been treated and solved, like the importance of the magnitude of corrections, the influence of delayed reaction, etc. The search is for somebody with sufficient knowledge of both population-dynamics and cybernetics to approach the problem of population regulation with the aid of the latter science.

The critical reader may remark that the scheme does not give anything which we didn't know before. This is exactly true, but I may remark that this is its very virtue, as it will therefore hardly give rise to serious disagreement. Now this admittedly is only a negative virtue; the advantages of the approach to population studies with the aid of the scheme are already discussed above.

Summarizing, we may state that the various conflicting theories are for the greater part connected with different stages of a "lengthy and arduous" ecological investigation, in which the emphasis shifts from one problem to the other. Such an ideal research will not often be made: generally the different investigators have good reasons for starting and ending their work at different points along this line, as their problems are different. This causes the well-known mutual reproaches: the "functional" ecologists blame the "evolutionary" ecologists for being too speculative, and on the other hand the latter blame the former for having only a very limited problem. Sometimes these reproaches are justified, but too often they are a result of a failure to see the important though different contribution both groups of workers make to ecology.

It is a pleasure to thank here in the first place Prof. Dr. C. J. van der Klaauw for his valuable and detailed criticism of the manuscript especially as regards its philosophical aspects. I am very grateful to Prof. Dr. D. J. Kuenen, Dr. P. J. den Boer, Mr. G. J. de Bruyn, Dr. W. Scharloo and Dr. A. D. Voûte for their interest and stimulating critical comments. Particulary since I have not always followed their suggestions I must emphasize that the responsibility for this paper is entirely my own. I am much indebted to my colleagues at the Zoölogisch Laboratorium at Leiden, to the members of our Ecological Discussion Group, and to the participants at the meeting of the Discussion Group Population Dynamics of the IUFRO in July 1963.

Zusammenfassung

Es wird der Versuch unternommen, die Ursachen der heutigen z. T. sehr starken Meinungsunterschiede in der Populationsdynamik-Forschung zu ermitteln. Nach Meinung des Verfassers lassen sich folgende, teilweise verwandte Quellen dieser Uneinigkeiten erkennen:

1. Die sehr unbestimmte Umschreibung des Untersuchungsgebietes der Ökologie, ihrer Fragestellung und ihrer Objekte.
2. Uneinigkeit hinsichtlich der Realität der Populationen selbst, die auf der Tatsache beruht, daß man nicht immer zwischen abstrakten Begriffen und konkreten Beispielen richtig unterscheidet.
3. Unzulässiger Ausbau von Analogien.
4. Unterschiede zwischen den Arbeitsgebieten der verschiedenen Autoren und ihrer Hauptinteressen (funktionelle und evolutionäre Ökologie im Sinne von Orians, 1962). Sie äußern sich in Unstimmigkeiten
   a. über die Frage, welche Begriffe aus der Evolution oder Selektionslehre für die Ökologie Bedeutung haben;
   b. über die Abgrenzung von Populationen, insbesondere ihrer Größe;
   c. in der Betonung direkt wirkender (proximativer) und über längere Zeiträume wirkender (ultimativer) Faktoren;
   d. über das Problem der Regulation im Gegensatz zu dem des Massenwechsels;
   e. über die Art des Problems, ob nämlich im wesentlichen eine kausale oder eine teleologische Frage vorliegt.
5. Verschiedene Wertung deduktiver Methoden in der Ökologie.
6. Unstimmigkeit über Sinn und Wert mathematischer Populationsmodelle.
7. Kontroversen hinsichtlich der Bedeutung biozönotischer Studien.
8. Sehr große Unterschiede zwischen den von den verschiedenen Forschern studierten Organismen und ihrer Umwelten.
9. Mißverständnisse zwischen den verschiedenen Autoren infolge ungenauer und ambivalenter Terminologie.

Es wird gezeigt, daß die meisten Streitfragen beseitigt werden können, wenn kein dogmatischer und starrer Gesichtspunkt in Bezug auf diese Fragen eingenommen wird. Die Fragestellung der verschiedenen Forscher ist nicht dieselbe, daher gehen auch die Ansichten über die Mittel zur Lösung

der Probleme auseinander. Die gegenseitigen Vorwürfe der Vertreter der
„funktionellen" und „evolutionären" Ökologie werden aufhören, wenn jede
der beiden Richtungen sich bewußt wird, daß auch die andere Richtung
wichtige Beiträge zum Aufbau der gemeinsamen Wissenschaft leistet.

Im zweiten Abschnitt wird versucht, mit Hilfe eines Schemas eine über-
sichtliche Darstellung des ökologischen Gefüges zu geben. Es wird betont,
daß die Population des untersuchten Organismus zentral gestellt werden
muß und nicht das Individuum oder die Biozönose. Die netzartige Bezie-
hungsstruktur des ökologischen Systems wird besonders hervorgehoben. Die
Umgebung wird in fünf Gruppen von Komponenten eingeteilt, wobei das
Wetter den anderen Komponenten übergeordnet ist. Es muß unterschieden
werden zwischen den Eigenschaften der Individuen und denjenigen der
Population, wobei die Gruppenmerkmale der Population, wie die Dichte,
die Mortalität, die genetische Struktur, der Altersaufbau usw. aus den Eigenschaften der die Population zusammensetzenden Individuen resultieren.

Appendix

The terms "functional" and "evolutionary" ecology used by ORIANS are
based on the terms functional and evolutionary biology, defined by MAYR
(1961). The problems discussed in MAYR's paper have a bearing on our subject, but as they are more "general" than specifically ecological I have decided to discuss them in this appendix, instead of incorporating them in the
paper.

MAYR starts with the old quarrel about the possibility of explaining
living beings and life processes causally in terms of physical and chemical
phenomena. Therefore it is obviously necessary to state what is meant by
"causality", and MAYR says: "Causality, no matter how it is defined in
terms of logic, is believed to contain three elements: (i) an explanation of
past events ("a posteriori causality"); (ii) prediction of future events; and
(iii) interpretation of teleological – that is "goal-directed" – phenomena".
He then proceeds to explain in which way biology can contribute to this
concept of causality. Biology is no uniform and unified science. It covers
two largely separate fields which differ in method, problems and basic concepts. These two fields are called "functional" and "evolutionary" biology.

"The functional biologist is vitally concerned with the operation and
interaction of structural elements, from molecules up to organs, and whole
individuals. His ever-repeated question is 'How?'

... The functional biologist attempts to isolate the particular component
he studies, and in any given study he usually deals with a single individual,
a single organ, a single cell, or a single part of a cell. He attempts to eliminate, or control, all variables and he repeats his experiments under constant
or varying conditions until he believes he has clarified the function of the
element he studies. The chief technique of the functional biologist is the
experiment, and his approach is essentially the same as that of the physicist
and the chemist ... In spite of certain limitations of this method, one must
agree with the functional biologist that such a simplified approach is an
absolute necessity for achieving his particular objectives".

"The evolutionary biologist differs in his method and the problems in which he is interested. His basic question is "Why?" This term is ambiguous – it may mean "What for?" and "How come?"

According to MAYR it is obvious that the evolutionist has the historical "How come?" in mind and not the finalistic "What for?" Apparently he thinks that the latter question is not interesting for the evolutionist. In my opinion this rejection does not apply to the whole of "evolutionary biology" because "What for?" can be a very meaningful and legitimate scientific question. This is even clear from MAYR's own words: in the course of his argument he says: "To find the *causes* for the existing characteristics and particularly *adaptations*, of organisms is the main preoccupation of the evolutionary biologists. He is impressed by the enormous diversity of the organic world. He wants to know the *reason* for this diversity as well as the *pathway*, by which it has been achieved" (italics mine).

In this paragraph MAYR clearly incorporates implicitly the "What for?" question in his "How come?" problem. That a "What for?" question, notwithstanding his earlier remarks, is for him legitimate is still more clear from his illustrative example of the difficulties of the concept of causality in biology. He writes: "Let us ask. . . . Why did the warbler on my summer place in New Hampshire start his southward migration on the night of the 25th of August?" and lists "four legitimate causes":

"1. *An ecological cause.* The warbler, being an insect eater, must migrate because it would starve to death if it should try to winter in New Hampshire".

This I would call an answer to the teleological "what for?" question. It is certainly not a "causal" explanation.

"2. *A genetic cause.* The warbler has acquired a genetic constitution in the course of the evolutionary history of its species which induces it to respond appropriately to the proper stimuli from the environment".

This is the answer to the historic-causal "how come?" question.

"3. *An intrinsic physiological cause.* The warbler flew south because its migration is tied in with photoperiodicity. It responds to the decrease in day length and is ready to migrate as soon as the number of hours of daylight have dropped below a certain level".

"4. *An extrinsic physiological cause.* Finally, the warbler migrated on the 25th of August because a cold air mass, with northerly winds, passed over our area that day. The sudden drop in temperature and the associated weather conditions affected the bird, already in a general physiological readiness for migration, so that it actually took off that particular day".

The first two "causes" are called "ultimate", the latter two are "proximate causes". The "ultimate causes have a history". "It is evident that the functional biologist would be concerned with analysis of the proximate causes, while the evolutionary biologist would be concerned with analysis of the ultimate causes".

As will be clear from this example, MAYR's concept "cause" is very broad. He even includes teleological explanations among the "causes". This incorporation does not clarify thinking about the different problems in biology, but I think we should consider it as a means to avoid the (wrong) impression that it would be MAYR's opinion that "goal-directed" phenomena cannot be explained causally. A teleological explanation can, however, never preclude a causal one.

The terms "functional" and "evolutionary" give rise to serious confusion, because other authors (see PITTENDRIGH, 1958) have used them in quite another meaning. PITTENDRIGH, following these authors, distinguishes three lines of explanation of biological phenomena open to the biologist. When dealing with the organization of a living system we may ask for:

1. *A causal analysis* of its operations. The answer is called the *physiological* explanation (This is the field of the *functional* biologist in the sense of MAYR). PITTENDRIGH says that no organization is ever fully explained by a causal analysis of its operations. The causal analysis leaves two fully meaningful questinos unanswered, namely the question of:

2. The *goal* of the organization. The answer to this question is called the *functional* explanation (This is the answer to the "What for?" question which was explicitly rejected by MAYR).

3. The *origin* of that information which underlies and causes the organization. The answer is called the *evolutionary* explanation (This is the field of the *evolutionary* biologist in the sense of MAYR).

The physiological explanation is called by others the "causal" explanation, but PITTENDRIGH prefers the former term because he wants to "avoid the possible overtone that "functional" and "evolutionary" explanation are antithetic to "causal". For those features of life at any horizon in time which demand functional and evolutionary explanation have developed by a process that is itself fully causal in the sense of being free from teleology".

On the subject of teleology PITTENDRIGH says: "It seems unfortunate that the term "teleology" should be resurrected ... The biologist's longstanding confusion would be more fully removed if all end-directed systems were described by some other term, like "teleonomic", in order to emphasize that the recognition and description of end-directedness does not carry a commitment to Aristotelian teleology as an efficient causal principle".

This proposal appears to be well worth considering.

References

ANDREWARTHA, H. G., and BIRCH, L. C. (1954): The distribution and abundance of animals. The University of Chicago Press.

ANDREWARTHA, H. G., and BROWNING, T. O. (1961): An analysis of the idea of „resources" in animal ecology. J. Theoret. Biol. 1, 83–97.

BAKKER, K. (1961): An analysis of factors which determine success in competition for food among larvae of *Drosophila melanogaster*. Arch. Néerl Zool. 14, 200–281.

BIRCH, L. C. (1957): The meanings of competition. Am. Nat. 91, 5–18.

BOER, P. J. DEN (1963): Pers. comm.

BRAUN-BLANQUET, J. (1928): Pflanzensoziologie.

BROWNING, T. O. (1962): The environments of animals and plants. J. Theoret. Biol. 2, 63—68.

CHAPMAN, R. N. (1931): Animal ecology. With especial reference to insects. McGraw Hill, New York & London.

CLEMENTS, F. E. (1905): Research methods in ecology. Lincoln, Nebraska.

— (1916): Plant succession. Carn. Inst. Wash. Publ. 242.

— (1931): The relict method in dynamic ecology. Jour. Ecol. 22, 39–68.

— (1949): Dynamics of vegetation. Wilson, New York.

CLEMENTS, F. E., and SHELFORD, V. E. (1939): Bio-ecology. Wiley & Sons, New York.

DU RIETZ, G. E. (1919): Referat: Clements, F. E. „Plant succession" 1916. Svensk Bot. Tidskr. 13, 117–121.

— (1921): Zur methodologischen Grundlagen der modernen Pflanzensoziologie. Uppsala.

EGLER, F. E. (1951): A commentary on American plant ecology, based on the textbooks of 1947–1949. Ecology **32**, 673–695.

FRANZ, J. (1961): Definitionen in der biologischen Schädlingsbekämpfung. Z. Pflanzenkrankh. Pflanzensch. **68**, 321–329.

— (1962): Definitions in biological control. XI. Int. Kongr. Entom., Wien, 1960, Bd. II, 670–674.

GAMS, H. (1918): Prinzipienfragen der Vegetationsforschung. Vierteljahrschr. Naturf. Ges. Zürich **63**, 293–493.

HEERING, H. (1956): Zur Biologie, Ökologie und zum Massenwechsel des Buchenprachtkäfers, *Agrilus viridis* (L.). Z. angew. Entom. **38**, 249–287 und **39**, 76–114.

HUFFAKER, C. B. (1958): The concept of balance in nature. Proc. Tenth. Int. Congr. Entom. **2**, 625–636.

KLAAUW, C. J. VAN DER (1936): Zur Aufteilung der Ökologie in Autökologie und Synökologie im Lichte der Ideen als Grundlage der Systematik der zoologischen Disziplinen. Acta Biotheoretica **2**, 195–241.

KLOMP, H. (1960): The concepts „similar ecology" and „competition" in animal ecology. Arch. Néerl. Zool. **14**, 90–102.

— (1962): The influence of climate and weather on the mean density level, the fluctuations and the regulation of animal populations. Arch. Néerl. Zool. **15**, 68–109.

KUENEN, D. J. (1954): Pers. comm.

— (1958): Some sources of misunderstandig in the theories of regulation of animal numbers. Arch. Néerl. Zool. **13**, Suppl. 1, 335–341.

LABEYRIE, V. (1963): Influence des hypothèses de travail sur la terminologie utilisée en dynamique des populations. IUFRO meeting, Lapland 1963.

LACK, D. (1954): The natural regulation of animal numbers. Clarendon Press, Oxford.

MAYR, E. (1961): Cause and effect in biology. Kinds of causes, predictability and teleology are viewed by a practising biologist. Science **134**, 1501–1506.

MILNE, A. (1957): Theories of natural control of insect populations. Cold Spring Harbor Symp. Quant. Biol. **22**, 253–271.

— (1961): Definition of competition among animals. Symp. Soc. Exp. Biol. **15**, Mechanisms in biological competition, 40–61.

— (1962): On a theory of natural control of insect population. J. Theoret. Biol. **3**, 19–50.

MORRIS, R. F. (1959): Single-factor analysis in population dynamics. Ecology **40**, 580–588.

NICHOLSON, A. J. (1933): The balance of animal populations. J. Anim. Ecol. **2**, 132–178.

— (1954): An outline of the dynamics of animal populations. Austr. J. Zool. **2**, 9–65.

— (1957): The self-adjustment of populations to change. Cold Spring Harbor Symp. Quant. Biol. **22**, 153–173.

— (1960): Mechanisms of population regulation and appropriate terminology. Paper presented to the Discussion Group Population Dynamics of the I. U. F. R. O., Zürich 1960.

ODUM, E. P. (1953): Fundamentals of ecology. Saunders, Philadelphia & London.

OOSTING, H. J. (1948): The study of plant communities. An introduction to plant ecology. Freeman, San Francisco.

ORIANS, G. H. (1962): Natural selection and ecological theory. Am. Nat. **96**, 257–264.

PARK, T. (1949): In Allee, et al.: Principles of animal ecology. Saunders, Philadelphia, London.

PEARCE, A. S. (1939): Animal ecology. McGraw Hill. New York & London.

PITTENDRIGH, C. S. (1958): Adaptation, natural selection and behavior. Behavior and evolution, edited by A. ROE and G. G. SIMPSON. Yale University Press.

RICHARDS, O. W. (1939): Review of „Animal Ecology" by A. S. Pearce. J. Anim. Ecol. **8**, 387–388.

— (1961): The theoretical and practical study of natural insect populations. Ann. Rev. Entom. **6**, 147–162.

SCHWENCKE, W. (1955): Ergebnisse und Aufgaben der ökologischen und biocönologischen Entomologie. 7. Wanderversamml. Deutscher Entomol. 8.–10. Sept. 1954, Berlin.

SCHWERDTFEGER, F. (1941): Über die Ursachen des Massenwechsels der Insekten. Z. ang. Entom. **28**, 254–303.

— (1958): Is the density of animal populations regulated by mechanisms or by chance? Proc. Tenth. Int. Congr. Entom. **4**, 115–122.

SOLOMON, M. E. (1949): The natural control of animal populations. J. Anim. Ecol. **18**, 1–35.

— (1955): Das Gleichgewicht von Insektenbevölkerungen und die chemische Schädlingsbekämpfung. Schädlingsvermehren als Folge von Insektizidbehandlung. Z. angew. Entomol. **37**, 110–121. Authorized translation by dr. J. Franz of the original paper in Chemistry & Industry (1953), 1143–1147.

— (1958): Meaning of density-dependence and related terms in population dynamics. Nature **181**, 1778–1781.

THOMPSON, W. R. (1929): On natural control. Parasitology **21**, 269–281.

— (1939): Biological control and the theories of the interactions of populations. Parasitology, **31**, 299–388.

— (1956): The fundamental theory of natural and biological control. Ann. Rev. Entom. **1**, 379–402.

ULLYETT, G. C. (1950): Competition for food and allied phenomena in sheep-blowfly populations. Phil. Trans. Roy. Soc. London, B: Biol. Sci. **234** (610), 77–174.

VARLEY, G. C. (1958): Meaning of density-dependence and related terms in population dynamics. Nature **181**, 1778–1781.

VARLEY, G. C., and GRADWELL, G. R. (1960): Key factors in population studies. J. Anim. Ecol. **29**, 399–401.

VOÛTE, A. D. (1946): Regulation of the density of the insect-populations in virgin-forests and cultivated woods. Arch. Néerl. Zool. **7**, 435–470.

WILBERT, H. (1959): Die langfristige Regulation von Insektenpopulationen. Verh. Deutsch. Zool. Ges. Münster 1959, 510–519.

— Über Festlegung und Einhaltung der mittleren Dichte von Insektenpopulationen. Z. Morph. Ökol. Tiere, **50**, 576–615.

12

Reprinted from *Am. Nat.* **101**(918):97–107 (1967)

THE "BALANCE OF NATURE" AND "POPULATION CONTROL"

P. R. EHRLICH* and L. C. BIRCH

Department of Biological Sciences, Stanford University, Stanford, California and
School of Biological Sciences, University of Sydney, Sydney, Australia

The idea that there is a "balance of nature" is commonly held by biologists. They feel that the organisms in a community are harmoniously adjusted to one another so that a state of dynamic equilibrium exists. In this equilibrium the numbers of the individuals of each species in the community remain relatively constant, and significant changes in numbers occur only when something upsets the natural "balance." This view of the "balance of nature" is perpetuated by popular magazines and nature films, and thus is part of the lore of the man-in-the-street. In our opinion, it is more difficult to explain why it persists in the writings of ecologists. In this paper we will first examine this idea as it appears in the ecological literature, and then present a realistic basis for models of "population control."

THE "BALANCE OF NATURE"

The existence of a supposed balance of nature is usually argued somewhat as follows. Species X has been in existence for thousands or perhaps millions of generations, and yet its numbers have never increased to infinity or decreased to zero. The same is true of the millions of other species still extant. During the next 100 years, the numbers of all these species will fluctuate; yet none will increase indefinitely, and only a few will become extinct. Furthermore, most species have at least some populations living in areas where they are well able to cope with the climate, yet even these populations never increase indefinitely. Such "observations" are made the basis for the statement that population size is "controlled" or "regulated," and that drastic changes in size are the results of upsetting the "balance of nature." Sometimes this is put in other ways, such as "on the average, the species just replaces its numbers in successive generations" or "on the average, the numbers of individuals over a long period of time are constant." An extreme version can be found in Slobodkin (1962, p. 46). "Despite this enormous variation in reproductive patterns, each female adult animal alive now—in every species, in almost every location—will be replaced by pre-

*National Science Foundation Senior Postdoctoral Fellow, University of Sydney, 1965–66.

cisely one female alive a generation from now. If this were not the case, the size of animal populations would be changing permanently and strikingly at a much greater rate than any existing evidence indicates.''

In this form, the ''balance of nature'' idea can be dealt with quite simply. Indeed, Slobodkin's statement may well be the most thoroughly falsified hypothesis still current in population biology. A survey of the literature fails to disclose a single case of a natural population behaving in the manner described. Even in those few situations in which the size of the population has been observed to remain relatively constant, ''precise'' one-for-one replacement does not occur.

A well-known statement about the balance of nature is ''population densities are continually changing, but their values tend to oscillate about a mean which is relatively stable, though itself subject to change'' (Smith, 1935, as quoted by Varley and Gradwell, 1958). Smith, unlike Slobodkin, at least recognized that numbers of organisms are continually changing; but the rest of his statement is almost meaningless for the following reasons. First, any set of values does not oscillate around a mean which is ''relatively stable.'' The values oscillate around a mean that is fixed. The only ways the mean can be subjected to change are by weighting values, adding values, or subtracting values (or, of course, by substituting a different kind of mean). Any set of numbers which is not generally increasing or decreasing will oscillate around its mean. This, indeed, is the total information content of the second part of Smith's statement. Second, Smith's statement has been taken to imply that mean population size has an objective existence separate from the observed population sizes. This cannot be so. Some have also implied that a population will ''strive'' to return to this ''mean.'' We are unable to attach any meaning to such an implication.

In saying that phrases such as ''balance of nature'' are rather meaningless, we are not denying that the numbers of some populations may be influenced by so-called ''regulatory factors,'' i.e., whose depressive effect on rate of increase is positively correlated with density (Solomon, 1964). We would deny that there is any convincing evidence that the numbers of all populations are primarily determined by density regulating factors. We do not deny the role such ''factors'' play in some populations. Indeed, it would be quite an interesting exercise as Solomon (1964, p. 9) suggests to measure the effects of density-regulating and nondensity-regulating factors in any particular case. There are substantial problems in designing practical tests of regulation in natural populations, but these may not be insurmountable. We would expect the role of regulatory factors to vary among species, among populations of the same species, and through time.

''BALANCE OF NATURE'' AND DECOMPOSERS

A deceptively different version of the ''balance of nature'' idea is presented in a well-known paper by Hairston, Smith, and Slobodkin (1960). This version has been accepted fairly widely without criticism except for a recent brief critique by Murdoch (1966) which appeared after a final draft of this manuscript had been completed. We agree with all of Murdoch's criticisms but would go further. It seems desirable to do this as Hairston and Smith in their brief reply to Murdoch's critique at the end of his paper "remain in complete disagreement." Hairston, Smith, and Slobodkin did not commence their argument with the constancy of numbers of organisms but with the constancy of the amount of organic matter on the earth. Organic matter does not appear to accumulate on the earth; there is no evidence of large amounts of fossil fuel being laid down, nor is the earth becoming a vast dung heap. So they infer that "the decomposers as a group must be food-limited, since by definition they comprise the trophic level which degrades organic debris." This is their starting point of a demonstration of "a pattern of population control in many communities which derives easily from a series of general, widely accepted observations." We are told further that, "The logic used is not easily refuted."

As we will show below, many of the "general, widely accepted observations" about different trophic levels, although they may be widely accepted, are quite likely wrong. We will further show that, even if these "widely accepted observations" are 100% accurate, the conclusions about "population control" stated in the summary of Hairston, Smith, and Slobodkin's paper, do not necessarily follow. This latter point is also made by Murdoch (1966).

In the passage quoted above, Hairston, Smith, and Slobodkin state that "the decomposers as a group must be food-limited . . . ." Unfortunately, they do not define what they mean by "food-limited." You could say that the Cabbage-white butterfly is food-limited because the world could be planted with more cabbages than it is; and if it were, there would be more individuals of the butterfly around. But this can hardly be their meaning of food-limited. Alternatively, it could mean that at all times decomposers are present in greater numbers than their food can support. Such cannot be the case, for then the rate of increase of these organisms would be always negative and they would become extinct. We presume they mean that, at some times, in almost all places, decomposers are in greater numbers than their food can support. Now this is certainly a possibility, but it is not the *only* possibility. We can construct alternative models.

1. The simplest alternative would be that the decomposers are "self-regulated" in the manner of an experimental grain weevil colony (e.g., Birch, 1953). The experiment commences with X grams of food in a vial together with a founding colony of beetles. Temperature and moisture are kept favorable. The food is replenished at regular intervals to the original quantity. The weevils increase rapidly until there are many of them in the vial. The experiment may be continued for years, yet the food is never completely used up between replenishings even though the beetles become very numerous. Factors other than the shortage of food limit the numbers of beetles. Mechanisms of "self-regulation," such as egg cannibalism, prevent the population from exhausting its food resource. The weevils do not die of starvation, yet the food resource does not accumulate. If food is added at a more rapid rate, the weevil colony grows larger; but food does not accumulate,

and weevils do not die of starvation. In short, the weevils are a model of a decomposer trophic level in which fossil fuel does not accumulate, and which is not "food-limited."

We have, of course, no basis for assuming that the weevil model can be used to generalize about the decomposer trophic level, any more than there is a basis for assuming that decomposers are "food-limited."

2. A second alternative model can be constructed on the following assumptions: (a) many different species of decomposers are involved in degrading organic matter in any one place, and (b) conditions favorable to one species may be unfavorable to another. Suppose that dead plants and animals are continually being deposited on a forest floor. Suppose, further, that some 100 different organisms are decomposers in the forest debris. It is realistic to assume that at some times organism A will be favored, at other times organism B will be favored, and so on. Suppose that in spring organism A increases in numbers and is then primarily responsible for the degradation of organic matter. But well before the organic matter is decomposed, the forest floor becomes too dry for A, which is killed off, except for some of its resistant spores. It is replaced by B, which is somewhat more resistant to dessication but less resistant to cold. Organism B, in turn, is replaced by C and D, which have somewhat different requirements, and so on throughout the year. Each population is prevented from continually increasing by the periodic arrival of unfavorable conditions. If conditions are unfavorable too long, the last spore may succumb and that population becomes extinct. It may then, of course, be replaced by another colony established by migrant spores. None of the populations of the 100 species are "food-limited," not one organism dies of starvation, food is continually added to the forest floor, and yet there is no significant accumulation of debris.

This sort of model is quite conceivable, but it is not at all favored by those ecologists who assume that all populations must be "controlled" by density-dependent factors.

This latter model can be made more realistic if the heterogeneity of the forest floor is taken into account. Different stages of the successional sequence would occur simultaneously at different places. Thus, A might persist in a moist depression, while C was building a large population at a nearby well-drained spot. The colony of species B might well become extinct when one area dried up completely; but, with the return of moisture, the colony of B in that area could quickly be reestablished by migration from the populations of B in places which remain moist throughout the year. This additional complexity in the model both increases the chance of survival of the species (though not of any particular local population), and also increases the probability that organic matter will not accumulate.

Finally, in our examination of this point let us ask the following question: What logical conclusions could be drawn if the present rate of accumulation of organic matter as fossil fuel was not "negligible"? The most likely conclusion would be that, in some manner, organic matter was being made rapidly unavailable to decomposers. This is the most likely explanation of past accumulations.

There would then be less food, not more food, available for the decomposers. This trend, if carried far enough, would increase the chances of decomposers running out of food. Hairston, Smith, and Slobodkin claim that nonaccumulation of fossil fuels means that decomposers as a group are "food-limited." This implies that if there were an accumulation of fossil fuel, then decomposers would not be "food-limited." As we have shown this does not follow.

There is, therefore, no compelling reason for making the assumption that decomposers are "food-limited" simply because organic matter does not seem to accumulate. Even if this assumption were in some sense correct, however, it tells us nothing about how populations of decomposers are "controlled" as Hairston, Smith, and Slobodkin claim. Suppose that there are 100 species of decomposers in a forest floor. According to Hairston, Smith, and Slobodkin at least one of them is "food-limited." Even if this were correct, the other 99 may be controlled by weather, predators, or they may be "self-regulated." This surely is not much of a contribution to the understanding of "population control."

"BALANCE OF NATURE" AND HERBIVORES AND CARNIVORES

What about the other trophic levels? Hairston, Smith, and Slobodkin assume that all green plants (producers) are "limited by their own exhaustion of a resource." As examples of their meaning of a resource, they mention water and light. Again, we must in part guess as to their meaning of "limited." In this case we will assume that they mean limited in density where weather is favorable, since weather is clearly one of the most potent factors limiting plant populations. The overall generalization of Hairston, Smith, and Slobodkin rests on the following two statements: (1) "cases of obvious depletion of green plants by herbivores are exceptions ..." and (2) "cases of obvious mass destruction by meteorological catastrophes are exceptional in most areas." Concerning (1), we can point to several cases where plants are known to be rare because of the presence of a successful herbivore in their environment. In each case, however, there is nothing "obvious" about the role the herbivore plays in keeping the plant rare. *Clidemia hirta* is relatively rare in the islands of Fiji. Its rarity is due to the herbivore *Liothrips urichi* which was introduced to Fiji from Hawaii. *Liothrips* is not common in Fiji today; it is not at all an obvious component in the environment of *Clidemia*. One would never guess from a casual visit that it keeps *Clidemia* rare. Nevertheless, *Clidemia* was abundant before *Liothrips* was introduced.

Similarly, a visitor to Eastern Queensland today would not guess that the rarity of Prickly-pear (*Opuntia*) was the direct result of the presence of an effective herbivore caterpillar, *Cactoblastis cactorum*, in its environment. One must search a great deal among the few *Opuntia* plants to find *Cactoblastis* today. Its role in keeping Prickly-pear rare is not at all obvious. Yet, we know the role of the herbivore because *Opuntia* covered thousands of square miles of Queensland before the caterpillar was introduced from South and Central America. Nor would a visit to South America today convince anyone that Prickly-pear is rare there because of a herbivore in its environment. We do not know enough about the effect of herbivores on the abundance of plants to say whether or not these examples are common. We must, however, avoid the simplistic assumption that because we do not see forest trees being defoliated before our eyes that herbivores are not a major factor in determining the density of plant populations. For instance, the most drastic effect of the grazing of game animals in East Africa and elsewhere is on young seedlings and may escape casual observation. This effect can be demonstrated by fencing off areas from game animals, or by otherwise reducing the herbivores. The great decline in numbers of rabbits in Australia following myxomatosis has had a dramatic effect in the regeneration of the native pine *Callitris* in Western New South Wales. Abundant evidence can be inferred on the important influence herbivores have had on plant evolution (e.g., Ehrlich and Raven, 1965). Any attempt to discount their influence on plant populations is, at best, premature.

Concerning the second statement of Hairston, Smith, and Slobodkin, we contend that weather may be primarily involved in determining the density of a plant population despite the absence of "obvious mass destruction by meteorological catastrophes." Two species of native palms are not uncommon in some places near Sydney, the Bangalow Palm, *Archontophoenix cunninghamiana,* and the Cabbage Tree Palm, *Livistona australis.* They are relatively common north of Sydney and are rare a little south of Sydney. Further south still they disappear. This is not due to a gradient in any resource. In the south, the weather is probably just too cold and the length of day too short for the plants to set seed. The chance of a seed germinating, of the seedling growing into a mature plant, and of the mature plant setting seed, becomes smaller and smaller as one proceeds south in Australia. This pattern of distribution is characteristic of many other species of rain forest trees in Australia. Similar changes in density doubtless occur in one place as the climate changes through relatively cool or warm periods. Again, the cause would not be obvious to the casual observer, especially in plants with a long length of life. Another of the many examples we could give is the distribution and abundance of the snow gum (*Eucalyptus pauciflora*) in the Australian Alps (Costin, 1954). On mountain slopes above the snow line, snow gums are common. However, in depressions on mountain slopes where cold air accumulates, the snow gums are sparse or absent altogether. They are not limited by resources, but simply by low temperature which kills the seedlings. A similar example is given by Watt (1950) for bracken, (*Pteridium aquilinum*) in England.

We do not deny that the density of plants may be limited by the amount of light or water available; numerous such cases have also been documented. We do deny that there is a basis for inferring that, in general, plants are "limited by their own exhaustion of a resource." We would suggest that there is only one way of knowing how plant populations in general are "limited." Having first defined "limited," it would then be necessary to sample a wide range of plant populations to see how they are "limited."

Turning to the trophic level of herbivores, Hairston, Smith, and Slobodkin further state "the usual condition is for populations of herbivores *not* to be limited by their food supply." They consider this to be a valid inference from the statement "causes of obvious depletion of green plants are exceptions...." As noted earlier, we must assume that Hairston, Smith, and Slobodkin do not refer to the meaning of "food-limited" that where there is no food for herbivores there are no herbivores. Presumably they mean that, in their view, it is rare for herbivores to reduce their food resources to the point where this reduction influences their chance to survive and multiply. With this we are inclined to agree, although one must be very careful in determining just what constitutes the "food supply." For instance, healthy Eucalypt trees may be a totally inadequate food for psyllids, which will starve to death in the presence of what appears to be a superabundant food supply (T.White, personal communication), or the spacing of plants may lead to starvation in the presence of food (Dethier, 1959). Furthermore, as Murdoch (1966) has noted, plants evolve characteristics, such as spines and secondary plant substances, that tend to prevent their being eaten (Ehrlich and Raven, 1965). However, if food does not ordinarily limit herbivore populations, what does? Hairston, Smith, and Slobodkin state that "although rigorous proof that herbivores are generally controlled by predation is lacking, supporting evidence is available, and the alternative hypothesis of control by weather leads to false or untenable implications." We would not deny that invasions, control of predators, and pesticides have given evidence that herbivore populations may be kept below a certain level by predators. When released from destruction by predators, introduced herbivores have increased and caused serious defoliation. But native species often do the same thing in the presence of their predators; this is well-documented, for instance, for forest Lepidoptera and grasshoppers. It is a basic error to assume that "control" by weather and "control" by predators are "alternative" hypotheses. There are others, some of which Murdoch (1966) lists and which we need not enumerate here. If we can draw any general conclusion from the work which has been done on natural populations, it is that single, neat "control" mechanisms are unlikely to explain fluctuations in the size of single populations, let alone numbers of all organisms of a trophic level.

Finally, Hairston, Smith, and Slobodkin assume that predators must generally be "food-limited." This conclusion falls down with the rest. There is no more reason to assume that predators are "food-limited" than to suppose that decomposers are "food-limited," or that herbivores are not "food-limited." The thesis of Hairston, Smith, and Slobodkin is an exercise based on premises which are very likely false. If they are indeed false, then the argument that rests on them is very likely false also. Even if the assumptions are completely true, however, it can be easily shown that conclusions on "population control" do not follow from them. This should be clear from the preceding discussion on decomposers.

"BALANCE OF NATURE" AND PERSISTENCE OF SPECIES

Following their argument about trophic levels, Hairston, Smith, and Slobodkin (1960, p. 424) draw the following conclusion: "Populations of producers, carnivores, and decomposers are limited by their respective resources in the classical density-dependent fashion.'' The literature on ''population control'' is so confused that it is not possible to assign a precise meaning to this statement. Considering the context of Hairston, Smith, and Slobodkin's paper, it seems safe to assume that their statement might be translated as follows: When populations at these three trophic levels grow too large, they begin to run out of energy or some essential resource. This leads to a decrease in numbers until resources are sufficiently abundant for the rate of increase once again to become positive. Thus, the population never becomes infinite, and rarely (perhaps in the case of catastrophe) becomes extinct.

Hairston, Smith, and Slobodkin make it clear that they consider it legitimate to argue logically from ''trophic level'' to ''population.'' But this procedure is not valid. In the first place, a ''trophic level'' exists only as an abstraction. As Murdoch (1966) has pointed out, tens of thousands of species of insects, for example, live in more than one trophic level; and, unlike populations, a trophic level has no properties that can be measured. Secondly, the argument from trophic level to population involves the idea that persistence of species can be used as an argument for ''population control.'' Since this proposition is one of the most common fallacies in population biology, we shall now examine it in some detail.

This is the supposition made by the so-called ''density-dependent'' school on ''population control.'' The basic idea of this school is that, for a species that persists, ''sooner or later'' or ''ultimately'' the density of the population is the determining factor in whether or not the rate of increase will be positive or negative. For this to be so, the size of the population must in some way affect the individuals in the population. Now, consideration of numbers of individuals in a species cannot ordinarily throw light on the question of density-dependence. To investigate this one must investigate changes in local populations. For example, satyrine butterflies of the species *Erebia magdalena* live, among other places, on rock slides in Alaska and in the Colorado Rockies. A population explosion in an Alaskan colony will have no effect on the Colorado colonies, and a Colorado extinction will not affect the Alaskan *Erebia magdalena*. Changes in the size of the Colorado population in no way affect the individuals in the Alaskan population, and vice versa. If we had mapped and censused all colonies of *Erebia magdalena*, we would know the population size for the species. But if we were magically handed the population size 2,328,456 for the species, we would know nothing about the sizes of the colonies. If we had information on rates of movement among colonies, and about the probabilities of colony extinction, we could make an estimate of the chance of species extinction per generation. But if we were told that the chance of species extinction was 10^{-7} per generation, we would know virtually nothing about the probabilities of extinction of individual colonies. In short, statements about species without reference to their component populations are unlikely to tell us much about ''population control.''

An example is the three populations of the checkerspot butterfly *Euphydryas editha* on Stanford University's Jasper Ridge Biological Experimental Area.

Over the five years 1960–64, a casual observer wandering along the ridge would find *E. editha* butterflies on the wing there every spring. "How precise is the control of natural populations" he might say, "for are there not butterflies here every year?" He might even guess at the number of butterflies present each year. He could then add up his estimates, divide by the number of years, and come up with an average adult population size. Superimposing this average on a chart of his yearly estimates he would find the average presented as a straight line parallel to the time axis. It could not, of course, be otherwise. "Nature" he would say, "keeps the average size of this population constant."

Only if our observer had taken the trouble to determine that the Ridge was actually occupied by three discrete populations of *E. editha* would he have found out what was actually going on; that, in fact, he had witnessed one population increase steadily in size, another fluctuate in size, and the third decrease to extinction (Ehrlich, 1965).

When movement of individuals is such that populations do not have clear-cut boundaries, then proper framing of questions concerning population size becomes much more difficult. It is nevertheless clear that careful consideration must be given to definition of the population units involved. A series of isolated populations with an array of different densities (including extinctions and reestablishment by migrants) may give the same superficial impression as a continuous population under rather tight "control." That is, to the casual observer, the species will be present each year. However, from the point of view of the way numbers change in nature, the two situations are entirely different.

It hardly seems necessary to add that the same arguments, which apply to statements made about population "control" on the basis of observations of species, apply even more forcefully to arguments drawn for all organisms at a particular trophic level.

A BASIS FOR MODELS OF "POPULATION CONTROL"

What, then, would be a reasonable set of propositions around which to build a theory concerned with the changes of numbers observed in populations?

The first might be a reversal of Slobodkin's statement quoted above. No female animal alive now, in any species or in any location, will be replaced by precisely one female alive a generation from now. A thorough search of the literature has failed to turn up a single case of exact replacement in a natural population, although admittedly the number of good studies is depressingly small. This surely is, however, a safer hypothesis than one which has been falsified in every single test known to us. The first proposition is, then, that all populations are constantly changing in size.

The second proposition is that the environments of organisms are constantly changing, with changes on different time scales (diurnal, seasonal, long-term, etc.) going on simultaneously.

The third proposition is that the local population, within which there is relatively free movement of individuals, must be recognized and investigated if changes in population size are to be understood. For example, if one is interested in the factors responsible for observed changes in numbers of individuals of a certain species, the first step in the investigation must be a study of the structure of the species population. Local populations must be identified by mapping, marking individuals, etc.; and some measure of the amount of migration among these populations must be obtained. The answer to the question at the "species level" will then be found in investigation of these local populations and the interactions among them.

The fourth proposition is that the influences of various components of the environment on population size will vary. That is, these components (weather, resources, etc.) will act differently on populations of different densities, on different populations of the same species, on populations of different species, and so on. Knowing what factors are primarily influencing the size of a Jasper Ridge *Euphydryas editha* population in 1966 will not necessarily tell us what the determinants of the size of that population will be in 1967. Nor will it necessarily tell us what factors are responsible for the size of the *E. editha* population at Woodside, California, in 1966. It is difficult enough to obtain the data necessary for generalizing about a single species, let alone for all the species at a particular trophic level. The most we can hope for in the way of broad generalizations are probabilistic statements such as "territorial animals are less likely to be limited by shortage of food than are non-territorial animals."

We are sympathetic with the goal of building simplified models to aid in our understanding of what determines the numbers of organisms. But such models are highly misleading if they are based on false assumptions and undefined terms such as "food-limited." It is our opinion that any realistic model must take into account the four propositions stated above. The necessary model will be stochastic, not deterministic. As digital computers become more sophisticated, it should be possible to advance from the pictorial model used by Andrewartha and Birch (1954, Chapter 14) to a more rigorous numerical treatment.

SUMMARY

1. The notion that nature is in some sort of "balance" with respect to population size, or that populations in general show relatively little fluctuation in size, is demonstrably false.

2. The thesis of Hairston, Smith, and Slobodkin that "populations of producers, carnivores, and decomposers are limited by their respective resources in the classical density-dependent fashion" is based on a series of assumptions about these trophic levels which are, in all probability, false. Even if the assumptions are true, this conclusion does not follow from them.

3. A realistic basis for building models dealing with the changes of numbers in populations would include the following propositions:

a. All populations are constantly changing in size.

b. The environments of all organisms are constantly changing.

c. Local populations must be recognized and investigated if changes in population size are to be understood.

d. The influence on population size of various components of environment varies with population density, among species, among local populations, and through time.

ACKNOWLEDGMENTS

The following persons read and criticized the manuscript, and we are grateful for their advice: Professor H. G. Andrewartha, University of Adelaide; Dr. M. A. Bateman, Joint Unit of Animal Ecology, University of Sydney; Professor LaMont C. Cole, Cornell University; Professors R. W. Holm and P. H. Raven, Stanford University; and Dr. P. A. Labine, University of Michigan.

LITERATURE CITED

Andrewartha, H. G., and L. C. Birch. 1954. The distribution and abundance of animals. Univ. of Chicago Press, Chicago. 782 p.

Birch, L. C. 1953. Experimental background to the study of distribution and abundance of insects. II. The relation between innate capacity for increase in numbers and the abundance of three grain beetles in experimental populations. Ecology 34:712–726.

Costin, A. B. 1954. A study of the ecosystems of the Monaro region of New South Wales. Soil Conservation Service, New South Wales. 860 p.

Dethier, V. G. 1959. Food-plant distribution and density and larval dispersal as factors affecting insect populations. Canadian Entomol. 91:581–596.

Ehrlich, P. R. 1965. The population biology of the butterfly *Euphydryas editha*. II. The structure of the Jasper Ridge Colony. Evolution 19:327–336.

Ehrlich, P. R., and P. H. Raven. 1965. Butterflies and plants: A study in coevolution. Evolution 18:586–608.

Hairston, N. G., F. E. Smith, and L. B. Slobodkin. 1960. Community structure, population control, and competition. Amer. Natur. 94:421–425.

Murdoch, W. W. 1966. Community structure, population control, and competition—a critique. Amer. Natur. 100:219–226.

Smith, H. S. 1935. The role of biotic factors in the determination of population densities. J. Econ. Entom. 28:873–898.

Slobodkin, L. B. 1962. Growth and regulation of animal populations. Holt, Rinehart, and Winston, New York. 184 p.

Solomon, M. E. 1964. Analysis of processes involved in the natural control of insects. Adv. Ecol. Res. 2:1–58.

Varley, G. C., and G. R. Gradwell. 1958. Balance in insect populations. Proc. Xth Int. Congr. Entomol. 2:619–624.

Watt, A. S. 1950. Contributions to the ecology of Bracken *Pteridium aquilinum*. V. Bracken and frost. New Phytol. 49:308–327.

Part V

BIOTIC MECHANISMS OF POPULATION REGULATION: PREDATION AND COMPETITION

Editor's Comments
on Papers 13 Through 16

PREDATION

This section, along with the next—which discusses competition—deals with particular theories of population regulation. While the general density-dependent/density-independent controversy may continue to some extent, there are particular instances where populations can be and are regulated by biotic, density-dependent factors. These studies are some of the more interesting that are encountered in the field of population ecology. While the weather can certainly regulate, if not cause, extinction of local populations (Ehrlich et al. 1972), biotic mechanisms of predation, competition, disease, and parasitism seem much more interesting to study. (Note that I am deferring until last the study of self-regulation, which is to me the most interesting method of regulation. We are in fact not only searching for the truth but also seeking the most interesting aspects of it.)

To me, biotic mechanisms are inherently more interesting than climatic mechanisms for two reasons. First, biotic mechanisms involve interactions of organisms that are inherently interesting to study. Second, biotic mechanisms are more subtle than abiotic mechanisms. Cold weather merely kills organisms; competition, on the other hand, can be scramble-type or contest-type. It also can concern any of a number of resources. But most important, its occurrence and effects are not self-evident. Weather can be freezing cold, but competition can be very subtle.

In this book, we are not setting aside particular sections for parasitism or disease. In some respects, disease is a cellular form of parasitism, and parasitism is merely predation where the predator is smaller than the prey. Pimentel (1963; 1966) has demonstrated stability in parasite systems as a function of heterogeneity in the environment, similar to what Gause (Paper 13) found in predator systems (see below).

From a theoretical viewpoint, the study of predation could be renamed "the quest for the periodic solution." Lotka (1925) and Volterra (1926) independently derived a set of equations showing how predator and prey populations will grow in each other's presence.

The predator–prey growth equations are as follows:

$$dN_1/dt = r_1N_1 - k_1N_1N_2 \quad \text{or } dN_1/N_1dt = r_1 - k_1N_2$$
$$dN_2/dt = k_2N_1N_2 - d_2N_2 \quad \text{or } dN_2/N_2dt = k_2N_1 - d_2$$

where N_2 = the number in the prey population
N_2 = the number in the predator population
r_1 = the intrinsic rate of prey increase
d_2 = the predator death rate
and
k_1, k_2 = predation constants

In these simple equations, an oscillation is established that neither converges nor diverges. That is, as the populations grow in each other's presence, first the prey increases, and with its increase, the predator population will increase because its food is increasing. Soon the predator population will overwhelm the prey population and cause it to decline. When the prey declines, the predator must also decline, and then the cycle repeats itself. Prima facie evidence for this cycle is the oscillation of predators and their prey, documented in fur returns of the Hudson Bay Company (Elton and Nicholson 1942). Biologists who tried to mimic this phenomenon in the laboratory ran into considerable difficulty, however.

Paper 13 is an excerpt from G. F. Gause's well-known *Struggle for Existence* (1934). Gause, whose principle of a competitive exclusion will be discussed in the next section, was a Russian biologist who attempted to test various ideas of competition and predation in the laboratory, primarily using microorganisms. In Paper 13 Gause shows the difficulty encountered in trying to produce a periodic oscillation in a test tube. He used *Paramecium* and its predator, *Didinium*. The only way to achieve success was to increase the "heterogeneity" of the environment by adding either a prey refuge or immigrants. Thus Gause believed that the theoretical oscillation could not be realized in nature without some sort of interference. Similar results were obtained by C. B. Huffaker (1958; Huffaker, Shea, and Herman 1963), who studied a system of mites; one was a predator of the other, which was phytophagous on oranges. By complex arrangements of oranges and by the use of various types of barriers, Huffaker was capable of generating oscillations. Here too we are dealing with refuges and migrants, however. In 1973, Ende demonstrated apparent stability in a very homogeneous culture vessel system. On closer examination, however, it appears that walls of the vessel can act as a refuge for bacteria. Apparently, the classical oscillation can be obtained, not as a result of the simple mathematics but rather as the result of interference: The prey must be allowed to keep one step ahead of the predators (see Murdoch and Oaten 1975 for a discussion and summary).

Rosenzweig and Mac Arthur present a further analysis of this problem, using graphical techniques, in Paper 14. They introduce the techniques of graphical analysis of predator–prey stability, and they deduce the way a community will interact by plotting the general form of the population densities of the two species. Lines are drawn, called isoclines, along whose locus of points the species will neither increase or decrease. By varying the conditions, and by noting whether populations are increasing or decreasing, it is possible to achieve interesting insights into the interactions of these populations. Rosenzweig and Mac Arthur added to Gause's conditions for the classical oscillation the importance of the regulation of the predator by more than just one prey resource.

Paper 15 is a classic paper by C. S. Holling, who analyzed the components of predation both with theory and with a study of three small mammal predators of the European pine sawfly. Solomon (1949) pointed out the difference between a functional and numerical response of predators to changing prey density; this dichotomy is a fundamental part of Holling's work (1961; 1963; Holling and Buckingham 1976). A numerical response occurs when the predator population enlarges as the prey enlarges. A functional response occurs when a single predator takes more prey when prey numbers increase. Holling believed both to be equally important to population regulation. Murdoch (1971) introduced the concept of a developmental response whereby a single predator grows in size as the prey increases and can thus eat more prey, as in a functional response.

The last paper in this section (Paper 16) is an article that recounts how a myth can be born. In this case the myth is the classical example of the balance produced between a predator and its prey. For many years the Kaibab deer story has been used as fact to illustrate what happens to a natural community when a predator is removed from a balanced system. In this case the pumas and coyotes that preyed on the Kaibab deer were removed. The basic problem, as analyzed originally by Caughley (1970) and pointed out in Paper 16, is that all the data are unreliable so that a myth about what has taken place has been disseminated by textbook writers. Burk's takehome lesson is caveat emptor, which is a good lesson any time. It is especially à propos when one deals with very old data.

The moose–wolf interaction on Isle Royale in Michigan may be another case in point. Mech (1966) documents a balance between the wolves and the moose, with both populations stable. More recent work seems to indicate that there is the possibility of errors in density estimates. In addition, recent density changes in both species may indicate an imbalanced system rather than a steady-state system (Belovsky, personal communication).

One more point. Earlier in these comments I referred to Elton's summary of some of the Hudson Bay Company data on Canadian fur returns, which included predators and prey (Elton and Nicholson 1942). I pointed out that there were cycles in the data of predators and their prey of the form predicted by theory. Several aspects need to be commented on. First, at best these data are correlative, not causal. That is, the predators can be cycling in response to an inherent prey cycle (see Parts VII and VIII). Second, the data base itself is biased. For example, the furs are a function of trapping effort, and trapping effort is a function of the value of certain species of fur pelts to the trappers. This point is discussed in more detail by Gilpin (1973).

The conclusion, then, is that theory predicts a classical oscillation, but practice has not found it commonly in nature. Predation can regulate a prey population, but whether predation actually regulates populations is still being vigorously debated (Pearson 1964; see Part VIII). It is important to examine specific cases each time, ensuring that the data are reliable.

COMPETITION

Since the Benchmark volume *Niche (Benchmark Papers in Ecology,* edited by Robert H. Whittaker and Simon A. Levin, 1975) deals with competition, I have not included any readings on this subject to avoid repeating much of what is covered there. However, let me just give a thumbnail sketch of the theory of competition as a regulating mechanism.

The key phrase in the study of competition has been the competitive exclusion principle. The original idea has been traced back to G. F. Gause's writing (Paper 13) and before that to Grinnell (1917), father of the niche concept. This principle, also called Gause's hypothesis, states that no two similar species can occupy the same niche forever. That is, sooner or later one will be victorious in competition and exclude the other.

At first, many laboratory and field studies were carried out to try to prove or disprove the competitive exclusion principle (Park 1948; Inger and Greenberg 1966; Istock 1966; Ayala 1971; etc.). These works proved valuable in dissecting interactions among species and in learning more about the ecology of interacting species. It soon became obvious, however, that the competitive exculsion principle cannot be disproved, for two reasons. First, we recognize more than one species, so there must be differences between them to begin with. Thus by the letter of Gause's hypothesis the groups are *not* similar to begin with. Second, when no differences are found between two closely related populations (assuming that could occur), the cynic can always contend that the investigator has not looked hard enough, and with further research, the critical differences will be uncovered.

In his *Geographical Ecology* (1972), Mac Arthur refers to Gause's hypothesis as obsolete. He suggests, however, that important work needs to be done to find out how much two species must differ in order to coexist. For example, Diamond (1973) found that for several species of New Guinea fruit pigeons to coexist, the larger birds must be about 1.5 times the size of the smaller ones. Mac Arthur has developed a simple model of competition where the degree of overlap is incorporated.

Mac Arthur points out that predation can influence a competitive community in either of two directions. On one hand, predators can increase the number of species living in an area by selectively eliminating the common species. For example, Janzen (1970) has given evidence that high species diversity of tropical trees is due to predation of the seeds, greatly lowering the probability for a seedling's survival near its parent. On the other hand, predators could eliminate species by their feeding habits (Patrick 1970). Thus while predation may limit the population of a given species, it also can disrupt the effects of competition. The interaction of predation and competition is clearly shown in work on intertidal invertebrate communities (Connell 1961; Menge 1976). The graphical analysis of competition is found in Mac Arthur (1958) and Slobodkin (1966).

REFERENCES

Ayala, F. J. 1971. Competition Between Species: Frequency Dependence. *Science* **171**:820–824.

Caughley, G. 1970. Eruption of Ungulate Populations, with Emphasis on Himalayan Thar in New Zealand. *Ecology* **51**:53–72.

Connell, J. H. 1961. The influence of Interspecific Competition and Other Factors on the Distribution of the Barnacle *Chthamalus stellatus*. *Ecology* **42**:710–723.

Diamond, J. M. 1973. Distributional Ecology of New Guinea Birds. *Science* **179**:759–769.

Ehrlich, P. R., D. Breedlove, P. Brussard, and M. Sharp. 1972. Weather and the "Regulation" of Subalpine Populations. *Ecology* **53**:243–247.

Elton, C., and M. Nicholson. 1942. The Ten-year Cycle in Numbers of the Lynx in Canada. *J. Anim. Ecol.* **11**:215–244.

Ende, P. van den. 1973. Predator–Prey Interactions in Continuous Culture. *Science* **181**:562–564.

Gilpin, M. E. 1973. Do Hares East Lynx? *Am. Nat.* **107**:727–730.

Grinnell, J. 1917. The Niche-Relationships of the California Thrasher. *Auk* **34**:427–433.

Holling, C. S. 1961. Principles of Insect Predation. *Ann. Rev. Ent.* **6**:163–182.

Holling, C. S. 1963. An Experimental Component Analysis of Population Processes. *Mem. Ent. Soc. Can.* **32**:22–32.

Holling, C. S., and S. Buckingham. 1976. A Behavioral Model of Predator–Prey Functional Responses. *Behav. Sci.* **21**:183–195.

Huffaker, C. B. 1958. Experimental Studies on Predation: Dispersion Factors and Predator–Prey Oscillations. *Hilgardia* **27**:343–383.

Huffaker, C. B., K. Shea, and S. Herman. 1963. Experimental Studies on Predation: Complex Dispersion and Levels of Food in an Acarine Predator–Prey Interaction. *Hilgardia* **34**:305–330.

Inger, R., and B. Greenberg. 1966. Ecological and Competitive Relations Among Three Species of Frogs (Genus *Rana*). *Ecology* **47**:746–759.

Istock, C. A. 1966. Distribution, Coexistence, and Competition of Whirligig Beetles. *Evolution* **20**:211–234.

Janzen, D. H. 1970. Herbivores and the Number of Tree Species in Tropical Forests, *Am. Nat.* **104**:501–529.

Lotka, A. J. 1925. Elements of Physical Biology. Baltimore: Williams and Wilkins.

Mac Arthur, R. H. 1958. Population Ecology of Some Warblers of Northeastern Coniferous Forests. *Ecology* **39**:599–619.

Mac Arthur, R. H. 1972. *Geographical Ecology*. New York: Harper & Row.

Mech, L. D. 1966. The Wolves of Isle Royale. Washington, D.C.: U.S. Govt. Printing Office.

Menge, B. A. 1976. Organization of the New England Rocky Intertidal Community: Role of Predation, Competition, and Environmental Heterogeneity. *Ecol. Monogr.* **46**:355–393.

Murdoch, W. W. 1971. The Developmental Response of Predators to Changes in Prey Density. *Ecology* **52**:132–137.

Murdoch, W. W., and A. Oaten. 1975. Predation and Population Stability. *Adv. Ecol. Res.* **9**:1–125.

Park, T. 1948. Experimental Studies of Interspecies Competition, I: Competition Between Populations of the Flour Beetles, *Tribolium confusum* Duval and *Tribolium castaneum* Herbst. *Ecol. Monogr.* **18**: 265–307.

Patrick, R. 1970. Benthic Stream Communities. *Am. Sci.* **58**:546–549.

Pearson, O. P. 1964. Carnivore–Mouse Predation: An Example of Its Intensity and Bioenergetics. *J. Mamm.* **45**:177–188.

Pimentel, D. 1963. Introducing Parasites and Predators to Control Native Pests. *Can. Ent.* **95**:785–792.

Pimentel, D. 1966. Wasp Parasite *(Nasonia vitripennis)* Survival on Its Housefly Host *(Musca domestica)* Reared on Various Foods. *Ann. Ent. Soc. Amer.* **59**:1031–1037.

Slobodkin, L. B. 1966. *Growth and Regulation of Animal Populations.* New York: Holt, Rinehart and Winston.

Solomon, M. E. 1949. The Natural Control of Animal Populations. *J. Anim. Ecol.* **18**:1–35.

Volterra, V. 1926. Fluctuations in the Abundance of a Species Considered Mathematically. *Nature* **118**:558–560.

13

Reprinted from pp. 114–128 of *The Struggle for Existence*, G. F. Gause, Hafner Publishing Co., 1934, 163 pp.

THE DESTRUCTION OF ONE SPECIES BY ANOTHER

G. F. Gause

I

(1) In the two preceding chapters our attention has been concentrated on the indirect competition, and we have to turn now to an entirely new group of phenomena of the struggle for existence, that of one species being directly devoured by another. The experimental investigation of just this case is particularly interesting in connection with the mathematical theory of the struggle for existence developed on broad lines by Vito Volterra. Mathematical investigations have shown that the process of interaction between the predator and the prey leads to periodic oscillations in numbers of both species, and all this of course ought to be verified under carefully controlled laboratory conditions. At the same time we approach closely in this chapter to the fundamental problems of modern experimental epidemiology, which have been recently discussed from a wide viewpoint by Greenwood in his Herter lectures of 1931. The epidemiologists feel that the spread of microbial infection presents a particular case of the struggle for existence between the bacteria and the organisms they attack, and that the entire problem must pass from the strictly medical to the general biological field.

(2) As the material for investigation we have taken two infusoria of which one, *Didinium nasutum*, devours the other, *Paramecium caudatum* (Fig. 27). Here, therefore, exists the following food chain: bacteria → *Paramecium* → *Didinium*. This case presents a considerable interest from a purely biological viewpoint, and it has more than once been studied in detail (Mast ('09), Reukauf ('30), and others). The amount of food required by *Didinium* is very great and, as Mast has shown, it demands a fresh *Paramecium* every three hours. Observation of the hunting of *Didinium* after the Paramecia has shown that *Didinium* attacks all the objects coming into contact with its seizing organ, and the collision with suitable food is simply due to chance (Calcins '33). Putting it into the words of Jennings ('15) *Didinium* simply "proves all things and holds fast to that which is good."

All the experiments described further on were made with pure lines of *Didinium* ("summer line") and *Paramecium*. In most of the experiments the nutritive medium was the oaten decoction, "with sediment" or "without sediment," described in the preceding chapter. Attempts were also made to cultivate these infusoria on a synthetic medium with an exactly controlled number of bacteria for the Paramecia, but here we encountered great difficulties in connection with differences in the optimal physicochemical conditions for our lines of *Paramecium* and *Didinium*. The introduction of a phosphate buffer and the increase of the alkalinity of the medium above pH =

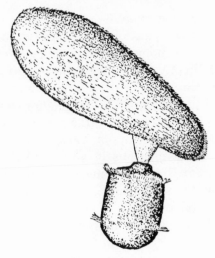

Fig. 27. *Didinium nasutum* devouring *Paramecium caudatum*

6.8–7.0 has invariably favored the growth of *Paramecium*, but hindered that of *Didinium*. Satisfactory results have been obtained on Osterhout's medium, but here also *Didinium* has grown worse than on the oaten medium. Therefore, absolute values of growth under different conditions can not be compared with one another though all the fundamental laws of the struggle for existence remained the same. The experiments were made in a moist thermostat at a temperature of 26°C.

(3) Let us first of all analyze the process of interaction between the predator and the prey from a qualitative point of view. It is well known that under natural conditions periodic oscillations in the numbers of both take place but in connection with the complexity of the

situation it is difficult to draw any reliable conclusions concerning the causes of these oscillations. However, quite recently Lotka (1920) and Volterra (1926) have noted on the basis of a purely mathematical investigation that the properties of a biological system consisting of two species one of which devours the other are such that they lead to periodic oscillations in numbers (see Chapter III). These oscillations should exist when all the external factors are invariable, because they are due to the properties of the biological system itself. The periods of these oscillations are determined by certain initial conditions and coefficients of multiplication of the species. Mathematicians arrived at this conclusion by studying the properties of the differential equation for the predator-prey relations which has already been discussed in detail in Chapter III (equation 21a). Let us now repeat in short this argument in a verbal form. When in a limited microcosm we have a certain number of prey (N_1), and if we introduce predators (N_2),[1] there will begin a decrease in the number of prey and an increase in that of the predators. But as the concentration of the prey diminishes the increase of the predators slows down, and later there even begins a certain dying off of the latter resulting from a lack of food. As a result of this diminution in the number of predators the conditions for the growth of the surviving prey are getting more and more favorable, and their population increases, but then again predators begin to multiply. Such periodic oscillations can continue for a long time. *The analysis of the properties of the corresponding differential equation* shows that one species will *never be capable of completely destroying another:* the diminished prey will not be entirely devoured by the predators, and the starving predators will not die out completely, because when their density is low the prey multiply intensely and in a certain time favorable conditions for hunting them arise. Thus *a population consisting of homogeneous prey and homogeneous predators in a limited microcosm, all the external factors being constant, must according to the predictions of the mathematical theory possess periodic oscillations in the numbers of both species.*[2] These oscillations may be

[1] It is assumed that all individuals of prey and predator are identical in their properties, in other words, we have to do with homogeneous populations.

[2] According to the theory, such oscillations must exist in the case of one component depending on the state of another at the same moment of time, as well as in the case of a certain delay in the responses of one species to the changes of the other.

called "innate periodic oscillations," because they depend on the properties of the predator-prey relations themselves, but besides these under the influence of periodic oscillations of external factors there generally arise "induced periodic oscillations" in numbers depending on these external causes. The classic example of a system which is subject to innate and induced oscillations is presented by the pendulum. Thus the ideal pendulum the equilibrium of which has been disturbed will oscillate owing to the properties of this system during an indefinitely long time, if its motion is not impeded. But in addition to that we may act upon the pendulum by external forces, and thereby cause induced oscillations of the pendulum.

If we are asked what proof there is of the fact that the biological system consisting of predator-prey actually possesses "innate" periodic oscillations in numbers of both species, or in other terms that the equation (21a) holds true, we can give but one answer: observations under natural conditions are here of no use, as in the extremely complex natural environment we do not succeed in eliminating "induced" oscillations depending on cyclic changes in climatic factors and on other causes. Investigations under constant and exactly controlled laboratory conditions are here indispensable. Therefore, in experimentation with two species of infusoria one of which devours the other the following question arose at the very beginning: does this system possess "innate" periodic oscillations in numbers, which are to be expected according to the mathematical theory?

(4) The first experiments were set up in small test tubes with 0.5 cm³ of oaten medium (see Chapter V). If we take an oaten medium without sediment, place in it five individuals of *Paramecium caudatum*, and after two days introduce three predators *Didinium nasutum*, we shall have the picture shown in Figure 28. After the predators are put with the Paramecia, the number of the latter begins to decrease, the predators multiply intensely, devouring all the Paramecia, and thereupon perish themselves. This experiment was repeated many times, being sometimes made in a large vessel in which there were many hundreds of thousands of infusoria. The predator was introduced at different moments of the growth of population of the prey, but nevertheless the same result was always produced. Figure 29 gives the curves of the devouring of Paramecia by *Didinium* when the latter are introduced at different moments of the growth of the prey population (in 0.5 cm³ of oaten medium without

sediment). This figure shows the decrease in the number of Paramecia as well as the simultaneous increase in number and in volume
of the population of *Didinium*. (We did not continue these curves
beyond the point where *Didinium* attained its maximal volume.) It
is evident that the Paramecia are devoured to the very end. As it is
necessary that the nutritive medium should contain a sufficient
quantity of bacteria in order to have an intense multiplication of
Paramecia, we arranged also experiments in the test tubes on a daily
changed Osterhout's medium containing *Bacillus pyocyaneus* (see
Chapter V). In Figure 30 are given the results of such an experiment which has led up, as before, to the complete disappearance of
both *Paramecium* and *Didinium*. Thus we see that in a homogeneous

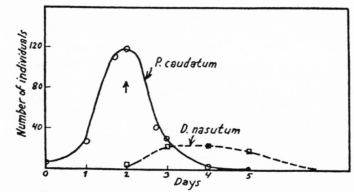

FIG. 28. The elementary interaction between *Didinium nasutum* and *Paramecium caudatum* (oat medium without sediment). Numbers of individuals
pro 0.5 c.c. From Gause ('35a).

nutritive medium under constant external conditions the system
Paramecium-Didinium has no innate periodic oscillations in numbers.
In other words, *the food chain:* bacteria → *Paramecium* → *Didinium*
placed in a limited microcosm, with *the concentration of the first link
of the chain kept artificially at a definite level, changes in such a direction that the two latter components disappear entirely and the food resources of the first component of the chain remain without being utilized
by any one.*

We have yet to point out that the study of the properties of the
predator-prey relations must be carried out under conditions favorable for the multiplication of both prey and predator. In our case,
there should be an abundance of bacteria for the multiplication of

Paramecia, and suitable physicochemical conditions for the very sensitive *Didinium*.   It is self-evident that if at the very beginning

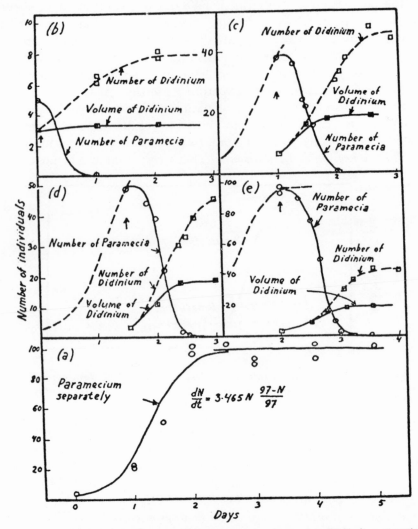

Fig. 29. The destruction of *Paramecium caudatum* by *Didinium nasutum*. (a) Growth of *P. caudatum* alone.   (b) *Didinium* is introduced at the very beginning of growth of Paramecia population.   (c) *Didinium* is introduced after 24 hours.   (d) *Didinium* is introduced after 36 hours.   (e) *Didinium* is introduced after 48 hours.   Numbers of individuals pro 0.5 c.c.

we set up unfavorable conditions under which *Didinium* begins to degenerate, and as a result is unable to destroy all the prey, or if the diminishing prey should perish not in consequence of their having been devoured by the predators but from other causes, we could not be entitled to draw any conclusions in respect to the properties of the predator-prey relations in the given chain.

(5) We may be told that after we have "snatched" two components out of a complex natural community and placed them under "artificial" conditions, we shall certainly not obtain anything valuable and shall come to absurd conclusions. We will therefore point out beforehand that under such conditions it is nevertheless possible to obtain periodic oscillations in the numbers of the predators and prey, if we but introduce some complications into the arrangement of the

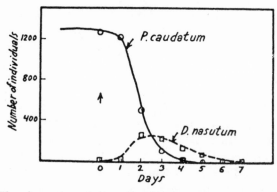

Fig. 30. The elementary interaction between *Didinium nasutum* and *Paramecium caudatum* (medium of Osterhout). The environment is not completely favorable for *Didinium*, and it begins to die out too early. Numbers of individuals pro 5 c.c. From Gause ('35a).

experiments. As yet we have only separated the elementary interaction between two species, and noted some of its fundamental properties.

However, why is the theoretical equation of the mathematicians not realized in our case? The cause of this is apparently that a purely biological property of our predator has not been taken into account in the equation (21a). According to this equation a decrease in the concentration of the prey diminishes the probability of their encounters with the predators, and causes a sharp decrease in the multiplication of the latter, and afterwards this even leads to their partly dying out. However, in the actual case *Didinium* in spite of the insufficiency of food continues to multiply intensely at the expense of a vast decrease in the size of the individual.   The following data give an idea of the diminution in size of *Didinium*: three normal individuals of this species placed in a medium free of Paramecia continue to multiply intensely, and in an interval of 24 hours give on an average 7.1 small individuals able to attack the prey.   This vast increase of the "seizing surface" represents, metaphorically speaking, those "tentacles by means of which the predators suck out the prey completely."   Translating all this into mathematical language, we can say: the function characterizing the consumption of prey by predators $[f_1(N_1, N_2)]$, as well as the natality and the mortality of predators $[F(N_1, N_2)]$,* are apparently more complicated than Lotka and Volterra have assumed in the equation (21a), and as a result the corresponding process of the struggle for existence has no periodic properties.   We shall soon return to a further analysis of this problem along mathematical lines.

II

(1) We have but to introduce a slight complication into the conditions of the experiment, and all the characteristic properties of our biological system will be altogether changed.   In order to somewhat approach natural conditions we have introduced into the microcosm a "refuge" where Paramecia could cover themselves.   For this purpose a dense oaten medium "with sediment" was taken (see Chapter V).   Direct observations have shown that while the Paramecia are covered in this sediment they are safe from the attack of predators. It must be noted that the *taxis causing the hiding of Paramecia in this "refuge" manifests itself in a like manner in the presence of the predators as in their absence.*

We must have a clear idea of the rôle which a refuge plays in the struggle for existence of the species under observation, as a lack of clearness can lead further on to serious misunderstandings.   If *Didinium* actively pursued a definite *Paramecium* which escaping from it hid in the refuge, the presence of the refuge would be a definite parameter in every elementary case of one species devouring another. In other words, the nature and the distribution of refuges would constitute an integral part of the expressions $f_1(N_1, N_2)$ and $F(N_1, N_2)$ of the corresponding differential equation of the struggle for existence.

* See Chapter III, equation (21).

Such a situation has recently been analyzed by Lotka ('32a). We might be told in this case that in experimenting with a homogeneous microcosm *without refuges* we have sharply disturbed the process of elementary interaction of two species. Instead of investigating "in a pure form" the properties of the differential equation of the struggle for existence we obtain a thoroughly unnatural phenomenon, and all the conclusions concerning the absence of innate oscillations in numbers will be entirely unconvincing. But for our case this is not true. We have already mentioned that *Dininium* does not actively hunt for Paramecia but simply seizes everything that comes in its way. In its turn *Paramecium* fights with the predator by throwing out trichocysts and developing an intense rapidity of motion, but *never hiding in this connection in the refuge of our type.* In this manner, we have actually isolated and studied "in a pure form" the elementary phenomenon of interaction between the prey and the predators in a homogeneous microcosm. The refuge in our experiment presents a peculiar "semipermeable membrane," separating off a part of the microcosm into which *Paramecium* can penetrate owing to its taxis, *in general quite independently of any pursuit of the predator*, and which is impenetrable for *Didinium*.

When the microcosm contains a refuge the following picture can be observed (see Fig. 31): if *Paramecium* and *Didinium* are simultaneously introduced into the microcosm, the number of predators increases somewhat and they devour a certain number of Paramecia, but a considerable amount of the prey is in the refuge and the predators cannot attain them. Finally the predators die out entirely owing to the lack of food, and then in the microcosm begins an intense multiplication of the Paramecia (no encystment of *Didinium* has been observed in our experiments). We must make here a technical note: the microcosm under observation ought not to be shaken in any way, as any shock might easily destroy the refuge and cause the Paramecia to fall out. On the whole it may be noted that when there appears a refuge in a microcosm, a certain threshold quantity of the prey cannot be destroyed by the predators. The elementary process of predator-prey interaction goes on to the very end, but the presence of a certain number of undestroyed prey in the refuge creates the possibility of the microcosm becoming later populated by the prey alone.

(2) Having in the experiment with the refuge made the microcosm a heterogeneous one, we have acquired an essential difference of the

corresponding process of the struggle for existence from all the elementary interactions between two species which we have so far examined. In the case of an elementary interaction between predator and prey in a homogeneous microcosm very similar results were obtained in various analogous experiments (see Table 6, Appendix). In any case the more attention we give to the technique of experimentation, the greater will be this similarity. In other terms, in a homogeneous microcosm the process of the struggle for existence in every individual test tube was exactly determined by a certain law, and this could be expressed by more or less complex differential equa-

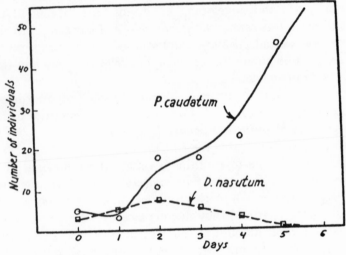

Fig. 31. The growth of mixed population consisting of *Didinium nasutum* and *Paramecium caudatum* (oat medium with sediment). Numbers of individuals pro 0.5 c.c.

tions. For every individual microcosm the quantities of the predator and the prey at a certain time t could be exactly predicted with a comparatively small probable error.

Such a deterministic process disappears entirely when a refuge is introduced into the microcosm, because the struggle for existence is here affected by a multiplicity of causes. If we take a group of microcosms with similar initial conditions the following picture is observed after a certain time: (1) in some of the microcosms in spite of the existence of a refuge all the prey are entirely devoured (they might have accidentally left the refuge, hidden inadequately, etc.).

Or else (2) as shown in Figure 31 a certain number of prey might have in the refuge been entirely out of reach of the predators, and the latter will perish finally from lack of food. (3) Lastly, prey may from time to time leave the refuge and be taken by the predators; as a result a mixed population consisting of prey and predators will continue to exist for a certain time. All this depends on the circumstance that in our experiments the absolute numbers of individuals were not large, and the amplitude of fluctuations connected with multiplicity of causes proved to be wider than these numbers.

(3) Let us consider the corresponding data. In one of the experiments 30 microcosms were taken (tubes with 0.5 cm³ of oaten medium with sediment), in each of them five *Paramecium* and three *Didinium* were placed, and two days after the population was counted. It turned out that in four microcosms the predators had entirely destroyed the prey whilst in the other 26 there were predators as well as prey. The number of prey fluctuated from two to thirty-eight. In another experiment 25 microcosms were examined after six days; in eight of them the predators had died out entirely and prey alone remained. Therefore, in the initial stage for every individual microcosm we can only affirm with a probability of $\frac{8}{25}$ that it will develop in the direction indicated in Figure 31. Certain data on the variability of populations in individual microcosms are to be found in Table 7 (Appendix). Further experimental investigations are here necessary. First of all we had to do with too complicated conditions in the microcosms owing to variability of refuges themselves. It is not difficult to standardize this factor and to analyze its rôle more closely.

In concluding let us make the following general remarks. When the microcosm approaches the natural conditions (variable refuges) in its properties, the struggle for existence begins to be controlled by such a multiplicity of causes that we are unable to predict exactly the course of development of each individual microcosm.[3] From the language of rational differential equations we are compelled to pass on to the language of probabilities, and there is no doubt that the corresponding mathematical theory of the struggle for existence may be developed in these terms. The physicists have already had to

[3] This means only that the development of each individual microcosm is influenced by a multiplicity of causes, and it would be totally fallacious to conclude that it is not definitely "caused." All our data have of course no relation to the concept of phenomenal indeterminism.

face a similar situation, and it may be of interest to quote their usual remarks on this subject: "Chance does not confine itself here to introducing small, practically vanishing corrections into the course of the phenomenon; it entirely destroys the picture constructed upon the theory and substitutes for it a new one subordinated to laws of its own. In fact, if at a given moment an extremely small external factor has caused a molecule to deviate very slightly from the way planned for it theoretically, the fate of this molecule will be changed in a most radical manner: our molecule will come on its way across a great number of other molecules which should not encounter it, and at the same time it will elude a series of collisions which should have taken place theoretically. All these 'occasional' circumstances in their essence are regular and determined, but as they do not enter into our theory they have in respect to it the character of chance" (Chinchin, '29, pp. 164–165).

(4) If we take a microcosm without any refuge wherein an elementary process of interaction between *Paramecium* and *Didinium* is realized, and if we introduce an artificial immigration of both predator and prey at equal intervals of time, there will appear periodic oscillations in the numbers of both species. Such experiments were made in glass dishes with a flat bottom into which 2 cm³ of nutritive liquid were poured. The latter consisted of Osterhout's medium with a two-loop concentration of *Bacillus pyocyaneus*, which was changed from time to time. The observations in every experiment were made on the very same culture, without any interference from without (except immigration) into the composition of its contents. At the beginning of the experiment and every third day thereafter one *Paramecium* + one *Didinium* were introduced into the microcosm. The predator was always taken when already considerably diminished in size; if it did not find any prey within the next 12 hours, it usually degenerated and perished. Figure 32 represents the results of one of the experiments. Let us note the following peculiarities: (1) At the first immigration into the microcosm containing but few Paramecia the predator did not find any prey and perished. An intense growth of the prey began. (2) At the time of the second immigration the concentration of the prey is already rather high, and a growth of the population of the predator begins. (3) The third immigration took place at the moment of an intense destruction of the prey by the predators, and it did not cause any essential changes. (4) Towards

the time of the fourth immigration the predator had already devoured all the prey, had become reduced in size and degenerated. The prey introduced into the microcosm originates a new cycle of growth of the prey population. Such periodic changes repeat themselves further on.

Comparing the results of different similar experiments with immigration made in a homogeneous microcosm, we come to the same conclusions as in the preceding paragraph. Within the limits of each cycle when there is a great number of both *Paramecium* and *Didinium* it is possible by means of certain differential equations to predict the course of the process of the struggle for existence for some time to

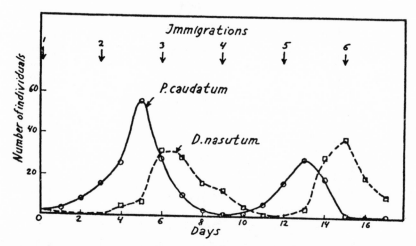

Fig. 32. The interaction between *Didinium nasutum* and *Paramecium caudatum* in a microcosm with immigrations (1 *Didinium* + 1 *Paramecium*). Causes of too low peak of *Didinium* in the first cycle of growth are known. From Gause ('34a).

come. However, at the critical moments, when one cycle of growth succeeds another, the number of individuals being very small, "multiplicity of causes" acquires great significance (compare first and second cycles in Fig. 32). As a result it turns out to be impossible to forecast exactly the development in every individual microcosm and we are again compelled to deal only with the probabilities of change.

(5) Let us briefly sum up the results of the *qualitative analysis* of the process of destruction of one species by another in a case of two infusoria. The data obtained are schematically presented in Figure

33. In a homogeneous microcosm the process of elementary inter-action between the predator and the prey led up to the disappearance of both the components. By making the microcosm heterogeneous

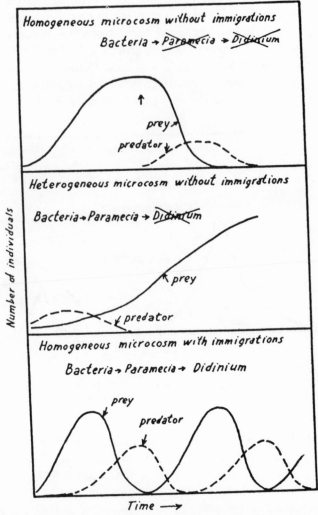

Fig. 33. A schematic representation of the results of a qualitative analysis of the predator-prey relations in the case of two Infusoria.

(refuge) and thus approaching the natural conditions we began to deal with a "probability" of change in various directions. The preda-tor sometimes dies out and only prey populate the microcosm. By introducing immigration into a homogeneous microcosm we obtain periodic oscillations in the numbers of both species.

[*Editor's Note:* In the original, material follows this excerpt.]

BIBLIOGRAPHY

[*Editor's Note:* Bibliography has been abridged to include only those references cited in the excerpt.]

19. CALCINS, G. N. 1933 The biology of Protozoa. Second Edition.
22. CHINCHIN, A. J. 1929 The principles of physical statistics. Progr. Phys. Sci. 9, p. 141 (in Russian).
45. GAUSE, G. F. 1934a. Experimental analysis of Vito Volterra's mathematical theory of the struggle for existence. Science. 79, p. 16.
49. GAUSE, G. F. 1935a Untersuchungen über den Kampf ums Dasein bei Protisten. Biol. Zentralbl. 55 (in press) also in Revue Zool. Russe, 13, p. 18 (1934).
56. GREENWOOD, M. 1932 Epidemiology. Historical and experimental. Baltimore.
65. JENNINGS, H. S. 1915 Behavior of the lower organisms. New York.
81. LOTKA, A. J. 1920a Undamped oscillations derived from the law of mass action. Journ. Americ. Chem. Soc. 52, p. 1595.
82. LOTKA, A. J. 1920b Analytical note on certain rhythmic relations in organic systems. Proc. Natl. Acad. 6, p. 410.
86. LOTKA, A. J. 1932a Contribution to the mathematical theory of capture. I. Conditions for capture. Proc. Nat. Ac. Sci. 18, p. 172.
91. MAST, S. O. 1909 The reactions of Didinium nasutum with special reference to the feeding habits and the function of trichocysts. Biol. Bull. 16, p. 91.
105. REUKAUF, E. 1930 Zur Biologie von Didinium nasutum. Zeitschr. Vergl. Physiol. 11, p. 689.
131. VOLTERRA, V. 1926 Variazioni e fluttuazioni del numero d'individui in specie animali conviventi. Mem. R. Accad. Naz. dei Lincei. Ser. VI, vol. 2.

14

Reprinted from Am. Nat. 97(895):209–223 (1963)

GRAPHICAL REPRESENTATION AND STABILITY CONDITIONS OF PREDATOR-PREY INTERACTIONS

M. L. ROSENZWEIG AND R. H. MACARTHUR

Department of Zoology, University of Pennsylvania, Philadelphia, Pennsylvania

INTRODUCTION

Investigators have employed two major pathways when inquiring into the nature of the predator-prey interaction. One of these has been to disassemble the interaction into as many component parts as possible and then characterize these for various specific predator-prey relationships. This approach is certainly necessary to a complete understanding of any given predator-prey interaction, but it does not stress, nor has it been fruitful at the task of making general statements about two central ecological problems. Does the interaction contribute to the observed stability of natural communities? In what direction, towards or away from a stable interaction, does the force of Natural Selection drive the predator and its prey? We shall herein embark on the second pathway, that of generalization, and attempt to begin to answer these two questions.

THE GRAPHICAL DESCRIPTION

One of the most common relationships between two populations involves the destruction by members of one population of members of the other for the purpose of obtaining food. This predator-prey relationship is marked by a mutual interaction of the two populations involved. To examine this interaction, let us make a graph with predator density as ordinate and prey density as abscissa. Each point on the graph will then represent a unique community composition; that is, prey at density x, predators at density y. Let us postulate that by ascertaining the community composition, we can unambiguously state the instantaneous rate of change of both the predator's and the prey's density.

Parenthetically speaking, this uniqueness is not absolutely true, as populations of identical density might differ in other characteristics which we do not show on the graph — and which are therefore items being held constant for the sake of the argument. Such characteristics as are probably important are average reproductive value (see Slobodkin, 1961), adrenal function (see Christian, 1961) and, undoubtedly, a host of other important items both discovered and awaiting discovery. This oversimplification, however, will not affect the qualitative outgrowths of the argument.

Let us now suppose that we run countless experiments by starting a predator-prey community at many different community compositions in identical environments, and recording whether the prey increased, decreased, or just maintained itself, and also noting the same information for the predator.

We plot all of the above data on our graph by inserting two arrows at each of the community composition points that we have tested. One arrow will be parallel to the x axis and will show us the magnitude and direction of change of the prey (toward y axis equals decrease; away from it equals increase; no arrow equals no change). The other arrow will be parallel to the y axis and will do the same for the predator.

Now we connect all the points at which the prey population just maintained itself, and call the resulting line the prey isocline $\left(\dfrac{d \text{ Prey}}{dt} = 0 \text{ for all points on the line} \right)$. Let us also connect the points at which the predator population just maintained itself and call this the predator isocline. If the lines intersect, neither population will be changing at the point of intersection. Such points, if any exist, are called the equilibrium points of the interaction.

Now we can proceed with a deduction of the general shape of each of the two isoclines, and from them make deductions about the stability of the interaction. Each population possesses a set of just-maintainable densities, $\dfrac{d \text{ pop.}}{dt} = 0$, for otherwise a population would be increasing or decreasing ad infinitum. If decreasing, we wouldn't observe it (it would be extinct); if increasing, it would eventually contradict the first law of thermodynamics. When a population is not at one of its just-maintainable densities, it is either increasing or decreasing. Also, in a continuous model, a population cannot pass from an increasing state to a decreasing one, or vice-versa, without attaining an equilibrium point en route.

We shall start with mental construction of the prey isocline to determine its general shape. First, consider what point(s) will result in the prey species just maintaining itself when there are no predators. Clearly, there will be a minimum maintainable density of prey associated with the minimum density of the prey species required for successful one-for-one reproduction; call this the minimum just-maintainable density, P_0, for the prey population with no predators. Also, there will be a point, Q_0, a maximum just-maintainable density for a prey population with no predators. Beyond this, the prey will be overcrowded; after all, the prey itself, since it is also animate, will depend on some limited source of life, be it solar energy, grass, or simple space. In experiments whose initial populations are represented by any point on the line between $(P_0, 0)$ and $(Q_0, 0)$, the prey will begin by increasing; at an initial point on the line to the left of $(P_0, 0)$, it will decrease to extinction; at an initial point to the right of $(Q_0, 0)$, it will begin by decreasing.

Assume the predators are able to eat the prey at every prey density between P_0 and Q_0. If we take a prey density, x, and hold it constant in a series of experiments like those previously outlined, the prey will begin by maintaining themselves or increasing if and only if the predators begin at or below a certain density. If the predators begin at too high a density, the prey population will begin by decreasing. This means that over every prey density between P_0 and Q_0, there exists a population composition at which the prey just maintain themselves. The set of all population compositions for which the prey just maintain themselves is thus a closed curve, such as that for $\dfrac{dPy}{dt} = 0$ in figure 1.

To prove that this curve is of a form similar to that in figure 1, that is, that it has one and only one peak, let us examine the interaction for constant predator densities and vary the prey. We add several members, i, of a

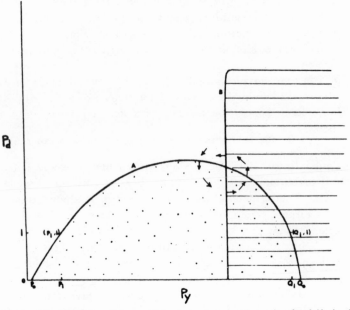

FIGURE 1. The instantaneous model of the interaction of a food-limited predator and its prey. Py = prey density; Pd = predator density. Line A is the prey iso-cline, that is, the set of all points for which $\dfrac{dPy}{dt} = 0$; line B is the predator iso-cline. Py increases in the dotted area only; Pd increases only in the shaded area. The vectors are the instantaneous (general) direction of change of the community at eight qualitatively-different points in the graph.

species of predator (which preys exclusively on our first species). These predators are living ultimately on the same resources as their prey. Since the prey's biomass can be limited by its own resources, then the additional onus on the resources (caused by the maintenance of the predator biomass), results in a decrease in the amount of prey biomass that can be maintained. Slobodkin (1962) has shown in superb laboratory studies that the amount of the "standing crop" of a Daphnia population which is limited by its resources is indeed decreased by the presence of predation. The maximum just-maintainable density, Q_i, at this population of predators, i, will thus usually be less than Q_0; it certainly can be no greater. On the other hand, due to the fact that the prey are being eaten, more prey will be necessary for successful one-for-one replacement of the prey population; that is, $P_i > P_0$. The prey will begin by increasing in experiments whose initial populations are represented by points on the horizontal line between (P_i, i) and (Q_i, i), and by decreasing at points on the line to the right of (Q_i, i). At initial points to the left of (P_i, i), the prey will no longer of necessity become extinct (although they will begin by decreasing), for the predators, too, may well be growing scarcer. A continuation of this type of reasoning leads to the inevitable conclusion that as we add more of the predators to the initial community, the minimum just-maintainable density increases and the maximum just-maintainable density decreases. The form of the prey isocline is thus confirmed to be the form of the curve in figure 1. The dotted area is the set of all points (population compositions) at which the prey are increasing; in the undotted area are all the points at which the prey are decreasing.

At $(Q_0, 0)$ when there are no predators, the prey are limited by their own resources; at $(P_0, 0)$ they are limited by their own reproductive ability. Increasing the numbers of predators in the community decreases the reproductive efficiency of the prey, and the amount of prey maintainable on the limited resource(s). As we pass from left to right, interference with reproduction becomes less important as a prey-limiting factor, and drain on prey resources becomes more important. Obviously, the slope of the isocline or its exact shape is not the same for every predator-prey relationship.

The predator isocline, $\dfrac{dPd}{dt} = 0$, is simpler to deduce. The predator is depending on the prey for its ability to increase. When the prey fall below a certain level, the predators decrease; when they are greater than this level, the predators increase. Since we are dealing with an instantaneous model, the predators will be increasing if and only if they are eating prey at the required rate (Andrewartha and Browning, 1961). Attainment of this rate depends only on the prey density. It is true that the greater the number of predators, the faster the density is reduced; still the instantaneous rate of change of the predator population depends only on the instantaneous rate of kill, which depends on the instantaneous density of prey. This results in the vertical line segment of $\dfrac{dPd}{dt} = 0$ in figure 1; that is, the predators increase if and only if the prey exist at or above a certain density. The shaded area is the region of predator increase; the unshaded area is the region of predator decrease. With vertebrate (and some other) predators, where increase is discontinuous and depends, in part, on accumulated food intake, greater densities of predators do indeed require greater densities of prey for increase. This model introduces a positive slope to the predator isocline $\left(\text{see lower part of } \dfrac{dPd}{dt} = 0 \text{ in figure 3}\right)$; that is, at greater predator densities, greater prey densities are required for predator increase.

The predator has other limitations (for example, standing room) besides food which he must eventually reach, and beyond which he may not increase, no matter what extravagant density the prey population might attain. This fact places a "ceiling" $\left(\text{the horizontal part of } \dfrac{dPd}{dt} = 0\right)$ on the predator's ability to increase, as in figures 1, 3, and 4.

Figure 1 gives us the instantaneous model of predator-prey interactions for a food-limited predator. Addition of the component population vectors to obtain the resultant community vectors at eight points in the graph demonstrates the nature of the community vectors in each of the graph's eight divisions. A community history is graphed by observing the numbers of the two populations at different times, and placing them as points on our graph. Due to the general direction of the community vectors in each of the eight "locations," we can predict that this history, if plotted on a graph like figure 1, might result in the arrow's forming an elliptic curve, that is, given a starting point, the community composition would return to a point at or near this starting point. If the community did not return to the precise point, then the vectors would describe a spiral with either inward (stable) or outward (unstable) flow. If the spiral ever got so large that one of the axes were intersected by a vector, the predators (in case of intersection with x axis) or both species (in case of intersection with y axis) would become extinct. Graphing the points of such spirals with predator and prey on the ordinate and time on the abscissa will demonstrate the fact that these spirals are just a different way of graphing "classical" predator-prey oscillations (see Huffaker, 1958, and Utida, 1957).

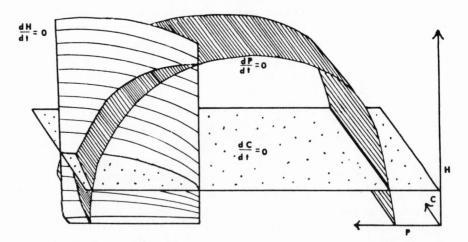

FIGURE 2. The interaction of a carnivore (C), and herbivore (H), and a plant (P). Dotted and shaded areas are the isosurfaces as marked. The plants increase their density at every point below the "airplane hangar" surface; the herbivores increase theirs at every point on the observer's side and to the left of their isosurface; the carnivores increase theirs at all points above their planar isosurface. Vectors, though applicable, are omitted for the sake of clarity.

As we shall later demonstrate, such spirals are not a necessary feature of every interaction. Some isoclines are so formed that both predator and prey approach an equilibrium value (be it zero or positive) asymptotically.

Graphical description of predation can readily be extended to the three species interaction. An interesting example of this is a graph (in three dimensions) of a carnivore eating an herbivore which is eating a plant. Figure 2 is a picture of such a graph. Dotted and shaded areas in this case are not regions of increase or decrease, but are the isosurfaces of the species involved. The present investigators are attempting analysis of such interactions similar to the one for two dimensions which follows below. Four-dimensional situations are unfortunately beyond our collective imagination, but it is hoped that analysis of the three-dimensional models and comparison with the two-dimensional ones will reveal trends which can be tested in the laboratory and the field.

VARIATIONS OF THE MODEL RESULTING IN GLOBAL STABILITY

A basic premise of all of these arguments has been that the rate of predation varies proportionately with the prey density. Holling (1957) has found at least one example, however, where increasing prey density has no effect on predation rate. Can our graphical system handle this instance?

Since the predation rate is constant at any level of prey density, the predator increases or decreases without regard to the prey density. It is thus limited by something other than prey density. This is the meaning of the horizontal segment of our isocline, and if such a situation pertains at the interaction equilibrium point, we may graph it by lowering our "ceiling" as

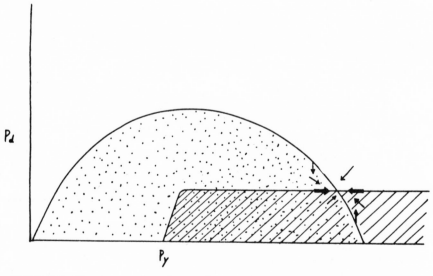

FIGURE 3. The interaction of a predator and its prey, where the predator is not limited at its equilibrium density by its supply of prey. Isoclines, coordinates, and markings as in figure 1. Vector construction demonstrates that oscillations are not present, but that a stable equilibrium is.

in figure 3.   Vector construction in this case shows us that we have a stable equilibrium with no oscillations.   Such stability, over the whole area of the graph will be termed global stability.

Since both figures 1 and 3 may well describe the incomplete utilization of a resource, we have a good reason for suspecting that each is perhaps modified towards figure 4, which represents a predator limited by more than one of his resources.   For instance, a predator that is not food-limited is permitting waste on his trophic level.   This provides an opportunity for some other predator to move in and "take up the slack," causing the density of food to become more important to our original predator.   If the second predator takes up all the slack, superficially one obtains exactly figure 4; however, due to the variation of a second predator, we must add it on a third axis.   Such multi-dimensional cases will be discussed later.

Similarly, a strictly food-limited predator is not utilizing some other feature of his "niche" to its utmost, a situation representable by figure 1. Addition of another species to utilize the wasted resource (for example, space) results in a lowering of the "ceiling" of the predator.   This phenomenon seems intuitively less potent than the maximization of food consumption discussed above.   Either force might also be channeled into a "ballooning" of the single predator "niche" as observed in Bermuda by Crowell (1960).   The net effect of this "nature abhors a vacuum" idea is

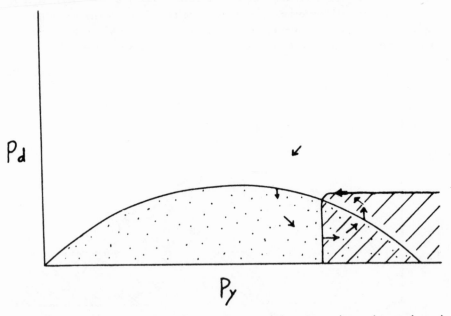

FIGURE 4. The interaction of a predator and its prey where the predator is limited at its equilibrium density both by its supply of prey and some other resource(s), for example, nesting sites or den space. Isoclines, coordinates, and markings as in figure 1. Vector construction demonstrates the fact that oscillations take place only in the extremely small area close to equilibrium, where they are probably unmeasurable.

the simultaneous limitation of the predator by all the resources of its environment (figure 4).

Vector construction in figure 4 shows how the horizontal segment of the predator's isocline causes a funnelling of the community vectors into interaction equilibrium. The limitation of the predator by multiple factors thus means that oscillations can take place only in the very small area around interaction equilibrium where the predator isocline is not horizontal. There they would probably be of undetectably small magnitude.

Another assumption we may negate with profit is that the predators are able to eat prey at any prey density between P_0 and Q_0. If we assume instead that the prey have some inviolable haven able to support a certain density of prey completely free of predation, then we get an open curve like that in figure 5. Vector construction in this system shows that because the community actually travels along the prey isocline when it is vertical, any series of community oscillations must eventually attain a maximum where one of the points reached is the point at which the prey isocline first begins to slope.

The only other line segment that remains, that is, the right side of the prey isocline, can also become vertical when there is no predation pressure at high prey and moderate predator densities. When this occurs, a maximum oscillation is similarly created. The community travels up along the isocline until it reaches the point where the isocline slopes. Therefore,

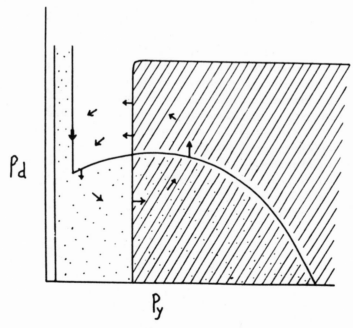

FIGURE 5. The interaction of a predator and its prey where the predator is unable to eat the prey at every prey density. Isoclines, coordinates, and markings as in figure 1. In this case, growing oscillations do not necessarily grow until one or both species becomes extinct, for a limiting oscillation may be reached.

this point will be reached in every oscillation after it is first reached, and we may describe the unique limiting oscillation by starting the community at this point and reporting its numbers until it returns there.

We do not mean to imply the necessity of a non-extinguishing oscillation, given either the "prey-hideaway" isocline or the "no-predation-pressure-at-moderate-predator-levels" isocline. The maximum oscillation may intersect one of the axes, in which case one or both species would become extinct (perhaps even before the maximum oscillation were attained). We suggest these isoclines merely as a possible means of control of some predator-prey oscillations. Their control will be exercised if and only if the oscillation is unstable close to community equilibrium, and the maximum oscillation intersects neither axis. All of these remarks apply equally well to the horizontal "ceiling" isocline of the predator, which isocline is also capable of limiting the oscillatory amplitude by inducing a maximum oscillation.

STABILITY OF LINEAR APPROXIMATION

A general theory of global stability of the food-limited predator's interaction with his prey is difficult to attain. Let us instead consider a lesser topic: stability of a linear approximation close to the interaction equilibrium point. Determination of this will at least enable us to answer the question: What are the graphical conditions which result in appearance of predator-prey oscillations? Regular oscillations should occur if the system is unstable at equilibrium (that is, the small oscillations are of increasing amplitude), but globally-stable. Recognizable oscillations of predictable period and large amplitude probably do not occur where the system is stable at community equilibrium (that is, the oscillations are of decreasing amplitude) and the natural complex of weather factors and chance is present.

Transposing the origin of our axes to community equilibrium, we note that new values for the abscissa are $x = py$ minus py_{eq}, and for the ordinate $y = pd$ minus pd_{eq}. At community equilibrium, $x = 0$ and $y = 0$. Here the rate of increase of the prey at any point is directly proportional to the distance down from the prey isocline (whose equation is approximately $y = k_1 x$), and the rate of increase of the predator at that point is directly proportional to its distance in the positive direction from the predator isocline (whose equation is approximately $y = k_2 x$, or when k_2 does not exist, $x = 0$). We can thus write differential approximations as follows:

(1)
$$\frac{dx}{dt} = a(k_1 x - y)$$

(2a)
$$\frac{dy}{dt} = \beta\left(x - \frac{y}{k_2}\right),$$

or when there is no slope (pd isocline has equation, x equals zero):

(2b)
$$\frac{dy}{dt} = \beta x.$$

210

α and β are positive constants involving the Malthusian parameters of the prey and the predator respectively. α is the change in dx/dt accompanying a unit change in the predator population. β is the change in dy/dt accompanying a unit change in the prey population.

Let us try to analyze situation (1) and (2b) where the predator's rate of increase is independent of his own density. We shall try to find a common parameter for the two populations, m. Since these are linear differential equations, we should be able to express their solutions as exponential functions:

(3a) $\qquad x = Ae^{mt}$, $\qquad\qquad$ (3b) $\quad \dfrac{dx}{dt} = mAe^{mt} = mx = \alpha(k_1 x - y)$.

(4a) $\qquad y = Be^{mt}$, $\qquad\qquad$ (4b) $\quad \dfrac{dx}{dt} = mBe^{mt} = my = \beta x$.

Using (4b), we obtain:

(5) $\qquad y = \beta x/m$, which upon substitution into (3b) yields

(6) $\qquad mx = \alpha(k_1 x - \beta x/m)$ $\quad$ or $\quad$ $x[m^2 - (\alpha k_1)m + \alpha\beta] = 0$.

Since we are not interested in the root, $x = 0$, of this equation (prey are at equilibrium and will by definition stay there), we eliminate it. We can thus solve for m in the usual way, obtaining

(7) $$m = \frac{\alpha k_1}{2} \pm \frac{\sqrt{\alpha^2 k_1^2 - 4\alpha\beta}}{2}.$$

Now from (6) when m is real (that is, when $k_1^2 \geq 4\beta/\alpha)m^2$ and $\alpha\beta$ are always positive, so that minus $\alpha k_1 m$ must be negative in equation (6). But minus α is always negative; therefore $k_1 m$ must be positive; therefore k_1 and m must have the same sign. From (3a) and (4a) we see that if m is positive, the interaction is unstable ($\lim_{t\to\infty}$ of both y and $x = \infty$); if it is negative, the interaction is stable ($\lim_{t\to\infty}$ of both x and $y = 0$). But k_1 must negative for m to be able to be negative; therefore k_1 must be negative for stability to exist close to community equilibrium when m is real. No oscillatory properties can be attributed to m when it is real.

When m is complex (that is, $k_1^2 < 4\beta/\alpha$), however, we can express x this way (from 3a):

(8) $\qquad x \propto e^{mt} = e^{(a+bi)t} = e^{at}(\cos bt + i \sin bt)$.

Note that the real part of m is the only part of m qualifying stability; the sin and cos functions contribute the oscillations. The oscillations decay if and only if the real part of m is negative. From (7) we note that the real part is just $\alpha k_1/2$ since we are dealing with the case where m is complex. Thus, for stability α and k_1 must differ in sign. But α is always positive; therefore the interaction is stable if and only if k_1 is negative. This is the same conclusion we reach for the real case, and we have constructed the following chart.

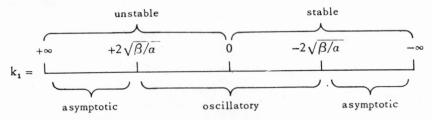

From (8) we note that x completes one oscillation when bt goes from zero to 2π, that is, when t goes from zero to $2\pi/b$. Thus x has period (from 7):

(9)
$$T = 2\pi/b = 4\pi/\sqrt{4a\beta - a^2 k_1^2}.$$

Now let us combine equations (1) and (2a) and search for an m in the same manner.

(10)
$$\frac{dx}{dt} = mAe^{mt} = mx = a(k_1 x - y), \quad \text{or} \quad (ak_1 - m)x = ay.$$

(11)
$$\frac{dy}{dt} = mBe^{mt} = my = \beta(x - y/k_2).$$

Solving (11) for x we obtain:

(12) $x = \dfrac{y(\beta/k_2 + m)}{\beta}$, which upon substitution into (10) gives us:

(13) $[m^2 + (\beta/k_2 - ak_1)m + a\beta(1 - k_1/k_2)] = 0.$

The two roots may be examined qualitatively by manipulating signs. Note that m^2 is always positive (for real m) as are a, β and k_2. As before, m must be negative for the system to be stable.

Case 1: If k_1 is negative, then $\left(1 - \dfrac{k_1}{k_2}\right)a\beta$ and $\left(\dfrac{\beta}{k_2} - ak_1\right)$ are positive, therefore m must be negative and the system is stable.

Case 2: k_1 is positive and $k_1 \leq k_2$ so that $a\beta(1 - k_1/k_2) \geq 0$:

(a) If $k_1 \leq \dfrac{\beta}{ak_2}$, so that $\left(\dfrac{\beta}{k_2} - ak_1\right) \geq 0$, then m must be negative and the system is stable.

(b) If $k_1 > \beta/ak_2$, so that $(\beta/k_2 - ak_1) < 0$, then m must be positive and the system is unstable. All of the above conditions also hold for m when it is complex. This may be proved by an analysis like that case for (1) + (2b).

Case 3: If $k_1 > k_2$, an isocline diagram reveals the instability most simply, but in this case another community equilibrium point is present which may have stable properties. In any event, this seems to be an unrealistic instance, for it implies that the predator is able to increase at the extremely low densities of prey where the prey themselves can no longer increase.

A summary of these stability properties is contained in figure 6. In general, decreasing the slope k_2 from infinity to some number, increases the number of possible stable systems.

Another way of modifying the continuous model is to insert vectors of discrete length at each point rather than view them as continuously changing. We are currently analyzing such a situation.

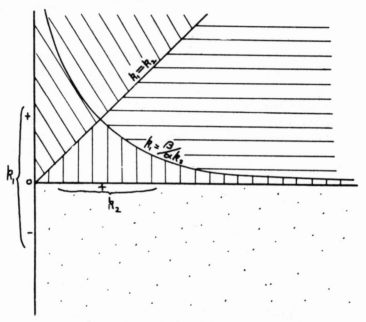

FIGURE 6. Comparative values of k_1 and k_2, and resultant stability close to interaction equilibrium (see text for complete analysis) for situation (1) and (2a). Dotted area is Case 1; vertical cross-hatching is Case 2a; horizontal cross-hatching is Case 2b; diagonal cross-hatching is Case 3.

Summarizing the stability properties around the community equilibrium point, we first note that the prey slope must almost always be negative for stability and the greater the negativity of k_1, the more stable the interaction. No relatively large positive k_1 value will support stability. In the second case, the mere presence of a predator isocline slope, k_2, increased the possible values of k_1 for which the relationship would be stable.

SOME RESULTS OF EVOLUTION ON THE STABILITY OF THE INTERACTION

Keeping these stability properties in mind, let us examine the evolutionary properties of our graph. A predator who can kill enough prey at a given prey density to maintain himself and enough offspring to replace himself will be more fit than a predator who cannot kill at a great enough rate to accomplish this (when given the same prey density). Natural selection will thus increase the predator's ability to kill prey; in other words, the predators are able to just maintain themselves at a constantly decreasing density of prey. The predator isocline moves left. This action always decreases stability.

However, the prey at this lower equilibrium density have suffered a decrease in the absolute number of offspring they can bring into the world and an increase in the rate at which they are being killed. They therefore will not usually be able to maintain themselves at the old predator density, let alone any higher one. This type of selection on the predator, therefore, also depresses the prey isocline. Due to this fact, increasing predator efficiency by increasing the predator's ability to kill may well result in decreasing the community equilibrium density of predators. Also, k_1 at equilibrium is certainly less steep. If the interaction was previously locally stable, stability is then decreased. If it was unstable before ($k_1 > 0$), it may become less unstable, but does not change to stability.

The opposite of this selective force is the selection of the prey which are best able to avoid being eaten. This tendency toward decreasing the rate of kill (or better, the rate of being killed) moves the predator isocline to the right and raises the prey isocline. It is thus a probable factor in increasing stability.

Efficiency of the predator may also be increased by selecting those better able to utilize the same amount of kill. This would still move the predator isocline left, but because the predation rates remain the same at each prey density, it would have no effect on the prey's isocline. In this way, the predators could increase their density at community equilibrium, but they are again decreasing the stability of the interaction.

Another method of increasing the interaction equilibrium value of the predator is to increase his absolute food supply. A priori, there seems to be only one way in which this can be done, and that is to increase or at least maximize the percentage of prey food turned into more prey. Graphically (if we plot prey biomass instead of number), this raises the prey isocline, steepening its slope and thus probably increasing stability. Although this seems far-fetched, it has actually been observed in the field by Connell (1961). The gastropod, *Thais lapillus*, which is able to open only a limited number of its prey, the barnacle, *Balanus balanoides*, per unit time, has naturally evolved in the direction of opening only the largest barnacles (these provide the most food per unit time). Coincidentally, these barnacles are the slowest growing of all (the growth rate of a barnacle decreases with age). This means that *Thais lapillus* was simultaneously evacuating the greatest barnacle space, and leaving the fastest growing barnacles. The predator was maximizing the amount of barnacle food converted to barnacle per unit time, though it accomplished this coincidentally with, and not directly by, natural selection. Of course, the predator, by opening the largest prey, was also increasing its efficiency, thus moving its isocline left, decreasing stability, and balancing (to an unknown extent) the effect of raising its prey isocline.

214

Such coincidences are probably rather widespread phenomena. Vertebrate predators may be seen to attack, preferentially, the dead and the dying (Allen, 1962), that is, those prey with the least reproductive value. This is coincidental with the fact that these are the very same prey which are least able to resist. Predators who can detect and preferentially attack such prey will be most efficient (MacArthur, 1960). A predator with this ability will most likely have little effect on the reproductive potential of its prey when he himself is scarce, that is, the lower right part of the prey's isocline will approach (or even reach) verticality. Thus this is also a force causing the approach to a maximum oscillation.

Natural selection, with regard to the continuous model, when acting on the predator, usually tends to increase its efficiency and destabilize the interaction; selection on the prey tends to increase stability. There is as yet no known force within the predator population acting specifically to conceive of and enforce the best strategies for maintaining the predator population at a maximum density. Efficiency selection on the predators appears to be blind with respect to the group, and changes the interaction in favor of the individual predator, even when doing so involves decrease of the total number of predators in the population.

SUMMARY

The general nature of the predator-prey interaction has been depicted as a graph of predator versus prey densities from which conditions for stability of the interaction are predicted. An example of a three-species interaction is also presented. Variations of the graph are introduced, and it is shown that an otherwise unstable interaction may be stabilized by the presence of either an inviolable prey hiding place, or extremely low predation pressure at moderate predator and high prey densities, or another predator-limiting resource. Stability is always conferred when the predator is severely limited at its equilibrium density by one of its resources other than its supply of prey. Predators should tend to be limited at their equilibrium densities by more than one of their resources. When either of the two foregoing situations pertains, regular predator-prey oscillations should not be observable.

The stability of the interaction close to equilibrium was found to depend exclusively, in the mathematically-continuous model, upon the slopes of two lines in the graph at equilibrium. Stability can be asymptotic rather than oscillatory in type. An equation for the period of oscillatory interactions is also advanced. The effects of Natural Selection on the isoclines, and thus the stability, is not clear-cut. Selection of the prey tends to stabilize the interaction; the opposite is true for selection on the predator.

ACKNOWLEDGMENTS

One author was supported by a graduate fellowship from the National Science Foundation, and the other by grant G-11575 from the same Foundation.

The authors both wish to thank Mrs. Rosenzweig, whose help and patience in typing and retyping their manuscript were infinite.

LITERATURE CITED

Allen, Durward L., 1962, Our wildlife legacy. Rev. ed. Funk and Wagnalls, New York. 422 pp.

Andrewartha, H. G., and T. O. Browning, 1961, An analysis of the idea of "resources" in animal ecology. J. Theoret. Biol., 1: 83–97.

Christian, J. J., 1961, Phenomena associated with population density. Proc. Nat. Acad. Sci. U. S., 47: 428.

Connell, J. H., 1961, Effects of competition, predation by Thais lapillus, and other factors on natural populations of the barnacle, Balanus balanoides. Ecol. Monographs, 31: 61–104.

Crowell, K., 1961, Effects of reduced competition in birds. Proc. Nat. Acad. Sci. U. S., 47(2): 240–3.

Holling, C. S., 1959, The components of predation as revealed by a study of small-mammal predation of the European sawfly. Can. Entomol., 91(5): 293–320.

Huffaker, C. B., 1958, Experimental studies on predation: dispersion factors and predator-prey oscillations. Hilgardia, 27: 343–383.

Lotka, A. J., 1932, The growth of mixed populations; two species competing for a common food supply. J. Wash. Acad. Sci., 22: 461–469.

MacArthur, R. H., 1960, On the relation between reproductive value and optimal predation. Proc. Nat. Acad. Sci. U. S., 46(1): 143–145.

Slobodkin, L. B., 1961, Growth and regulation of animal populations. Holt, Rinehart, and Winston, New York. 184 pp.

Utida, S., 1957, Population fluctuation, an experimental and theoretical approach. Cold Spring Harbor Symp. Quant. Biol., 22: 139–151.

15

Reprinted from *Can. Ent.* **91**(5):293–320 (1959)

The Components of Predation as Revealed by a Study of Small-Mammal Predation of the European Pine Sawfly[1]

By C. S. Holling

Forest Insect Laboratory, Sault Ste. Marie, Ont.

INTRODUCTION

The fluctuation of an animal's numbers between restricted limits is determined by a balance between that animal's capacity to increase and the environmental checks to this increase. Many authors have indulged in the whimsy of calculating the progressive increase of a population when no checks were operating. Thus Huxley calculated that the progeny of a single *Aphis* in the course of 10 generations, supposing all survived, would "contain more ponderable substance than five hundred millions of stout men; that is, more than the whole population of China", (in Thompson, 1929). Checks, however, do occur and it has been the subject of much controversy to determine how these checks operate. Certain general principles—the density-dependence concept of Smith (1955), the competition theory of Nicholson (1933)—have been proposed both verbally and mathematically, but because they have been based in part upon untested and restrictive assumptions they have been severely criticized (e.g. Andrewartha and Birch 1954). These problems could be considerably clarified if we knew the mode of operation of each process that affects numbers, if we knew its basic and subsidiary components. Predation, one such process, forms the subject of the present paper.

Many of the published studies of predation concentrate on discrete parts rather than the whole process. Thus some entomologists are particularly interested in the effect of selection of different kinds of prey by predators upon the evolution of colour patterns and mimicry; wildlife biologists are similarly interested in selection but emphasize the role predators play in improving the condition of the prey populations by removing weakened animals. While such specific problems should find a place in any scheme of predation, the main aim of the present study is to elucidate the components of predation in such a way that more meaning can be applied to considerations of population dynamics. This requires a broad study of the whole process and in particular its function in affecting the numbers of animals.

Such broad studies have generally been concerned with end results measured by the changes in the numbers of predator and prey. These studies are particularly useful when predators are experimentally excluded from the environment of their prey, in the manner adopted by DeBach and his colleagues in their investigations of the pests of orchard trees in California. This work, summarized recently (DeBach, 1958) in response to criticism by Milne (1957), clearly shows that in certain cases the sudden removal of predators results in a rapid increase of prey numbers from persistently low densities to the limits of the food supply. Inasmuch as these studies have shown that other factors have little regulatory function, the predators appear to be the principal ones responsible for regulation. Until the components of predation are revealed by an analysis of the processes leading to these end results, however, we will never know whether the conclusions from such studies apply to situations other than the specific predator–prey relationship investigated.

Errington's investigations of vertebrate predator–prey situations (1934, 1943, 1945 and 1956) suggest, in part, how some types of predation operate. He has

[1]Contribution from the Dept. of Zoology, University of British Columbia and No. 547, Forest Biology Division, Research Branch, Department of Agriculture, Ottawa, Canada. Delivered in part at the Tenth International Congress of Entomology, Montreal, 1956.

postulated that each habitat can support only a given number of animals and that predation becomes important only when the numbers of prey exceed this "carrying capacity". Hence predators merely remove surplus animals, ones that would succumb even in the absence of natural enemies. Errington exempts certain predator-prey relations from this scheme, however, and quotes the predation of wolves on deer as an example where predation probably is not related to the carrying capacity of the habitat. However logical these postulates are, they are only indirectly supported by the facts, and they do not explain the processes responsible.

In order to clarify these problems a comprehensive theory of predation is required that on the one hand is not so restrictive that it can only apply in certain cases and on the other not so broad that it becomes meaningless. Such a comprehensive answer requires a comprehensive approach, not necessarily in terms of the number of situations examined but certainly in terms of the variables involved, for it is the different reactions of predators to these variables that produce the many diverse predator-prey relations. Such a comprehensive approach is faced with a number of practical difficulties. It is apparent from the published studies of predation of vertebrate prey by vertebrate predators that not only is it difficult to obtain estimates of the density of predator, prey, and destroyed prey, but also that the presence of many interacting variables confuses interpretation.

The present study of predation of the European pine sawfly, *Neodiprion sertifer* (Geoff.) by small mammals was particularly suited for a general comprehensive analysis of predation. The practical difficulties concerning population measurement and interpretation of results were relatively unimportant, principally because of the unique properties of the environment and of the prey. The field work was conducted in the sand-plain area of southwestern Ontario where Scots and jack pine have been planted in blocks of up to 200 acres. The flat topography and the practice of planting trees of the same age and species at standard six-foot spacings has produced a remarkably uniform environment. In addition, since the work was concentrated in plantations 15 to 20 years of age, the closure of the crowns reduced ground vegetation to a trace, leaving only an even layer of pine needles covering the soil. The extreme simplicity and uniformity of this environment greatly facilitated the population sampling and eliminated complications resulting from changes in the quantity and kind of alternate foods of the predators.

The investigations were further simplified by the characteristics of the prey. Like most insects, the European pine sawfly offers a number of distinct life-history stages that might be susceptible to predation. The eggs, laid in pine needles the previous fall, hatch in early spring and the larvae emerge and feed upon the foliage. During the first two weeks of June the larvae drop from the trees and spin cocoons within the duff on the forest floor. These cocooned sawflies remain in the ground until the latter part of September, when most emerge as adults. A certain proportion, however, overwinter in cocoons, to emerge the following autumn. Observations in the field and laboratory showed that only one of these life-history stages, the cocoon, was attacked by the small-mammal predators, and that the remaining stages were inaccessible and/or unpalatable and hence completely escaped attack. These data will form part of a later paper dealing specifically with the impact of small mammal predation upon the European pine sawfly.

Cocooned sawflies, as prey, have some very useful attributes for an investigation of this kind. Their concentration in the two-dimensional environment of the duff-soil interface and their lack of movement and reaction to predators considerably simplify sampling and interpretation. Moreover, the small mammals' habit of making a characteristically marked opening in the cocoon to permit removal of the insect leaves a relatively permanent record in the ground of the number of cocooned sawflies destroyed. Thus, the density of the destroyed prey can be measured at the same time as the density of the prey.

Attention was concentrated upon the three most numerous predators—the masked shrew, *Sorex cinereus cinereus* Kerr, the short-tail shrew, *Blarina brevicauda talpoides* Gapper, and deer mouse, *Peromyscus maniculatus bairdii* Hoy and Kennicott. It soon became apparent that these species were the only significant predators of the sawfly, for the remaining nine species trapped or observed in the plantations were either extremely rare or were completely herbivorous.

Here, then, was a simple predator-prey situation where three species of small mammals were preying on a simple prey—sawfly cocoons. The complicating variables present in most other situations were either constant or absent because of the simple characteristics of the environment and of the prey. The absence or constancy of these complicating variables facilitated analysis but at the expense of a complete and generally applicable scheme of predation. Fortunately, however, the small-mammal predators and the cocoons could easily be manipulated in laboratory experiments so that the effect of those variables absent in the field situation could be assessed. At the same time the laboratory experiments supported the field results. This blend of field and laboratory data provides a comprehensive scheme of predation which will be shown to modify present theories of population dynamics and to considerably clarify the role predators play in population regulation.

I wish to acknowledge the considerable assistance rendered by a number of people, through discussion and criticism of the manuscript: Dr. I. McT. Cowan, Dr. K. Graham and Dr. P. A. Larkin at the University of British Columbia and Dr. R. M. Belyea, Mr. A. W. Ghent and Dr. P. J. Pointing, at the Forest Biology Laboratory, Sault Ste. Marie, Ontario.

FIELD TECHNIQUES

A study of the interaction of predator and prey should be based upon accurate population measurements, and in order to avoid superficial interpretations, populations should be expressed as numbers per unit area. Three populations must be measured—those of the predators, prey, and destroyed prey. Thus the aim of the field methods was to measure accurately each of the three populations in terms of their numbers per acre.

Small-Mammal Populations

Since a complete description and evaluation of the methods used to estimate the density of the small-mammal predators forms the basis of another paper in preparation, a summary of the techniques will suffice for the present study.

Estimates of the number of small mammals per acre were obtained using standard live-trapping techniques adapted from Burt (1940) and Blair (1941). The data obtained by marking, releasing and subsequently recapturing animals were analysed using either the Lincoln index (Lincoln, 1930) or Hayne's method for estimating populations in removal trapping procedures (Hayne, 1949). The resulting estimates of the number of animals exposed to traps were converted to per acre figures by calculating, on the basis of measurements of the home range of the animals (Stickel, 1954), the actual area sampled by traps.

The accuracy of these estimates was evaluated by examining the assumptions underlying the proper use of the Lincoln index and Hayne's technique and by comparing the efficiency of different traps and trap arrangements. This analysis showed that an accurate estimate of the numbers of *Sorex* and *Blarina* could be obtained using Hayne's method of treating the data obtained from trapping with bucket traps. These estimates, however, were accurate only when the populations had not been disturbed by previous trapping. For *Peromyscus*, Lincoln-index estimates obtained from the results of trapping with Sherman traps provided an ideal way of estimating numbers that was both accurate and unaffected by previous trapping.

N. sertifer Populations

Since small-mammal predation of *N. sertifer* was restricted to the cocoon stage, prey populations could be measured adequately by estimating the number of cocoons containing living insects present immediately after larval drop in June. This estimate was obtained using a method outlined and tested by Prebble (1943) for cocoon populations of the European spruce sawfly, *Gilpinia hercyniae* (Htg.), an insect with habits similar to those of *N. sertifer*. Accurate estimates were obtained when cocoons were collected from sub-samples of litter and duff distributed within the restricted universe beneath the crowns of host trees. This method was specially designed to provide an index of population rather than an estimate of numbers per acre. But it is obvious from this work that any cocoon-sampling technique designed to yield a *direct* estimate of the number of cocoons per acre would require an unpractically large number of sample units. It proved feasible in the present study, however, to convert such estimates from a square-foot to an acre basis, by stratifying the forest floor into three strata, one comprising circles with two-foot radii around tree trunks, one comprising intermediate rings with inner radii two feet and outer radii three feet, and one comprising the remaining area (three to five feet from the tree trunks).

At least 75 trees were selected and marked throughout each plantation, and one or usually two numbered wooden stakes were placed directly beneath the crown of each tree, on opposite sides of the trunk. Stakes were never placed under overlapping tree crowns. The four sides of each stake were lettered from A to D and the stake was placed so that the numbered sides bore no relation to the position of the trunk. Samples were taken each year, by collecting cocoons from the area delimited by one-square-foot frames placed at one corner of each stake. In the first year's sample the frames were placed at the AB corner, in the second year's at the BC corner, etc. Different-sized screens were used to separate the cocoons from the litter and duff.

Cocoons were collected in early September before adult sawflies emerged and those from each quadrat were placed in separate containers for later analysis. These cocoons were analysed by first segregating them into "new" and "old" categories. Cocoons of the former category were a bright golden colour and were assumed to have been spun in the year of sampling, while those of the latter were dull brown in colour and supposedly had been spun before the sampling year. These assumptions proved partly incorrect, however, for some of the cocoons retained their new colour for over one year. Hence the "new" category contained enough cocoons that had been spun before the sampling year to prevent its use, without correction, as an estimate of the number of cocoons spun in the year of sampling. A correction was devised, however, which reduced the error to negligible proportions.

This method provided the best available estimate of the number of healthy cocoons per acre present in any one year. The population figures obtained ranged from 39,000 (Plot 1, 1954) to 1,080,000 (Plot 2, 1952) cocoons per acre.

Predation

Small-mammal predation has a direct and indirect effect on *N. sertifer* populations. The direct effect of predation is studied in detail in this paper. The indirect effect, resulting from the mutual interaction of various control factors (parasites, disease, and predators) has been discussed in previous papers (Holling, 1955, 1958b).

The direct effect of predation was measured in a variety of ways. General information was obtained from studies of the consumption of insects by caged animals and from the analysis of stomach contents obtained from animals trapped in sawfly-infested plantations. More particular information was obtained from the analysis of cocoons collected in the regular quadrat samples and from laboratory experiments which studied the effect of cocoon density upon predation.

The actual numbers of *N. sertifer* cocoons destroyed were estimated from cocoons collected in the regular quadrat samples described previously. As shown in an earlier paper (Holling, 1955), cocoons opened by small mammals were easily recognized and moreover could be classified as to species of predator. These estimates of the number of new and old cocoons per square foot opened by each species of predator were corrected, as before, to provide an estimate of the number opened from the time larvae dropped to the time when cocoon samples were taken in early September.

It has proved difficult to obtain a predation and cocoon-population estimate of the desired precision and accuracy. The corrections and calculations that had to be applied to the raw sampling data cast some doubt upon the results and conclusions based upon them. It subsequently developed, however, that a considerable margin of error could be tolerated without changing the results and the conclusions that could be derived from them. In any case, all conclusions based upon cocoon-population estimates were supported and substantiated by results from controlled laboratory experiments.

LABORATORY TECHNIQUES

Several experiments were conducted with caged animals in order to support and expand results obtained in the field. The most important of these measured the number of cocoons consumed by *Peromyscus* at different cocoon densities. These experiments were conducted at room temperature (ca. 20°C) in a screen-topped cage, 10' x 4' x 6". At the beginning of an experiment, cocoons were first buried in sand where the lines of a removable grid intersected, the grid was then removed, the sand was pressed flat, and a metal-edged levelling jig was finally scraped across the sand so that an even 12 mm. covered the cocoons. A single deer mouse was then placed in the cage together with nesting material, water, and an alternate food—dog biscuits. In each experiment the amount of this alternate food was kept approximately the same (i.e. 13 to 17 gms. dry weight). After the animal had been left undisturbed for 24 hours, the removable grid was replaced, and the number of holes dug over cocoons, the number of cocoons opened and the dry weight of dog biscuits eaten were recorded. Consumption by every animal was measured at either four or five different densities ranging from 2.25 to 36.00 cocoons per sq. ft. The specific densities were provided at random until all were used, the consumption at each density being measured for three to six consecutive days. Ideally the size of the cage should remain constant at all densities but since this would have required over 1,400 cocoons at the highest density, practical considerations necessitated a compromise whereby the cage was shortened at the higher densities. In these experiments the total number of cocoons provided ranged from 88 at the lowest density to 504 at the highest. At all densities, however, these numbers represented a surplus and no more than 40 per cent were ever consumed in a single experiment. Hence consumption was not limited by shortage of cocoons, even though the size of the cage changed.

221

The sources and characteristics of the cocoons and *Peromyscus* used in these experiments require some comment. Supplies of the prey were obtained by collecting cocoons in sawfly-infested plantations or by collecting late-instar larvae and allowing them to spin cocoons in boxes provided with foliage and litter. Sound cocoons from either source were then segregated into those containing healthy, parasitized, and diseased prepupae using a method of X-ray analysis (Holling, 1958a). The small male cocoons were separated from the larger female cocoons by size, since this criterion had previously proved adequate (Holling, 1958b). To simplify the experiments, only male and female cocoons containing healthy, living prepupae were used and in each experiment equal numbers of cocoons of each sex were provided, alternately, in the grid pattern already described.

Three mature non-breeding male deer mice were used in the experiments. Each animal had been born and raised in small rearing cages 12 x 8 x 6 in. and had been isolated from cocoons since birth. They therefore required a period to become familiar with the experimental cage and with cocoons. This experience was acquired during a preliminary three-week period. For the first two weeks the animal was placed in the experimental cage together with nesting material, water, dog biscuits and sand, and each day was disturbed just as it would be if an experiment were in progress. For the final week cocoons were buried in the sand at the first density chosen so that the animal could learn to find and consume the cocoon contents. It has been shown (Holling, 1955, 1958b) that a seven-day period is more than ample to permit complete learning.

THE COMPONENTS OF PREDATION

A large number of variables could conceivably affect the mortality of a given species of prey as a result of predation by a given species of predator. These can conveniently be classified, as was done by Leopold (1933), into five groups:

(1) density of the prey population.
(2) density of the predator population.
(3) characteristics of the prey, e.g., reactions to predators, stimulus detected by predator, and other characteristics.
(4) density and quality of alternate foods available for the predator.
(5) characteristics of the predator, e.g., food preferences, efficiency of attack, and other characteristics.

Each of these variables may exert a considerable influence and the effect of any one may depend upon changes in another. For example, Errington (1946) has shown that the characteristics of many vertebrate prey species change when their density exceeds the number that the available cover can support. This change causes a sudden increase in predation. When such complex interactions are involved, it is difficult to understand clearly the principles involved in predation; to do so we must find a simplified situation where some of the variables are constant or are not operating. The problem studied here presents such a situation. First, the characteristics of cocoons do not change as the other factors vary and there are no reactions by the cocooned sawflies to the predators. We therefore can ignore, temporarily, the effect of the third factor, prey characteristics. Secondly, since the work was conducted in plantations noted for their uniformity as to species, age, and distribution of trees, there was a constant and small variety of possible alternate foods. In such a simple and somewhat sterile environment, the fourth factor, the density and quality of alternate foods, can therefore be initially ignored, as can the fifth factor, characteristics of the predator, which is really only another way of expressing factors three and four. There are thus only two basic variables affecting predation in this instance, i.e., prey density and predator density. Furthermore, these are the only essential ones, for the remainder, while possibly important in affecting the amount of predation, are not essential to describe its fundamental characteristics.

The Basic Components

It is from the two essential variables that the basic components of predation will be derived. The first of these variables, prey density, might affect a number of processes and consumption of prey by individual predators might well be one of them.

The data which demonstrate the effect of changes of prey density upon consumption of cocooned sawflies by *Peromyscus* were obtained from the yearly cocoon quadrat samples in Plots 1 and 2. In 1951, Dr. F. T. Bird, Laboratory of Insect Pathology, Sault Ste. Marie, Ont., had sprayed each of these plots with a low concentration of a virus disease that attacked *N. sertifer* larvae, (Bird 1953). As a result, populations declined from 248,000 and 1,080,000 cocoons per acre, respectively, in 1952, to 39,000 and 256,000 in 1954. Thus predation values at six different cocoon densities were obtained. An additional sample in a neighbouring plantation in 1953 provided another value.

Predation values for *Sorex* and *Blarina* were obtained from one plantation, Plot 3, in one year, 1952. In the spring of that year, virus, sprayed from an aircraft flying along parallel lines 300 feet apart, was applied in three concentrations, with the lowest at one end of the plantation and the highest at the other. An area at one end, not sprayed, served as a control. When cocoon populations were sampled in the autumn, a line of 302 trees was selected at right angles to the lines of spray and the duff under each was sampled with one one-square-foot quadrat. The line, approximately 27 chains long, ran the complete length of the plantation. When the number of new cocoons per square foot was plotted against distance, discrete areas could be selected which had fairly constant populations that ranged from 44,000 to 571,000 cocoons per acre. The areas of low population corresponded to the areas sprayed with the highest concentration of virus. In effect, the plantation could be divided into rectangular strips, each with a particular density of cocoons. The width of these strips varied from 126 to 300 feet with an average of 193 feet. In addition to the 302 quadrats examined, the cocoons from another 100 quadrats were collected from the areas of lowest cocoon densities. Thus, in this one plantation in 1952, there was a sufficient number of different cocoon densities to show the response of consumption by *Sorex* and *Blarina* to changes of prey density.

The methods used to estimate predator densities in each study plot require some further comment. In Plots 1 and 2 this was done with grids of Sherman traps run throughout the summer. In Plot 3 both a grid of Sherman traps and a line of snap traps were used. This grid, measuring 18 chains by 4 chains, was placed so that approximately the same area sampled for cocoons was sampled for small mammals. The populations determined from these trapping procedures were plotted against time, and the number of "mammal-days" per acre, from the start of larval drop (June 14) to the time cocoon samples were made (Aug. 20-30), was determined for each plot each year. This could be done with *Peromyscus* and *Blarina* since the trapping technique was shown to provide an accurate estimate of their populations. But this was not true for *Sorex*. Instead, the number of *Sorex*-days per acre was approximated by dividing the number of cocoons opened at the highest density by the known number consumed by caged *Sorex* per day, i.e. 101. Since the number of cocoons opened at the highest cocoon density was

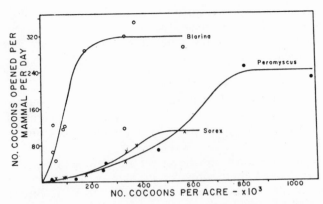

Fig. 1. Functional responses of *Blarina*, *Sorex* and *Peromyscus* in plots 1, 2, and 3.

151,000 per acre, then the number of *Sorex*-days per acre should be 151,000/101 = 1,490. This is approximately 10 times the estimate that was obtained from trapping with Sherman traps. When the various trapping methods were compared, estimates from Sherman trapping were shown to underestimate the numbers of *Sorex* by about the same amount, i.e. one-tenth.

With estimates of the numbers of predators, prey and destroyed prey available, the daily number of prey consumed per predator at different cocoon densities can be calculated. As seen in Fig. 1, the number of cocoons opened by each species increased with increasing cocoon density until a maximum daily consumption was reached that corresponded approximately to the maximum number that could be consumed in any one day by caged animals. For *Sorex* this of course follows from the method of calculation. The rates at which these curves rise differ for the different species, being greatest for *Blarina* and least for *Peromyscus*. Even if the plateaus are equated by multiplying points on each curve by a constant, the rates still decrease in the same order, reflecting a real difference in species behaviour.

The existence of such a response to cocoon density may also be demonstrated by data from the analysis of stomach contents. The per cent occurrence and per cent volume of the various food items in stomachs of *Peromyscus* captured immediately after larval drop and two months later is shown in Table I. When cocoon densities were high, immediately after larval drop, the per cent occurrence and per cent volume of *N. sertifer* material was high. Two months later when various cocoon mortality factors had taken their toll, cocoon densities were lower and

TABLE I

Stomach contents of *Peromyscus* trapped immediately before larval drop and two months later

Time trapped	Approx. no. cocoons per acre	No. of stomachs	Analysis	Plant	*N. sertifer*	Other insects	All insects
June 16–21	600,000	19	% occurrence	37%	95%	53%	100%
Aug. 17–19	300,000	14		79%	50%	64%	86%
June 16–21	600,000	19	% volume	5%	71%	24%	95%
Aug. 17–19	300,000	14		47%	19%	34%	53%

TABLE II

Occurrence of food items in stomachs of *Microtus* trapped before and after larval drop

Time trapped	Plant		*N. sertifer*		All insects	
	No. of stomachs	% occurrence	No. of stomachs	% occurrence	No. of stomachs	% occurrence
before larval drop	25	100%	2	8%	2	8%
after larval drop	29	100%	8	28%	11	38%

N. sertifer was a less important food item. The decrease in consumption of *N. sertifer* was accompanied by a considerable increase in the consumption of plant material and a slight increase in the consumption of other insect material. Plants and other insects acted as buffer or alternate foods. *Microtus*, even though they ate few non-plant foods in nature, also showed an increase in the per cent occurrence of *N. sertifer* material in stomachs as cocoon density increased (Table II). Before larval drop, when cocoon densities were low, the incidence of *N. sertifer* in *Microtus* stomachs was low. After larval drop, when cocoon densities were higher, the incidence increased by 3.5 times. Even at the higher cocoon densities, however, *N. sertifer* comprised less than one per cent of the volume of stomach contents so that this response to changes in prey density by *Microtus* is extremely low.

The graphs presented in Fig. I and the results of the analyses of stomach contents leave little doubt that the consumption of cocooned sawflies by animals in the field increases with increase in cocoon density. Similar responses have been demonstrated in laboratory experiments with three *Peromyscus*. As shown in Fig. 2, the number of cocoons consumed daily by each animal increased with increase in cocoon density, again reaching a plateau as did the previous curves. Whenever the number of prepupae consumed did not meet the caloric requirements, these were met by consumption of the dog biscuits, the alternate food provided. Only one of the animals (A) at the highest density fulfilled its caloric requirements by consuming prepupae; the remaining animals (B and C) consumed

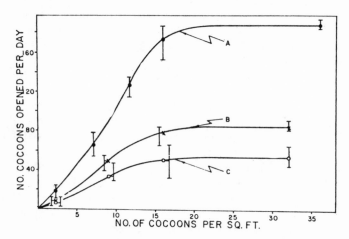

Fig. 2. Functional responses of three caged *Peromyscus* (means and ranges shown).

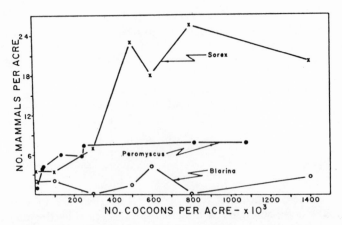

Fig. 3. Numerical responses of *Blarina, Sorex* and *Peromyscus*.

less than one-half the number of sawflies they would consume if no alternate foods were present. The cocoons used in experiments involving animals B and C, however, had been spun 12 months earlier than those involving animal A. When the characteristics of the functional response are examined in another paper, it will be shown that the strength of stimulus from older cocoons is less than that from younger cocoons, and that these differences are sufficient to explain the low consumption by animals B and C. The shape of the curves and the density at which they level is very similar for all animals, so similar that multiplying points along any one curve by the proper constant will equate all three. These curves are very similar to the ones based upon field data. All show the same form, the essential feature of which is an S-shaped rise to a plateau.

The effect of changes of prey density need not be restricted exclusively to consumption of prey by individual predators. The density of predators may also be affected and this can be shown by relating the number of predators per acre to the number of cocoons per acre. Conclusions can be derived from these relations but they are tentative. The data were collected over a relatively short period of time (four summers) and thus any relationship between predator numbers and prey density may have been fortuitous. Only those data obtained in plantations over 12 years old are included since small mammal populations were most stable in these areas. The data for the three most important species of predators are shown in the curves of Fig. 3, where each point represents the highest summer population observed either in different plantations or in the same plantation in different years.

The densities of *Blarina* were lowest while those of *Sorex* were highest. In this situation, *Blarina* populations apparently did not respond to prey density, for its numbers did not noticeably increase with increase in cocoon density. Some agent or agents other than food must limit their numbers. Populations of *Peromyscus* and *Sorex*, on the other hand, apparently did initially increase with . increase in cocoon density, ultimately ceasing to increase as some agents other than food became limiting. The response of *Sorex* was most marked.

Thus two responses to changes of prey density have been demonstrated. The first is a change in the number of prey consumed per predator and the second is a change in the density of predators. Although few authors appear to recognize the existence and importance of *both* these responses to changes of prey density, they have been postulated and, in the case of the change of predator density, demonstrated. Thus Solomon (1949) acknowledged the two-fold nature of the response to changes of prey density, and applied the term *functional response* to the change in the number of prey consumed by individual predators, and the term *numerical response* to the change in the density of predators. These are apt terms and, although they have been largely ignored in the literature, they will be adopted in this paper. The data available to Solomon for review did not permit him to anticipate the form the functional response of predators might take, so that he could not assess its importance in population regulation. It will be shown, however, that the functional response is as important as the numerical.

It remains now to consider the effect of predator density, the variable that, together with prey density, is essential for an adequate description of predation. Predator density might well affect the number of prey consumed per predator. Laboratory experiments were designed to measure the number of cocoons opened by one, two, four, and eight animals in a large cage provided with cocoons at a density of 15 per square foot and a surplus of dog biscuits and water. The average number of cocoons opened per mouse in eight replicates was 159, 137, 141 and 159 respectively. In this experiment, therefore, predator density apparently did not greatly affect the consumption of prey by individual animals. This conclusion is again suggested when field and laboratory data are compared, for the functional response of *Peromyscus* obtained in the field, where its density varied, was very similar to the response of single animals obtained in the laboratory.

In such a simple situation, where predator density does not greatly affect the consumption by individuals, the total predation can be expressed by a simple, additive combination of the two responses. For example, if at a particular prey density the functional response is such that 100 cocoons are opened by a single predator in one day, and the numerical response is such that the predator density is 10, then the total daily consumption will be simply 100 x 10. In other situations, however, an increase in the density of predators might result in so much competition that the consumption of prey by individual predators might drop significantly. This effect can still be incorporated in the present scheme by adopting a more complex method of combining the functional and numerical responses.

This section was introduced with a list of the possible variables that could affect predation. Of these, only the two operating in the present study — prey and predator density — are essential variables, so that the basic features of predation can be ascribed to the effects of these two. It has been shown that there are two responses to prey density. The increase in the number of prey consumed per predator, as prey density rises, is termed the functional response, while the change in the density of predators is termed the numerical response. The total amount of predation occurring at any one density results from a combination of the two responses, and the method of combination will be determined by the way predator density affects consumption. This scheme, therefore, describes the effects of the basic variables, uncomplicated by the effects of subsidiary ones. Hence the two responses, the functional and numerical, can be considered the basic components of predation.

The total amount of predation caused by small mammals is shown in Fig. 4, where the functional and numerical responses are combined by multiplying the number of cocoons opened per predator at each density by the number of effective mammal-days observed. These figures were then expressed as percentages opened. This demonstrates the relation between per cent predation and prey density during the 100-day period between cocoon formation and adult emergence. Since the data obtained for the numerical responses are tentative, some reservations must be applied to the more particular conclusions derived

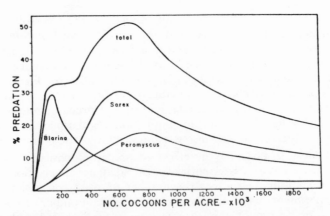

Fig. 4. Functional and numerical responses combined to show the relation between per cent predation and cocoon density.

from this figure. The general conclusion, that per cent predation by each species shows an initial rise and subsequent decline as cocoon density increases holds, however. For this conclusion to be invalid, the numerical responses would have to decrease in order to mask the initial rise in per cent predation caused by the S-shaped form of the functional responses. Thus from zero to some finite cocoon density, predation by small mammals shows a direct density-dependent action and thereafter shows an inverse density-dependent action. The initial rise in the proportion of prey destroyed can be attributed to both the functional and numerical responses. The functional response has a roughly sigmoid shape and hence the proportion of prey destroyed by an individual predator will increase with increase in cocoon density up to and beyond the point of inflection. Unfortunately the data for any one functional response curve are not complete enough to establish a sigmoid relation, but the six curves presented thus far and the several curves to be presented in the following section all suggest a point of inflection. The positive numerical responses shown by *Sorex* and *Peromyscus* also promote a direct density-dependent action up to the point at which predator densities remain constant. Thereafter, with individual consumption also constant, the per cent predation will decline as cocoon density increases. The late Dr. L. Tinbergen apparently postulated the same type of dome-shaped curves for the proportion of insects destroyed by birds. His data were only partly published (1949, 1955) before his death, but Klomp (1956) and Voûte (1958) have commented upon the existence of these "optimal curves". This term, however, is unsatisfactory and anthropocentric. From the viewpoint of the forest entomologist, the highest proportion of noxious insects destroyed may certainly be the optimum, but the term is meaningless for an animal that consumes individuals and not percentages. Progress can best be made by considering predation first as a behaviour before translating this behaviour in terms of the proportion of prey destroyed. The term "peaked curve" is perhaps more accurate.

Returning to Fig. 4, we see that the form of the peaked curve for *Blarina* is determined solely by the functional response since this species exhibited no numerical response. The abrupt peak occurs because the maximum consumption of prepupae was reached at a very low prey density before the predation was "diluted" by large numbers of cocoons. With *Sorex* both the numerical and functional responses are important. Predation by *Sorex* is greatest principally because of the marked numerical response. The two responses again determine the form of the peaked curve for *Peromyscus*, but the numerical response, unlike that of *Sorex*, was not marked, and the maximum consumption of cocoons was reached only at a relatively high density; the result is a low per cent predation with a peak occurring at a high cocoon density.

Predation by all species destroyed a considerable number of cocooned saw-flies over a wide range of cocoon densities. The presence of more than one species of predator not only increased predation but also extended the range of prey densities over which predation was high. This latter effect is particularly important, for if the predation by several species of predators peaked at the same prey density the range of densities over which predation was high would be slight and if the prey had a sufficiently high reproductive capacity its density might jump this vulnerable range and hence escape a large measure of the potential control that could be exerted by predators. Before we can proceed further in the discussion of the effect of predation upon prey numbers, the additional components that make up the behaviour of predation must be considered.

The Subsidiary Components

Additional factors such as prey characteristics, the density and quality of alternate foods, and predator characteristics have a considerable effect upon predation. It is necessary now to demonstrate the effect of these factors and how they operate.

There are four classes of prey characteristics: those that influence the caloric value of the prey; those that change the length of time prey are exposed; those that affect the "attractiveness" of the prey to the predator (e.g. palatability, defence mechanisms); and those that affect the strength of stimulus used by predators in locating prey (e.g. size, habits, and colours). Only those characteristics that affect the strength of stimulus were studied experimentally. Since small mammals detect cocoons by the odour emanating from them (Holling, 1958b), the strength of this odour perceived by a mammal can be easily changed in laboratory experiments by varying the depth of sand covering the cocoons.

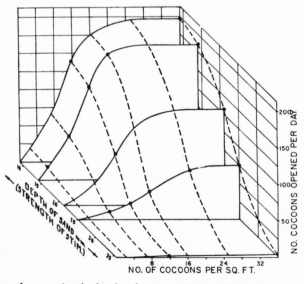

Fig. 5. Effect of strength of stimulus from cocoons upon the functional response of one caged *Peromyscus*. Each point represents the average of three to six replicates.

One *Peromyscus* was used in these experiments and its daily consumption of cocoons was measured at different cocoon densities and different depths of sand. These data are plotted in Fig. 5. Since the relation between depth of sand and strength of stimulus must be an inverse one, the depths of sand are reversed on the axis so that values of the strength of stimulus increase away from the origin. Each point represents the mean of three to six separate measurements. Decreasing the strength of the perceived stimulus by increasing the depth of sand causes a marked decrease in the functional response. A 27 mm. increase in depth (from nine to 36 mm.), for example, causes the peak consumption to drop from 196 to four cocoons per day. The daily number of calories consumed in all these experiments remained relatively constant since dog biscuits were always present as alternate food. The density at which each functional-response curve levels appear to increase somewhat as the strength of stimulus perceived by the animal decreases. We might expect that the increase in consumption is directly related to the increase in the proportion of cocoons in the amount of food available, at least up to the point where the caloric requirements are met solely by sawflies. The ascending portions of the curves, however, are S-shaped and the level portions are below the maximum consumption, approximately 220 cocoons for this animal. Therefore, the functional response cannot be explained by random searching for cocoons. For the moment, however, the important conclusion is that changes in prey characteristics can have a marked effect on predation but this effect is exerted through the functional response.

In the plantations studied, cocoons were not covered by sand but by a loose litter and duff formed from pine needles. Variations in the depth of this material apparently did not affect the strength of the perceived odour, for as many cocoons were opened in quadrats with shallow litter as with deep. This material must be so loose as to scarcely impede the passage of odour from cocoons.

The remaining subsidiary factors, the density and quality of alternate foods and predator characteristics, can also affect predation. The effect of alternate foods could not be studied in the undisturbed plantations because the amount of these "buffers" was constant and very low. The effect of quality of alternate foods on the functional response, however, was demonstrated experimentally using one *Peromyscus*. The experiments were identical to those already described except that at one series of densities an alternate food of low palatability (dog biscuits) was provided, and at the second series one of high palatability (sunflower seeds) was provided. When both foods are available, deer mice select sunflower seeds over dog biscuits. In every experiment a constant amount of alternate food was available: 13 to 17 gms. dry weight of dog biscuits, or 200 sunflower seeds.

Fig. 6 shows the changes in the number of cocoons opened per day and in the amount of alternate foods consumed. The functional response decreased with an increase in the palatability of the alternate food (Fig. 6A). Again the functional response curves showed an initial, roughly sigmoid rise to a constant level.

As cocoon consumption rose, the consumption of alternate foods decreased (Fig. 6B) at a rate related to the palatability of the alternate food. Each line indicating the change in the consumption of alternate food was drawn as a mirror image of the respective functional response and these lines closely follow the mean of the observed points. The variability in the consumption of sunflower seeds at any one cocoon density was considerable, probably as a result of the extreme variability in the size of seeds.

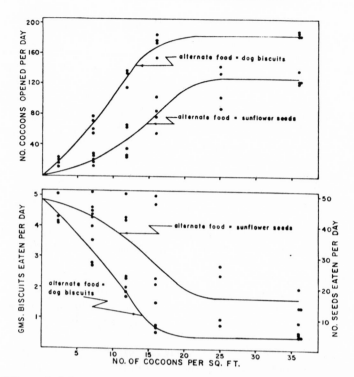

Fig. 6.   Effect of different alternate foods upon the functional response of one *Peromyscus*. *A* (upper) shows the functional responses when either a low (dog biscuits) or a high (sunflower seeds) palatability alternate food was present in excess. *B* (lower) shows the amount of these alternate foods consumed.

Again we see that there is not a simple relation between the number of cocoons consumed and the proportion of cocoons in the total amount of food available. This is most obvious when the functional response curves level, for further increase in density is not followed by an increase in the consumption of sawflies. The plateaus persist because the animal continued consuming a certain fixed quantity of alternate foods. L. Tinbergen (1949) observed a similar phenomenon in a study of predation of pine-eating larvae by tits in Holland. He presented data for the consumption of larvae of the pine beauty moth, *Panolis griseovariegata*, and of the web-spinning sawfly *Acantholyda pinivora*, each at two different densities. In each case more larvae were eaten per nestling tit per day at the higher prey density. This, then, was part of a functional response, but it was that part above the point of inflection, since the proportion of prey eaten dropped at the higher density. It is not sufficient to explain these results as well as the ones presented in this paper by claiming, with Tinbergen, that the predators "have the tendency to make their menu as varied as possible and therefore guard against one particular species being strongly dominant in it". This is less an explanation than an anthropocentric description. The occurrence of this phenomenon depends upon the strength of stimulus from the prey, and the amount and quality of the alternate foods. Its proper explanation must await the collection of further data.

We now know that the palatability of alternate foods affects the functional response. Since the number of different kinds of alternate food could also have

TABLE III

The effect of alternate foods upon the number of cocoons consumed per day by one *Peromyscus*

Alternate food	No. of exp'ts	No. of cocoons opened	
		$\overline{X}$	S.E.$\overline{x}$
none...............................	7	165.9	11.4
dog biscuits.........................	5	143.0	8.3
sunflower seeds......................	8	60.0	6.2
sunflower seeds and dog biscuits........	8	21.5	4.2

an important effect, the consumption of cocoons by a caged *Peromyscus* was measured when no alternate foods, or one or two alternate foods, were present. Only female cocoons were used and these were provided at a density of 75 per sq. ft. to ensure that the level portion of the functional response would be measured. As in the previous experiments, the animal was familiarized with the experimental conditions and with cocoons for a preliminary two-week period. The average numbers of cocoons consumed each day with different numbers and kinds of alternate foods present are shown in Table III. This table again shows that fewer cocoons were consumed when sunflower seeds (high palatability) were present than when dog biscuits (low palatability) were present. In both cases, however, the consumption was lower than when no alternate foods were available. When two alternate foods were available, i.e., both sunflower seeds and dog biscuits, the consumption dropped even further. Thus, increase in both the palatability and in the number of different kinds of alternate foods decreases the functional response.

DISCUSSION

General

It has been argued that three of the variables affecting predation—characteristics of the prey, density and quality of alternate foods and characteristics of the predators — are subsidiary components of predation. The laboratory experiments showed that the functional response was lowered when the strength of stimulus, one prey characteristic, detected from cocoons was decreased or when the number of kinds and palatability of alternate foods was increased. Hence the effect of these subsidiary components is exerted through the functional response. Now the numerical response is closely related to the functional, since such an increase in predator density depends upon the amount of food consumed. It follows, therefore, that the subsidiary components will also affect the numerical response. Thus when the functional response is lowered by a decrease in the strength of stimulus detected from prey, the numerical response similarly must be decreased and predation will be less as a result of decrease of the two basic responses.

The density and quality of alternate foods could also affect the numerical response. Returning to the numerical responses shown in Fig. 3, if increase in the density or quality of alternate foods involved solely increase in food "per se", then the number of mammals would reach a maximum at a lower cocoon density, but the maximum itself would not change. If increase in alternate foods also involved changes in the agents limiting the numerical responses (e.g. increased cover and depth of humus), then the maximum density the small mammals could attain would increase. Thus increase in the amount of alternate foods could increase the density of predators.

Increase in alternate foods *decreases* predation by dilution of the functional response, but *increases* predation by promoting a favourable numerical response. The relative importance of each of these effects will depend upon the particular problem. Voûte (1946) has remarked that insect populations in cultivated woods show violent fluctuations, whereas in virgin forests or mixed woods, where the number of alternate foods is great, the populations are more stable. This stability might result from alternate foods promoting such a favourable numerical response that the decrease in the functional response is not great enough to lower predation.

The importance of alternate foods will be affected by that part of the third subsidiary component — characteristics of the predators — that concerns food preferences. Thus an increase in plants or animals other than the prey will most likely affect the responses of those predators, like the omnivore *Peromyscus*, that are not extreme food specialists. Predation by the more stenophagous shrews, would only be affected by some alternate, animal food.

Food preferences, however, are only one of the characteristics of predators. Others involve their ability to detect, capture, and kill prey. But again the effect of these predator characteristics will be exerted through the two basic responses, the functional and numerical. The differences observed between the functional responses of the three species shown earlier in Fig. 1 undoubtedly reflect differences in their abilities to detect, capture, and kill. The amount of predation will similarly be affected by the kind of sensory receptor, whether visual, olfactory, auditory, or tactile, that the predator uses in locating prey. An efficient nose, for example, is probably a less precise organ than an efficient eye. The source of an undisturbed olfactory stimulus can only be located by investigating a gradient in space, whereas a visual stimulus can be localized by an efficient eye from a single point in space — the telotaxis of Fraenkel and Gunn (1940). As N. Tinbergen (1951) remarked, localization of direction is developed to the highest degree in the eye. Thus the functional response of a predator which locates prey by sight will probably reach a maximum at a much lower prey density than the response of one that locates its prey by odour. In the data presented by Tothill (1922) and L. Tinbergen (1949), the per cent predation of insects by birds was highest at very low prey densities, suggesting that the functional responses of these "visual predators" did indeed reach a maximum at a low density.

The Effect of Predation on Prey Populations

One of the most important characteristics of mortality factors is their ability to regulate the numbers of an animal — to promote a "steady density" (Nicholson, 1933; Nicholson and Bailey, 1935) such that a continued increase or decrease of numbers from this steady state becames progressively unlikely the greater the departure from it. Regulation in this sense therefore requires that the mortality factor change with change in the density of the animal attacked, i.e. it requires a direct density-dependent mortality (Smith, 1935, 1939). Density-independent factors can affect the numbers of an animal but alone they cannot *regulate* the numbers. There is abundant evidence that changes in climate, some aspects of which are presumed to have a density-independent action, can lower or raise the numbers of an animal. But this need not be regulation. Regulation will only result from an interaction with a density-dependent factor, an interaction

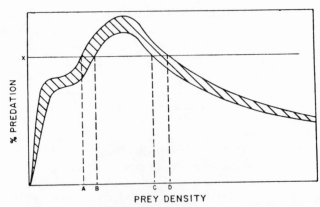

Fig. 7. Theoretical model showing regulation of prey by predators. (see text for explanation).

that might be the simplest, i.e. merely additive. Recently, the density-dependent concept has been severely criticized by Andrewartha and Birch (1954). They call it a dogma, but such a comment is only a criticism of an author's use of the concept. Its misuse as a dogma does not militate against its value as a hypothesis.

We have seen from this study that predation by small mammals does change with changes in prey density. As a result of the functional and numerical responses the proportion of prey destroyed increases from zero to some finite prey density and thereafter decreases. Thus predation over some ranges of prey density shows a direct density-dependent action. This is all that is required for a factor to regulate.

The way in which predation of the type shown in this study can regulate the numbers of a prey species can best be shown by a hypothetical example. To simplify this example we will assume that the prey has a constant rate of reproduction over all ranges of its density, and that only predators are affecting its numbers. Such a situation is, of course, unrealistic. The rate of reproduction of real animals probably is low at low densities when there is slight possibility for contact between individuals (e.g. between male and female). It would rise as contacts became more frequent and would decline again at higher densities when the environment became contaminated, when intraspecific stress symptoms appeared, or when cannibalism became common. Such changes in the rate of reproduction have been shown for experimental populations of *Tribolium confusum* (MacLagan, 1932) and *Drosophila* (Robertson and Sang, 1944). Introducing more complex assumptions, however, confuses interpretations without greatly changing the conclusions.

This hypothetical model is shown in Fig. 7. The curve that describes the changes in predation with changes in prey density is taken from the actual data shown earlier in Fig. 4. It is assumed that the birth-rate of the prey at any density can be balanced by a fixed per cent predation, and that the variation in the environment causes a variation in the predation at any one density. The per cent predation necessary to balance the birth-rate is represented by the horizontal line, x%, in the diagram and variation in predation is represented by the thickness of the mortality curve. The death-rate will equal the birth-rate at two density ranges, between A and B and between C and D. When the densities of the prey are below A, the mortality will be lower than that necessary to balance reproduction and the population will increase. When the densities of the animal are between B and C, death-rate will exceed birth-rate and the populations will decrease. Thus, the density of the prey will tend to fluctuate between densities A and B. If the density happens to exceed D, death-rate will be lower than birth-rate and the prey will increase in numbers, having "escaped" the control exerted by predators. This would occur when the prey had such a high rate of reproduction that its density could jump, in one generation, from a density lower than A to a density higher than D. If densities A and D were far apart, there would be less chance of this occurring. This spread is in part determined by the number of different species of predators that are present. Predation by each species peaks at a different density (see Fig. 4), so that increase in the number of species of predator will increase the spread of the total predation. This will produce a more stable situation where the prey will have less chance to escape control by predators.

Predation of the type shown will regulate the numbers of an animal whenever the predation rises high enough to equal the effective birth-rate. When the prey is an insect and predators are small mammals, as in this case, the reproductive rate of the prey will be too high for predation *alone* to regulate. But if other mortality occurs, density-independent or density-dependent, the total mortality could rise to the point where small mammals were contributing, completely or partially, to the regulation of the insect.

Predation of the type shown will produce stability if there are large numbers of different species of predators operating. Large numbers of such species would most likely occur in a varied environment, such as mixed woods. Perhaps this explains, in part, Voûte's (1946) observation that insect populations in mixed woods are less liable to show violent fluctuations.

I cannot agree with Voûte (1956 and 1958) that factors causing a peaked mortality curve are not sufficient for regulation. He states (1956) that "this is due to the fact that mortality only at low densities increases with the increase of the population. At higher densities, mortality decreases again. The growth of the population is at the utmost slowed down, never stopped". All that is necessary for regulation, however, is a rise in per cent predation over some range of prey densities and an *effective* birth-rate that can be matched at some density by mortality from predators.

Neither can I agree with Thompson (1930) when he ascribes a minor role to vertebrate predators of insects and states that "the number of individuals of any given species (i.e. of vertebrate predators) is . . . relatively small in comparison with those of insects and there is no reason to suppose that it varies primarily in function of the supply of insect food, which fluctuates so rapidly that it is impossible for vertebrates to profit by a temporary abundance of it excepting to a very limited extent". We know that they do respond by an increase in numbers and even if this is not great in comparison with the numerical response of parasitic flies, the number of prey killed per predator is so great and the increase in number killed with increase in prey density is so marked as to result in a heavy proportion of prey destroyed; a proportion that, furthermore, increases initially with increase of prey density. Thompson depreciates the importance of the numerical response of predators and ignores the functional response.

In entomological literature there are two contrasting mathematical theories of regulation. Each theory is based on different assumptions and the predicted results are quite different. Both theories were developed to predict the interaction between parasitic flies and their insect hosts but they can be applied equally well to predator-prey relations. Thompson (1939) assumes that a predator has a limited appetite and that it has no difficulty in finding its prey. Nicholson (1933) assumes that predators have insatiable appetites and that they have a specific capacity to find their prey. This searching capacity is assumed to remain constant at all prey densities and it is also assumed that the searching is random.

The validity of these mathematical models depends upon how closely their assumptions fit natural conditions. We have seen that the appetites of small mammal predators in this study are not insatiable. This fits one of Thompson's assumptions but not Nicholson's. When the functional response was described, it was obvious that predators did have difficulty in finding their prey and that their searching ability did not remain constant at all prey densities. Searching by small mammals was not random. Hence in the present study of predator-prey relations, the remaining assumptions of both Thompson and Nicholson do not hold.

Klomp (1956) considers the damping of oscillations of animal numbers to be as important as regulation. If the oscillations of the numbers of an animal affected by a delayed density-dependent factor (Varley, 1947) like a parasite, do increase in amplitude, as Nicholson's theory predicts (Nicholson and Bailey, 1935), then damping is certainly important. It is not at all certain, however, that this prediction is true. We have already seen that the assumptions underlying Nicholson's theory do not hold in at least some cases. In particular he ignores the important possibility of an S-shaped functional response of the type shown by small mammal predators. If the parasites did show an S-shaped functional response, there would be an *immediate* increase in per cent predation when host density increased, an increase that would modify the effects of the delayed numerical response of parasites emphasized by Nicholson and Varley. Under these conditions the amplitude of the oscillations would not increase as rapidly, and might well not increase at all. An S-shaped functional response therefore acts as an intrinsic damping mechanism in population fluctuations.

Oscillations undoubtedly do occur, however, and whether they increase in amplitude or not, any extrinsic damping is important. The factor that damps oscillations most effectively will be a concurrent density-dependent factor that reacts immediately to changes in the numbers of an animal. Predation by small mammals fulfils these requirements when the density of prey is low. The consumption of prey by individual predators responds immediately to increase in prey density (functional response). Similarly, the numerical response is not greatly delayed, probably because of the high reproductive capacity of small mammals. Thus if the density of a prey is low, chance increases in its numbers will immediately increase the per cent mortality caused by small mammal predation. When the numbers of the prey decrease, the effect of predation will be immediately relaxed. Thus, incipient oscillations can be damped by small-mammal predation.

We have seen that small mammals theoretically can regulate the numbers of prey and can damp their oscillations under certain conditions. Insufficient information was obtained to assess precisely the role of small mammals as predators of *N. sertifer* in the pine plantations of southwestern Ontario, however. Before the general introduction of a virus disease in 1952 (Bird, 1952, 1953), the sawfly was exhausting its food supplies and 70 to 100% defoliation of Scots, jack and red pines was observed in this area. Predators were obviously not regulating the numbers of the sawfly. After the virus was introduced, however, sawfly populations declined rapidly. In Plot 1, for example, their numbers declined from 248,000 cocoons per acre in 1952 to 39,000 per acre in 1954. The area was revisited in 1955 and larval and cocoon population had obviously increased in this plot, before the virus disease could cause much mortality. It happened, however, that *Peromyscus* was the only species of small mammal residing in Plot 1 and it is interesting that similar increases were not observed in other plantations where sawfly numbers had either not decreased so greatly, or where shrews, the most efficient predators, were present. These observations suggest that predation by shrews was effectively damping the oscillations resulting from the interaction of the virus disease with its host.

Types of Predation

Many types of predation have been reported in the literature. Ricker (1954) believed that there were three major types of predator-prey relations, Leopold (1933) four, and Errington (1946, 1956) two. Many of these types are merely minor deviations, but the two types of predation Errington discusses are quite different from each other. He distinguishes between "compensatory" and "noncompensatory" predation. In the former type, predators take a heavy toll of individuals of the prey species when the density of prey exceeds a certain threshold. This "threshold of security" is determined largely by the number of secure habitable niches in the environment. When prey densities become too high some individuals are forced into exposed areas where they are readily captured by predators. In this type of predation, predators merely remove surplus animals, ones that would succumb even in the absence of enemies. Errington feels, however, that some predator-prey relations depart from this scheme, so that predation occurs not only *above* a specific threshold density of prey. These departures are ascribed largely to behaviour characteristics of the predators. For example, he does not believe that predation of ungulates by canids is compensatory and feels that this results from intelligent, selective searching by the predators.

If the scheme of predation presented here is to fulfill its purpose it must be able to explain these different types of predation. Non-compensatory predation is easily described by the normal functional and numerical responses, for predation of *N. sertifer* by small mammals is of this type. Compensatory predation can also be described using the basic responses and subsidiary factors previously demonstrated. The main characteristic of this predation is the "threshold of security". Prey are more vulnerable above and less vulnerable below this threshold. That is, the strength of stimulus perceived from prey increases markedly when the prey density exceeds the threshold. We have seen from the present study that an increase in the strength of stimulus from prey increases both the functional and numerical responses. Therefore, below the "threshold of security" the functional responses of predators will be very low and as a result there will probably be no numerical response. Above the threshold, the functional response will become marked and a positive numerical response could easily occur. The net effect will result from a combination of these functional and numerical responses so that per cent predation will remain low so long as there is sufficient cover and food available for the prey. As soon as these supply factors are approaching exhaustion the per cent predation will suddenly increase.

Compensatory predation will occur (1) when the prey has a specific density level near which it normally operates, and (2) when the strength of stimulus perceived by predators is so low below this level and so high above it that there is a marked change in the functional response. Most insect populations tolerate considerable crowding and the only threshold would be set by food limitations. In addition, their strength of stimulus is often high at all densities. For *N. sertifer* at least, the strength of stimulus from cocoons is great and the threshold occurs at such high densities that the functional responses of small mammals are at their maximum. Compensatory predation upon insects is probably uncommon.

Entomologists studying the biological control of insects have largely concentrated their attention on a special type of predator — parasitic insects. Although certain features of a true predator do differ from those of a parasite, both predation and parasitism are similar in that one animal is seeking out another. If insect parasitism can in fact be treated as a type of predation, the two basic responses to prey (or host) density and the subsidiary factors affecting these responses should describe parasitism. The functional response of a true predator is measured by the number of prey it destroys; of a parasite by the number of hosts in which eggs are laid. The differences observed between the functional responses of predators and parasites will depend upon the differences between the behaviour of eating and the behaviour of egg laying. The securing of food by an individual predator serves to maintain that individual's existence. The laying of eggs by a parasite serves to maintain its progenies' existence. It seems likely that the more a behaviour concerns the maintenance of an individual, the more demanding it is. Thus the restraints on egg laying could exert a greater and more prolonged effect than the restraints on eating. This must produce differences between the functional responses of predators and parasites. But the functional responses of both are similar in that there is an upper limit marked by the point at which the predator becomes satiated and the parasite has laid all its eggs. This maximum is reached at some finite prey or host density above zero. The form of the rising phase of the functional response would depend upon the characteristics of the individual parasite and we might expect some of the same forms that will be postulated for predators at the end of this section. To summarize, I do not wish to imply that the characteristics of the functional response of a parasite are identical with those of a predator. I merely wish to indicate that a parasite has a response to prey density — the laying of eggs — that can be identified as a functional response, the precise characteristics of which are unspecified.

The effects of host density upon the number of hosts parasitized have been studied experimentally by a number of workers (e.g., Ullyett, 1949a and b; Burnett, 1951 and 1954; De Bach and Smith, 1941). In each case the number of hosts attacked per parasite increased rapidly with initial increase in host density but tended to level with further increase. Hence these functional response curves showed a continually decreasing slope as host density increased and gave no indication of the S-shaped response shown by small mammals. Further information is necessary, however, before these differences can be ascribed solely to the difference between parasitism and predation. It might well reflect, for example, a difference between an instinctive response of an insect and a learned response of a mammal or between the absence of an alternate host and the presence of an alternate food.

The numerical response of both predators and parasites is measured by the way in which the number of adults increases with increase in prey or host density. At first thought, the numerical response of a parasite would seem to be so intimately connected with its functional response that they could not be separated. But the two responses of a predator are just as intimately connected.

238

The predator must consume food in order to produce progeny just as the parasite must lay eggs in order to produce progeny.

The agents limiting the numerical response of parasites will be similar to those limiting the response of predators. There is, however, some difference. During at least one stage of the parasites' life, the requirements for both food and niche are met by the same object. Thus increase in the amount of food means increase in the number of niches as well, so that niches are never limited unless food is. This should increase the chances for parasites to show pronounced numerical responses. The characteristics of the numerical responses of both predators and parasites, however, will be similar and will range from those in which there is no increase with increase in the density of hosts, to those in which there is a marked and prolonged increase.

A similar scheme has been mentioned by Ullyett (1949b) to describe parasitism. He believed that "the problem of parasite efficiency would appear to be divided into two main phases, viz.: (a) the efficiency of the parasite as a mortality factor in the host population, (b) its efficiency as related to the maintenance of its own population level within the given area". His first phase resembles the functional response and the second the numerical response. Both phases or responses will be affected, of course, by subsidiary components similar to those proposed for predation—characteristics of the hosts, density and quality of alternate hosts, and characteristics of the parasite. The combination of the two responses will determine the changes in per cent parasitism as the result of changes in host density. Since both the functional and numerical responses presumably level at some point, per cent parasitism curves might easily be peaked, as were the predation curves. If these responses levelled at a host density that would never occur in nature, however, the decline of per cent parasitism might never be observed.

The scheme of predation revealed in this study may well explain all types of predation as well as insect parasitism. The knowledge of the basic components and subsidiary factors underlying the behaviour permits us to imagine innumerable possible variations. In a hypothetical situation, for example, we could introduce and remove alternate food at a specific time in relation to the appearance of a prey, and predict the type of predation. But such variations are only minor deviations of a basic pattern. The major types of predation will result from major differences in the form of the functional and numerical responses.

If the functional responses of some predators are partly determined by their behaviour, we could expect a variety of responses differing in form, rate of rise, and final level reached. All functional responses, however, will ultimately level, for it is difficult to imagine an individual predator whose consumption rises indefinitely. Subsistence requirements will fix the ultimate level for most predators, but even those whose consumption is less rigidly determined by subsistence requirements (e.g., fish, Ricker 1941) must have an upper limit, even if it is only determined by the time required to kill.

The functional responses could conceivably have three basic forms. The mathematically simplest would be shown by a predator whose pattern of searching was random and whose rate of searching remained constant at all prey densities. The number of prey killed per predator would be directly proportional to prey density, so that the rising phase would be a straight line. Ricker (1941) postulated this type of response for certain fish preying on sockeye salmon, and De Bach and Smith (1941) observed that the parasitic fly, *Muscidifurax raptor,* parasitized puparia of *Musca domestica*, provided at different densities, in a similar fashion. So few prey were provided in the latter experiment, however, that the initial linear rise in the number of prey attacked with increase in prey density may have been an artifact of the method.

A more complex form of functional response has been demonstrated in laboratory experiments by De Bach and Smith (1941), Ullyett (1949a) and Burnett (1951, 1956) for a number of insect parasites. In each case the number of prey attacked per predator increased very rapidly with initial increase in prey density, and thereafter increased more slowly approaching a certain fixed level. The rates of searching therefore became progressively less as prey density increased.

The third and final form of functional response has been demonstrated for small mammals in this study. These functional responses are S-shaped so that the rates of searching at first increase with increase of prey density, and then decrease.

Numerical responses will also differ, depending upon the species of predator and the area in which it lives. Two types have been demonstrated in this study. *Peromyscus* and *Sorex* populations, for example, increased with increase of prey density to the point where some agent or agents other than food limited their numbers. These can be termed direct numerical responses. There are some cases, however, where predator numbers are not affected by changes of prey density and in the plantations studied *Blarina* presents such an example of no numerical response. A final response, in addition to ones shown here, might also occur. Morris *et al.* (1958) have pointed out that certain predators might decrease in numbers as prey density increases through competition with other predators. As an example of such inverse numerical responses, he shows that during a recent outbreak of spruce budworm in New Brunswick the magnolia, myrtle, and black-throated green warblers decreased in numbers. Thus we have three possible numerical responses — a direct response, no response, and an inverse response.

The different characteristics of these types of functional and numerical responses produce different types of predation. There are four major types conceivable; these are shown diagramatically in Fig. 8. Each type includes the three possible numerical responses — a direct response (a), no response (b), and an inverse response (c), and the types differ because of basic differences in the functional response. In type 1 the number of prey consumed per predator is assumed to be directly proportional to prey density, so that the rising phase of the functional response is a straight line. In type 2, the functional response is presumed to rise at a continually decreasing rate. In type 3, the form of the functional response is the same as that observed in this study. These three types of predation may be considered as the basic ones, for changes in the subsidiary components are not involved. Subsidiary components can, however, vary in response to changes of prey density and in such cases the basic types of predation are modified. The commonest modification seems to be Errington's compensatory predation which is presented as Type 4 in Fig. 8. In this figure the vertical dotted line represents the "threshold of security" below which the strength of stimulus from prey is low and above which it is high. The functional response curves at these two strengths of stimulus are given the form of the functional responses observed in this study. The forms of the responses shown in Types 1 and 2 could also be used, of course.

The combination of the two responses gives the total response shown in the

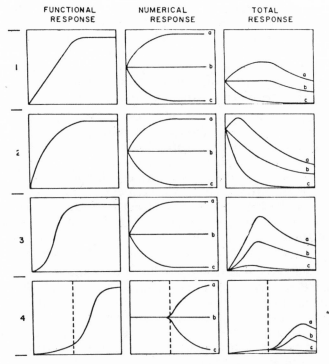

Fig. 8. Major types of predation.

final column of graphs of Fig. 8. Both peaked (curves 1a; 2a; 3a, b, c; 4a, b, c) and declining (1b, c; 2b, c) types of predation can occur, but in the absence of any other density-dependent factor, regulation is possible only in the former type.

This method of presenting the major types of predation is an over-simplification since predator density is portrayed as being directly related to prey density. Animal populations, however, cannot respond *immediately* to changes in prey density, so that there must be a delay of the numerical response. Varley (1953) pointed this out when he contrasted "delayed density dependence" and "density dependence". The degree of delay, however, will vary widely depending upon the rate of reproduction, immigration, and mortality. Small mammals, with their high reproductive rate, responded so quickly to increased food that the delay was not apparent. In such cases the numerical response graphs of Fig. 8 are sufficiently accurate, for the density of predators in any year is directly related to the density of prey in the same year. The numerical response of other natural enemies can be considerably delayed, however. Thus the density of those insect parasites that have one generation a year and a low rate of immigration results from the density of hosts in the preceding generation.

In these extreme cases of delay the total response obtained while prey or hosts are steadily increasing will be different than when they are steadily decreasing. The amount of difference will depend upon the magnitude and amount of delay of the numerical response, for the functional response has no element of delay.

SUMMARY AND CONCLUSIONS

The simplest and most basic type of predation is affected by only two variables — prey and predator density. Predation of cocooned *N. sertifer* by small mammals is such a type, for prey characteristics, the number and variety of alternate foods, and predilections of the predators do not vary in the plantations where *N. sertifer* occurs. In this simple example of predation, the basic components of predation are responses to changes in prey density. The increase in the number of prey consumed per predator, as prey density rises, is termed the functional response. The change in the density of predators, as a result of increase in prey density, is termed the numerical response.

The three important species of small mammal predators (*Blarina*, *Sorex*, and *Peromyscus*) each showed a functional response, and each curve, whether it was derived from field or laboratory data, showed an initial S-shaped rise up to a constant, maximum consumption. The rate of increase of consumption decreased from *Blarina* to *Sorex* to *Peromyscus*, while the upper, constant level of consumption decreased from *Blarina* to *Peromyscus* to *Sorex*. The characteristics of these functional responses could not be explained by a simple relation between consumption and the proportion of prey in the total food available. The form of the functional response curves is such that the proportion of prey consumed per predator increases to a peak and then decreases.

This peaked curve was further emphasized by the direct numerical response of *Sorex* and *Peromyscus*, since their populations rose initially with increase in prey density up to a maximum that was maintained with further increase in cocoon density. *Blarina* did not show a numerical response. The increase in density of predators resulted from increased breeding, and because the reproductive rate of small mammals is so high, there was an almost immediate increase in density with increase in food.

The two basic components of predation — the functional and numerical responses — can be affected by a number of subsidiary components: prey characteristics, the density and quality of alternate foods, and characteristics of the predators. It was shown experimentally that these components affected the amount of predation by lowering or raising the functional and numerical responses. Decrease of the strength of stimulus from prey, one prey characteristic, lowered both the functional and numerical responses. On the other hand, the quality of alternate foods affected the two responses differently. Increase in the palatability or in the number of kinds of alternate foods lowered the functional response but promoted a more pronounced numerical response.

The peaked type of predation shown by small mammals can theoretically regulate the numbers of its prey if predation is high enough to match the effective reproduction by prey at some prey density. Even if this condition does not hold, however, oscillations of prey numbers are damped. Since the functional and numerical responses undoubtedly differ for different species of predator, predation by each is likely to peak at a different prey density. Hence, when a large number of different species of predators are present the declining phase of predation is displaced to a higher prey density, so that the prey have less chance to "escape" the regulation exerted by predators.

The scheme of predation presented here is sufficient to explain all types of predation as well as insect parasitism. It permits us to postulate four major types of predation differing in the characteristics of their basic and subsidiary components.

REFERENCES

Andrewartha, H. G. and L. C. Birch. 1954. The distribution and abundance of animals. *The Univ. of Chicago Press*, Chicago.

Bird, F. T. 1952. On the artificial dissemination of the virus disease of the European saw-fly, *Neodiprion sertifer* (Geoff.). *Can. Dept. Agric., For. Biol. Div., Bi-Mon. Progr. Rept.* 8(3): 1-2

Bird, F. T. 1953. The use of a virus disease in the biological control of the European pine sawfly, *Neodiprion sertifer* (Geoff.). *Can. Ent.* 85: 437-446.

Blair, W. F. 1941. Techniques for the study of mammal populations. *J. Mamm.* 22: 148-157.

Buckner, C. H. 1957. Population studies on small mammals of southeastern Manitoba. *J. Mamm.* 38: 87-97.

Burnett, T. 1951. Effects of temperature and host density on the rate of increase of an insect parasite. *Amer. Nat.* 85: 337-352.

Burnett, T. 1954. Influences of natural temperatures and controlled host densities on oviposition of an insect parasite. *Physiol. Ecol.* 27: 239-248.

Burt, W. H. 1940. Territorial behaviour and populations of some small mammals in southern Michigan. *Misc. Publ. Univ. Mich. Mus. Zool.* no. 45: 1-52.

De Bach, P. 1958. The role of weather and entomophagous species in the natural control of insect populations. *J. Econ. Ent.* 51: 474-484.

De Bach, P., and H. S. Smith. 1941. The effect of host density on the rate of reproduction of entomophagous parasites. *J. Econ. Ent.* 34: 741-745.

De Bach, P., and H. S. Smith. 1947. Effects of parasite population density on rate of change of host and parasite populations. *Ecology* 28: 290-298.

Errington, P. L. 1934. Vulnerability of bob-white populations to predation. *Ecology* 15: 110-127.

Errington, P. L. 1943. An analysis of mink predation upon muskrats in North-Central United States. *Agric. Exp. Sta. Iowa State Coll. Res. Bull.* 320: 797-924.

Errington, P. L. 1945. Some contributions of a fifteen-year local study of the northern bob-white to a knowledge of population phenomena. *Ecol. Monog.* 15: 1-34.

Errington, P. L. 1946. Predation and vertebrate populations. *Quart. Rev. Biol.* 21: 144-177, 221-245.

Fraenkel, G., and D. L. Gunn. 1940. The orientation of animals. Oxford.

Hayne, D. W. 1949. Two methods for estimating population from trapping records. *J. Mamm.* 30: 339-411.

Holling, C. S. 1955. The selection by certain small mammals of dead, parasitized, and healthy prepupae of the European pine sawfly, *Neodiprion sertifer* (Goeff.). *Can. J. Zool.* 33: 404-419.

Holling, C. S. 1958a. A radiographic technique to identify healthy, parasitized, and diseased sawfly prepupae within cocoons. *Can. Ent.* 90: 59-61.

Holling, C. S. 1958b. Sensory stimuli involved in the location and selection of sawfly cocoons by small mammals. *Can. J. Zool.* 36: 633-653.

Klomp, H. 1956. On the theories on host-parasite interaction. *Int. Union of For. Res. Organizations, 12th Congress,* Oxford, 1956.

Leopold, A. 1933. Game management. Charles Scribner's Sons.

Lincoln, F. C. 1930. Calculating waterfowl abundance on the basis of banding returns. *U.S. Dept. Agric.* Circular 118.

MacLagan, D. S. 1932. The effect of population density upon rate of reproduction, with special reference to insects. *Proc. Roy. Soc. Lond.* 111: 437-454.

Milne, A. 1957. The natural control of insect populations. *Can. Ent.* 89: 193-213.

Morris, R. F., W. F. Chesire, C. A. Miller, and D. G. Mott. 1958. Numerical response of avian and mammalian predators during a gradation of the spruce budworm. *Ecology* 39(3): 487-494.

Nicholson, A. J. 1933. The balance of animal populations. *J. Anim. Ecol.* 2: 132-178.

Nicholson, A. J., and V. A. Bailey. 1935. The balance of animal populations. Part 1, *Proc. Zool. Soc. Lond.* 1935, p. 551-598.

Prebble, M. L. 1943. Sampling methods in population studies of the European spruce saw-fly, *Gilpinia hercyniae* (Hartig.) in eastern Canada. *Trans. Roy. Soc. Can.,* Third Series, Sect. V. 37: 93-126.

Ricker, W. E. 1941. The consumption of young sockeye salmon by predaceous fish. *J. Fish. Res. Bd. Can.* 5: 293-313.

Ricker, W. E. 1954. Stock and recruitment. *J. Fish. Res. Bd. Can.* 11: 559-623.

Robertson, F. W., and J. H. Sang. 1944. The ecological determinants of population growth in a *Drosophila* culture. I. Fecundity of adult flies. *Proc. Roy. Soc. Lond.,* B., 132: 258-277.

Solomon, M. E. 1949. The natural control of animal populations. *J. Anim. Ecology* 18: 1-35.

Stickel, L. F. 1954. A comparison of certain methods of measuring ranges of small mammals. *J. Mamm.* 35: 1-15.

Thompson, W. R. 1929. On natural control. *Parasitology* 21: 269-281.

Thompson, W. R. 1930. The principles of biological control. *Ann. Appl. Biol.* 17: 306-338.

Thompson, W. R. 1939. Biological control and the theories of the interactions of populations. *Parasitology* 31: 299-388.

Tinbergen, L. 1949. Bosvogels en insecten. *Nederl. Boschbouue. Tijdschr.* 21: 91-105.

Tinbergen, L. 1955. The effect of predators on the numbers of their hosts. *Vakblad voor Biologen* 28: 217-228.

Tinbergen, N. 1951. The study of instinct. Oxford.

Tothill, J. D. 1922. The natural control of the fall webworm (*Hyphantria cunea* Drury) in Canada. *Can. Dept. Agr. Bull.* 3, new series (Ent. Bull. 19): 1-107.

Ullyett, G. C. 1949a. Distribution of progeny by *Cryptus inornatus* Pratt. (Hym. Ichneumonidae). *Can. Ent.* 81: 285-299, 82: 1-11.

Ullyett, G. C. 1949b. Distribution of progeny by *Chelonus texanus* Cress. (Hym. Braconidae). *Can. Ent.* 81: 25-44.

Varley, G. C. 1947. The natural control of population balance in the knapweed gall-fly (*Urophora jaceana*). *J. Anim. Ecol.* 16: 139-187.

Varley, G. C. 1953. Ecological aspects of population regulation. *Trans. IXth Int. Congr. Ent.* 2: 210-214.

Voûte, A. D. 1946. Regulation of the density of the insect populations in virgin forests and cultivated woods. *Archives Neerlandaises de Zoologie* 7: 435-470.

Voûte, A. D. 1956. Forest entomology and population dynamics. *Int. Union For. Res. Organizations*, Twelfth Congress, Oxford.

Voûte, A. D. 1958. On the regulation of insect populations. *Proc. Tenth Int. Congr. of Ent.* Montreal, 1956.

16

The Kaibab Deer Incident:
A Long-persisting Myth

C. John Burk

One of the most cherished fables of modern biology is the tale of the Kaibab deer. The myth goes basically as follows: Before 1906, a population of Rocky Mountain mule deer shared a portion of the Kaibab plateau in northern Arizona with cattle, sheep, and an array of predatory creatures. The deer provided coyotes, wolves, mountain lions, bears, and bobcats with venison and were compensated in return by a carnivorous mode of zero population growth which prevented overgrazing on their range. In 1906, however, Theodore Roosevelt proclaimed the Kaibab a federal game refuge, and his minions proceeded to disrupt nature's delicate balance, dispersing the cattle and sheep which had competed with the deer for forage and eradicating many of the predators. The deer population, about 4,000 when the refuge was established, freed from its usual checks and balances, multiplied vigorously, reaching, in 1924, a peak of an estimated hundred thousand animals, only to be punished for gross biotic hubris in the classic manner. With the range worn out by overgrazing, starvation and attendant illnesses reduced the herd, quite ruthlessly and in a few years, to slightly more than its size at the turn of the century.

These events have been interpreted theoretically as a "classic instance" where "the effects of disruption of prey-predator relationship can be readily seen" (Kormondy 1969), or even more theoretically as a typical example of a delayed density-dependent death rate (Lack 1954). Practical conservationists view the situation as "perhaps the most celebrated of such cases" where predator control injures the species wildlife biologists are attempting to

The author is at the Department of the Biological Sciences, Smith College, Northampton, Massachusetts.

protect (Owen 1971), while one popular commentator has noted, "The lesson of the Kaibab had to be learned over and over again throughout the West" (Mattheissen 1964).

What actually happened to the real deer out there on the Kaibab is not, apparently, quite so well understood as the myth would lead us to believe. Caughley (1970), reviewing ungulate irruptions, in general, within a more specific study of the Himalyan thar,[1] concludes, "data on the Kaibab deer herd ... are unreliable and inconsistent, and the factors that may have resulted in an upsurge of deer are hopelessly confounded." Readers should consult the Caughley article and its sources for full details of the sequence of oversimplifications and distortions which have resulted in the Kaibab story as it now exists. Reinspecting the original documents and publications on the topic, Caughley discovered that the extent of the initial population irruption is not clear. Without question an increase in deer occurred, followed by overgrazing and decline. During 1924, however, the period when the deer were presumably most numerous, various observers estimated their population as high as 100,000, as low as 30,000, with guesses of 50,000, 60,000, and 70,000 bridging the interval. A dramatically explicit graph, reprinted in many textbooks, the latest to cross my desk being *Invitation to Biology* (Curtis 1972), is based on the maximum estimate and evolved by unjustified tamperings with an original which was itself based on a number of speculations and dubious assumptions.

[1] Definitions may be in order here − the sort of rapid population increase which the Kaibab deer achieved has been termed an *eruption* or, by purists, an *irruption*, the latter term distinguishing the biotic event from what volcanoes do. A Himalayan that looks something like a goat.

Moreover, while pumas and coyotes were, without question, removed from the range throughout the crucial period, sheep and cattle were also banished; the reduction in sheep alone from 1889 to 1908 might have totaled 195,000 animals, more than the mule deer at the height of their profligacy. Hence the irruption of deer, whatever its extent, may in large part have resulted from an increased food supply after removal of other herbivores which had competed with the deer for browse. A description of the fate of the Kaibab deer as "a well-documented example of what can happen when predators are removed" (Platt and Reid 1967) or "a case where the role of the predator is plainly seen" (Johnson, Delaney, Cole, and Brooks 1972) is scarcely justified.

Nonetheless, the incident has exercised an irresistibly attractive force. A survey of 28 general biology texts[2] which have accumulated on my bookshelves since 1965 yielded 17 accounts of the Kaibab episode. Of these latter, 16 clearly stress the primary importance of the reduction of predators in causing the upsurge in deer population and 7 contain variants of the faulty graph. The use to which the episode is put is in many ways as serious a problem as the inaccuracy of the data from which the saga is derived. If the facts are in question and the role of the predator uncertain, extensive theorizing and extrapolations to issues of morality would seem unwise.

Some retellings are indeed lowkeyed while others are written in highly colored language. Simpson and Beck (1969) for instance interpret the Kaibab events as an illustration of "unforeseen and disastrous possibilities of ignorant interference in natural communities"

[2] List available upon request; I have quoted here only one edition of each text.

245

while Nelson, Robinson, and Boolotian (1970) see them as an example of a "common consequence of man's attempts to reorganize ecosystems to suit his whims". Phillips (1971) subheads a paragraph "The Kaibab Deer Disaster" and Baker and Allen (1971) find the Kaibab ecosystem "caught in a vicious cycle". Keeton, in his 1972 edition, continues to define the case as a "classical example" of what happens "when people set out to protect the prey from their 'enemies' (sometimes only to preserve them for their human ones) by killing the predators," dropping his 1967 description of the villains of the piece as "well-meaning and misguided" and man as "the most destructive predator alive." These are clearly milder days on campus and with simple exaggeration Etkin, Devlin, and Bouffard (1972) strike the cadences of an old-fashioned dormitory bull-session in their claim that "... the deer almost destroyed the plant cover by overgrazing. Whole herds were wiped out in winter and the species might have been lost if they had not been rescued by bringing in cattle fodder for them."

I personally blench recalling instances — at least yearly for more than a dozen years — when I myself used, often dramatically and with gestures, the Kaibab example in a classroom situation. Science contains a self-correcting element, and authors of general texts cannot be blamed for accepting the conclusions of specialists much more than the teacher in the lecture hall. Still, if as now seems evident, what these writers claimed is not justified by the facts of what happened there in Arizona, the myth retains at least some value for our times. With the recent upsurge of interest in the environmental aspects of biology, so great a number of similar texts in general biology, ecology, and wildlife conservation are being produced that it is difficult to choose the best among them. The rapidity with which, in subsequent editions of these works, our authors and/or editors respond to demonstrations of faulty examples and spurious interpretations of dubious facts might well be a very useful criterion for our selection. One still cannot contemplate the Kaibab incident without extracting some moral from its consequences; all things considered, *Caveat emptor* would seem as good as any.

REFERENCES

Baker, Jeffrey J. W. and Garland E. Allen. 1971. *The Study of Biology*, 2nd ed. Addison-Wesley Publishing Co., Reading, Massachusetts.

Caughley, Graeme. 1970. Eruption of ungulate populations, with emphasis on Himalyan thar in New Zealand. *Ecology*, 51: 53-72.

Curtis, Helena. 1972. *Invitation to Biology*. Worth Publishers, Inc.

Etkin, William, Robert M. Devlin, and Thomas G. Bouffard. 1972. *A Biology of Human Concern*. J. B. Lippincott Co., New York.

Johnson, Willis H., Louis E. Delaney, Thomas A. Cole, and Austin C. Brooks. 1972. *Biology*, 4th ed. Holt, Rinehart, and Winston, Inc., New York.

Keeton, William. 1972. *Biological Science*, 2nd ed. W. W. Norton and Co., New York.

Kormondy, Edward J. 1969. *Concepts of Ecology*. Prentice-Hall, Inc., Englewood Cliffs, New Jersey.

Lack, David. 1954. *The Natural Regulation of Animal Numbers*. Oxford University Press, Ely House, London.

Matthiessen, Peter. 1964. *Wildlife in America*. Viking Press, Inc., New York.

Nelson, Gideon E., Gerald G. Robinson, and Richard A. Boolootian. 1970. *Fundamental Concepts of Biology*, 2nd ed. John Wiley and Sons, Inc. New York.

Owen, Oliver S. 1971. *Natural Resource Conservation*. MacMillan Co., New York.

Phillips, Edwin A. 1971. *Basic Ideas in Biology*. MacMillan Co., New York.

Platt, Robert B. and George K. Reid. 1967. *BioScience*, Reinhold Publishing Corp., New York.

Simpson, George G. and William S. Beck. 1969. *Life: An Introduction to Biology, Shorter Edition*. Harcourt, Brace, and World Inc., New York.

Part VI

KEY-FACTOR ANALYSIS

Editor's Comments
on Papers 17 and 18

17   **MORRIS**
     Predictive Population Equations Based on Key Factors

18   **VARLEY and GRADWELL**
     Key Factors in Population Studies

Key-factor anslysis is a specific technique developed by R. F. Morris (forest entomologist in New Brunswick, Canada) to determine if density-dependent population regulation is taking place and which parameters influencing the population are responsible for that regulation. The logarithm of population density at time $n + 1$ is graphed against the logarithm of population density at time n. If there is no density-dependent regulation, then the percentage increase will stay the same regardless of the density at time n, and the graph will be a straight line with a slope of 1. If, however, there is density-dependent population control, the increase in density will be a decreasing percentage as density increases, and consequently the graph will be a straight line with slope less than 1. The slope's value will indicate the degree of density dependence. By the addition of different factors into the regression, their effects can be examined individually.

Paper 17, a 1963 paper by Morris, is a step-by-step instruction on how to use his technique. Paper 18, a 1960 paper by Varley and Gradwell, gives modifications of the basic technique. According to Morris, the value of the technique is that all one need know is how to use the simple statistical technique of regression analysis. Several other authors have devised techniques similar to key-factor analysis, including the Varley and Gradwell modification (Paper 18; 1963) and a modification by Watt (1961). In 1963, Morris edited a symposium, *The Dynamics of Epidemic Spruce Budworm Populations*. Since Morris originally worked on the budworm, this volume is interesting in terms of both key-factor analysis and the ecology of the budworm.

Key-factor analysis has been criticized, however. Eberhardt (1970) and St. Amant (1970) show that under certain circumstances, when a series of random numbers is analyzed by key-factor analysis, it will give a density-dependent line. Kuno (1973) points out some of the problems involved when time-series data are used. A good survey paper on the problems and applications of the key-factor methods is by Ito (1972). More recently, Royama (1977) has differentiated "statistical" and "causal" density-dependence and pointed to some of the problems with using simple linear regression.

REFERENCES

Eberhardt, L. L. 1970. Correlation, Regression, and Density Dependence. *Ecology* **51**:306–310.

Ito, Y. 1972. On the Methods for Determining Density-Dependence by Means of Regression. *Oecologia* **10**:347–372.

Kuno, E. 1973. Statistical Characteristics of the Density-Independent Population Fluctuation and the Evaluation of Density-Dependence and Regulation in Animal Populations. *Res. Popul. Ecol.* **15**:99–120.

Morris, R. F. (ed.). 1963. The Dynamics of Epidemic Spruce Budworm Populations. *Mem. Ent. Soc. Can.* **31**:1–332.

Royama, T. 1977. Population Persistence and Density Dependence. *Ecol. Monogr.* **47**:1–35.

St. Amant, J. 1970. The Detection of Regulation in Animal Populations. *Ecology* **51**:823–828.

Varley, G. C., and G. R. Gradwell. 1963. The Interpretation of Insect Population Changes. *Ceylon Ass. Adv. Sci.* **18**:142–156.

Watt, K. E. F. 1961. Mathematical Models for Use in Insect Pest Control. *Can. Ent., Suppl.* **19**:1–62.

17

Reprinted from *Mem. Ent. Soc. Can.* **32**:16–21 (1963)

Predictive Population Equations Based on Key Factors[1]

By R. F. MORRIS

Forest Entomology and Pathology Laboratory, Fredericton, New Brunswick

In the analysis of population data for some forest insects in the Maritime Provinces, it was discovered that the measurement of only one or two mortality factors often made it possible to predict population changes from one generation to the next with surprising success. This led to the proposal of the term "key factor" and to the suggestion that changes in population density, although *affected* to some extent by many variables, may be essentially *determined* by only a few variables (Morris 1959). A method of developing simple predictive equations based on key factors was proposed for the black-headed budworm, *Acleris variana* (Fern.), and the European spruce sawfly, *Diprion hercyniae* (Htg.), (*op. cit.*) and recently extended to the more difficult spruce budworm, *Choristoneura fumiferana* (Clem.), (Morris 1962).

This work has elicited some rather interesting responses. The term "key factor" has gained some degree of acceptance in population literature, and this is perhaps a direct result of its vagueness. It can be applied, by definition, to any factor that is useful in the prediction of population changes, with no commitment as to the precise mode of operation of the factor. The usefulness of such a general term may be attributed to the fact that we can often recognize the importance of certain variables, and even use them in predictive equations, before we understand their modes of action well enough to apply such precise terms as those proposed by Nicholson (1954). The suggested method of analysis, which employed only simple linear regression, seemed too involved or laborious for some entomologists, but at the same time too lacking in sophistication for others. For example, a few workers have asked me to apply the analysis to their field data instead of attempting it themselves, and Varley and Gradwell (1960) have proposed a simplified method of detecting key factors based on purely graphical procedures. On the other hand Smith (1961) prefers partial regression analyses based on logarithmic changes in population and Watt, in his contribution for this Symposium, accepts the concept of key factors but prefers partial regression analyses and differential equations for modelling their effects. Finally, it was the opinion of a few workers (unpublished) that the method used by the writer was based on the Nicholson and Bailey model, and therefore subject to any assumptions or limitations contained in the model.

In the present paper it is proposed to review and extend the analysis, with a view to establishing three points: (1) That it is basically simple and can be applied by anyone who has done a simple regression analysis. (2) That although it produces only empirical predictive equations, the approach is biologically meaningful and provides a very useful framework for the development of population models. (3) That the analysis represents a test of different ideas on population regulation, not an acceptance of any one theory. In the interests of brevity it will be convenient to present a hypothetical rather than a real example. I may say, however, that population work in progress on the fall webworm, *Hyphantria cunea* (Dru.), was primarily in my mind when the sketches were drawn, and the figures therefore represent the sequence of regressions to be applied to the webworm data after a sufficient number of generations has been studied. The sketches are described in the following paragraphs.

[1]Contribution No. 854, Forest Entomology and Pathology Branch, Department of Forestry, Ottawa, Canada.

Fig. 1 represents the type of population behaviour exhibited by the webworm, which is being studied in six census areas from northern New Brunswick to the southern coast of Nova Scotia. It has only one generation a year throughout this region. For the sake of simplicity only the two extreme areas are shown. The scale is not realistic; actually the mean density (broken lines) in Area 6 is nearly 40 times higher than that in Area 1. Even in Area 6, however, the webworm does not reach the limit of its food supply. Although the mean densities are different, the oscillations appear to be well synchronized in all six areas and vary in length from 9 to 13 generations. In Figs. 2-7, the sketches will be restricted to a proposed form of analysis for each individual area and in Fig. 8 the six areas will again be considered.

Fig. 2 shows how N_{n+1} is related to N_n. For populations that oscillate in a fairly regular manner, this forms a series of ellipses in a clockwise sequence (Morris 1959) but for present purposes the points are treated as a scatter diagram. The relationship is curvilinear and the variance increases with population density, as shown by the broken lines. This would complicate any analysis of N_{n+1} and N_n without transformation.

Fig. 3 shows the same relationship after the population data have been converted to logarithms. For the forest insect populations analysed by this method to date, involving some six species, this transformation has been effective both in providing linearity and in stabilizing variance. The r^2 of .3, a hypothetical figure that is really lower than the value obtained for some insects, shows that 30% of the variation in $\log N_{n+1}$ is explained by $\log N_n$ alone. This arises simply from the fact that the rate of change from one generation to the next is generally limited, so that, knowing only N_n, we can predict that N_{n+1} will fall within certain limits, plus or minus. The necessity for this regression will now be clear. If it were omitted, this block of variance could easily be credited, artifactitiously, to the first mortality factor that is tested. The succeeding steps in the analysis are therefore designed to learn what improvements in predictability over the $r^2 = .3$ are gained by adding the effect of the suspected key factors, one at a time. Before leaving Fig. 3, however, note that the slope, $b = .5$, which is a reasonably average value for forest insects, provides an index of the degree of density dependence in the system. If the rate of increase in population did not decrease with density, the slope would of course be 1.0.

In *Fig. 4*, $N_n p$ represents the number of larvae that escape parasitism. It is reasonable to test this factor first because parasitism is easily measured in defoliator populations and the work can often be combined with the population sampling if N is based on the larval stage. The degree of improvement in predictability depends, of course, upon the insect and varies from none in outbreak populations of the spruce budworm to an r^2 as high as .85 for the black-headed budworm. The hypothetical example shows a modest gain to $r^2 = .6$. It also shows that the slope has increased to $b = .8$; but as it is still less than unity, there are clearly other density-dependent factors in the system.

In *Fig. 5*, the object is to add the effect of predation. In situations where no shortage of foliage occurs, this seems like a reasonable factor to be tested next. When predation and other residual sources of density dependence are difficult to measure directly, their effects can sometimes be assessed by indirect methods, as outlined earlier (Morris 1959). But for the sake of simplicity in the present illustration, let us assume that predation can be measured, that the interaction between parasitism and predation is of the form pq, and that the use of $N_n pq$ improves correlation and takes care of all density dependence by bringing the

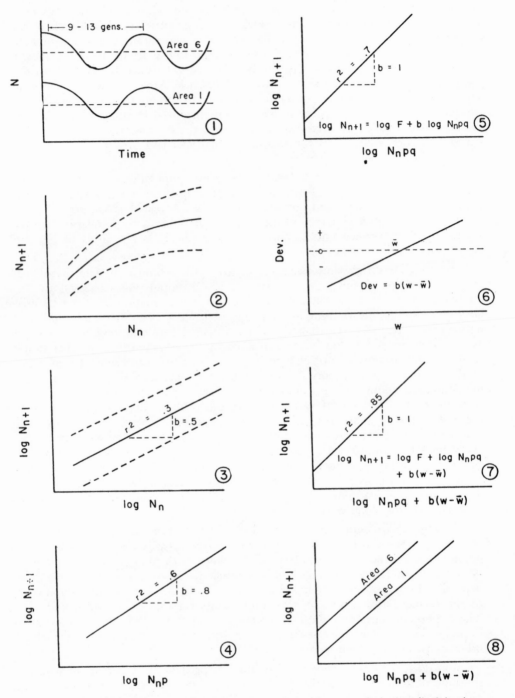

Figs. 1-8. Illustration of the successive steps in key-factor analysis described in the text. N_n = number of insects in any generation; N_{n+1} = number of insects in next generation at same point in life cycle; p = proportion of N_n surviving parasitism; q = proportion of N_n surviving predation; F = intercept = effective rate of increase; w = weather index; r = correlation coefficient; b = slope.

slope to unity. The intercept of the regression line on the ordinate is log F.
The formula for the line, in its arithmetic form, simply states that population in
the next generation is equal to the number of survivors from parasites and
predators in this generation multiplied by the effective rate of increase, F. More
will be said about F later on. In actual field examples the slope may remain
significantly less than unity, even after parasitism, predation, and food supply
have been included. This simply means that there are other sources of compensatory mortality in the system that have not been detected, and that b must be
retained in the predictive equations.

Fig. 6, the next step in the analysis, represents an attempt to explain the
deviations of the individual points from the regression line of Fig. 5. Weather
and phenology have very important effects on insect populations, and predicted
values of N_{n+1} based on N_npq can be expected to deviate more or less from the
actual values, depending upon the sensitivity of the species to weather. In the
black-headed budworm, for example, these deviations are rather small while in
the spruce budworm they are very wide and comprise most of the variation in the
system. The synchronization of webworm oscillations in the three Maritime
Provinces, separated as they are by bodies of water, suggests that a broad influence
such as weather may largely determine the timing. In Fig. 6 the positive and
negative deviations from regression in Fig. 5 are plotted over some synoptic index
of weather, and w is simply the weather index at zero deviation. Appropriate
indices to test will be suggested by our knowledge of the insect. In some situations we get rectilinear regressions as in Fig. 6; in others, where weather on both
sides of an optimum is experienced, it is necessary to fit a curve. Since the
deviations have been obtained from the logarithmic scale of Fig. 5, variance should
remain stable because population is likely to change by a proportion for each
weather increment, not by an absolute number of insects.

Fig. 7 merely adds the regression of Fig. 6 to that of Fig. 5 to show how
much additional variance has been explained by weather. Some workers will
prefer a multiple regression analysis in place of the intermediate step represented
by Fig. 6, but the end result will be similar. The slope in Fig. 7 should be unity
because all we are really doing, except for the intercept, is testing observed against
predicted values. Residual variation from the regression line may now be
examined in relation to population sampling error, in order to decide whether or
not it is worth while to test additional independent variables.

Fig. 8 shows what may happen when the final regression lines, of the Fig. 7
type, are plotted for different areas. This is speculative because, so far as I know,
no field study has yet been completed in which oscillations about a mean density
have been studied simultaneously over areas experiencing wide differences in
mean density. However, the fall webworm data gathered so far suggest that
differences in mean density among the six areas may be related more to F, the
effective rate of increase, than to differences in such factors as parasitism; and F in
turn seems to be related to mean weather, or climate, and perhaps to vegetation.
It seems to me that the study of differences in mean density in different areas and
in different stand or crop environments deserves more attention than it has
received, since it is the basis of any attempt to reduce insect damage through
cultural methods.

The relationships shown in Figs. 7 and 8 represent descriptive or predictive
equations, not explanatory population models. However, the analysis is extremely
useful in determining what factors, among the host of factors causing some
mortality to a species, are mainly responsible for the observed changes in popula-

tion; and hence what factors are deserving of more detailed study. For example, if it turns out that p and q explain significant blocks of variance, we would no doubt try to model them as functions of host density along with the density and characteristics of the parasites or predators involved, following the lead of Holling's (1961) component analysis or Watt's (1959) deductive-inductive attack models. Similarly, if a single index of weather is shown to improve predictability, we would be tempted to do some detailed work to model the operation of the specific meteorological factors involved. Thus, although the webworm population data do not yet cover a sufficient number of generations, preliminary key-factor analyses have led to concomitant experimental work on the parasites and predators, and particularly on the role of weather in both temporal and spatial changes in density.

It is clear that equations of the Fig. 7 type, although empirical, provide a biologically meaningful framework into which detailed models can be incorporated. The first term concerns the effective rate of increase in different places, as determined perhaps by climate and environment, while the second concerns the density-dependent factors and the third the density-independent factors that are involved in oscillations. In the more detailed modelling, of course, we might expect to find interactions between the last two terms, and perhaps among all three. If it is possible through more detailed work to gain an understanding of the precise mode of action of the recognized key factors affecting a given species, the simple terms of the predictive equation may be gradually expanded into the more complex expressions of a model, viz:

Equation $\longrightarrow$	*Model*
p $\longrightarrow$	f (host density, attacking parasite density, parasite characteristics, weather, etc.)
q $\longrightarrow$	f (prey density, predator density and characteristics, etc.)
w $\longrightarrow$	f (temperature, humidity, etc.)
F $\longrightarrow$	f (*mean* temperature, humidity, density and distribution of host plants, etc.)

However, the distinction between predictive equations and real biological models is not a sharp one. Models can be constructed in widely different levels of complexity and usually represent some sort of compromise between the description of ecological events and the explanation of them. The investigator may be satisfied with the sort of parameters listed above on the right, or he may wish to subdivide some of them into such physiological components as hunger states, perceptual fields, etc. (cf. Holling, in this Symposium). In any case the ability to predict population changes, even one generation in advance, is the real test of how well we have detected the key factors in a given situation, and the detection of these factors seems the logical first step on the road to understanding the population dynamics of an insect pest.

In a broad sense, the key-factor approach described here is based on Nicholsonian concepts of regulation. However, since each step can be tested statistically for improvements in correlation and for significant changes in both slope and intercept, it should be obvious that it represents a critical test of those concepts rather than an uncritical acceptance of them.

Finally, it is not proposed that the approach is preferable to more detailed life-table work in which all stages of the insect are sampled and studied. Even when earlier work on a species provides some useful leads, as it does in the case of the fall webworm, there is a calculated risk in restricting sampling and mortality studies to one stage. However, some insects do not lend themselves to life-table work, at least with existing techniques, while others sometimes reach such low population levels that the sampling of more than one stage becomes impractical. Also, when life tables for more amenable species show that a certain period in the life cycle, and a few factors, essentially determine the rate of population change, there is no merit in the continued study of all age intervals and mortality factors for such species. In these situations the key-factor approach can be very useful.

Summary

By analysis of long-term population data on some forest insects in the Maritime Provinces, it was found possible to predict population changes with a surprising degree of success. In this paper a method of analysis based on the measurement of one or two mortality factors in the population, and employing only simple linear regression, is reviewed and extended to establish the following points: (1) That it is basically simple and can be applied by anyone who has done a simple regression analysis. (2) That although it produces only empirical predictive equations, the approach is biologically meaningful and provides a very useful framework for the development of population models. (3) That the analysis represents a test of different ideas on population regulation, not an acceptance of any one theory. A drawback to the method is that for one-generation-a-year species it will require several years to accumulate enough points for regression analyses.

Résumé

A la suite de l'analyse de données, accumulées au cours de plusieurs années et se rapportant à certains insectes de la forêt dans les Provinces Maritimes, l'auteur a trouvé que l'estimation d'un ou de deux facteurs de mortalité permettaient, à maintes reprises, d'établir avec beaucoup de succès des prévisions sur les mouvements des populations. Une méthode d'analyse, basée sur l'emploi de simples lignes de régression et appliquée à l'étude des "facteurs déterminants", est résumée dans la présente communication qui en outre apporte des précisions sur les points suivants: (1) la méthode est fondamentalement facile et accessible à quiconque peut effectuer une analyse de régression simple; (2) elle ne donne que des équations empiriques de prédiction, mais son usage sur le plan biologique est logique et fournit des cadres utiles au développement des formes de population; (3) l'analyse met à l'essai différentes idées sur le mécanisme régulateur des populations, mais n'adopte en fait aucune théorie. La méthode comporte comme objection principale l'apport de données abondantes pour effectuer avec précision des analyses de régression et de ce fait nécessite plusieurs années de recherches spécialement pour les espèces univoltines.

References

Holling, C. S. 1961. Principles of insect predation. *Ann. Rev. Ent.* 6: 163-182.
Morris, R. F. 1959. Single-factor analysis in population dynamics. *Ecology* 40: 580-588.
Morris, R. F. 1962. The development of predictive equations for the spruce budworm based on key-factor analysis. *In* On the dynamics of epidemic spruce budworm populations. *Canadian Ent. Supplement* (in press).
Nicholson, A. J. 1954. An outline of the dynamics of animal populations. *Australian J. Zool.* 2: 9-65.
Smith, F. F. 1961. Density dependence in the Australian thrips. *Ecology* 42: 403-407.
Varley, G. C., and G. R. Gradwell. 1960. Key factors in population studies. *J. Anim. Ecol.* 29: 399-401.
Watt, K. E. F. 1959. A mathematical model for the effect of densities of attacked and attacking species on the number attacked. *Canadian Ent.* 91: 129-144.

18

Reprinted from *J. Anim. Ecol.* **29**:399–401 (1960)

KEY FACTORS IN POPULATION STUDIES

By G. C. VARLEY AND G. R. GRADWELL

Hope Department of Entomology, Oxford

(With 1 Figure in the Text)

Morris (1959) has introduced the term *key-factor* for mortality factors which 'cause a variable … mortality and appear to be largely responsible for the observed changes in population' density in successive generations. In his paper Morris illustrates a statistical method designed to determine whether or not mortality at one stage is, at least in part, caused by a key factor. Here we give a simple alternative method of identifying the stage at which a key factor is operating using an extention of Haldane's (1949) logarithmic method for comparing the different killing powers of a series of successive mortality factors acting on a population. Haldane wrote an equation for the total mortality $K = k_1 + k_2 + k_2 \ldots$ where the k-value for each mortality is the difference between logarithms of numbers per unit area before and after its action. In his example he used Napierian logarithms but we prefer to use common logarithms.

Our method is to calculate the k-values for each estimated mortality over a number of years and plot them against time. The contribution of each mortality to the variation in K can be seen by inspection, or can be studied statistically. Mortality caused wholly or in part by a key factor is recognized since its k-values will change with time in the same way as the changes in the total mortality. If this method is applied to cases like those considered by Morris where the only available information is a series of annual counts of population and the percentage parasitism it will reveal whether the parasites are the key factor or not.

In our study of the population dynamics of the winter moth (*Operophtera brumata* (L.)) at Wytham, Berkshire, we have estimated the numbers at two stages of the life cycle each year, and can calculate the k-values between each estimate. The k-value of the mortality caused by some parasites has been separately assessed, but often many factors contribute to the measured mortality over a certain period. Fig. 1 shows plots of these k-values, and we see immediately that the shape of the curve of k_1 is very like that of K, hence the mortality which we call winter disappearance includes that which is due to the key factor. Winter disappearance includes all the mortality from the time the adult moths are sampled in November and December to the subsequent count of fully fed larvae in May, and is calculated on the basis of an assumed constant egg production. It thus includes variations in female mortality and in egg production as well as mortality in the eggs and newly hatched larvae. In a previous paper (Varley & Gradwell 1958) we found that winter moth suffers 'the greatest proportionate loss in the first larval stage. Survival at this stage is very variable from year to year, probably owing to weather factors. These differences go far to explain the big

256

changes in population density, which are often synchronous over a wide area.' This new method of presenting the observations, now extended for a further 4 years, serves to confirm this earlier conclusion.

The graphs show also that the change in k_1 the winter disappearance is usually greater than the change in K, and that pupal predation k_5 is partly compensating for changes in winter disappearance. This effect has already been reported (Varley

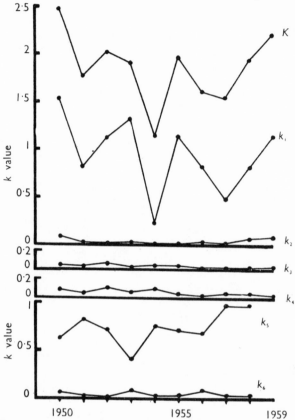

Fig. 1. Mortality affecting winter moth 1950-9 at Wytham, Berkshire, on logarithmic scale.
K, total mortality $= k_1 + k_2 \ldots k_6$;
k_1, winter disappearance;
k_2, Tachinid parasite of larva, *Cyzenis albicans* (Fall.);
k_3, other larval parasites;
k_4, disease (Microsporidian);
k_5, pupal predators;
k_6, pupal parasite, *Cratichneumon culex* (Müll.).

& Gradwell 1958, Table 1) since pupal predation in any one year was higher under trees with a high pupal population than under adjacent trees with low populations. The graphs of the k-values provide a simple alternative method of revealing it.

A further discussion of the nature and role of the mortality factors in the population dynamics of winter moth will be published at a later date, but we hope that this illustration of our method for identifying the cause of population change will be of immediate use to other workers.

REFERENCES

Haldane, J. B. S. (1949). Disease and evolution. In Symposium sui fattori ecologici e genetici della speciazone negli animali. *Ric. Sci.* 19 (suppl.), 3-11.

Morris, R. F. (1959). Single-factor analysis in population dynamics. *Ecology,* 40, 580-8.

Varley, G. C. & Gradwell, G. R. (1958). Oak defoliators in England. *Proc. Xth Int. Congr. Ent.* 1956, 4, 133-6.

Part VII

THEORIES OF SELF-REGULATION

Editor's Comments
on Papers 19 Through 24

In all the theories mentioned so far, outside agents acted on the particular "regulated" population. No importance was given to the quality, or differences in quality, of individuals within a population. That is, *Thrips* were regulated by the weather, great tits were regulated by food, snowshoe hares were regulated by Canada lynx, Isle Royale moose were regulated by wolves, and so on. Although biotic systems of competition, predation, parasitism, and disease tend to be integrated systems where regulation depends on the interaction between a regulated and a regulating species—or between two interregulating species, one can still treat the regulated populations as community compartments that are being acted on by outside forces, be they other species or the environment in general. This section, however, considers theories where populations are self-regulated. In the broadest terms, self-regulation means that the density of the regulated population is kept at or below the level of resource shortage by the behavior of the individuals in the population.

"Extrinsic regulation" is a term often used to refer to regulation by outside forces, as we have so far outlined, whereas self-regulation is often called "intrinsic regulation." Intrinsic mechanisms, the subjects of this section, can be broadly classified as either phenotypic of genotypic (Krebs 1972). In phenotypic mechanisms, every individual in the population can be considered capable of changing the same way; an example is found in Paper 23 by Christian and Davis. Genotypic mechanisms, on the other hand, are mechanisms that take into account micro-evolutionary phenomena. These phenomena occur when natural selection acts on a population, and by changing the gene pool of that population, brings about regulation. An example of this is discussed in Paper 21 by Pimentel.

We were first introduced to the importance of natural selection and adaptation to population regulation by Orians (Paper 10). In this section, the role of adaption in population regulation is reaffirmed in Paper 19 by L. C. Birch. This is the same Birch of Andrewartha and Birch (Paper 5), who clearly developed and expounded a view of population regulation primarily by the weather, and of Ehrlich and Birch (Paper 12), who argued against a Nicholsonian concept of competitive population regulation.

Since the publication of *The Distribution and Abundance of Animals* (see Paper 5), Birch has been concerned with the genetic structure of populations (Birch and Ehrlich 1967; Birch and Vogt 1970). He has successfully bridged the gap between ecology and genetics to become one of the first true "population biologists." In Paper 19, Birch argues for the importance of looking at the genetic plasticity of populations and at the influence of genetic changes on population regulation.

E. B. Ford was one of the first to suggest genetic causes of population regulation (1931). As he said in the first edition of his *Ecological Genetics*, "Consequently, numerical increase with diversity prepares the way for numerical decline with relative uniformity. . . ." (1964, page 12). As the environment becomes favorable, numbers will increase. With the relaxed selection pressure of a favorable environment, genotypes that normally could not survive do survive. Thus when the environment returns to normal, these less fit genotypes will be removed. As Birch points out in Paper 19, Franz (1949) suggested a similar mechanism to explain oscillations in insect pests.

261

In his 1962 book, *Animal Dispersion in Relation to Social Behavior*, Wynne-Edwards developed the controversial hypothesis of "group selection." The argument is that individuals of a species will stop reproducing to keep numbers below the environment's carrying capacity to avoid starvation by all. To demonstrate that animals do this, Wynne-Edwards cites many examples of displays and behaviors, primarily of birds, to show that they are cognizant of their own population density and can thus know when to cease reproducing. Although this is basically a comprehensive theory of population regulation that depends on competition (see Milne, Paper 7), Wynne-Edwards adds the proviso that the competition is artificial to keep numbers below the carrying capacity (Paper 20). This makes very good sense for the species, however evolution and natural selection act on individuals. It is difficult to imagine a system where it is beneficial for an individual to cease reproducing as a favor to the rest of the population. Individuals that did so would produce fewer offspring and would actually be selected against.

Currently, most population biologists do not accept group selection. An in-depth critique of the theory is presented in the *Adaption and Natural Selection—A Critique of Some Current Evolutionary Thought* by G. C. Williams (1966). Also of great value for an in-depth analysis of group selection and for the arguments against it is Wilson's 1975 book, *Sociobiology: The New Synthesis*, especially chapter 5. Current theory does allow for apparent altruistic behavior, but only if the altruistic act is for a relative. In this case, it is called "kin selection." Because kin selection is especially interesting in insects that have sterile castes of workers, a fair amount of thought has gone into the population genetics of social insects (see, for example, Alexander and Sherman 1977; Hamilton 1972; Wilson 1975). Sometimes the term "group selection" is used synonymously with interdemic selection where some local populations go extinct. Interdemic selection provides a possible mechanism for the action of what Wynne-Edwards would call group selection. A classic case of this involves the T-locus in house mice where sterile or lethal alleles are maintained in natural populations at high frequencies (Lewontin and Dunn 1960; Lewontin 1962). Presumably, this is due to segregation distortion where male heterozygotes produce more t-bearing sperm than normal sperm. Local extinctions take place, but populations are re-established by migrants. More recently, the concept of interdemic selection has been applied to grain beetles (Wade 1976), a group where cannibalism is believed to play an important role in self-regulation (Lloyd 1968; Park et al. 1965).

In Paper 21, David Pimentel, an entomologist at Cornell University, has suggested a mechanism of population regulation that involves interactions between herbivore and plant, predator and prey, parasite and host, or two competitors. He outlines what he refers to as the "genetic feed-back mechanism." Pimentel theorizes that those organisms being eaten, parasitized, or outcompeted will be under pressure to improve their resistance to their predators, parasites, or competitors. For example, if two species are competing and one begins to win, that species will increase in numbers in relation to the losing species. The population will then consist mainly of the winners. At this point, the winners are competing against themselves, but the losers are mainly competing against winners because of the disparity between numbers. The result is selection within the loser population to gain a competitive edge over the winners. After a sufficient period of selection, the numbers should reverse so that the losers become winners, and vice versa. This reversal should produce a long-term oscillation in numbers and competitive ability. Pimentel has gathered some proof of this in studies of competition between blowflies and houseflies (Pimentel et al. 1965). The herbivore–plant system is gaining attention because there is an interest in the production of secondary products by plants and their effects on animal populations (Swain 1977).

Let me digress a moment to continue on the theme of plant–animal interactions. Another classic study of self-regulation is that of the western tent caterpillar, work done primarily by W. G. Wellington (1957; 1965). The populations are probably regulated by differential dispersal where active larvae give rise to active adults who disperse, whereas less active larvae—if they survive—give rise to nondispersing, sluggish adults. As an outbreak proceeds in a given area, the populations consist more and more of the sluggish type because active individuals disperse. Various explanations have been given for how these different types are produced. It is probably a simple function of nutrition in the eggs, which in a sense is inherited because active adults produce a greater proportion of active larvae. However, let me return to the reason for my digression. We were discussing the production of secondary products by plants that have an effect on animal populations. The latest work being done on the tent caterpillars involves the hypothesis that the sluggishness of larvae is a function of the ingestion of plant secondary products (Orians, personal communication). Also, Lloyd and Dybas (1966) suggest the possibility of resistant trees in regulating periodical cicadas. These studies show a current interest in plant–animal interactions as potential regulators of animal population density. More will be said about this in Part VIII.

The last group of papers in this section deal with ideas touched on by Wynne-Edwards but not adequately explained by his group-selection theory—that is, the concept that social organization, primarily in mammalian populations, can control population density. For example, Lack (1954) suggests that birds can be regulated effectively by competition for food if there are compressible territories. When food supply is high, territories will be small; conversely, when food is scarce, territories will be larger.

The next two papers in this section deal with phenotypic behavior mechanisms, and the last paper deals with a genotypic behavior mechanism. Paper 22, by J. B. Calhoun, is a 1949 work entitled "A Method of Self-Control of Population Growth Among Mammals Living in the Wild." Calhoun was one of the first to suggest that ". . . social conditioning may be a potent factor in population control among mammals." Looking for the factors that cause a decreasing population growth rate as density increases, he set up an experimental enclosure of Norway rats *(Rattus norvegicus)* to demonstrate that maternal physiology can be upset by high density and would then cause reduced population growth. A specific group of rats who were receiving the hostility of others had a low weaning success rate. Thus we get the sequence of increased density leading to increased hostility, which disturbs the psychology and physiology of the population members and leads to decreased reproductive output. Southwick (1955a; 1955b) followed up Calhoun's work in a study of house mice *(Mus musculus)*; he found that many types of interactions will lead to lowered population growth. Others, such as Barnett (1975), and Calhoun (1962; 1963) followed up and expanded on this work.

This then leads us directly into Paper 23, "Endocrines, Behavior and Population," by J. J. Christian and D. E. Davis (1964), who summarize their concept of the behavior-endocrine feedback system that can regulate populations. They are getting at the physiological mechanisms of the events described by Calhoun, Southwick, Barnett, and others. Basically, they are dealing with the effects of Hans Selye's (1946) "general adaptation syndrome" (GAS) wherein organisms put under continued stress will show a syndrome of symptoms caused by endocrine disorders. That is, any sort of prolonged stress will invoke the GAS with increasing encounters at high density providing the stress involved in mammal population regulation. The syndrome involves an overstimulation, and thus exhaustion, of the adreno-pituitary axis. This leads to decreased reproduction (diminished production of sex hormones), increased mortality due to hypoglycemia, and any number of specific symptoms generally labelled "shock disease." Christian and Davis cite examples of data both from the laboratory and from wild populations to support their hypothesis.

The last paper in this section (Paper 24), by Dennis Chitty, complements as well as contrasts the Christian and Davis paper because Chitty views the same process from a genotypic rather than a phenotypic point of view. That is, Chitty views the increase in population density the same way that Christian and Davis do: as an increased stress on the individuals. Unlike Christian and Davis, however, Chitty believes that natural selection will favor certain types of behaviors over others rather than causing a general endocrine breakdown in all individuals. That is, as density increases, aggressive behavior may be selected for, a population will become full of aggressive individuals, and an aggressive population will have curtailed population growth. Thus in both mechanisms, density increase is viewed as stressful. However, the two interpretations disagree over whether there is a phenotypic or a genotypic response. This disagreement is another interesting example of how the same phenomenon can be viewed in such different ways by population biologists and emphasizes the necessity of keeping an open mind and attempting to devise unambiguous tests of hypotheses to separate various mechanisms.

REFERENCES

Alexander, R., and P. Sherman. 1977. Local Mate Competition and Parental Investment in Social Insects. *Science* **196**:494–500.

Barnett, S. A. 1975. *The Rat* (rev. ed.). Chicago: University of Chicago Press.

Birch, L. C., and P. R. Ehrlich. 1967. Evolutionary History and Population Biology. *Nature* **214**:349–352.

Birch, L. C., and W. G. Vogt. 1970. Plasticity of Taxonomic Characters of the Queensland Fruit Flies *Dacus tryoni* and *Dacus neohumeralis* (Tephritidae). *Evolution* **24**:320–343.

Calhoun, J. B. 1962. *The Ecology and Sociology of the Norway Rat.* Washington, D.C.: U.S. Govt. Printing Off.

Calhoun, J. B. 1963. The Social Use of Space. *Physiol. Mamm.* **1**:1–187.

Ford, E. B. 1931. *Mendelism and Evolution.* London: Methuen.

Ford, E. B. 1964. *Ecological Genetics.* London: Methuen.

Franz, J. 1949. Über die genetischen Grundlagen des Zusammenbruchs einer Massenvermehrung aus inneren Ursachen. *Z. Angew. Ent.* **31**: 228–260.

Hamilton, W. D. 1972. Altruism and Related Phenomena, Mainly in Social Insects. *Ann. Rev. Ecol. Syst.* **3**:193–232.

Krebs, C. J. 1972. *Ecology*. New York: Harper & Row.

Lack, D. 1954. *The Natural Regulation of Animal Numbers*. London: Oxford University Press.

Lewontin, R. C. 1962. Interdeme Selection Controlling a Polymorphism in the House Mouse. *Am. Nat.* **96**:65–78.

Lewontin, R. C., and L. C. Dunn. 1960. The Evolutionary Dynamics of Polymorphism in the House Mouse. *Genetics* **45**:705–722.

Lloyd, M. 1968. Self-Regulation of Adult Numbers by Cannibalism in Two Laboratory Strains of Flour Beetles *(Tribolium castaneum)*. *Ecology* **49**:245–259.

Lloyd, M., and H. Dybas. 1966. The Periodical Cicada Problem, I: Population Ecology. *Evolution* **20**:133–149.

Park, T., D. B. Mertz, W. Grodzinski, and T. Prus. 1965. Cannibalistic Predation in Populations of Flour Beetles. *Physiol. Zool.* **38**:289–321.

Pimentel, D., E. Feinberg, P. Wood, and J. Hayes. 1965. Selection, Spatial Distribution, and the Coexistence of Competing Fly Species. *Am. Nat.* **99**:97–109.

Selye, H. 1946. The General Adaptation Syndrome and the Disease of Adaptation. *J. Clin. Endocrin.* **6**:117–230.

Southwick, C. H. 1955a. The Population Dynamics of Confined House Mice Supplied with Unlimited Food. *Ecology* **36**:212–225.

Southwick, C. H. 1955b. Regulatory Mechanisms of House Mouse Populations: Social Behavior Affecting Litter Survival. *Ecology* **36**:627–634.

Swain, T. 1977. Secondary Compounds as Protective Agents. *Ann. Rev. Plant Physiol.* **28**:479–501.

Wade, M. 1976. Group Selection Among Laboratory Populations of *Tribolium*. *Proc. Nat. Acad. Sci. USA* **73**:4604–4607.

Wellington, W. G. 1957. Individual Differences as a Factor in Population Dynamics: The Development of a Problem. *Can. J. Zool.* **35**:293–323.

Wellington, W. G. 1965. Some Maternal Influences on Progeny Quality in the Western Tent Caterpillar *Malacosoma pluviale* (Dyar.). *Can. Ent.* **97**:1–14.

Williams, G. C. 1966. *Adaptation and Natural Selection—A Critique of Some Current Evolutionary Thought*. Princeton, N.J.: Princeton University Press.

Wilson, E. O. 1975. *Sociobiology*. Cambridge, Mass.: Harvard University Press.

Wynne-Edwards, V. C. 1962. *Animal Dispersion in Relation to Social Behavior*. Edinburgh: Oliver and Boyd.

19

Reprinted from *Am. Nat.* **94**(874):5–24 (1960)

THE GENETIC FACTOR IN POPULATION ECOLOGY

L. C. BIRCH

Department of Zoology, University of Sydney, Sydney, Australia

INTRODUCTION

The ecological problem of populations has to do with the numbers of animals and what determines these numbers. The genetical problem of populations has to do with the kind or kinds of animals and what determines kind. These two disciplines meet when the questions are asked, how does the kind of animal (i.e., genotype) influence the numbers and how does the number of animals influence the kind, i.e., the genetical composition of the population? These questions are as much ecological as they are genetical.

GENETIC AND PHENOTYPIC PLASTICITY

Chapman (1928) made a fundamental contribution to animal ecology when he introduced the important idea that the ecological characteristics of a species can be measured and regarded as constants in the sense in which chemical substances can be defined precisely in terms of certain constant characteristics. Such were birth-rate, death-rate, rate of development and so on. He considered these as characteristics of the species in the same way in which a taxonomist might regard certain morphological features as characterizing the species. Chapman had the idea that one day the ecologist would have at his disposal a table of ecological constants for the different species he worked with. Since Chapman's day some ecologists have attempted to measure quantitatively these qualities of ecological importance. The initial problem was to define them precisely. We need only recall Chapman's concept of "biotic potential" and the changes this concept has undergone, to appreciate the time and thought that was necessary to transform this into something that was both measurable and meaningful. The concept of dispersal is another example. At one time dispersal was the subject of anecdotes and little more. Today it can be studied precisely with the tools of statistics and chemistry.

It was perhaps fortunate that the attention of ecologists was directed by Chapman toward the end of defining more precisely ecological characteristics of animals, before they became confused by the fact that such qualities are not really constants at all. They are probably not constant even for a particular genotype, particularly if the genotype has phenotypic plasticity, by which is meant the ability of the genotype to survive and multiply in a wide range of environments. However, populations consist of an array of genotypes and we now know, at least for quite a number of species, that this array changes both in space and in time. Instead of thinking of ecological characteristics of species as constants, we have been forced by genetics to think of them as fluctuating between certain values or even drifting in time to different mean values. Likewise we have to think of a transect in the spatial distribution of the species as revealing a spectrum of values corresponding to a spatial genetic spectrum. From a long term evolutionary point of view this characteristic of genetic plasticity has made evolution or transformation of species possible. From a short term ecological point of view it enables a species to live in a wide range of environments. And in a changing environment it enables the species to cope with change by changing itself. A change in environment may mean a new "ecological opportunity" for a species which has genetic plasticity. Genetic plasticity and phenotypic plasticity are two ways in which species are adapted to survive and multiply in a wide range of environments or, which amounts to the same thing, are adapted to cope with a change in environment. Since change is a more characteristic feature than stability in environments, these two sorts of plasticity are of fundamental significance for the ecologist to recognize and study.

The basis of genotypic plasticity is diversity of genotypes on which selection can operate. As a mechanism of adaptation to changing environment it can only be effective when the length of generation is shorter than the time within which the environment changes. For example, it is of no use to an elephant as an adaptive mechanism to seasonal change in the environment. But it is for Drosophila which can complete several generations in a season. On the other hand, it could presumably be of value to the elephant in adapting the species to long term changes in its environment such as must have occurred in the evolution of elephants.

Adaptation through genotypic plasticity is only possible when there is considerable genetic variability available at all times. The source of such variability is twofold: mutation and, in sexual organisms, recombination of genes. Recurrent mutation is the main source of genetic variability in bacteria, algae and protozoa. But mutation rates are, for the most part, so low that the effectiveness of mutation on its own has been questioned for all but such organisms as these which multiply at a prodigious rate. A high rate of increase combined with intense selection can lead to rapid change despite relatively low mutation rates. With sexual organisms mutation rate is reinforced with the element of stored variability which means that there is a reserve of variability over and above that which mutation alone can provide. This important aspect of adaptation in sexual organisms has been discussed in detail by Dobzhansky (1951) and Waddington (1957) and others, to whom reference should be made for details. Suffice it to indicate here the main genetic mechanisms involved in stored or concealed variability.

(a) Genes which have no phenotypic expression will be stored in the gene pool since it is the phenotype which is selected. Two mechanisms are involved, dominance and canalizing selection. Recessive genes concealed by dominant alleles will only become expressed phenotypically when homozygous. A tremendous store of recessive genes is concealed in heterozygotes. This was first shown by Tschetwerikoff in 1927 (see Dobzhansky, 1951) in natural populations of *Drosophila melanogaster* and has been amply confirmed for numerous other species by Dobzhansky (1951) and others since. Canalizing selection tends toward a stability of the phenotype through selection of genes which make the organism insensitive to abnormal environments (Waddington, 1957). Genes for a canalized character will inevitably be stored.

(b) Polygenic inheritance favors stored variability (Mather, 1941, 1943). This variability becomes released in linked polygene complexes when crossing over occurs and such released variability can be adaptive when environment changes.

(c) Heterosis or superiority of heterozygote over the homozygotes. This is the essential condition for balanced polymorphism in Mendelian populations. If a mutant produces a heterotic heterozygote, natural selection will retain this mutant in the population even if the homozygote is lethal. This mechanism has been extensively studied by Dobzhansky (1951) and his colleagues in Drosophila populations which exhibit polymorphism in chromosomal inversions. Heterosis is the mechanism by means of which a diversity of chromosomal inversions is maintained in the population. This diversity adapts the species to a wider variety of environments than would otherwise be possible (Dobzhansky et al., 1950). The existence of heterosis of single pairs of genes is more difficult to establish. The superiority of the heterozygote carrier of sickle-cell anaemia in malarial environments may be such an example (Allison, 1955). Other examples may occur in man (Dobzhansky, 1958) and Drosophila (Wallace, 1958).

A striking example of the release of stored variability with change in environment is Waddington's (1957) experiment in which he finds that in some flies of *Drosophila melanogaster* a cross-vein in the wing is missing when they are reared at a high temperature. The abnormality does not occur at normal temperatures. By selecting for cross-veinless flies at high temperature, Waddington found that the character was genetically determined. In his selected stock the character appeared irrespective of whether they were raised at low or high temperatures. The capacity to respond to high temperature in this way is resident in the normal unselected flies. The character cannot however be selected until environment favors its phenotypic expression. From this experiment Waddington argues for the genetic assimilation of adaptive characters induced by environment. One need only suppose that cross-veinlessness was adaptive at high temperatures to see his point. The capacity for response to environment is inherited. All the environment does

269

is to cause the genes already present, but concealed, to be expressed. Once expressed the new phenotypes can be selected. This mechanism would be far more effective in adapting a species to changed environment than reliance on random recurrent mutation alone.

Genetic plasticity and diversity of genotype is of no advantage in an environment which is constant in its properties except as an insurance against possible change in the future. Lewontin (1958) has pointed out that in a constant environment if a homozygote arose which was superior or equal in fitness to the heterozygote then fixation of that allele would result. This he claims to have demonstrated in a population cage of *Drosophila pseudoobscura* which initially contained two chromosomal inversions but after 1000 days the population was nearly homozygous for one inversion. The homozygous population is the "narrow specialist"; the heterozygous population may be less fit in any one environment but this is the price it pays for being able to live in a variety of environments by virtue of the diversity of its genotypes.

A balance between flexibility and stability of the genetic composition of a population is attained by a variety of genetic mechanisms. Chromosomal inversions are one way of tying up blocks of genes which have been proved to be of adaptive value in selection. Inversions suppress crossing over with consequent reduction in variability. This would be advantageous in some environments. But where the environment is constantly providing new challenges, such as on the periphery of the distribution of a species, greater genetic flexibility may be necessary for survival. This is borne out by the finding of a decreased number of inversions at the periphery of the distribution as compared with the center in certain populations of Drosophila (see later). Another mechanism for maintenance of a balance between stability and flexibility of the genotypic composition of the population is the alternation of sexual and asexual generations. In the asexual generation genotypes are kept stable. The change from asexual to sexual phase is related to change in environment. The sexual generation occurs when the environment becomes unfavorable and so provides the species at this stage with an increase in genetic variability (see Lewontin, 1957, for examples of this).

Huxley (1942) and more recently Lewontin (1957) have argued that there has been a general trend in evolution in which genotypic plasticity is gradually supplanted or replaced by phenotypic plasticity. Man's ability to alter his environment instead of being altered by it is an example of phenotypic plasticity, for this enables man to live in a wide variety of environments. Phenotypic plasticity does not necessarily involve the ability to alter the environment but more importantly the ability of a genotype to survive and reproduce in a wide variety of environments. Examples of this may be found more readily in the higher animals than in the lower. However it is not as yet possible to say to what extent one does supercede the other in passing from lower to higher organisms. Genotypic plasticity is, no doubt, the main method of adaptation in bacteria, protozoa and algae. It is a feature of many insects which have a high rate of increase (see Dobzhansky, 1951; Andrewartha and Birch, 1954; De Bach, 1958). Bullock (1955) has shown that plasticity of one sort or another is common amongst a variety of marine invertebrates but he makes no distinction between genetic and phenotypic plasticity in his review. Battaglia (1958) provided an example of genetic plasticity in a marine copepod and suggested a number of others. Nevertheless phenotypic adaptation to temperature alone in lower organisms has been demonstrated in bacteria, planaria, crayfish, crab, clam, limpet, various annelids and a great variety of insects (Fry, 1958). In the vertebrates genetic plasticity is well illustrated by races with different tolerances to temperature in the frog *Rana pipiens* (Moore, 1949) and in fish in the two-spined stickleback (Heuts, 1956). The stickleback also has races with different tolerances to salinity. The existence of genotypic plasticity in fishes is also evident from the success of fish culturists in selecting for higher fecundity and faster growth rates. On the other hand the great amount of work on acclimatization of fishes has been singularly unsuccessful in revealing much genetic plasticity. This may simply mean that genetic diversity is more difficult to detect in fish than in other animals. Some reasons why this may be so have been given by Fry (1957). Hart's (1952) study of freshwater fishes in the North American continent from widely different environments showed very little conclusive evidence for genetic diversity; on the other hand, his work and that of Fry (1957, 1958) shows that phenotypic plasticity in relation to temperature is common in freshwater fishes. Homoiothermy confers a high degree of phenotypic plasticity in birds and mammals making genetic plasticity less necessary in some circumstances. But of course genetic plasticity is still a feature of homoiotherms and without it evolution could not occur.

There is a succession of levels at which adaptation could be studied; the genes involved, the chemical intermediaries between the genes and the immediate phenotypic effects they produce, such as increased resistance to cold or increased ability to disperse, and the ultimate effect of these phenotypic changes on birth-rate and death-rate. The purpose of this paper is to relate genetics with birth-rate and death-rate, for it is birth-rate and death-rate which ultimately determine the number of animals. The immediate phenotypic expression of the genes is also the province of genetics and ecology but this will not be considered further here.

THE INFLUENCE OF GENETIC COMPOSITION ON THE RATE OF INCREASE "r"

Species differ in their capacity to increase in numbers during favorable periods when increase is possible. One species can be compared to another in this respect by comparing their innate capacities for increase or intrinsic rates of natural increase, r_m (Andrewartha and Birch, 1954, chapter 3). Such comparisons show quite clearly that species differ genetically in their capacities to increase in numbers. When we come to question how capacity for increase is selected in evolution it is necessary to discuss the rate of increase in terms of the actual rate of increase, r, characteristic of the natural environment in which the species lives. The statistic r_m is an abstraction from nature in so far as it is a measure of a rate of increase when certain components of environment are excluded.

Natural selection will tend to maximize r for the environment in which the species lives, for any mutation or gene combination which increases the chance of genotypes possessing them contributing more individuals to the next generation (that is, of increasing r) will be selected over genotypes contributing fewer of their kind to successive generations. This is the usual meaning of fitness of a genotype. The tendency of natural selection to maximize r does not necessarily mean that natural selection will tend to make the numbers of the species a maximum. The maximization of r would tend to this end except in so far as mechanisms have evolved which put a limit to the numbers in unit space, irrespective of rates of increase. The extent to which such mechanisms may exist is discussed below.

The rate of increase is the difference between the two components of increase: birth-rate and death-rate. The maximization of r through selection does not necessarily imply that natural selection will tend to increase birth-rate or to decrease death-rate, but that it will tend to maximize the difference between them. An animal has a certain amount of energy to dissipate in its life. Some of this energy will go into functions associated with reproduction, some of it will go into activities such as dispersal and escape from predators and some of it will go into the functions associated with just being alive. The partitioning of energy between these various functions will be such as to maximize the chance for survival and multiplication. Selection for clutch size in birds and litter size in mammals are rather special examples as we shall see later. An increase in the size of the clutch or litter to numbers so great that offspring cannot get enough food for survival from the parents is unadaptive. There is good evidence that selection will tend to produce a clutch size corresponding to the number of young that can be successfully reared. This may vary from one part of a bird's range to another (Lack, 1956; Moreau, 1944). Similarly a balance has to be struck between the number of eggs laid by an animal such as a fish and the size of the egg. Survival of fry hatched from large eggs may be greater than survival of fry hatched from small eggs. Selection may favor a small number of large eggs rather than a greater number of small eggs (Svardson, 1949; Rodd, 1946). Tsetse flies have a birth-rate which is probably the lowest of any insect. The offspring are laid as mature larvae about to pupate and only one larva is produced at a time. Their energy is concentrated into a few offspring born in a mature stage of development rather than in a large number of eggs. Survival of the immature stages is made maximum by virtue of the advanced stage at which the young are born.

Evidence that natural selection has not pushed birth rates to the attainable maximum is provided by those domestic and laboratory animals in which artificial selection has been effective in increasing the birth rate or egg-laying rate. But this gain is purchased at the expense of other traits that would be important in survival in nature (see Cole, 1957; Smith, 1954).

In contrast to the tsetse fly, adult Mayflies (Ephemeroptera) produce a large number of eggs and then die after a brief adult life without feeding at all. There is presumably in these insects a selective advantage in concentrating the energy of life into early egg-production in the adult and survival of the long-lived immature stages, rather than in survival of the adult with egg production covering a longer period. An insect which can mature eggs without feeding, such as the Mayfly, has an evolutionary advantage when adult food is scarce over an adult which has to feed to mature its eggs. The adults of blowflies normally require protein in their adult diet for maturation of eggs. But Nicholson (1957) has produced a strain of the blowfly *Lucilia cuprina* which can mature some eggs without protein in its diet (from protein taken in the larval diet) by raising them in very crowded cultures where protein is in short supply. Insects which do not feed at all as adults have evidently taken this step some stages further.

These are a few of the variety of ways in which the life history of a species is patterned by selection and presumably in each case to maximize the difference between birth-rate and death-rate. Early production of litters, larger litters, closer spacing of litters and biassing of the sex-ratio in favor of females and higher survival of pre-reproductive and reproductive stages would each (other things remaining the same) increase r. Cole (1954, 1957) has pointed out that which particular ones which would be most effective depends upon the pattern of life history of the species. For example, species that reach maturity early can gain more from increasing litter size than from living longer and producing more litters. In species that mature more slowly it may be more advantageous to live longer and produce more litters than to increase litter size. Life history changes that involve a biassing of the sex-ratio are peculiar in the payment exacted from an evolutionary point of view. An increase in the proportion of females in the population may decrease the chance of females finding a mate. An answer to this may be found in asexual reproduction. But this would usually involve loss in genetic plasticity. A combination of the two may be best both from an ecological point of view (Cole, 1957) and from an evolutionary point of view (Wright, 1931). Whatever change occurs in the pattern of the life history a balance has to be found between the most appropriate reproductive and survival pattern.

Direct evidence of selection for rate of increase is provided by Bateman's (unpublished thesis, 1958) study of populations of the trypetid fruit fly *Dacus tryoni* collected from different geographic areas in Australia. He measured the innate capacity for increase r_m of population from four places along a 2,000 mile stretch of coastal country in Eastern Australia. In this example there is reason to suppose that the statistic r_m reflects the real capacity of the species to increase in numbers in the places where they live. There were significant differences in the capacities for increase of the four populations. These differences have probably developed through selection in the last fifty years, for evidence suggests that the fly has spread from its tropical home into temperate latitudes during this period. The differences which he found were correlated with differences in temperature in the four places from which the populations came. For example, the most northern population (from Cairns in the tropics) had the lowest value of r_m at 20°C. and the highest at 30°C. The population from Sydney 1500 miles south had the highest value of r_m at 20°C. and the lowest at 30°C. Increase in the innate capacity for increase at 20°C. was doubtless one factor which enabled the species to become established in Sydney. The main evolutionary changes which occurred in the life history pattern to bring this about were increase in the number of progeny and in the life expectancy of the adult. For example, if we compare the populations from Cairns and Sydney we find that at 20°C. the number of progeny produced is greater for the Sydney population at all ages of the parent female and that they start laying eggs several weeks earlier. In the tenth week the Sydney strain lays nearly 30 times as many eggs as the Cairns strain. By the 20th week it lays about twice as many eggs. This may be an illustration of the principle that a rise in the innate capacity for increase can be most readily obtained by increasing the rate of egg production early in a female's life. The survivorship of adults of the Sydney strain is also greater at all ages than that of the Cairns strain at this temperature. The Sydney climate has evidently imposed a selection at 20°C. whereas in Cairns selection at such a temperature could hardly occur.

It would be a fascinating field of study to investigate the genetics of such evolutionary changes in life history patterns. A possible lead in this direction has been given by Carson's (1958) striking experiment with *Drosophila melanogaster*. He established experimental populations of flies over several generations in which the numbers fluctuated around a fairly constant level. He then introduced a "foreign" gene into these populations. There was a rapid three-fold increase in size of the population which was maintained for fifteen generations, after which the experiment was terminated. The increase in total numbers of the populations involves an increase in birth-rate or a decrease in death-rate or both. One gene was responsible for the change. His evidence was in favor of the hypothesis that these changes were the result of new heterotic combinations of genes produced after the foreign gene was introduced.

The evolution of heterosis following recombination and consequent change in fitness of genotypes has also been demonstrated in laboratory cultures of *Drosophila pseudoobscura* by Dobzhansky (1957). Seasonal changes in the frequency of chromosomal inversions in natural populations of this species in California (Wright and Dobzhansky, 1946) suggest that the rate of increase r of populations of *D. pseudoobscura* is a function of the different kinds of inversions in the third chromosome. Some combinations permit increase in the spring, others permit increase in the summer. In some unpublished experiments of my own I have found that when the trypetid fruit fly *Dacus tryoni tryoni* was bred together with the color variant known as *D. tryoni neohumeralis* in the one population cage, and provided that its initial frequency was only 20 per cent, its rate of increase in the population declined until none were left after 35 weeks at 25°C. But when the initial frequency of *tryoni* was 80 per cent the rapid decline in numbers was halted after 20 weeks and this coincided with an increase in frequency of hybrids. From then on for the 100 weeks in which the experiment has continued *tryoni* has persisted in the population together with *neohumeralis* and their hybrids. The initial high frequency of *tryoni* gave this variant sufficient time to introduce its genes into the populations through the hybrids that were formed, so permitting a balanced population of the two types and their hybrids to evolve. Both *tryoni* and *neohumeralis* have changed genetically in this experiment, for the degree of sexual isolation that exists between the original populations had largely disappeared after 100 weeks. A genetic change in *tryoni* in this experiment has altered its rate of increase permitting it to persist in the mixed population whereas in the initial experiment its rate of increase decreased in the course of the experiment.

Family selection. The tendency of natural selection to maximize the rate of increase r poses a dilemma. It is easy to imagine that a low rate of increase could be advantageous under some circumstances in which large numbers would result in serious depletion of resources of food and space, with consequent starvation and death. The chance of annihilation from this cause would be reduced if the birth-rate were lowered and this resulted in greater chance of offspring surviving. However, selection for lower birth-rate can only occur when parents and progeny remain as a family during the rearing stages or in circumstances which are strictly analagous to a family situation. Selection for clutch size in birds is a classic example of selection operating on the individuals of a family unit. It is the families of optimum size that are selected. In social insects sterility for the bulk of the colony has evolved. This has happened because the colony is a family. Here it is the parents whose family organization is best for survival who are selected. Darwin recognized that sterile castes of social insects could only evolve as a result of selection operating on a family kept together as a unit. If the progeny of one colony mixed freely with the progeny from another then sterility could hardly evolve. This is sometimes called, with a lot of other unrelated things, selection in which the population is the unit of selection. This however is a misleading phrase for what is always selected are individuals. In selection for clutch size the individuals selected are those whose parents laid neither too many nor too few eggs. The regulation of the fecundity of the queen bee and the regulation of the number of reproductive individuals in the colony of the termite *Kalatermes flavicollis* are further examples of evolution of lowered birth-rate (Emerson, 1958).

Can selection favor the individual with a low birth-rate (other things being equal) in cases other than the closely knit family? The following hypothetical example is perhaps one sort of situation in which selection might operate in this direction. Let us suppose that a species of mosquito lays its eggs in pools of water with insufficient food for more than a few larvae. If each pool received eggs from one female only then the female which laid the smaller number of eggs would tend to be selected. We shall suppose that those which laid large numbers of eggs produced no living progeny because of overcrowding in the pool. If different females laid their eggs together in the same pool then selection will not favor the mosquito which lays the smaller number of eggs. This would be analagous to mixing the clutches of several birds. However we could imagine an intermediate situation in which, despite the fact that mosquitoes laid their eggs in the same pools, some pools by chance might have eggs laid in them by mosquitoes of low fecundity. In so far as this occurred selection might favor the genotype of low fecundity especially if the smaller number of eggs is also correlated with larger eggs. In this model the pool is analogous to a family. I find some difficulty in supposing that this could be at all common in nature. The possibility should not however be overlooked. In these examples in which selection operates on individuals in a family, or something analogous to a family, selection still favors those genotypes with higher r, though in these cases the higher r is achieved by lowered birth-rate.

The general statement that selection will tend to maximize r is quite consistent with the fact that genotypes of low adaptive value may not be selected out of a population. In balanced polymorphism the homozygotes have lower adaptive values than the heterozygote. Similarly a genotype may have qualities of advantage to the species but of no advantage to itself. The theoretical concept of the "altruistic gene" (Haldane, 1932; Wright, 1949) is an example of this. Such a gene would increase in the population so long as the presence of such genotypes increased the chance of the population as a whole to survive and multiply. Too many of them might of course be disadvantageous. But even in this case selection still tends to maximize r for the population.

Territoriality. The tendency of selection is to bring r to a maximum. Yet there are numerous disadvantages in overcrowding and a high rate of increase would tend to produce overcrowding. The disadvantages of high numbers would be overcome if there were mechanisms to stop increase when density reached a certain critical maximum. Some forms of territoriality may serve this end. This does not involve selection for a low rate of increase but selection for cessation of increase when numbers are high. Such mechanisms would have the advantages which a high rate of increase confers without the disadvantage of high total numbers. Intraspecific strife in territorial muskrats may serve such an end. By fighting when their numbers reach a certain density in relation to cover muskrats prevent further increase in numbers (Errington, 1943). Muskrats only tolerate a certain number of their kind in any one marsh but when numbers are low they can increase at a fast rate and without serious intraspecific strife. Territoriality may in some cases serve to conserve resources, though there is no general agreement among ecologists that this is so. However, it does seem to result in lower numbers per unit area than would be the case without it. Territoriality is common in birds and mammals (Gibb, 1956; Hinde, 1956). But apart from ants (Brian, 1955) it seems to be rarely recorded in invertebrates with a few possible exceptions such as dragon flies (Moore, 1952; Jacobs, 1955) and crabs (Crane, 1941).

The slaughter of drones in Apidae and Meliponidae has a similar effect of getting rid of excess individuals in the colony (Emerson, 1958). These are examples of special mechanisms which will tend to keep population density at a low level, possibly even at an optimum level. They are in a different category from the more common effects of increased density in reducing birth-rate and increasing death-rate such as is observed in crowded experimental cultures of beetles and blowflies. A characteristic of these cultures is the enormous number of insects per unit space despite the effect of high density in reducing r.

We may then have to think of natural selection as having two tendencies, on the one hand to increase the rate of increase (with its attendant advantages) and on the other toward the evolution of mechanisms which stop increase when a critical density is reached.

THE INFLUENCE OF THE NUMBER OF ANIMALS ON GENETICAL COMPOSITION

In laboratory populations of insects the birth-rate falls and the death-rate rises with increase in density. This has been demonstrated also in some natural populations of certain birds and mammals which exhibit territorial behavior (Andrewartha and Birch, 1954, chapter 9). It has often been assumed that selection will be greatest in crowded populations because mortality rate is greater. There are however selective differences between some genotypes which exist whether the individuals live in a crowd or not. Genotypes homozygous for lethal or semilethal genes are examples of this. Furthermore the selective differences between genotypes may be a function of density and instead of disappearing at low densities the selective values may even be reversed. In uncrowded populations of *Drosophila pseudo-obscura* the inversion Chiracahua was favored over Standard. When larvae only or larvae and adults were crowded at a high density the Standard arrangement of the genes was favored over Chiracahua. When larvae and adults were crowded there was selective mortality of larvae but not of adults. When neither were crowded and there was no opportunity for selective mortality there were selective differences evidently in the rate of egg-laying (Birch, 1955). Similarly I have found a reversal of selective values in two color variants of the Queensland fruit fly *Dacus tryoni tryoni* and *D. tryoni neohumeralis* depending upon whether the adults and larvae were crowded or not. In a population cage at 25°C. the type *neohumeralis* was favored and increased in frequency when adults and larvae were crowded. In relatively uncrowded cages the type *tryoni* was favored over *neohumeralis* and increased in frequency.

Nicholson (1957) kept cultures of the blowfly *Lucilia cuprina* under crowded conditions supplying the population with a fixed amount of larval and adult food at regular intervals. In all ten of his cultures the character of the oscillations in numbers changed about the 400th day. Nicholson showed that this was due to a genetic change in the population. Acute shortage of protein in the experiments had resulted in the selection of flies which could produce and lay eggs in complete absence of protein. Such flies would have a selective advantage in these experiments as there was a severe shortage of protein. Normal adults require protein for production of eggs. Presumably the flies which do not need it in adult food can mature eggs on the protein in their bodies which was derived from larval food. The shortage of protein was in this case caused by high density of flies in relation to the amount provided daily. Nicholson's experiments were not designed to tell if this peculiar quality of flies would be selected when flies were uncrowded but on a diet lacking protein.

Laboratory experiments with *Drosophila melanogaster* have demonstrated that selective differences in survival of larvae are a function of both the density of larvae and the genotype of larvae with which they are crowded. Lewontin (1955) found that a particular genotype was favored in the presence of certain genotypes but at a disadvantage in the presence of others. Parsons (1958) has since demonstrated the same thing.

The complexity of selection of a particular genotype in relation both to density and kind of genotypes with which it lives has been unravelled in a series of complex experiments with *Drosophila pseudoobscura* by Dobzhansky (1957), Levene, Dobzhansky and Pavlovsky (1954), Levene, Pavlovsky and Dobzhansky (1958). They have shown that the selective values of flies carrying a particular chromosomal inversion is a function of both the kind and number of other chromosomal inversions in the population. In population cages containing flies with different chromosomal inversions the selective values of the inversions change as the frequency of the different inversions change. The selective values of a particular inversion will depend not only on its own frequency but on the frequency and kind of the other inversions present in the population.

Oscillations. These considerations of laboratory experiments suggest that change in genetic composition in relation to density may provide a clue to the vexed problem of the causes of oscillations in numbers in certain animal populations. Oscillations are characteristic of confined populations of the beetles Tribolium and Calandra studied in the laboratory and also of some natural populations. Park has consistently found that when populations of *Tribolium confusum* are maintained in vials for long times with regular renewal of food the numbers undergo a long term oscillation. The time between successive peaks was about 500 days when cultures were kept at 29°C. Birch found that two species of Calandra grain weevils gave similar long term oscillations with about 280 days between successive peaks at 25°C. (see Andrewartha and Birch, 1954, chapter 9). These oscillations appear to be quite different in nature from the short term oscillations obtained by Nicholson with Lucilia which appear to be explained quite satisfactorily by the massive deaths of larvae or adults when food was completely exhausted. This never happened in Park's or Birch's experiments. It is conceivable that such oscillations as they found could be due to selection favoring certain genotypes at high density and others at low density. As yet experiments have not been done to test this.

This hypothesis has been suggested as an explanation of outbreaks and declines of certain insect pests in Europe (Franz, 1950) and as a possible explanation of the unsolved problem of four year cycles in the vole *Microtus agrestis* in Wales (Chitty, 1957). Chitty has evidence of the existence of a hemolytic disease which is common when voles are dense and numbers are declining and rare when voles are increasing in numbers. There is some evidence that the disease may be genetic. Chitty postulates a gene or genes for the disease which confer some advantage on the voles living under crowded conditions at least upon heterozygotes and which is at a disadvantage when voles are not crowded.

When we come to examine the evidence from natural populations for the influence of density on selection and therefore on genetical composition little is to be found. This may simply mean that it has not been looked for. Williamson (1958) reviewed such evidence as is available and concluded from a number of suggestive cases that the only substantial one was Gershenson's (1945) work in Russia on change in proportion of black forms of the hamster *Cricetus cricetus* with change in number.

Drift. Fluctuations in numbers also suggests the possibility of genetic drift in isolated populations of small absolute size. Kerr and Wright (1954 a, b, c) demonstrated the operation of random drift as well as selection in populations of very small size (four pairs). Dobzhansky and Pavlovsky (1957) have shown experimentally that the results of selection were different in populations of *Drosophila pseudoobscura* containing different chromosomal inversions, depending upon whether the initial population consisted of 20 or 4000 flies. Variability in chromosome frequency was very much greater between populations initiated with the smaller number of flies. Their explanation is that natural selection started with populations which were more like one another in the experiments initiated with many flies but with populations which were less like one another in the populations initiated with only 20 flies.

Extinction. A final aspect of small numbers is the problem of extinction. Because ecologists study species that are extant on the face of the earth today and not the much greater number of species that are extinct they are inclined to regard the existence of extinct species as a peculiar problem. They tend to pose the question thus—what prevents species from becoming extinct? In view of the fact that extinction seems to be the inevitable fate of all species it might be more realistic to put the question thus—what it is that enables species to remain extant for as long as they do in the face of changing environment? Ecologists have attempted to answer this type of question largely in the terms of ecology. It is claimed for example by some of the adherents of the so-called "density-dependent" school of thought that in the absence of "density-dependent" factors populations would quickly become extinct. An alternative point of view has been that the chance of extinction during a low phase in fluctuation in numbers is reduced by the patchiness of the environment or the discontinuity of the population in space. The genetic factor which may be all important in this discussion is the capacity of species to change genetically during unfavorable periods when its numbers are drastically reduced. Combinations of genes which will enhance the chance for survival and multiplication will tend to be selected. During such exigencies genetic plasticity is a safety factor reducing the chance of extinction. It is not of course a guarantee of the continuance of the species any more than either of the ecological arguments can guarantee survival of the species (Birch, 1957). In an environment subject to change, populations of the polymorphic species will become extinct less often than the monomorphic one.

The peculiar characteristics of diapause, hibernation and migration are adaptations which have presumably been evolved in relation to such adverse influences as extreme dryness and cold. Similarly peculiarities of behavior such as aggregation and the instincts which serve to bring the sexes together in sparse populations are evidently adaptations evolved to overcome the hazards of low numbers.

THE INFLUENCE OF OTHER SPECIES ON GENETICAL COMPOSITION

The genetical composition of a population may change in space and time as a result of the selective action of almost any component of environment (Andrewartha and Birch, 1954, chapter 15). Most of the examples in preceding sections were concerned with genetic change in relation to the numbers of the animal present and to weather. The numbers of another species present in an animal's environment may also be a selective agency. This has now been well established for a number of predators but as yet little direct evidence has been found of selection due to non-predators in an animal's environment.

The outstanding examples of the selective action of predators are Cain and Sheppard's work on predation by birds on the land snail *Cepaea nemoralis*, summarized by Sheppard (1958); the work of Ford and Kettlewell on industrial melanism in moths summarized by Kettlewell (1956, 1958, 1959); and Brower's (1958a, b, c) studies on selective predation on mimetic and non-mimetic butterflies. In each of these examples the authors have succeeded in demonstrating that predators tend to select the conspicuously colored prey so conferring an advantage on the cryptically colored individuals. Over 70 species of moths have evolved black populations in industrial areas in the last 100 years. Kettlewell (1959) has found a number of genetic mechanisms responsible for the dark forms. In some species a single dominant gene changes the animal from white to black in one step. In some populations of *Gonodontis bidentata* polygenes are responsible for darkness. In some populations of *Lymantria monacha* three dominant genes are responsible for producing the black forms. Kettlewell also quotes one case of blackness being due to a recessive gene and another where the gene was incompletely dominant.

Concerning the possible selective role of non-predators in the environment of an animal Brown and Wilson (1956) cite a number of examples of several species with overlapping ranges. They refer to various species of ants, frogs and birds in which the related species show more divergence in various characters in the region of overlap than elsewhere. Most of the variations they refer to are morphological but some are physiological. They suggest that the differences have been evolved in the region of overlap as a means of preventing gene flow between two related species. These may be ex- amples of change in genetic composition as a result of the presence of an- other sort of animal, the change having taken place before the two forms were completely sexually isolated. However there is not any evidence on which to make a judgment as to whether this is simply a case of evolution of isolating mechanisms in the region of overlap or whether genetic change was promoted by selection in response to direct interference of one form by the other or in relation to shortage of common resource. Brown and Wilson assume the latter. It may have been either or both.

PERIPHERAL POPULATIONS

Populations on the periphery of the distribution present some special eco- logical and genetical problems. Usually the environment is more severe at the periphery. The ecological problem is how the species manages to sur- vive there and secondly how it sometimes spreads from there to previously uncolonized regions. The occupancy of some peripheral areas is temporary or is reinforced by invasions from within the distribution. Thus the moth *Heliothis armigera* is found in places where it can not overwinter, such as in the state of Minnesota, as a result of migrations of adults from the south. At the periphery the species is usually rarer than elsewhere, a fact which Andrewartha and Birch (1954) interpret as being due to the shortness of the favorable period when numbers can increase before an unfavorable period and a negative rate of increase supervene. This is merely an intensification of factors which operate in a less extreme way elsewhere in the distribution. But the severity of the environment must impose extremely severe selection and this would seem to be corroborated by the findings of Townsend (1952) for *Drosophila willistoni* and Carson (1955) for *Drosophila robusta* that homozygosis, so far as chromosomal inversions are concerned, increases from the center of the distribution to the margins. In the marginal areas where environment is hostile few chromosomal inversions are successful. But those that are successful enable the species to survive there. Another aspect of this hypothesis is that a species with many chromosomal inver- sions can occupy a greater variety of environments than one with few. This concept is supported by the wide distribution of *Drosophila willistoni* and *D. paulistorum* which have 44 and 34 chromosomal inversions respectively and the very restricted distribution of its sibling species *D. tropicalis* and *D. equinoxialis* which have each only four chromosomal inversions (da Cunha et al., 1950; Dobzhansky et al., 1950). Chromosomal inversions con-

fer adaptability on the species in an environment which varies either in time
or in space. Polymorphism in the center of the distribution is maintained at
the expense of a certain degree of genetic plasticity which crossing over
confers and which is presumably of greatest advantage at the margins of the
distribution. There the species is on the frontier of its distribution and is
subject to the constant threat of extinction. It is there that variability has
to be welded into new combinations to meet a constantly changing and hostile environment. Speculation as to the importance of peripheral populations
in evolution on a grand scale has been made by Mayr (1954) and Brown
(1957) but these considerations go beyond the scope of this paper.

SUMMARY

The genetic plasticity of populations implies that the numbers of animals,
which is what the population ecologist studies, may be a reflection of
change in genetic composition either in space or in time. Alternatively the
number of animals may itself be a cause of genetic change. These genetic
aspects of ecology will be more important when genetic plasticity is more
characteristic than phenotypic plasticity. In relation to changing environment genetic plasticity can only be adaptive when the length of the generation is less than the time the environment takes to change. Both types of
plasticity exist throughout the animal and plant kingdoms. In some groups
of animals in which phenotypic plasticity is common, as in fishes, it is extremely difficult to establish the extent to which genetic plasticity exists.
Adaptation through genetic plasticity depends upon a continuous source of
genetic variability. The source is mutation and in addition, in sexual organisms, recombination of genes. Sex also introduces the possibility of stored
variability which is another source of variability available to the species.
The sources of stored variability are, dominance, canalizing selection, linked
polygenes in which crossing over occurs and heterosis. A balance between
flexibility and stability of genetic composition is attained by a variety of
genetic mechanisms of which chromosomal inversions and alternation of
sexual and asexual generations are two.

From an ecological point of view the significance of change in genetical
composition of a population is its effect on the rate of increase r, that is on
birth-rate and death-rate. The tendency of natural selection is to maximize
r. This does not mean that natural selection will tend to increase birth-rate
to the absolute maximum possible and to reduce death-rate to the absolute
minimum possible. But it will tend to maximize the difference between them.
Life histories have been patterned by natural selection to this end. The
rate of increase r can be increased by a variety of alterations to the life
history pattern. The ones which will be useful will depend upon the environment the animal lives in. An increase in r may be achieved through
natural selection by a decrease in the birth-rate. This can occur in one sort
of situation only and that is when progeny and parents remain together as a
family, at least during the rearing stage. This sort of selection has resulted
in characteristic clutch sizes in birds and sterile castes in the social in-

sects. Selection for low birth-rate could, in theory, occur in non-family organisms under special circumstances in which the offspring of the one or a few parents tended to be reared in isolation from those of other parents. Although selection cannot favor a low rate of increase, it may favor the development of mechanisms which cause a cessation of increase when a certain critical density is reached. Some forms of territoriality may serve this end.

Concerning the influence of numbers of animals on their genetic composition, there is experimental evidence that some genotypes are favored in a crowd and others are favored when sparse. Further the survival value of a genotype is a function not only of the number of other genotypes around it but also of their kind. These findings in experimental populations may be important in resolving the causes of oscillations in numbers in some experimental and possibly in some natural populations; and secondly they suggest a role for genetic plasticity in reducing the chance of extinction.

ACKNOWLEDGMENTS

Earlier drafts of this paper were read and criticized by Dr. M. A. Bateman, Joint Unit of Animal Ecology, University of Sydney; Professor L. C. Cole, Cornell University; Professors Th. Dobzhansky, Columbia University, A. E. Emerson and Thomas Park, University of Chicago; and Dr. J. M. Rendel, C.S.I.R.O. Section of Genetics, University of Sydney, to all of whom I acknowledge a debt of gratitude. As a result of their help and criticism much of the paper was rewritten but this does not mean that any one of them will necessarily agree with all the concepts put forward nor can they be held responsible for what is in the paper.

LITERATURE CITED

Allison, A. C., 1955, Aspects of polymorphism in man. Cold Spring Harbor Symp. Quant. Biol. 20: 239-255.

Andrewartha, H. G., and L. C. Birch, 1954, The distribution and abundance of animals. University of Chicago Press, Chicago, Ill.

Bateman, M. A., 1958, Ecological adaptations in geographic races of the Queensland fruit-fly *Dacus (Strumeta) tryoni. Frogg.* Unpublished thesis, University of Sydney, Sydney, Australia.

Battaglia, Bruno, 1958, Balanced polymorphism in *Tisbe reticulata*, a marine copepod. Evolution 12: 358-364.

Birch, L. C., 1955, Selection in *Drosophila pseudoobscura* in relation to crowding. Evolution 9: 389-399.

  1957, The role of weather in determining the distribution and abundance of animals. Cold Spring Harbor Symp. Quant. Biol. 22: 203-218.

Brian, M. V., 1955, Food collection by a Scotch ant community. J. Animal Ecol. 24: 336-351.

Brower, J. Z., 1958a, Experimental studies of mimicry in some North American butterflies. Part 1. The Monarch *Danaus plexippus*, and Viceroy *Limenitis archippus archippus*. Evolution 12: 32-47.

  1958b, Experimental studies of mimicry in some North American butter-

flies.   Part 2.   *Battus philenor* and *Papilo troilus, P. polyxenes*
and *P. glaucus.* Evolution 12: 123-136.

1958c, Experimental studies of mimicry in some North American butterflies.   Part 3.   *Danaus gilippus berenice* and *Limenitis archippus
floridensis.* Evolution 12: 273-285.

Brown, W. L., 1957, Centrifugal speciation. Quart. Rev. Biol. 32: 247-277.

Brown, W. L., and E. O. Wilson, 1956, Character displacement. Syst. Zool.
5: 49-64.

Bullock, T., 1955, Compensation for temperature in the metabolism and activity of poikilotherms. Biol. Revs. 30: 311-342.

Carson, H. L., 1955, The genetic characteristics of marginal populations of
Drosophila. Cold Spring Harbor Symp. Quant. Biol. 20: 276-287.

1958, Increase in experimental populations resulting from heterosis.
Proc. Nat. Acad. Sci. 44: 1136-1141.

Chapman, R. N., 1928, The quantitative analysis of environmental factors.
Ecology 9: 111-122.

Chitty, D., 1957, Self regulation of numbers through changes in viability.
Cold Spring Harbor Symp. Quant. Biol. 22: 277-280.

Cole, L. C., 1954, The population consequences of life history phenomena.
Quart. Rev. Biol. 29: 103-137.

1957, Sketches of general and comparative demography.   Cold Spring
Harbor Symp. Quant. Biol. 22: 1-15.

Crane, J., 1941, Crabs of the genus Uca from the west coast of Central America. Zoologica 26: 297-310.

Cunha, A. B. da, H. Burla and Th. Dobzhansky, 1950, Adaptive chromosomal polymorphism in *Drosophila willistoni.* Evolution 4: 212-235.

De Bach, P., 1958, Selective breeding to improve adaptations of parasitic
insects. Proc. 10th Int. Cong. Ent. 4: 759-768.

Dobzhansky, Th., 1951, Genetics and the origin of species. Columbia University Press, New York, N. Y.

1957, Mendelian populations as genetic systems.   Cold Spring Harbor
Symp. Quant. Biol. 22: 385-393.

1958, Evolution at work. Science 127: 1091-1098.

Dobzhansky, Th., H. Burla and A. B. da Cunha, 1950, A comparative study
of chromosomal polymorphism in sibling species of the *willistoni*
group of Drosophila. Amer. Nat. 84: 229-246.

Dobzhansky, Th., and O. Pavlovsky, 1957, An experimental study of interaction between genetic drift and natural selection. Evolution 11:
311-319.

Emerson, A. E., 1958, The evolution of behavior among social insects. *In*
Evolution and behavior, eds., A. Rowe and G. G. Simpson. pp.
311-335.

Errington, P. L., 1943, Analysis of mink predation upon muskrats in north
central United States. Res. Bull. Iowa Agr. Exp. Sta. 320:797-924.

Franz, J. von, 1950, Über die genetischen Grundlagen des Zusammenbruchs
einer Massenvermehrung aus inneren Ursachen. Zeit f. angen. Entomologie 31: 228-260.

Fry, F. E. J., 1957, The lethal temperature as a tool in taxonomy. Colloq.
Int. de Biol. Mar. Stn. Biol de Roscoff Ann. Biol. 33: 205-219.

1958, Temperature compensation. Ann. Rev. Physiol. 20: 207-224.

Gershenson, S., 1945, Evolutionary studies on the distribution and dynamics of melanism in the hamster (*Cricetus cricetus* L.). Genetics 30: 207-251.

Gibb, J., 1956, Territory in the genus Parus. Ibis 98: 420-429.

Haldane, J. B. S., 1932, The causes of evolution. Harper & Brothers, New York and London.

Hart, J. S., 1952, Geographic variations of some physiological and morphological characters in certain freshwater fish. Publ. Ont. Fish Res. Lab. 72: 1-79.

Heuts, M. J., 1956, Temperature adaptation in *Gasterosteus aculeatus* L. Publ. Stazione Zool. Napoli 28: 44-62.

Hinde, R. A., 1956, The biological significance of territories of birds. Ibis 98: 340-369.

Huxley, J., 1942, Evolution: the modern synthesis. Allen & Unwin, London.

Jacobs, M. E., 1955, Studies on territorialism and sexual selection in dragonflies. Ecology 36: 566-587.

Kerr, W. E., and S. Wright, 1954 a, Experimental studies of the distribution of gene frequencies in very small populations of *Drosophila melanogaster*. I. Forked. Evolution 8: 172-177.

1954 b, Experimental studies of the distribution of gene frequencies in very small populations of *Drosophila melanogaster*. II. Bar. Evolution 8: 225-240.

1954 c, Experimental studies of the distribution of gene frequencies in very small populations of *Drosophila melanogaster*. III. Aristapedia and spineless. Evolution 8: 293-302.

Kettlewell, H. B. D., 1956, A resume of investigations on the evolution of melanism in the Lepidoptera. Proc. Roy. Soc. London B 145: 297-303.

1958, A survey of the frequencies of *Biston betularia* and its melanic forms in Great Britain. Heredity 12: 51-72.

1959, New aspects of the genetic control of industrial melanism in the Lepidoptera. Nature 183: 918-921.

Lack, D., 1956, The evolution of reproductive rates. In Evolution as a process, eds., J. Huxley, A. C. Hardy and E. B. Ford. pp. 143-156.

Levene, H., O. Pavlovsky and Th. Dobzhansky, 1958, Differences in the adaptive values of certain genotypes in *Drosophila pseudoobscura* on the composition of the gene pool. Evolution 12: 18-23.

1954, Interactions of the adaptive values in polymorphic experimental populations of *Drosophila pseudoobscura*. Evolution 8: 335-349.

Lewontin, R. C., 1955, The effects of population density and composition on viability in *Drosophila melanogaster*. Evolution 9: 27-41.

1957, The adaptations of populations to varying environments. Cold Spring Harbor Symp. Quant. Biol. 22: 395-408.

1958, Studies on heterozygosity and homeostasis. II. Loss of heterosis in a constant environment. Evolution 12: 497-503.

Mather, K., 1941, Variation and selection of polygenic characters. J. Genetics 41: 159-193.

1943, Polygenic inheritance and natural selection. Biol. Rev. 18: 32-62.

Mayr, E., 1954, Change of genetic environment and evolution. In Evolution as a process, eds., J. Huxley, A. C. Hardy and E. B. Ford. pp. 157-180.

Moore, J. A., 1949, Geographic variation of adaptive characters in *Rana pipiens*. Evolution 3: 1-24.

Moore, N. W., 1952, On the so called territories of dragonflies. Behaviour 4: 85-100.

Moreau, R. E., 1944, Clutch size; a comparative study, with special reference to African birds. Ibis 86: 286-347.

Nicholson, A. J., 1957, The self adjustment of populations to change. Cold Spring Harbor Symp. Quant. Biol. 22: 153-173.

Parsons, P. A., 1958, Competition between genotypes in *Drosophila melanogaster*. Nature 182: 271.

Rodd, J. A., 1946, Big trout from big eggs. A Canadian experiment. Salmon and Trout Mag. 116: 32-36.

Sheppard, P. M., 1958, Natural selection and heredity. Hutchinson, London.

Smith, F. E., 1954, Quantative aspects of population growth. *In* Dynamics of growth processes, ed., E. J. Boell. Princeton University Press, Princeton, N. J.

*Svardson, G., 1949, Fish Bd. Inst. Freshwater Res. Drottingholm. Rept. 29: 115-122.

Townsend, J. I., 1952, Genetics of marginal populations of *Drosophila willistoni*. Evolution 6: 428-442.

Waddington, C. H., 1957, The strategy of the genes. Allen & Unwin, London.

Wallace, B., 1958, Average effect of radiation-induced mutations on viability in *Drosophila melanogaster*. Evolution 12: 532-556.

Williamson, W. H., 1958, Selection, controlling factors and polymorphism. Amer. Nat. 92: 329-335.

Wright, S., 1931, Evolution in Mendelian populations. Genetics 16: 97-159.
    1949, Adaption and selection. *In* Genetics, paleontology and evolution, eds, G. L. Jepson, E. Mayr and G. G. Simpson. pp. 365-389.

Wright, S., and Th. Dobzhansky, 1946, Genetics of natural populations. XII. Experimental reproduction of some of the changes caused by natural selection in certain populations of *Drosophila pseudoobscura*. Genetics 31: 125-156.

*Known by reference only.

20

Reprinted from *Science* **147**:1543–1548 (1965)

Self-Regulating Systems in Populations of Animals

A new hypothesis illuminates aspects of animal behavior that have hitherto seemed unexplainable.

V. C. Wynne-Edwards

I am going to try to explain a hypothesis which could provide a bridge between two biological realms (*1*). On one side is that part of the "Balance of Nature" concerned with regulating the numbers of animals, and on the other is the broad field of social behavior. The hypothesis may, I believe, throw a bright and perhaps important sidelight on human behavior and population problems. I must emphasize, however, that it is still a hypothesis. It appears to be generally consistent with the facts, and it provides entirely new insight into many aspects of animal behavior that have hitherto been unexplainable; but because it involves long-term evolutionary processes it cannot be put to an immediate and comprehensive test by short-term experiments.

Human populations are of course increasing at compound interest practically all over the world. At the overall 2 percent annual rate of the last decade, they can be expected to double with each generation. In the perspective of evolutionary time such a situation must be extremely short-lived, and I am sure we are going to grow more and more anxious about the future of man until we are able to satisfy ourselves that the human population explosion is controllable, and can be contained.

Populations of animals, especially when they are living under primeval undisturbed conditions, characteristically show an altogether different state of affairs; and this was equally true of man in the former cultural periods of the stone age. These natural popula-

tions tend to preserve a continuing state of balance, usually fluctuating to some extent but essentially stable and regulated. The nature of the regulatory process has been the main focus of study and speculation by animal ecologists during the whole of my working life, and in fact considerably longer.

Charles Darwin (*2*) was the first to point out that though all animals have the capacity to increase their numbers, in fact they do not continuously do so. The "checks to increase" appeared to him to be of four kinds—namely, the amount of food available, which must give the extreme limit to which any species can increase; the effects of predation by other animals; the effects of physical factors such as climate; and finally, the inroads of disease. "In looking at Nature," he tells us in the *Origin of Species*, "it is most necessary . . . never to forget that every single organic being may be said to be striving to the utmost to increase in numbers." This intuitive assumption of a universal resurgent pressure from within held down by hostile forces from without has dominated the thinking of biologists on matters of population regulation, and on the nature of the struggle for existence, right down to the present day.

Setting all preconceptions aside, however, and returning to a detached assessment of the facts revealed by modern observation and experiment, it becomes almost immediately evident that a very large part of the regulation of numbers depends not on Darwin's hostile forces but on the initiative taken by the animals themselves; that is to say, to an important extent it is an intrinsic phenomenon.

Forty years ago Jespersen (*3*)

showed, for example, that there is a close numerical agreement between the standing crop of planktonic organisms at the surface of the North Atlantic Ocean and the distribution density of the various deep-sea birds that depend on these organisms for food. Over the whole of this vast area the oceanic birds are dispersed in almost constant proportion to the local biomass of plankton, although the biomass itself varies from region to region by a factor of about 100; the actual crude correlation coefficient is 85 percent. This pro rata dispersion of the birds must in fact depend solely on their own intrinsic efforts and behavior. Even though the dispersion directly reflects the availability of food, the movements of the birds over the ocean are essentially voluntary and not imposed against their will by hostile or other outside forces.

Turning to the results of repeatable experiments with laboratory animals, it is a generally established principle that a population started up, perhaps from one parental pair, in some confined universe such as an aquarium or a cage, can be expected to grow to a predictable size, and thereafter to maintain itself at that ceiling for months or years as long as the experimenter keeps the conditions unchanged. This can readily be demonstrated with most common laboratory animals, including the insects *Drosophila* and *Tribolium*, the water-flea *Daphnia*, the guppy *Lebistes*, and also mice and rats. The ceiling population density stays constant in these experiments in the complete absence of predators or disease and equally without recourse to regulation by starvation, simply by the matching of recruitment and loss. For example, a set of particularly illuminating experiments by Silliman and Gutsell (*4*), lasting over 3 years, showed that when stable populations of guppies, kept in tanks, were cropped by removal of a proportion of the fish at regular intervals, the remainder responded by producing more young that survived, with the consequence that the losses were compensated. In the controls, on the other hand, where the stocks were left untouched, the guppies went on breeding all the time, but by cannibalism they consistently removed at birth the whole of the surplus produced. The regulating methods are different in different species; under appropriate circumstances in mice, to take another example, ovulation and reproduction can

The author is Regius Professor of Natural History, Marischal College, University of Aberdeen, Aberdeen, Scotland. This article is based on a lecture presented 26 December 1964 at the Montreal meeting of the AAAS.

decline and even cease, as long as the ceiling density is maintained.

Here again, therefore, we are confronted by intrinsic mechanisms, in which none of Darwin's checks play any part, competent in themselves to regulate the population size within a given habitat.

The same principle shows up just as clearly in the familiar concept that a habitat has a certain carrying capacity, and that it is no good turning out more partridges or planting more trout than the available habitat can hold.

Population growth is essentially a density-dependent process; this means that it tends to proceed fastest when population densities are far below the ceiling level, to fall to zero as this level is approached, and to become negative, leading to an actual drop in numbers, if ever the ceiling is exceeded. The current hypothesis is that the adjustment of numbers in animals is a homeostatic process—that there is, in fact, an automatic self-righting balance between population density and resources.

I must turn briefly aside here to remind you that there are some environments which are so unstable or transitory that there is not time enough for colonizing animals to reach a ceiling density, and invoke their regulatory machinery, before the habitat becomes untenable again or is destroyed. Populations in these conditions are always in the pioneering stage, increasing freely just as long as conditions allow. Instability of this kind tends to appear around the fringes of the geographical range of all free-living organisms, and especially in desert and polar regions. It is also very common in agricultural land, because of the incessant disturbance of ploughing, seeding, spraying, harvesting, and rotating of crops. In these conditions the ecologist will often look in vain for evidences of homeostasis, among the violently fluctuating and completely uncontrollable populations typical of the animal pests of farms and plantations. Homeostasis can hardly be expected to cope unerringly with the ecological turmoil of cultivated land.

I return later to the actual machinery of homeostasis. For the present it can be accepted that more or less effective methods of regulating their own numbers have been evolved by most types of animals. If this is so, it seems logical to ask as the next question: What is it that decides the ceiling level?

Food Supply as a Limiting Factor

Darwin was undoubtedly right in concluding that food is the factor that normally puts an extreme limit on population density, and the dispersion of oceanic birds over the North Atlantic, which so closely reflects the dispersion of their food supply, is certain to prove a typical and representative case. Just the same, the link between food productivity and population density is very far from being self-evident. The relationship between them does not typically involve any signs of undernourishment; and starvation, when we observe it, tends to be a sporadic or accidental cause of mortality rather than a regular one.

Extremely important light is shed on this relationship between population density and food by our human experience of exploiting resources of the same kind. Fish, fur-bearing animals, and game are all notoriously subject to overexploitation at the hands of man, and present-day management of these renewable natural resources is based on the knowledge that there is a limit to the intensity of cropping that each stock can withstand. If we exceed this critical level, the stock will decline and the future annual crops will diminish. Exactly parallel principles apply to the exploitation of natural prairie pastures by domestic livestock: if overgrazing is permitted, fertility and future yields just as fatally decline.

In all these situations there is a tendency to overstep the safety margin while exploitation of the resource is still economically profitable. We have seen since World War II, for example, the decimation of stocks of the blue and the humpback whale in the southern oceans, under the impetus of an intense profit motive, which persisted long after it had become apparent to everyone in the industry that the cropping rate was unsupportably high. The only way to protect these economically valuable recurrent resources from destruction is to impose, by agreement or law, a man-made code of rules, defining closed seasons, catch limits, permitted types of gear, and so on, which restrict the exploitation rate sufficiently to prevent the catch from exceeding the critical level.

In its essentials, this is the same crucial situation that faces populations of animals in exploiting their resources of food. Indeed, without going any further one could predict that if the food

supplies of animals were openly exposed to an unruly scramble, there could be no safeguard against their overexploitation either.

Conventional Behavior in Relation to Food

When I first saw the force of this deduction 10 years ago, I felt that the scales had fallen from my eyes. At once the vast edifice of conventional behavior among animals in relation to food began to take on a new meaning. A whole series of unconnected natural phenomena seemed to click smoothly into place.

First among these are the territorial systems of various birds (paralleled in many other organisms), where the claim to an individual piece of ground can evoke competition of an intensity unequaled on any other occasion in the life of the species concerned. It results, in the simplest cases, in a parceling out of the habitat into a mosaic of breeding and feeding lots. A territory has to be of a certain size, and individuals that are unsuccessful in obtaining one are often excluded completely from the habitat, and always prevented from breeding in it. Here is a system that might have been evolved for the exact purpose of imposing a ceiling density on the habitat, and for efficiently disposing of any surplus individuals that fail to establish themselves. Provided the territory size is adequate, it is obvious that the rate of exploitation of the food resources the habitat contains will automatically be prevented from exceeding the critical threshold.

There are other behavioral devices that appear, in the light of the food-resource hypothesis we are examining, equally purposive in leading to the same result—namely, that of limiting the permitted quota of participants in an artificial kind of way, and of off-loading all that are for the time being surplus to the carrying capacity of the ground. Many birds nest in colonies—especially, for example, the oceanic and aerial birds which cannot, in the nature of things, divide up the element in which they feed into static individual territories. In the colony the pairs compete just as long and keenly for one of the acceptable nest sites, which are in some instances closely packed together. By powerful tradition some of these species return year after year to old-established resorts, where the perimeter of the colony is closely drawn like an imaginary fence around the occupied sites. Once again there is not always room to accommodate all the contestants, and unsuccessful ones have to be relegated to a nonbreeding surplus or reserve, inhibited from sexual maturation because they have failed to obtain a site within the traditional zone and all other sites are taboo.

A third situation, exemplifying another, parallel device, is the pecking order or social hierarchy so typical of the higher animals that live in companies in which the individual members become mutually known. Animal behaviorists have studied the hierarchy in its various manifestations for more than 40 years, most commonly in relation to food. In general, the individuals of higher rank have a prior right to help themselves, and, in situations where there is not enough to go round, the ones at the bottom of the scale must stand aside and do without. In times of food shortage—for example, with big game animals—the result is that the dominant individuals come through in good shape while the subordinates actually die of starvation. The hierarchy therefore produces the same kind of result as a territorial system in that it admits a limited quota of individuals to share the food resources and excludes the extras. Like the other devices I have described, it can operate in exactly the same way with respect to reproduction. In fact, not only can the hierarchical system exclude individuals from breeding, it can equally inhibit their sexual development.

It must be quite clear already that the kind of competition we are considering, involving as it does the right to take food and the right to breed, is a matter of the highest importance to the individuals that engage in it. At its keenest level it becomes a matter of life and death. Yet, as is well known, the actual contest between individuals for real property or personal status is almost always strictly conventionalized. Fighting and bloodshed are superseded by mere threats of violence, and threats in their turn are sublimated into displays of magnificence and virtuosity. This is the world of bluff and status symbols. What takes place, in other words, is a contest for conventional prizes conducted under conventional rules. But the contest itself is no fantasy, for the losers can forfeit the chance of posterity and the right to survive.

Conventionalized Rivalry and Society

It is at this point that the hypothesis provides its most unexpected and striking insight, by showing that the conventionalization of rivalry and the foundation of society are one and the same thing. Hitherto it has never been possible to give a scientific definition of the terms *social* and *society*, still less a functional explanation. The emphasis has always been on the rather vague element of companionship and brotherhood. Animals have in the main been regarded as social whenever they were gregarious. Now we can view the social phenomenon in a new light. According to the hypothesis the society is no more and no less than the organization necessary for the staging of conventional competition. At once it assumes a crisp definition: a society is an organization of individuals that is capable of providing conventional competition among its members.

Such a novel interpretation of something that involves us all so intimately is almost certain to be viewed at first sight a bit skeptically; but in fact one needs no prompting in our competitive world to see that human society is impregnated with rivalry. The sentiments of brotherhood are warm and reassuring, and in identifying society primarily with these we appear to have been unconsciously shutting our eyes to the inseparable rough-and-tumble of status seeking and social discrimination that are never very far to seek below the surface, bringing enviable rewards to the successful and pitiful distress to those who lose. If this interpretation is right, conventional competition is an inseparable part of the substance of human society, at the parochial, national, and international level. To direct it into sophisticated and acceptable channels is no doubt one of the great motives of civilized behavior; but it would be idle to imagine that we could eliminate it.

A corollary of the hypothesis that deserves mention is the extension of sociality that it implies, to animals of almost every kind whether they associate in flocks or seek instead a more solitary way of life. There is no particular difficulty of course in seeing, for example, cats and dogs as social mammals, individually recognizing the local and personal rights of acquaintances and strangers and inspired by obviously conventional codes of rivalry when they meet. In a different setting, the territory-holding birds that join in

the chorus of the spring dawn are acting together in social concert, expressing their mutual rivalry by a conventional display of exalted sophistication and beauty. Even at the other extreme, when animals flock into compact and obviously social herds and schools, each individual can sometimes be seen to maintain a strict individual distance from its companions.

Social Organization and Feedback

We can conveniently return now to the subject of homeostasis, in order to see how it works in population control. Homeostatic systems come within the general purview of cybernetics; in fact, they have long been recognized in the physiology of living organisms. A simple model can be found in any thermostatic system, in which there must of course be units. capable of supplying or withdrawing heat whenever the system departs from its standard temperature and readjustment is necessary. But one also needs an indicator device to detect how far the system has deviated and in which direction. It is the feedback of this information that activates the heating or cooling units.

Feedback is an indispensable element of homeostatic systems. There seems no reason to doubt that, in the control of population density, it can be effectively provided simply by the intensity of conventional competition. Social rivalry is inherently density-dependent: the more competitors there are seeking a limited number of rewards, the keener will be the contest. The impact of stress on the individuals concerned, arising from conventional competition and acting through the pituitary-adrenal system, is already fully established, and it can profoundly influence their responses, both physiological and behavioral.

One could predict on theoretical grounds that feedback would be specially important whenever a major change in population density has to take place, upsetting the existing balance between demand and resources. This must occur particularly in the breeding season and at times of seasonal migrations. Keeping this in mind, we can obtain what we need in the way of background information by examining the relatively long-lived vertebrates, including most kinds of birds and mammals, whose individual members live long enough to constitute a standing population all the year round. The hypothesis of course implies that reproduction, as one of the principal parameters of population, will be subject to control—adjusted in magnitude, in fact, to meet whatever addition is currently required to build up the population and make good the losses of the preceding year. *Recruitment* is a term best used only to mean intake of new breeding adults into the population, and in that sense, of course, the raw birth rate may not be the sole and immediate factor that determines it. The new-born young have got to survive adolescence before they can become recruits to the breeding stock; and even after they attain puberty, social pressures may exclude them from reproducing until they attain a sufficiently high rank in the hierarchy. Indeed, there is evidence in a few species that, under sufficient stress, adults which have bred in previous years can be forced to stand aside.

There are, in fact, two largely distinct methods of regulating reproductive output, both of which have been widely adopted in the animal kingdom. One is to limit the number of adults that are permitted to breed, and this is of course a conspicuous result of adopting a territorial system, or any other system in which the number of permissible breeding sites is restricted. The other is to influence the number of young that each breeding pair is conditioned to produce. The two methods can easily be combined.

What we are dealing with here is a part of the machinery for adjusting population density. What we are trying to get at, however, is the social feedback mechanism behind it, by which the appropriate responses are elicited from potential breeders.

Birds generally provide us with the best examples, because their size, abundance, and diurnal habits render them the most observable and familiar of the higher animals. It is particularly easy to see in birds that social competition is keenest just before and during the breeding season, regardless of the type of breeding dispersion any given species happens to adopt. Individuals may compete for and defend territories or nest sites, or in rarer cases they may engage in tournaments in an arena or on a strutting ground; and they may join in a vocal chorus especially concentrated about the conventional hours of dawn and dusk, make mass visits to colony sites, join in massed flights, and share in other forms of communal displays. Some of these activities are more obviously competitive than others, but all appear to be alike in their capacity to reveal to each individual the concentration or density level of the population within its own immediate area.

Communal Male Displays

Some of these activities, like territorial defense, singing, and the arena displays, tend to be the exclusive concern of the males. It has never been possible hitherto to give a satisfactory functional explanation of the kind of communal male displays typified by the arena dances of some of the South American hummingbirds and manakins, and by the dawn strutting of prairie chickens and sharp-tailed grouse. The sites they use are generally traditional, each serving as a communal center and drawing the competitors from a more or less wide surrounding terrain. On many days during the long season of activity the same assembly of males may engage in vigorous interplay and mutual hostility, holding tense dramatic postures for an hour or more at a stretch without a moment's relaxation, although there is no female anywhere in sight at the time. The local females do of course come at least once to be fertilized; but the performance makes such demands on the time and energy of the males that it seems perfectly reasonable to assume that this is the reason why they play no part in nesting and raising a family. The duty they perform is presumably important, but it is simply not credible to attribute it primarily to courting the females. To anyone looking for a population feedback device, on the other hand, interpretation would present no difficulty: he would presume that the males are being conditioned or stressed by their ritual exertions. In some of the arena species some of the males are known to be totally excluded from sexual intercourse; but it would seem that the feedback mechanism could produce its full effect only if it succeeded in limiting the number of females fertilized to an appropriate quota, after which the males refused service to any still remaining unfertilized. I hope research may at a not-too-distant date show us whether or not such refusal really takes place.

The conclusion that much of the social display associated with the breeding season consists of males competing with males makes necessary a reappraisal of Darwinian sexual selection. Whether the special organs developed for display are confined to the males, as in the examples we have just considered, or are found in both sexes, as for instance in most of the colony-nesting birds, there is a strong indication that they are first and foremost status symbols, used in conventional competition, and that the selective process by which they have been evolved is social rather than sexual. This would account for the hitherto puzzling fact that, although in the mature bullfrog and cicada the loud sound is produced by the males, in both cases it is the males that are provided with extra-large eardrums. There does not seem much room for doubt about who is displaying to whom.

Communal displays are familiar also in the context of bird migration, especially in the massing and maneuvering of flocks before the exodus begins. A comparable buildup of social excitement precedes the migratory flight of locusts. Indeed, what I have elsewhere defined as *epideictic* phenomena—displays, or special occasions, which allow all the individuals taking part to sense or become conditioned by population pressure—appear to be very common and widespread in the animal kingdom. They occur especially at the times predicted, when feedback is required in anticipation of a change in population density. The singing of birds, the trilling of katydids, crickets, and frogs, the underwater sounds of fish, and the flashing of fireflies all appear to perform this epideictic function. In cases where, as we have just seen, epideictic behavior is confined in the breeding season to the male sex, the presumption is that the whole process of controlling the breeding density and the reproductive quota is relegated to the males. Outside the breeding season, when the individuals are no longer united in pairs and are all effectively neuter in sex, all participate alike in epideictic displays—in flighting at sundown, like ducks; in demonstrating at huge communal roosts at dusk, like starlings, grackles, and crows; or in forming premigratory swarms, like swallows. The assumption which the hypothesis suggests, that the largest sector of all social behavior must have this fundamentally epideictic or feedback function, gives a key to understanding a vast agglomeration of observed animal behavior that has hitherto been dubiously interpreted or has seemed altogether meaningless.

Maintaining Population Balance

Having outlined the way in which social organization appears to serve in supplying feedback, I propose to look again at the machinery for making adjustments to the population balance. In territorial birds, variations in the average size of territories from place to place and year to year can be shown to alter the breeding density and probably also the proportion of adults actually participating in reproduction. In various mammals the proportion of the females made pregnant, the number and size of litters, the survival of the young and the age at which they mature may all be influenced by social stress. Wherever parental care of the young has been evolved in the animal kingdom, the possibility exists that maternal behavior and solicitude can be affected in the same way; and the commonly observed variations in survival rates of the newborn could, in that case, have a substantial functional component and play a significant part in regulating the reproductive output. This would, among other things, explain away the enigma of cannibalism of the young, which we noticed earlier in the guppies and which occurs sporadically all through the higher animals. Infanticide played a conspicuous part in reducing the effective birth rate of many of the primitive human peoples that survived into modern times. Not infrequently it took the form of abandoning the child for what appeared to be commendable reasons, without involving an act of violence.

Reproduction is of course only one of the parameters involved in keeping the balance between income and loss in populations. The homeostatic machinery can go to work on the other side of the balance also, by influencing survival. Already, in considering the recruitment of adults, we have taken note of the way this can be affected by juvenile mortality, some of which is intrinsic in origin and capable of being promoted by social pressures. Conventional competition often leads to the exclusion of surplus individuals

from any further right to share the resources of the habitat, and this in turn compels them to emigrate. Research conducted at Aberdeen in the last 8 years has shown how important a factor forced expulsion is in regulating the numbers of the Scottish red grouse. Every breeding season so far has produced a population surplus, and it is the aggressive behavior of the dominant males which succeeds in driving the supernumeraries away. In this case the outcasts do not go far; they get picked up by predators or they mope and die because they are cut off from their proper food. Deaths from predation and disease can in fact be substantially "assisted" under social stress.

On the income side, therefore, both reproductive input and the acquisition of recruits by immigration appear to be subject to social regulation; and on the loss side, emigration and what can be described as socially induced mortality can be similarly affected. Once more it appears that it is only the inroads of Darwin's "checks to increase," the agents once held to be totally responsible for population regulation, which are in fact uncontrollable and have to be balanced out by manipulation of the other four components.

Attention must be drawn to the intimate way in which physiology and behavior are entwined in providing the regulatory machinery. It seems certain that the feedback of social stimulation acts on the individual through his endocrine system, and in the case of the vertebrates, as I have said, this particularly involves the pituitary and adrenal cortex or its equivalent. Sometimes the individual's response is primarily a physiological one—for example, the inhibition of spermatogenesis or the acceleration of growth; sometimes it is purely behavioral, as in the urge to return to the breeding site, the development of aggressiveness, or the demand for territory of a given size. But often there is a combination of the two—that is to say, a psychosomatic response, as when, for instance, the assumption of breeding colors is coupled with the urge to display.

Sources of Controversy

There is no need for me to emphasize that the hypothesis is controversial. But almost all of it is based on

well-established fact, so that the controversy can relate solely to matters of interpretation. Examples have been given here which show the ability of the hypothesis to offer new and satisfying interpretations of matters of fact where none could be suggested before. Some of these matters are of wide importance, like the basic function of social behavior; some are matters of everyday experience, like why birds sing at dawn. Very seldom indeed does the hypothesis contradict well-founded accepted principles. What, then, are the sources of controversy?

These are really three in number, all of them important. The first is that the concept is very wide-ranging and comprehensive; this means that it cannot be simply proved or disproved by performing a decisive experiment. There are of course dubious points where critical tests can be made, and research is proceeding, at Aberdeen among many other places, toward this end. Relevant results are constantly emerging, and at many points the hypothesis has been solidified and strengthened since it was first formulated. On the other hand, there has been no cause yet to retract anything.

The second source of controversy is that the hypothesis invokes a type of natural selection which is unfamiliar to zoologists generally. Social grouping is essentially a localizing phenomenon, and an animal species is normally made up of countless local populations all perpetuating themselves on their native soil, exactly as happens in underdeveloped and primitive communities of man. Social customs and adaptations vary from one local group to another, and the hypothesis requires that natural selection should take place between these groups, promoting those with more effective social organizations while the less effective ones go under. It is necessary, in other words, to postulate that social organizations are capable of progressive evolution and perfection as entities in their own right. The detailed arguments (5) are too complex to be presented here, but I can point out that intergroup selection is far from being a new concept: It has been widely accepted for more than 20 years by geneticists. It is almost impossible to demonstrate it experimentally because we have to deal with something closely corresponding to the rise and fall of nations in history, rather than with success or failure of single genes over a few generations; it is therefore the time scale that prevents direct experiment. Even the comparatively rapid process of natural selection acting among individuals has been notoriously difficult to demonstrate in nature.

The third objection is, I think, by far the most interesting. It is simply that the hypothesis does not apply to ourselves. No built-in mechanisms appear to curb our own population growth, or adjust our numbers to our resources. If they did so, everything I have said would be evident to every educated child, and I should not be surveying it here. How is this paradox to be explained?

The answer, it seems clear, is that these mechanisms did exist in primitive man and have been lost, almost within historic times. Man in the paleolithic stage, living as a hunter and gatherer, remained in balance with his natural resources just as other animals do under natural conditions. Generation after generation, his numbers underwent little or no change. Population increase was prevented not by physiological control mechanisms of the kind found in many other mammals but only by behavioral ones, taking the form of traditional customs and taboos. All the stone age tribes that survived into modern times diminished their effective birth rate by at least one of three ritual practices—infanticide, abortion, and abstention from intercourse. In a few cases, fertility was apparently impaired by surgery during the initiation ceremonies. In many cases, marriage was long deferred. Mortality of those of more advanced age was often raised through cannibalism, tribal fighting, and human sacrifice.

Gradually, with the spread of the agricultural revolution, which tended to concentrate the population at high densities on fertile soils and led by degrees to the rise of the town, the craftsman, and the merchant, the old customs and taboos must have been forsaken. The means of population control would have been inherited originally from man's subhuman ancestors, and among stone age peoples their real function was probably not even dimly discerned except perhaps by a few individuals of exceptional brilliance and insight.

The continually expanding horizons and skills of modern man rendered intrinsic limitation of numbers unnecessary, and for 5,000 or 10,000 years the advanced peoples of the Western world and Asia have increased without appearing to harm the world about them or endanger its productivity. But the underlying principles are the same as they have always been. It becomes obvious at last that we are getting very near the global carrying capacity of our habitat, and that we ought swiftly to impose some new, effective, homeostatic regime before we overwhelm it, and the ax of group selection falls.

References

1. V. C. Wynne-Edwards, *Animal Dispersion in Relation to Social Behaviour* (Hafner, New York, 1962).
2. C. Darwin, *The Origin of Species* (Murray, London, 1859) (quoted from 6th edition, 1872).
3. P. Jespersen, "The frequency of birds over the high Atlantic Ocean," *Nature* 114, 281 (1924).
4. R. P. Silliman and J. S. Gutsell, "Experimental exploitation of fish populations," *U.S. Fish Wildlife Serv. Fishery Bull.* 58, 214 (1958).
5. V. C. Wynne-Edwards, "Intergroup selection in the evolution of social systems," *Nature* 200, 623 (1963).

21

ANIMAL POPULATION REGULATION BY THE GENETIC
FEED-BACK MECHANISM*

DAVID PIMENTEL

Cornell University, Ithaca, New York

Natural population regulation has its foundation in the process of evolution. One such process described herein is called the genetic feed-back mechanism. This mechanism through genetic evolution integrates herbivore and plant, parasite and host, and predator and prey in the community. It functions as a feed-back system through the dynamics of density pressure, selective pressure, and genetic changes in the interacting populations. Density influences selection; selection influences genetic make-up; and in turn, genetic make-up influences density. The actions and reactions of the interacting populations in the food chain cycling in this mechanism result in the evolution and regulation of animal populations.

E. B. Ford (1930 and 1931) was the first to point out the importance of genetic changes in population dynamics and specifically as a cause of population fluctuations. He proposed that "numerical increase inevitably prepares the way for reduction, and the reverse; so giving rise to fluctuations in numbers, with alternating periods of high and low variability" (Ford, 1931). During mass increases caused by the changing environment variability increases, and many inferior genetic types result. "These are eliminated, and the numbers reduced when conditions become more rigorous again" (Ford, 1956). A genetic system of population regulation suggested by Franz (1949) proposes that population waves are generated both by inbreeding and the fixation of deleterious genes during mass increases. These are followed by declines initiated by the consequent weakening of the population. The relation between density regulation and natural selection was explored by Haldane (1956), who showed that genetic changes and adaptation for some environmental selective factor may cause a population to increase or decrease to a new stable level. Chitty (1957 and 1960) presented evidence to support the fact that changes in the genetics and viability of field mice are responsible for the population cycles of this species. That "the role of individual differences in population dynamics has been relatively neglected" was emphasized by Wellington (1957), and in a later paper

*This study is supported by research grants of the National Science Foundation (G-8903) and National Institutes of Health (E-2914).

(1960) he explained how individual differences might influence populations. Recently, Turner (1960) proposed that population outbreaks follow cross-breeding between isolated inbreeding populations.

From this evidence, it is clear that genetic changes play some role in population regulation, but the manner in which they function is not known. The genetic feed-back mechanism may provide an insight into the nature of this problem.

When a species population enters a new biotic community in which it is not integrated and in which no ecological barrier exists, it reaches outbreak levels a short while after introduction. The following cases amply illustrate this point: Japanese beetle introduced into the United States (Smith and Hadley, 1926), European rabbit introduced into Australia (Stead, 1935), and European gypsy moth introduced into eastern United States (Forbush and Fernald, 1896). The Hessian fly was still another species to reach high density within a short time after its introduction into the United States. In this instance, through genetic change of wheat plants and the consequent alteration of food quality, the density of the herbivore or Hessian fly population was controlled. Previous to 1942, when only susceptible varieties of wheat were grown in Kansas, the Hessian fly population occurred in large numbers across Kansas. When the flies were fed on certain resistant varieties, they suffered high mortality in the larval populations from time of hatching to pupation. If development did take place, growth of the larvae was slow on these resistant varieties (Painter, 1951). When the resistant varieties of wheat were introduced into Kansas in 1942, the Hessian fly population declined in a few years to the point where the flies were too scarce to be used in resistant wheat tests (Painter, 1954). Thus, by changing the genetic make-up of the plant population type this herbivore was feeding upon, the animal population was significantly reduced. If the resistant wheat were exchanged for the original susceptible variety, an increase in the Hessian fly population could be predicted.

The interaction of oysters and a pathogen found in the waters off Prince Edward Island further demonstrates the importance of genetic mechanisms in natural populations. Before 1915, oysters in the Malpeque Bay abounded. During 1915, however, the oyster population was struck by disease. Nearly 90 per cent of the oyster population was infected with the yellowish-green pustules during the first wave (Needler and Logie, 1947). The population of oysters decreased rapidly, and by 1926 no oysters were harvested (figure 1).

Subsequently in 1929, fishermen noticed an increase in oysters, and nearly 500 barrels were removed during 1930. By 1940 production approached the 1915 level of 4000 barrels (figure 1). An investigation to determine if this increase was due to genetic resistance developing in the oyster led Needler and Logie (1947) to import oyster spat from the disease-free Hillsborough River. Over 90 per cent of the Hillsborough spat died of disease whereas the Malpeque Bay spat treated in a similar manner in the bay survived. Malpeque Bay spat were also compared with Enmore River spat. The Enmore River region received the disease about two years previous to this test.

294

Under the infective conditions at Enmore only 30 per cent of the Enmore River spat survived whereas 98 per cent of the resistant Malpeque Bay spat survived.

Since the pathogen was not isolated, no tests were made of the parasite to determine if any changes in its reproduction and pathogenicity occurred. The oyster itself, however, was well adapted for rapid evolutionary change when it is considered that an oyster produces nearly 60,000,000 young per year (Galtsoff, 1930). This natural event with oysters showed that parasite pressure resulted in genetic change in the oyster-host, and this regulated the density of the parasite itself.

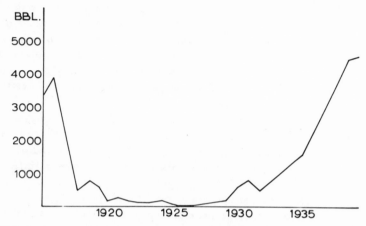

FIGURE 1. Annual yields of oysters from Malpeque Bay and associated regions off Prince Edward Island. (After Needler and Logie, 1947.)

The myxomatosis outbreak in the rabbit population in Australia is another example of the genetic changes functioning in the adjustment of a natural parasite and host population. At Christmas, 1859, the European rabbit (*Oryctolagus cuniculus*) was introduced into Australia and increased rapidly during the next 20 years (Stead, 1935). The extent of the damage caused by these animals prompted the Australian Government to investigate the possibility of introducing some biotic agent which would reduce the density of the rabbit to a less harmful level. The myxomatosis virus obtained from South American rabbits was introduced into the Australian rabbit population. During the first epizootic, myxomatosis was fatal to between 97 and 99 per cent of the rabbits; the second epizootic resulted in 85 to 95 per cent mortality; and the third epizootic resulted in 40 to 60 per cent mortality (Fenner, et al., 1953). The effect on the rabbit population was less severe with each succeeding epizootic, suggesting that the two populations were becoming integrated and adjusted to one another in the ecosystem.

In this adjustment between virus and rabbit, attenuated genetic strains of virus have evolved by mutation and are tending to replace the virulent strains (Thompson, 1954). In addition, passive immunity to myxomatosis is

conferred to kittens born of immune does (Fenner, 1953). Finally, a genetic
change has occurred in the rabbit population, and this is providing intrinsic
resistance to myxomatosis (Marshall, 1958). Here definitely is illustrated
the functioning of the feed-back of density, selection, and genetic change
which has in turn altered the density of both populations. In this particular
association, genetic change seems to be taking place in both populations.
The virulent genetic strain of virus has an apparent advantage in that it reproduces quickly and can rapidly convert rabbit protoplasm into itself. This
is an advantage only when this virus is compared to another which has a
slower rate of increase within the rabbit. The virus strains, however, must
be evaluated in the ecosystem to determine which strain ultimately has the
adaptive advantage. As Li (1955) points out, "adaptability is a response of
populations rather than of the individual." If the virulent strain were to become 100 per cent effective in attacking the rabbit in the ecosystem, it
would destroy itself by destroying its food supply. A less virulent strain in
this case would tend to have greater survival value when the strains are
separated diversely in space. The non-pathogenic strain observed in Australia has a selective advantage in this region.

Transmission of the myxomatosis virus depends upon mosquitoes (Aedes
and Anopheles) which feed only on living animals (Day, 1955). Rabbits infected with the virulent strain of virus live for a shorter period of time than
those infected with the less virulent strain. Because rabbits infected with
the less virulent strain live for longer periods of time, mosquitoes have access to that virus for longer periods of time. This provides the non-virulent
strain a competitive advantage over the virulent strain. In addition, in regions where the non-virulent strain is located, rabbits are more abundant,
and this allows more total virus to be present than in a comparable region
infected with the virulent virus. Thus, the virus with the greatest rate of
increase and density within the rabbit is not the virus selected for, but it is
the virus whose demands are balanced against supply which has survival
value in the ecosystem.

The above mentioned natural populations were regulated by genetic
changes operating in the feed-back mechanism. The interactions and trends
which operated in this mechanism are translated into biomathematics and
explained in the following model using a herbivore-plant system. This proposed feed-back mechanism functions through polygenic action, but to illustrate the process two alleles (A, a) at one locus are adequate. The alleles
in various proportions $(p^2 + 2pq + q^2 = 1)$ in the diploid plant determine
whether an animal population feeding on the plant increases or decreases,
where p^2 is the proportion of homozygous dominants (AA), $2pq$ is the proportion of heterozygotes (Aa), and q^2 is the proportion of homozygous reces-
sives (aa) in the plant population. The animals distribute themselves
equally on the individual plants, and animal reproduction (R) varies according to the plant genotype on which they are feeding. For example, on the
AA plant animal reproduction (R_p) is 2, on the Aa plant animal reproduction
(R_{pq}) is 1, and on the aa plant animal reproduction (R_q) is 0.5. Thus animal

density (N) at an initial time (N_{to}) increases or decreases in the following generation (N_{t1}) depending on the proportion of the AA, Aa, and aa plant genotypes. In this case then

(1) $$N_{t1} = p^2 R_p N_{to} + 2pq R_{pq} N_{to} + q^2 R_q N_{to} \cdot$$

Environmental selective pressure (S), or survival (1 − S), and animal density pressure determines the genotypic proportions of the plant population at the next generation. For this example, environmental selective pressure on the AA plant (S_p) is 0.001, on the Aa plant (S_{pq}) is 0.2, and on the aa plant (S_q) is 0.6. In a situation without the animal the "relative fitness" (Li, 1955) of the genotypes is such that the AA plants are better than the Aa plants, and the Aa plants are better than the aa plants ($p^2 > 2pq > q^2$). Plant tolerance for animal density varies according to plant genotype. At one maximal animal density (b) none of the AA plants survive; at another density (c) none of the Aa plants survive; and still at another density (d) none of the aa plants survive. Pressure by the animal on the AA, Aa, and aa plant genotypes is proportional to animal density as $\dfrac{b - N}{b}$, $\dfrac{c - N}{c}$, and $\dfrac{d - N}{d}$, respectively. Thus the selective pressure against the plant genotypes exerted by animal density and the other environmental factors in the ecosystem is

(2) $$p^2(1 - S_p)\frac{(b - N)}{b} + 2pq(1 - S_{pq})\frac{(c - N)}{c} + q^2(1 - S_q)\frac{(d - N)}{d} = G,$$

The total proportion of the plant population surviving is G. Following the selection, the proportions of the surviving plant genotypes are

(3) $$\frac{p^2(1 - S_p)\frac{(b - N)}{b}}{G} + \frac{2pq(1 - S_{pq})\frac{(c - N)}{c}}{G} + \frac{q^2(1 - S_q)\frac{(d - N)}{d}}{G} = 1.$$

The proportion of the A allele (p) surviving is $p^2 + \frac{1}{2}(2pq) = p$ and the proportion of the surviving a allele (q) is $q^2 + \frac{1}{2}(2pq) = q$. By random mating the surviving allelic proportions,

(4) $$(p + q)^2 = 1.$$

The proportions of the plant genotypes present in the next generation are

(5) $$p^2 + 2pq + q^2 = 1.$$

For the present example, the maximum animal density (b) for survival of the AA plants is 1075; the maximal animal density (c) for the Aa plants is 1500; and the maximal density for survival of the aa plants is 3000. Logically the genotype destroyed by the lowest maximum animal density is the genotype on which the animal has the highest reproduction rate. If we now imagine 150 animals being introduced into the ecosystem and the proportions of the plant genotypes are .360 AA plants, .500 Aa plants, and .140 aa plants and the numerical example is fed into a digital computer and cycled through equations 1, 2, 3, 4, and 5 for 100 generations, we find that the animal population fluctuations decrease in amplitude with each generation and stability is reached at an animal density of 795 in 72 generations (figure 2). The genotypic plant proportions at stability are .172 AA plants, .485 Aa plants, and .343 aa plants.

The model was revised and made more complex to allow the genetics of the animal population to vary in addition to density. Changes in the plant population remained similar to those in the previous model. The relation of animal genetics in this system is represented by two alleles (Z, z) at one locus in the animal. The proportions of ZZ are indicated by x^2, of Zz by $2xy$, and zz by y^2. It is assumed that the three animal genotypes (ZZ, Zz, zz) reproduce differently on each of the three plant genotypes (AA, Aa, aa).

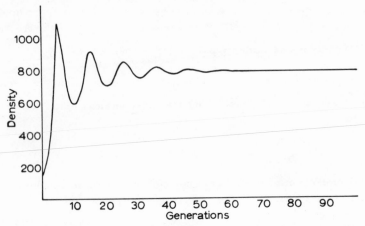

FIGURE 2. Animal population regulation resulting from the interaction of plants and animals in the genetic feed-back mechanism. Starting conditions: p^2 (.360), $2pq$ (.500), q^2 (.140), N_{to} (150), S_p (.001), S_{pq} (.2), S_q (.6), b (1075), c (1500), d (3000), R_p (2), R_{pq} (1), 2nd R_q (.5).

Hence, on the AA plants the ZZ animals reproduce I_x, the Zz animals reproduce I_{xy}, and the zz animals reproduce I_y. On the Aa plants, the ZZ animals reproduce J_x, the Zz animals reproduce J_{xy}, and the zz animals reproduce J_y; and on the aa plants the ZZ animals reproduce L_x, the Zz animals reproduce L_{xy}, and the zz animals reproduce L_y. Reproduction of the animal and survival of the animal types depends on the proportion of the plant genotypes. Animal reproduction, of course, on the various plant genotypes depends on the proportion of the animal genotypes. Thus the proportion of the animal population on the AA plants produce the following animal numbers

$$N_{t1p} = N_{to} P^2 x^2 I_x + N_{to} P^2 2xy I_{xy} + N_{to} P^2 y^2 I_y$$

and on the Aa plants the animals produce

$$N_{t1pq} = N_{to}\, 2\, pqx^2 J_x + N_{to}\, 4\, pqxy J_{xy} + N_{to}\, 2\, pqy^2 J_y$$

and on the aa plants the animals produce

$$N_{toq} = N_{to}\, q^2 x^2 L_x + N_{to}\, q^2 2\, xy L_{xy} + N_{to}\, q^2 y^2 L_y\,.$$

Animal density for the following generation is

(6)
$$N_{t1} = N_{t1p} + N_{t1pq} + N_{t1q}\,.$$

The proportions of the surviving animal genotypes x^2, $2\,xy$, and y^2 respectively are

$$\frac{N_{to}\, p^2 x^2 I_x + N_{to}\, 2\, pqx^2 J_x + N_{to}\, q^2 x^2 L_x}{N_{t1}}$$

(7)
$$+\, \frac{N_{to}\, p^2 2\, xy I_{xy} + N_{to}\, 4\, pqxy J_{xy} + N_{to}\, q^2 2\, xy L_{xy}}{N_{t1}}$$

$$+\, \frac{N_{to}\, p^2 y^2 I_y + N_{to}\, 2\, pqy^2 J_y + N_{to}\, q^2 y^2 L_y}{N_{t1}} = 1\,.$$

The proportion of the Z allele (x) of the animals surviving is $x^2 + \tfrac{1}{2}(2\,xy) = x$ and the proportion of the surviving z allele (y) is $y^2 + \tfrac{1}{2}(2\,xy) = y$. By random mating the surviving allelic proportions of the animal,

(8)
$$(x + y)^2 = 1$$

the proportions of the animal genotypes in the next generation are

(9)
$$x^2 + 2\,xy + y^2 = 1\,.$$

Then with the animal density (N_{t1}) we pass through equations 2, 3, 4, and 5 as in the first model. Starting with the conditions listed in figure 3 and cycling these data through equations 6, 7, 8, 9, 2, 3, 4, and 5, population cycles result for 2100 generations. Only 100 generations are graphed in figure 3. During the 2100 generations the amplitude of the cycles decreased by only four individuals. By extrapolation, the population would continue to cycle for about 20,000 generations.

Starting with conditions similar to those listed in figure 3, except that $S_{pq} = 0.2$ and $S_q = 0.6$, the population stabilizes in 100 generations, and there results a population trend similar to that graphed in figure 2.

Numerous other models were constructed. In one the animal passed through ten generations while in the plant there was one generation; in another, animal reproduction was made density-dependent, and in another, plant density varied in addition to its genetic changes. The feed-back mechanism regulated in all cases.

A longer time is required for the model to stabilize when the starting animal density is relatively far from the stable value, when the starting genotypic proportions are far from the stable values, and if the differences in either the environmental selective pressure or the maximum animal densities

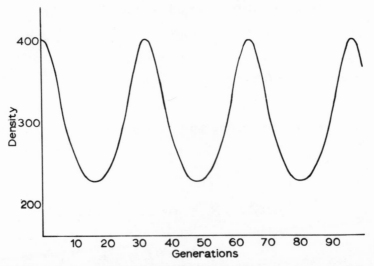

FIGURE 3. Animal population cycles resulting from the interaction of plants and animals in the genetic feed-back mechanism. Starting conditions: p^2 (.172), $2pq$ (.485), q^2 (.343), x^2 (.250), $2xy$ (.500), y^2 (.250), N_{to} (400), S_p (.001), S_{pq} (.1), S_q (.2), b (1075), c (1500), d (3000), I_x (2.8), I_{xy} (2.2), I_y (.8), J_x (1), J_{xy} (1), J_y (1), L_x (.1), L_{xy} (.4), and L_y (1.1).

for the survival are small between each plant genotype. For example, using 0.001, 0.100, and 0.200 for environmental selection pressures for the respective genotypes, AA, Aa, and aa, has greater instability than larger differences such as 0.001, 0.200, and 0.600, respectively. Similarly the maximum densities, 1000, 2000, and 3000, contribute less stability than larger differences such as 1000, 3000, and 9000. Any change occurring in the environmental pressure, in the animal reproduction on the plant genotypes, or in the maximum animal density for the survival of each genotype will change the stabilizing density of the animal to a new level or change the stable values for both the animal density and the plant genotypic proportions.

The feed-back mechanism will regulate under any number of combinations of starting conditions if (1) animal reproduction on the AA plant is greater than that on the aa plant, (2) the animal reproduces greater than one on any one of the genotypes and less than one on another, and (3) the AA plants have a greater survival value than the aa plants in the ecosystem without the animal. Conditions with the homozygous plant genotypes, of course, can be reversed.

The biomathematical models allowed simplification and thus a better understanding of the functioning and action of the feed-back mechanism. In nature the feed-back mechanism would be based most likely on a multifactorial system instead of the unifactorial genetic system used in the models. A multifactorial system would have greater flexibility, and, of course, greater complexity. Obviously the evolution of population regulation in nature would be most difficult to follow because of the nearly infinite number of changing environmental factors. The addition of these other factors will not change the course of evolution in population regulation, but these factors will make the course devious.

With the biomathematics as a base of understanding the function of the mechanism, further details are needed to relate it to biological systems. In all cases, the density of the herbivore populations is a function of both birth rate and death rate, excluding dispersal. Both birth rate and death rate of the herbivore are a function of the quality of food provided by the plant. The food quality is a function of the genetic characteristics of the plant population which in turn are a function of the selective pressure exerted on the plant by the herbivore. Therefore, herbivore density at an initial time determines herbivore density at some future time. So the cycle continues with the density-dependent mechanism regulating the size of the herbivore population.

It is natural that animal reproduction on the AA plants in the models is greater than that on the aa plants and at the same time the AA plants possess a greater survival value than the aa plants in the ecosystem without the animal. If the animal-resistant aa plant possessed greater survival value than the animal-susceptible AA plants, then the animal could not have established itself because of this initial ecological barrier. Whenever the animal is absent or at low density, the plant population gradually shifts until there exists a higher proportion of AA plants than aa plants. In the ecosystem without the animal, the AA plant has an advantage because it has greater survival value than the aa plant. In contrast, when animal density is high, the aa plant has greater advantage than the AA plant because it is more resistant to animal attack.

Man's selection, which operates to produce plants and animals adapted to artificial environments, has sacrificed characters which are necessary to the animals if they are to compete and survive with natural forms in the wild (Srb and Owen, 1953). Because the resistant genes which would allow a plant or animal to survive in an ecosystem that now includes some attacking animal were existing at low frequency in the original ecosystem, it must be assumed that these resistant genes at high frequency are to some extent disadvantageous — if this were not so, then the genes would have been common in the population in the original ecosystem (Crow, 1957).

Organisms only maintain characters important to their survival. Degeneration of skin pigmentation and eyes in cave fishes results from decreased selection for these characters and increased selection for sensory barbels and other characters which lead to better adaptation to the cave environment (Hubbs, 1938). An organism adapting itself to some special feature of the environment, like resistance to animal attack, must sacrifice certain organs or functions for the greater efficiency of others (Huxley, 1943). This efficiency is basic to the economy of the organism itself. Because the dominant selective pressures receive special attention, they tax the other systems of the organism for support.

Then with relaxation of the new selective pressure, a reversion to original genetic type will result, following the principle of "genetic homeostasis" (Lerner, 1954). Darwin (1859) was aware that domesticated animals if not under continuous selection tended to revert to original wild stocks. Examples of reversion following the withdrawal of selective pressures on laboratory populations are numerous. Mather and Harrison (1949) and Streams (1960) found that Drosophila selected for high bristle number tended to return to their original low bristle number when selection ceased. Resistance to insecticides by house flies was lost when this selective pressure was removed from the populations (Pimentel et al., 1953; Varzandeh et al., 1954; Barbesgaard and Keiding, 1955). Populations of microorganisms lost their high level of resistance to drugs when cultured under normal conditions without the drug (Cardot and Laugier, 1923; Morgenroth, 1924; Dettwiler and Schmidt, 1940; Schmidt et al., 1942; Davies and Hinshelwood, 1943; Fulton and Yorke, 1943).

The genetic change in the plant necessary to reduce the herbivore population itself is determined by the nature of the environment. When environmental pressure is severe then only slight genetic change is needed in the plant to reduce the herbivore population. However, when the environment is highly favorable for the herbivore, the pressure on the plants becomes more intense, and the change in the plant has to be significant to reduce the herbivore population to a point of balanced supply and demand.

The rabbit-virus model mentioned earlier presents evidence concerning the question of differential rates of evolution between the eaten and eating species — this is also true of the interactions between cynipids and their oak-tree hosts. Because cynipids pass through more generations than oak trees per unit time, a faster rate of evolutionary change in the cynipids is possible than in oak trees. Similarly, the myxomatosis virus has a greater capacity for change in a short period when compared with rabbits. Natural selection does not favor the cynipids or virus which evolves and destroys its host, but favors the cynipids or virus which allows survival of its host. Through individuals and colonies selection favors the balanced supply-demand system. The evolution of the virus-rabbit association substantiates this fact.

In some cases where animal pressure is severe and the animal must contend with competitive and other environmental factors, the plant may evolve faster than the animal. This, however, is not a requisite for the successful operation of the system. Evolution in each animal is toward survival and the leaving of reproductively successful progeny. Beyond a certain point, the animal gains no advantage in overcoming the plant's resistance to leave more progeny. Selection does not favor a high reproductive rate per se but a reproductive rate profitable from the standpoint of producing successful progeny. Fair apportionment of nutriment must be made between that devoted to maintenance of the parent and production of young (Fisher, 1930) and in some cases maintenance of these young upon birth. Therefore, any increase in fertility is made at the expense of other survival traits (Smith, 1954; Cole, 1957). Selection for lower reproductive rates has been documented by Lack (1956). He found that in "Switzerland, the alpine swift (*Apus melba*) normally lays three eggs"; the number of young which fly from broods initially consisting of one, two, three, and four young was respectively, 1.0, 1.7, 2.4, and 2.2. Thus, the largest brood (four) produced fewer successful young than the smaller brood of three.

Selection for the most productive birth rates, not necessarily the highest, occurs in family units (Birch, 1960; Emerson, 1960), colonies (Emerson, 1958), and individuals (Root, 1960). Fundamental to optimal reproduction is the supply and demand economy which exists between individuals or colonies of the herbivores and plants, parasites and hosts, and predators and prey. On partially isolated trees an insect colony which evolves to reproduce at a high rate by converting the trees into insect protoplasm at a rapid rate may destroy the trees and in the end produce fewer successful young than another colony with a lower reproductive rate (Wright, 1960). Viruses and bacteria, which attack relatively long-lived plants and animals, do not evolve rapidly to high reproductive types and greater pathogenicity. Thus, the drift of evolution is toward optimal reproductive types which will provide a balanced economy of supply and demand between the eating and eaten species.

Population birth rate of the animal is influenced either by alterations in the quality of the food or alterations in the intrinsic nature of the eating individuals themselves. Beadle (1945) has experimentally developed genetic strains of Neurosopora which were unable or inefficiently able to synthesize various necessary vitamins and amino acids from a minimal medium. Some of the genetic strains were unable to grow while others grew at reduced rates on such medium. Thus, by altering the genetic make-up of the individual and correspondingly the biochemical structure of the organism, its functional rate of growth can be changed, and, of course, this will influence the dynamics of such a population.

The feed-back mechanism is in accord with the fact that the majority of animal species are rare in nature (Darwin, 1859; Andrewartha and Birch, 1954; Milne, 1960). The herbivore, parasite, or predator population cannot be abundant compared with its respective plant, host, or prey population. In the balanced economy, the eating species feed on only the interest (excess individuals of the eaten population) and do not touch the capital (those individuals necessary for the maintenance of the population of the eaten species).

That the genetic feed-back mechanism functions as a regulatory system in herbivore-plant and parasite-host relationships is supported by evidence from the biomathematics of population dynamics and studies of natural populations. The principles of the mechanism also apply to predator-prey systems. The importance of the feed-back mechanism as a regulatory system is substantiated by its wide application to such diverse interacting systems; however, the significance of the mechanism lies in the fact that it has its foundation in evolution. The mechanism follows Dr. A. E. Emerson's view that evolution is toward increased homeostasis within populations and the ecosystem (Emerson, 1960).

The task which lies ahead is to determine how the feed-back mechanism functions in regulating natural populations and what its relationship is to the other regulatory theories like "competition" (Nicholson, 1933; Varley, 1947; Solomon, 1949; DeBach, 1958; Morris, 1959; Holling, 1959; Watt, 1959), and "environmental randomness" (Thompson, 1929; Andrewartha and Birch, 1954; Milne, 1957). I do not propose that the feed-back mechanism is the only means of population regulation, nor that this mechanism is independent of the "competition" and "environmental randomness" ideas. The three are interdependent, and I suspect that upon the introduction of a new animal type into a new ecosystem there is an evolution of regulation from both the "competition" and "environmental randomness" conditions to the feed-back mechanism. That is, before sufficient change takes place in the eating population and eaten population, the principal means of regulation is through "competition" and "environmental randomness."

In well-designed experiments lie the challenge and necessary evidence concerning the various control mechanisms. The validity of the feed-back mechanism is under experimental investigation both in the laboratory and field by myself and students of ecology at Cornell University.

I wish to acknowledge the stimulating and pleasant discussion in person and through the mails with Drs. H. G. Andrewartha, W. L. Brown, L. C. Cole, A. E. Emerson, J. Franz, A. Milne, A. J. Nicholson, T. Park, and B. Wallace and Mr. F. R. Streams. Their arguments have helped me clarify my own concept of this mechanism. These discussions have underscored the need for research, and as Claude Bernard (1865) emphasized, "we shall reach really fruitful and luminous generalizations about vital phenomena only insofar as we ourselves experiment and, in hospitals, amphitheaters, or laboratories, stir the fetid or throbbing ground of life."

SUMMARY

That a genetic feed-back mechanism functions to regulate populations of herbivores, parasites, and predators is supported by evidence from the biomathematics of population dynamics and studies of natural populations. The mechanism functions as a feed-back system through the dynamics of density pressure, selective pressure, and genetic changes in interacting populations. In a herbivore-plant system, animal density influences selective pressure on plants; this selection influences genetic make-up of plant; and in turn, the genetic make-up of plant influences animal density. The actions and reactions of interacting populations in the food chain cycling in the genetic feed-back mechanism result in the evolution and regulation of animal populations.

LITERATURE CITED

Andrewartha, H. G., and L. C. Birch, 1954, The distribution and abundance of animals. 782 pp. University of Chicago Press, Chicago, Ill.

Beadle, G. W., 1945, Genetics and metabolism in *Neurospora*. Physiol. Revs. 25: 643–663.

Barbesgaard, P., and J. Keiding, 1955, Crossing experiments with insecticide-resistant houseflies (*Musca domestica* L.). Vidensk. Medd. fra Dansk. naturh. Foren. 117: 84–116.

Bernard, C., 1865, An introduction to the study of experimental medicine, translated by Henry C. Greene, United States. 226 pp. Dover Publications, Inc., New York, N. Y.

Birch, L. C., 1960, The genetic factor in population ecology. Amer. Nat. 94: 5–24.

Cardot, H., and H. Laugier, 1923, Adaptation, transmission des caractéres acquis, sélection par concurrence vitale chez le ferment lactique. C. R. Acad. Sci., Paris 176: 1087–1090.

Chitty, D., 1957, Self-regulation of numbers through changes in viability. Cold Spring Harbor Symp. Quant. Biol. 22: 227–280.

    1960, Population processes in the vole and their relevance to general theory. Canad. J. Zool. 38: 99–113.

Cole, L. C., 1957, Sketches of general and comparative demography. Cold Spring Harbor Symp. Quant. Biol. 22: 227–280.

Crow, J. F., 1957, Genetics of insect resistance to chemicals. Ann. Rev. Entomol. 2: 227–246.

Darwin, C. R., 1859, The origin of species. 488 pp. J. M. Dent and Sons Ltd., London, England.

Davies, D. S., and C. N. Hinshelwood, 1943, The adaptation of Bact. lactis aerogenes to growth in the presence of sulphonamides. Trans. Faraday Soc. 39: 431–444.

Day, M. F., 1955, Factors influencing the transmissibility of myxoma virus by mosquitoes. J. Austral. Inst. Agr. Sci. 21: 145–151.

DeBach, P., 1958, The role of weather and entomophagous species in the natural control of insect populations. J. Econ. Entomol. 51: 474–484.

Dettwiler, H. A., and L. H. Schmidt, 1940, Observations on the development of resistance to sulfapyridine. J. Bact. 40: 160–161.

Emerson, A. E., 1958, The evolution of behavior among social insects. *In* Behavior and evolution, ed. by A. Roe and G. G. Simpson. pp. 311–335. Yale University Press, New Haven, Conn.

    1960, The evolution of adaptation in population systems. *In* Evolution of life, ed. by Sol Tax. 629 pp. University of Chicago Press, Chicago, Ill.

Fenner, F., 1953, Host-parasite relationships in myxomatosis of the Australian wild rabbit. Cold Spring Harbor Symp. Quant. Biol. 18: 291–294.

Fenner, F., I. D. Marshall and G. M. Woodroffe, 1953, Studies on the epidemiology of infectious myxomatosis of rabbits. I. Recovery of Australian wild rabbits (*Oryctolagus cuniculus*) myxomatosis under field conditions. J. Hyg. 51: 225–244.

Fisher, R. A., 1930, The genetical theory of natural selection. 268 pp. Clarendon Press, Oxford, England.

Forbush, E. H., and C. H. Fernald, 1896, The Gypsy moth, *Porthetria dispar* (Linn.). 459 pp. Wright and Potter, Boston, Mass.

Ford, E. B., 1931, Mendelism and evolution. 122 pp. Methuen and Co. Ltd., London, England.

——— 1956, The study of organic evolution by observation and experiment. Endeavor 15: 149–152.

Ford, H. D., and E. B. Ford, 1930, Fluctuation in numbers, and its influence on variation, in *Melitaea aurinia*, Rott. (Lepidoptera). Trans. Entomol. Soc. London 78: 345–351.

Franz, J., 1949, Über die genetischen Grundlagen das Zusammenbruchs einer Massenvermehrung aus inneren Ursachen. Z. angew. Ent. 31: 228–260.

Fulton, J. D., and W. Yorke, 1943, Further observations on plasmoquine-resistance in *Plasmodium knowlesi*. Ann. Trop. Med. Parasit. 37: 41–47.

Galtsoff, P. S., 1930, The fecundity of the oyster. Science 72: 97–98.

Haldane, J. B. S., 1956, The relation between density regulation and natural selection. Proc. Roy. Soc. London (B) 145: 306–308.

Holling, C. S., 1959, The components of predation as revealed by a study of small mammal predation of the European pine sawfly. Canad. Entomol. 91: 293–320.

Hubbs, C. L., 1938, Fishes from caves of Yucatan. 261 pp. Publ. Carnegie Instn. No. 491.

Huxley, J., 1943, Evolution the modern synthesis. 645 pp. Harper & Brothers Publishers, New York and London.

Lack, D., 1956, Variations in the reproductive rate of birds. Proc. Roy. Soc. London (B) 145: 329–333.

Lerner, I. M., 1954, Genetic homeostasis. 134 pp. Oliver and Boyd, London, England.

Li, C. C., 1955, Population genetics. 366 pp. University of Chicago Press, Chicago, Ill.

Marshall, I. D., 1958, Studies in the epidemiology of infectious myxomatosis of rabbits. V. Changes in the innate resistance of Australian wild rabbits exposed to myxomatosis. J. Hyg. 56: 288–302.

Mather, K., and B. J. Harrison, 1949, The manifold effect of selection. Heredity 3: 1–52.

Milne, A., 1957, The natural control of insect populations. Canad. Entomol. 84: 193–213.

——— 1960, On a theory of natural control of insect population. 22 pp. Agricultural Research Council, Newcastle upon Tyne, England.

Morgenroth, J., 1924, Die Bedeutung der Variabilität der Microorganismen für die Therapie. Z. Bact., Orig. 93: 94–113.

Morris, R. F., 1959, Single-factor analysis in population dynamics. Ecology 40: 580–588.

Needler, A. W. H., and R. R. Logie, 1947, Serious mortalities in Prince Edward Island oysters caused by a contagious disease. Trans. Roy. Soc. Canada, 3d ser., Sect. V 41: 73–94.

306

Nicholson, A. J., 1933, The balance of animal populations. J. Anim. Ecol. 2: 138–178.

Painter, R. H., 1951, Insect resistance in crop plants. 520 pp. Macmillan Company, New York, N. Y.

1954, Some ecological aspects of the resistance of crop plants in insects. J. Econ. Entomol. 47: 1036–1040.

Pimentel, D., H. H. Schwardt and J. E. Dewey, 1953, Development and loss of insecticide resistance in the housefly. J. Econ. Entomol. 46: 295–298.

Root, R. B., 1960, An estimate of the intrinsic rate of natural increase in the planarian, *Dugesia tigrina.* Ecology 41: 369–372.

Schmidt, L. H., C. Sesler and H. A. Dettwiler, 1942, Development of sulfapyridine resistance by pneumococci. J. Pharmacol. 74: 175–189.

Smith, F. E., 1954, Quantitative aspects of population growth. *In* Dynamics of growth processes, ed. by E. J. Boell. pp. 277–294. Princeton University Press, Princeton, N. J.

Smith, L. B., and C. H. Hadley, 1926, The Japanese beetle. Dept. Cir. U.S. Dept. Agric. 363: 1–66.

Solomon, M. E., 1949, The natural control of animal populations. J. Anim. Ecol. 18: 1–35.

Srb, A. M., and R. D. Owen, 1958, General genetics. 561 pp. Freeman and Co., San Francisco, Calif.

Stead, D. G., 1935, The rabbit in Australia. 108 pp. Winn, Sydney, Australia.

Streams, F. A., 1960, Effects of immigration on the evolution of populations. 68 pp. M.S. Thesis, Cornell University, Ithaca, N. Y.

Thompson, H. V., 1954, The rabbit disease: myxomatosis. Ann. Appl. Biol. 41: 358–366.

Thompson, W. R., 1929, On natural control. Parasitology 21: 269–281.

Turner, N., 1960, The effect of inbreeding and crossbreeding on numbers of insects. Ann. Entomol. Soc. Amer. 35: 686–688.

Varley, G. C., 1947, The natural control of population balance in the knapweed gall-fly (*Urophora jaceana*). J. Anim. Ecol. 16: 139–187.

Varzandeh, M., W. N. Bruce and G. C. Decker, 1954, Resistance to insecticides as a factor influencing the biotic potential of the housefly. J. Econ. Entomol. 47: 129–134.

Watt, K. E. F., 1959, A mathematical model for the effect of densities of attacked and attacking species on the number attacked. Canad. Entomol. 91: 129–144.

Wellington, W. G., 1957, Individual differences as a factor in population dynamics: The development of problem. Canad. Zool. 35: 293–323.

1960, Qualitative changes in natural populations during changes in abundance. Canad. J. Zool. 35: 289–314.

Wright, S., 1960, Physiological genetics, ecology of populations, and natural selection. *In* Evolution of life, ed. by Sol Tax. 629 pp. University of Chicago Press, Chicago, Ill.

22

Reprinted from *Science* **109**(2831):333–335 (1949)

A Method for Self-Control of Population Growth among Mammals Living in the Wild[1]

John B. Calhoun
Rodent Ecology Project, Johns Hopkins University

It is a common observation that the numbers of most organisms in a reproducing population reach an equilibrium with the conditions of their environment. In approaching this upper limit of the logistic of the population, Pearl (*2*) has pointed out that ''the rate of reproduction or fertility is negatively correlated with density of population.'' This is merely a statement of fact which prompts the study of the mode by which the reduction in contribution of progeny to the population

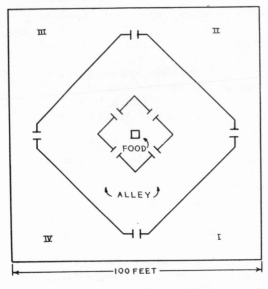

FIG. 1. Diagram of pen in which rats are housed: outer, central, and middle fences which prevent rats from passing over or under them; 8 passages through fences (3″ clay drain tiles); food and water continuously and abundantly available in central pen; 9 harborage boxes in each of the 4 triangular corner areas; rats allowed to dig burrows in alley and in triangular areas.

occurs. Whatever the means of reduction, the result is that there are less adults to compete for the existing supply of food and harborage.

A recent note in *Science* by Mirone, *et al.* (*1*) suggests one possible way in which the increment to a population may be effectively reduced. They observed in mice that newborn young of mothers on a poor diet frequently fail to survive past the fourth day. From the fact that these

[1] The work reported in this paper was conducted under a grant from the International Health Division of the Rockefeller Foundation.

same mothers may successfully rear adopted litters born to mothers on an adequate diet, they conclude that failure of the litters to survive is due to inadequate nutrition during gestation. This conclusion suggests that any environmental conditions which affect the maternal physiology to the extent that foetal nutrition is lowered will slow down the rate of population growth due to early post-parturition mortality.

Recent observations on the growth of a colony of wild Norway rats (*Rattus norvegicus*) indicates that this process of upsetting maternal physiology may be one of the limiting factors in population growth. This experimental colony is maintained in a 100′-square pen where abundant food (Purina fox checkers) is continually available in a 20′-square central pen to which the rats gain access by four narrow passages. Fig. 1 shows details of the pen.

The colony in the pen was begun with five pairs of rats, which are assumed to have been as genetically homozygous as it is possible to trap them in the wild

TABLE 1

PHYSICAL STATE AND REPRODUCTIVE CONTRIBUTION*
(January 1 to September 25, 1948)

		Average wt. (gms)	Average wounds	No. of pregnancies	Litters weaned
Born in an Area Harborage Box	♀ 17	379[7]	14[6]	3	1?
	♀ 20	388[4]	14[4]	4†	0
	♀ 25	371[7]	15[9]	5†	0
	L – 3 ♀♀	379	14.3	12	1?
Born in Alley Burrow	♀ 33	451[4]	1[3]	3	2 (3rd?)
	♀ 37	411[4]	0.6[5]	5	4
	♀ 43	426[5]	3[4]	4	4
	L – 5 ♀♀	429	1.5	12	10

* Superscripts denote number of observations from which averages were determined.
† Each includes 2 pregnancies for the fall of 1947.

state. This assumption is made on the following inferential grounds. The rats were trapped in February 1947 on Parsons Island, a 150-acre tract of land in the Chesapeake Bay. Its land bridge with the mainland was severed about 40 years ago, since which time the rats have been effectively isolated. The number of rats on the island has fluctuated widely both on an annual basis and on the basis of changes in agricultural practices. An experimental reduction by poison in 1923 was conducted by the Fish and Wildlife Service. A second experimental reduction was conducted in the spring of 1946 by J. T. Emlen and D. E. Davis, of the Rodent Ecology Project. Estimations of numbers: (a) pre-poisoning, 670; (b) post-poisoning, 220. At the time of trapping in February 1947 surveys indicated that there were probably no more than 150 rats on the island. Under these circumstances of fluctuation in population size, it might be anticipated that considerable homozygosity would have been reached through gene drift (*3*). It is from this inference that the conditions here reported are judged to arise from environmental rather than hereditary differences.

Rats living in the triangular areas were further from the food source than were those living in the alley. There was thus produced a simple gradient of availabilty of food in which one group of rats had an advantage over another group. This gradient of availability of food was intensified by the social life of the rats. Rats become attached to certain areas of the pen and their movements are mainly confined to these areas and from it to the food pen and back. In order to get to the food pen, rats living in the triangular areas frequently must pass near the burrows of rats living in the alley. At such times they may be repulsed by the resident rats. Such repulsion is particularly severe when the resident alley rat is a lactating female. With frequent repulsions the individual's growth rate is slowed down, and since weight is a major factor in winning combats, such individuals occupy a low position in the social hierarchy, and in extreme cases the individual becomes so inhibited that it approaches the food pen with great caution, even when no other rats are about.

To illustrate the effect of social conditioning on physical well-being and reproduction the histories of three females from each of two litters are given in Table 1. Litter 3 .(L-3) was born May 30, 1947, in one of the triangular areas. Litter 5 (L-5) was born August 16, 1947, in the alley near the food pen. Though born 2½ months later the L-5 females average 50 gms heavier than the L-3 females as adults. As individuals, the upper

asymptote of their growth curves was reached in 8 months by L-5 females, but not until 12 months by L-3 females, when weight is used as the criterion. The degree of social inhibition is reflected in the number of fresh wounds recorded at each time of handling. It is the loser in a combat which usually receives wounds as it turns to flee. L-3 females received nearly 10 times as many wounds as L-5 females.

It so happened that the total number of pregnancies for the females in each litter to the last date of handling was the same. The contrast between the two groups in their reproductive history lies in the fate of their litters. Although the socially dominant, larger females were known to have weaned 10 litters from their 12 pregnancies, the socially inhibited individuals with a retarded growth rate definitely weaned no more than one litter. These observations give no direct evidence as to the cause of the differential survival rate of the young of these two groups of females. However, the histories of the mothers indicate that there is a physiological and psychological disturbance in socially inhibited individuals which might have a deleterious effect on the progeny either through poor foetal nutrition or from breakdown of maternal instincts. At any rate, social conditioning may be a potent factor in population control among mammals.

References

1. MIRONE, LEONORA, PANZARELLA, F. P., and CERECEDO, L. R. *Science*, 1948, **101**, 139–140.
2. PEARL, RAYMOND. *The biology of population growth.* New York : Alfred Knopf, 1925.
3. WRIGHT, S. In J. HUXLEY. *The new statistics.* Oxford : Clarendon Press, 1940. Pp. 161–183.

23

Copyright © 1964 by the American Association for the Advancement of Science

Reprinted from *Science* 146(3651):1550–1560 (1964)

Endocrines, Behavior, and Population

Social and endocrine factors are integrated in the regulation of growth of mammalian populations.

John J. Christian and David E. Davis

For several decades the spectacular increase and decrease of certain arctic mammals has stimulated research on populations. The crashes of rabbits were dramatized by Seton (*1*), and the suicidal movements of lemmings were publicized by many authors. However, as is so often the case, the conspicuous features turn out to be merely an extreme case of a very general phenomenon—namely, the fluctuations of a population. Investigators first sought an explanation for the "crash," but now most of them search for a description and understanding of the interaction and relative importance of the many factors that influence the ups and downs of populations.

In this article we describe the current status of our understanding of population fluctuations, emphasizing the regulatory features that prevent populations from destroying the habitat. The research discussed is limited to work with mammals, since the mechanisms are best known for that class. It is assumed that the reader has knowledge of ecological principles such as density dependence and limiting factors.

For many years it was assumed that epizootics, famine, and climatic factors terminated the explosive rises in population size and precipitated the often spectacular crashes (*2*). However, by the early 1940's it had become apparent that none of these mechanisms explained some of the observed declines in population, and it was suggested that factors intrinsic to the population were involved in its regulation

(*3*). The skepticism toward earlier explanations was reflected further in a review by Clarke in 1949 (*4*), as well as in Elton's classic earlier work (*5*). Probably the greatest shift in emphasis has occurred since 1949; there has been an upsurge of investigations in which density-dependent changes in the animals themselves have been explored, and of theories in which the observed phenomena of population growth and decline (*6–9*) are explained in terms of biological mechanisms intrinsic in the populations and not only as results of the action of external factors. It is clear that food, climatic factors, and disease may cause population change. Indeed, it would be foolish to state that these factors do not, under certain circumstances, limit population growth or produce spectacular decline. The early investigations of Emlen, Davis, and their co-workers (*8*) on populations of Norway rats demonstrated clearly that environmental factors can reduce a population. For example, a drought followed by excessive rain resulted in a notable decline in rats in Baltimore (*8*). However, as early as 1946 spectacular declines in rat populations were found to be coincident with social disturbances rather than with environmental changes.

The suspicion that social phenomena were involved prompted a search for mechanisms that could regulate the growth of populations in a density-dependent manner. No longer is attention focused exclusively on spectacular crashes and the causes of death. Instead, an attempt is made to integrate the social actions and the well-known habitat factors into a scheme that will explain the changes in populations. Since social or behavioral

features are density-dependent, they become evident only at high population levels. Nevertheless, such features are present in low populations, but inconspicuous. Purely ecological factors, such as food and climatic conditions, also affect populations and, indeed, may prevent a population from attaining a level where social forces can become important. Hence, examination was begun of a theory which states that, within broad limits set by the environment, density-dependent mechanisms have evolved within the animals themselves to regulate population growth and curtail it short of the point of suicidal destruction of the environment (*6, 10–13*). Milne (*12*) has summarized this point of view as follows: "The *ultimate* capacity of a place for a species is the maximum number of individuals that the place could carry without being rendered totally uninhabitable by utter exhaustion or destruction of resources. . . . The environmental capacity cannot be greater than ultimate capacity; it could, conceivably be equal to ultimate capacity but . . . is usually somewhat smaller." We would modify the "somewhat" to "considerably," in view of the situation most often observed for mammals (here we are talking primarily of herbivores and rodents). Milne goes on to say that "the one and only perfectly density-dependent factor [is] intraspecific competition."

While some investigators ascribe all regulation and limitation of populations to direct effects of environmental factors, others recognize that a feedback control of population growth exists. However, there is not complete agreement on the mechanisms by which these results are achieved. In the rest of this article we review the more recent results of experiments made to test the hypothesis that a behavioral-physiological mechanism operates to control population growth in mammals, and we consider criticisms of this view in the light of the evidence on which they are based. The acceptability of the hypothesis should be considered from the viewpoint of what would constitute disproof. To prove that behavioral mechanisms *never* affect population growth is of course impossible. To cite one or more cases in which some habitat factor controlled the population is merely an elaboration of the obvious. Thus, proof or disproof of the hypothesis reduces to the problem of finding how frequently and under what circumstances

Dr. Christian is affiliated with the Research Laboratories of the Albert Einstein Medical Center, Philadelphia, Pa.; Dr. Davis is professor of zoology at Pennsylvania State University, University Park.

the behavioral mechanism does operate. The discovery of other physiological mechanisms [for example, pregnancy block caused by the proximity of strange males (14) or direct block of reproduction organs in *Peromyscus* (15)] does not alter the situation. Similarly, the absence of the mechanism in certain mammals would not prove its absence in rodents. The problem, then, is not that of proving the existence of a behavioral-physiological mechanism but that of proving the importance of such a mechanism in the regulation of populations.

Physiological Mechanisms

On the basis of the knowledge of pituitary-adrenocortical physiology available prior to 1950, it was proposed (16) that stimulation of pituitary-adrenocortical activity and inhibition of reproductive function would occur with increased population density. It was suggested, further, that increased adrenocortical secretion would increase mortality indirectly through lowering the resistance to disease, through parasitism or adverse environmental conditions, or, more directly, through "shock disease," although it soon became evident that unwarranted emphasis was being placed on "shock disease." Implicit in this theory and in the design of experiments to test it was the theory that behavioral factors (aggressive competition, for example) comprised the only stimulus to the endocrine responses which would invariably be present in every population. Experiments to test the theory were conducted on animals which were provided with (or known to have) more food, cover, and other environmental assets than they could utilize, and were thus in populations either totally free of predation or having a minimum degree of predation (17–19).

The endocrine responses were first assessed through measurement of changes in the weights of the adrenals, the thymus, the reproductive organs, and certain other organs. Interpretations of adrenal weights are reliable and simple in species that have been adequately studied in the laboratory— for example, in rats and mice, whose adrenal physiology and morphology have been examined in detail under a variety of circumstances. In particular, the immature zonation (X-zone) of mice and its changes with respect to age and sex had been thoroughly ex-

plored (20). An important point was the lack of evidence of function for this zone. Where adrenal weight could be reliably interpreted in terms of function, it seemed better, in the study of populations, to use an indicator of long-term conditions, rather than indicators highly sensitive to acute stimuli. For example, concentrations of ascorbic acid in the adrenal gland and concentrations of corticosteroid in plasma respond very rapidly to acute stimuli. Furthermore, the interpretation of changes in adrenal weight was supported by other morphological criteria of increased corticosteroid secretion, such as involution of the thymus, though the possible role of other factors in the alteration of these other organs was not overlooked. Nevertheless, even in rats and mice, changes in adrenal weight can only be considered strong presumptive evidence of changes in adrenocortical function until validation is obtained by direct functional studies.

Adrenal weights are not valid indices of function unless certain precautions are observed. The presence of immature zones (X-zones) complicates the use of adrenal weights as indices of function, since evidence that such zones contribute to cortical function is lacking. Another complication is the possibility of weight loss with sudden or excessive stimulation. Moreover, there may be a misleading increase in adrenal weight due to accumulation of lipids with cessation of adrenocorticotropic hormone (ACTH) stimulation. Also misleading is the hypertrophy of the adrenal medulla which occurs in some instances, but this usually is not important (21). In addition, qualitative changes in the corticosteroids secreted may require modification of interpretations based on adrenal weight. Finally, sexual maturation or activity may alter cortical function and adrenal weight. Androgens involute the X-zone or decrease adrenal weight in adult animals, whereas estrogens commonly increase adrenal weight. It is axiomatic that, in comparing changes in adrenal weight with changes in population, one must consider adrenal changes due to reproductive condition, and that only adrenals from animals of similar reproductive status can properly be compared.

In addition to these physiological considerations, there is the problem of obtaining adequate samples. Since there are two sexes and at least two age groups, the sample must contain

enough animals in each of four categories for appropriate analysis. This requirement may seem obvious, but it often has been neglected.

The foregoing principles regarding the interpretation of adrenal weights have been presented because in many studies one or more of these principles has been neglected. Earlier work on physiological responses to changes in populations has been reviewed elsewhere (6, 17–19) and is only summarized here. In experiments with mice in the laboratory, progressive adrenocortical hypertrophy and thymic involution were observed to occur with increasing size of population. Somatic growth was suppressed and reproductive function was curtailed in both sexes. Sexual maturation was delayed or, at higher population densities, totally inhibited. Spermatogenesis was delayed, and the weights of the accessory sex organs declined with increasing population density. In mature females, estrous cycles were prolonged and ovulation and implantation were diminished; intrauterine mortality of the fetuses increased. Recent results in rabbits show an increase in intrauterine mortality in association with increased population density, especially in the fetuses of socially subordinate females (22). In another study a similar increase in intrauterine mortality was noted, but no difference in rate of resorption of embryos relative to social rank was observed (23). Increased resorption of embryos also followed grouping of *Peromyscus* (24). However, in mice, the importance of resorption of embryos in regulating birthrates may vary considerably from population to population (17). Also, increased population density resulted in inadequate lactation in mice, so that nurslings were stunted at weaning. This effect was seen again, though to a lesser degree, in animals of the next generation not subjected to additional crowding (25). It has since been found that crowding of female mice prior to pregnancy results in permanent behavioral disturbances in subsequently conceived young (26). Particularly interesting in this regard is the observation that increased concentrations of corticosterone may permanently affect the development of the brain in mice (27). Increased population size also delayed or totally inhibited maturation in females, as well as in males, so that in some populations no females reached normal sexual maturity. The combination of these responses, believed to result from inhibition of gonadotrophin secretion, resulted in a decrease in birthrate, or an increase in infant mortality, or both, as populations increased, until increase of the population through the production of young ceased. Concentrations of gonadotrophins in relation to changes in population size have not been measured. However, increase in the number of rats per cage was found to alter responses to injected gonadotrophins, even when the area per rat was kept constant (*28*).

Increased population density may affect reproductive function in male and female house mice differently in different populations. The growth of one population was slowed and eventually stopped mainly by a decline in birthrate due to (i) failure of the young to mature and (ii) decrease in the reproductivity of mature animals (*17*). Infant mortality was a negligible factor in this population. In several others a decline in the survival of nurslings was largely responsible for a slowing and stopping of population growth, although a lowering of the birthrate also occurred (*17, 19*). In most populations both a decrease in birthrate and a decrease in the survival of nurslings contributed importantly to slowing of the rate of population growth and limitation of numbers, but, as one might expect, the relative importance of these two factors varied among populations. In populations in which a change in birthrate was the main regulating factor, other measurements indicated that it was the males which were primarily affected by increased population density, the effect on females being slight. When increasing mortality of nurslings was the main regulating factor, the females were severely affected and the males were relatively less affected than in other populations (*17*). These results imply that effects on the male may be important in producing declining birthrates, although failure of females to mature also would contribute to a decline in birthrate in any population and cannot be excluded. Final conclusions regarding this problem must await further investigation.

For many years it has been known that disease sometimes becomes rampant when populations reach peak levels (*5*). However, the belief that disease usually is a primary cause in the reduction of populations has not been supported (*5, 11*). A change in host resistance has been suggested as an

underlying condition leading to increased mortality from epizootics (*6, 11, 17*). It is well known that glucocorticoids reduce resistance to infectious disease by inhibiting the normal defense reactions. They may also be involved to some extent in the pathogenesis of other disease, such as glomerulonephritis as seen in woodchucks (*17*). Furthermore, grouping, presumably through adrenal stimulation, augments adrenal-regeneration hypertension in rats (*29*). Experiments have shown that, with increased population density, there is a marked depression of inflammatory responses, and of formation of antibodies, and of other related defenses, with a resultant increase in susceptibility to infection or parasitism. For example, in a confined population of rabbits a highly lethal epidemic of myxomatosis occurred coincident with attainment of a high density (*22*). During this epidemic dominant animals and their descendants had the highest survival rate, implying a breakdown in host resistance following increased social competition. Similar results were observed in a population of deer, associated with high densities and subsequent decline in population (*30*). Increased density also enhances mortality from other causes —for example, radiation, amphetamine toxicity, and toxicity due to other pharmacologic agents (*31*). Decreased resistance to amphetamine following grouping is probably due to increased secretion of epinephrine and not to increased secretion of corticosteroids (*32*). Emotional stress also enhances mortality from disease, probably through the same endocrine mechanisms (*33*). These results suggest that at high population densities an epidemic occurs in part because resistance is lowered. Thus, disease is a consequence of high population rather than a primary cause of a decline in population.

Behavioral Aspects

What basic behavioral factors result in these profound effects? It seemed to us that any density-dependent effects would be related to social rank. Experiments made to test this hypothesis showed that adrenal weight and somatic growth were related to social rank (*18, 34*). Other experiments, in which adrenocortical function was assessed from counts of circulatory eosinophils (*35*), confirmed these re-

sults. Adrenal cortical activity is similarly related to social rank in rats and dogs, as determined by lipid and cholesterol concentrations in the adrenals of rats and by hydrocortisone secretion in dogs (*36*). In several somewhat related experiments it has been shown that the degree of response to changes in population size is dependent on the behavioral aggressiveness of the strain or species involved (*19, 37*). In the highly aggressive house mouse (*Mus musculus*), changes in adrenal weight, ascorbic acid content, and cholesterol content demonstrated the important role of behavioral factors in the responses to changes in population density. In contrast, deer mice (*Peromyscus maniculatus bairdii*) failed to respond, due to behavioral characteristics and not to an inherently unresponsive endocrine system (*37*). The two species responded equally when exposed to trained fighters of their own species or when subjected to cold.

In most studies of social rank an indirect measure of adrenocortical function was used, such as the weights of adrenal and thymus, cholesterol and ascorbic acid content of the adrenal, and numbers of circulating eosinophils. Recently, a number of investigators have observed increases in adrenocortical function with increases in population density. There is an appreciably greater in vitro production of corticosteroids by adrenals in grouped mice than in singly caged mice (*38*). Albino laboratory rats show an increase in plasma corticosterone concentrations from 6.7 to 22 micrograms per 100 milliliters when they are maintained in colonies rather than in groups of four to a cage (*39*). There was also a fivefold increase in the in vitro production of corticosteroids by the adrenals of the colony-maintained rats. Barrett and Stockham (*40*) reported a 73-percent increase in plasma corticosterone concentrations, as measured fluorometrically, in albino rats kept in groups of 20 as compared with concentrations in singly caged animals. Pearson (*41*) found that, in general, plasma corticosterone levels increased with increasing density in freely growing populations of mice, although there was considerable scatter in the results, possibly because of capture and handling procedures. Thus, direct measurement of corticosteroid levels confirms conclusions from experiments in which morphological criteria were used to assess adrenocortical function in Norway rats and house mice.

Increases in the weight of the spleen in response to increased population density have been reported in mice and voles (6, 42, 43). In house mice the increase in splenic weight is due to increased hematopoiesis involving all blood-forming elements, and not solely to erthyropoiesis, as in voles (43). The increase probably is related to social rank (44), although a response to injuries from fighting could not be ruled out.

The problem of the role of food invariably arises in discussion of changes in population. A shortage of food might have the direct effect of causing starvation or an indirect effect by increasing competition among animals. Contrary to a widely held belief, chronic inanition per se (as opposed to acute starvation) appears not to result in increased adrenal weight or increased cortical function in rats, mice, and men (45, 46). Experiments with mice showed that chronic inanition had no effect on adrenal weight, either directly or indirectly (46). However, inanition curtailed reproductive function independently of its effects on the pituitary-adrenocortical system. In some species, limitation of the food supply apparently increases competition (22, 47, 48), and thus subordinate animals are more affected by the shortage than dominant ones. Resistance to starvation (and thus survival) is greater in dominant or older animals than in subordinate or younger animals (22). Also, the decreased need for protein seen in deer during winter and early spring is frequently overlooked (49). It is possible that some microtines or other rodents also have mechanisms for taking advantage of bacterial protein synthesis during periods when proteins and natural plant foods are scarce. On the basis of existing evidence (11, 50), the direct effect of food shortages cannot be considered a common denominator in the regulation and limitation of growth of populations of herbivorous mammals. Studies of populations of *Clethrionomys* (51, 52), lemmings (53), voles (11, 19), woodchucks (54), *Apodemus* (52), and other mammals have shown that a deficiency of food either was not a factor in population decrease or else had an effect complementary to behavioral changes associated with changes in population density (47). From evidence currently available it

appears that the effects of restricting water intake over a long period can be regarded in the same fashion as the effects of chronic inanition. In a thorough study of food requirements and availability of food in relation to populations of small mammals, it was shown that food was not a limiting factor in the area studied (50). More critical studies of this sort are needed before a final evaluation can be made of the relative importance of food shortages in limiting population growth and of the degree to which such limitation, when it does occur, is associated with increasing competition within existing hierarchical structures.

The important point, in assessing the effects of behavioral factors on adrenal function, is the number of interactions between individuals rather than density of population per se. Thus, age, sex, previous experience, local distribution, and other factors may be critical in producing effects (6, 17–19, 55). The development of the adrenal responses may be produced by very brief encounters with other animals. Experiments showed that 1-minute exposure to trained fighter mice 1, 2, 4, and 8 times a day for 7 days produced increases in adrenal weight and increases in adrenal and plasma concentrations of corticosterone (56). As few as two 1-minute exposures per day resulted in a 14-percent increase in adrenal weight, and eight exposures daily resulted in a 29-percent increase. Plasma corticosterone increased by 67 percent. Adrenal levels of corticosterone increased in proportion to adrenal weight, so corticosterone concentrations per gram of adrenal tissue remained constant. These results validate, for mature male house mice, the use of adrenal weight as an index of cortical function. Thus, a few short daily exposures to aggressive mice produced a greater increase in adrenal weight than caging male mice of the same strain together in groups of eight continuously for a week (37, 56). These results should serve as an answer to the criticism that laboratory experiments on populations are not realistic because of artificially high densities.

Differences in basic aggressiveness of the strain or species must be considered in a comparison of relative population densities. For example, albino mice are extremely docile in contrast to some strains maintained in the laboratory (57). *Peromyscus maniculatus*

bairdii also is nonaggressive—even more so than albino *Mus* (37). Recently Southwick has demonstrated the importance of behavioral factors in eliciting an adrenocortical response in *P. leucopus* by showing that grouped animals had no adrenal response when they were "compatible" but did if they were "incompatible" (58). Thus, to compare absolute densities in the laboratory with those of feral populations is not a justifiable procedure.

It is often said that fighting per se, or injury from fighting, produces the endocrine changes that occur with change in rank and number (59). However, data from a large number of populations of mice demonstrate that the endocrine responses to grouping are identical whether or not there is fighting or injury (6). Fighting is another symptom of social competition. It seems clear that the basic stimulus to the endocrine changes are sociopsychological, or "emotional," and not physical in nature. Pearson has made the interesting observation that in freely growing populations a few excessively submissive, thoroughly beaten-up, badly scarred mice have low plasma concentrations of corticosterone (41). This result agrees with our observations that mice that sink to this level are so abjectly submissive that the more dominant animals no longer pay any attention to them. Because they no longer interact with other members of the population, they cease to be part of it. Also, their continuing existence is probably the result of an artificial situation created by confinement, as in natural populations such animals would doubtless have been forced to move continually; hence most of them would have become mortality statistics. Such submissive animals have been observed and repeatedly captured in a population of woodchucks.

Criticisms of Theory

The criticism has been made, as stated earlier, that results from studies on populations in the laboratory cannot be extrapolated to natural populations because of the excessive densities in the laboratory (11, 60–62). The work cited above (56) showed that mice exposed to crowding for very short periods each day had an increase in adrenal function. In addition, data on density for most natural populations are often misleading, as many

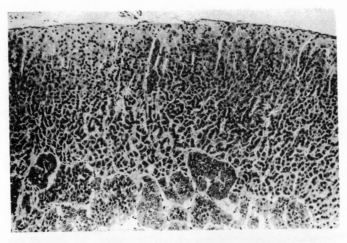

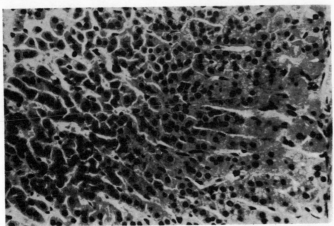

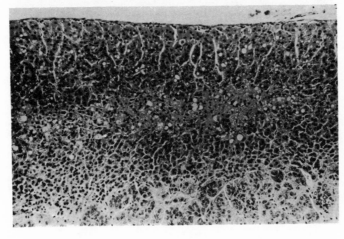

species of rodents, especially rats, voles, and mice, often occur in local "colonies" that may be rather crowded even though areas around them may be very sparsely inhabited. Localized groups of rats in natural populations apparently behave like independent populations, with different degrees of crowding, until the numbers and movement increase sufficiently to fill the general area, at which time the colonies lose their identity and become part of a larger population (6). Furthermore, comparable endocrine changes have been observed in natural populations of a number of other species—voles, rats, Japanese deer (sika), woodchucks, and rabbits (30, 53, 63–65). Increased social strife produced by the introduction of aliens into a population of rats will induce movements, increase mortality, and, if the original population was high, cause a striking decline from original densities (18, 66). Conversely, artificial reduction of a population or alteration of its social structure in a way that

Fig. 1 (top left). Adrenal of an immature 15-gram male *Microtus pennsylvanicus*, trapped 15 June, illustrating zonation of the cortex. The cortical zone next to the medulla is composed of compact, lipid-free cells with moderately hyperchromatic nuclei. Between this zone and the typical fasciculata is a zone of small cells containing some lipid (its distinctiveness is more clearly apparent in the original sections than in black and white photomicrographs). These two zones appear to differ morphologically from the X-zone of *Mus*, although both involute with attainment of sexual maturity. Spermatogenesis had nowhere advanced beyond primary spermatocytes in the testes of this vole. The seminal vesicles and coagulating glands together weighed 2.3 milligrams. (Five-micron section stained with hematoxylin and eosin; × 143)

Fig. 2 (center left). Same adrenal as in Fig. 1 at higher magnification, showing cellular details more clearly. Outer cortex at the right. (× 358)

Fig. 3 (bottom left). Adrenal of a more mature male *Microtus pennsylvanicus* than that of Fig. 1. Two distinct cortical zones of degeneration may be seen, one juxtamedullary and the other midcortical. The midcortical zone results from involution of the central cortical zone shown in Figs. 1 and 2, while the juxtamedullary involution arises from involution of the innermost zone. This involution occurs when spermatogenesis is complete, with sperm in the epididymis, but before the seminal vesicles have attained mature size. The seminal vesicles and coagulating glands together weighed 434 milligrams. (Five-micron section stained with hematoxylin and eosin; × 143) reduces competition will reduce adrenal weight and incidence of disease accordingly (*17, 22, 67*). This reduction has been observed in rats, deer, and woodchucks (*30, 65, 67*).

In some situations no correlation has been shown between adrenocortical function and changes in population, but so far the cases fall into two categories. The first is that where the sample is too small to demonstrate any correlation. For instance, Negus (see *61*, Table 4) studied only 98 animals over a 2-year period, of all ages and both sexes (*61*). A second cause of lack of correlation is inaccuracy of population measurement, primarily because currently available census methods are notoriously poor and confidence limits of the estimates have been disregarded (*61*).

Since changes in adrenal weight occur with reproductive activity, several authors have concluded that adrenal weight cannot be used as an index of adrenocortical function in the study of populations (*68, 69*). It was implied in these accounts that these changes in adrenal weight with changes in reproductive status were overlooked when conclusions concerning population were drawn from changes in adrenal weight in earlier studies of house mice or other species (*62, 68, 70, 71*). Our published data show that these factors were taken into consideration in our studies (*64, 72*). On the other hand, a number of workers may have failed to find a correlation between population status and adrenal weight because changes with sexual function were disregarded. It is well known that adrenal weight increases during pregnancy or with estrogen

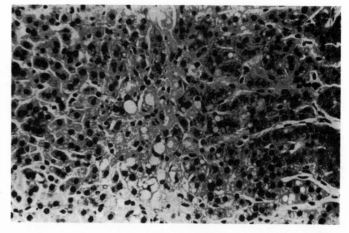

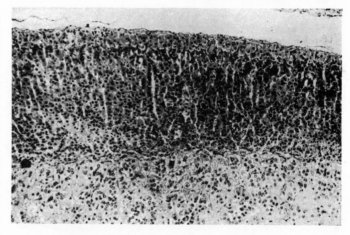

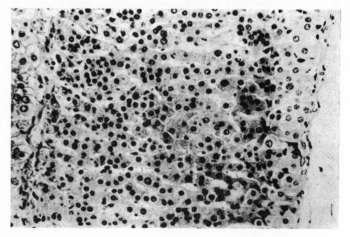

Fig. 4 (top right). Same adrenal as in Fig. 3, showing more clearly the unique mid-cortical zone of degeneration which closely resembles the fatty type of degeneration of the X-zone often seen in female *Mus*. Outer cortex at the right. (× 358)

Fig. 5 (center right). Adrenal of a fully mature male *Microtus pennsylvanicus* captured on 15 June, typical of a mature adrenal cortex in males of this species, having a conspicuous zona glomerulosa and zona fasciculata and a central, rather thin zona reticularis. The seminal vesicles and coagulating glands together weighed 1479 milligrams. (Five-micron section, stained with hematoxylin and eosin; × 143)

Fig. 6 (bottom right). Same adrenal as in Fig. 5 at higher magnification, showing more clearly the details of zonation of the mature cortex of *Microtus pennsylvanicus*. Outer cortex at the right. (× 358)

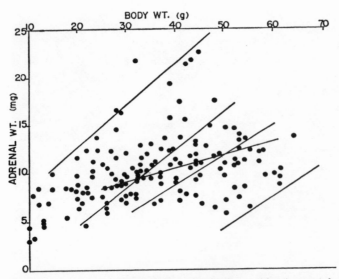

Fig. 7. A plot of adrenal weights (in milligrams) against body weights (in grams) for male *Microtus pennsylvanicus*. The lines were not fitted but were drawn in approximately as follows. The two parallel lines at upper left enclose points for immature animals whose adrenals showed typical immature zonation, as shown in Figs. 1 and 2. The two parallel lines at lower right enclose points for fully mature animals resembling those of Figs. 5 and 6. The points between (and inevitably to some extent some points enclosed by the parallel lines) are for animals in the process of maturing. The single line corresponds roughly to the mean adrenal weights of maturing animals; however, this is not a fitted line and only suggests the direction of transition. It was found impossible to fit regressions of adrenal weight relative to body weight (or body length) for these data in defining starting or end points of zonal involution.

stimulation in some species, but it is not always remembered that changes in adrenal weight due to population changes can be superimposed on these increases (*19, 64, 65, 70*). Changes in adrenal weight with change in reproductive status fall into two categories: (i) change in weight when there is immature zonation which later disappears, and (ii) change in weight in fully mature animals which is associated with reproductive activity. Obviously, only changes in adrenal weight or function in animals in the same reproductive condition can be properly compared or correlated with changes in population. Chitty and Clarke (*71*) have claimed that a marked increase in the size of the adrenal in female voles (*Microtus agrestis*) is restricted to pregnant animals. However, McKeever reported similar increases in nonpregnant, nulliparous, but sexually mature, females of *M. montanus* (*69*). Our results with *M. pennsylvanicus* are similar, although mature nonpregnant, nulliparous females are scarce, as one would expect. It appears, at least in the North

American voles, that the striking increase in the size of the adrenal is associated with maturation and estrogen secretion and is not limited to pregnancy. However, we have long been aware that adrenal size increases during pregnancy in many species and that this must be considered in using adrenal weights as indices of adrenal function. In other cases, a change in adrenal weight is related to seasonal behavioral changes (*64*), as originally suggested for muskrats (*73*) and later for *Microtus* (*70*).

Further criticism of the theory that behavioral-endocrine mechanisms are operative in the control of population growth is based on recent reports of a lack of correlation between adrenal weight and changes in population size, from which it has been concluded that endocrine mechanisms do not affect population growth (*61, 68, 69*). In another report it was stated that there is no evidence of a "stress mechanism" in a collapse of a lemming population, as no related changes in adrenal weight were found (*74*). First, it must be noted that failure to demonstrate

a correlation, without consideration of pertinent relationships, is not disproof of a correlation. Second, these criticisms have been based on observed adrenal weights in voles or rice rats (*Oryzomys*), primarily in the former, without critical evaluation and validation, microscopic or otherwise, of the weight changes. While such conclusions may eventually prove correct in some instances, the inappropriate use, in the studies reported, of adrenal weight as an index of adrenocortical function in these rodents invalidates the conclusions. A basic error in the studies was failure to recognize that many rodents have zones in the adrenal cortex which in many ways resemble the X-zone in house mice, and that these zones are without known function. The use, as indices of function, of the weights of adrenals which include these zones is not appropriate. Delost has published numerous reports on the existence of an "X-zone" in the adrenals of voles (*Clethrionomys, Pitymys,* and *Microtus*) which involutes at maturity in males and regenerates during sexual quiescence (see *6*). Chitty and Clarke (*71*) have further explored this problem in *M. agrestis*. On morphological grounds and because we have observed two immature zones in male *M. pennsylvanicus*, we do not entirely agree with Delost that these should be called X-zones, but the basic observation that in immature voles there are zones which later involute, spontaneously or on administration of testosterone, remains valid. Male *M. pennsylvanicus* appears to have two distinct zones which involute at maturity (Figs. 1–6), neither one of which appears to be entirely comparable morphologically to the X-zone of house mice. The male *Pitymys, Synaptomys,* and *Clethrionomys* that we have examined, and possibly other voles, have similar zonation, although the probability of differences between species or genera must be kept in mind. These zones persist with inhibition of maturation, so that in such voles adrenal weight is relatively much greater in immature than in mature males (Fig. 7). The converse is true for the adrenals of female voles (Figs. 8–10), which undergo a striking hypertrophy at maturity, probably as an exaggerated effect of estrogens, as described for many species, although this has not been tested as yet (*74a*). McKeever (*69*) has demonstrated changes in adrenal weight with age and maturation in

Microtus, illustrating changes occurring with maturation, but he failed to recognize the zonal changes and probably typical, but enhanced, responses to estrogen, and so arrived at unjustified conclusions. In addition, the picture is confounded by the fact that all gradations between the immature and the fully mature condition of the adrenals occur, as shown in Figs. 8 to 11.

Further complicating the picture is the fact that most small mammals born in the fall, and probably even those born at the end of the spring and in the early summer breeding season in a period of relatively high population density, overwinter in the im-

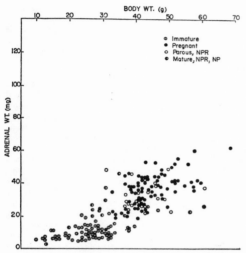

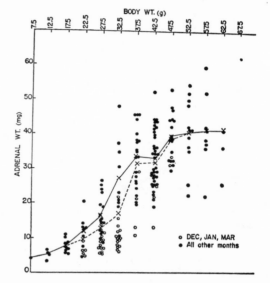

Fig. 8 (top left). A plot of adrenal weights (in milligrams) against body weights (in grams) for female *Microtus pennsylvanicus* captured at all seasons of the year. Reproductive status is indicated as shown (NPR, nonpregnant; NP, nulliparous). It may be seen that adrenal weight increases sharply with sexual maturation whether or not the animal is pregnant or parous, although most were pregnant. As may be seen in Fig. 9, most of the immature animals were captured in the late fall and early winter and mainly represent suppressed maturation in young of the preceding breeding season.

Fig. 9 (top right). Weights of adrenals from the animals of Fig. 8 plotted against body weights, with season of capture indicated. A large number of the adrenal weights for immature females are for animals captured between December and March, as indicated in Fig. 8. (Solid line) Mean adrenal weight for animals captured in any month other than December, January, and March; (dotted line) mean adrenal weight for all animals. Figures 8 and 9 show that only the weights of adrenals from mature animals can properly be used for comparing changes in weight with changes in population; in the main, this means that only the weights of adrenals of animals weighing more than 35 grams can be used, but in the winter one finds a few immature females even in this weight range. For this reason the values for mean adrenal weight that we previously published (*18*) for female *Microtus montanus* captured in winter are probably too low, although we used only weights of the adrenals of animals weighing 37.5 grams or more in the study, thus largely, but not entirely, avoiding this pitfall.

Fig. 10 (right). Plot of adrenal weights against body weights for female *Microtus pennsylvanicus* and *M. montanus*. Regression curves were fitted to points for fully mature females (upper curve) and to points for immature females (lower curve).

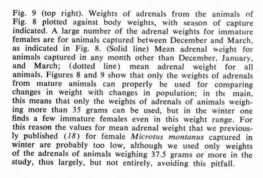

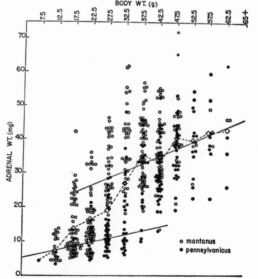

Weights of adrenals from maturing females form a continuum between these end stages. This plot again illustrates the problems one encounters in using adrenal weight of voles to assess adrenocortical function in relation to population changes unless one uses only fully mature animals. It appears from this diagram that female *M. montanus* mature somewhat earlier than female *M. pennsylvanicus*, but a number of other factors, including differences in populations, confound the data and make it impossible to draw a definite conclusion.

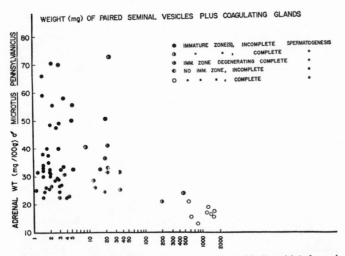

Fig. 11. Plot of adrenal weight (in milligrams per 100 g of body weight) for male *Microtus pennsylvanicus* against the logarithms of values for combined weights (in milligrams) of seminal vesicles and coagulating glands. The state of sexual maturity is indicated in the key. This plot depicts the difficulties encountered in using adrenal weight to assess adrenocortical function in male microtines because of the presence of immature cortical zones.

mature condition (*17, 19, 75, 76*), so that a persistence of immature zonation in males and, in females, the small size of the adrenals unstimulated by estrogen (or whatever factors stimulate the hypertrophy associated with maturation) would be expected (Figs. 8 and 9). The basic error in the conclusions of several investigators was the assumption that adrenal weight is always synonymous with cortical function. In addition, nothing is yet known about the steroids secreted by these species or the possible relation of steroid secretory patterns to changes in zonation. Obviously, if adrenal weight is to be used as an index of adrenocortical function in these species, comparisons can be made only between animals in the same state of reproductive function and with the same degree of involution of immature adrenal zones. Thus, for practical purposes, comparisons are limited to fully mature, sexually active animals. This means, in our experience, that in *Microtus (pennsylvanicus* or *montanus*) one usually is limited to the use of animals weighing 35 to 40 grams or more and having uninhibited reproductive function. The relationship between adrenal weight and reproductive function in terms of the weight of seminal vesicles in *M. pennsylvanicus* is shown in Fig. 11. These data

illustrate problems one encounters in attempting to make comparisons of adrenal weight for other than fully mature, sexually active males (Figs. 7 and 11).

Another cause of failure to demonstrate a correlation between adrenal weight and population density is failure to consider the social rank of individuals in the samples examined. Since high-ranking individuals generally do not have enlarged adrenals, comparisons of high-ranking individuals at low and high population densities will reveal no changes in adrenal weight or function. McKeever may have made this error when he divided animals into sexually nonactive and active categories (*69*). At high population densities maturation of subordinate animals would be delayed, and these animals would be called nonactive. McKeever's Table 2 (*69*) may simply show that high-ranking animals have similar adrenal weights at low and high population densities, and that low-ranking animals do also. However, comparisons between sexually inactive animals in this case are very probably invalid because of the persistence of immature zonation. Another example of failure to consider social rank is Rudd and Mullen's consideration of only the survivors from groups of pocket gophers (*77*).

In most instances, failure to find a correlation between adrenal weight and population density is due to inclusion of immature animals in samples in progressively larger numbers with seasonal progression. Seasonal or maturational changes in the adrenals do not invalidate the use of adrenal weights as indicators of adrenocortical function if the weights are used critically, but comparisons must be made between comparable animals at comparable times. For example, it has been possible to show a significant decrease in the size of adrenals of woodchucks with alteration of social structure and diminution of competition during the time of rapid increase in adrenal weight by making the appropriate adjustments (*64, 65*); however, there is no complicating zonation in this mammal.

So far we have discussed primarily the restriction of increases of populations due to the effects of high densities. In addition, this explanation should provide some understanding of the increased mortality of young that occurs in subsequent generations. One of the striking aspects of both a natural and a confined population is the observation that young animals have a higher mortality than adults coincident with high population and in, in natural populations, also after population density has fallen to relatively low levels (*7*). Chitty (*7*) explained these losses of young in two ways: losses in the year of peak population he attributed to attacks by adults, and losses in the following spring he attributed to some unknown congenital condition acquired *in utero*. Evidence consistent with this view was presented by Godfrey (*78*). Body weights that were low as compared with those in the peak year have been reported in these studies (*79*), and we have observed a similar nonoccurrence of large animals following a peak in population (*19*).

Chitty (*79, 80*) invoked genetic selection to explain how later generations might be influenced by conditions existing before they were born. Therefore, he postulates an effect of social behavior different from that proposed by us (*17, 19*). Thus, he and his colleagues—for example, Krebs (*74*) and H. Chitty (*70*)—differ from us on the *kind* of physiological and behavioral changes they postulate, but not on the question of whether behavioral changes play an essential part in the regulation of numbers. We find

Chitty's explanation for the events in natural populations difficult to accept because it requires genetic selection acting rapidly for a year or two with a subsequent return to, or close to, the original genetic status. In contrast, we believe there is ample evidence of endocrine mechanisms which have the prolonged effects necessary to account for the increased mortality of young during, and for a considerable time after, episodes of maximum density. We have mentioned some of these effects, but we should also call attention to the life-long effects on reproductive function of single injections of androgens into mice or rats less than 10 days old (see *81*); the behavioral effects produced *in utero* reported by Keeley (*26*); the effects of the injection of corticosteroids or other hormones during pregnancy on later behavior (*82*); and the effects of corticosteroids on brain development (*27*). Undernutrition during nursing also has profound and permanent effects on offspring (*83*), which are consistent with the observed reduced growth at high population levels. Actually neither the endocrine nor the genetic selection explanations have been adequately tested, but there appears to be more evidence in support of the former. However, selection must play a long-range role, if not a short-term one (*19*). Whatever the mechanisms accounting for the observed increased mortality of young during and following episodes of high density, it seems evident that the altered status, which we believe to be physiological, will increase susceptibility to adverse environmental conditions, and that behavioral factors are of primary importance in the genesis of the altered status. It is clear that, in a general way, we arrive at the same ultimate conclusions as Chitty, but we place more emphasis on decreased productivity than on increased mortality, although one would anticipate various combinations of these two factors to occur in different populations and under different circumstances. One would expect altered reproductive function to be of greater importance in mammals with a high reproductive rate than in those with a much lower reproductive rate, such as woodchucks. Woodchucks exhibit decreased reproductive function with increased social pressure, brought about by an increased failure to mature in their first year, and increased intrauterine mortality (*84, 85*), but this is less important in regulating their population

than movement of young or mortality (*17, 84*). Of interest in this regard is the finding that young woodchucks become more seriously affected by renal disease at high population densities, and that this probably results in appreciable mortality (*17*).

These comments lead to consideration of another recent discovery of direct pertinence to the question of the greater effects of high population density on young than on adult mice. First, we repeat that the young in general are subordinate animals and thus, other things being equal, more seriously affected by crowding. However, immature house mice secrete appreciable quantities of 17-hydroxycorticoids, especially hydrocortisone, and, when they are grouped, not only does the total adrenal corticosteroid production increase but the hydrocortisone-corticosterone ratio increases as well (*38, 86*). With sexual maturation of male mice, the ability to produce hydrocortisone is greatly reduced. Also, if there is delayed maturation accompanying increase in numbers, the secretion of appreciable amounts of hydrocortisone is prolonged. The importance of this finding is that hydrocortisone is a much more potent glucocorticoid than corticosterone, which is the principal compound secreted by adult mice, adult rats, and probably a number of other adult rodents (see *6*). Therefore, similar degrees of stimulation of the adrenals of immature and adult mice should result in more profound effects in the immature animals even if there were no difference in social rank. This difference has been observed biologically in the much greater degree of thymic involution and growth suppression produced in immature mice either by ACTH or by grouping than can be produced in adults by similar treatment or by the injection of relatively high amounts of corticosterone (*18, 19, 87, 88*). Similarly, gonadotrophin secretion is suppressed by much smaller doses of steroids in immature than in mature mice and rats (*89*), so that inhibition of maturation of the young in experimental and natural populations may be explained on this basis.

In attempting to explain the mechanisms of the progressive inhibition of reproductive function with increasing population density we postulated that increased secretion of adrenal androgens in response to increased secretion of ACTH might be sufficient to inhibit gonadotrophin secretion, especially in immature mice, and thus explain the

observed declines in reproductive function (*6, 90*). Indeed, the injection of adrenal androgens at nonvirilizing physiological concentrations suppresses gonadotrophin secretion and inhibits normal maturation in immature female mice (*91*). Injection of ACTH in intact immature mice also totally inhibits normal maturation (*87*). Surprisingly, ACTH has a similar effect in adrenalectomized mice maintained on hydrocortisone (*88, 92*); thus it appears that ACTH has a direct suppressive effect on reproductive function and therefore on maturation (the site of action is as yet unknown) of immature female mice. Consequently there are at least two distinct mechanisms capable of inhibiting maturation, whose relative importance in the intact animal is unknown. There also remains the distinct possibility that the central nervous system, in response to emotional stimuli, may inhibit gonadotrophin secretion even more directly. In any event, there is ample explanation, including both behavioral and physiological mechanisms, for the differences in the effects of high population levels or increased competition on reproduction, growth, and mortality of the young in contrast to adult animals.

Conclusions

The experimental results suggest that there are mechanisms for the regulation of many populations of mammals within the limits imposed by the environment, including food. We subscribe to the view that density-dependent mechanisms have evolved in many forms, and probably in most mammals (*11–13, 19, 93*). Thus, mammals avoid the hazard of destroying their environment, and thus the hazard of their own extinction. We believe that the evidence, as summarized here, supports the existence of endocrine feedback mechanisms which can regulate and limit population growth in response to increases in overall "social pressure," and which in turn are a function of increased numbers and aggressive behavior. Neither increased numbers nor increased aggressiveness can operate wholly independently. Furthermore, we believe that environmental factors in most instances probably act through these mechanisms by increasing competition. A good example of this would be the situation described by Errington for muskrats (*94*). A drought causes the animals to concentrate in areas of remaining water, with the result that competition and social strife are greatly increased. It follows that increased strife, with increased movement, will also increase losses through predation, another way of increasing mortality of subordinate animals (22, 47, 94).

Finally, we might paraphrase Milne's statements (12) regarding density-dependent regulation of population growth as follows: Environmental factors (food, predation, disease, physical factors) may limit population growth, but if they do not, as appears more often than not to be the case in mammals, the physiologic mechanisms outlined above will. And finally, the action of these mechanisms is always proportional to changes that depend on changes in population density, behavior, or both. The fact that a sigmoid growth form requires the operation of such a "density-dependent damping factor" supports this conclusion, whereas external limiting factors, unless they operate through the density-dependent damping mechanism, will characteristically truncate a growth curve. Truncation is seldom seen, but the best example of such a curve for mammals that we have seen is that given by Strecker and Emlen (95).

In summary, we believe that the behavioral-endocrine feedback system is important in the regulation of populations of rodents, lagomorphs, deer, and possibly other mammals. One would expect other factors to occasionally limit population growth, but, when these fail to do so, the feedback mechanism acts as a safety device, preventing utter destruction of the environment and consequent extinction. Because of time-lag effects, this feedback system should not be expected to work perfectly in every situation.

References

1. E. T. Seton, *The Arctic Prairies* (Scribner, New York, 1911).
2. J. R. Dymond, *Trans. Roy. Soc. Can. Sect. 5* 41, 1 (1947).
3. P. H. Leslie and R. M. Ransom, *J. Animal Ecol.* 9, 27 (1940).
4. C. H. D. Clarke, *J. Mammal.* 30, 21 (1949).
5. C. Elton, *Voles, Mice and Lemmings* (Clarendon, Oxford, 1942).
6. J. J. Christian, in *Physiological Mammalogy*, W. V. Mayer and R. G. Van Gelder, Eds. (Academic Press, New York, 1963).
7. D. Chitty, *Trans. Roy. Soc. London* B236, 505 (1952).
8. D. E. Davis, *Quart. Rev. Biol.* 28, 373 (1953).
9. P. L. Errington, *Am. Naturalist* 85, 273 (1951).
10. A. J. Nicholson, *Ann. Rev. Entomol.* 3, 107 (1958).
11. D. Chitty, *Can. J. Zool.* 38, 99 (1960).
12. A. Milne, *J. Theoret. Biol.* 3, 19 (1962).
13. V. C. Wynne-Edwards, *Ibis* 101, 436 (1959).
14. H. M. Bruce, *J. Reprod. Fertil.* 1, 96 (1960).
15. C. R. Terman, *Ecol. Bull.* 44, 123 (1964).
16. J. J. Christian, *J. Mammal.* 31, 247 (1950).

17. ——, *Military Med.* 128, 571 (1963).
18. ——, *Proc. Columbia Univ. Symp. Comp. Endocrinol.*, A. Gorbman, Ed. (Wiley, New York, 1959), p. 31.
19. ——, *Proc. Natl. Acad. Sci. U.S.* 47, 428 (1961).
20. I. C. Jones, *The Adrenal Cortex* (Cambridge Univ. Press, Cambridge, 1957).
21. P. V. Rogers and C. P. Richter, *Endocrinology* 42, 46 (1948).
22. R. Myktowycz, *Australia Commonwealth Sci. Ind. Res. Organ. Wildlife Res.* 6, 142 (1961).
23. K. Myers and W. E. Poole, *Australian J. Zool.* 10, 225 (1962).
24. R. L. Helmreich, *Science* 132, 417 (1960).
25. J. J. Christian and C. D. LeMunyan, *Endocrinology* 63, 517 (1958).
26. K. Keeley, *Science* 135, 44 (1962).
27. E. Howard, *Federation Proc.* 22, 270 (abstr.) (1963).
28. M. R. A. Chance, *Nature* 177, 228 (1956).
29. L. L. Bernardis and F. R. Skelton, *Proc. Soc. Exptl. Biol. Med.* 113, 952 (1963).
30. J. J. Christian, V. Flyger, D. E. Davis, *Chesapeake Sci.* 1, 79 (1960).
31. J. A. Gunn and M. R. Gurd, *J. Physiol. London* 97, 453 (1940); M. R. A. Chance, *J. Pharmacol. Exptl. Therap.* 87, 214 (1946); ——, *ibid.* 89, 289 (1947); E. A. Swinyard, L. D. Clark, J. T. Miyahara, H. H. Wolf, *ibid.* 132, 97 (1961); G. B. Fink and R. E. Larson, *ibid.* 137, 361 (1962); R. Ader, A. Kreutner, Jr., H. L. Jacobs, *Psychosomat. Med.* 25, 60 (1963).
32. E. A. Swinyard, N. Radhakrishnan, L. S. Goodman, *J. Pharmacol. Exptl. Therap.* 138, 337 (1962); B. Weiss, V. G. Laties, F. L. Blanton, *ibid.* 132, 366 (1961).
33. J. T. Marsh and A. F. Rasmussen, Jr., *Proc. Soc. Exptl. Biol. Med.* 104, 180 (1960).
34. D. E. Davis and J. J. Christian, *ibid.* 94, 728 (1957).
35. J. G. Vandenbergh, *Animal Behavior* 8, 13 (1960).
36. S. A. Barnett, *Nature* 175, 126 (1955); K. Eik-Nes, *Record Progr. Hormone Res.* 15, 380 (1959).
37. F. H. Bronson and B. E. Eleftheriou, *Physiol. Zool.* 36, 161 (1963).
38. H. H. Varon, J. C. Touchstone, J. J. Christian, *Endocrinology*, in press.
39. W. Eechaute, G. Demeester, E. LaCroix, I. Leusen, *Arch. Intern. Pharmacodyn.* 136, 161 (1962).
40. A. M. Barrett and M. A. Stockham, *J. Endocrinol.* 26, 97 (1963).
41. P. G. Pearson, *Bull. Ecol. Soc. Am.* 43, 134 (abstr.) (1962).
42. J. R. Clarke, *J. Endocrinol.* 9, 114 (1953).
43. J. Dawson, *Nature* 178, 1183 (1956).
44. J. P. Rapp and J. J. Christian, *Proc. Soc. Exptl. Biol. Med.* 114, 26 (1963).
45. R. A. Huseby, F. C. Reed, T. E. Smith, *J. Appl. Physiol.* 14, 31 (1959); K. A. Khaleque, M. G. Muazzam, R. I. Choadhury, *J. Trop. Med. Hyg.* 64, 277 (1961); G. G. Slater, R. F. Doctor, E. G. Kollar, paper presented at the 44th meeting of the Endocrine Society (1962).
46. J. J. Christian, *Endocrinology* 65, 189 (1959).
47. R. M. Lockley, *J. Animal Ecol.* 30, 385 (1961).
48. C. Kabat, N. E. Collias, R. C. Guettinger, *Wis. Tech. Wildlife Bull. No. 7* (1953).
49. L. C. McEwan, C. E. French, N. D. Magruder, R. W. Swift, R. H. Ingram, *Trans. North Am. Wildlife Conf.* 22, 119 (1957); H. Silver and N. F. Colovos, *Proc. Northeast. Wildlife Conf., Portland, Me.* (1963).
50. W. Grodzinski, *Proc. Intern. Congr. Zool., 16th* (1963), vol. 1, p. 257.
51. O. Kalela, *Ann. Acad. Sci. Fennicae* A-IV, No. 34 (1957).
52. A. Gorecki and Z. Gebcaynska, *Acta Theriol.* 6, 275 (1962).
53. K. Curry-Lindahl, *J. Mammal.* 43, 171 (1962).
54. J. A. Lloyd and J. J. Christian, *Proc. Intern. Conf. Wildlife Distr., 1st* (1963).
55. B. Welch, *Proc. Intern. Congr. Zool., 16th* (1963), vol. 1, p. 269.
56. F. H. Bronson and B. E. Eleftheriou, *Gen. Comp. Endocrinol.* 4, 9 (1964).
57. J. J. Christian, *Am. J. Physiol.* 182, 292 (1955).
58. C. H. Southwick, *Science* 143, 55 (1964).
59. —— and V. P. Bland, *Am. J. Physiol.* 197, 111 (1959).
60. P. Crowcroft and F. P. Rowe, *Proc. Roy. Zool. Soc. London* 131, 357 (1958).
61. N. C. Negus, E. Gould, R. I. Chipman, *Tulane Studies Zool.* 8, 95 (1961).

62. R. Tanaka, *Bull. Kochi Women's Univ.* 10, 7 (1962).
63. B. L. Welch, *Proc. Natl. Deer Distr. Symp., 1st* (Univ. of Georgia Press, Athens, 1962); K. Wodzicki and H. S. Roberts, *New Zealand J. Sci.* 3, 103 (1960); E. F. Patric, *J. Mammal.* 43, 200 (1962).
64. J. J. Christian, *Endocrinology* 71, 431 (1962).
65. J. A. Lloyd, J. J. Christian, D. E. Davis, F. H. Bronson, *Gen. Comp. Endocrinol.* 4, 271 (1964).
66. D. E. Davis, *Trans. North Am. Wildlife Conf., 14th* (1949), p. 225.
67. J. J. Christian and D. E. Davis, *Trans. North Am. Wildlife Conf., 20th* (1955), p. 177.
68. D. A. Mullen, *J. Mammal.* 41, 129 (1960).
69. S. McKeever, *Anat. Record* 135, 1 (1959).
70. H. Chitty, *J. Endocrinol.* 22, 387 (1961).
71. —— and J. R. Clarke, *Can. J. Zool.* 41, 1025 (1963).
72. J. J. Christian, *Ecology* 37, 258 (1956).
73. J. R. Beer and R. K. Meyer, *J. Mammal.* 32, 173 (1951).
74. C. J. Krebs, *Science* 140, 674 (1963).
74a. Note added in proof: Results from a recent study of the relationships between sexual maturity, the adrenal glands, and population density in female *M. pennsylvanicus* from a natural population suggest that *female* voles of this species have no X-zone as it is defined for house mice (20). Apparently it is a hypertrophic reticularis and inner fasciculata [resembling the adrenals of woodchucks in this respect (54, 64)] which have been labeled an X-zone. There is no involution at pregnancy. The cells contain lipids, and the hyperplasia occurs with maturation, as pointed out by Chitty and Clarke (71). Adrenal weight relative to body weight is a discontinuous function in these animals as a result of the sudden increase at maturation. Therefore, regressions of adrenal weight relative to body weight or body length are invalid if the data come from both immature and mature females. When these facts are taken into account it is clear that there is no change in adrenal weight relative to body weight with reproductive status in mature females, and that there is a remarkable parallelism between mean adrenal weight of mature females and population size.
75. A. van Wijngaarden, *Verslag Landbouwk. Onderzoek No. 66.22* (1960), pp. 1-68.
76. D. A. Spencer "The Oregon Meadow Mouse Irruption of 1957–58," *Fed. Coop. Expt. Serv., Corvallis, Publ.* (1959), p. 15; K. A. Adamczewska, *Acta Theriol.* 5, 1 (1961); W. Sheppe, *J. Mammal.* 44, 180 (1963); D. R. Breakey, *ibid.*, p. 153.
77. R. L. Rudd and D. A. Mullen, *J. Mammal.* 44, 451 (1963).
78. G. R. Godfrey, *ibid.* 36, 209 (1955).
79. D. Chitty, *Cold Spring Harbor Symp. Quant. Biol.* 22, 277 (1958).
80. H. Chitty and D. Chitty, *Symp. Theriol., Prague* (Czechoslovak Academy of Science, Prague, 1962), p. 77.
81. R. A. Gorski and C. A. Barraclough, *Endocrinology* 73, 210 (1963).
82. M. W. Lieberman, *Science* 141, 824 (1963).
83. E. M. Widdowson and G. C. Kennedy, *Proc. Roy. Soc. London* B156, 96 (1962); E. M. Widdowson and R. A. McCance, *ibid.* B158, 329 (1963).
84. D. E. Davis, *J. Wildlife Management* 26, 144 (1962).
85. R. L. Snyder, *Ecology* 43, 506 (1962).
86. H. H. Varon, J. C. Touchstone, J. J. Christian, *Federation Proc.* 22, 164 (abstr.) (1963).
87. J. J. Christian, *Endocrinology*, 74, 669 (1964).
88. ——, *ibid.* 75, 653 (1964).
89. W. W. Byrnes and R. K. Meyer, *ibid.* 48, 133 (1951); W. W. Byrnes and E. G. Shipley, *Proc. Soc. Exptl. Biol. Med.* 74, 308 (1950); D. Ramirez and S. M. McCann, *Endocrinology* 72, 452 (1963).
90. J. J. Christian, *Proc. Soc. Exptl. Biol. Med.* 104, 330 (1960).
91. H. H. Varon and J. J. Christian, *Endocrinology* 72, 210 (1963); G. E. Duckett, H. H. Varon, J. J. Christian, *ibid.*, p. 903.
92. J. J. Christian, *Federation Proc.* 22, 507 (abstr.) (1963).
93. F. A. Pitelka, *Cold Spring Harbor Symp. Quant. Biol.* 22, 237 (1958).
94. P. L. Errington, *Agr. Expt. Sta. Iowa State Coll., Ames, Res. Bull.* 320 (1943).
95. R. L. Strecker and J. T. Emlen, *Ecology* 35, 249 (1953).

24

Reprinted from pp. 136–170 of *Natural Regulation of Animal Populations*,
I. A. McLaren, ed., Lieber–Atherton Inc., 1971, 195 pp.

*The Natural Selection of
Self-Regulatory Behavior
in Animal Populations*

DENNIS CHITTY

The object of this paper is to discuss ways of testing the hypothesis that all species of animals have a form of behavior that can prevent unlimited increase in population density (Chitty, 1960, 1964, 1965). "Behavior" is taken to include the numerous manifestations of hostility discussed by Tinbergen (1957), and the first assumption is that all species have some form of dispersion mechanism, or method of spacing themselves out by avoiding, threatening, or otherwise influencing certain other members of the same species. The pattern of dispersion is assumed to depend partly on the properties of the individuals (genotype, age, experience, hormone balance, etc.), and partly on the properties of their environment (weather; amount, kind, and distribution of food and cover; number and kind of other animals present, etc.). The second assumption is that this behavior persists only because it has survival value for the individual and is constantly being selected for.

While assuming that this behavior occurs in all *species*, the hypothesis does not imply that all *populations* are thereby self-regulated: merely that within any species one can expect to find a class of population whose rate of increase is slowed down and finally stopped because of the way its members interact with one another. The hypothesis also recognizes that this supposed self-regulatory mechanism is not always effective in preventing populations from reaching outbreak proportions such as those sometimes observed in rodents and defoliating insects; the problem is to explain why such outbreaks do not occur more often. Thus no claim is made that the mechanism is either necessary to prevent the increase of all populations, or sufficient to prevent others from depleting their food supply; we cannot, in fact, make any statements that can be tested on all populations of all species. Yet a *sine qua non* for any scientific hypothesis is that it be stated in a way that can be tested, which means that some form of generalization is required. Testing consists of trying to falsify this generalization, since evidence in favor of a hypothesis is generally useless except when it results from the failure of such attempts (Cohen and Nagel, 1934; Medawar, 1957; Popper, 1959, 1963; Platt, 1964).

Generalizations, then, do not necessarily assert the truth, but become part of a logical device for discovering falsity. The more widely a hypothesis can be tested, the greater the chance of evidence being found that not only contradicts it but explains its failure. Most of the evidence for the present hypothesis comes from tests of this sort carried out on small mammals; but really crucial evidence is lacking, since neither individual behavior nor population genetics has so far received much attention from those working on mammal populations. It is thus fortunate that the assumptions on which the hypothesis depends are completely general; hence, contradictory evidence, regardless of the species from which it is obtained, should enable one to test the present interpretation: it cannot both be true for the relevant populations of small mammals and false for those of other groups. This being so, it is clearly advisable to study those species best suited for an experimental attack on the problem. An attempt to enlist the help of entomologists has already been made (Chitty, 1965); as Klomp (1964) has shown, self-regulation occurs among the insects.

The argument in the following pages is set forth as follows: (a) many small mammal populations have a recognizably distinct form of fluctuation, which is not explained by conventional hypotheses; (b) these fluctuations are consistent with the idea that there are changes with population density in the survival value of certain kinds of behavior; (c) this and all other hypotheses must be tested by methods designed to refute them and thus to avoid mere confirmation of *a priori* ideas; (d) the testing of hypotheses about the more stationary populations is complicated by changes in numbers due to changes in irrelevant variables, and by lack of adequate comparative data between regulated and unregulated populations.

The Phenomenon in Certain Mammal Populations

The present ideas have developed from an attempt to explain the recurrent declines in numbers in populations of the Field Vole, *Microtus agrestis* (Elton, 1931, 1942). Lack of success in finding a solution to this problem is partly due to the difficulties illustrated in Table 1, which is based on an early study (Chitty, 1952). As shown, a decline to scarcity occurred after the second of two winters of abundance on area A, but not after the first. Only 10 per cent instead of 40 per cent of the animals survived this second winter, and they did not grow to full size; yet survival and growth were good at the same time on other areas. Clearly, then, high numbers in autumn and winter are not a sufficient condition for a decline; indeed it can occur among overwintered populations that are relatively sparse (Chitty and Chitty, 1962a). Since Hamilton (1937, 1941) had already observed this pattern of change, I described it as the H type of decline (Chitty, 1955), to distinguish it from the G type (after Godfrey, 1955), which

TABLE 1: *Changes in Numbers and Body Weight of* Microtus Agrestis
(*from Chitty, 1952*)

		1936	1937		1938	
		Sept	May	Sept	May	Sept
Area A						
Approx. no./acre		300	120	300	30	1?
	males		29.06		24.04	
			± 0.42		± 0.48	
			n = 62		n = 53	
Mean body wt (g.) ± s.e.						
	females		24.07		18.42	
			± 0.46		± 0.33	
			n = 44		n = 46	
Other areas						
Abundance		—	—	—	high	high
	males		—		30.45	
			—		± 0.81	
			—		n = 51	
Mean body wt (g.) ± s.e.			—			
	females		—		26.19	
			—		± 0.73	
			—		n = 34	

continues unchecked throughout the breeding season. Krebs (1964b) observed both patterns among lemmings (Figure 1), and has described others in populations of *Microtus californicus* (Krebs, 1966). High rates of loss also occur among relatively sparse populations of Snowshoe Hares (Figure 2). Although there are many differences between populations, yet where enough data are available they suggest that a common class of events is involved. Not only are these declines recurrent phenomena, but they are attended by characteristic changes in the distribution of body weights and survival rates. Thus one advantage of studying these declines is that they are easily recognizable instances of the phenomenon we want to explain. In addition they occur fairly often, are sufficiently pronounced to be relatively unaffected by irrelevant environmental variables, and may occur when other

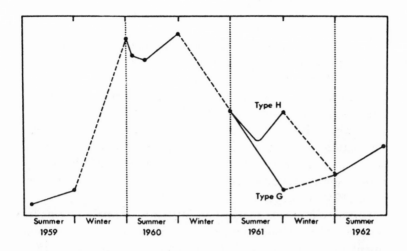

FIGURE 1: Generalized changes in population density of the lemmings *Lemmus trimucronatus* and *Dicrostonyx groenlandicus*; log scale. (From Krebs, 1964b.)

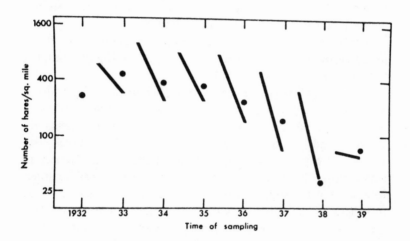

FIGURE 2: Population density of Snowshoe Hares (*Lepus americanus*) in February 1932–9 (•). Sloping lines show the difference between estimates of the numbers born and numbers alive the following February. (From Chitty, 1964, based on Green and Evans, 1940.)

populations are increasing or stationary, thus permitting one to obtain properly comparative data (Table 1; also Figures 4 and 5 discussed below).

Since declines of this type are uncommon elsewhere in the animal kingdom it is fair to ask whether their study has any general significance. The assumption made here is that these particular fluctuations are simply well-marked effects of a general process, whose more familiar effect is to keep numbers fairly stationary, a state sometimes observed even in vole populations (Summerhayes, 1941, Table 5).

One may, of course, make quite different assumptions, provided one tests their implications. Ford (1961) writes: "Considerable attention has in the past been directed to a limited group of special instances in which alternating periods of abundance and rarity coincide over extensive areas. Such cycles are doubtless climatic in origin, and have been associated among other things with the waxing and waning of sun-spots. Yet they have in fact been detected in very few species, a small selection of rodents and animals of value to the fur trade, and they are of negligible importance compared with the automatic fluctuations in numbers to which organisms in general are subject." A slightly updated version is given by Ford (1964).

The present interpretation of this phenomenon differs from that put forward by Chitty (1960). At that time I still supposed that interactions between animals had their main effects on viability, and that declines in the numbers of Field Voles were sufficiently explained by the consequent increase in severity of action of the normal forces of mortality, such as bad weather. In other words I supposed there was a systematic change in the properties of the individuals but not of their environment. This idea was found to be inadequate (Newson and Chitty, 1962), since animals were clearly not in a serious pathological condition just prior to their decline in numbers. It therefore seemed that some environmental component, not previously taken into account, was probably responsible for the changes in survival; and of those not already excluded the most likely was that attributable to the activities of the animals themselves.

Andrewartha and Birch (1954) have written that "The difficulty of thinking of the 'environment of the population' is that it leaves out half the picture." Even this may be an understatement. Early vole studies had shown that the "environment of the population" seemed to be favorable during the declines; and although I had assumed that the "environment of the individual" was unfavorable at the high densities prior to a decline, I had not imagined that this condition would persist at the lower densities during the decline itself, especially during that of type H.

One other point should be made about my 1960 paper, namely that it dealt with the occurrence of qualitative changes and their ecological implications (cf. Wellington, 1960) and not with their explanation in terms of selective advantage. At the time it was difficult to imagine what selective advantage to look for, other than some unknown physiological property that enabled certain individuals to be relatively unaffected by interference (Chitty, 1958). Even so it was difficult to see how selection could act so drastically in such a short number of generations. It is worth emphasizing this difficulty, which has been the main barrier to looking for a solution in terms of population genetics, especially as there is also a great difference in mean adult body weight between a peak population and one that has suffered a severe decline (Chitty, 1952; Chitty and Chitty, 1962b; Newson and Chitty, 1962; Krebs, 1964b, 1966). The animals with the low body weights in Table 1 were either the F_1 progeny of the animals of the previous spring, or the backcrosses between the F_1 females and the parental males. How then were such big qualitative differences to be accounted for?

The most likely solution came from finding that declining populations consisted of a mixture of animals with potentially good and potentially poor growth rates (as revealed by their performance when taken into the laboratory), and from the suggestion that in the field "some unknown aspect of their own behavior may have been at least partly responsible for the poor survival, growth, and reproduction of the voles" (Newson and Chitty, 1962). From this grew the idea that the animals with the inherently poor growth rates were inhibiting the growth and

327

survival of the others. Thus one could now conceive of large population effects, partly phenotypic and partly genotypic, resulting from the behavior of a few individuals. One highly aggressive animal that could deny living space to many others, or inhibit their growth or reproduction, would clearly have a huge selective advantage. Even so it would have been difficult to entertain this idea had there not, since the earlier days of these studies, been a fundamental change in outlook on the part of the population geneticists. Ford (1964) refers to "the recent recognition that advantageous qualities are frequently favored or balanced in particular environments by far greater selection-pressures than had hitherto been envisaged."

A summary of present ideas has already been given by Krebs (1964b); here we shall refer to two points only. First, the loop in Figure 3, indicating a systematically increasing selection pressure, explains how a declining population might come to contain a high proportion of aggressive animals. The effects of interaction would thus be more severe than those in a higher density population of more docile animals. The increasingly severe loss of young Snowshoe Hares (Figure 2) is also consistent with such selection becoming more pronounced after the initial years of high numbers.

Secondly, this selection is shown as having an adverse effect on viability. Tinbergen (1957) has discussed some of the disadvantages to which highly aggressive animals are subject; and the time lost in fighting or guarding the nest and the difficulties between mates are well illustrated in the Gannet, *Sula bassana* (Nelson, 1964, 1965). Clearly, then, selection cannot go too far in this direction, especially if there are associated disadvantages in attributes other than behavior.

If the "environment of the individual" in stationary or declining populations is indeed different from that of the individual in an expanding population, then it is reasonable to suppose that animals best fitted for the one environment are less well fitted for the other. The generally good reproductive performance of expanding populations (Davis, 1951; Chitty and Chitty, 1962b; Newson, 1963; Krebs, 1964b, 1966) is consistent with this idea,

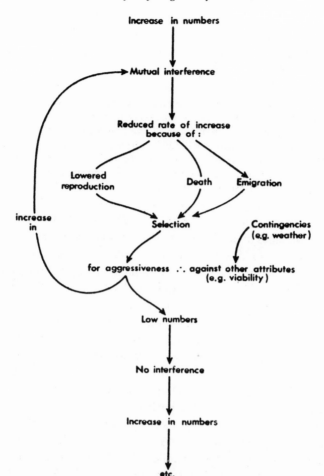

FIGURE 3: Postulated self-regulatory feedback system in small mammal populations. (From Krebs, 1964b.)

but also with many others (Christian and Davis, 1964; Smyth, 1966). Genotypes that are usually eliminated may also survive better during these periods of rapid increase (Ford, 1961), but there is no reason to suppose that they will increase faster than genotypes already adapted to the local hazards.

Despite the evidence against the original belief that declining populations are markedly less viable than normal (Chitty, 1952), there is some theoretical justification for believing that adverse changes in attributes are still worth looking for. Mather (1961) has stated the case as follows:

> selection arising from competition does not necessarily make succeeding generations of individuals of that species more fit to meet circumstances other than those of the competition itself. Selection arising from competition will favor nothing but the ability to survive that particular type of competition. Indeed the selective rise of a special type of competitive power may be accompanied by a reduction in other components of fitness.

The scheme represented by Figure 3 differs from two somewhat similar schemes in at least the following ways: it differs from that of Christian, Lloyd, and Davis (1965), who claim that phenotypic changes alone are adequate to explain why populations decline in numbers; it differs from that of Koskimies (1955), Kalela (1957), Snyder (1961), Brereton (1962), Wynne-Edwards (1962), and others who explain regulation in terms of mechanisms produced by group selection. Differences from other explanations are that (1) population density is assumed to be only one of many environmental variables affecting population trends and not necessarily the best for predicting them, and (2) mortality factors are assumed to be among the local variables about which predictions of rather limited value can be made from one population to another or from one year to the next. But while I attribute no special relevance to the so-called density-dependent mortality factors, and thus agree with Andrewartha and Birch (1954), I differ from them in assuming that feedback mechanisms are commoner than they think likely.

These are fairly basic differences in point of view; but rather than add to discussions such as those of Milne (1962), Bakker (1964), and Lack (1966), I shall review some of the methods that can be employed to decide empirically between rival points of view.

SOME PROBLEMS OF TESTING

Falsifiability

There are many reasons why it is difficult to decide between rival hypotheses. One of them is that if an event is considered in isolation, and explained without implications to other events, there is no way of disputing whatever interpretation the author cares to adopt (Medawar, 1957). Few ecologists state what they will accept as evidence against their point of view, some merely claim that a factor is "important" without describing the empirical procedures by which this belief may be tested. It is equally difficult to see how to test the claim of an author such as Huffaker (1966), who writes that "food may be a limiting and regulating factor for a given population even if utilization of supply at equilibrium is low." Few populations can be excluded from this category. There are also practical difficulties in testing theories that are satisfied by some percentage effect that is much smaller than the effect of the supposedly irrelevant variables.

If our aim is to produce some sort of unity out of the chaos of our field observations we must obviously get rid of superfluous hypotheses and stick to those that explain the greatest variety of instances. It is systematic simplicity of this sort that we should be searching for, rather than simplicity in the sense of familiarity. Pitelka (1958) misunderstands the principle of parsimony when he writes: "it may be a strain on Occam's razor to suggest genetical hypotheses regarding such fluctuations as long as more directly ecological explanations can be invoked and tested." Moreover these simpler explanations were invoked, tested, and rejected at an early stage of the enquiry into the fluctuations in numbers of small mammals (Summerhayes, 1941; Elton, 1942, 1955; Chitty, 1952, 1960).

Cole (1954) has another idea about simplicity: "The hypotheses of random population fluctuations has the further advantage of being probably the simplest possible explanation for population cycles." Simplicity in this sense is obtained by ignoring the associated biological changes and accepting any one of an infinite number of explanations for the purely numerical changes. Cole's interpretation may be justified, however, where population densities depart only slightly and irregularly from their mean (see below).

"When in doubt, appeal to experiment" wrote Eddington, and there can be few subjects to which this advice is more applicable than to population ecology. Varley (1957) and Varley and Gradwell (1963) discuss some of the possibilities and limitations of an experimental approach. We should be clear, however, that an experiment is a test of hypotheses and does not necessarily entail setting up artificial conditions (Medawar, 1957). The essence of an experiment is an active search for evidence against one's hypothesis; and though some implications are best observed in the laboratory, the logical form of a null hypothesis is unaffected by being applied to "mere observations" made under natural conditions (Lloyd, 1960). As a rule an investigator will wish to test a wide variety of predictions under both natural and artificial conditions, for no single type of result can be decisive, even when it goes against the hypothesis (Cohen and Nagel, 1934; Popper, 1959). The reason for this is that in any subject, but particularly in one as complex as population ecology, auxiliary hypotheses are also involved in the testing; thus authors wishing to protect their own point of view can always blame these other conditions for an otherwise contradictory result. The logical chain between hypothesis and observations should therefore be as simple as possible. Predictive equations (Morris, 1963) are not much use if they do not predict; fitting them retrospectively to the data merely tests the ingenuity of the author, not the empirical content of the model. "Irrefutability is not a virtue of a hypothesis (as some people seem to think), but a vice" (Popper, 1963).

Irrelevant Variables

At an early stage in any investigation one's first task will usually be the purely empirical one of eliminating irrelevant variables. Having noticed an association between events we must find out whether or not this association is invariant. At least four possibilities must be recognized: (1) the association was mere co-incidence; (2) the events were concomitant effects of antecedent circumstances; (3) the antecedents were both necessary and sufficient for the phenomenon, or were (4) either necessary or sufficient but not both.

The first line of defense against faulty interpretations is to replicate the observations, varying the circumstances as much as possible. An investigation, if confined in its early stages to a detailed study of a single population, may be less instructive than a more superficial study of several. For preference both approaches should be used. Quite simple observations (e.g., Elton, 1955) often show that possibly relevant factors are not invariably associated with the phenomenon, a finding that saves one from building theoretical structures on unsound empirical foundations.

More troublesome than mere coincidence — for example, that of a hot summer with a rise (or fall) in numbers — are those possibly relevant factors that tend to vary, or necessarily vary, with a sharp rise or fall in numbers. Self-regulatory herbivore populations, as they become more abundant, will almost always have a smaller surplus of food; and as they become less abundant will usually provide a smaller surplus for their predators. More damage to the vegetation and a higher proportion of prey eaten by predators are thus among the expected consequences of this type of fluctuation. From correlations alone one could not decide between self-regulation and the rival interpretations that herbivores increase until they starve (Lack, 1954), or alternatively that they are eaten before they do so (Hairston, Smith, and Slobodkin, 1960). A reduced food supply and a higher ratio of predators to prey will affect the course of events; but the inference that they, or a higher incidence of disease (Elton, 1942; Chitty, 1954), play any necessary part in them cannot be drawn from such data. Practical difficulties should not blind us to the limited explanatory value of studies which are not designed to distinguish between causes and effects.

Let us suppose, however, that we have found many instances in which some factor, process, or supposed cause (C) is present when the phenomenon, event, or supposed effect (E) is present, and which is absent when the phenomenon is absent. We then have the entries CE and $\overline{C}$E in two of the four possible cells of the following 2 × 2 contingency table (Chitty, 1954):

		Supposed Cause (C)	
		Present	Absent
Supposed Effect (E)	Present	CE	$\overline{C}$E
	Absent	C$\overline{E}$	$\overline{C}\overline{E}$

To show that we have correctly identified a cause as both necessary and sufficient we must next produce evidence of failure to find it without its effect (C$\overline{E}$), or the effect without its supposed cause ($\overline{C}$E). If further study shows that C is not necessary for E we may be able to eliminate it from the relevant variables, or we may conclude that it is one of several that are sufficient to produce the effect (CE) without being necessary ($\overline{C}$E). This brings us up against the problem of the "plurality of causes."

To take an example: a change in food supply, predators, competitors, disease, weather, or any one of a long list of physical factors may be sufficient to alter the average level of abundance of a population; but none of them may be necessary. Again, let us suppose that a population declines and that the bare numerical change is the only observation recorded. Clearly anything may have caused the decline, and we can no more carry out a crucial test than we can diagnose a disease merely from knowing that a man's temperature has gone up. Yet doctors do diagnose a patient's troubles; they do so by taking account of his symptoms; and in general the solution to this well-known problem is through getting an accurate definition of the object or effect. A useful discussion is given by von Wright (1957). Suppose we wanted to check certain statements about phosphorus. Then, says von Wright: "The fundamental condition is that we have reliable criteria which enable us to decide when it is with a piece of phosphorus that we are dealing and when not." Cohen and Nagel (1934) put the matter as follows: "When a plurality of causes is asserted for an effect, the *effect* is not analyzed very carefully.

Instances which have significant differences are taken to illustrate the *same effect*. These differences escape the untrained eye, although they are noticed by the expert."

We can now see the peculiar merit of the typical decline in numbers of small mammal populations. This is a reasonably specific effect for which we are justified in trying to find a reasonably specific explanation; we can therefore eliminate hypotheses that fail to provide it. In a later section we shall see that, where populations are normally stationary, we do not have the same reliable criteria to help us when we are trying to distinguish between equally plausible but mutually incompatible hypotheses.

Possibly Relevant Variables

Methods of elimination, while serving to narrow one's choice of alternatives, cannot be guaranteed to work as methods of discovery; and in claiming otherwise Platt (1964) bids us revive our faith in Baconian induction. While failures may spur invention, many of the best ideas owe little to logic; but by common consent we adopt a "didactic dead-pan" style (Watkins, 1964) and conceal the irrational ways in which we find the relevant variables and start getting positive results. The part played by luck, by errors that turned out to be useful, and by the work of colleagues and students, is an aspect of this story I can only briefly acknowledge.

A great deal of the work prior to 1959 was of the type illustrated in Figures 4 and 5, and is unlikely to be published; it consisted of unsuccessful attempts to find an association between population trends and changes in some organ or function that would indicate a pathological condition.

Figure 4 shows that two populations were out of phase from 1953 until 1957; Figure 5 shows that there was no difference between them in standardized mean adrenal weight — either in 1954, when numbers were low on one area and high on the other, or in 1955 when numbers were similar on both areas but going in opposite directions. Between years there was a difference in adrenal weight, which could have been misleading if either area

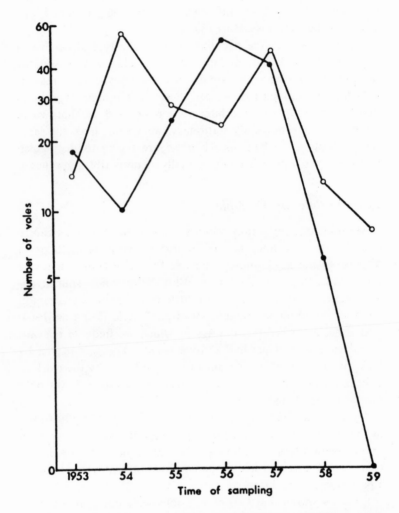

FIGURE 4: Population trends in two independent populations of the vole, *Microtus agrestis*, at Lake Vyrnwy, Wales, in April-May, 1953–59. The ordinate shows the number of voles taken per 100 traps in two days. (From Chitty and Chitty, 1962a. Scale: log n – 1.) o — Area F, • — Area R.

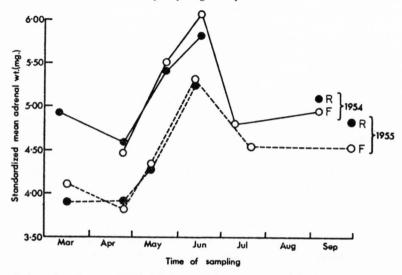

FIGURE 5: Seasonal and annual differences in standardized mean adrenal weights of male voles at Lake Vyrnwy, Wales, illustrating the need for comparative data to eliminate errors due to differences between years. Since the populations were out of phase (Figure 4) the null hypothesis was accepted that there was no relation between population trend and adrenal weight. (From H. Chitty, 1961.)

had been studied alone; seasonally there were differences that were probably due to changes in the amount of intraspecific strife (H. Chitty, 1961).

Although much time was spent in testing *mechanisms* that were wholly or partly false, there is still no reason to abandon the original *concept* that populations can regulate their own numbers through qualitative changes. The role of behavior in bringing about these changes was first studied in the Field Vole by Clarke (1953, 1956) and in the Partridge, *Perdix perdix*, by Jenkins (1961a, b); but the idea that behavior might be polymorphic is still too recent for us to know how fruitful it will be (Andrewartha, 1959; Krebs, 1964b; Chitty, 1964, 1965). Some of its implications have been looked into, however, and I shall refer briefly to a few of the results.

The most comprehensive studies have been carried out by

Krebs (1964b, 1966) on two species of lemmings in the Arctic and on *M. californicus*. He concluded that the observations to be explained were essentially the same as those previously described for *Microtus* spp. and were consistent with the scheme outlined in Figure 3. Skull proportions of the lemmings varied with the stage of their cycle in numbers, which also supported the idea that fundamental qualitative changes were taking place (Krebs, 1964a). Krebs himself did not study the behavior of his animals, though he noted that wounding occurred even at very low densities in lemmings, and refers to a study carried out on aggressive behavior in male *M. californicus*. These latter results did not turn out the way they were expected to (Krebs, pers. comm.), a warning that if behavior has the relevance predicted, we do not yet know what form it takes. Certainly we should not confine our observations to the grosser forms of aggression. Among other aspects the part played by odors in the defense of territories is likely to repay further study (Lyne, Molyneux, Mykytowycz, and Parakkal, 1964).

Other types of field experiments were carried out by Krebs (1966). An introduced population made rapid growth in an area on which a decline had occurred, which showed that the area itself was favorable. The introduced animals had been removed from an expanding population on another area, which confirmed one part of the prediction that "numbers should continue to increase if animals from an increasing population are successfully transferred to an area from which a declining population has been removed; but numbers should continue to decline if animals from a declining population are transferred to a new area" (Chitty, 1960).

However, when this prediction was made I thought that declining populations consisted predominantly of animals in which some adverse physiological change had occurred. Now that the change seems to consist of an increase in the proportion of aggressive animals it is less likely that a declining population would continue to decline if moved to a new area. Established social patterns might be sufficiently disrupted for results to go either way. Petruscewicz (1963) found that putting a stationary population of white mice into a different cage of the same size was sometimes enough to make their numbers go up.

Krebs (1966) also tested the idea that a heavily cropped population would retain the chief characteristics of an expanding population. Unfortunately, he could not prevent the numbers from being made up again by immigrants; but this at least showed that animals had previously avoided or been kept out of the area, and that the number of replacements was fairly predictable. Smyth (1966), in a similar attempt at cropping the Bank Vole (*Clethrionomys glareolus*), also found that in most months the animals he killed were almost all replaced by immigrants.

Sadleir (1965), using the deermouse, *Peromyscus maniculatus*, quantified the aggressive behavior of adult males and concluded that survival and recruitment of juveniles could be explained by seasonal changes in aggressive behavior of the adults. Both he and Britton (1966), by removing adults, increased the proportion of subadults reaching maturity. [Snyder (1961, 1962) had produced the same effect by cropping a population of woodchucks, *Marmota monax*.]

Healey (1966) tested Sadleir's conclusions by first establishing adult populations of aggressive and docile *Peromyscus* in the wild and then introducing a cohort of juveniles. There was usually a much greater loss of juveniles from the plots containing the aggressive adults, but Healey was unable to say that the aggressive and docile adults were genetically different.

The most crucial test of all has yet to be carried out (Chitty and Phipps, 1966, Appendix 1). According to hypothesis the animals present in stationary or declining populations have been selected for their superior ability to survive the effects of mutual interference. Animals in expanding populations, by contrast, are assumed not to have been so selected, but to be better fitted to withstand all other hazards of their environment. Therefore if animals of these different origins are placed together in the wild we should find the following differences in their respective contributions to the gene pool of later generations.

1. Let us first assume that the "environment of the population" remains favorable; then (a) at high population densities the

selective advantage should be with the supposedly aggressive individuals from the stationary or declining populations, but (b) the reverse should be true at very low population densities.

2. Now let us assume that there is a climatic catastrophe of the sort to which animals from the expanding population are supposed to be the more resistant. (a) According to the model previously discussed (Leslie, 1959), the direct effects of weather will be to remove a relatively low proportion of these resistant animals. However, the failure to find any evidence of reduced viability in voles now makes it less likely that weather has direct effects of the magnitude required. A second mechanism is therefore worth considering. (b) Let us suppose that the effect of the weather is on the habitat, which is made either more or less favorable. In relation to the new conditions, individuals will now find themselves either less crowded or more crowded, and may be expected to change their dispersion accordingly. This in turn may result in numbers either increasing or decreasing, or at least changing at a different rate from that expected.

Two vole populations that came into phase during the mild winter of 1956–57 may have followed this latter pattern: the denser population failed to decline until a year later than expected, while the expanding population reached its peak in three instead of the usual four years (Figure 4 and Chitty and Chitty, 1962a). Another mild winter, that of 1960–61, was also associated with an unexpected peak year instead of a further decline (Chitty and Phipps, 1966). These habitats were perhaps more than usually favorable when the surplus animals would normally have been eliminated.

The success of Krebs and Healey in setting up artificial populations in the wild suggests that we may now look forward to having populations out of phase when we want them. If so we can make an experimental attack on the problem of how weather affects the individuals, and what part it plays in the tendency of populations to keep in step. The idea that the effects of weather are independent of population density is so firmly rooted in ecological thinking that no one seems to have made the necessary observations to find out (cf. Moran, 1954).

The technique of setting up populations in the wild is not new: Einarsen (1945), Sheppard (1953, 1956), Sheppard and Cook (1962), and Miller (1958) are among those who have applied it; Morris (1960) quotes other examples.

THE PROBLEM IN STATIONARY POPULATIONS

A frequent source of confusion is that the problem of accounting for differences in population density *between* areas is often identified with the problem of accounting for the relatively stationary state of populations *within* areas. One often meets the non sequitur that because parasites can reduce average population density, as in successful biological control, therefore they are also necessary to prevent such populations from reaching abnormally high densities. The problem of explaining differences in population density between areas, and of explaining the regulation of numbers within areas, may or may not be entirely separate problems; they certainly cannot be assumed to be the same, and the difficulty is to know how to study the variables relevant to one of these problems in spite of the uncontrolled variables which are relevant only to the other. The technical problem is much the same as that encountered in agricultural field trials of removing effects due to differences between areas from effects within areas due to treatments or varieties of crop. "It would be common for the yields on individual plots in a field to vary by as much as $\pm$ 30 per cent from their mean, and a systematic difference of 5 per cent between varieties might be of considerable practical importance. We shall be concerned with methods for arranging the experiment so that we may with confidence and accuracy separate the varietal differences, which interest us, from the uncontrolled variations, which do not" (Cox, 1958).

In population ecology we are of course interested in differences in abundance both between and within areas. We need to know why, on the average, population densities are higher in some areas than in others, i.e., why one environment is more or less favorable than another, or what change is sufficient to make it so

(Morris, 1963; Geier, 1966). In either case the answer can be sought in comparative terms: by finding out what factors are associated with observed differences in population density, or what changes occur when a factor is artificially varied. In the present context, however, this problem concerns us only to the extent already discussed: that uncontrolled changes in certain aspects of the environment make conditions either more or less favorable. Some population changes are adjustments to such environmental changes; others are not; the difficulty is to tell one from the other. If we cannot distinguish between different sorts of numerical change we cannot draw valid inferences about regulatory mechanisms; on the other hand if populations do not fluctuate at all we have no worthwhile comparative data whatever.

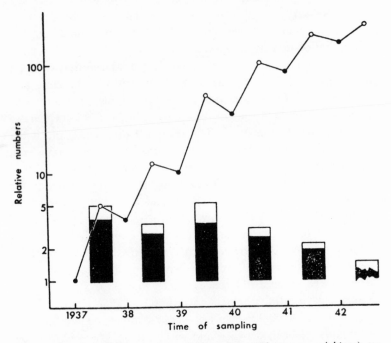

FIGURE 6: Estimated number of Pheasants (*Phasianus colchicus*) on Protection Island, Washington, in March and November 1937–42 (•). Histograms show the relative size of spring and fall populations, and (in black) the net annual rates of increase. (From Einarsen, 1945.)

Figure 6 shows one of the relatively few instances in which a pronounced increase in numbers has been measured on a population released under natural conditions. Eight artificially reared Pheasants, *Phasianus colchicus*, liberated on an island in the state of Washington, increased within six seasons to the abnormally high density of about nine birds per suitable acre (Einarsen, 1945). Had the population become stationary, as it seemed about to, the problem would have been to compare this regulated state with the previous one, which must have been as near to being unregulated as one is likely to find. And had the population subsequently declined of its own accord we might have found an even more obvious contrast with its unregulated state. As it happened, however, the environment was rudely disturbed, and the decline that occurred was irrelevant to the problem of natural regulation.

The histograms show the net annual increase expressed as the

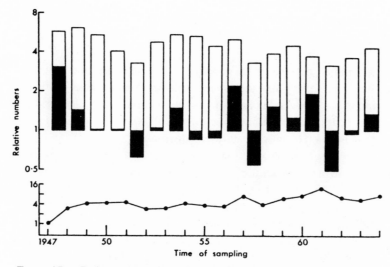

FIGURE 7: Estimated number of Great Tits (*Parus major*) breeding in Marley Wood Oxfordshire in 1947–65 (•). Histograms show the relative sizes of spring and summer populations, and (in black) the net annual changes in numbers. The breeding population varied between 14 in 1947 and 172 in 1961. (From Lack, 1966, pp. 60–61.)

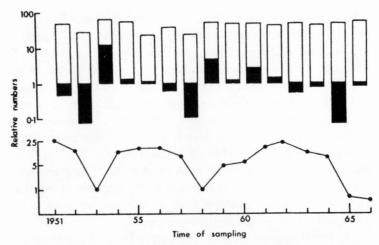

FIGURE 8: Estimated numbers of adult Pine Loopers (*Bupalus pini-arius*) in De Hoge Veluwe, the Netherlands in June 1951–66 (•). Histograms show the relative sizes of adult and egg populations, and (in black) the net annual changes in numbers. The adult population varied between 2.7 per sq. m. in June 1950 and 0.05 (max.) per sq. m. in June 1966. Unity = 0.1 per sq. m. (From Klomp, 1966, pp. 268–70, and personal communication for data for 1965–66.)

difference between the proportionate increase and decrease. Between spring and fall these birds were capable of a fivefold increase; between fall and spring their decrease was always slight. The reduced rates of increase after 1939 were thus due to factors that interfered with recruitment during the summer.

Figures 7 and 8 offer a sharp contrast to the previous example in showing how seldom these particular populations made any appreciable departure from a relatively stationary state. The breeding population of Great Tits (Lack, 1966) increased three-fold between 1947 and 1948 and doubled between 1956 and 1957: all other changes were between + 69 per cent and 50 per cent of the numbers breeding the previous year. The adult population of Pine Loopers (*Bupalus piniarius*) also remained fairly stationary (Klomp, 1966): by comparison with an elevenfold increase in 1953–54 and an almost fivefold increase in 1958–59, all other increases were slight. These studies thus provide many examples

344

of the phenomenon — a more or less stationary state — but few comparative observations on the state of rapid expansion from low numbers. It is not surprising, therefore, to find Lack (1966, p. 26) dismissing the high clutch sizes of 1947 and 1948 as abnormal, or including them with data collected at later stages of population growth, which make the averages "more reliable."

In both studies reproduction was adequate throughout, and the problem is to explain why the progeny failed to survive in sufficient numbers to produce a continual expansion, comparable to that observed among Einarsen's pheasants. Lack believed the Great Tits lost their young because of starvation, but was unable to find any evidence. Klomp believed that larval interference in *Bupalus* was responsible for reducing viability in the next generation; but even before getting the unpublished evidence for 1965–66 (Figure 8) he was unable to find a statistically significant relation between larval density in one year and egg or juvenile mortality the next.

After the mild winters of 1956–57 and 1960–61, not only in England but also in Holland (Lack, 1966), breeding populations of Great Tits were higher than expected; certain *Microtus* populations were also unexpectedly high in the spring of these same years (p. 14). Unfortunately we do not know whether or not these associations of events were fortuitous.

According to Klomp (1966): "The study of the population dynamics of insects has progressed further than that of any other animal group excepting perhaps the birds." Klomp does not suggest how this belief should be tested; but an appropriate null hypothesis might be that there is no difference between ecologists in their ignorance of why populations behave as they do.

I will conclude this section by referring to another study carried out on a normally stationary class of populations. Smith (1965) carried out a two-year study on chickadees (*Parus atricapillus*), a resident species usually found in fair numbers on the southwest coast of British Columbia. In this study the habitat was chosen in advance as likely to be favorable for their survival and reproduction; it was thus expected that the effects to be measured would be large in comparison with those of the irrelevant variables. The area was residential, partly surrounded by woods; it provided good cover, nesting sites, and food — the latter supplemented by several feeding tables maintained throughout the winter. Little predation seemed likely; only one kill was reported. The birds were nearly all colorbanded, and counts were made of the numbers alive at two-weekly intervals.

During fall and winter an average of over 95 per cent of the

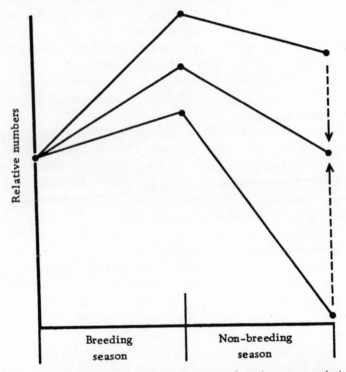

FIGURE 9: Seasonal increase and decrease of stationary populations living under hypothetically favorable, unfavorable, and intermediate conditions. Self-regulatory behavior might be obvious only if good reproduction and survival were followed by a sudden drop in numbers (cf. Jenkins, 1961a, Smith, 1965), though not necessarily at the time shown. Under other conditions numbers might be less obviously regulated through behavior restricting the amount of immigration.

birds present at the start of each two-week period were alive at the start of the next; but during a single period in February 1964 and again in March 1965, when the flocks broke up into pairs, only 60–70 per cent of the birds remained on the area. No such sharp change in numbers could have been expected, however, if reproduction had been less successful or if the autumn and winter survival rate had been just slightly lower (90 per cent period without immigration); and in less favorable habitats there might even have been an increase in numbers after the break-up of flocks on better areas (Figure 9).

These observations are an example of the self-regulatory behavior to be expected in a habitat where the chances of surviving the purely contingent mortality factors are extremely good. But because individuals of this species are capable of spacing themselves out in a way that limits their breeding density one does not infer that all populations of chickadees are self-regulating. Those that are and those that are not must be determined empirically (cf. Kluyver and Tinbergen, 1953); predictions appropriate to the testing of various other hypotheses must then be stated in their own operational terms. These other classes of population possibly do behave in the manner postulated by authors such as Nicholson (1954), Hairston, Smith, and Slobodkin (1960), or Lack (1966); but the relation of a population to its requisites cannot be deduced from unsubstantiated principles (Murdoch, 1966).

DISCUSSION

The principal claim in this paper is that population densities, while obviously varying in response to numerous environmental factors, are further affected by a continual process of selection. If we can demonstrate that interference has severe effects on survival and reproduction it is less reasonable to assume that all genotypes suffer equally than to assume they are affected non-randomly. Selective advantage is measured in terms of *relative* contribution to the gene pool of later generations; hence a form of behavior that reduces an individual's absolute contribution would nevertheless be selected for if at the same time it reduced still further the contribution of other individuals. This explanation certainly does less violence to present ideas about natural selection than does Wynne-Edwards's view (1962) that reduced fecundity has been evolved because of its advantages to the population. Dispersion, then, and its effect on population density, should be explained in the ultimate terms of its evolutionary significance, not in terms of its proximate advantages, either to the individual or the group.

These proximate advantages are sometimes obvious — less crowding means more food, for example — but we cannot infer that dispersion mechanisms have been selected for this sort of reason, a point emphasized by Hinde (1956). Territorial behavior is the most obvious of these mechanisms, but Lack (1954, p. 263) doubts that territorial behavior "is important in maintaining a food supply or in limiting numbers." "If territorial behavior as such limits population density" he writes on page 260, "then the size of the territories should be nearly constant in each species." Unfortunately he does not explain why size of territory should differ from most other expressions of activity in being unaffected by environmental variables.

Territorial behavior probably has many functions that are not selected for, and in some instances perhaps its only selective advantage is in excluding other animals from the best breeding places. Brown (1964) seems to hold a minority view when he writes: "As long as counter selection against aggressiveness were weak, *aggressiveness per se would be maintained in the population merely by the exclusion of less aggressive birds from breeding.*"

In some species the selective advantages of dispersion may be confined to a short period in the life of the organism, which for the rest of the time may lead a social life (Barnett, 1964; Brereton, 1966) and be subjected to strong selective pressures of other sorts. The effects of selection should also vary according to the habitat, owing to differences in the proportions eliminated by intraspecific behavior (Chitty, 1965, Figure 1). These expected differences might be reduced by gene flow, although immigrants to the worst habitats should consist mainly of animals selected for avoidance of the more crowded areas (Lidicker, 1962). During a general decline in their numbers, Bank Voles (*Clethrionomys glareolus*) survived better in the habitats that had been least crowded (Evans, 1942). Such habitats, Evans suggested, might be essential for the survival of the species.

The sudden removal of a mortality factor, such as an effective parasite, that had minimized the frequency of intraspecific interactions, should be followed by unusually good survival, high abundance, and damage to resources. Subsequent peaks should be appreciably lower after the strong selection presumably exerted during the first decline. Similar results might occur after the introduction of animals raised in captivity, where wildness is presumably selected against. Outbreaks might also occur after any long period of expansion into a relatively empty universe. Such opportunities often follow invasions; they should also follow severe catastrophes other than those due to the animal's own behavior. Watt (1963) recognizes that genetic changes may have occurred after DDT spraying against Spruce Budworm (*Choristoneura fumiferana*): "A striking feature of budworm survival data has been the rise in survival the season after a time of great adversity for budworm. It does not seem to matter what causes the adversity.... Two examples of post-adversity rises in survival ... one resulting from spraying and the other from starvation, are typical of many in our data." The unusual abundance of pheasants observed by Einarsen (1945) may have exemplified the combined effects of previous domestication and a long period of expansion in the absence of wild residents (cf. Miller, 1958).

Some years ago Ford (1955) wrote that ecologists all too often "deal with what are essentially genetic phenomena but rarely attempt to investigate them genetically." There is much justice in this criticism, though it is equally clear that the traffic in ideas must flow both ways. Birch (1960) and Milne (1962) summarize many of the ideas of ecologists about the role of selection in determining animal numbers; two more recent papers are those of Wilbert (1963) and Pimentel (1964).

349

Studies on the pathological effects of crowding, reviewed or carried out by Christian and Davis (1964), and Myers (1966), show that the "environment of the individual" can be very harsh in artificially crowded populations. Many of these effects are probably gross exaggerations of one part of what goes on in nature, or are complete artifacts. Nevertheless, given field evidence of unexplained reductions in breeding success and survival, we can be reasonably sure that these experimental results indicate that powerful intraspecific processes of some kind are at work in the wild. If so, the chances of them being non-selective seem remote, and we may expect population parameters to vary according to the number of generations exposed to these stresses.

It seems, then, that behavior, physiology, and genetics must be of increasing concern to population ecologists, who have probably spent too long already on purely descriptive studies.

Summary

1. Mechanisms for the self-regulation of animal numbers are thought to be a consequence of selection, under conditions of mutual interference, in favor of genotypes that have a worse effect on their neighbors than vice versa. This idea is highly speculative and is therefore presented in conjunction with operational tests of its implications. Evidence for the idea is reviewed only briefly, the aim of the paper being to elaborate the consequences of this hypothesis to make it more readily falsifiable.

2. Populations of small mammals, during their periodic declines in numbers, present a clearly recognizable phenomenon, whose most puzzling feature is the severity of the losses at relatively low densities after peak abundance. There is no evidence that the animals are less viable than normal, though a decrease in some components of fitness may reasonably be inferred.

3. For a crucial test of these ideas it will be necessary to measure the selective advantage of the supposed behavioral polymorphs — when they occur together both in crowded

and uncrowded conditions and exposed both to good and to bad weather. Various workers have now quantified behavior and made preliminary tests on populations specially established in the wild.

4. In populations that remain fairly stationary, many slight changes in numbers are due to changes in variables that are irrelevant to the problem of what prevents unlimited increase — an example of the need for comparative observations between any phenomenon and its control. Instances of rapid expansion in numbers sometimes provide the requisite contrasts with the stationary state.

5. Since we cannot yet analyze all stationary populations into recognizable classes we do not have specific phenomena whose explanation we can test by prediction, nor can we unify our explanations for differences in abundance between areas. However, in habitats that temporarily become more or less favorable than usual (e.g., through changes in weather) there may be associated changes in the amount of crowding that animals will tolerate. Such changes might explain why some populations tend to fluctuate in step.

6. Individuals that have not been selected under conditions of intraspecific strife are likely to be mutually tolerant, and populations composed of such individuals should reach abnormal abundance before such selection takes place. If conditions are otherwise favorable we might find such populations (a) when new areas are invaded, especially if (b) the animals released into a vacant niche are from stocks reared under conditions that select against aggressive behavior; (c) when an existing source of heavy mortality is removed; (d) when populations have been seriously reduced by natural or artificial catastrophes.

7. These ideas, whether themselves true or false, may suggest further work on behavior, physiology, and genetics that will contribute to the solution of ecological problems.

REFERENCES

Andrewartha, H. G. (1959). Self-regulatory mechanisms in animal populations. *Aust. J. Sci.*, 22:200–205.

———, and Birch, L. C. (1954). "The distribution and abundance of animals." (Univ. Chicago Press.)

Bakker, K. (1964). Backgrounds of controversies about population theories and their terminologies. *Z. ang. Ent.*, 53:187–208.

Barnett, S. A. (1964). Social stress. *Viewpoints in Biol.*, 3:170–218.

Birch, L. C. (1960). The genetic factor in population ecology. *Amer. Nat.*, 94:5–24.

Brereton, J. Le Gay (1962). Evolved regulatory mechanisms of population control. In "The evolution of living organism," ed. G. W. Leeper (Melbourne Univ. Press), pp. 81–93.

———. (1966). The evolution and adaptive significance of social behaviour. *Proc. ecol. Soc. Aust.*, 1:14–30.

Britton, M. M. (1966). Reproductive success and survival of the young in *Peromyscus.* M.Sc. Thesis, Univ. British Columbia.

Brown, J. L. (1964). The evolution of diversity in avian territorial systems. *Wilson Bull.*, 76:160–169.

Chitty, D. (1952). Mortality among voles (*Microtus agrestis*) at Lake Vyrnwy, Montgomeryshire in 1936–39. *Phil. Trans. B.*, 236:505–552.

———. (1954). Tuberculosis among wild voles: with a discussion of other pathological conditions among certain mammals and birds. *Ecology*, 35:227–237.

———. (1955). Adverse effects of population density upon the viability of later generations. In "The numbers of man and animals," eds. J. B. Cragg and N. W. Pirie. (Oliver & Boyd, Edinburgh), pp. 57–67.

———. (1958). Self-regulation of numbers through changes in viability. *Cold Spring Harbor Symp. Quant. Biol.*, 22:277–280.

———. (1960). Population processes in the vole and their relevance to general theory. *Canad. J. Zool.*, 38:99–113.

———. (1964). Animal numbers and behaviour. In "Fish and wildlife: A memorial to W. J. K. Harkness," ed. J. R. Dymond. (Longmans, Canada), pp. 41–53.

———. (1965). Predicting qualitative changes in insect populations. *Proc. 12th Int. Congr. Ent. Lond.*, 384–386.

———, and Chitty, H. (1962a). Population trends among the voles at Lake Vyrnwy, 1932–60. *Symp. Theriologicum, Brno. 1960*:67–76.

———, and Phipps, E. (1966). Seasonal changes in survival in mixed populations of two species of vole. *J. Anim. Ecol.*, 35:313–331.

Chitty, H. (1961). Variations in the weight of the adrenal glands of the field vole, *Microtus agrestis. J. Endocrin.*, 22:387–393.

———, and Chitty, D. (1962b). Body weight in relation to population phase in *Microtus agrestis. Symp. Theriologicum, Brno. 1960*:77–86.

Christian, J. J., and Davis, D. E. (1964). Endocrines, behaviour, and population. *Science*, 146:1550–1560.

———, Lloyd, J. A., and Davis, D. E. (1965). The role of endocrines in the self-regulation of mammalian populations. *Recent. Progr. Hormone Res.*, 21:501–571.

Clarke, J. R. (1953). The effect of fighting on the adrenals, thymus and spleen of the vole (*Microtus agrestis*). *J. Endocrin.*, 9:114–126.

———. (1956). The aggressive behaviour of the vole. *Behaviour*, 9:1–23.

Cohen, M. R., and Nagel, E. (1934). "An introduction to logic and scientific method." (Routledge, London.)

Cole, L. C. (1954). Some features of random population cycles. *J. Wildlife Manag.,* 18:2–24.

Cox, D. R. (1958). "Planning of experiments." (Chapman & Hall, London.)

Davis, D. E. (1951). The relation between level of population and pregnancy of Norway rats. *Ecology,* 32:459–461.

Einarsen, A. S. (1945). Some factors affecting ring-necked pheasant population density. *Murrelet,* 26:2–10; 39–44.

Elton, C. S. (1931). The study of epidemic diseases among wild animals. *J. Hyg., Camb.,* 31:435–456.

———. (1942). "Voles, mice and lemmings: problems in population dynamics." (Clarendon Press, Oxford.)

———. (1955). Discussion. In "The numbers of man and animals," eds. J. B. Cragg & N. W. Pirie. (Oliver & Boyd, Edinburgh), pp. 82–83.

Evans, F. C. (1942). Studies of a small mammal population in Bagley Wood, Berkshire. *J. Anim. Ecol.,* 11:182–197.

Ford, E. B. (1955). "Moths." (Collins, London.)

———. (1961). "Mendelism and evolution." 7th ed. (Methuen, London.)

———. (1964). "Ecological genetics." (Methuen, London.)

Geier, P. W. (1966). Management of insect pests. *Ann. Rev. Ent.,* 11:471–490.

Godfrey, G. K. (1955). Observations on the nature of the decline in numbers of two *Microtus* populations. *J. Mammal.,* 36:209–214.

Green, R. G., and Evans, C. A. (1940). Studies on a population cycle of snowshoe hares on the Lake Alexander Area. *J. Wildlife Manag.,* 4:220–238, 267–278, 347–358.

Hairston, N. G., Smith, F. E., and Slobodkin, L. B. (1960). Community structure, population control, and competition. *Amer. Nat.,* 94:421–425.

Hamilton, W. J. (1937). The biology of microtine cycles. *J. agric. Res.,* 54:779–790.

———. (1941). Reproduction of the field mouse *Microtus pennsylvanicus* (Ord). Mem. Cornell Univ. agric. exp. Sta. No. 237.

Healey, M. C. (1966). Aggression and self-regulation of population size in deermice. M.Sc. thesis, Univ. British Columbia.

Hinde, R. A. (1956). The biological significance of the territories of birds. *Ibis,* 98:340–369.

Huffaker, C. B. (1966). Competition for food by a phytophagous mite: the roles of dispersion and superimposed density-independent mortality. *Hilgardia,* 37:533–567.

Jenkins, D. (1961a). Population control in protected partridges (*Perdix perdix*). *J. Anim. Ecol.,* 30:235–258.

———. (1961b). Social behaviour in the partridge, *Perdix perdix. Ibis,* 103 A:155–188.

Kalela, O. (1957). Regulation of reproduction rate in subarctic populations of the vole *Clethrionomys rufocanus* (Sund.). *Ann Acad. Sci. Fenn. Ser. A., Sect. 4, No. 34.*

Klomp, H. (1964). Intraspecific competition and the regulation of insect numbers. *Ann. Rev. Ent.,* 9:17–40.

———. (1966). The dynamics of a field population of the pine looper, *Bupalus piniarius* L. (Lep., Geom.) *Adv. Ecol. Res.,* 3:207–305.

Kluyver, H. N., and Tinbergen, L. (1953). Territory and the regulation of density in titmice. *Archs. Néerl. Zool.,* 10:265–289.

Koskimies, J. (1955). Ultimate causes of cyclic fluctuations in numbers in animal populations. *Papers Game Res., Helsinki,* 15:1–29.

Krebs, C. J. (1964a). Cyclic variation in skull-body regressions of lemmings. *Canad. J. Zool.*, 42:631–643.

——. (1964b). The lemming cycle at Baker Lake, Northwest Territories, during 1959–62. Arctic Inst. N. Amer. Tech. Paper No. 15.

——. (1966). Demographic changes in fluctuating populations of *Microtus californicus*. *Ecol. Monog.*, 36:239–273.

Lack, D. (1954). "The natural regulation of animal numbers." (Clarendon Press, Oxford.)

——. (1966). "Population studies of birds." (Clarendon Press, Oxford.)

Leslie, P. H. (1959). The properties of a certain lag type of population growth and the influence of an external random factor on a number of such populations. *Physiol. Zool.*, 32:151–159.

Lidicker, W. Z. (1962). Emigration as a possible mechanism permitting the regulation of population density below carrying capacity. *Amer. Nat.*, 96:29–33.

Lloyd, M. (1960). Statistical analysis of Marchant's data on breeding success and clutch-size. *Ibis*, 102:600–611.

Lyne, A. G., Molyneux, G. S., Mykytowycz, R., and Parakkal, P. F. (1964). The development, structure and function of the submandibular cutaneous (chin) glands in the rabbit. *Aust. J. Zool.*, 12:340–348.

Mather, K. (1961). Competition and co-operation. *Symp. Soc. exp. Biol.*, 15:264–281.

Medawar, P. B. (1957). "The uniqueness of the individual." (Methuen, London.)

Miller, R. B. (1958). The role of competition in the mortality of hatchery trout. *J. Fish. Res. Bd. Canada*, 15:27–45.

Milne, A. (1962). On a theory of natural control of insect population. *J. Theoret. Biol.*, 3:19–50.

Moran, P. A. P. (1954). The logic of the mathematical theory of animal populations. *J. Wildlife Manag.*, 18:60–66.

Morris, R. F. (1960). Sampling insect populations. *Ann. Rev. Ent.*, 5:243–264.

——. (1963). Predictive population equations based on key factors. *Mem. Ent. Soc. Canada*, 32:16–21.

Murdoch, W. M. (1966). "Community structure, population control, and competition"—a critique. *Amer. Nat.*, 100:219–226.

Myers, K. (1966). The effects of density on sociality and health in mammals. *Proc. ecol. Soc. Aust.*, 1:40–64.

Nelson, J. B. (1964). Factors influencing clutch-size and chick growth in the North Atlantic gannet, *Sula bassana*. *Ibis*, 106:63–77.

——. (1965). The behaviour of the gannet. *Brit. Birds*, 58:233–288; 313–336.

Newson, J., and Chitty, D. (1962). Haemoglobin levels, growth and survival in two *Microtus* populations. *Ecology*, 43:733–738.

Newson, R. (1963). Differences in numbers, reproduction and survival between two neighbouring populations of bank voles (*Clethrionomys glareolus*). *Ecology*, 44:110–120.

Nicholson, A. J. (1954). An outline of the dynamics of animal populations. *Aust. J. Zool.*, 2:9–65.

Petruscewicz, K. (1963). Population growth induced by disturbance in the ecological structure of the population. *Ekol. Polska A*, 11:87–125.

Pimentel, D. (1964). Population ecology and the genetic feed-back mechanism. In "Genetics Today": Proc. 11th Int. Congr. Genetics, pp. 483–488.

Pitelka, F. A. (1958). Some aspects of population structure in the short-term cycle of the brown lemming in northern Alaska. *Cold Spr. Harb. Symp. Quant. Biol.*, 22:237–251.

Platt, J. R. (1964). Strong inference. *Science*, 146:347–353.

Popper, K. R. (1959). "The logic of scientific discovery." (Hutchinson, London.)

———. (1963). "Conjectures and refutations: the growth of scientific knowledge." (Routledge and Kegan Paul, London.)

Sadleir, R. M. F. S. (1965). The relationship between agnostic behaviour and population changes in the deermouse, *Peromyscus maniculatus* (Wagner). *J. Anim. Ecol.*, 14:331–352.

Sheppard, P. M. (1953). Evolution in bisexually reproducing organisms. In "Evolution as a process," eds. J. S. Huxley, A. C. Hardy, and E. B. Ford. (Allen & Unwin, London), pp. 201–218.

———. (1956). Ecology and its bearing on population genetics. *Proc. Roy. Soc. B.*, 145:308–315.

———, and Cook, L. M. (1962). The manifold effects of the *medionigra* gene in the moth *Panaxia dominula* and the maintenance of a polymorphism. *Heredity*, 17:415–426.

Smith, S. M. (1965). Seasonal changes in the survival of the black-capped chickadee. M.Sc. Thesis, Univ. British Columbia.

Smyth, M. (1966). Winter breeding in woodland mice, *Apodemus sylvaticus*, and voles, *Clethrionomys glareolus* and *Microtus agrestis*, near Oxford. *J. Anim. Ecol.*, 35:471–485.

Snyder, R. L. (1961). Evolution and integration of mechanisms that regulate population growth. *Proc. Nat. Acad. Sci.*, 47:449–455.

———. (1962). Reproductive performance of a population of woodchucks after a change in sex ratio. *Ecology*, 43:506–515.

Summerhayes, V. S. (1941). The effect of voles (*Microtus agrestis*) on vegetation. *J. Ecol.*, 29:14–48.

Tinbergen, N. (1957). The functions of territory. *Bird Study*, 4:14–27.

Varley, G. C. (1957). Ecology as an experimental science. *J. Anim. Ecol.*, 26:251–261.

———, and Gradwell, G. R. (1963). The interpretation of insect population changes. *Proc. Ceylon Ass. Adv. Sci.*, 1962, 18:142–156.

Watkins, J. W. W. (1964). Confession is good for ideas. In "Experiment: a series of scientific case histories . . . ," ed. D. Edge. (B.B.C., London), pp. 64–70.

Watt, K. E. F. (1963). The analysis of the survival of large larvae in the unsprayed area. *Mem. Ent. Soc. Canada*, 31:52–63.

Wellington, W. G. (1960). Qualitative changes in natural populations during changes in abundance. *Canad. J. Zool.*, 38:289–314.

Wilbert, H. (1963). Können Insektenpopulationen durch Selektionsprozesse reguliert werden? *Z. ang. Ent.*, 52:185–204.

von Wright, G. H. (1957). "The logical problem of induction." (Blackwell, Oxford.)

Wynne-Edwards, V. C. (1962). "Animal dispersion in relation to social behaviour." (Oliver & Boyd, Edinburgh.)

ERRATA

Page 160, line 20 should read: "certain *Microtus* populations were also unexpectedly high in the spring of these same years (p. 155)." Page 162, line 7 should read: "winter survival rate had been just slightly lower (90 per cent per period without immigration); and in . . ."

Part VIII

POPULATION CYCLES

Editor's Comments
on Paper 25

25   KREBS et al.
Population Cycles in Small Rodents

The study of population cycles is a microcosm of the study of population regulation, which is why the topic is a separate section in this volume. Much research is currently being done on cyclic species. Populations undergoing cycles show an interesting twist above and beyond the general problems of regulation; that is, certain populations undergo very regular declines in density.

Two types of population cycles are generally recognized: the three- to four-year "short-term" cycle, found primarily in lemmings, field mice, and voles (Elton 1942; Krebs and Myers 1974; Tapper 1976; Keith 1974) and the nine- to ten-year "long-term" cycle of snowshoe hares and muskrats (Keith 1963, 1974; Errington 1963). Predators of these species and several species of tetraonid birds also undergo these same types of cycles (Watson 1964; Watson and Moss 1970; Jenkins, Watson, and Miller 1964). Recently data have been accumulated on species of forest rodents and birds that apparently fluctuate in synchrony with the mast output of the forest trees (Bock and Lepthien 1976). Why the forest trees undergo these cycles is another problem entirely (unless, of course, some type of plant–animal interaction is involved). In this section I shall confine my remarks to the short-term cycle. Many of the statements will hold for the long-term cycle, about which a bit less is known, partially because of the larger time commitment that is necessary for research.

In the short-term cycle, populations of voles, field mice, and lemmings increase in density until the growth curve levels off. The populations then often remain at high density for a while and then decline, often almost to extinction. The populations may or may not stay at a low level for a while. The shortest natural cycles were about two years (Krebs 1966) and the longest reported cycles have been five or six years (Krebs and Myers 1974). In the past there has been some controversy about whether these cycles actually exist. In several articles, Cole (the author of Paper 1 in this volume) presented evidence that random numbers will generate cyclicity (1951; 1954); however, although his random number cycles with serial correlations produced cycles in wavelength that could be interpreted as vole-like, the amplitude changes were not similar to natural animal cycles. His work serves more as a caveat that the burden of demonstrating cycles can lie with the observer. In general, the consensus of population biologists is that the short-term cycle is a real event.

Explanations of the vole cycle have run the gamut of possible extrinsic and intrinsic mechanisms, including a correlation of the long-term cycle with the sunspot cycle (Elton 1924) and a quasi-science fiction "lunar" theory (Siivonen and Koskimies 1955). Eliminating unsupported hypotheses leaves basically five mechanisms currently under investigation (food, predation, endocrine-stress, genetic-stress, and multifactorial). Lack (1954) originally suggested that food supply could regulate populations. As density increased, the voles ate the grass—their food supply—and became more open to predation: the voles' food is also their habitat because they make runways in the grass, so when the grass is eaten, both food and habitat are gone. This interaction of food and predation has also been studied extensively by Frank Pitelka and his students at the University of California at Berkeley (Batzli and Pitelka 1971).

In addition to food quantity, food quality has also been considered because abundant grass that is low in nutrients will support neither reproduction nor good health. This has led to a "nutrient recovery hypothesis" that has supportive evidence primarily from lemming interactions with tundra vegetation (Schultz 1964).

Freeland (1974) has suggested that voles could be regulated by being forced to eat foods that contain toxic substances when they exhaust their prime food choices. Although the particular case to which he referred was refuted (Batzli and Pitelka 1975), it is still an enticing idea. Pearson (1964; 1966; 1971), also at Berkeley, has been a proponent of predation as a regulating mechanism and has shown that several California vole populations have declined in the presence of heavy predation.

Two of the remaining general hypotheses, the two intrinsic behavior theories, have been treated in Part VII: the phenotypic endocrine-stress hypothesis (Christian and Davis, Paper 23), and the genotypic behavior-stress hypothesis (Chitty, Paper 24). Finally, recently there have also been suggestions of "community models" of population regulation where the interaction of many parameters control population density in voles (Lidicker 1975; Petrusewicz et al. 1971).

I present Paper 25 because, after a brief summary of vole cycles, it proceeds to examine Chitty's genetic behavior hypothesis, and it concludes with future experiments. This paper clearly presents a methodology of approach: experimentation and testing of hypotheses. But the question of how to distinguish between all these models remains.

Obviously, careful experiments need to be designed whose outcomes will definitely support or disprove one or another of the various theories (Popper 1959). Two problems with this attack arise: (1) most community-type models (also called "multifactor hypotheses") are not really testable (Lidicker 1977; Tamarin 1977); and (2) if we confine ourselves to single-factor hypotheses, we still run into enormous technical difficulties in doing experiments. Paper 25 describes some fencing experiments that were done in order to have an arena for manipulating populations. However, although the fencing regime produced informative results, it showed that we do not yet know enough about populations to enclose them and yet to expect them to behave normally. Experimenting on open populations produces problems of outside swamping by immigrants (Krebs 1966), but in lieu of any other technique, Krebs and his colleagues have had some recent success with open population manipulation (LeDuc and Krebs 1975; Krebs, Halpin, and Smith 1977). Concomitantly, some investigators are attempting to manipulate fences in order to permit dispersal (Personal communications by Getz, University of Illinois; Gaines, University of Kansas; Riggs, University of California at Berkeley). A third approach has been to examine naturally isolated populations, usually on islands (Lidicker 1973; Petrusewicz et al. 1971; Tamarin 1978). These works have proved useful in the study of populations isolated both from dispersal and from some of the complexity found in mainland populations. Both Lidicker (1973) and Tamarin (1978) have developed models of population regulation based on their island studies, both of which remain to be tested.

Thus in the next few years, we may have some breakthroughs in understanding the short-term cycle if the problem of manipulation can be overcome and if critical experiments are then performed. At least there is some light at the end of this tunnel.

REFERENCES

Batzli, G., and F. A. Pitelka. 1971. Condition and Diet of Cycling Populations of the California Vole, *Microtus californicus. J. Mamm.* **52**:141–163.

Batzli, G. and F. Pitelka. 1975. Vole Cycles: Test of Another Hypothesis. *Am. Nat.* **109**:482–487.

Bock, C., and L. Lepthien. 1976. Synchronous Eruptions of Boreal Seed-Eating Birds. *Am. Nat.* **110**:559–571.

Cole, L. C. 1951. Population Cycles and Random Oscillations. *J. Wildl. Manage.* **15**:233–252.

Cole, L. C. 1954. Some Features of Random Population Cycles. *J. Wildl. Manage.* **18**:2–24.

Elton, C. 1924. Periodic Fluctuations in the Numbers of Animals: Their Causes and Effects. *Br. J. Exp. Biol.* **2**:119–163.

Elton, C. 1942. *Voles, Mice and Lemmings.* Oxford, England: Clarendon Press.

Errington, P. 1963. *Muskrat Populations.* Ames: Iowa State University Press.

Freeland, W. 1974. Vole Cycles: Another Hypothesis. *Am. Nat.* **108**:238–245.

Jenkins, D., A. Watson, and G. Miller. 1964. Predation and Red Grouse Populations. *J. Appl. Ecol.* **1**:183–195.

Keith, L. 1963. *Wildlife's Ten-Year Cycle.* Madison: University of Wisconsin Press.

Keith, L. 1974. Some Features of Population Dynamics in Mammals. *Proc. Int. Congr. Game Biol.* **11**:17–58.

Krebs, C. J. 1966. Demographic Changes in Fluctuating Populations of *Microtus californicus. Ecol. Monogr.* **36**:239–273.

Krebs, C. J., Z. Halpin, and J. Smith. 1977. Aggression, Testosterone, and the Spring Decline in Populations of the Vole *Microtus townsendii. Can. J. Zool.* **55**:430–437.

Krebs, C. J., and J. Myers. 1974. Population Cycles in Small Mammals. *Adv. Ecol. Res.* **8**:267–399.

Lack, D. 1954. *The Natural Regulation of Animal Numbers.* London: Oxford University Press.

LeDuc, J., and C. Krebs. 1975. Demographic Consequences of Artificial Selection at the LAP Locus in Voles *(Microtus townsendii). Can. J. Zool.* **53**:1825–1840.

Lidicker, W. Z. Jr. 1973. Regulation of Numbers in an Island Population of the California Vole, a Problem in Community Dynamics. *Ecol. Monogr.* **43**:271–302.

Lidicker, W. Z. Jr. 1975. The Role of Dispersal in the Demography of Small Mammals. In F. Golley, K. Petrusewicz, and L. Ryskowski (eds.), *Small Mammals: Their Productivity* and Population Dynamics, pp. 103–134. Cambridge, England: Cambridge University Press.

Lidicker, W. Z., Jr. 1977. *Regulation of Numbers in Small Mammal Populations.* In D. Snyder (ed.), Pymatuning Laboratory of Ecology, Symposium no. 5. Ann Arbor, Mich.: Edwards Brothers.

Pearson, O. P. 1964. Carnivore-Mouse Predation: An Example of Its Intensity and Bioenergetics. *J. Mamm.* **45**:177–188.

361

Pearson, O. P. 1966. The Prey of Carnivores During One Cycle of Mouse Abundance. *J. Anim. Ecol.* **35**:217–233.

Pearson, O. P. 1971. Additional Measurements of the Impacts of Carnivores on California Voles *(Microtus californicus)*. *J. Mamm.* **52**:41–49.

Petrusewicz, K., G. Bujalska, R. Anderzejewski, and J. Gliwicz. 1971. Productivity Processes in an Island Population of *Clethrionomys glareolus*. *Ann. Zool. Fennici* **8**:127–132.

Popper, K. 1959. (Harper Torchbook edition, 1965.) *The Logic of Scientific Discovery*. New York: Harper & Row.

Schultz, A. 1964. The Nutrient-Recovery Hypothesis for Arctic Microtine Cycles, II: Ecosystem Variables in Relation to the Arctic Microtine Cycles. In D. Crisp (ed.), *Grazing in Terrestrial and Marine Environments*, pp. 57–68. Oxford, England: Blackwell.

Siivonen, L., and J. Koskimies. 1955. *Population Fluctuations and the Lunar Cycle*. Finnish Game Foundation, Papers on Game Research, no. 14.

Tamarin, R. 1977. *A Defense of Single-Factor Models of Population Regulation*. IN D. Snyder (ed.), Pymatuning Laboratory of Ecology, Symposium no. 5. Ann Arbor, Mich.: Edwards Brothers.

Tamarin, R. 1978. Dispersal, Population Regulation and K-selection in Field Mice. *Am. Nat.*

Tapper, S. C. 1976. Population Fluctuations of Field Voles *(Microtus)*: A Background to the Problems Involved in Predicting Vole Plagues. *Mamm. Rev.* **6**:93–117.

Watson, A. 1964. Aggression and Population Regulation in Red Grouse. *Nature* **202**:506–507.

Watson, A., and R. Moss. 1970. Dominance, Spacing Behavior and Aggression in Relation to Population Limitation in Vertebrates. In A. Watson (ed.), *Animal Populations in Relation to Their Food Resources*. Oxford, England: Blackwell.

Reprinted from *Science* 179:35–41 (1973)

Population Cycles in
Small Rodents

Demographic and genetic events are closely coupled
in fluctuating populations of field mice.

Charles J. Krebs, Michael S. Gaines, Barry L. Keller,
Judith H. Myers, Robert H. Tamarin

Outbreaks of small rodents were recorded in the Old Testament, in Aristotle's writings, and in the pages of European history. Charles Elton (*1*) summarized the colorful history of rodent plagues, and described the general sequence of outbreaks, from rapid multiplication to the destruction of crops and pastures, and the decline of the plague into scarcity. This cycle of abundance and scarcity is a continuing rhythm in many small rodents, although not all high populations reach plague proportions. The population cycles of small rodents have always been a classic problem in population ecology, and speculation on the possible causes of rodent outbreaks has long outstripped the available scientific data. Both for practical reasons and because of our innate curiosity we would like to understand the mechanisms behind the rise and fall of these rodent populations.

Population cycles present an ideal situation in which to study population regulation. One question that has occupied biologists since the time of Malthus and Darwin has been this: What stops population increase? Cyclic populations, which follow a four-step pattern of increase–peak–decline–low, are thus useful in presenting a sequence of contrasting phases and then repeating the phases again and again. In small rodents the period of this cycle (*2*) is usually 3 to 4 years, although 2-year and 5-year cycles sometimes occur.

Since Charles Elton first kindled interest in population cycles in 1924 (*3*), a great amount of effort has been expended in trying to describe and to explain these fluctuations. Two general facts have emerged from this work. First, many species of microtine rodents

(lemmings and voles) in many different genera fluctuate in numbers. These species have not all been studied for long time-periods, but it is striking that in no instance has a population been studied in detail and found to be stable in numbers from year to year. Second, these cycles are found in a variety of ecological communities: lemmings on the tundras of North America and Eurasia, red-backed voles in the boreal forests of North America and Scandinavia, meadow voles in New York, field voles in coastal California, New Mexico, Indiana, Britain, Germany, and France. The list grows long and includes rodents from north temperate to arctic areas. No cyclic fluctuations have been described for tropical rodents or for South American species, but almost no population studies have been done on these species.

The phenomenon of population cycles is widespread but there is disagreement about whether we should seek a single explanation for the variety of situations in which it occurs. We adopt here the simplest hypothesis, that a single mechanism underlies all rodent cycles, from lemming cycles in Alaska to field vole cycles in southern Indiana. The only empirical justification we can give for this approach is that demographic events are similar in a variety of species living in different climates and in different plant communities; but the expectation of a single explanation for rodent cycles is only an article of faith.

There are two opposing schools of thought about what stops population increase in small rodents. One school looks to extrinsic agents such as food supply, predators, or disease to stop populations from increasing. The other looks to intrinsic effects, the effects of

one individual upon another. We have abandoned a search for extrinsic agents of control for reasons discussed elsewhere (*4, 5*). This is not to say that extrinsic factors such as weather and food are not influencing microtine populations to varying degrees, but we believe that more important than the variable effects of extrinsic factors are the intrinsic factors which act in a common way in cycling rodents. We have turned our attention toward intrinsic effects, particularly those of behavior and genetics hypothesized by Chitty (*6*). Two essential elements of Chitty's hypothesis are (i) that the genetic composition of the population changes markedly during a cycle in numbers; and (ii) that spacing behavior (or hostility) is the variable which drives the demographic machinery through a cycle.

The suggestion that genetical mechanisms might be involved in the short-term changes in rodent populations has opened a new area of investigation. Population ecologists have traditionally been concerned with quantity rather than quality, and have only recently begun to realize the importance of individual variation (*7*). The genetical basis of the control of population size was discussed as early as 1931 by Ford (*8*) but most geneticists have assumed that population control is an ecological problem and not a genetic one. Lerner (*9*) attempted to bridge the gap between genetics and ecology by showing how the solution of ecological problems might be helped by genetical insights. Although population genetics and population ecology have developed as separate disciplines, we have tried to utilize both these disciplines in our attempts to determine the causes of population cycles in rodents.

From 1965 to 1970 we studied the relationships among population dynamics, aggressive behavior, and genetic composition of field vole populations in southern Indiana. The two species of *Microtus* (*M. pennsylvanicus* and *M. ochrogaster*) that we studied fluctuate strongly in numbers with peak densities recurring at intervals of 2 or 3 years (*10*). The purposes of our investigations were to (i) describe the mechanics of the fluctuations in population size, (ii) monitor genetic changes with polymorphic marker loci, and (iii) measure changes in male aggressive behavior

Dr. Krebs is at the University of British Columbia, Vancouver 8; Dr. Gaines is at the University of Kansas; Dr. Keller is at Idaho State University; Dr. Myers is at the University of British Columbia; and Dr. Tamarin is at Boston University.

during a population fluctuation. We here synthesize our findings on the demography and genetic composition of *Microtus* populations, and summarize the results of our behavioral studies that have been reported elsewhere (*11*).

Demographic Changes

In *M. pennsylvanicus* changes in population size can be grouped into three phases, each of which lasts several months or more: an increase phase in which the rate of population increase (*r*) is greater than 0.03 per week (maximum observed, 0.13 per week); a peak phase in which the rate of increase is zero (between −0.02 and +0.03 per week) and density is high and essentially constant; and a decline phase in which *r* is negative (−0.03 per week or less; maximum observed, −0.12 per week). Figure 1 illustrates these phases for one population of *M. pennsylvanicus*.

Detailed information on changes in population size is available for several species of voles (*4, 5, 10, 12*). The increase phase is typically the most constant phase of the cycle, and once begun may continue through the winter, as shown in Fig. 1. The peak phase often begins with a spring decline in numbers, and a summer or fall increase restores the population to its former level. The

Table 1. Components of population fluctuations in *M. pennsylvanicus* in southern Indiana, 1965 to 1970. The data are expressed as mean values for more than 2000 individuals from four populations. The survival of early juvenile animals is determined from the number of unmarked young per lactating female; survival of subadults and adults is measured as a probability of survival per 14 days.

Phase	Birth rate (% lactating females)	Survival		
		Early juveniles	Subadult and adult	
			Males	Females
Increase	45	1.31	0.78	0.86
Peak	29	0.96	0.79	0.85
Decline	27	0.88	0.71	0.72

decline phase is most variable. It may begin in the fall of the peak year or be delayed until the next spring. The decline may be very rapid, so that most of the population disappears over 1 to 2 months, but often the decline is gradual and prolonged over a year or more. A phase of low numbers may or may not follow the decline, and little is known of this period, which may last a year or longer.

Changes in birth and death rates are the immediate cause of the population fluctuations in *M. pennsylvanicus* in Indiana. Table 1 shows that the birth rate, measured by the percentage of adult females captured that are visibly lactat-

ing, is reduced both in the peak phase and in the decline phase. The principal reason for this is that the breeding season is shortened in the peak and decline phases. Changes in weight at sexual maturity also contribute to a reduced birth rate in peak populations (*13*).

The death rate of small juvenile animals seems to increase dramatically in the peak and declining populations of *M. pennsylvanicus*. By contrast, the death rate of subadult and adult animals is not increased in peak populations but is increased in declining populations. Thus, in a peak population, if an animal is able to survive through the early juvenile stage, it has a high survival rate as an adult. Declining populations suffer from a low birth rate and a high mortality rate of both juveniles and adults (*14*).

What is the nature of the mortality factor acting during the population decline? The older animals seem to bear the brunt of the increased mortality during the population decline. Also, periods of high mortality during the decline are not always synchronous in males and females (see Fig. 2). Therefore, the mortality factors can be very selective, which argues against the overwhelming influence of extrinsic agents such as predation and disease.

These changes in birth and death rates are not unique to *M. pennsylvanicus*. Birth rates are higher in the phase of increase for all vole and lemming populations that have been studied (*5, 12, 13, 15*). The most common method of increasing the reproductive rate is by extending the breeding season, which may continue through the winter in both lemmings and voles. Extended breeding seasons are also accompanied by lowered ages at sexual maturity in some species. These trends are reversed in peak and declining populations, and the breeding season may be particularly short in some peak populations. Litter sizes seem to be essentially the same during the increase phase and the decline phase.

Death rate measurements are available for relatively few small rodent populations (*4, 5, 10, 16*). Juvenile losses are often high in peak populations and especially high in declining populations. Adult death rates are not unusually high in dense populations, but may be very high during the decline phase. The demographic changes which cause these rodent populations to fluctuate are thus a syndrome of reproduc-

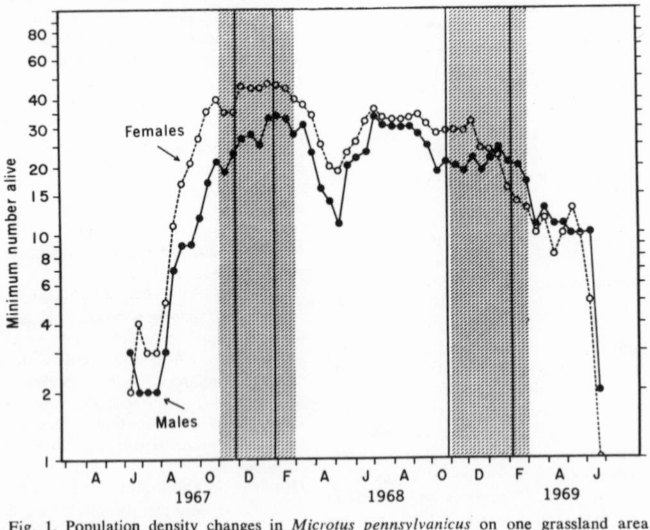

Fig. 1. Population density changes in *Microtus pennsylvanicus* on one grassland area in southern Indiana. Winter months are shaded. Vertical lines separate "summer" breeding period from "winter" period. An increase phase occurred from June to October 1967, and a decline phase from November 1968 to June 1969. [By permission of the Society for the Study of Evolution]

Fig. 2. Detailed breakdown of a population decline in *M. pennsylvanicus* during the spring of 1969. The critical observation is the difference in timing of male losses (highest in early March) and female losses (highest in mid-April). This timing is reflected in the gene frequency changes shown on the lowest graph (*r* is the instantaneous rate of population increase).

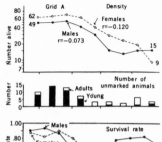
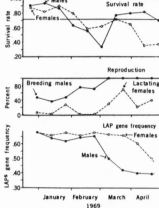

tive shifts and mortality changes. Reproduction and early juvenile survival seem to deteriorate first, and only later is adult survival impaired. This syndrome of changes is common to situations as diverse as lemmings in northern Canada, voles in England, and field voles in Indiana.

Growth rates of individual animals are also affected by the population fluctuations. Both males and females in increasing populations grow more rapidly than individuals in peak populations, who in turn grow more rapidly than individuals in declining populations. Figure 3 illustrates this change in growth for *M. pennsylvanicus* from southern Indiana. The higher growth rates of individuals in increasing populations, coupled with higher survival rates, produce animals of larger than average body size in increasing and peak populations (*10*). These large animals are characteristic of all peak populations of small rodents.

Fencing Experiments

The first hint we obtained about how the demographic changes are brought about in field populations came from an experiment designed to answer the question: Does fencing a population of *Microtus* effect its dynamics? We constructed three mouse-proof enclosures in the field, each measuring 2 acres (0.8 hectare), and used these to study populations constrained by the fence, which allowed no immigration or emigration of *Microtus*. Figure 4 shows population changes on two adjacent fields, one of which was fenced in July 1965. Both populations increased in size but diverged sharply in the early peak phase. The fenced population (grid B) continued to increase in the summer of 1966 to 310 animals on the 2-acre plot, a density about three times as high as that on control grid A. The overpopulation of the fenced *M. pennsylvanicus* on grid B resulted in habitat destruction and overgrazing, and led to a sharp decline with symptoms of starvation. The result was

the same with enclosed populations of *M. ochrogaster* (*10*), and during the course of our studies four introductions of *M. ochrogaster* to the fenced areas resulted in abnormally high densities. Thus we conclude that fencing a *Microtus* population destroys the regulatory machinery which normally prevents overgrazing and starvation.

Dispersal (immigration and emigration) is the obvious process which is

prevented by a fence, and we suggested that dispersal is necessary for normal population regulation in *Microtus*. We could see no indication that predation pressure was changed by the small fence around the large areas we studied. Foxes, cats, weasels, and snakes were known to have entered the fenced areas, and hawks and owls were not deterred.

Dispersal Experiments

If dispersal is important for population regulation, how might it operate? We could envisage two possible ways. First, dispersal might be related to population density, so that more animals would emigrate from an area in the peak phase and especially in the decline phase. These emigrants we would presume to be at a great disadvantage from environmental hazards such as other voles, predators, and bad weather. Second, the number of dispersers might not be as important as the quality of the dispersers. If only animals of a certain genetic type are able to tolerate high densities, dispersal may be one mechanism for sorting out these individuals.

We measured dispersal by maintaining two areas free of *Microtus* by trapping and removing all animals caught for 2 days every second week. Voles were free to colonize the areas for 12 days between each episode of trapping. We defined dispersers as those animals colonizing these vacant habitats (*17*). We thus determined the loss rate of individuals from control populations and the number of colonizers entering the trapped areas, and could calculate the

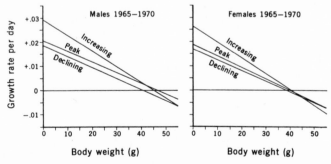

Fig. 3. Instantaneous relative growth rates for *M. pennsylvanicus* in southern Indiana. Regression lines for increase, peak, and decline phases are based on 691, 1898, and 333 observations for males and 776, 1696, and 322 observations for females (all pregnant animals excluded). Slope and elevation of the three regression lines are significantly different (*P* < .01) in both sexes.

38   C. J. Krebs et al.

fraction, in control populations, of losses attributable to dispersal.

Dispersal was most common in the increase phase of a population fluctuation and least common in the decline phase (Fig. 5). Most of the loss rate in increasing populations seems to be due to emigration (Table 2). Conversely, little of the heavy loss in declining populations is due to animals dispersing into adjacent areas, and hence most losses must be deaths in situ.

Thus dispersal losses from *Microtus* populations were not heaviest during the peak and decline, which supports the view that the role of dispersal is related to the quality of dispersing animals. We present evidence of genetic differences in dispersing *Microtus* in the next section.

Genetic Changes

Polymorphic serum proteins have been used as genetic markers to study the possible role of natural selection in population fluctuations of *Microtus*. We have used the genes *Tf* (transferrin) and *LAP* (leucine aminopeptidase) as markers (*18, 19*). The electrophoretically distinguishable forms of the products of these genes are inherited as if controlled by alleles of single autosomal loci.

We have found evidence of large changes in gene frequency at these two loci in association with population changes. Some of these changes are

Table 2. Percentage of losses known to be due to dispersal for control populations of *M. pennsylvanicus* in southern Indiana. Total numbers lost are shown in parentheses.

Population phase	Males (%)	Females (%)
Increase	56(32)	69(16)
Peak	33(157)	25(127)
Decline	15(53)	12(42)

repetitive and have been observed in several populations (*18, 19*). Figure 2 shows the details of one decline in *M. pennsylvanicus* in the late winter and early spring of 1969. The survival rate of males during this decline dropped to a minimum in early March; female survival dropped 6 weeks later. These periods of poor survival coincided with the onset of sexual maturity in many of the adult males and the approximate dates of weaning first litters in adult females. The frequency of the LAP^S allele (distinguished by slow electrophoretic mobility) dropped about 25 percent in the males beginning at the time of high losses, and 4 to 6 weeks later declined an equal amount in the females. This type of observation supports strongly the hypothesis that demographic events in *Microtus* are genetically selective and that losses are not distributed equally over all genotypes. Because we may be studying linkage effects and because we do not know how selection is acting, we cannot describe the mechanisms which would explain the associations shown in Fig. 2. We

cannot therefore assign cause and effect to the observations.

We have also used the *Tf* and *LAP* variation to investigate possible qualitative differences between dispersing *Microtus* and resident animals. Since dispersal is particularly important in the increase phase (Fig. 5, Table 2), we looked for qualitative differences at this time. Figure 6 shows the genotypic frequencies at the locus of the *Tf* gene for control populations and dispersing animals during an increase phase. Heterozygous females (Tf^C/Tf^E, where C and E are alleles of the *Tf* gene) are much more common in dispersing *Microtus* than in resident populations and 89 percent of the loss of heterozygous females from the control populations during the population increase was due to dispersal. Certain genotypes thus show a tendency to disperse, a possibility suggested by several authors (*20*) but not previously demonstrated in natural populations.

The polymorphic genes that we have used for markers in *M. pennsylvanicus* and *M. ochrogaster* are subject to intensive selection pressure, but we have not been able to determine how these polymorphisms are maintained. For example, let us consider the *Tf* polymorphism in *M. ochrogaster*. Two alleles are found in Indiana populations. The common allele Tf^E has a frequency of 97 percent in female and 93 percent in male *M. ochrogaster*. This polymorphism does not seem to be maintained by heterosis. We have not found any component of fitness (survival, reproduction, or growth) in which heterozygote voles (Tf^E/Tf^F) are superior to homozygote voles (Tf^E/Tf^E), except in declining and low populations when the male heterozygotes survive better than the homozygotes. Increasing populations are always associated with strong selection for the Tf^E allele (*18, 19*). Homozygote Tf^F/Tf^F females had higher prenatal mortality in field experiments (*21*). We do not know if this *Tf* polymorphism is maintained by density-related changes in fitness or by frequency-dependent variations in fitness (*22*).

An alternative explanation for the associations we have described between population density changes and gene frequency changes has been provided by Charlesworth and Giesel (*23*). Population fluctuations result in continual shifts in age structure. Genotypes with differing ages at sexual maturity and differing survival rates will thus change in frequency as a result of population fluctuations, and genetic changes could

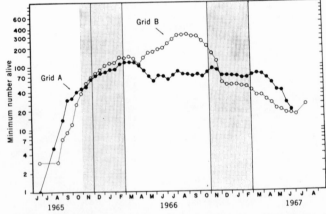

Fig. 4. Changes in population density of *M. pennsylvanicus* on unfenced grid A (control) and fenced grid B. Both are 2-acre (0.8-hectare) grassland fields. Grid B is surrounded by a mouse-proof fence extending 2 feet (0.6 meter) into the soil and projecting 2 feet above the ground. Signs of severe overgrazing were common on grid B by August 1966. [By permission of the Ecological Society of America]

366

Fig. 5. Rate of population change in *M. pennsylvanicus* control population from southern Indiana in relation to dispersal rate from that population, 1968 to 1970. Rate of population change is the instantaneous rate of change per week, averaged over "summer" and "winter" periods shown in Fig. 1. Dispersal rate is the mean number of voles dispersing from the control population to the trapped grid per 2 weeks, averaged over the same time periods. Populations increasing rapidly show the highest dispersal rates.

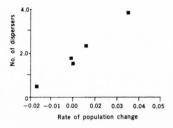

thus be the side effect of population cycles caused by any mechanism. We do not know whether the genetic changes we have described are causally related to population changes or merely side effects, but we question whether they are adequately explained by the Charlesworth and Giesel model. The size of the changes in gene frequency we observed (for example, Fig. 2) is several times larger than the size of the changes obtained in the Charlesworth and Giesel model (1 to 9 percent). Also, Charlesworth and Giesel obtained relatively little effect on gene frequencies by changing death rates in their model; we have found that changes in death rates of different genotypes are a major component of shifts in gene frequency (*11, 19*). We suggest that field perturbation experiments may help to resolve these alternative explanations (*24*).

Behavioral Changes

If behavioral interactions among individual voles are the primary mechanism behind population cycles, the behavioral characteristics of individuals would change over the cycle. We have tested this hypothesis only for male *M. pennsylvanicus* and *M. ochrogaster* in our Indiana populations. Males were tested by paired round-robin encounters in a neutral arena in the laboratory. Males of both species showed significant changes in aggressive behavior during the population cycle, so that individuals in peak populations were most aggressive (*11*). Male *M. pennsylvanicus* which dispersed during periods of peak population density tended to be even more aggressive than the residents on control areas (*17*).

Laboratory measurements of behavior can be criticized because we have no way of knowing how such measures might apply to the field situation. There is no doubt that aggression does go on in field populations of voles and lemmings because skin wounds are found,

particularly in males (*5, 25*). Field experiments could be designed to test the effects of aggression on mortality and growth rates, but none has been done yet on lemmings or voles. In the deer mouse (*Peromyscus maniculatus*) field experiments have demonstrated that aggressive adult mice can prevent the recruitment of juveniles into the population (*26*).

Conclusions

We conclude that population fluctuations in *Microtus* in southern Indiana are produced by a syndrome of changes in birth and death rates similar to that found in other species of voles and lemmings. The mechanisms which cause the changes in birth and death rates are demolished by fencing the population so that no dispersal can occur. Dispersal thus seems critical for population regulation in *Microtus*. Because most dispersal occurs during the increase phase of the population cycle and there is little dispersal during the decline phase, dispersal is not directly related to population density. Hence the quality of the dispersing animals must be important, and

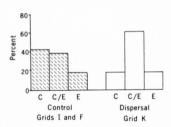

Fig. 6. The increase phase of *M. pennsylvanicus*, fall 1969. Transferrin genotype frequencies of dispersing females on trapped grid K (*N = 39*) compared with those of resident females on control grids immediately adjacent in the same grassland (*N = 224*). Dispersing voles in the increase phase are not a random sample from the control population. C, CIE, and E represent the three transferrin genotypes.

we have found one case of increased dispersal tendency by one genotype.

The failure of population regulation of *Microtus* in enclosed areas requires an explanation by any hypothesis attempting to explain population cycles in small rodents. It might be suggested that the fence changed the predation pressure on the enclosed populations. However, the fence was only 2 feet (0.6 meter) high and did not stop the entrance of foxes, weasels, shrews, or avian predators. A striking feature was that the habitat in the enclosures quickly recovered from complete devastation by the start of the spring growing season. Obviously the habitat and food quality were sufficient to support *Microtus* populations of abnormally high densities, and recovery of the habitat was sufficiently quick that the introduction of new animals to these enclosed areas resulted in another population explosion. Finally, hypotheses of population regulation by social stress must account for the finding that *Microtus* can exist at densities several times greater than normal without "stress" taking an obvious toll.

We hypothesize that the prevention of dispersal changes the quality of the populations in the enclosures in comparison to those outside the fence. Voles forced to remain in an overcrowded fenced population do not suffer high mortality rates and continue to reproduce at abnormally high densities until starvation overtakes them. The initial behavioral interactions associated with crowding do not seem sufficient to cause voles to die in situ.

What happens to animals during the population decline? Our studies have not answered this question. The animals did not appear to disperse, but it is possible that the method we used to measure dispersal (movement into a vacant habitat) missed a large segment of dispersing voles which did not remain in the vacant area but kept on moving. Perhaps the dispersal during the increase phase of the population cycle is a colonization type of dispersal, and the animals taking part in it are likely to stay in a new habitat, while during the population decline dispersal is a pathological response to high density, and the animals are not attracted to settling even in a vacant habitat. The alternative to this suggestion is that animals are dying in situ during the decline because of physiological or genetically determined behavioral stress.

Thus the fencing of a population prevents the change in rates of survival and reproduction, from high rates in the increase phase to low rates in the decline phase, and the fenced populations resemble "mouse plagues." A possible explanation is that the differential dispersal of animals during the phase of increase causes the quality of the voles remaining at peak densities in wild populations to be different from the quality of voles at much higher densities in enclosures. Increased sensitivity to density in *Microtus* could cause the decline of wild populations at densities lower than those reached by fenced populations in which selection through dispersal has been prevented. Fencing might also alter the social interactions among *Microtus* in other ways that are not understood.

The analysis of colonizing species by MacArthur and Wilson (*27*) can be applied to our studies of dispersal in populations of *Microtus*. Groups of organisms with good dispersal and colonizing ability are called *r* strategists because they have high reproductive potential and are able to exploit a new environment rapidly. Dispersing voles seem to be *r* strategists. Young females in breeding condition were over-represented in dispersing female *Microtus* (*17*). The Tf^C/Tf^E females, which were more common among dispersers during the phase of population increase (Fig. 6), also have a slight reproductive advantage over the other *Tf* genotypes (*19*). Thus in *Microtus* populations the animals with the highest reproductive potential, the *r* strategists, are dispersing. The segment of the population which

remains behind after the selection-via-dispersal are those individuals which are less influenced by increasing population densities. These are the individuals which maximize use of the habitat, the *K* strategists in MacArthur and Wilson's terminology, or voles selected for spacing behavior. Thus we can describe population cycles in *Microtus* in the same theoretical framework as colonizing species on islands.

Our work on *Microtus* is consistent with the hypothesis of genetic and behavioral effects proposed by Chitty (*6*) (Fig. 7) in that it shows both behavioral differences in males during the phases of population fluctuation and periods of strong genetic selection. The greatest gaps in our knowledge are in the area of genetic-behavioral interactions which are most difficult to measure. We have no information on the heritability of aggressive behavior in voles. The pathways by which behavioral events are translated into physiological changes which affect reproduction and growth have been carefully analyzed by Christian and his associates (*28*) for rodents in laboratory situations, but the application of these findings to the complex field events described above remains to be done.

Several experiments are suggested by our work. First, other populations of other rodent species should increase to abnormal densities if enclosed in a large fenced area (*29*). We need to find situations in which this prediction is not fulfilled. Island populations may be an important source of material for such

an experiment (*30*). Second, if one-way exit doors were provided from a fenced area, normal population regulation through dispersal should occur. This experiment would provide another method by which dispersers could be identified. Third, if dispersal were prevented after a population reached peak densities, a normal decline phase should occur. This prediction is based on the assumption that dispersal during the increase phase is sufficient to ensure the decline phase 1 or 2 years later. All these experiments are concerned with the dispersal factor, and our work on *Microtus* can be summarized by the admonition: study dispersal.

References and Notes

1. C. Elton, *Voles, Mice and Lemmings: Problems in Population Dynamics* (Clarendon Press, Oxford, 1942).
2. The term "cycle" is used here as a convenient shorthand for the more technically correct term "periodic fluctuation." We do not mean to imply a physicist's meaning of the word "cycle" because both the amplitude and the period of population fluctuations in small rodents are variable.
3. C. S. Elton, *Brit. J. Exp. Biol.* **2**, 119 (1924).
4. D. Chitty, *Phil. Trans. Roy. Soc. London Ser. B* **236**, 505 (1952); *Can. J. Zool.* **38**, 99 (1960).
5. C. J. Krebs, *Arctic Inst. N. Amer. Tech. Pap. No. 15* (1964).
6. D. Chitty, *Proc. Ecol. Soc. Aust.* **2**, 51 (1967).
7. L. C. Birch, *Amer. Natur.* **94**, 5 (1960); W. G. Wellington, *Can. J. Zool.* **35**, 293 (1957); *Can. Entomol.* **96**, 436 (1964).
8. E. B. Ford, *Mendelism and Evolution* (Methuen, London, 1931).
9. I. M. Lerner, *Proc. Int. Congr. Genet. 11th* **2**, 489 (1965).
10. C. J. Krebs, B. L. Keller, R. H. Tamarin, *Ecology* **50**, 587 (1969).
11. C. J. Krebs, *ibid.* **51**, 34 (1970); *Proceedings of the NATO Advanced Study Institute, Oosterbeek, 1970*, P. J. den Boer and G. R. Gradwell, Eds. (Center for Agricultural Publishing and Documentation, Wageningen, Netherlands, 1971), pp. 243–256.
12. D. Chitty and H. Chitty, in *Symposium Theriologicum, Brno, 1960*, J. Kratochvil and J. Pelikan, Eds. (Czechoslovak Academy of Sciences, Prague, 1962), pp. 67–76; F. B. Golley, *Amer. Midland Natur.* **66**, 152 (1961); O. Kalela, *Ann. Acad. Sci. Fenn. Ser. A* **4**, 34 (1957); C. J. Krebs, *Ecol. Monogr.* **36**, 239 (1966); E. P. Martin, *Univ. Kans. Publ. Mus. Natur. Hist.* **8**, 361 (1956); J. Zejda, *Zool. Listy* **13**, 15 (1964); G. O. Batzli and F. Pitelka, *J. Mammalogy* **52**, 141 (1971).
13. B. L. Keller and C. J. Krebs, *Ecol. Monogr.* **40**, 263 (1970).
14. We describe here our findings on *M. pennsylvanicus*. We have similar results for *M. ochrogaster* in Indiana, but we do not present these data here because they provide essentially the same conclusions.
15. G. S. Greenwald, *Univ. Calif. Publ. Zool.* **54**, 421 (1957); W. J. Hamilton, Jr., *Cornell Univ. Agric. Exp. Stat. Mem.* **237** (1941); T. V. Koshkina, *Bull. Moscow Soc. Nat. Biol. Sect.* **71**, 14 (1966); G. O. Batzli and F. A. Pitelka, *J. Mammal.* **52**, 141 (1971).
16. D. Chitty and E. Phipps, *J. Anim. Ecol.* **35**, 313 (1966); G. O. Batzli, thesis, Univ. of California, Berkeley (1969).
17. J. H. Myers and C. J. Krebs, *Ecol. Monogr.* **41**, 53 (1971).
18. R. H. Tamarin and C. J. Krebs, *Evolution* **23**, 183 (1969).
19. M. S. Gaines and C. J. Krebs, *ibid.* **25**, 702 (1971).
20. W. E. Howard, *Amer. Midland Natur.* **63**, 152 (1960); W. Z. Lidicker, *Amer. Natur.* **96**, 29 (1962).
21. M. S. Gaines, J. H. Myers, C. J. Krebs, *Evolution* **25**, 443 (1971).

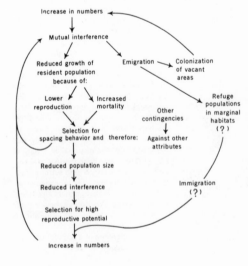

Fig. 7. Modified version of Chitty's hypothesis to explain population fluctuations in small rodents. Density-related changes in natural selection are central to this hypothesis. Our data indicate that selection through dispersal is more important than originally proposed by Chitty.

22. Density-related changes in fitness might be mediated by dispersal. The very rare Tf^p/Tf^p homozygote in *M. ochrogaster* occurred more frequently among dispersing males than in resident populations (*17*).

23. B. Charlesworth and J. T. Giesel, *Amer. Natur.* **106**, 388 (1972).

24. R. P. Canham and D. G. Cameron (personal communication) have obtained evidence for selection against certain *Tf* genotypes in declining populations of *Clethrionomys* and *Peromyscus* which have discrete annual generations in northern Canada. The Charlesworth and Giesel model (*23*) can apply only to species with overlapping generations.

25. J. J. Christian, *J. Mammal.* **52**, 556 (1971).

26. R. M. F. S. Sadleir, *J. Anim. Ecol.* **34**, 331 (1965); M. C. Healey, *Ecology* **48**, 337 (1967).

27. R. H. MacArthur and E. O. Wilson, *The Theory of Island Biogeography* (Princeton Univ. Press, Princeton, N.J., 1967).

28. J. J. Christian, *Biol. Reprod.* **4**, 248 (1971); J. J. Christian, J. A. Lloyd, D. E. Davis, *Recent Progr. Hormone Res.* **21**, 501 (1965); J. J. Christian, *Proc. Nat. Acad. Sci. U.S.A.* **47**, 428 (1961).

29. J. R. Clarke, *Proc. Roy. Soc. London Ser. B* **144**, 68 (1955); P. Crowcroft and F. P. Rowe, *Proc. Zool. Soc. London* **129**, 359 (1957); J. B. Gentry, *Res. Population Ecol.* **10**, 21 (1968); W. Z. Lidicker, *ibid.* **7**, 57 (1965); K. Petrusewicz, *Ekol. Pol. Ser. A* **5**, 281 (1957); R. L. Steecker and J. T. Emlen, *Ecology* **34**, 375 (1953).

30. The population of *M. californicus* on Brooks Island in San Francisco Bay may be acting in the same way as a fenced population, maintaining densities higher than mainland populations (W. Z. Lidicker, personal communication).

31. This research was conducted when all of us were at Indiana University. We thank the National Science Foundation and the Public Health Service for financial support of the research.

CONCLUDING REMARKS

I should have retitled this book *Animal Population Regulation* because there was not enough space to include material on plant populations. Several references have been made to plant–animal interactions as important in animal population regulation (Pimentel, Paper 21; Freeland 1974; Janzen 1970). Plant population biology, however, is coming into its own now, and some articles serve as a valuable introduction to this area. In particular, John Harper (University College of North Wales), a leader in the field of plant demography and population regulation, has written two excellent reviews (Harper 1968; Harper and White 1974), both of which emphasize that one cannot simply carry over animal demography methodologies to plant demography. Instead, the study of plants requires its own techniques and concepts. The 1974 article with its 348 references is an excellent, topical review article with which to enter the field of plant demography.

The field of population regulation seems to be heading in a positive direction. Field, laboratory, and theoretical biologists are combining their energies increasingly to work out many of the problems in the field (see for example May 1976). In addition there is an increasing interaction with allied fields: population genetics, endocrinology, nutrition, biochemistry, and so on. Thus we are making strides in understanding many of the interactions occurring in natural populations. Remembering, however, that our unit of measure is the natural population, it is discouraging that little experimentation and manipulation are being done in the field. As mentioned in Part VIII, much effort is being

371

expended in an effort to overcome the impasse of manipulation. The overwhelming spatial and temporal magnitude of many ecological problems makes manipulation unpromising at this time. More pessimistically, there seems to be a fundamentally deeper problem: the lack of a unified theory.

On one hand, the study of lemming cycles is interesting because there is still the possibility that a single factor underlies all these cyclic phenomena; that is, a predictive model may be developed, and what we learn from one population may be carried over to other populations. On the other hand, this may not be true in the wider field of population regulation. Recently, at a symposium at the University of Pittsburgh Pymatuning Laboratory of Ecology (edited by Snyder, 1977) on population regulation in small mammals, Lidicker reiterated some of the classical models (see Parts II, III, and IV of this book) and ended by defining a theory that he said he hoped would result in a new field of comparative demography. This theory is a compromise model reminiscent of Thompson (Paper 6) and Milne (Paper 7). At this time, I think that Lidicker is probably correct, with the exception of the lemming cycles. This leaves us with only one great concept in the area of population regulation: that all animal populations are regulated. Any population under study may be very interesting in regard to learning what regulates its numbers; it is impossible to generalize to all species, however. This simple fact may be at the root of most of the controversy that has pervaded and, to a lesser extent, still does pervade the field of population regulation. Thus Morris (Paper 17) suggests that we use key-factor analysis to determine what factors provide the greatest density-dependent regulation of a population; yet we have very little theory on which to base an *a priori* prediction of what these factors should be.

R. H. Peters stated this pessimism more eloquently:

> . . . I was led to wonder if competitive exclusion, succession, and diversity are tractable scientific problems—that is, if they can be resolved or if by their nature they are beyond resolution. I cannot prove my suspicions, but we must be aware of the possibility of intractable problems and not be surprised if another mode of thought produces more fruitful science than these. Perhaps the existence of so much logic and so little theory indicates that this is infertile ground on which to raise predictive hypotheses. If this is the case, then the dedication of so much ecology to these topics is wasted energy. (Peters 1976, p. 10)

REFERENCES

Freeland, W. 1974. Vole Cycles: Another Hypothesis. *Am. Nat.* **108**:238–245.

Harper, J. 1968. The Regulation of Numbers and Mass in Plant Populations. In R. C. Lewontin (ed.), *Population Biology and Evolution*, pp. 139–158. Syracuse, N.Y.: Syracuse University Press.

Harper, J., and J. White. 1974. The Demography of Plants. *Ann. Rev. Ecol. Syst.* **5**:419–463.

Janzen, D. H. 1970. Herbivores and the Number of Tree Species in Tropical Forests. *Am. Nat.* **104**:501–529.

May, R. M. (ed.). 1976. *Theoretical Ecology.* Philadelphia: Saunders.

Peters, R. 1976. Tautology in Evolution and Ecology. *Am. Nat.* **110**:1–12.

Snyder, D. (ed.). 1977. *Populations of Small Mammals Under Natural Conditions.* Pymatuning Laboratory of Ecology, Symposium no. 5. Ann Arbor, Mich.: Edwards Brothers.

AUTHOR CITATION INDEX

SUBJECT INDEX

About the Editor

ROBERT H. TAMARIN, Associate Professor of Biology at Boston University, teaches courses in ecology, genetics, and population biology. He received the B.S. in biology from the City University of New York, Brooklyn College, in 1963, and the Ph.D. in zoology from Indiana University (where he was a student of Charles Krebs) in 1968. From 1968 to 1970, Tamarin served as a postdoctoral fellow at the University of Hawaii's Department of Genetics, working with Geoffrey Ashton, and from 1970 to 1971, he was a Ford Foundation Research Associate at Princeton University, working with Robert Mac Arthur. Since 1971 he has been at Boston University, where his research has been concerned with population regulation in small rodents, primarily on islands.